Verbum Caro

An Encyclopedia on Jesus, the Christ

Michael O'Carroll, C.S.Sp.

A Michael Glazier Book
THE LITURGICAL PRESS
Collegeville, Minnesota

A Michael Glazier Book published by The Liturgical Press

Cover illustration by Placid Stuckenschneider, O.S.B.

1   2   3   4   5   6   7   8   9

Library of Congress Cataloging-in-Publication Data

O'Carroll, Michael.
  Verbum caro : an encyclopedia on Jesus, the Christ / Michael O'Carroll.
      p.   cm.
  "A Michael Glazier book."
  Includes bibliographical references.
  ISBN 0-8146-5017-1
  1. Jesus Christ—Encyclopedias.   I. Title.
BT199.023   1992
232'.03—dc20   92-1216
                                                   CIP

Contents

Foreword

This work follows the pattern of the other encyclopedias which I have composed. I have sought to return to the sources, to record and explain the important interventions of the Church's Teaching Authority in the continuous reflection and debate on Jesus Christ, to choose for presentation the significant authors who have written on him, and the principal themes that have emerged thus far in all this thinking.

This is a daunting task. More has been written on Jesus Christ in the last fifty years than in all the previous Christian centuries. I hope that in dealing with this vast literature I have been fair to writers, ancient and modern. I have provided ample bibliographies to allow readers to pursue personal study of the topic that interests them.

I have thought that it would be useful for students, especially students for the priesthood, to have available in my work the full text of the Tome of Leo, an epoch-making document, and of recent, illuminating statements from the Biblical Commission and the International Theological Commission.

I have deferred consideration of subjects which do have an impact on Christology, gnosticism, for example, and feminist theology; they will be dealt with in *Gloria Deo,* a comprehensive study of systems of thought, institutions, agencies, personalities, religions which are in one way or another related to the idea of God revealed directly or indirectly, rationally or intuitively discovered, sustained or opposed: more than a summary of comparative religions.

Work on the present composition has progressively shown me the claim of the mystics to be included in any enlightened reflection on Jesus Christ. From a historical standpoint they have had immeasurable effect throughout Christendom, stirring individuals of every cultural origin and output to a more lively consciousness of him and a readiness to respond to his call. From an anthropological viewpoint they envelop, within their human personality, a deep, subtle, rich potentiality on which he and he alone can directly act. Any one of the great mystics whom I have briefly studied in the following pages, from Origen to Vassula Ryden, would, without the thrust of Christ into the heart of their being, be, on objective analysis, a different person: a psyche ordinary in scope and power in contrast with the complete, fulfilled, creative personality known to us. This is almost a paraphrase of Henri Bergson's well-known tribute to the mystics. What history and anthropology clearly indicates, theology clarifies and develops.

As I complete this work I am left with a feeling which at first may appear superficial, but which the reader may find as valid and profound as I do. The immense volume of writing and speaking, not all of this kept on record, constitutes an incontrovertible testimony to the magnitude and uniqueness within human experience and the flow of history of the One we call Jesus Christ.

Jesus Christ has stirred the human heart to depths unknown, motivated the human will to super-human achievement, released the resources of the human mind and activated its powers, whether intuitive, discursive, or mystical, in a way that no other human being can remotely rival. The most sophisticated systems of thought have been used to attempt the impossible, to imprison in mental categories this sublimely enigmatic figure. He eludes every such effort. He prompts incessant renewal of the task, and he is himself the reward of those who undertake it.

For all that we think we know about Jesus Christ, for all the progress we seem to have made working with the intellectual tools of varied cultures, we have as yet so much to discover that the enterprise in being constantly renewed seems always both satisfying and endlessly challenging. For Jesus Christ removes the unbearable burden of his mystery by being a presence. He stimulates the most rigorous historical and philosophical inquiry to the point where we feel like retiring exhausted, until we realize that he is beside us. He defies and transcends time as a constraint; he assumes moments of time into his existence to transmute them into the eternal. He dissolves time and, with the elements, creates a reality that will endure forever.

I have done my best in the following pages to set out what may help those embarking upon or already well into study of the mystery of Jesus Christ. I have a debt of gratitude to those who have helped me, principally the librarians of Milltown Park, Dublin, the Bibliotheca Bollandiana in Brussels, Les Fontaines, Chantilly and Trinity College, Dublin. I thank Michael Glazier who encouraged me to write this book, as did others, and Dr. John Craghan for his very many valuable suggestions on the manuscript.

Michael O'Carroll, C.S.Sp.

Abbreviations

AAS	*Acta Apostolicae Sedis*
ACO	*Acta Conciliorum Oecumenicorum*, ed. E. Schwartz
AER	*American Ecclesiastical Review*
AGreg	*Analecta Gregoriana*
ASS	*Acta Sanctae Sedis*
AugMag	*Augustinus Magister* (Congrès international augustinien) Paris, 1954
Bauer	*An Encyclopedia of Biblical Theology*, ed. J. B. Bauer, 3 vols.
BB	*Biblica*
BeO	*Bibbia e Oriente*
BETL	*Bibliotheca ephemeridum theologicarum lovaniensium*
BJRL	*Bulletin of the John Rylands Library*
BLE	*Bulletin de littérature ecclésiastique*
BR	*Biblical Research*
BTB	*Biblical Theology Bulletin*
BZ	*Byzantinische Zeitschrift*
CBQ	*Catholic Biblical Quarterly*
CCCM	*Corpus Christianorum. Continuatio Medievalis*
CCSG	*Corpus Christianorum. Series Graeca*
CCSL	*Corpus Christianorum. Series Latina*
Chalkedon	*Das Konzil von Chalkedon*, 3 vols., 1951–1954, ed. A. Grillmeier, S.J. (qv) -H. Bacht, S.J.
ClavisG	M. Geerard, *Clavis Patrum Graecorum*, Turnhout, 1974
Contemporary Theologies	N. Ormerod, *Introducing Contemporary Theologies*, Newtown, New South Wales, 1990
Corpus Christi	M. O'Carroll, *A Theological Encyclopedia of the Eucharist*, Wilmington, 1989
CSCO	*Corpus Scriptorum Christianorum Orientalium*

CSEL	*Corpus Scriptorum Ecclesiasticorum Latinorum*
CSNT	*Christ and Spirit in the New Testament: Studies in Honor of C. F. D. Moule,* eds. B. Lindars and S. S. Smalley, Cambridge, 1973
DACL	*Dictionnaire d'Archéologie Chrétienne et de Liturgie*
DBS	*Dictionnaire de la Bible, Supplément*
DCath	*La Documentation Catholique*
DHGE	*Dictionnaire d'Histoire et de Géographie Ecclésiastiques*
DOP	*Dumbarton Oaks Papers*
DS	*Enchiridion Symbolorum,* Denziger-Bannwart, ed. 33, A. Schönmetzer, S.J.
DSp	*Dictionnaire de Spiritualité*
DTC	*Dictionnaire de Théologie Catholique*
EB	Enchiridion Biblicum
EO	*Echos d'Orient*
EphMar	*Ephemerides Mariologicae*
EstBibl	*Estudios Biblicos*
ET	English Translation
ETL	*Ephemerides Theologicae Lovanienses*
Etudes mariales	Bulletin of the French Society for Marian Studies
EvTh	*Evangelische Theologie*
ExT	*Expository Times*
Fliche-Martin	H. Fliche, V. Martin, ed., *Histoire de l'Eglise,* 1935
FS	*Franciscan Studies*
GCS	*Die griechischen christlichen Schriftsteller der ersten drei Jahrhunderte*
Greg.	*Gregorianum*
Grillmeier	A. Grillmeier, *Christ in Christian Tradition,* 1965, 2nd ed. 1973; reference to each
HJ	*Historische Jahrbuch*
HTR	*Harvard Theological Review*
IER	*Irish Ecclesiastical Record*
ITQ	*Irish Theological Quarterly*
JB	*La Bible de Jérusalem*
JBL	*Journal of Biblical Literature*
JJS	*Journal of Jewish Studies*
JSJ	*Journal for the Study of Judaism*
JSNT	*Journal for the Study of the New Testament*
JTS	*Journal of Theological Studies*
KD	*Kerygma und Dogma*
Kelly, Doctrines	J. N. D. Kelly, *Early Christian Doctrines, 1958*

LNPF	*Library of Nicene and Post-Nicene Fathers*
LTK	*Lexikon für Theologie und Kirche*, 2nd ed.
LumV	*Lumière et Vie*
LV	*Lumen Vitae*
Mansi	J. D. Mansi, *Sacrorum Conciliorum Nova et Amplissima Collectio*, Florence, 1759–98
MSCA	*Miscellanea Augusteniana*
MiscFr	*Miscellanea Franciscana*
Modern Theologians	*The Modern Theologians*, ed. D. F. Ford, Oxford 1989
MSR	*Mélanges de Science Religieuse*
Mus	*Le Muséon*
NCE	The New Catholic Encyclopaedia
NJBC	The New Jerome Biblical Commentary
NovT	*Novum Testamentum*
NRT	*Nouvelle Revue Théologique*
NT	The New Testament
NTS	*New Testament Studies*
OCP	*Orientalia Christiana Periodica*
OT	The Old Testament
Patrology IV	Supplement of Quasten, Patrology
PG	*Patrologia Graeca*
PL	*Patrologia Latina*
Quasten	J. Quasten, Patrology, I, II, III, 1950–1960
RAM	*Revue d'Ascétique et de Mystique*
RAug	*Revue d'Etudes Augustiniennes*
RB	*Revue Biblique*
REB	*Revue d'Etudes Byzantines*
RET	*Revista Española de Teologia*
RevSR	*Revue des Sciences Religieuses*
RHE	*Revue d'Histoire ecclésiastique*
RSPT	*Revue des Sciences Philosophiques et Théologiques*
RSR	*Recherches de Science Religieuse*
RSV	Revised Standard Version of the Bible
RTP	*Revue de Théologie et de Philosophie*
SC	*Sources Chrétiennes*
SE	*Sciences Ecclésiastiques*
SF	*Studi Franciscani*

SJT	*Scottish Journal of Theology*
SNTS	*Society for New Testament Studies, Monograph Series*
SPCC	*Studiorum Paulinorum Congressus Catholicus,* 2 vols., Rome, 1963
ST	St. Thomas Aquinas, *Summa Theologiae*
STh	*Studia Theologica*
TDNT	*Theological Dictionary of the New Testament*
Theotokos	M. O'Carroll, *A Theological Encyclopedia of the Blessed Virgin Mary,* Wilmington, 1983
ThQS	*Theologische Quartalschrift*
ThS	*Theological Studies*
TLZ	*Theologische Literaturzeitung*
TOB	*Traduction Oecuménique de la Bible*
Trinitas	M. O'Carroll, *A Theological Encyclopedia of the Holy Trinity,* Wilmington, 1987
TTZ	*Treier Theologische Zeitschrift*
TU	*Texte und Untersuchungen zur Geschichte der altchristlichen Literatur*
TZ	*Theologische Zeitschrift*
Veni Creator Spiritus	M. O'Carroll, *A Theological Encyclopedia of the Holy Spirit,* Wilmington, 1990
VS	*La Vie Spirituelle*
VT	Vetus Testamentum
Why Christ?	J. B. Carol, O.F.M., *Why Jesus Christ? Thomistic, Scotistic and Conciliatory Perspectives.* Manassas, Virginia 1986
Young, F.M.	F.M. Young, *From Nicaea to Chalcedon,* London, 1983
ZKT	*Zietschrift fur Katholische Theologie*
ZNW	*Zeitschrift fur die neutestamentliche Wissenschaft*
ZTK	*Zeitschrift fur Theologie und Kirche*

A

ABBA

The great biblical scholar, Joachim Jeremias, had the merit of focusing attention on the significance of Jesus' Abba prayer. His opinion still commands respect, though other scholars have examined the evidence to reach somewhat different, at least marginally different, conclusions. Let Jeremias be heard first: "The complete novelty and uniqueness of *Abba* as an address to God in the prayers of Jesus shows that it expresses the heart of Jesus' relationship to God. He spoke to God as a child to its father: confidently and securely, and yet, at the same time, reverently and obediently."[1] Jeremias rejected the idea that by using this word Jesus was adopting the language of a tiny child. The fact that in the period before the NT grown-up sons and daughters addressed their fathers as *Abba* rules out any such limitation. But there seems to be a kind of popular liking for such a meaning. "To his disciples," says Jeremias, "it must have been something quite extraordinary that Jesus addressed God as 'my Father.' Moreover not only do the four Gospels attest that Jesus used this address, but they report unanimously that he did so in all his prayer."[2] The single exception, as the author points out, is the cry from the cross, "My God, my God, why hast thou forsaken me?" (Mk 15:34; Mt 27:46), which is a quotation from Ps 22:1.

Still, in the context of biblical reflection, account must be taken of J. Barr's research, along with that of J. A. Fitzmyer. Barr entitled his study, "Abba Isn't 'Daddy.' " His position, argued with a wealth of erudition and precision, is thus summarized: "(1) In Jesus' time *abba* belonged to a familiar or colloquial register of language, but it was not a childish expression comparable with 'Daddy'; it was a more solemn, responsible, adult address to a father. (2) While it is possible that all cases in which Jesus addresses God as 'father' derive from an original *'abba,'* it is impossible to prove that this is so since alternative hypotheses fit the evidence equally well. (3) The use of the word *abba* could in principle be within Hebrew or Aramaic speech. (4) Although the use of *abba* in address to God may have been first originated by Jesus, it remains difficult to prove how constant and pervasive this element was in his expression of himself; and it is therefore difficult to prove that it is a quite central keystone in our total understanding of him."[3]

On the theological level E. Schillebeeckx (qv) makes the *abba* experience the starting point of Trinitarian theory: "Only in the light of Jesus' life, death and resurrection can we know that the Trinity is the divine mode of God's perfect unity of being. Only of Jesus of Nazareth, his *abba* experience—source and soul of his message, ministry, and death—and his resurrection, is it possible to say anything meaningful about Father, Son and Spirit. For what matters in the *abba* experience of Jesus is that this unique turning of Jesus to the Father in absolute priority is 'preceded' and inwardly supported by the unique turning of the Father himself to Jesus. Now early Christian tradition calls this self-communication of the Father—ground and source of Jesus' peculiar *abba* experience, 'the Word.' This implies that the Word of God is the undergirding ground of the whole Jesus phenomenon."[4]

---

[1]*New Testament Theology,* London, 1971, 67; *id., Abba,* Göttingen, 1966, 15–67; *id., The Central Message of the New Testa-*

1

ment, London, 1965, 9–30; id., Abba, Jésus et son Père, Paris, 1972; J. Barr, "Abba Isn't 'Daddy,'" JTS 39 (1988) 28–47; J. A. Fitzmyer, S.J., "Abba and Jesus' Relation to God" in A cause de l'évangile (Festschrift J. Dupont, LD 123, ed. R. Gantoy) Paris, 1985, 57–81; ²Ibid., ³NTA 33 (1989) 61, 11; ⁴Jesus: An Experiment in Christology, London, 1979, 658; cf. also TDNT, Abba, Pater, I, 5–6, Kittel; V, 945–1022, Quell, Schrenk; J. A. Fitzmyer, A Christological Catechism, New York, 1982, 24–25.

ADAM, KARL (1876–1966)

In the inter-war years A. was probably the best-known German theologian outside his native country. A Bavarian priest, he did pastoral work and then held professorial posts in Munich and Strasbourg before being appointed Professor of Dogmatic Theology in Tübingen University. He held the post until 1949 and was the teacher of important academic and pastoral figures. The inspiring quality of the lecture room or hall passed into his written work and won him very many translations. In the English-speaking world he was fortunate to have the service of a publisher of genius, Frank Sheed of Sheed and Ward. He was not an aloof academic; he paid a price in terms of personal harassment for his stand against Nazi incursions into religion. He was a true and highly influential pioneer in the ecumenical movement in Germany in the decades before Vatican II and John XXIII. He had shown his scholarly aptitude in monographs on the ecclesiology of Tertullian (qv) and the Eucharistic theology of St. Augustine (qv). As an enlightened teacher of the public, Catholics and Christians of other denominations, especially German Lutheran, the focus of his thinking was Jesus Christ, in his Mystical Body and in his Person and human existence. He excelled in presenting a solid core of doctrine, amply enlarged from Sacred Scripture, combined with high readability. He had a novel approach at times, as in the chapter, "The Mental Stature of Jesus," in The Son of God, or in "The Self-Revelation of Jesus," in the same work. His Christological teaching is contained in this work with The Spirit of Catholicism, Christ and the Western Mind, Christ our Brother, and The Christ of Faith. All but the last title appeared in English in the 1930s. The Christ of Faith has a more scholarly structure and was published in German, Der Christus des Glaubens, some years after his retirement.

¹Cf. Catholic Authors, ed. M. Hoehm, O.S.B., I, St. Mary's Abbey, Newark, 1948, 2–3; Abhandlungen über Theologie und Kirche: Festgabe für Karl Adam, ed. M. Reding, Dusseldorf, 1952, bibl. of Karl Adam, 319f; Vitae et Veritati, Festgabe für Karl Adam, ibid., 1956.

ADAM, THE NEW

The two basic texts in regard to this doctrine are as follows: Rom 5:12-21. "For if while we were enemies we were reconciled to God by the death of his Son, much more, now that we are reconciled, shall we be saved by his life. Not only so, but we also rejoice in God through our Lord Jesus Christ, through whom we have now received our reconciliation. Therefore as sin came into the world through one man and death through sin, and so death spread to all men because all men sinned—sin indeed was in the world before the law was given, but sin is not counted where there is no law. Yet death reigned from Adam to Moses, even over those whose sins were not like the transgression of Adam, who was a type of the one who was to come. But the free gift is not like the trespass. For if many died through one man's trespass, much more have the grace of God and the free gift in the grace of that one man Jesus Christ abounded for many. And the free gift is not like the effect of that one man's sin. For the judgment following one trespass brought condemnation, but the free gift following many trespasses brings justification. If, because of one man's trespass death reigned through that one man, much more will those who receive the abundance of grace and the free gift of righteousness reign in life through the one man Jesus Christ. Then as one man's trespass led to condemnation for all men, so one man's act of righteousness leads to acquittal and life for all men. For as by one man's disobedience many were made sinners, so by one man's obedience many will be made righteous. Law came in, to increase the trespass; but where sin increased, grace abounded all the more, so that, as sin reigned in death, grace also might reign through righteousness to eternal life through Jesus Christ our Lord." 1 Cor 15:21-22, 44-49. "For as by a man came death, by a man has come also the resurrection of the dead. For as in Adam all die, so also in Christ shall all be made alive. . . . It is sown a physical body, it is raised a spiritual body. If there is a physical body, there is also a spiritual body. Thus it is written, 'The first man Adam became a living being'; the last Adam became a life-giving spirit. But it is not the spiritual which is first but the physical, and then the spiritual. The first man was from the earth, a man of dust; the second man is from heaven. As was the man of dust, so are those who are of the dust; and as is the man of heaven, so are those who are of heaven. Just as we have borne the image of the man of dust, we shall also bear the image of the man of heaven.''

There are certain broad ideas in these passages which have formed the traditional Adam-Christ typology[1]: sin and death came into the world through one man, with whom all had some solidarity; justice and life were made available to all by one man, through the free gift of God. The two orders are outlined, the old vitiated and lost by sin, the new embodying an abundance of grace. Christ, in his role as the last Adam, stands at the head of all mankind. He is superior to Adam not only because he includes Adam in the cosmic sweep of his beneficence, but because Adam's legacy of death is surpassed by the justification brought by the free gift, because ''the abundance of grace and the free gift of righteousness'' lift men to ''reign through the one man Jesus Christ.'' It is not only acquittal he gives but life.

The Common Bible here used translates *eph ho* in v. 12 by ''because'' (all men sinned). It is well known that the Vulgate uses *in quo* (*omnes peccaverunt*). ''Because'' presents an obvious difficulty: it imputes responsibility to each human being for death. There are these other suggested translations: ''on the grounds of which,'' ''because of the one by whom,'' ''in view of the fact that,'' ''on condition that.'' It is for scholars to decide. One of them, Msgr. L. Cerfaux, writes: ''Since Adam's sin must be modelled on Christ's salvific act, the one influencing the many, the sense will be as follows. Necessarily (*dia touto*) just as sin (and through sin, death) came into the world through one man, death must likewise touch all men, beginning with the one through whom all have sinned. As with salvation, the starting-point is one man, and the term is all men. Thus we have on the one hand reconciliation and life, and on the other, sin and death. For the same reason we have to admit that the Vulgate is right when it translates '*in quo omnes peccaverunt*.' It is obvious that *eph ho* does not mean *in quo,* but in this context, given the constant comparison of Christ and Adam, and the respective origins of life and sin, we cannot say that the expression does not imply a relationship between the state of sin and its initiator, Adam.'' Cerfaux rejects ''because'' for the reason already given. As he says, criticism of *in quo* has been excessive since Erasmus; he suggests ''because of the one by whom.''[2]

Cerfaux makes another point: ''We are in the habit of reversing St. Paul's order. To us it seems rather that redemption is universal because sin had affected all men. But for Paul, the new life of participation in Christ's life is prior in God's intention.''[3] It is the fall that is modelled on salvation, not vice versa. We

enter here the mystery of divine goodness, transcendent, munificent. This opinion of the great exegete would bring this Pauline passage into line with the others cited in support of the universal primacy (qv) of Christ. The concept of the new creation, rightly emphasized latterly, has to be given a dimension which releases it from any intrinsic dependence on the first creation and its headship in Adam.

Msgr. Cerfaux traces echoes of the Adam-Christ theme elsewhere in St. Paul and in Ephesians, the antithesis between the sinful, or outer, man and the inner man renewed by the Christian life (Rom 7:22; 2 Cor 4:16; Col 3:9-10; Eph 4:22-24).[4] J. D. G. Dunn (qv), with his customary scholarly thoroughness, probes all the Pauline texts which could have relevance and show an influence of Gen 1-3 (Rom 1:18-25; 3:23; 7:7-11; 8:19-22). These show the influence of the Adam concept on Pauline anthropology. Dunn offers insights on Pss 110 and 8, which enlighten. More directly related to Adam-Christ theology, and thoroughly investigated by Dunn is the well-known hymn used by Paul in Phil 2:6-11; he also considers 2 Cor 8:9. There is depth upon depth in this junction of the key figures in the old and the new creation. Dunn sums up his findings: ''We have traced the Pauline (and pre-Pauline) Adam Christology backwards from a Christology focusing only on the risen Christ ('image' and 'glory'), through the transition afforded by Ps 8, to a Christology of Christ, the one man who fulfilled God's purpose for man—a Christology embracing the earthly as well as the exalted Christ. Can we trace this Adam Christology still further backwards to an earlier stage of pre-existence? Can we detect in Paul not just a two-stage Adam Christology (Adam = earthly Jesus; last Adam = exalted Jesus) but a three-stage Adam Christology (pre-existent Man, Adam, last Adam)?''[5] The reader must follow Dunn's closely argued reply to his question.

The Fathers, seeking to elaborate a theological system, used the concept of Christ, the last Adam. St. Irenaeus (qv), the great pathfinder, with it wrought his doctrine of recapitulation (qv). ''There shall be required all the righteous blood which is shed on earth, from the blood of righteous Abel. Here he signifies that there would be a gathering up of the blood to be saved; neither would the Lord have gathered up all this into himself, unless he himself also had been made flesh and blood, saving finally in himself that which had originally perished in Adam.''[6]

''Let us recall some aspects in which Adam is presented as the figure of Christ,'' writes J. Daniélou of St. Irenaeus. ''As we have said, these are to a certain extent made up of oppositions. As Adam's disobedience is the cause of our sinful state, so it is through Christ's obedience that we are redeemed. 'If he had not been made flesh, and as flesh had not obeyed, his works would not have been true. So he had 'to recapitulate the former creation.' '"[7]

This is already in St. Paul; but one text adds a further thought. Adam "who was first formed from virgin earth" is likened to Christ who was born of a Virgin Mother. So we find a likeness between the birth of Adam and that of Jesus. St. Irenaeus puts it thus: "And as the first-formed Adam had his substance of the rude and yet virgin earth (for God had not yet rained and man had not yet tilled) and was molded by the Hand of God, that is by the Word, for all things were made by him; and the Lord took clay from the earth, and molded man; so when the Word himself, being of Mary who was yet a virgin, was gathering into himself what relates to Adam, it was meet that he should receive a birth suitable to this gathering up of Adam. And so, if the first Adam had a man for his father and was born of a man's seed, it were meet that the second Adam was also born of Joseph. But if the former was taken out of earth and God was his Framer, it was meet that he also, being summed up as part of Adam—I mean the man framed by the Almighty—should have the same resemblance of birth with him. Why then did not God a second time take dust, but wrought so that the birth should be of Mary? That it might not be a different formation, nor merely another being to be saved, but that the very same might be gathered in, thus preserving the similitude."[8] Christ re-enacts everything that Adam did, but on a higher plane, and his solidarity with Adam is assured by his birth, though miraculously, from a daughter of Adam.

The Adam-Christ typology has not in Christian literature the same prominence as the Eve-Mary parallel. Of this St. Irenaeus is one of the first exponents, possibly still the greatest. The doctrine was expounded by his near contemporaries, St. Justin Martyr (qv) and Tertullian (qv). None of the three found it in the Pauline texts on Adam and Christ; they all appeal to the parallel—and difference—between the temptation of Eve as told in Genesis and the Annunciation narrative as found in Luke's infancy narrative: Eve, the tempter, disobedience; Mary, the archangel, obedience. Eve's title, "Mother of the Living" is transferred, in the supernatural order, to Mary, to whom some medieval theologians also applied the Gen 2:18 text: "a helper like himself."

The teaching Authority has been sparing in treatment of the theme, as it presented no controversial danger. Trent invoked Rom 5:12 in regard to Original Sin, did not advert explicitly to the Adam-Christ parallel.[9] Pius XII spoke of the new Adam in the context of the new Eve. The passages are in important doctrinal documents: "We must remember especially that since the second century the Virgin Mary has been designated by the Holy Fathers as the new Eve, who, although subject to the new Adam, is most intimately associated with him in that struggle against the infernal foe which, as foretold in the *Protoevangelium,* would finally result in that most complete victory over sin and death which are always mentioned together in the writings of the Apostle of the Gentiles."[10] "Mary, in the work of redemption, was by God's will joined with Jesus Christ, the cause of salvation. . . . the Blessed Virgin is Queen not only as Mother of God but also because she was associated as the second Eve with the new Adam."[11] Pius brought together two traditions, Mary as the new Eve and the Woman in Gen 3:15, as a passage in *Mystici Corporis Christi* (qv) shows: "(Mary) offered him on Golgotha to the eternal Father together with the holocaust of maternal rights and motherly love, like a new Eve, for all the children of Adam contaminated through his unhappy fall."[12]

St. Augustine (qv) who did not deal at length with the Eve-Mary parallel, did have a place in his synthesis for the Adam-Christ idea.[13] Vatican II (qv) barely sketched an anthropology which would take in the concept: "In reality it is only in the mystery of the Word made flesh that the mystery of man truly becomes clear. For Adam, the first man was a type of him who was to come.[14] Christ the Lord, Christ the new Adam, in the very revelation of the mystery of the Father and of his love, fully reveals man to himself and brings to light his most high calling. It is no wonder, then, that all the truths mentioned so far should find in him their source and their most perfect embodiment. He who is the 'image of the invisible God' (Col 1:15; cf. 2 Cor 4:4) is himself the perfect man who has restored in the children of Adam that likeness to God which has been disfigured ever since the first sin. Human nature, by the very fact that it was assumed, not absorbed, in him, has been raised in us also to a dignity beyond compare. For, by his incarnation, he, the Son of God, has in a certain way united himself with each man."[15]

A fully satisfactory Adam-Christ theology will draw on the elements thus far set forth and unify and expend them with the help of new insights. One great modern theologian seemed to see the need for such a development. M. J. Scheeben returned to the theme more than once in his great work, *The Mysteries of Christianity.* He was seized by the idea of Christ's headship of the human race. In that framework he elaborates firmly the difference between Christ and Adam. "Therefore the difference between the supernational condition of the first Adam and that of the second consists precisely in this, that the first Adam possessed it not of himself, not by reason of the power and right of his person, but out of sheer grace whereas the second Adam possesses it of himself, that is by the power and right of his Person, and hence by nature. . . . The divine life flowed to the humanity of the first Adam from a source widely separated from it, situated outside it. The humanity of Christ receives that divine life from a source interiorly united to it, just as life is conveyed to the members of the body from the head, or to the branches from the vine to which they are joined.''[16]

Christ's humanity, in its substance and nature, had no greater privileges than in the nature of the first man: ''the prerogatives of sanctity and integrity were gifts added to it by God; but the right to these privileges and the source from which they sprang were embodied in it by virtue of this union (with a divine Person).'' Adam was called by grace but was for a while in an intermediate stage, ''a transition point between the rank of God's servants and that of his fully reborn children.'' No such separation is thinkable for the second Adam; his ''soul's participation in the divine nature meant not merely holiness and grace; it meant fully achieved glory and beatitude from the very first instant.''[17]

Adam could sin; Christ was impeccable. Studying the two Adams from the standpoint of integrity, Scheeben concedes that the second Adam's humanity, though immensely superior to that of the first Adam in holiness, seemed to be inferior in integrity, integrity meaning that the lower faculties could not be stimulated apart from and contrary to his will. But in reality ''in his own right and by his own power Christ was able to impede any modification of his nature that did not accord with his will, and so he was able to keep all suffering and death at a distance from himself. He suffered and died not because he had to, not because he could not prevent it, but because he willed to.''[18] According to the more probable opinion of theologians, Adam could not have done this. Adam had perfect dominion of will over all his proclivities and appetites, but this depended on his continuing uprightness of will. But Christ possesses such dominion necessarily.

Scheeben also shows the different grounds for applying the title ''head of the human race'' to Adam and to Christ. ''The first Adam was himself only an adopted child of God. By nature he was no more than the rest of men. . . . He was chosen and commissioned by the grace of God to be no more than the point of departure from which the dignity of divine sonship was to be extended to his posterity. He could not give it because it was not his own; he could only lose it. . . . The God-man, on the contrary, is the

principle of the supernatural order in virtue of his personal and natural dignity.''[19] Christ has grace essentially as his own, through him it belongs to the race. He can give it, cannot lose it for himself or for others.

Such are perspectives opened by Scheeben. Others will be seen: the question of Christ's awareness of his continuity with Adam, the kind of priesthood Adam possessed, the meaning of his lordship over creation in comparison with the kingship of Christ (qv), how he received divine revelation—to mention some. We may not entirely overlook the dramatic manner in which Adam's encounter with Christ or his Blessed Mother is portrayed by poets and homilists. Romanos the Singer (c. 490-c. 556) pictures the meeting in the underworld thus: ''Adam says to Mary: 'See me at your feet, Virgin Mother without stain, and in my person the whole race is attached to your steps. Eve—Hope of my soul, listen to me, Eve also, drive shame far from her who gave birth in pain, for you see that miserable as I am, Adam's laments still crush my heart.' ''[20]

An ancient homilist thus expresses his idea: ''He goes to free the prisoner Adam and his fellow-prisoner Eve from their pains, he who is God and Adam's son. The Lord goes into them holding his victorious weapon, his cross. When Adam, the first created man, sees him, he strikes his breast in terror and calls out to all: 'My Lord be with you all.' And Christ in reply says to Adam: 'And with your spirit.' And grasping his hand he raises him up, saying: 'Awake, O sleeper, and arise from the dead, and Christ shall be your light. I am your God, who for your sake became your son, who for you and your descendants now speak and command with authority those in prison: Come forth; and those in darkness: Have light; and those who sleep: Rise.''[21]

[1]With commentaries on the Pauline passages cf. esp. A. Vitti, Christus-Adam, BB 7 (1926), 384–401; F. Prat, S. J., The Theology of St. Paul, London, 1927, and later ed., I, 438–42, II, 171–79; M. J. Scheeben, The Mysteries of Christianity, English tr. C. Vollert, S. J., London, 1951; M. Black, ''The Pauline Doctrine of the Second Adam,'' SJT 7 (1954) 170–79; M. J. Nicolas, ''La théologie du Christ Nouvel Adam dans St. Thomas d'Aquin,'' Etudes Mariales, Bulletin de la Société Française d'Etudes Mariales, 13 (1955), 1–13; A. Gelin, ''La doctrine paulinienne du Nouvel Adam,'' ibid., 15–23; H. Rondet, S. J., ''Le Christ Nouvel Adam dans la théologie de St. Augustine,'' ibid., 25–41; J. Jervell, Imago Dei: Gen 1:26f. im Spätjudentum, in der Gnosis und in den paulinischen Briefen, Göttingen, 1960; E. Brandenburger, Adam und Christus: exegetisch-religionsgeschtliche Untersuchung zu Rom 5:12-21, 1 Kor 15, Neukirchen, 1962; C. K. Barrett, From First Adam to Last, A. and C. Black, 1962; R. Scroggs, The Last Adam, A Study in Pauline Anthropology, Blackwell, 1966; H. Müller, ''Der rabbinische Qal-Wachomer-Schluss in paulinischer Typologie zur Adam-Christus Typologie in Rom V,'' ZNW 58 (1967), 73–92; C. E. B. Cranfield, ''Some of the Problems in the Interpretation

of Romans 5:12," *SJT,* 22 (1969) 324–41; H. Haag, *Is Original Sin in Scripture?* New York, 1969, 95–108; G. Barth, "Erwägungen zu 1 Kor 15:20-28," *EvT,* 30 (1970) 515–27; J. (Cardinal) Daniélou, S. J., *From Shadows to Reality,* London, 1960, ch. I; A. J. M. Wedderburn, "The Theological Structure of Romans V," 12, *NTS* 19 (1972–73) 339–54; P. Grelot, *Péché originel et rédemption,* Paris, 1973; M. E. Thrall, "Christ Crucified or Second Adam," *CSNT* (1973) 143–56; J. D. G. Dunn, (qv) "1 Corinthians 15:45—Last Adam, Life-giving Spirit," *CSNT* 127–41; *id., Christology in the Making,* 2nd ed., 1989, 98–128; G. R. Castellano, "Il peccato di Adamo," *BeO* 16 (1974) 45–62; A. Vanneste, "Où en est le problème du péché originel?" *ETL* 52 (1976) 143–67; U. Wickens, "Christus der 'letzte Adam' und der Menschensohn," *JMAV* (1975) 387–403; J. Murphy-O'Connor, O.P., "Christological Anthropology in Phil 2:6-11," *RB* 83 (1976) 25-50; D. M. Stanley, "Paul's Interest in the Early Chapters of Genesis, in *Studiorum Paulinorum Congressus Internationalis Catholicus,* Analecta Biblica 17, Rome, 1963, 241–52; J. Lambrecht, "Paul's Christological use of Scripture in 1 Cor 15:20-28," *NTS* 28 (1982) 302–27; J. Muddiman, "Adam, the Type of the One to Come," *Theology* 87 (1984) 101–10; C. C. Caragounis, "Romans 5:15-16 in the Context of 5:12-21: Contrast or Comparsions," *NTS* 21 (1985) 142–48; article "Eve" in M. O'Carroll, *Theotokos,* Wilmington, 1983, 139–41; [2]L. Cerfaux, *op.cit.,* 231f; J. Fitzmyer, S. J., *NJBC,* 845–47; [3] L. Cerfaux, *ibid.,* 231; [4]*Op. cit.,* 239ff; [5]*Op. cit.,* 113; [6]*Adv. Haer.,* V. 14, *PG* 7, 1161AB; [7]*Op. cit.,* 40, St. Irenaeus, III, 18, 6, *PG* 7, 938B; [8]*Adv. Haer.* III, 21, 955B; [9]*DS* 1512; cf. 223, 372, 1514, 1521; [10]*DS* 3900; Apostolic Constitution, *Munificentissimus Deus,* on the dogma of the Assumption, 1 November 1950, repr. *Papal Teachings, Our Lady,* Boston, 317; [11]Encyclical, *Ad Caeli Reginam* on the Queenship of Mary, October 11, for November, 1954, *Papal Teachings,* 393, 94; [12]Encyclical, June 29, 1943, *DS* 3815; *Papal Teachings,* 253; [13]*Opus imperfectum* I, 49, 1651; III, 38, 1265; VI, 22, 1553, 24, 1557; [14]Reference in text to Tertullian, *De carnis resurrectione,* 6 *PL* 2, 282; *CSEL* 47, p. 33, 1. 12–13; [15]Church in the Modern World, 22, A. Flannery, ed., I, 922; [16]*Op. cit.,* 323f; [17]*Op. cit.,* 325; [18]*Op.cit.,* 329; [19]*Op. cit.,* 386; [20]Hymns of Romanos, *Mary at the Cross,* 110, 98; [21]Reading for Holy Saturday, *The Divine Office,* II, 1974, 321.

AGONY OF JESUS, THE

"Then Jesus went with them to a place called Gethsemane, and he said to his disciples,[1] 'Sit here, while I go yonder and pray.' And taking with him Peter and the two sons of Zebedee, he began to be sorrowful and troubled. Then he said to them, 'My soul is very sorrowful, even to death; remain here and watch with me.' And going a little farther he fell on his face and prayed, 'My Father, if it be possible, let this cup pass from me; nevertheless, not as I will, but as thou wilt.' And he came to the disciples and found them sleeping; and he said to Peter, 'So, you could not watch one hour with me? Watch and pray that you may not enter into temptation; the spirit indeed is willing, but the flesh is weak.' Again, for the second time he went away and prayed, 'My Father, if this cannot pass unless I drink it, thy will be done.' And again he came and found them sleeping, for their eyes were heavy. So, leaving them again, he went away and prayed for the third time, saying the same words. Then he came to the disciples and said to them, 'Are you still sleeping and taking your rest? Behold, the hour is at hand, and the Son of Man is betrayed into the hands of sinners. Rise, let us be going; see, my betrayer is at hand' " (Mt 26:36-46).

"And they came to a place which was called Gethsemane; and he said to his disciples, 'Sit here while I pray.' And he took with him Peter and James and John, and began to be greatly distressed and troubled. And he said to them, 'My soul is very sorrowful, even to death; remain here, and watch.' And going a little farther, he fell on the ground and prayed that, if it were possible, the hour might pass from him. And he said, 'Abba, Father, all things are possible to thee; remove this cup from me; yet not what I will, but what thou wilt.' And he came and found them sleeping, and he said to Peter, 'Simon, are you asleep? Could you not watch one hour? Watch and pray that you may not enter into temptation; the spirit indeed is willing, but the flesh is weak.' And again he went away, and prayed, saying the same words. And again he came and found them sleeping, for their eyes were very heavy; and they did not know what to answer him. And he came the third time, and said to them, 'Are you still sleeping and taking your rest? It is enough; the hour has come; the Son of man is betrayed into the hands of sinners. Rise, let us be going; see, my betrayer is at hand' " (Mk 14:32-42).

"And he came out, and went, as was his custom, to the Mount of Olives; and the disciples followed him. And when he came to the place he said to them, 'Pray that you may not enter into temptation.' And he withdrew from them about a stone's throw, and knelt down and prayed, 'Father, if thou art willing, remove this cup from me; nevertheless, not my will, but thine be done,' and there appeared to him an angel from heaven, strengthening him. And being in an agony he prayed more earnestly; and his sweat became like great drops of blood falling down upon the ground. And when he rose from prayer he came to the disciples and found them sleeping for sorrow, and he said to them, 'Why do you sleep? Rise and pray that you may not enter into temptation' " (Lk 22:39-46).

"Now is my soul troubled. And what shall I say: 'Father, save me from this hour? No, for this purpose I have come to this hour. Father, glorify thy name.' Then a voice came from heaven, 'I have glorified it, and I will glorify it again.' The crowd standing by heard it, and said that it had thundered. Others said, 'An angel has spoken to him.' Jesus answered, 'This voice has come for your sake, not for mine. Now is the judgment of this world, now shall the ruler of this world be cast out; and I when I am lifted up from the earth, will draw all men to myself'" (Jn 12:27-32).

"In the days of his flesh, Jesus offered up prayers and supplications, with loud cries and tears, to him who was able to save him from death, and he was heard for his godly fear" (Heb 5:7).

Reading the synoptic accounts one notes that Lk differs from Mt and Mk as to the place; at the same point Jn says that Jesus "went forth with his disciples across the Kidron valley, where there was a garden, which he and his disciples entered" (18:1). The name Gethsemane means an oil press. Jn has no account of the agony in the Passion record, though he has a similar passage elsewhere in his Gospel. The Johannine passage and that from Heb manifest the Savior in a way that proves increasingly baffling the deeper the analysis goes.

The event in Gethsemane closes the story of the public ministry and is a prelude to the Passion (qv). Certain things are clear: certain themes or motifs have occurred to theologians. We are at a point where the human and divine meet in a manner unique in the whole range of religious history, so that the total content of this moment must be beyond our comprehension.

Jesus had celebrated a meal, the paschal meal if we follow the Synoptics, with his disciples. Is the story of the dramatic episode, of such a very different kind, which followed this meal, historically reliable? R. Bultmann (qv) spoke of its "wholly legendary character"; and M. Goguel thought it an "admirable allegory," which expresses what took place in the soul of Jesus. The general consensus favors historicity, with divergent views possible on some details. Lk omits Jesus' revelation of his state of soul to the disciples, as he does the description of his mental agony which precedes it, which raises the crucial problem. Mk is variously translated: "il commença à être saisi d'effroi et d'abattement" (Lagrange); RÇV "greatly amazed"; RSV here used; Moffat, "appalled": TOB "Il commença à ressentir frayeur et effroi"; JB "Il commença à ressentir effroi et angorsse"; A. Chouraqui, "Il commença à être étreint, envahi d'effroi, en détresse."

Lk puts the accent, characteristically, on prayer and he adds important details: the appearance of the angel and the sweat of blood. There are textual problems here as the verses giving these elements are absent from important manuscripts. This does not prevent scholars from taking them as authentic.

What suddenly induced the changed attitude in Jesus? From the atmosphere of festivity, though festivity with overtones of seriousness, to the access of sorrow, "even to death." Was it the departure of

Judas from the table to betray him (Mk 14:20; Mt 26:25; Lk 22:22-23; Jn 13:30)? A point mostly passed over is the wound to Jesus caused by the outrageous conduct of Judas. The betrayal has become an abstract stereotype. It was wrought in flesh and blood: a blow to the friendship of the most perfect friend (qv) imaginable; a failure in a vocation of immense significance.

But even if the action of Judas initiated the crisis, it could not cause the profound psychic convulsion which Jesus suffered. The phrase "unto death" has prompted different interpretations, sorrow which kills, acceptable; as another—death is a friend which ends unbearable grief—is not. Much more effort has been expended on the nature of the inner distress which Jesus endured. Here we must surely proceed with great care. We have to bear in mind the individual consciousness of Christ, his knowledge, his sense of destiny, even as we are increasingly reminded latterly in so many aspects of his life and lifework, his Jewishness (qv): he was of the race of Judas Maccabeus, "let us die bravely for our brethren" (1 Macc 9:10).

We may bear this last point in mind when we read what a great Catholic exegete, one who is influential regarding this problem, Fr. M. J. Lagrange, writes: "The subject of Jesus' sadness was his Passion and his death."[2] He dismisses the opinion of St. Ambrose and St. Jerome (qqv) and quotes Knabenbauer against them and against mystics (qv) and ascetics who see no other cause for Jesus' sadness than the sight of men's sins, the futility of his sufferings for a large number: "We should beware," says Knabenbauer, "of forming an idea of the piety and glory of Christ which does not agree with Sacred Scripture."

Some Catholic publicists may see an advantage in depicting Jesus afraid of death. The opinion is characterized by a contemporary exegete, Fr. André Feuillet, as the most superficial of all that have been expressed on this subject, the least in agreement with Sacred Scripture. There are texts to be considered, with attention to three witnesses chosen by Jesus. Peter, James, and John had witnessed the raising of the daughter of Jairus (Mk 5:37; Lk 8:51), the Transfiguration (qv), and a miraculous catch of fish (Lk 5:10) when they heard the words, "You will be fishers of men." To Peter the Lord had spoken these words, "And do not fear those who kill the body but cannot kill the soul; rather fear him who can destroy both soul and body in hell" (Mt 10:28). Having taught Peter thus, would he bring him to see himself frightened of death?

There is another serious objection to the thesis. Shortly before the agony Jesus spoke serenely of his death, ". . . my blood of the covenant, which is poured out for many for the forgiveness of sins," (Mt 26:28); in the long ordeal of torture which was part of death by crucifixion (qv) he did not flinch—his cry, "My God, my God, why has thou forsaken me?" as yet not explained, was a spiritual reaction, better related to his final word, "Father, into thy hands I commit my spirit" (Lk 23:46). Here, too, his total self-control is evident. It is equally so in the Johannine account, where the truly altruistic character of Jesus is manifest. The view that he was expressing his own private fear in the garden takes no account of the altruism which dominated his outlook and behavior. But, and this is the immediate point, it is not reconcilable with his attitude from the Supper to the moment of death. Why, in this moment of prayer should he show fear which is so notably absent where it would be expected?

Here we rejoin A. Feuillet's interpretation. The episode must be seen in a messianic context. Jesus did not cease to be the Messiah in the very moment when his full messianic vocation was to attain fulfillment. Feuillet speaks of the "incontrovertible truth which has been too often forgotten: he who suffers in the garden of the agony is not an ordinary man, nor merely the greatest of men, but the 'Son of Man,' the 'Servant' who bears the weight of the sins of the world."[3] Jesus was true in this moment to his word: "I have a baptism to be baptized with; and how am I constrained until it is accomplished!" (Lk 12:50). "Are you able to drink the cup that I am to drink?" (Mt 20:22). These last words were spoken to James and John who were now present in the garden. They had been followed by the assurance, "You will drink my cup."

The lifework of Jesus Christ was based essentially on his solidarity with mankind. Could he possibly be thought to disengage himself from this solidarity as the supreme crisis approached? What meaning then would his act of submission have, "Thy will be done"? Therein was also expressed his solidarity with men. He had given them this principle as the norm of their conduct in the prayer, "Thy will be done on earth, as it is in heaven." He had taken into the closest relationship with him those obedient to his precept: "For whosoever does the will of my Father in heaven is my brother, and sister, and mother" (Mt 12:50).

A facile case can be made for the fear of death theory. He had to suffer to redeem us, and as he saw this suffering, massive in view of his sensibility, approach, his sensitive nature could recoil. Or he shrank from death, with intensity incalculable, because death was, to one all perfect, an unthinkable evil. He was not made to die and of himself did not have in him the seeds of death, as do we. There is here a plausible idea, but by no means the real explanation. It is not irrelevant to recall that in the death of Jesus and the resurrection which followed it, countless Christians through the ages have found sublime fortitude; like St. Felicity, as she gave birth to a child on the eve of her martyrdom and cried out in the birth-pangs, but could say: "Tonight, it is Felicity who suffers; tomorrow another will suffer in Felicity, for Felicity wishes to suffer for him." Or St. Thomas More, who joked with the executioner. It is a constant in history that those totally possessed of a cause face death with equanimity, if death is seen to serve the cause. Who could equal the dedication of Jesus Christ, his whole being concentrated on the achievement of our salvation? Here truly Judas Maccabeus was his prototype. Fear was utterly dissolved in love for us. Honor was integral, with the mother directly involved.

His prayer (qv) of petition combined with resignation has been pronounced the most perfect ever framed by human lips. Its perfection lies in its plenary expression of his character as the Messiah, the suffering Servant: "Then I said, 'Lo, I come; in the roll of the book it is written of me; I delight to do thy will, O my God; thy law is within my heart'" (Ps 40:7, 8; cp. Heb 10:5-7). It fulfilled the noblest aspiration of the Ancient Covenant and it ushered in the new. Nothing less was at issue than the entire plan of salvation willed by God the Father, and only to be achieved by the free will of his eternal Son made man. We come back to the mystery of the God-man.

---

[1]Cf. NT commentaries, e.g., Anchor Bible, *Matthew*, W. F. Albright, and C. S. Mann (1971) 325-27; *Mark*, C. S. Mann (1986) 587-94; *Luke*, J. A. Fitzmyer, S.J., II (1985) 1436-46, bibl., R. E. Brown, "Incidents that Are Units in the Synoptic Gospels but Dispersed in John," *CBQ* 23 (1961); Y. B. L. Tremiel, *L'Agonie de Jésus, Lumen Vitae* 13 (1964) 79-103; R. S. Barbour, "Gethsemane in the Tradition of the Passion," *NTS* 16 (1969–70) 231-51; J. W. Holleran, "The Story of Gethsemane. A. Critical Study," *AGreg* (1973) 191; A. Feuillet, P.S.S., "Le récit lucanien de l'agonie de Gethsémani," *NTS* 22 (1975–76) 397-417; *id.* esp., L'Agonie de Gethsémani, Paris, 1977; P. L. Carle, "L'Agonie de Gethsémani. Exégèse et théologie du P. Feuillet," *Divinitas* 21 (1977) 429-32; D. M. Stanley, *Jesus in Gethsemane,* New York, 1980; esp., M. J. Lagrange, *Evangile selon St. Marc,* Paris, 1947, 386-92; esp., V. Taylor, *The Gospel According to St. Mark,* London, 1959, 551-57; A. Durand, *DTC* I, 615-19; K. T. Schäfer, *LTK* II, 546-47; N. M. Flanagan, *NCE* I, 210-12; J. Neyrey, *The Passion According to Luke: A Redaction Study of Luke's Soteriology,* New York, 1985 = *BB* 61 (1980) 153-71; M. L. Soards, *The Passion According to Luke: The Special Material of Luke 22,* Sheffield, 1987; D. Senior, *The Passion of Jesus in the Gospel of Luke,* Wilmington, 1989, 81-89; [2]*Op. cit.,* 387; [3]*Op. cit.,* 190.

ALBERT THE GREAT, ST., DOCTOR OF THE CHURCH (c. 1200–1280)

In the encyclopedic work of A., vastly engaged in questions of science, the theology of Christ has not a large place.[1] He dealt with the subject in the Commentary on the Sentences, in the *Summa Theologiae*, and in the work recently published, *De incarnatione*. He accepted the doctrine already consecrated by tradition since the early Councils and did not consider making any special contribution. In the exhaustive bibliography compiled for the special commemorative issue of the *Revue Thomiste* in 1931, there is no mention of a work on Christology. An article by B. Lavaud, O.P. on the Gifts of the Holy Spirit in A.'s writings briefly mentions the Gifts in Christ's life.

[1]Works, *Super libros Sententiarum,* ed. Borgnet, 25–30; ed. Cologne, 29–32; *Summa Theologiae,* B. 31–3, C. 34–5; *De incarnatione,* C. 26; cf. P. Mandonnet, O.P., *DTC* I, 666–74; M. Viller, *DSp* I 277–83; J. H. Weishipl, *NCE* I 254–58; *Revue Thomiste*; special number, 1931, 224–468; bibl. M. H. Laurent, O.P., and M. J. Congar, O.P., 424–62.

AMBROSE, ST., DOCTOR OF THE CHURCH (c. 339–397)

Ambrose did not delve very deeply into Christology; he had other concerns.[1] However, his orthodoxy is patent in the great works which deal with doctrinal questions: *De fide ad Gratianum* (5 books) which deals with the divinity of the Son; *De Spiritu Sancto,* indebted to Athanasius, Didymus the Blind, and Basil the Great (qqv); and *De incarnationis dominicae sacramento.* All three works manifest A.'s resolute opposition to Arianism. In dealing with the easterns of his time he may have read too much into terminology not yet fully developed. A. reacted strongly thus to any suspicion of Apollinarianism. He insists on the nature of the complete man. Christ has a body with a perfect soul and spirit, but he is not subject to his human desires. The soul of Christ is of importance in the human and in the theological context; it is united with the Godhead, is the real principle of suffering, of progress, and of our redemption. A. was misquoted in the Middle Ages on the question of Christ's knowledge. He was clear on the real distinction between divine and human knowledge, but Christ is one and the same God and man—*non enim alter ex Patre et alter ex Maria sed qui erat ex patre carnem sumpsit ex virgine.* Duality in Christ is evident in his works, which are divine or human. There is no difference of Person, *non varietate personae.*

[1]Cf. F. H. Dudden, *The Life and Times of St. Ambrose,* 2 vols., Oxford, 1935, 591–605; K. Schwerdt, *Studien zur Lehre des hl. Ambrosius von der Person Christi,* Buckeburg, 1937; W. Seibel, *Fleisch und Geist beim Hl Ambrosius,* Munich, 1958, 152ff; A. Morgan, *Light in the Theology of Saint Ambrose,* Dissert., Gregorian University, (1963); G. Matt, *Fons Vitae,* Dissert., *ibid.,* (1964); *Patrology* IV, 404;   [2]*PL* 16, 873B.

ANNUM SACRUM, May 25, 1900

The encyclical in which Leo XIII gave the reason why he was to consecrate the whole human race to the Sacred Heart of Jesus on June 11, 1899.[1] The Pope without lengthy development uses arguments to show how this consecration is due to Christ endowed with universal power, not unlike those on which Pius XI would draw to demonstrate the universal kingship (qv) of Christ. He is the Son of God and has an acquired right to such authority. Leo states that already twenty-five years previously request had been made to Pius IX for the consecration, by bishops as well as private individuals. He is content to speak of the Heart of Jesus as "the symbol and image of his infinite love." He hopes for benefits to follow the act, which, as he intends, will be repeated everywhere on the same day, after special prayers for three days. Even those outside the Church will, he trusts, profit by the act of consecration. He thinks especially, recalling one of the great themes of his pontificate, of the blessings to come to civil governments, to States. A "wall has been erected between Church and State" in places—"the most solid foundations of public order are shaken when religion is despised." Leo sent the formula which he wished to serve for the act of consecration to all the bishops.

It is well known that a Good Shepherd nun, Sister Droesch-Vichering, sent from Portugal to the Pope a message saying that the consecration was desired by the Lord himself.

[1]Text. *Acta Leonis,* 19 (1900) 70–78; *Lettres Apostoliques, Encicliques, Brefs, de Léon XIII,* with French Tr., VI, Paris, 24–35.

ANSELM, ST., DOCTOR OF THE CHURCH (1033–1109)

A forerunner of the great Scholastic Doctors, A. set a landmark in the theology of the Redemption by his work *Cur Deus Homo?*[1] He eliminated an idea that had come down from early patristic speculation, that the devil had a right over sinful man. "God owes the devil only punishment, man owes him only conflict. All that had been demanded of man he owed to God, not to the devil."[2] A. accepted the truth of our solidarity with Adam (qv) and the consequent transmission of Original Sin. He knew of the Latin tradition which emphasized Christ's sacrifice offered for sins. But he did not integrate his ideas of the redemption with the doctrine of the Mystical Body of Christ, which he could have learned from St. Augustine (qv). Nor does he give any lengthy consideration to divine grace by which we are identified with Christ.

The theory elaborated by A. led him to assume a certain necessity in the Incarnation, a necessity which followed from God's initial, immutable plan for men, one issuing from divine love. This was contrary to Augustine's teaching, which preserved the idea of God's total independence in his gifts: "In God," says A., "there is not the least possibility of any disagreement, and the weakest reason, if it is not overcome by any greater one, is accompanied by necessity."[3] "It is necessary that the goodness of God complete what it begins in man, although every good that God does is a grace on his part."[4] A. deems it inconceivable that the whole human race should fail to reach its assigned goal, the eternal vision of God. But sin impedes this: sin inherited or committed.

In sinning, man refuses to submit to the will of God and denies to God the glory which is his due, incurring thereby a debt in regard to divine justice. The way of redress is either by punishment or satisfaction. "It is impossible for God to lose honor. Either the sinner spontaneously renders what he owes (this is satisfaction), or God takes it from the sinner against the latter's will (this is punishment)."[5] Since A. thinks that it is impossible for a sinner to justify a sinner, and since the evil of man's sin is so great, only a God-man could offer the required satisfaction. "You do not make satisfaction unless you render something superior to that for which you should not have committed sin."[6] By a completely free acceptance of the cross Jesus made satisfaction which, because he was God, had infinite value. A. did not think that Christ merited for himself, forgetting that he merited his glory, so the merit accrues to us, in terms of pardon.

There has been considerable research into the prehistory of the word "satisfaction." It was in existence for some time, is found in Tertullian (qv) but never with the same application. A. may have been influenced by German feudal law. He does hold a truth stated by St. Paul: "For as by one man's disobedience many were made sinners, so by one man's obedience many will be made righteous" (Rom 5:19). This is not to say that the whole meaning of the Redemption is thus explained (see article Redeemer, Christ the).

A. cleared the ground and stated the problem. He presented the Redemption, however, as motivating the Incarnation as a demand for the rights of God, whereas it was initiated by God as a manifestation of his love and mercy. For Scotists it was decreed independently of the first sin, and mankind's need for forgiveness (see article Primacy of Christ).[1]

[1]*Cur Deus Homo?* Works, *PL* 158, critical ed. F. S. Schmitt, Edinburgh, (1946) Vol. II, references by section numbers; cf. J. Hopkins, *A Companion to the Study of St. Anselm,* Minneapolis, (1972); J. Rivière, *The Doctrine of the Atonement, A Historical Essay,* St. Louis, (1909) I, 124–25; *id.,* "Sur les premières applications du terme 'satisfactio' à l'oeuvre du Christ," *Bulletin de Littérature Ecclésiastique* (Toulouse) 25 (1924) 285–97, 353–69; *id., Le dogme de la Rédemption au début du moyen-âge,* Paris, (1934) 293–302; *id.,* "Le mérite du Christ d'après le magistère ordinaire de l'Eglise," *RevSR,* 21 (1947) 56–7, 22 (1948) 225–26; A. M. Jacquin, "Les 'Rationes Necessariae' de saint Anselm," in *Mélanges Mandonnet,* Paris, 1930, II, 66–78; J. B. Reeves, in *The Atonement,* ed. C. Lattey, S.J., Cambridge, 1928, 149–52; esp., J. McIntyre (Protestant), *St. Anselm and His Critics, A Reinterpretation of the 'Cur Deus homo,'* Edinburgh, (1954); L. Richard, *The Mystery of the Redemption,* Baltimore-Dublin, (1965) 175–83; [2]2, 20; [3]1, 10; [4]2, 5; [5]1, 14; [6]1, 21.

APOLLINARIANISM

Taking its origin in Apollinarius (c. 310-c. 390), son of a grammarian of Beirut of the same name, author of many theological works now lost, and of others circulating for some time under other names, the heresy denied the complete manhood of Jesus Christ.[1] He opposed the Arians (qv), and known as a close friend of St. Athanasius (qv), was appointed Bishop of Laodicea c. 360. Ideas similar to those he was to expound were condemned at the Council of Alexandria, 362; but he apparently justified himself later. The great historian of patristic Christology, A. Grillmeier, S.J., thinks that the historical origins of Apollinarianism have not been fully investigated. Apollinarius was zealous to establish fully the Godhead of Jesus Christ and, at the same time, to show the unity of divinity and manhood in Christ.

Though eventually involved in the first Christological heresy, a new departure after the Trinitarian debates, A. was handicapped by lack of precise terminology and, despite his heretical character, stimulated or provoked a discussion which would clear the air for the definitive formulation of Chalcedon (qv). He tried to work with the Platonic division of body, sensitive soul and rationality. What had preceded him in application of these terms, *sarx, psyche sarkike, psyche logike* remains obscure. He appears as a committed *Logos-sarx* Christologist, insisting on a literal interpretation of Jn 1:14, "The Word became flesh." To affirm fullness of manhood in Christ would, he thought, compromise the unity of divinity and humanity in him; there must, he argued, be some lessening of manhood. He saw the solution in making the *Logos* replace the spirit of man, or the rational soul (*nous*), so that the Word of God did not assume a complete human nature, but only a body and what is needed to give it life, a sensitive soul. "Another concept which is to be as important in the future, *ousia,* should be regarded as equivalent or approximate to the *physis* concept. This, too, is incorporated into the truly Apollinarian interpretation of the substantial unity in Christ. The body and the flesh are joined to the *Logos* by being made his *organon,* into which the *energeia* of the *Logos,* its sole and exclusive source, flows, in order to excite *kinesis* there. It is a question not only of the energy of the will and purely spiritual impulses, but also of all the life-energy. One should not therefore simply equate 'unity of *energeia*' with 'unity of person.' In all this, the one *ousia,* the one substantial and functional unity in Christ, is formed. So Apollinarius explains the connection between the terms in his *Logos Syllogistikos* against Diodore (qv). The God-man, then, is one *physis,* one *ousia,* because one life-giving power, which completely permeates the flesh, goes out from the *Logos* and unites the two in a living and functional unity, in a *kath enoteta zotikenenothen.* The *Logos-sarx* Christology is carried through to its last principles."[2]

The same author summarizes thus "the basic thought" of the Christology of Apollinarius: "Man is a hypostasis by virtue of his *nous,* which is the principle of life. His animal soul (*psyche*) and his body have their hypostasis in and through this *nous.* If then the Word as divine *nous* and divine *pneuma* has taken a human *nous,* there are two hypostases in Christ, which is impossible. If, on the other hand, he took only an animal body and soul, then they are necessarily hypostatized in him and Christ is only a single hypostasis."[3] Words were used here which would be refined and given precision later, especially *hypostasis.*

A. was also fearful that to concede a full human nature to Christ would possibly imply that he was not free from sin, for sin, A. thought, resided in the will which was part of the spirit.

The condemnation at Alexandria had been in virtue of the theological axiom sacred in the East that "that which is not assumed (by the divine Word) is not healed." The redemption would not then benefit human souls if the divine Logos had not assumed a soul. Apollinarius was not named. Later a disciple, Vitalis, after the Meletian schism, founded an Apollinarian party at Antioch, 375. Damasus I was at first misled but on better information, in a Rome Synod in 377, warned Vitalis to repudiate Apollinarianism; the Pope also urged the deposition of Apollinarius and the bishops heretical with him. A. replied to all criticism with a statement of his views in the *Demonstration of the Divine Incarnation,* 376. He further defied the Pope by consecrating Vitalis bishop in Antioch and promoting another follower, Timotheus, to the episcopate. Synods at Alexandria in 378, Antioch in 379, and the Council of Constantinople in 381 confirmed the Roman condemnation. Imperial decrees from Theodosius I outlawed the Apollinarians, exiled important representatives. The heresy continued nonetheless, but did not last much longer than A.

---

[1]Cf. G. Voisin, *L'Apollinarisme,* Louvain, 1901; H. Lietzmann, *Apollinaris von Laodicea und seine Schule,* Tübingen, 1904; C. E. Raven, *Apollinarianism,* Cambridge, 1923; M. Richard, "L'Introduction du mot 'hypostase' dans la théologie de l'Incarnation," *Melánges de Science Religieuse,* 2 (1945) 5–32, 243–70; H. de Riedmatten, "Some Neglected Aspects of Apollinarist Christology," *Dominican Studies,* 1 (1948) 239–60; *id.,* "La correspondance entre Basile de Césarée et Apollinaire de Laodicée," *JTS NS* 6 (1955) 199–210, 7 (1956) 53–70; *id., La Christologie d'Apollinaire de Laodicée, Studia patristica* II (TU 64) Berlin, (1957); E. Muhlenberg, *Apollinaris von Laodicéa,* (Forschungen zur Kirchen—und *Dogmengeschichte,* 23), (1969); esp. Grillmeier, 329–47; R. Aigrain, *DHGE,* III, 962–82; *Chalkedon,* I, 102–12, 203–12; Quasten, III, 377–83; F. Chiovaro, *NCE,* I, 665–67; F. M. Young, *From Nicaea to Chalcedon,* London, 1983, 182–99; [2]Grillmeier (1964) 228;   [3]*Ibid.,* 232.

ARCHAEOLOGY AND JESUS CHRIST

A theologian's interest in the immense labors expended for some time on the archaeology of Christian origins is related to the Jesus of history controversy and transcends it.[1] There are controversies about Jerusalem sites, with some certainties, little or no disagreement about Bethlehem and Nazareth, interesting views about other localities mentioned in the NT, Cana and Capernaum notably. The research and judgment belong to scholars and work continues, as the publications of the American Schools of Oriental Research, the British School of Archaeology, and the Ecole Biblique et Archéologique Française de Jérusalem abundantly show. J. H. Charlesworth adds significantly: "The role played by Israeli archaeologists is now becoming of great importance in Jesus research." The same author continues: "The archaeological discoveries are not known outside sophisticated circles; yet, few areas of research prick the imagination and stir the excitement of scholars and students so much as new archaeological discoveries. In the past three decades, spectacular discoveries are proving significant for research on the historical Jesus."[2]

This author relates all the recent, exciting finds to the Jesus of history research. This archaeological interest and its results have a wider significance. All things were made through the Word, and the Word made flesh enters into his material creation adding to it a mysterious new dimension, imprinting the sacred seal of his divine Person on that which is subject to decay, conferring on that so touched a fresh capacity to awaken mental curiosity, religious awe.

[1]G. Cornfeld, *The Historical Jesus. A Scholarly View of the Man and His Work*, London, 1982; J. Murphy-O'Connor, O.P., *The Holy Land: An Archaeological Guide from Earliest Times to 1700*, Oxford, 1986; J. Jeremias, *Jerusalem in the Time of Jesus*, London, 1969; N. Avigad, *Discovering Jerusalem*, Nashville, 1983; esp., J. H. Charlesworth, *Jesus within Judaism*, London, 1988, 103–30; [2]*Ibid.*

ARIUS (d. 336)

One of the principal heresiarchs of all Church history, A. is not well known; his extant writings are slight.[1] Much research has in recent times gone into his career, his writings, and his place in the tumultuous doctrinal history of his time (see articles Athanasius; Nicaea, Council of). A. was probably born in Libya; he appears first in the exegetical school founded by St. Lucian of Antioch (qv), then became head of the exegetical school at Alexandria, the city which was still the intellectual capital of the Roman world. The Bishop of Alexandria, St. Peter (d. 312), excommunicated him for membership in the Melitian sect. Restored to communion with the Church, he was ordained a priest by Peter's successor, Achillas. Eloquent and ascetic, he exerted considerable influence. But he clashed with his bishop on a fundamental point of the Christian faith, the relationship between God the Father and the Logos, that is Jesus Christ. The divergence came into the open in the years 319–323; A. was condemned by a synod at Alexandria in 320, and again excommunicated. He continued to spread his teaching and won the support of a number of bishops.

The Church was entering the Constantinian era, with Church and State closely enmeshed. Constantine himself was to set the style. Sole ruler of the empire after 324, he wished to settle the dispute in Alexandria, to which end he sent his principal ecclesiastical advisor, Hosius (Ossius) of Cordova, to the city to effect a reconciliation between priest and bishop. When the attempt failed, the emperor, probably on the advice of Hosius, decided to call a General Council of the Church to deal with the theological question. The Council, held at Nicaea in 325, repeated the condemnation of A. which had been made by bishops meeting under Hosius at Antioch. He was banished to Illyricum. But he was gradually brought back to acceptable status, to the point where a Council held at Jerusalem in 336 decided to reinstate him formally; his death intervened to impede the ceremony fixed by the emperor.

The essence of his heresy was in a Trinitarian context. What affected his Christology was the opinion that in Christ the Logos took the place of the human soul; but this was less stressed. The Trinitarian controversy was settled at Nicaea (qv).

[1]*Trinitas*, 23–28, bibl., E. Boularand, *L'hérésie d'Arius et la foi de Nicée*, Paris, 1972; R. P. C. Hanson, *The Search for the Christian God*, Edinburgh, 1989; Grillmeier, 219–48; F. M. Young, *From Nicaea to Chalcedon*, London, 1983, 58–64; M. O'Carroll, *Trinitas*, 23–28.

ASCENSION, THE

A good deal of recent writing is influenced by the remarkable study of the Ascension by Fr. Pierre Benoit, O.P., the great French biblical scholar.[1] To deal adequately with different theories proposed about the mystery, this author divides the documents to be considered as follows: (A) those which do not explicitly mention the Ascension; (B) those which mention it, but as a purely theological fact; and (C) those which speak of it as a historical fact, give it a position in time, and sometimes even describe it.

(A) Omission of the fact of the Ascension is most striking in the Pauline epistles; the two references (Eph 4:8; 1 Tim 3:16) are theological in content. The author of Eph and 1 Tim, otherwise, is abundantly explicit on Christ's exaltation to God's right hand, where he enjoys a celestial, even a supercelestial glory, ruler of a kingdom. The apostle does not tell us how or when Christ reached this heavenly abode. A somewhat similar result is obtained from examination of the *Catholic epistles*; again the one reference, 1 Pet 3:22, is theological. The book of Rev gives concrete detail about the ascension of the two prophets in 11:12. But, though Christ's triumphant position in heaven is fully affirmed (1:13ff; 3:12; 3:21; 5:6ff; 7:17; 14:14; 21:22f), we are not told how he made entry to this glorious kingdom. Mt and Mk make no contribution, for Mk 16:19, which states the Ascension, is found in a conclusion added to the gospel after it was finished, and though inspired and canonical, this "cannot, on the plane of historical evidence, confer on it the status of an independent witness."[2]

Acts, apart from 1:2 and 1:9-11, emphasizes Christ's presence in heaven, or refers to the Ascension in theological terms (2:33f; 5:30ff).

Fr. Benoit notes the same silence on the Ascension as a physical event, visibly manifest, in the writings of the Apostolic Fathers: it is not mentioned by Clement of Rome, the Didache, St. Ignatius of Antioch, St. Polycarp or Hermas.

(B) Texts which mention the Ascension in terms of theology. Rom 10:6 does not refer specifically to the Ascension. In Eph, 4:10 clearly does, but to balance Christ's descent to earth, under the earth, to hell with his reascending above all the heavens. The context is more cosmic than limited to an ascent of Jesus from the Mount of Olives.

1 Tim 3:16 is a fragment of a liturgical hymn: "He was manifested in the flesh, vindicated in the Spirit, seen by angels, preached among the nations, believed on in the world, taken up in glory." The different expressions interpret Christ's life theologically. It terminates in his ascent to God in the glory of his Resurrection. The time and manner of this final moment are not stated.

The Epistle to the Hebrews celebrates throughout as a clear assumption Christ's ascent from his state of obedient sufferer to the glorious state of High Priest. Christ is seated at the right hand of God above all creatures, even angels (1:3, 13; 2:7-9; 8:1; 10:12; 12:2). To reach his heavenly throne he passed through the heavens as the High Priest passed through the Holy Place in order to enter the Holy of Holies (4:14; 6:19f; 9:24). The context is again cosmic. The heavenly triumph of Christ is confirmed by the physical reality, but the emphasis is theological; this is not the description of a historical scene. The very nature of the ascent to the right hand of the Father is outside the world of sense perception exercised by the apostles in the scene on the Mount of Olives. 1 Pet 3:22 calls for the same comment: "Jesus Christ who has gone into heaven and is at the right hand of God with angels, authorities, and powers subject to him."

(C) Texts which show the Ascension as an established historical fact. Two forms are distinguishable: the first is exemplified in Acts 1:9-11: "And when he had said this, as they were looking on, he was lifted up, and a cloud took him out of their sight. And while they were gazing into heaven as he went, behold two men stood by them in white robes, and said, 'Men of Galilee, why do you stand looking into heaven? This Jesus, who was taken up from you into heaven, will come in the same way as you saw him go into heaven.' " This description of the scene is not widely found. Fr. Benoit mentions *The Gospel of Peter, The Ascension of Isaiah,* the *Epistola Apostolorum, The Apocalypse of Peter,* and *Pistis Sophia.*

Differing from these descriptive passages are those which make the Ascension part of history by fixing a date for it. The NT texts here present a problem. The passage quoted from Acts is preceded by a reference to forty days interval between the Resurrection and the Ascension (1:1-3). Luke, author of Acts, on the other hand, in his gospel, narrates a number of happenings, with the general impression that they all took place on the same day, the day the Lord rose from the dead (Lk 24:36-50). Jn agrees if we take the apparition to Mary Magdalene as comprehensive: "Jesus said to her, 'Do not hold me, for I have not yet ascended to the Father; but go to my brethren and say to them, I am ascending to my Father and your Father, to my God and your God.' Mary Mag-

dalene went and said to the disciples, 'I have seen the Lord'; and she told them that he had said these things to her" (Jn 20:17, 18). Fr. Benoit concludes that the "message indisputably announces a glorification which is to take place immediately."[3]

The author of the *Epistle to Barnabas* seems to concur. To show why Christians attach importance to the eighth day, he says that it was on this day that Jesus rose from the dead: "Wherefore we also celebrate with gladness the eighth day in which Jesus also rose from the dead, and was made manifest, and ascended into heaven."[4] This is a clear statement of the fact that Jesus ascended on the Sunday of the Resurrection (qv). The *Gospel of Peter* expresses the same truth in this manner: "Wherefore are you come?" says the angel to the women at the tomb. "Whom seek you? Not him that was crucified. He is risen and gone. But if you believe not, stoop this way and see the place where he lay for he is not here. For he is risen and is gone thither whence he was sent."[5] It is put more succinctly in a Christian interpolation in the *Testament of the Twelve Patriarchs*: "And he shall ascend from Hades and shall pass from earth to heaven. I understand how humble he will be on earth and how splendid in heaven."[6]

With the passage of time we find the possibility seen by some writers of holding two views, an immediate glorification on the day of the Resurrection and a delay, of the order fixed by Acts (1:3, 9-10) and only by this text, of forty days. This, without too much precision, was an opinion held by the Apologists; it was formulated with more clarity by St. Jerome.

There has been a recall to the sense of the event as the exaltation of Jesus. This meant so much for the NT writers that they sometimes spoke of Christ going to his glory without any reference to the Resurrection. Theologically it must be taken as one with the Resurrection, for Jesus' whereabouts during the forty days traditionally thought of between the Resurrection and the Ascension is not indicated. Our belief has been influenced wrongly by the fact that the feast is celebrated forty days after Easter. Fr. Benoit has shown that the Christophanies up to the fortieth day—even if this figure be a rounded one in the biblical manner—and then the final visible Ascension are understandable along with the immediate exaltation which we must associate with the Resurrection. There was a visible and an invisible Ascension and he comments thus: "It is clear that the invisible and transcendent entrance of the risen Christ into the divine world is the essential part of the mystery, the part which is of sovereign importance for the faith. His visible departure from the earth is only a secondary aspect, which was not even necessary in itself. It was possible for Jesus not to have made the compassionate concession to the eyes of the disciples, by which they saw and made certain of his departure to heaven; the faithful would not have believed in his heavenly exaltation any the less; it had been foretold in the Scriptures, asserted by himself, and finally proved by the miraculous and visible gift of the Spirit.'' The great scholar goes on to use language like ''an indulgent concession to our weakness,'' ''the essential assertion of the heavenly triumph,'' and ''the imperfect and inessential manifestation of it granted to a few witnesses.''[7]

While admitting the author's main thesis, one may have reservations on the way he emphasizes the true meaning of the Ascension, basing his view on the early tradition. It appears almost as an arbitrary appendage, more adapted to the subjective state of the disciples than to the objective chain of events. The latter it was that dictated the visible Ascension. It must be seen in relation not only to the Resurrection but to the forthcoming momentous event of Pentecost. The Lord's words are important: ''And while staying with them he charged them not to depart from Jerusalem, but to wait for the promise of the Father, which he said 'you heard from me, for John baptized with water, but before many days you shall be baptized with the Holy Spirit.' '. . . But you shall receive power when the Holy Spirit has come upon you; and you shall be my witnesses in Jerusalem and in all Judea and Samaria and to the end of the earth. And when he had said this, as they were looking on, he was lifted up, and a cloud took him out of their sight'' (Acts 1:4, 5, 8, 9). Later in the same chapter occurs the story of the Spirit's descent: ''And suddenly a sound came from heaven like the rush of a mighty wind, and it filled all the house where they were sitting. And there appeared to them tongues as of fire, distributed and resting on each one of them. And they were all filled with the Holy Spirit and began to speak in other tongues, as the Spirit gave them utterance'' (Acts 2:2-4). It would then appear that there had to be one moment of encounter between the risen Jesus and the disciples, which would match the forthcoming event of Pentecost.

Fr. J. A. Fitzmyer has given, from the NT and Qumran documents, especially the Temple Scroll, important background information on Pentecost, showing the harmony in the ''first-fruits'' bound up with the feast and the ''first-fruits'' of the Church. In fact, the visible Ascension, narrated by Luke, significantly in Acts, not in the gospel, is in close-knit harmony with the sequence of events, the aftermath of the Spirit's descent. This is notable in Peter's speech, the key phrase being, ''Being therefore exalted at the right hand of God, and having received ırom the Father the promise of the Holy Spirit, he has poured out this which you see and hear.'' Just before this statement of the Ascension in its plenary meaning, Peter had said, ''This Jesus God raised up and of that we all are witnesses'' (Acts 2:32). All three mysteries meet on the same high level, the Resurrection, the Ascension, and Pentecost.

---

[1]In extensive bibliography cf. G. Bertram, ''Die Himmelfahrt Jesu vom Kreuz aus und der Glaube an seine Auferstehung,'' in *Festgabe für Adolf Deissman*, Tübingen, 1927, 187–217; Morton Enslin, ''The Ascension Story,'' *JBL* 47 (1928) 60–73; U. Holzmeister, S.J., ''Der Tag der Himmelfahrt des Herrn,'' *ZKT*, 55 (1931) 44–82; esp. the most complete work, V. LarraNaga, S.J., *L'Ascension dans le Nouveau Testament*, Rome, 1938; W. Michaelis, *Die Erscheinungen des Auferstandenen*, Basel, 1944; A. M. Ramsey, ''What Was the Ascension?'' *SNTS Bulletin* 2 (1951); G. Kretschmar, ''Himmelfahrt, und Pfingsten,'' *Zeitschrift für Kirchengeschichte*, 66 (1954–55) 209–12; J. G. Davies, *He Ascended into Heaven*, London, 1958; P. A. van Stempvoort, ''The Interpretation of the Ascension in Luke and Acts, *NTS* 5 (1958–59) 30–42; P. Miquel, ''Le Mystère de l'Ascension,'' *Questions liturgiques et paroissiales*, 40 (1959) 105–26; E. Schillebeeckx, O.P., ''Ascension and Pentecost,'' *Worship* 35 (1960–61) 336–63; G. Schille, ''Die Himmelfahrt,'' *ZNW* 57 (1966) 183–99; S. G. Wilson, ''The Ascension, a Critique and an Interpretation,'' *ZNW* 59 (1968) 269–81; G. Lohfink, *Die Himmelfahrt Jesu. Untersuchungen zu den Himmelfahrts-und Erhöhungstexten bei Lukas*, (*SANT* 26, Munich) (1971); J. E. A. Alsop, *The Post-Resurrection Appearance Stories of the Gospel Tradition*, (Calwer Theologische Monographien 5), Stuttgart, (1975); esp. P. Benoit, O.P., ''The Ascension,'' in *Jesus and the Gospel*, London, (1973) 209–53; id., *DBS*, 24–27; esp. J. Fitzmyer, S.J., *The Ascension of Christ and Pentecost*, ThS 45 (1984) 209–39, bibl.; [2]P. Benoit, *op. cit.*, 213; [3]*Op. cit.*, 218; [4]*Epistle to Barnabas* XV, 9; cf. P. Benoit, *op. cit.*, 218, n. 3; [5]P. Benoit, *op. cit.*, 219, n. 1; [6]Benjamin IX, 5; [7]*Op. cit.*, 244f.

ATHANASIUS, ST., DOCTOR OF THE CHURCH (c. 295-373)

Born in Alexandria, A. benefitted from the excellent classical and biblical schooling then available in the city, as he assimilated its distinctive theological traditions.[1] Ordained a deacon in 318 by Bishop Alexander, who chose him as his secretary, he was from the outset totally involved in the anti-Arian struggle. He was present at Nicaea, the close confidant of his bishop, and may have had a hand in the textual drafting. He was named by Alexander to succeed him in office; this he did, despite Arian and Meletian opposition, in 328. Before long he was in the wars. In 331 he was called to the court of Constantine to answer charges laid against him by the Meletians. Then he had to face the campaign mounted by Eusebius of Nicomedia, an Arian sympathizer, who had already worked successfully for the deposition of Eustathius of Antioch and other pro-Nicene bishops. First summoned to the Council of Tyre (335) and seeing that it was packed by bishops opposed to him, A. went to Constantinople to appeal to the emperor. The result, whatever took place in the city, was his first exile: Constantine banished him to Trier in northern Gaul. The power, which this emperor and his successors used freely, of banishing and recalling bishops, was an unfortunate feature of the Church-State relationship then in force, one obviously influenced by Roman custom and institutions.

Indomitable in spirit, A. took the opportunity of his exile to spread monastic ideals in the west. Here we touch a source of his phenomenal spiritual courage, his close links with consecrated souls, and the interaction between their contemplative prayer and his incessant intellectual and administrative activity. This is a chapter which awaits exploration, as it does in the careers of the great Latin Doctors, Ambrose and Augustine (qqv). Testimony to the personal insight of A. to the reality will be found in the *Letter to the Virgins,* as in the *Life of St. Anthony*; the former text was taken over literally by St. Ambrose.

Though A.'s chief impact was in Trinitarian theology, his Christology also calls for attention. It is found in the early works, the *Contra Gentes* and *De Incarnatione,* and in passages through some of the later writings, esp. the *Festal Letters,* the *Discourses Against the Arians* and the *Letter to the Church at Antioch (Tomus ad Antiochenos).* His terminology could not have the precision which would be acquired in the generations after him, on the way to Ephesus and Chalcedon.

A.'s thinking on this subject had a strong tendency towards soteriology: "For the signs which actually took place show that he who was in a body was God, and also the Life and Lord of death. For it became the Christ, when giving life to others, himself not to be detained by death; but this could not have happened, had he, as you suppose, been a mere man. But in truth he is the Son of God, for men are all subject to death. Let no one therefore doubt, but the whole house of Israel know assuredly that this Jesus, whom you saw in shape a man, doing signs and such works, as no one ever yet had done, is himself the Christ and Lord of all. For though made man and called Jesus, as we said before, he received no loss by that human passion, but rather, in being made man, he is manifested as Lord of the living and the dead. For since, as the Apostle said, 'in the wisdom of God the world by wisdom knew not God, it pleased God by the foolishness of preaching to save them that believe' (1 Cor 1:22). And so since we men would not acknowledge God through his Word, nor serve the Word of God, our natural Master, it pleased God to show in man his own lordship, and to draw all men to himself. But to do this by a mere man was not appropriate, lest having man for our Lord, we should become worshippers of man. Therefore the Word himself became flesh, and the Father called his name Jesus, and so 'made' him Lord and Christ, as much as to say, 'He made him to rule and to reign,' that while in the name of Jesus, whom you crucified, every knee should bow, we may acknowledge as Lord and King both the Son and through him the Father.''[2]

Comparable is this passage from the Easter Letter, 342: "The gladness of our feast, my brethren, is always near at hand, and never fails those who wish to celebrate it. For the Word is near, who is all things on our behalf, even our Lord Jesus Christ, who having promised that his habitation with us would be perpetual, in virtue thereof cried out, saying, 'Lo, I am with you all the days of the world.' For as he is the Shepherd, and the High Priest, and the Way and the Door, and everything at once to us, so again, he is shown to us as the Feast, and the holyday, according to the Blessed Apostle, 'Our Passover, Christ, is sacrificed.' He it was who was expected, he caused a light to shine at the prayer of the psalmist, who said, 'My joy, deliver me from those who surround me.' ''[3]

A.'s anthropology emphasized man's corruption and divine incorruption. The Greek doctrine of the divine image is also part of his theological outlook. Hence he can write: "the Word was made flesh in order to offer up this body for all, and that we, partaking of his Spirit, might be deified, a gift which we could not otherwise have gained than by his clothing himself in our created body, for hence we derive our name of 'men of God' and 'men in Christ.' But as we, by receiving the Spirit do not lose our own proper substance, so the Lord, when made man for us, and bearing a body, was not less God; for he was not lessened by the envelopment of the body, but rather deified it and rendered it immortal.''[4]

In the earlier work on the Incarnation A. had elaborated this doctrine in somewhat similar terms: "For the Word, perceiving that in no other way could the corruption of men be undone save by death as a necessary condition, while it was impossible for the Word to suffer death, being immortal and Son of the Father; to this end he takes to himself a body capable of death, that it, by partaking of the Word who is above all, might be worthy to die instead of all, and might, because of the Word which was come to dwell in it, remain incorruptible, and that henceforth corruption might be stayed from all by the grace of the Resurrection. Whence, by offering unto death the body he himself had taken, as an offering and sacrifice free from any stain, straightway he put away death from all his peers by the offering of an equivalent. For being over all, the Word of God naturally by offering his own temple and corporeal instrument for the life of all, satisfied the debt by his death. And thus he, the incorruptible Son of God, being conjoined with all by a like nature, naturally clothed all with incorruption, by the promise of the resurrection.''[5]

A. saw a second reason for the Incarnation—that men should know God: "Nay, why did God make them at all, as he did not wish to be known by them? Whence, lest this should be so, being good, he gives them a share in his own image, our Lord Jesus Christ, and makes them after his own image and after his likeness; so that, by such grace perceiving the image, that is the Word of the Father, they may be able through him to get an idea of the Father, and knowing their maker, live the happy and truly blessed life.''[6]

One passage summarizes his thought brilliantly: "We have, then, now stated in part, as far as it was possible, and as ourselves had been able to understand, the reason of his bodily appearing; that it was in the power of none other to turn the corruptible to incorruption, except the Savior himself that had, at the beginning, also made all things out of nought; and that none other could create anew the likeness of God's image for men, save the image of the Father; and that none other could render the mortal immortal, save our Lord Jesus Christ, who is the very life; and that none other could teach men of the Father, and destroy the worship of idols, save the Word, that orders all things and is alone the true Only-begotten Son of the Father. But since it was necessary also that the debt owing from all should be paid again: for, as I have already said, it was owing that all should die, for which especial cause indeed, he came among us: to this intent, after the proofs of his Godhead from his works, he next offered up his sacrifice also on behalf of all, yielding his temple to death instead of all, in order firstly to make men quit and free of their old trespass, and further to show himself more powerful even than death, displaying his own body incorruptible, as first-fruits of the resurrection of all.''[7]

L. Bouyer thought the following passage the keystone to A.'s whole synthesis: "For man had not been deified if joined to a creature, or unless the Son were very God; nor had man been brought into the Father's presence, unless he had been his natural and true Word who had put on the body. And as we had not been delivered from sin and the curse, unless it had been by nature human flesh which the Word put on (for we should have had nothing in common with what was foreign), so also the man had not been deified unless the Word who became flesh had been by nature from the Father and true and proper to

him. For therefore the union was of this kind, that he might unite what is man by nature to him who is in the nature of the Godhead, and his salvation and deification might be sure.''[8]

A.'s vindication of the *homousios,* which was a gigantic landmark in theological development, belongs to his Trinitarian doctrine. We may note that he saw clearly the possibility of *communicatio idiomatum* (qv), as he also saw the primacy—though not absolute, as Franciscans claim—of Christ: "For as he was ever worshipped as being the Word and existing in the form of God, so being what he ever was though become man and called Jesus, he nonetheless has the whole creation under foot, and bending their knees to him in this name, and confessing that the Word's becoming flesh, and undergoing death in flesh, has not happened against the glory of his Godhead, but to the glory of God the Father. For it is the Father's glory that man, made and then lost, should be found again; and when dead, that he should be made alive, and should become God's temple. For whereas the powers in heaven, both Angels and Archangels, were ever worshipping the Lord, as they are now worshipping him in the name of Jesus, this is our grace and high exaltation, that even when he became man, the Son of God is worshipped, and the heavenly powers will not be astonished at seeing all of us, who are of one body with him, introduced into their realms.''[9]

A tortuous question arises about A.'s doctrine of the soul of Christ. The reader must follow the arguments for and against in A. Grillmeier's authoritative work—he will note that scholarly opinion is sharply divided. A.'s language needs strict interpretation. His central Christological formula—"(The Word) became man, and did not come into a man"—might imply a denial of the soul of Christ, but this is certainly not made explicit, and A. probably had his own deep meaning for the words. In general the argument turns on silence. Specialists argue that in sections of his work where he should have mentioned the soul of Christ, he does not do so. But they must concede that he never says that Jesus Christ did not have a human soul. A. Grillmeier includes him among those who defended the *Logos-sarx* (Word-flesh) Christological framework. The *Tomas ad Antiochenos* constitutes a problem of interpretation, because of textual difficulties. The crucial sentence runs thus: "For they confessed also that the Savior had not a body without a soul, nor without sense or intelligence; for it was not possible, when the Lord had become man for us, that his body should be without intelligence: nor was the salvation effected in this Word himself a salvation of body only, but of soul also.''[10] A. Grillmeier seeks to distinguish A.'s use of the soul in a theological sense and a physical sense. Grillmeier sees difficulties in attributing belief in a soul in Christ: he may have seen, after 362, that recognition of a soul in Christ was in accordance with tradition, but may not have drawn all the conclusions; "his idea of a positive, vital, dynamic influence of the Logos on the flesh of Christ and his interpretation of the death of Christ seem to go beyond a mere silence about the soul of Christ; the debate with the Arians was of such a character that silence over the soul of Christ was tantamount to a denial."[11] One may be tempted to argue that A. distinguished what Christ knew as God from what he knew or did not know as man, but when he makes the contrast it is again the contrast between the divine nature and the flesh: "And concerning the day and the hour he was not willing to say according to his divine nature, 'I know' but after the flesh, 'I know not' for the sake of the flesh which was ignorant as I have said before; lest they should ask him further, and then either he should have to pain the disciples by not speaking, or by speaking might act to the prejudice of them and us all. For whatever he does, that altogether he does for our sakes, since also for us, 'the Word became flesh.' "[12]

---

[1]Bibl., *Trinitas*, 37f; article 31–37; cf. esp. critical ed. *De Incarnatione*, C. Kannengiesser, *SC* 199; *Epp. to Serapion*, J. Lebon, *SC* 15; cf. G. Müller, *Lexicon Athanasianum*, Berlin, 1944–52; X. le Bachelet, *DTC* I, 2: 2143–78; G. Bardy, *DHGE*, IV, 1313–40; J. Quasten III, 20–79; *ClavisG*, II, 12–60; V. C. DeClercq, *NCE* I:996-99; on A.'s Christology, E. Weigl, *Untersuchungen zur Christologie des hl. Athanasius*, Paderborn, 1914; A. Stulcken, *Athanasiana. Literatur und dogmengeschichtliche Untersuchungen*, TU, NF 4, 4, Leipzig, 1899; G. Voisin, "La doctrine christologique de saint Athanase," *RHE* 1 (1900) 226–48; J. Lebon, "Une ancienne opinion sur la condition du corps du Christ dans la mort," *RHE* 23 (1927) 5–43; 209–41; A. Gaudel, "La théologie du Logos chez saint Athanase," *RevSR* 9 (1929) 524–39; 11 (1931) 1–26; L. Bouyer, *L'incarnation et l'Église—Corps du Christ dans la théologie de saint Athanase*, Paris, 1943, 52–58; M. Richard, *Saint Athanase et la psychologie du Christ selon les Ariens*, MSR 4 (1947) 5–54; I. Ortiz de Urbina, S.J., "L'anima umana di Cristo secondo s. Atanasio," *OCP* 20 (1954) 27–43; P. Galtier, "Saint Athanase et l'âme humaine du Christ," *Greg* 36 (1955) 553–89; Grillmeier, 249–73; F. M. Young, *From Nicaea to Chalcedon*, London, 1983, 65–83; Grillmeier, 193–219, 308–328; [2]*Or. Arianos*, II, 16, *LNPF*, IV, 357; [3]*Letter XIV*, 1, *LNPF*, 541f; [4]*De Decretis* 3, *LNPF* IV, 159; [5]*De Incarn.*, 9, *LNPF* 41; [6]*Ibid.*, 11, 42; [7]*Ibid.*, 20, 46f; [8]*C. Arianos*, II, 70, *LNPF* 386; [9]*C. Arianos*, I, 42, 330f; [10]*Tomus ad Antiochenos*, 7, *LNPF* 485; [11]*Op. cit.*, 215; [12]*C. Arianos*, III, 48, 420.

AUGUSTINE, ST., DOCTOR OF THE CHURCH (354–430)

A. died on the eve of the Council of Ephesus (qv), twenty-one years before the Council of Chalcedon (qv).[1] He was grappling not so much with the problems these assemblies would solve, but with questions of terminology and conceptualization closely related to them. His orthodoxy is not open to question. He used the word 'person' but had to think out its meaning as things became clearer to him. He wished to safeguard Christ's transcendence. Nature he thought of as something which is had in common, person as *aliquid singulare atque individuum*—thus he writes in *De Trinitate*. He is clearer, too, with the passage of time and further reflection on the unity of subject in Christ and on the distinction of the natures. From the immense concentration of his study of the Trinity he worked his way to the problems of Christology. The principle of unity of subject, of person, in Christ was not merely the result of a synthesis of two natures. "It is rather the pre-existent person of the Word who is the focal point of this unity and who 'takes up' the human nature 'into the unity of this Person' (*in unitatem personae suae, Unigeniti, Verbi assumere*). In this way Augustine eventually comes to make a definitive improvement in the Latin Christological formula: *Persona una ex duabus substantiis constans; una utraque natura persona.*"[2] A. points to the substantial character of the union of Godhead and manhood by insisting that it cannot be dissolved, by placing Christ above any prophet on whom the Spirit had descended, and by showing the profound difference between God's presence in the world, his presence in 'inspired' saints and his presence in Christ.[3]

In an attempt to expound the mystery of the unity of God and man in Christ, A. used the analogy of the unity of body and soul in man, with some influence on his thinking of Neo-Platonic anthropology. A. develops this analogy in an important document in the Christological dossier, the letter to a pagan Volusian, written at the instance of Marcellinus: "A human person is a mingling (*mixtura*) of soul and body, but the Person of Christ is a mingling (*mixtura*) of God and of man; as the Word of God is mingled with a soul which has a body, it took at the same time a soul and body; (the union of soul and body takes place daily in the procreation of human beings, (what Christ did) was done once for the liberation of men."

The letter generally shows an advancement in A.'s thought. Elsewhere he is faced with a different problem: was the Godhead stained, polluted, by contact with humanity in this intimate union? His solution is that the union was effected through the soul, *mediante anima*.[4]

A.'s thinking is difficult to interpret when he enters the context of the *Totus Christus*, speaking of the mystical marriage between Christ and humanity in the womb of Mary, implying a relationship between

Christ and the Church, making it difficult to differentiate between the historical Christ and the mystical Christ.

A. was firm against the heresies of the time, Docetists and Apollinarianists (qqv), Photinians and Manicheans: "The entire Christ is true man and God, God and man. This is the Catholic faith. Whoever denies that Christ is God is a Photinian. Whoever denies that Christ is man is a Manichean. Whoever confesses that Christ is God equal to the Father and true man . . ."[5] "The Arian who does not believe that he is equal does not believe that he is the Son. If he does not believe that he is the Son, he does not believe that he is the Christ."[6] "Whoever denies that he is like the Father denies that he is Christ"[7]—this against the Eunomians.

Christ for A. was essentially a Redeemer (qv); he was mediator because Redeemer. He thought that there was no other reason why God should have become man but to save men from their sins—though proponents of the absolute primacy of Christ (qv) search, not altogether without success, for some texts which would indicate a relationship between him and the whole universe. From the universality of the Redemption A. argued to the universality of original sin. He expressed his soteriology willingly through the Adam-Christ typology: "Through this Mediator there is reconciled to God the mass of the entire human race which is alienated from him through Adam."[8] "One man and one man; one who leads to death, one who gives life."[9] "Each man is Adam, just as in those who believe each man is Christ."[10] Those unduly influenced by A.'s idea of the *massa damnata* must not overlook the *massa redempta*, the basis of his optimism.

The work of redemption is elaborated by A. into a doctrine of the priesthood (qv) and sacrifice. Christ was anointed priest "when the human nature was united with the Word in the womb of Mary." He willed to be not only priest but sacrifice: "For us, in your sight, priest and sacrifice, and priest inasmuch as sacrifice."[11] A. never speaks of a ransom paid by Christ to the devil: He died "to fulfil the will of a good Father, not to pay a debt to an evil principle."[12]

[1]C. Andresen, *Bibliographia Augustiniana,* Darmstadt, 1962; T. van Bavel, O.E.S.A., *Repertoire bibliographique de S. Augustin,* 1950–1960, The Hague, 1963; O. Scheel, *Die Anschaung Augustins über Christi Person und Werk,* Tübingen, 1901; C. van Crombrugge, "La doctrine christologique et sotériologique de St. Augustin et ses rapports avec le néo-platonisme," *RHE* 5 (1904) 237–57, 477–503; J. Rivière (qv), *Le dogme de la rédemption chez St. Augustin,* Paris, 1933; H. Paissac, *Théologie du Verbe, St. Augustin et St. Thomas,* Paris, 1951; E. Scano, *Il cristocentrismo e i suoi fondamenti dommatici in S. Agostino,* Turin, 1951; T. J. van Bavel, *Recherches sur la christologie de St. Augustin,* Fribourg, 1954; "G. Philips, "L'influence du Christ-Chef sur son Corps mystique suivant St. Augustin," *AugMag* II, 805–15; id., "Le mystère du Christ,' ibid., III, 213–29; J. Lécuyer, C.S.Sp., "Le sacrifice selon St. Augustin," *AugMag* II, 905–14; L. Galati, *Cristo la Via nel pensiero di S. Agostino,* Rome, 1956; A. Piolanti, "Il mistero del 'Cristo totale' in S. Ag," *AugMag* III, 453–69; J. Pintard, *Le sacerdoce selon St. Augustin,* Tours, 1960; F. Arsenault, *Le Christ, plenitude de la révélation selon St. Augustin,* Rome, 1965; O. Brabant, *Le Christ, centre et source de la vie morale chez St. Augustin,* Gembloux, 1971; W. Geerlings, *Christus exemplum. Studien zur Christologie und Christusverkündigung Augustins,* Mainz, 1978; G. Remy, *Le Christ médiateur dans l'oeuvre de Saint Augustin,* Lille-Paris, 1979; B. Studer, "Le Christ notre justice selon St. Augustine," *RAug* 15 (1980) 99–143; Grillmeier, 319–328, 406–13; Patrology IV, A. Trape, 431–62; [2]*In Joh. Ev* tr. 99, 1 *PL* 35, 1886; [3]*Ibid.,* tr 99, 2 *PL* 35, 1886; [4]*De fide et symbolo,* IV, 10, *CSEL* 41, 13; [5]*Sermo* 92, 3, 3 *PL* 38, 573; [6]*Sermo* 183, 4, 5, *PL* 38, 990; [7]*Ibid.* 6, 990; [8]*Sermo* 293, 8; [9]*Sermo* 151, 5; [10]In ps 70, 2, 1; [11]*Confessions* X, 43, 69; [12]Serm. Morin, *MSCA* 1, 662.

B

BAPTISM OF JESUS, THE

"Behold my servant, whom I uphold, my chosen in whom my soul delights: I have put my Spirit upon him, he will bring forth justice to the nations" (Is 42:1; cp. 11:2; 61:1). The messianic mission announced by the prophet was solemnly inaugurated in the setting of the Baptism of Jesus in the Jordan by John the Baptist.[1] Mk's account, the primitive one, shows how the servant (qv) theme merges into that of the sonship: "In those days Jesus came from Nazareth of Galilee and was baptized by John in the Jordan. And when he came out of the water, immediately he saw the heavens opened and the Spirit descending upon him like a dove; and a voice came from heaven, 'Thou art my beloved Son; with thee I am well pleased' " (Mk 1:9-11). This, as A. Feuillet makes clear, is not to be read as artificial embellishment. What we have is the record of a capital moment in the history of humankind, what Pere Lagrange did not hesitate to call the beginning of Christianity. It is not yet fully understood, which should not astonish as the immense change in Jesus' life marks it with deep, manifold meaning.

Before the Baptism Jesus was a village carpenter, unknown to the world outside his village. After it he is launched on a career which will affect the destinies of humankind until it ceases to exist. The heavens were "opened," which was a sign of revelation (Ez 1:1; Is 64:1). Before considering this we have to deal with an objection raised about the possible misunderstanding due to the penitential nature of John's baptism; it was a ritual washing for sinners. Was the early Christian community embarrassed that Jesus should submit to the rite, as the Baptist himself was so embarrassed, though on grounds of Jesus' superiority? Did Jn omit the actual baptism from his account for this reason? While respecting the opinions of biblical scholars, one may suggest that it is hazardous to dogmatize on the mentality of the early Christians. There are interesting variants in the accounts; Mt records the Baptist's protest (3:14); Lk characteristically mentions Jesus' prayer (3:21); Jn, again characteristically, emphasizes that the Spirit "remained" on Jesus (1:32-33) and Jn was prepared for the event by a divine message (1:33). Note that there is not the slightest utterance of any kind by Jesus to suggest that he sought release from sin. His sinlessness was accepted by the first Christians (2 Cor 5:21; Jn 8:46; Heb 4:15; 7:21).

What has not been fully seen in the Baptism story is the importance of the descent of the Spirit on Jesus. Neglect of this mystery is part of the neglect of the Spirit which has been a defect in the Latin Church in recent times. Let us note that this is the only outpouring of the Spirit which is narrated in all four Gospels and in the Acts of the Apostles (Mt 3:16; Mk 1:10; Lk 3:22; Jn 1:32; Acts 10:37-38), a unique collective testimony commanding attention and profound reflection. H. Mühlen, a great theologian of the Holy Spirit, sees in this moment the key to a whole doctrine which he discovered, the presence of the Spirit in Christ and in the faithful, "one Person in many persons," *Una mystica persona*. Whether his theory be accepted or not, we shall not have a satisfactory understanding of the event until we see in it not John the Baptist as central, not Jesus in his humanity as central, but the Holy Spirit, one with the Word incarnate in Jesus, but now and henceforth dominant in his human life, ruling all that he thinks, says, does. This is the thesis of the present work, reached after much research and reflection. Once it is accepted, the problem of a baptism which might too closely associate Jesus with sinners sinks to insignificance. Hence the phrase used earlier "in the setting of the Baptism of Jesus in the Jordan by John." The Baptism was in no way intrinsically linked with the mighty theophany of the Spirit. It was chosen as an acceptable circumstance, nothing more. Such a circumstance was needed to mark the divine intervention which would initiate a chain of events, made up of public temptation (qv), discourses, intimate teaching, instruction, dialogue with enemies, miracles, apostolic prayer (qv), culminating in the final duel with the powers of evil, the Passion, death by torture, burial, resurrection, glorification. It is impossible to grasp the divine thread running through this saving program apart from the vital presence of the Spirit in the life of Jesus. Without such an understanding, Pentecost loses most of its creative meaning.

Seen thus, Christ, the new Adam (qv), is undertaking a new creation; the Logos, through whom all things were made (Jn 1:3) works steadily towards a "new heaven and a new earth" (Rev 21:1). As in the first creation "the Spirit moved over the surface of the waters" (Gen 1:3) so it is the Spirit directing, sustaining, fulfilling the words and deeds of Christ who activates him from the moment at the Jordan to the final glory.

---

[1]Commentaries on NT passages, Mt 3:13-17; Mk 1:9-11; Lk 3:21-22; Jn 1:32-34; Acts 10:37-38; J. Kosnetter, *Die Taufe Jesu,* Vienna, 1936; A. Feuillet, "Le baptême de Jésus d'après l'évangile selon St. Marc," *CBQ* 2 (1939) 468-90; *id.,* "Le symbole de la colombe dans les récits évangéliques du baptême," *RSR* 32 (1958) 524-94; *id.,* "Le baptême de Jésus," *RB* 64 (1971) 321-52; J. Schneider, *Die Taufe in NT,* Berlin, 1952; G. W. H. Lampe, *The Seal of the Spirit,* London, 1951; M. E. Boismard, "La révélation de l'Esprit Saint," *RT* 63 (1955) 5-21; *id., Du baptême à Cana,* Paris, 1956; *id., Les traditions johanniques concernant le baptême, RB* 70 (1963) 5-42; C. E. D. Cranfield, *The Baptism of Our Lord, SJT* 8 (1955) 53-63; J. A. T. Robinson, "The Baptism as a Category of NT Soteriology," *SJT* 6 (1955) 257-74; *id.,* "The Baptism of Jesus and the Qumran Community," *HTR* 50 (1957) 183-87; H. Bouman, "The Baptism of Jesus with Special Reference to the Gift of the Spirit," *Concordia Theol. Monthly* 28 (1957) 1-14; I. Buse, "The Markan Account of the Baptism of Jesus and Is 63," *JTS* (1956) 74-75; I. de la Potterie, S.J., "L'onction du Christ," *NRT* 80 (1958) 225-52; J. Lebreton, S.J., *DBS* IV, 987-90; H. Cazelles, *Catholicisme* I, 1228, 1229; J. Blinzler, Bauer, I, 62-66; A. Michel, *DTC* I, 1184-85; H. Houbaut, *DTC* I, 646-56; J. A. Fitzmyer, *A Christological Catechism: New Testament Answers,* New York, 1982, 39-43; *id., The Gospel According to Luke,* I-IX, Anchor Bible, New York, 1981, 479-87, bibl. 486, 487; *Veni Creator Spiritus,* articles Baptism of Jesus, Mühlen, Heribert; J. Jeremias, *New Testament Theology,* I, London, 1971, 51-55.

BARTH, KARL (1886-1968)

The giant of Calvinist theology, so remarkable in the evolution of his thinking, is of prime interest to all students of the theology of Christ.[1] For he reached the view that only in Jesus Christ is God revealed. He reacted against any idea of natural religion as found in Scholastic theology as he did against a theology rooted in experience; he saw the Word of God as the unique divine communication. How B. elaborates his gigantic synthesis, incorporating in it all that he can discover by analysis of the data of Sacred Scripture, investing classic Christian ideas like creation and covenant with a meaning that he finds acceptable, is one of the great personal achievements of modern theology. The Incarnation of the Son of God affords God the mode of expression of his self-giving, the effect of his eternal choice. There are subtleties in the understanding of God's choice of us, sinful that we are, for fellowship with him. There are still deeper subtleties in the reality whereby, as B. sees it, Jesus Christ is not only what God chooses, he is also God who effectively chooses: " 'Jesus Christ is the electing God.' It is high on the long list of B.'s controversial propositions: between the 'eternal being' of the 'second Person' and the temporal reality of Jesus the Christ there is a 'third' reality, the occurrence of that choice in which the Son is chosen to be, and himself chooses to be, the man Jesus, and in which the Son therefore is the man Jesus. The Incarnation, B. said, to the consternation of all standard Protestants, *happened* in God before all time."[2] The test is, all through, the truthfulness of God's self-revelation in Christ. Jesus presents the face of God, as he is. So equipped, B. seeks to enter more and more into the mystery of God's dealing with mankind, on the pre-existence of Jesus Christ, on God and history, God as history, divine transcendence, how God's triune existence makes history, with at the core of eternal history God in Jesus Christ, the ultimate explanation of all that happens.

---

[1]Cf. R. Jenson, *God after God: The God of the Past and the God of the Future, Seen in the Work of Karl Barth,* Indianapolis, 1969; F. Schmid, *Verkündigung und Dogmatik in der Theologie Karl Barth,* Munich, 1964; H. Urs von Balthasar, *The Theology of Karl Barth,* New York, 1971; S. W. Sykes (ed.), *Karl Barth; Studies of His Theological Method,* Oxford, 1979; D. G. Bloesch, *Jesus is Victor! Karl Barth's Doctrine of Salvation,* Nashville, 1976; D. F. Ford, *Barth and God's Story. Biblical Narrative and Theological Method of Karl Barth in the Church Dogmatics,* New York, 1981; *id.,* Modern Theologians, I, 23-49; K. Runia, "Karl Barth's Christology," in *Christ the Lord. Studies Presented to D. Guthrie,* ed. H. H. Rowdon, Leicester, 1982, 299-310; B. Marshall, "The Identity of the Savior in Rahner and Barth," *Christology in Conflict,* Oxford, 1987, 115-42;   [2]Apud R. W. Jenson, *The Modern Theologians,* I, 39.

BASIL THE GREAT,
ST., DOCTOR OF THE CHURCH (c. 330–379)

The great Cappadocian did not develop an elaborate Christology.[1] He had, like his fellow Cappadocians, Gregory of Nazianzus and Gregory of Nyssa, reaped the fruits of the Council of Nicaea (qv). He was concerned, in an important doctrinal letter to the people of Sozopolis, to combat any lingering Docetism (qv): "But who has the hardihood now once again to renew by the help of sophisticated arguments and, of course, by scriptural evidence, that old dogma (i.e., heresy, for so the word was used) of Valentinus long since silenced? For this impious doctrine of the seeming (i.e., Docetism) is no novelty. It was started long ago by the feeble-minded Valentinus, who, after tearing off a few of the Apostle's statements, constructed for himself this impious fabrication, asserting that the Lord assumed the 'form of a servant' himself, and that he was made in the 'likeness' but that the actual manhood was not assumed by him."[2]

B. wished to clarify the divine and human characteristics in Christ. There was no question of suffering in the Godhead: "As to the statement that human feelings are transmitted to the actual Godhead, it is one made by men who preserve no order in their thoughts, and are ignorant that there is a distinction between the feelings of flesh, of flesh endowed with soul and of soul using a body. It is the property of flesh to undergo division, diminution, dissolution; of flesh endowed with soul to feel weariness, pain, hunger, thirst, and to be overcome by sleep; of soul using body to feel grief, heaviness, anxiety, and such like. Of these, some are natural and necessary to every living creature; others come of evil will, and are superinduced because of life's lacking proper discipline and training for virtue. Hence it is evident that Our Lord assumed the natural affections to establish his real Incarnation, and not by way of semblance of incarnation, and that all the affections derived from evil that besmirch the purity of our life, he rejected as unworthy of his unsullied Godhead. It is on this account that he is said to have been 'made in the likeness of flesh of sin'; not, as these men hold, in likeness of flesh, but flesh of sin. It follows that he took our flesh with its natural affections, but 'did not sin.' Just as the death which is in the flesh, transmitted to us through Adam, was swallowed up by the Godhead, so was the sin taken away by the righteousness which is in Christ Jesus, so that in the resurrection we receive back the flesh neither liable to death nor subject to sin."[3]

B. grapples with the problem of Christ's knowledge (qv) in a letter, 236, to his friend Amphilochius, Bishop of Iconium. He is particularly exercised by the much debated text on "that day and that hour no one knows, not even the angels in heaven, nor the Son, but only the Father" (Mk 13:32; Mt 24:36). He suggests this ingenious explanation: "Now as to the words of Mk, who appears distinctly to exclude the Son from the knowledge, my opinion is this. No man knoweth, neither the angels of God; nor yet the Son would have known unless the Father had known; that is, the cause of the Son's knowing comes from the Father. To a fair hearer there is no violence in this interpretation, because the word 'only' is not added as it is in Mt. Mk's sense, then, is as follows: of that day and of that hour knoweth no man, nor the angels of God; but even the Son would not have known if the Father had not known, for the knowledge he naturally his was given by the Father." B. sums up thus: "This is very decorous and becoming the divine nature to say of the Son, because he has, his knowledge and his being, beheld in all the wisdom and glory which become his Godhead, from him with whom he is consubstantial."[4]

---

[1]Cf. Grillmeier, 278f; Quasten III, 230; B. Otis, "Cappadocian Thought as a Coherent System," *DOP* 12 (1958) 95–124; Grillmeier, 367–68; F. M. Young, *From Nicaea to Chalcedon,* London, 1983, 106–09; [2]*Letter* 261, 2, *LNPF* VIII, 300; [3]*Ibid.,* 3; [4]*Letter* 236, 2, *LNPF* VIII, 277.

BEATITUDES, THE

"Blessed are the poor in spirit for theirs is the kingdom of heaven. Blessed are those who mourn, for they shall be comforted. Blessed are the meek, for they shall inherit the earth. Blessed are those who hunger and thirst for righteousness, for they shall be satisfied. Blessed are the merciful, for they shall obtain mercy. Blessed are the pure in heart, for they shall see God. Blessed are the peacemakers, for they shall be called sons of God. Blessed are those who are persecuted for righteousness' sake, for theirs is the kingdom of heaven. Blessed are you when men revile you and persecute you and utter all kinds of evil against you falsely on my account. Rejoice and be glad, for your reward is great in heaven, for so men persecuted the prophets who were before you" (Mt 5:3-11).

"Blessed are you poor, for yours in the kingdom of God. Blessed are you that hunger now, for you shall be satisfied. Blessed are you that weep now, for you shall laugh. Blessed are you when men hate you, and when they exclude you and revile you, and cast out your name as evil, on account of the Son of Man! Rejoice in that day, and leap for joy, for behold, your reward is great in heaven; for so their fathers did to the prophets" (Lk 6:20-22).

We are not here concerned with the many strictly biblical questions which arise in regard to these passages from Mt and Lk.[1] The reader can see at once certain obvious differences in content, mode of formulation and number of beatitudes. Mt has eight, or nine if 5:10 is separated from 5:11; Lk has four, which are followed by four maledictions: "Woe to you . . ." Mt reports the words of Jesus in the third person, Lk has him addressing his audience directly. Mt outlines a program of action in many of his items, with a consequent reward; Lk speaks more of a transformation in men's lot.

Despite these differences, there is basic resemblance, almost identity in certain of the Beatitudes as framed by one and the other evangelist. The language used is easily paralleled from the OT. Lk is thought to have eliminated certain very Jewish elements—he was a Gentile Christian writing for Gentile Christians.

What concerns us is the theological and especially the Christological implications of the teaching here recorded. Theological: this series of encouraging exhortations or promises must be seen in the context of the Good News announced by Jesus, "The kingdom of God is at hand." The conception of God's kingdom was colored by traditional royalist ideology. God is a just and merciful king, who will ensure the triumph of the unfortunate and oppressed. Jesus appears as God's supremely authorized legate, a messenger of relief assured for the poor, the afflicted, the starving. God, for whom he speaks with such clarity and certainty, is the Creator and Sovereign Lord of all, rich and poor, powerful and weak, oppressors and oppressed. But God is prompted by his infinite mercy to take the side of the deprived, the underprivileged, the marginalized. In his kingdom the poor are privileged.

Jesus totally accepts this divine choice and makes the fact clear in the first statement of policy which gives the key to his entire mission. He is on the side of the poor, the disinherited, the victims of institutional, social injustice. He is essentially, in the Beatitudes, in the whole Sermon on the Mount, to which they serve as an exordium, the Liberator (qv). Lk emphasizes this important truth by the very mode of enunciation. Jesus speaks directly to those whom he will release from their particular bondage.

Mt's interest is not opposed to this, but complementary. He shows the pastoral orientation which enlarges the meaning of the Beatitudes, gives them a creative dimension, offers through them an inspiring program of life. This is carried to its ultimate conclusion: a whole Christocentric spirituality. Hence the refinements which Mt adds: it is not poverty of itself which ensures entry to the Kingdom, but poverty of spirit; it is not hunger but hunger for justice which counts; it is persecution for "righteousness' sake" which is meritorious; there must be a positive program of meekness, of mercy, and of peacemaking.

Especially Mt enjoins purity of heart, total detachment from all that sullies. This beatitude has been called, by St. Thomas Aquinas (qv) among others, the summary of the gospel: the reward is on the same scale, vision of God, source of inexhaustible happiness. Did Mt make the additions or, as already affirmed, did Lk reduce the list? A question for biblical scholars; they seem to have divergent answers.

There can be no doubt on the plenary message of the Beatitudes. This is a proclamation of happiness. It is the answer to those who think that Jesus proposed only a negative program of life. What he speaks of here is fulfillment. This is the complement to his stringent call to take up one's daily cross and follow him. Those who follow him will solve the problem of happiness, the crucial problem in every sense of the word. It is not a solution promised in terms of an immediate recipe, but of profound future hope. It is a charter which Jesus underwrites solemnly, publicly; it is universal in its application.

One biblical commentator has sought in the word of the Master, "Unless you become as little children, you shall not enter the kingdom of heaven" (Mt 18:3), further light on the meaning of the Beatitudes. Whether the Master is explicitly teaching in the Beatitudes the doctrine of spiritual childhood or not, Jesus' words agree admirably with this outlook, which was characteristic of him. Clearly it must be understood in a sense that is free of the sentimental, the mawkish or the childish.

[1]Bibl. C. W. Votaw, Hastings *Dictionary of the Bible,* extra vol., *Sermon on the Mount,* V, 44f; H. Foston, *The Beatitudes and the Contrasts,* London, 1911; A. Lemonnyer, "Le Messianisme des Béatitudes," *RSPT* 11 (1922) 272–89; G. Strecker, "Die Makarismen der Bergpredigt," *NTS* 17 (1970–71) 255–75; E. Jacquemin, "Les Béatitudes," *Assemblées du Seigneur* 89 (1963); A. Gardeil, *DTC* II (1905) 515–17; L. Pirot, *DBS* I, 927–39; esp., J. Dupont, O.S.B., *Les Béatitudes,* 2 vols., Louvain, 1958–73; commentaries on Mt and Lk; W. D. Davies, *The Setting of the Sermon on the Mount,* Cambridge, 1964; id., *The Sermon on the Mount,* Cambridge, 1966; O. S. Brooks, *The Sermon on the Mount: Authentic Human Values,* Lanham, Maryland, 1985; University Press of America, 19–29; C. G. Vaught, *The Sermon on the Mount: A Theological Interpretation,* New York, 1986, 12–38; G. Strecker, *The Sermon on the Mount: An Exegetical Commentary,* Nashville, 1988, 27–47; D. Hamm, *The Beatitudes in Context: What Luke & Matthew Meant,* Wilmington, 1990.

BEAUTY OF JESUS CHRIST, THE

As God incarnate, Jesus Christ embodies divine beauty.[1] The transcendent beauty of God is known to us by analogy, but this analogical knowledge, though valid, does not remove the mystery which confronts and surrounds us in all our thinking on divine reality. This mystery permeates the very structure of our thought patterns about God.

Beauty is an emanation of splendor perceived by the aesthetic sense with an immediate accompaniment of satisfaction, of pleasure in its most profound sense. Hence the ancient simple definition of the beautiful, *quod visum placet*. Analysis of the components of beauty and of the required response from the aesthetic sense leads deep into philosophical theory and discussion. Fathers of the Church, notably St. Gregory of Nyssa and St. Augustine (qqv) saw the relevance of a theory of beauty to theological speculation.

St. Thomas (qv) insists on integrity, proportion, and clarity as elements contributing to beauty: order is fundamental. All that is in the object. In the subject who perceives what is beautiful a proper exercise of the aesthetic sense is needed. It must discern splendor in its required form, eliminate what is disorderly, evaluate all the attributes needed. This calls for training, experience, self-correction or guidance, self-discipline. The confusion so often spoken of between objective beauty and subjective interpretation of the beautiful is often the result of inadequate education; this means lack of the humility which great beauty commands.

In reflecting on the beauty of Jesus Christ we suffer a certain handicap. Theology and spirituality have been starved of the beautiful, of beauty with a valid place in theological syntheses, of beauty as a source of perfection in prayer, a language through which God, the Spirit of God, speaks to the soul. A crude form of this error would be the refusal to allow any place for works of art in personal or communal practice of religion. A more sophisticated variation on the same negative theme would be rejection of beauty as part of the divine scheme—it would be considered a purely human adjunct to be discarded as the soul made its way to the heights.

The result was a dichotomy at times apparent; artists of genius strove to depict Christian themes, but in a social area kept apart from the high intellectual arena of the theologians; the two did occasionally meet, but almost by accident.

So we have to reflect on the evidence afforded by Sacred Scripture. We have no direct evidence on the physical beauty of Christ. If the Shroud of Turin is genuine, then we have a representation of this man which is indeed beautiful. The physical exhaustion and the torture which he endured before his death marked his bodily frame and are reflected in his countenance; but the splendid features remain to impress. With due contemplation they prompt adver-

tence to the spiritual beauty of Jesus Christ, to the harmonious consistency of all his faculties, powers, and individual habits about a center wherein resides some source of mysterious supernatural stability and energy.

Attempts have been made to analyze the character (qv) of Jesus Christ; they rightly stress the heroic temperament which was a permanent frame of his decision, volition, and activity; they point to the striking contrasts in his teaching and behavior; the uncompromising exalted idealism, which could allow compassion and tenderness towards the wayward and the weak; the fountain of miracles which he could set in motion and the entire absence of any such superhuman or extraordinary device in the moment of his Passion; the deep attachment to the ideals, traditions, and destiny of his own people and the sense of universal mission which would lead him to break the mold of Jewish exclusiveness; the warning that "not on bread alone" does man live, with a willingness to provide bread for the hungry thousands.

These contrasts, so far from disrupting the essential psychological harmony, which was the sign of his flawless moral beauty, do but point to the accuracy and richness of his response to the varying situations, problems, challenges of life. He summed up his personal beauty in the simple, powerful metaphor of light: "I am the Light of the world" (Jn 8:12; 9:5). Light is free from that which disfigures; to be totally light means to be pure splendor. This is the splendor which the Father glorified (Jn 8:54; 17:1), which the Spirit of truth will glorify (Jn 16:14).

Again Jesus, seeking to instruct his disciples on his essential solidarity with them, chose a plant which is beautiful in its appearance and in its fruitfulness, even ultimately in the wine that will be distilled from its grapes: "I am the true vine and my Father is the vinedresser" (Jn 15:1). Vitality which is intrinsic to Jesus Christ, the plenitude of vitality, in his lifetime and through the ages in the lives of his faithful, stirs admiration. This is an invitation, from the inner logic of reality, to pray and look for that intuition which would enlighten us on the fairest of the sons of men. We have ample testimony in age after age from the great mystics (qv) to the commanding excellence of Jesus Christ; the greatest artists and writers have sought to give it some expression, failing in each case through the inadequacy of the medium used, to depict one who is unique, to direct the attention of the spectator from the physical appearance of Jesus to his interior totally compelling beauty.

[1]Cf. Hans Urs von Balthasar, *The Glory of the Lord, A Theological Aesthetics,* vol. VII, Edinburgh, 1990; *id.,* "Transcendentality and Gestalt," *Communio* 11 (1984) 4–12; P. A. Mellor, *The Virgin Birth and the Theology of Beauty, ITQ* 57, 3 (1991) 196–208.

BÉRULLE, PIERRE DE (1575–1629)

A key figure in the French school of spirituality, B. had an important role in the establishment in France of Reformed Carmel and founded the French Oratory, which was not dependent on the Congregation founded by St. Philip Neri, though he was inspired by it.[1] Pope Urban VIII, in a much-quoted phrase, called B. the "Apostle of the Word Incarnate." The substance of his rich spirituality is derived from contemplation of the Word Incarnate, expressed in his major works, *Discours de l'état et des grandeurs de Jésus,* 1623, and *Vie de Jésus,* 1629. Why an author like Brémond could call him original in this respect, since Christian spirituality from its very name is Christocentric, needs some explanation. It was the capacity of B. and the whole school which he influenced to put forward the two elements, the Word and his incarnate life, so compellingly, that was singular. It is not here a question of the Jesus of history (qv) or the Christ of faith, but the second Person of the Holy Trinity in the flesh as an object of contemplation, admiration, imitation. B. showed that the totality of the mystery of the Incarnation can become a living ideal. He concentrates on adoration and considers Christ in a threefold aspect as adorer or adored. He is the term or object of our adoration: "We adore an eternal God but one who has made himself mortal; an invisible God, but who has made himself visible; an impassible God, but who made himself subject to heat, cold, the Cross and death . . . We have a Child God, a mortal God, one suffering, trembling, weeping in the crib."[2]

Entering more deeply into the mystery, B. sees the Word incarnate as the means of adoration: "From all eternity there was a God infinitely adorable, but there was not yet an infinite adorer; there was a God worthy of being infinitely loved and served, but there was no man, no servant, infinite, fit to give infinite service and love. You are now, O Jesus, this adorer, this man, this servant, infinite in power, in quality, in dignity, to satisfy this duty fully, to render this divine homage. You are this man loving, adoring, and serving the supreme majesty as it is worthy of being loved, served, and honored. And as there is a God worthy of being adored, served, and loved, there is in you, O my Lord Jesus, a God adoring, loving, and serving him for all eternity in the nature which was united to your Person in the fullness of time."[3]

B., as others of the French school, chose the priestly office of Christ for consideration, rather than that of King (qv), Shepherd, or Judge (qv), for he sees the priest giving supreme homage, as was due, to Almighty God. With this turning of Christ towards God, B. thought of him as priest thinking of himself that he should sacrifice himself, and of souls that he should sanctify them. He was broadly in agreement with St. Thomas (qv) on the motive of the Incarnation—Christ came to save sinners—but could still see the mystery enclosed in God's eternal mind. "In him God wishes to include and conclude his greatness, his power, his goodness, and the ineffable communication of himself."[4]

When B. comes to speak of Jesus as the example of our adoration, he propounds one of the great doctrines of the French school; the Christian must seek to imitate all the actions of Jesus, by entering into his state, by a kind of assimilation with the mysteries of his life: Christ is not only our model, he is the fulfillment of our being; our being is to be in him, to belong to him, to be, to live, and to act through him—Jesus is to be our life, our repose, our strength, and all our power to act. He saw this quasi-identification achieved most perfectly in Mary, Mother of God, whom he saw as the spouse, not of the Holy Spirit, as did St. Louis Marie de Montfort, but of God the Father. In his elaboration of the close spiritual union between Jesus and Mary he used the language of the Hearts, which St. John Eudes (qv) would make more explicit and plenary.

[1] H. Brémond, *Histoire littéraire du sentiment religieux en France,* III, 1913, 3–279; P. Pourrat, *La spiritualité chrétienne,* III, 1918, 491–515; A. Molien, *DSp,* I (1539–1581); *Theotokos,* 79–80; M. Dupoy, *Bérulle, Une spiritualité de l'adoration,* Paris, 1964; id., *Bérulle et le sacerdoce,* Paris, 1969; W. M. Thompson, "A Study of B.'s Christic Spirituality," *Jesus, Lord and Savior,* Paulist, 1988, 227–49; [2] *Oeuvres,* 938–940; [3] *Ibid.,* 153, *Grandeurs,* II, 12; [4] *Ibid.,* 161, *Grandeurs,* II, 2, 222.

BIBLICAL CHRISTOLOGY: THE PONTIFICAL BIBLICAL COMMISSION

In 1984 the Pontifical Biblical Commission published a document of somewhat unusual character for that body, though an intimation of its change in style of publication had been given twenty years previously with the Instruction on *The Historical Truth of the Gospels.*[1] The way in which the document was issued was unique for a text emanating from a Roman body; it appeared in Paris over an ordinary publisher's imprint as *Bible et Christologie,* with a preface by the very great biblical scholar, Henri Cazelles, P.S.S., then professor at the Catholic Institute in Paris, appointed later in that year to secretary of the Biblical Commission.[2] The text is given in Latin and French. An English translation has appeared from the American biblical scholar, Joseph Fitzmyer, S.J., in *Theological Studies,*[3] and since in book form, with a detailed commentary by the translator; another English translation has been made by M. J. Wrenn.[4] The French edition carried essays relevant to the subject of the official document by nine members of the Biblical Commission. Fifteen members had voted on the final text in April, 1983: Jean Dominique Barthélemy, O.P. (France/Switzerland), Pierre Benoit, O.P. (France/Israel), Henri Cazelles, P.S.S. (France), Guy Couturier, C.S.C. (Canada), Alfons Deissler (Germany), Jacques Dupont, O.S.B. (Belgium), Joachim Gnilka (Germany), John Greehy (Ireland), Pierre Grélot (France), Augustyn Jankowski, O.S.B. (Poland), Antonio Moreno Casamitjana (Chile), Laurent Nare (Upper Volta), Ignace de la Potterie, S.J. (Belgium/Italy), Matthew Vellanickal (India), Benjamin Wambacq, O.Praem. (Belgium). The secretary was Marino Maccarelli, O.S.M. The five members who helped draft the document, but were absent from the voting for different reasons were: Bishop Albert Descamps (Belgium) and Angelo Penna (Italy), who had died; José Alonso Diaz (Spain), and Jerome D. Quinn (U.S.A.), for reasons of illness; Carlo Maria Martini (Italy), promoted to Cardinal Archbishop of Milan.

Fr. Fitzmyer's valuable commentary on the official text carries important bibliographical information; both the document and his commentary are used, with references, in articles throughout the present work.

---

[1]For text and commentary, cf. J. Fitzmyer, S.J., "The Biblical Commission's Instruction on the Historical Truth of the Gospels," *ThS* 25 (1964) 386–408; separate issue, revised, *Scripture and Christology: A Statement of the Biblical Commission with a Commentary,* New York, 1986; id., *A Christological Catechism: New Testament Answers,* New York, 1982, 97–140; [2]Paris, Cerf (1984); [3]"The Biblical Commission and Christology," *ThS* 46 (1985) 407–79; [4]"Bible and Christology," *The Wanderer* 118/11-14 (March 14, 21, 28 and April 4, 1985) 8–9, 10–11, 9, 10–11.

BIRTH OF JESUS, THE

It is narrated in the two infancy narratives as taking place in Bethlehem (Mt 2:1; Lk 2:4, 6-7).[1] Each evangelist places the infancy in the days of King Herod (Mt 2:1; Lk 1:5) and since he died in 4 B.C., Jesus must have been born before that date. From the second century, tradition in the Apocrypha mentions Bethlehem. St. Justin Martyr, a Palestinian in the same age, refers to a "certain cave nigh the village."

Mary (qv), Mother of Jesus, had conceived him virginally. From early times there has been a tradition that her virginity was preserved, through a special divine action, in the moment of childbirth; she did not lose the physical signs of virginity. The fact is described on the evidence of midwives, in the Protevangelium of James (XIX, XX);[2] it is insinuated as a painless birth in the *Odes of Solomon* (XIX), and by St. Irenaeus in the *Demonstration of the Apostolic Preaching.*[3] Tertullian accepted the idea while, at about the same time, Clement of Alexandria accepted it from the Apocrypha. Zeno of Verona (d. c. 372) is the earliest explicit voice on the subject in the West: "O great mystery! Mary, an incorrupt virgin conceived, after conception she brought forth as a virgin, after childbirth she remained a virgin."[4]

St. Jerome avoided the subject because it had been treated by the *Apocrypha* of which he had a horror; his phrase dismissing the story of the midwives was *deliramenta apocryphorum,* ravings of the apocrypha. Fourth-century eastern Fathers asserted the doctrine, the Cappadocians and St. Epiphanius notably. St. Ambrose was explicit: "Mary kept the seals of her virginity."[5] Augustine still more so and repeatedly, as, for example: "She had conceived without male seed, brought forth without corruption, retained her integrity after childbirth."[6] Pope Leo the Great (qv) in the Tome (qv) wrote: "Mary brought him forth with her virginity intact, as with her virginity intact she had conceived him." Pope Hormisdas (d. 523) used the words, "Not opening his Mother's womb in birth, by the power of the deity not undoing his Mother's virginity."[7] The idea is found in the third canon of the first Lateran Council, and some theologians argue that because Pope Martin I, in a letter to the "holy pleroma," gave his support to the Council, the decree is a dogma of faith though the Council was not ecumenical. The essential words are: "(Mary) in the fullness of time and without male seed, conceived by the Holy Spirit God the Word himself, who before all time was born of God the Father and incorruptibly brought him forth, and after his birth preserved her virginity intact."[8] Paul IV in the Bull *Cum quorumdam,* 1555, condemned those who denied the virginal conception and who taught that Joseph was the father of Jesus. The Pope ended with the assertion that Mary's virginity was threefold: "before birth, in birth, and perpetually after birth."[9]

Ten years before Vatican II met, A. Mitterer had in a book which caused some stir in Catholic circles, questioned the *virginitas in partu - Dogma und Biologie der heiligen Familie.* The first Marian schema, which never came to the Council assembly, contained the words "who (the Son) willed the bodily integrity of his Mother to remain, in the moment of birth (*in ipsomet partu*), incorrupt and untouched. . . ."; the notes to the text said that this phrasing was intended to counter Mitterer's theory.[10] The final schema carried a sentence similar to that proposed by Msgr. G.

Philips of Louvain, in a schema he had submitted before the conciliar proceedings. He was now, with Fr. Karl Balic, O.F.M., an official draftsman of the text: "The Mother of God showed her first-born Son, who did not lessen her virginal integrity, but sanctified it (sacravit) to the shepherds and the Magi." The words were retained in the Constitution on the Church, 57.

Lk gives the very human detail, "And she gave birth to her first-born Son and wrapped him in swaddling cloths, and laid him in a manger" (2:7, 12). Thus the danger of Docetism was forestalled. The same evangelist tells of the angel of the Lord who appeared to the shepherds "and the glory of the Lord shone around them. . . . And suddenly there was with the angel a multitude of the heavenly host praising God and saying, 'Glory to God in the highest, and on earth peace among men with whom he is pleased'" (2:9, 13-14). Here the presence of angels signifies the presence of the Godhead, appropriate to the divinity of the new-born Child.

The miraculous birth was due to an intervention of the Spirit (qv). This is consonant with his essential role in the conception of Jesus, a logical sequel, complementary rather to the divine work of the Annunciation, a continuation of the intrinsic bond, showing his control of the life of the God-man, which was to be continuous, reaching a pinnacle in the Baptism (qv), consummation in the Resurrection, public manifestation in Pentecost.

---

[1]Bibl. to article, Virginity in partu, Theotokos, 361, 2; Cf. esp. E. P. Nugent, C.M.F., "The Closed Womb of the Blessed Mother of God," EphMar 8 (1958) 249–70; J. Crehan, S.J., "Mary's Virginity and the Painless Birth of Christ," The Clergy Review 45 (1960) 718–25; R. Laurentin, "Le mystère de la naissance virginale," EphMar 10 (1960) 345–74; J. de Aldama, S.J., "Natus ex maria Virgine," Greg 42 (1961) 37–62; id. "La virginida 'in partu' en la exegesis patristica," Salmanticensis 9 (1962) 113–53; M. Hurley, S.J., "Born Incorruptibly," Heythrop Journal 2 (1961) 217–23; K. Rahner, S.J., "Virginitas in partu," Theol. Investigations IV (1966) 134–62; [2]Papyrus Bodmer V, ed. M. Testuz, 1958, 38–41; [3]SC 62, 115; [4]Tractatus lib. 2, tr. 8, 2, PL 11, 415; [5]Epist. 63, 33 PL 16, 1198C; [6]Sermo 215, 3 PL 38, 1073; [7]Leo I, ACO 2, 2, 1 25; PL 54, 759; Hormisdas Epist. 137 (79), PL 63, 514; [8]Mansi 10, 1152; [9]DS 1880; Bullarium Marianum, Bourassé, VII, 60; [10]Schema Constitutionis de B.M.V., Matre Dei et Matre hominum, Vatican Press, 1962, n. 4.

BLOOD OF CHRIST, THE PRECIOUS

Blood was sacred in the OT.[1] From this character came the prohibition to kill, and the ban on human consumption of blood (Lev 17:10). This sacred character also explains the importance attached to blood in cult. A rite of blood seals the covenant of Yahweh with his people. "And Moses took half of the blood and put it into basins, and half of the blood he threw against the altar. Then he took the book of the covenant, and read it in the hearing of the people; and they said, 'All that the Lord has spoken we will do, and we will be obedient.' And Moses took the blood and threw it upon the people and said, 'Behold the blood of the covenant which the Lord has made with you in accordance with all these words'" (Ex 24:6-8; cp. Zech 9:11; Heb 9:16-21).

Blood had a most important place in sacrifices (Lev 1:5; 9:12). The blood of the Paschal Lamb saved lives, "For the Lord will pass through to slay the Egyptians; and when he sees the blood on the lintel and the two doorposts, the Lord will pass over the door, and will not allow the destroyer to enter your houses to slay you" (Ex 12:23). Blood rites have an essential role in the liturgy of expiation, "For the life of the flesh is in the blood; and I have given it for you upon the altar to make atonement for your souls; for it is the blood that makes atonement, by reason of the life" (Lev 17:11). Blood in the consecration rites of priests (Ex 29:20f; Lev 8:23f, 30) and of altars (Ex 24:6-8; Lev 9:12) signified that they belong to God.

As the very idea of prophet (qv) becomes inadequate to describe the mission of Christ, the Son of God, who was the fulfillment of all prophecy, so the prescriptions and incidents featuring blood in the OT are totally surpassed, rendered irrelevant by that which they prefigured. The new dispensation hinges on the one supreme offering of "the precious blood of Christ, like that of a lamb (qv) without blemish or spot" (1 Pet 1:19). Here is the origin of the traditional phrase, "Precious Blood." It is abundantly clear in the NT that the blood of Christ is the price of our ransom. Especially in St. Paul: "Since all have sinned and fall short of the glory of God, they are justified by his grace as a gift through the redemption which is in Christ Jesus, whom God put forward as an expiation by his blood, to be received by faith" (Rom 3:24f); "Since therefore we are now justified by his blood, much more shall we be saved by him from the wrath of God" (Rom 5:9). "For in him all the fullness of God was pleased to dwell, and through him to reconcile to himself all things, whether on earth or in heaven, making peace by the blood of his cross" (Col 1:19f). In Eph we read, "in him we have redemption through his blood, the forgiveness of our trespasses, according to the riches of his grace which he lavished upon us" (1:7f). Paul, in his final recommendations to the elders at Ephesus, assured them: "Take heed to yourselves and to all the flock, in which the Holy Spirit has made you overseers, to care for the church of God, which he obtained with the blood of his own Son" (Acts 20:28).

1 Jn 1:7 invokes the theme to support fidelity, "but if we walk in the light, as he is in the light, we have fellowship with one another and the blood of Jesus his Son cleanses us from all sin." The same idea occurs early in Rev, "To him who loves us and has freed us from our sins by his blood and made us a kingdom of priests to his God and Father, to him be glory and dominion for ever and ever. Amen" (1:5f; cp. 5:9; 7:12; 12:11; 19:13). The conceptual framework here is the Lamb of God (qv).

It varies in Heb consonant with the Christology and priestly theology of that letter: "But when Christ appeared as a high priest of the good things that have come, even through the greater and more perfect tent (not made with hands, that is, not of this creation), he entered once for all into the Holy Place, taking not the blood of goats and calves but his own blood, thus securing an eternal redemption" (Heb 9:11f). This comes after a description of the ancient ritual, which is superseded, sublimated in the new act of Christ. We are accordingly enjoined, "Therefore, brethren, since we have confidence to enter the sanctuary by the blood of Jesus . . . (10:19). The responsibility is great, as we learn from the comparison with the law of Moses: "A man who has violated the law of Moses dies without mercy at the testimony of two or three witnesses. How much worse punishment do you think will be deserved by the man who has spurned the Son of God, and profaned the blood of the covenant by which he was sanctified, and outraged the Spirit of grace?" (10:29). We are finally reminded that "Jesus suffered outside the gate in order to sanctify the people through his blood" (13:12). Innocent blood (Mt 23:23-30), as even Judas would testify (Mt 27:3-4).

Blood which we are bidden to consume (Jn 6:13; 1 Cor 10:10), whereby the OT prohibition is ignored, while, at the same time, total meaning is given to blood as the symbol of life, now belonging to God as does life. For the association of blood with religious rites is brought to its highest point in the institution of the Eucharist, wherein Christ speaks of "the new covenant in my blood" (1 Cor 11:25; Lk 22:20), or according to Mt (26:28) and Mk (14:24), "my blood of the covenant." Here he assumes fully his role of the new and immeasurably greater Moses (see article, Transfiguration, The); here the typology of the Paschal Lamb was fully realized, the new and everlasting Passover begun, the entire thrust of the OT attained its goal and its glory.

Since Christ's sacrifice was effected by the shedding of his blood, this is rightly spoken of as the price of our redemption. M. J. Scheeben suggests that Christ's sacrifice and the shedding of his blood to the last drop may be seen "as the highest expression of the Trinitarian relations and the most perfect vehicle of their extension to the outer world." The Holy Spirit issues from the mutual love of the Father and the Son, "from their common heart," the one to whom they give themselves as the pledge of their infinite love. "In order worthily to represent this infinitely perfect surrender to his Father, the Logos wished in his humanity to pour forth his blood from his heart to the last drop, the blood in which and through which the Holy Spirit gave life to his humanity, the blood that was pervaded, sanctified, and scented with heavenly loveliness, and so ascended to God with such pleasing fragrance. The Holy Spirit himself is portrayed as the agent of this sacrifice. He is the agent in this sense: that in his capacity of *amor sacerdos* he urges on the God-man to his sacrifice, and brings the oblation itself into the presence of the Father, uniting it to the eternal homage of love, which is he himself."[2]

The highest religious act we can make towards the Precious Blood of Christ is to receive it in the sacrifice of the Mass, wherein it is truly present. But great saints, especially from medieval times, notably St. Bonaventure, St. Gertrude, and especially St. Catherine of Siena, have expressed their piety towards the Blood of Christ in a singular way. In 1747 Benedict XIV approved a feast to honor it liturgically; for the nineteenth centenary of the Redemption, Pius XI raised the feast to a Double of the First Class.

An ardent apostle of the devotion, St. Gaspar de Bufalo (1786–1837) founded the Society of the Precious Blood for priests and brothers in 1815; that year also saw the beginning of the Archconfraternity of the Precious Blood. John XXIII approved the litany of the Precious Blood and issued an Apostolic Exhortation, *Inde a primis,* June 30, 1960, to encourage the devotion, linking it with the Name of Jesus (qv) and the Sacred Heart (qv). Notable centers of the devotion are at Mantua since 553, Weingarten since 1090, and Bruges since 1158.

[1]Cf. F. Faber, C. Orat., *The Precious Blood,* new ed., Philadelphia, 1959; F. Rusche, *Blut, Leben und Seele,* Paderborn, 1930; J. H. Rohling, *The Blood of Christ in Christian Latin Literature before the Year 1,000,* Washington, 1932; C. M. Schröder, *Blutglaube in der Religionsgeschichte,* Munich, 1936; E. F. Siegman, "The Blood of the Covenant," *AER* 136 (1951) 167–74; C. Greisner, *Das Kostbare Blut Christi: Gedanken und Gebete,* Mindelheim, 1957; L. Dewar, "The Biblical Use of the Term Blood," *JTS* 4 (1951) 204–08; J. L. Morris, "The Biblical Use of the Term Blood," *JTS* 5 (1952) 216–27; A. J. Pollack, *The Blood of Christ in Christian Greek Literature Till the Year 444,* Carthagena, Ohio, 1956; L. Moraldi, *Espiazione sacrificale e riti espiatori,* Analecta Biblica 5, Rome, 1956; J. Siebeneck, "The Precious Blood and St. John," *Proceedings of the First Precious Blood Study Week,* Carthagena, Ohio, 1959, 65–92; G. Lefebvre, *Redemption through the Blood of Jesus,* tr. E. A. Maziare, Westminster, 1960; E. G.

Kaiser, "Theology of the Precious Blood," *AER* 145 (1961) 190–201; J. Siebeneck, "The Precious Blood and St. Peter," *Proceedings of the Second Precious Blood Study Week,* Carthagena, Ohio, 1962, 36–56; E. F. Siegman, "The Blood in St. Paul's Soteriology," *ibid.,* 11–35; J. Behm, Kittel, *TheolWörterbuch* I, 171–76; A. Vögtle, *LTK* II, 539–41; R. Haubst, *ibid.,* 544–45; A. Grillmeier, *ibid.,* 1156–66; *NCE* XI, 705–08; R. T. Siebeneck, The Bible; E. G. Kaiser, Theology; J. H. Rohling, Devotion; text of *Inde a primis, AAS* 52 (1960) 545–60; D. J. McCarthy, "The Symbolism of Blood and Sacrifice, *JBL* 88 (1969) 166–76; *id.* "Further Notes on the Symbolism of Blood and Sacrifice, *JBL* 92 (1973) 205–10; J. Schmid in Bauer I, 79–81; R. Gregoire in *DSp* XIV, 319–33; ²*The Mysteries of Christianity,* English tr., C. Vollert, S.J., London, St. Louis, 1951, 445.

BONAVENTURE, ST., DOCTOR OF THE CHURCH (c. 1218–1274)

Predominantly a mystic in the golden age of scholasticism, B. showed as Master General of the Franciscan Order, in its early phase of gigantic expansion, high qualities of administration, sure judgment, and holiness. The corpus of his writing is extensive, with a leaning towards St. Augustine and Alexander of Hales.[1] He turns to the figure of the Savior at many places in the course of his writings or sermons. He treats of Christological questions formally: in his commentary on the third book of the Sentences, *De incarnatione Verbi et Humani Generis Reparatione,* which occupies more than 460 folio pages of the Quaracchi ed., III; in part IV of the *Breviloquium De incarnatione Verbi,* pp. 241–52, and in *Quaestiones Disputatae, De scientia Christi,* pp. 3–43.

B. ranges over the whole area of Christology "from above," dealing with the hypostatic union (qv), analyzing and justifying the various suitabilities of the mystery, e.g., why the Son was incarnate, dealing at length with the predestination of Christ and its relation to ours. "Praedestinatio Christi ratione connotati dici potest causa nostrae praedestinationis dispositiva per meritum et excitativa per exemplum sed non proprie effectiva."[3] Again on divine omnipotence, whether the human soul of Christ may be said to be omnipotent, he writes: "Nec animae Christi nec alicui creaturae potest omnipotentia communicari ut proprietas ei inhaerens."[4]

B. wrote a great deal on the knowledge of Christ, attracted to the subject no doubt by his own superb mystical gifts. He was intrigued by the way Christ's soul interacted with the Word of God.[5] He sums up: "Cognitio qua mediate Christi anima cognoscit Verbum sibi unitum non est ipsum Verbum sed effectus Verbi et quid creatum."[6]

[1]E. Smeets, *DTC* II, 962–82; I. C. Brady *NCE* II, 658–64; A. Sepinski, O.F.M., *La psychologie du Christ chez St. Bonaventure,* Paris, 1948; ²Quaracchi ed., V; ³D. XI, a. 1, q. 3, p. 247; ⁴XIV, 3, 3, p. 324; ⁵cf. *ibid.* XIV a. 2, q. 3; a. 3, q. 1, pp. 312–21; ⁶Vol III, 296.

BONHOEFFER, DIETRICH (1906–1945)

B.'s thinking on Christ was expressed in lectures in Berlin University in the 1930s, before the dramatic events which thrust him into conflict with the secular powers as a committed Christian; he was victimized in his academic career, and eventually, after the failure of his effort to negotiate peace, joined the German resistance, accepting the need for tyrannicide.[1] Imprisoned, he was a victim of the attempt on the tyrant's life; he died a martyr's death by hanging, on April 9, 1945.

B. was influenced by Barth's (qv) works; eventually they became personal friends, though there was a moment of divergent thinking. Barth, in the *Church Dogmatics,* acknowledges the merit of B.'s treatment of the Church in *Sanctorum Communio* and of discipleship in *Nachfolge,* English tr., *The Cost of Discipleship.*[2]

The lectures on Christology were put together on the basis of student notes; they were published posthumously as *Wer ist und wer war Jesus Christus?*[3] Though insights on Christ occur in passages here and there through his other works, it is in this work that we come nearest to a synthesis. Christ is present with us in the form of Word, Sacrament, and Church. He is the center not only of human existence but of history and of the world. The fundamental question for B. is not how Jesus Christ can be both God and man, but who Christ is. We are challenged by his claim to be the Word of God and we are forced to decide who he is. B. thought the question of Christ's personal identity antecedent to discussion of his works. He rejected any cleavage between Jesus and Christ. But Christ is known to us with the certainty of faith through his own witness as the risen One.

The lectures were divided into three parts, on the present Christ, the historical Christ, and the eternal Christ, but only the first two were delivered, as the semester ended then. The approach is existential; one must begin with Christ living in the Church and seek to understand who he is from how he is for me; the essential meaning of Christ is to be not in and for himself but for me. B. went on to deal with the humiliation of Christ; as humiliated he is the object of offense. In a certain way he is still so, as we meet him not in the condition of his resurrection and exaltation, but in proclamation, which is unworthy of his dignity.

These ideas would have been more fully developed and we should have also no doubt in elaborate form, the third part of the Christology which B. planned.

Instead, the author was learning more profoundly what Christ means to a disciple exposed to the ordeal of injustice and punishment for his name's sake. That fidelity in discipleship set a special seal on B.'s *fides quaerens intellectum.* His work and his theology will survive certain misunderstandings which have come from a misreading of his texts divorced from their full context, and from the context, enlightening in its way, of his very special witness.

¹Cf. J. D. Godsey, *The Theology of Dietrich Bonhoeffer,* Philadelphia, 1960; *id.* "Barth and Bonhoeffer: The Basic Difference," *Quarterly Review,* 7 (1987) 9–27; J. A. Philips, *The Form of Christ in the World. A Study of Bonhoeffer's Christology,* London, 1967; J. Moltmann (qv) "The Lordship of Christ and Human Society," in Moltmann and Weissbach, *Two Studies in the Theology of Bonhoeffer,* New York, 1967, 21–94; R. Mayer, *Christuswirklicheit. Grundlagen, Entwicklung und Konsequenzen der Theologie Dietrich Bonhoeffer,* 1969; E. Bethge, *Dietrich Bonhoeffer, Theologian, Christian, Contemporary,* New York, London, 1970; E. Feil, *The Theology of Dietrich Bonhoeffer,* Philadelphia, 1984; J. D. Godsey, in *The Modern Theologians,* 150–70; B. de Margerie, S.J., in *Christ for the World. The Heart of the Lamb,* Chicago, 1973; *The Early Bonhoeffer, Christ Logos, Anti-Logos,* 140–50; *The Later Bonhoeffer, The This-World Christ Man for Others,* 151–169;   ²New York, 1963, London, 1964;   ³*Christology,* London, 1978; U.S. title: *Christ the Center,* New York 1978.

BULTMANN, RUDOLF (1884–1976)

Enmeshed at every point with the world of the German universities, B. succeeded, by his writings, in mesmerizing intellectually biblical scholars throughout the world.¹ The details of this vast achievement do not concern us, save insofar as they determined his ideas about Jesus Christ. He took up ardently the historical-critical approach to the Bible, Form Criticism (qv), though with emphasis on the motive that determined entry of different elements into the gospel tradition—hence the title of one of his principal works: *Die Geschichte der synoptischen Tradition* (ET *The History of the Synoptic Tradition*). B. is also one of the great names in the development of *Demythologizing* (qv). To understand him in this subject which proved explosively controversial after his lecture on *Neues Testament und Mythologie,* April 21, 1941, one has to bear in mind the influence on him of Martin Heidegger, as in other areas of his thinking and literary production he was influenced by Barth, and by Luther's (qv) *sola fide.* With his deep concern for the existentialist situation went a noble desire to make the Christian message of the gospel meaningful, relevant to modern man. The gospel, as he understood it, is not myth and needs no myth to support it. On these simple assertions arose much debate, even on the meaning of the very word myth.

B.'s ideas about Jesus Christ are found in several works, principally in the work on the synoptic tradition, in *Jesus and the Word,* 1934 (ET of *Jesus,* 1926) and in the 1951 Shaffer Lectures given at Yale, *Jesus Christ and Mythology,* issued in 1958. He saw the mission of Jesus as a call to his contemporaries to a decision to accept his proclamation and his sweeping demand. But this Jesus we really know only through the Church, which gives us his message.

What of the historical Jesus? The great biblical scholar, Fr. Pierre Benoit, under the title "The anti-historical aspect of Form-criticism: Everything invented by Tradition," gives the results of B.'s study of the life of Jesus as follows: "Here it is Bultmann who is the most radical. Reading his work produces a disconcerting effect. All, or nearly all, of the material of the gospels is there attributed to the creative genius of the primitive community. These rules for fasting, for keeping the sabbath, were not uttered by Jesus: they were invented by the first Christians in Jerusalem in their controversies with the Jews and put into the Master's mouth to give them proper authority. This healing of a leper, this raising of a young man at Naim—Jesus had no hand in these. It was the Christians of Damascus or of Antioch who attributed them to him, in order to put the miracles of the heathen gods into the shade. The brief descriptions of the setting which figure in the Apothegms are pure fiction, created to suit the saying which they enclose. That Peter and Andrew were engaged in fishing when Jesus called them is not a real recollection at all; it is the work of the imagination, basing itself on the words, 'I will make you fishers of men.' And so on."²

Fr. Benoit further comments: "And when we express astonishment, Bultmann replies with a certain candor: Sure enough, Jesus *could* have uttered this saying, Jesus *could* have performed this action. But what means have we of knowing? Between him and us comes the community; it is from the community that we receive tradition, it is the community that has interpreted the historical reality. We can find out what the community said about Jesus; but we can no longer find out what Jesus really said and did."³

B.'s insistence on faith freed from any basis in historical record is a powerful throw-back to Luther's *sola fide*; it is the strange twist given to the Reformer's basic principle by the addition of Form Criticism and demythologizing; far from what Luther himself would have thought, for his belief in *Scriptura sola* would not tolerate doubt on the historical framework of Jesus. He certainly did not reduce the yield of the gospel narratives to mere stark facts that Jesus existed and was crucified. B. stripped the kerygma of any historical element but this *Dass*: a unique skepticism in the world wherein he was so honored, where many looked to him as a pathfinder.

Inevitably such an approach and end-result provoked a counter-attack, which at times went almost to the point of demythologizing B.; these developments are beyond our scope. Though he saw Jesus as one who realized God's eschatological act in him, and though he took account of the Jewish background, thinking Jesus "an existentialist apocalyptic preacher challenging his contemporaries to radical obedience in view of the imminent coming of the reign of God," he could still relegate the Savior to "one presupposition among others for the theology of the New Testament. Thus the historical Jesus is not of constitutive significance for theology, for Christian faith is not a response to the message of Jesus but to the Church's message about him."[4]

It is these presuppositions and others supporting them which vitiate much of B.'s theorizing. It is for experts to unravel the various strands and trace their origin, the history of religions school, not forgetting its attention to a presumed gnostic mentality in the NT world; in a word, there is need to achieve an impartial assessment of the man and his work. There is further need to apply source criticism to the impressive corpus of writing as Fr. Benoit has partially done—it would presumably be improper to speak of Form Criticism. Recent attention to the Jewishness of Jesus (qv) brings a sense of concrete reality to what B. had raised to misty theory; recent existentialist claims on the gospel from Latin America so far from reducing the historical Christ, exalt him and give him priority over the kerygma; an existentialist test not foreseen by B.

B.'s commentary on St. John, generally considered his masterpiece, emphasizes the revelation embodied in Jesus, who is truth, who illuminates and must be accepted, to know whom is to be saved. Throughout all his work runs the influence of Luther, of Barth to a lesser extent, certainly of his Marburg colleague, Martin Heidegger.

[1]Cf. S. M. Ogden, *Christ without Myth,* London, 1962; A. Malet, *La pensée de Rudolf Bultmann,* Geneva, 1962; ET, *The Thought of Bultmann,* Dublin, 1969; C. W. Kegley (ed), *The Theology of Rudolf Bultmann,* London, 1966; W. Schmitals, *An Introduction to the Theology of Rudolf Bultmann,* London, 1968; J. Macquarrie, *An Existentialist Theology: A Comparison of Heidegger and Bultmann,* London, 1970; P. J. Cahill, "The Theological Significance of Rudolf Bultmann," *ThS* 38 (1977) 231–74; H. D. McDonald, "Christ the Lord," in *Studies Presented to D. Guthrie,* ed. H. Rowdeon, Leicester, 1982, 311–326; E. C. Hobbs, ed. *Bultmann, Retrospect and Prospect,* Philadelphia, 1985; R. Morgan, *The Modern Theologians,* I, 109–33; T. J. Ryan, *NCE,* XVII, 59f; B. de Margerie, S.J., *Christ for the Word: The Heart of the Lamb,* Chicago, 1973, 121–39; [2]*Jesus and the Gospel,* London, 1973, 28f; [3]*Ibid.;* [4]T. J. Ryan, *op. cit.,* 59.

C

CAROL, JUNIPER, O.F.M. (1911–1990)

This Franciscan has rendered precious services to Marian theology in the United States by his own contributions, especially in the area of Mary's role in the redemption of humankind; as editor of an important three-volume collective work, to which he also contributed, *Mariology*; and as founder of the American Mariological Society, of which he also edited for years the annual proceedings. His written work as a whole recalls a remark made by Newman. The great Tractarian had been taught that Catholics minimize Jesus Christ by their devotion to Mary. He found in practice that it was the regions that cherished the Mother which had retained their faith in the divinity of her Son. In the Franciscan tradition it has been great Marian theologians like Duns Scotus (qv) and St. Lawrence of Brindisi who vigorously championed the primacy of Christ. In the present century, along with other Franciscans like M. Meilach and J. M. Bonnefoy, C. is in that great tradition. His work, *Why Jesus Christ?* has a scope, thoroughness, and erudite foundation unequalled in the relevant literature: it was preceded in his research and publication by other studies, also impressive. Most remarkable of these is *The Absolute Primacy and Predestination of Jesus and his Virgin Mother*, Chicago, 1981. Of some relevance also is *A History of the Controversy over the Debitum Peccati,* St. Bonaventure, New York, 1978, as would his *magnus opus* among many contributions to Marian Theology, *De Corredemptione B.V.M,* Vatican City, 1950 (see also article, Primacy of Christ, in the present work, entirely indebted to C.)

---

[1]Cf. also "The Absolute Predestination of the Blessed Virgin Mary," *Marian Studies,* 31 (1980) 172–238: "Cur Deus Homo,"

Homiletic and Pastoral Review, 82 (August-September 1982) 8–9; "Duns Scotus on the Incarnation," *Ibid.* (June 1983) 4; cf. *Carol, Juniper* in *Theotokos,* M. O'Carroll, 98.

CATHERINE OF SIENA, ST., DOCTOR OF THE CHURCH (1347?–1380)

No critical study of the sources for St. Catherine's life and doctrine can seriously challenge the claim that she had one of the richest endowments of charisms in the history of mankind: miracles, ecstasies, visions, divine communications including a whole treatise of theological substance taken in dictation, charismatic leadership at the highest level of the Church, the stigmata, spiritual and bodily sustenance derived from the Eucharist.[1] There is no one quite like her in this domain so privileged. And the explanation? Totally consummated union with Jesus Christ in the supreme grace of spiritual marriage. Like Teresa of Avila (qv) and others, she is, in terms of mystical anthropology, Christ's vicar. Through her, Christ accomplished his program, an epoch-making one. This is her first, primary interest for the student of Jesus the Christ. She shows how he can, through one individual, release into the whole corporate entity which is his Mystical Body, an enormous new spiritual dynamism, with effects beyond time and space limitations. The totality of his possession of her being is exemplified in his word, "I am he who is and you are she who is not." The full resources of modern psychology have not yet been deployed in the study of her amazing life and life-work. Her confessor once saw her transfigured into Christ in her facial features.

Her principal work, *The Dialogue,* dictated by her divine Spouse, coheres on a key concept, that the Word Incarnate is the bridge between God and man;

she has subtle analyses of the progress made by souls on that bridge. In her thinking on Christ it is his mystery as the crucified One, the wounded side which reveals his Heart, that particularly attracts her. Above all the mystery of his Blood (qv) seized on her in a very profound way, becoming not a mere devotion but a central intuition of the Savior; it singles her out among those who have pondered the mystery of Christ. "It is in the blood" of the Redeemer, she wrote, "that we know the truth in the light of our most holy faith, which enlightens the eye of the mind." The words were addressed to Pedro de Luna, the future Benedict XII. Catherine had the experience of feeling her soul bathed in blood. Her last audible words were "Blood! Blood!" She saw the Church in the function of bringing souls under the influence of the Blood.[2]

It is the personality imbued with this conviction, taken over by Christ, who effected such mighty things in the course of her short life, making peace between warring cities, leading the group attracted to her, the *Catherinati,* to high holiness, prevailing on sinners to repent, and finally, achieving the goal of her spiritual yearning, the return of the Papacy to its rightful see and seat, the Eternal City.

[1] L. Zanini, "Bibliografia analitica di Santa Caterina da Siena 1901-19," in *Miscellanea del Centro di Studi Medievali,* Pubblicazioni dell'Universita Cattolica del Sacro Cuore, 58 (1956) 325-74; *id.,* 62 (1958) 265-367; M. M. Gorce, O.P., *DSp* II (1953) 327-48; R. Fawtier, *Sainte Catherine de Sienne, Essai de critique des Sources* (Bibliotheque des écoles francaises d'Athenes et de Rome, 121, 135, 1921, 1930) *id.,* with L. Canet, *La double experience de Catherine Benincasa,* Paris, 1948; A. Donaine, O.P. "Sainte Catherine de Sienne et Nicoldo Toldo," *Archivum Fratrum Praedicatorum* 19 (1949) 169-207 (critique of Fawtier); [2] On the Precious Blood, cf. Letters 25, 28, 73, 102, 273, *The Dialogue,* ch. 75; G. Cavallini, "Caterina da Siena. La luce del Sangue," in *Il Sangue che rivela l'Amore,* Centro Studi Sanguinis Christi, Rome, 1987, 309-20.

CHALCEDON, THE COUNCIL OF, 451

A very important landmark in the history of Christology, as in the history of the Papacy.[1] Pope Leo had formerly sought a Council to settle doctrinal questions in the Church; the Emperor Theodosius II had given him little heed for a while and when a Council did take place, it went very wrong. So when the pope heard from the Emperor Marcian, successor to Theodosius and much more cooperative, that he had summoned a Council to meet in Nicaea in August, 451, he felt no enthusiasm; he had asked the emperor to delay action, but the decision was now taken and though an assembly in the East caused him some apprehension, he decided to make the best of it. His view expressed to Marcian had been that bishops could not leave their dioceses because of war. In the event, besides the three papal legates, Paschasinus of Lilybaeum, Lucinus of Ascoli, and the priest Boniface, there were two Africans. Therefore the overwhelming majority of the 500 or more episcopal participants were eastern. The emperor was directly represented by 19 commissioners. He had changed the venue to Chalcedon. Here the first session took place October 8, 451.

There was much contention over personalities, which makes tedious reading nowadays. Doctrinally, the first important date was the second session, during which the assembly heard the letters of Cyril to Nestorius (qv) and to John of Antioch, and the "Tome" of Leo. The reading was greeted by acclamation and cries in which "Peter has thus spoken through Leo" was heard.

Next, on October 22 a formula of belief was presented. It was the work of a commission under the presidency of Anatolius. It did not take sufficient account of the "Tome" (qv) so the Roman legates refused to accept it, threatening to leave and seek transference of the Council to Italy. The commissioners faced with opposition from the "monophysites" who saw some hope for their case in the formula under consideration, sought the emperor's advice. He supported the idea of a new committee. It was formed and produced the Chalcedonian definition (qv), a balanced statement which reflected the "Tome" predominantly, but with a reasonable acceptance of other formulations and phrasing.

[1] A. Grillmeier, S.-H. Bacht, S. J., *Chalkedon,* 3 vols. (1951-1954); T. Jalland, *The Life and Times of St. Leo the Great,* London, 1941, ch. XII, "The Council of Chalcedon," 288-302; R. V. Sellers, *The Council of Chalcedon,* London, 1953; P. Hughes, *The Church in Crisis,* London, 1960, ch. IV, "The General Council of Chalcedon," 53-75; P. T. Camelot, O.P., *Ephèse et Chalcédoine (Histoire des Conciles Oecuméniques)* Paris, 1962; *id., NCE,* III, 423-26; Grillmeier, 543-54; F. M. Young, *From Nicaea to Chalcedon,* London, 1983.

CHALCEDONIAN DEFINITION, THE, 451

"Following then the Holy Fathers, we all with one accord teach that it should be confessed that our Lord Jesus Christ is one and the same Son, the same perfect in Godhead, the same perfect in humanity, true God and true man, with a rational soul and body; consubstantial with the Father, as to his Godhead, and the same consubstantial with us as to his humanity, in all things like unto us, sin only excepted; begotten of the Father before the ages, as to his Godhead, but in the last days, for us and for our salvation, of Mary, of the Virgin *Theotokos,* as to his humanity; one and the same Christ, Son, Lord, only-begotten, recognized in two natures, without confusion, without change, without division, without separation; the difference of the natures being in no way removed by the union, rather the distinctive character of each nature being preserved and coming together in one Person and hypostasis, not parted or divided into two persons, but one and the same Son and only-begotten God the Word, the Lord Jesus Christ; just as the prophets of old and the Lord Jesus Christ himself taught us, and as the creed of the Fathers has handed down to us."[1]

[1]*ACO* II, 1, 2, 129–30; Latin, *ACO* II, 3, 2, 137–38; *DS* 301; English tr. *The Sources of Catholic Dogma,* tr. R. J. Deferrari, 60, 61; R. V. Sellers, *The Council of Chalcedon,* London, 1953, 210f; G. O'Collins, *Interpreting Jesus,* London, 1983, 172; see articles Chalcedon, Council of; Leo the Great, St., Doctor of the Church.

CHARACTER OF JESUS, THE

If the history of Jesus (qv) presents problems, still more so does any attempt to assess his human character scientifically.[1] Unconsciously the student succumbs to certain temptations. One is to adopt a schematic approach. We know what the Christian virtues are. The founder of Christianity exemplified them to the highest degree: we can then seek evidence in the record of Jesus' life for one virtue after another. Another danger is the tendency to project on to the life of Jesus the ideological or moral preferences of a particular age or ethnic grouping, or individual temperament. Whereas the first approach will list one virtue after another and produce facts, not all accepted as such by biblical experts, to exemplify the claim made by the author, the second method will make Jesus Christ appear to live and behave according to the ideals, the longings, and the dictates of one specific social and cultural community: emphasizing, for instance, the mystic if it is from a milieu predominantly mystical, the social reformer in a world conscious of inequality, of widespread structured inequality which seems immune from redress; he is the doctrinaire idealist where people suffer from excessive pragmatic regimentation, the miracle of innocence and candor to those harassed or obsessed by the wickedness and follies of men, the fully integrated human being to those suffering from psychic disorder or deficiency.

Those who believe that Jesus Christ is God incarnate can never think too highly of him. Whatever of praise is expressed with the use of these different methods will still, for the believer, fall short of a reality which is beyond us, as all our attempts to penetrate the inner citadel of his mind, his consciousness (qv), must meet some kind of final frustration. We can, nonetheless, and ought, with the record established for us by sound biblical exegesis, seek to compose a psychological and moral portrait of the historical Jesus Christ; for this is an avenue that, for many, may lead to an interest in his divine personality, in his teaching, in his essential meaning in the flow of human events, in the entire cosmos. Divine Providence has surely intended things thus by manifesting certain historical facts about him.

With a significant lacuna. Apart from one brief episode after he had reached twelve years, we know nothing directly about his life until he takes up his task of public teaching and preaching. He was then in his thirties, the prime of life for a Mediterranean Jew (see article Jewishness of Jesus, The). The change in his life and life-style at the inception of his public career confronts us with the most striking character riddle in history: how did one whose previous education, experience, and training were in the context and requirements of a village tradesman, a carpenter or small house contractor in that limited world, suddenly, with no hiatus, firmly step into a role where articulate exposition of religious truth was a paramount demand, where challenge from sophisticated dissenters was to be expected, from men long practiced in their trade, thoroughly professional? If he succeeded in such a performance once, or for a short while, it would be a tour de force. Nothing of the kind: he took up and maintained this way of life as if it were a family inheritance, or a calling for which he had been meticulously prepared. He is one day a manual worker in a remote village, totally unknown in his country; he goes through what could be styled an initiation ceremony in the Baptism (qv) and then he is a public teacher, entering a privileged preserve, that of religious instruction in a society closed, tightly regimented, insulated with protective defenses.

Did his physique help? For those who, like the present writer, accept the authenticity of the Shroud of Turin (qv), he was a man of superb appearance, a beautifully proportioned body, a countenance such as no artist has ever been able to portray, with features of compelling power, a countenance which even in death speaks of noble lineage, reflects uniquely the features of one parent only. Without running to any such excess as talk about an athletic Christ, we can say confidently that Jesus was physically strong. He was reared to an outdoor life, in a district rich in nutriment, among a people with very sound dietary customs. In the years through which we can follow him, not only does he never show any sign of physical weakness or ill-health, he could fulfill tiring programs, go without sleep, travel on foot over considerable distances. He was never tense or strained, could switch from one kind of encounter to another with no respite: he was continuously available to those who sought him, with no insistence on timetables.

Jesus' social life was relaxed, free of any sort of taboo, religious or class snobbery. With him persons came first, as persons, without a publicized demand. When he had established a bond of trust, shown his astonishing insight, he would then set forth his teaching, nuanced only to gain faith and afford time, never bent to please. He was delicate, sensitive, gracious with the weak: mysteriously so with sinners. And what strange people met him, consorted with him: the religious establishment figures, scribes and Pharisees, on one notable occasion an official of the Roman occupying army (Mt 8:5-13; Lk 7:1-10), the hated tax collectors (Mt 9:9-13 par), the sick and handicapped, children, whom he welcomed (Mt 19:13-15 par), whom he proposed as models in his kingdom (Mt 18:3; 19:14; Lk 9:46), women (qv), some of whom followed him to minister to him (Lk 8:2), those perplexed such as the rich young man or Nicodemus; even those who sought to catch him out on questions of the law or on payment of taxes, he dealt with; he did not dismiss them as another might have done. His capacity to identify with the sick and suffering was inexhaustible.

In the one-to-one situations described by St. John, and any confrontation recorded by him or in the synoptic gospels, Jesus excelled in character analysis. It was not only his amazing capacity to combine two very different modes of communication, a public address or discourse and thinking on his feet to handle an objection, or to answer a loaded question; it was his ability to read men, to penetrate the bluff or the camouflage, and lay bare the inner drive and objective. With such equipment he never had to postpone an argument, play for time, just as he never needed notice beforehand of a statement expected of him.

He was a superb communicator, even, as with Pilate or the Sanhedrin, in what he did not wish to communicate because he had measured their power of assimilation. In his day-to-day teaching and preaching he was and still is unrivaled; he still communicates and the impact now as then is the word and the man at one as never by anyone else. As he assumed his public role with no training remotely commensurate, so he astonishes by his total self-assurance.

If we take the great "I" assertions related by John with all the care that exegetes suggest, they do represent the kind of didactic authority which Jesus exercised, which popular memory associated with him. The immense tolerance exhibited toward the sick and sinners did not prompt a dilution of doctrine, hesitation on essentials, reluctance to make an intransigent claim. And it all came out from the man himself. There was no research unit, no drafting committee,

no back-up team. There was no arranged setting, no staging for effect. The message could be given anywhere: in the fields, on a hillside, in the streets, by the water's edge, or from a boat, in the places of religious observance, a synagogue or the Temple. He was all that was needed; and with his unshakable self-assurance he knew this with certainty: "You have heard that it was said to the men of old . . . But I say to you . . . (Mt 5:21, etc.). Hence he never went back on an assertion, never apologized for an opinion, never withdrew from a position he had taken up.

His self-discipline and integrity placed him beyond any reproach, "Which of you will convince me of sin?" (Jn 8:46); "He was tempted as we are but without sin" (Heb 4:15); not a shadow of guilt complex, not the slightest indication of any feeling of personal inadequacy. But he was no recluse, he was not afraid to risk self-exposure; he was very sociable and accepted invitations to eat and drink with people of diverse quality and social backgrounds.

There is in the series of episodes put together by the evangelists a recurring impression of innovation; over every new page one expects something hitherto unknown. Yet it was not change for the sake of change; it was not thoughtless destruction; it certainly was not physical violence. This man could push forward the tracks of progress with a minimum of social upset. In practice he created the beneficial principles of healthy change: do not remove what serves its purpose; do not remove what you cannot replace by something better; in things organic, retain what will grow in the new reality.

Jesus was a perfect innovator because he was totally free. He owed his position to no man, to no previous bargain with powerful or vested interests. And he was without self-interest or merely human ambition; he rejected any attempt to give him a political position; he never touched money, never even hinted at anything like financial remuneration.

How did his human character enmesh with the lifework he undertook, and with the specifically religious ideas, ideals, achievements which were his? It is, of course, through this entire program, planned and executed, that his character was revealed. His teaching placed a heavy emphasis on interior, spiritual attitudes, and from such attitudes his own entire conduct drew its coherence and power. He summoned others to total commitment, "Thou shalt love the Lord thy God . . ." "If any man will come after me let him take up his cross and follow me." From that coherent depth sprang the unifying principle of his whole life, his unique singleness of purpose, obedience to the will of the Father: "My food is to do the will of him who sent me, and to accomplish his work" (Jn 4:34). "I do nothing on my own authority but speak thus as the Father taught me. And he who sent me is with me; he has not left me alone, for I always do what is pleasing to him'' (Jn 8:28-29).

There is no evidence that Jesus interpreted his Father's will in any sense of a frustrating regulation, a set of prohibitions only. The Agony in the Garden (qv) has to be considered separately. In public acts and gestures he knew how to reflect the munificence of the Godhead: he gave between 120 and 180 gallons of wine as a wedding gift; he gave an open-air banquet to five thousand people; finally, with a generous consciousness of the gift, it was his own life-blood that he poured out for all of us, but not before he had ensured in the mystery of the last meal, that his body and blood would be his constant gift to us until the end of time.

Jesus had a creative, optimistic outlook in what we would now call human relations. He gave people hope; he could see the best in everyone, which means anyone, refused to be tied to anyone's past in dealing with him, could transform a human life in the course of a single encounter. For many who met him, life would never be the same again. He had inexhaustively and immeasurably the magnetism which great leaders have had, which, when they are good, leaves a trail of illumination through the dull, at times obscure, spaces of history.

With his followers collectively his teaching had a positive, uplifting effect, as in the Beatitudes (qv); it searched out and exposed the vagaries of human conduct, as in the Parables (qv) which have an authentic ring across the ages; but it never sank into pessimism on the human condition, however stern his warning might be on the vicious habits he deplored, hypocrisy, institutional hardness, and pride.

In one-to-one relationships we meet something not often found in religious founders, a genius for friendship. "Greater love has no man than this, that a man lay down his life for his friends. You are my friends if you do what I command you. No longer do I call you servants, for the servant does not know what his master is doing; but I have called you friends, for all that I have heard from my Father I have made known to you" (Jn 15:13-15). This exalted friendship wonderfully. Jesus lived up to his ideal; so many of the attributes we look for in friends: tolerance, affection, trust, deep-seated concern, protection against evildoers are exemplified in Jesus. The family at Bethany is rightly cited in evidence: "Then Mary, when she came where Jesus was and saw him, fell at his feet, saying to him, 'Lord, if you had been here, my brother would not have died.' When Jesus saw her weeping, and the Jews who came with her also weeping, he was deeply moved in spirit and troubled; and he said, 'Where have you laid him?' They said

to him, 'Lord, come and see.' Jesus wept. So the Jews said, 'See how he loved him!' " (Jn 11:32-36). An act of friendship and an apologetic and messianic sign; Jesus had a plenitude of spirit which engaged him to act fully at different levels. His uniqueness raises him above the whole stream of history; his richness of character enabled him to enter history in his time and all time, as no one has ever done or ever will do.

---

[1]Cf. L. de Grandmaison, S.J., *Jésus Christ. Sa personne, ses messages, ses preuves*, 2 vol., 1928, ET 1935; V. Taylor, *The Life and Ministry of Jesus*, London, 1954; J. Guitton, *Jesus: The Eternal Problem*, 1958; C. H. Dodd, *The Founder of Christianity*, London, 1971; esp. K. Adam (qv) "The Mental Stature of Jesus," "The Interior Life of Jesus," "The Self-Revelation of Jesus," in *The Son of God*, London, 1934, 87–206; esp. E. Leen, C.S.Sp., "The Tenderness of Jesus to Those Who Fail," and "The triumph of failure," in *In the Lifeness of Christ*, 12th printing, 1956, 196–241; R. Orlett, *Jesus Christ in the Bible*, NCE VII, 909–18, esp. 913; J. A. Fitzmyer, *A Christological Catechism: New Testament Answers*, New York, 1982, 11–17; J. P. Meier, *NJBC*, 1316–1328.

CHRISTOLOGY FROM ABOVE

This approach to the theology of Christ, a methodology proceeding from such routine traditional positions that it is not consciously articulated, begins from God's action.[1] As a source of ideas almost automatically the preference is given to the Teaching Authority, and prominence is assumed for the dogma of Chalcedon (qv). The starting point is the Incarnation, and the interpretation of this has been given in scholastic theology; there is a high degree of conceptualization logically consequent on the Hellenistic intellectual milieu in which the first reflection on the truths of Christianity was undertaken, the first formulas fashioned and set. From the dogmatic definitions of the fourth and fifth centuries, which themselves gave a capital importance to earlier thinking on the Logos, development followed on clearly marked routes. The high point was reached in the twelfth and thirteenth centuries with the profound assimilation of Aristotelian philosophy into speculative theology.

It would be a caricature of this vast theological endeavor and the literature it produced to say that Sacred Scripture and Tradition were not investigated or explored to yield truth, but considered adjuncts to the essential project; bits and pieces would, on this view, have been picked to make a theologically respectable patchwork. Such caricature might be justified in regard to the manualistic treatment of theological theses, especially in certain instances where it was degenerate and desiccated. The thesis absorbed the attention, and passages from Scripture and Tradition were sought to buttress its content.

But there were excellent textbooks representing this manner of studying and presenting Christology: L. Billot's *De Verbo incarnato,* work of a great Jesuit professor in the Gregorian University in Rome in the early decades of the century, and *De Verbo incarnato* by his more recent successor in the same chair, Bernard Lonergan, S.J., though already a change in certain methodical modes is here evident. The fear that Sacred Scripture and Tradition would be automatically misinterpreted is not justified. The Incarnation which was deemed initial, essentially illuminating and normative, is a reality evident in Sacred Scripture; Chalcedon represented a vast achievement of Tradition. Wolfhart Pannenberg, whose option is a Christology "from below" nevertheless takes account of the fact that a giant of modern, indeed all-time, Calvinist theology, Karl Barth (qv), follows the procedure "from above to below"; so for a while did Emil Brunner; so did Heinrich Vogel.[2]

Pannenberg takes it that Christologies from above presuppose the doctrine of the Trinity and face this question: "How has the second Person of the Trinity (the Logos) assumed a human nature?"[3] He does not think the method feasible for these reasons: 1) A Christology from above presupposes what requires to be investigated and established, confession of Jesus' divinity; 2) A Christology which takes the divinity of Christ as its starting-point cannot give proper importance to "the historical man Jesus in his historical particularity," with its many diverse aspects; even the mysteries of Christ's humiliation and exaltation, his offices, and the very meaning of his death may not be rightly appreciated; 3) Such a Christology would mean that one "would have to stand in the position of God himself in order to follow the way of God's Son into the World." We cannot, the author thinks, get over the limitation of thinking "from the context of a historically determined situation."[4]

However, the author nuances his position and promises to show later "a relative justification for such a way of approaching the question." He does not think that the incarnational Christology which for so long ruled the development of Christology was "a mistake." He thinks it restricted the "historical reality of Jesus" and this "must be made fruitful today in its fullness."

To clarify the antithesis is helpful; to force it to the point of imposing a choice between options considered mutually exclusive is unjustifiable. As with so many approaches to theology this would seek to evade the mystery; it would ignore or misrepresent an immense literature, fruit of human genius enlightened by faith, of diverse authorship, method, insights, and conclusions.

[1]Cf. W. Pannenberg, "The Method of Christology," in *Jesus, God and Man,* London, 1968, 33–37; R. H. Fuller, "The Approach to New Testament Christology," in *The Foundations of New Testament Christology,* Fontana ed., 1972, 15–22; O. Cullman, "The Method to be Followed," in *Christology of the New Testament,* London, 1959, 6–10; W. Kasper, "The Problematics of Contemporary Christology," "The Historical Quest for Jesus Christ," in *Jesus the Christ,* 1977 ed., London, 14–40; J. Bowden, "History, Doctrine and Miracle," in *Jesus, The Unanswered Questions,* London, 1988, 148–64; C. F. D. Moule, *The Origin of Christology,* Cambridge, 1977; I. H. Marshall, *The Origins of New Testament Christology,* London, 1977; M. Hengel, *The Son of God: The Origin of Christology and the History of Jewish-Hellenistic Religion,* Philadelphia, 1976; J. Sobrino, *Christology at the Crossroads,* London, 1978, Ch. I and II; W. J. Thompson, *The Jesus Debate,* New York, 1985, passim; [2]W. Pannenberg, *Jesus, God and Man,* London, 1968, 33; [3]*Ibid.,* 34; [4]*Ibid.,* 35.

CHRISTOLOGY FROM BELOW

This is an approach to the study of Jesus Christ as he can be known from the Bible and all the ancillary disciplines which it uses.[1] The emphasis from the beginning of research is on the human existence of Jesus Christ, the historical setting, the deeds and words which can be established as his, the forces at work in and about him during his life, the spiritual and cultural legacy which he inherited, the meaning of statements and events in the light of his people with their unique religious belief and cultural ethos. Attention is absorbed by exegesis and hermeneutics, all theological or ideological presuppositions are excluded or thought to be so.

Can presuppositions be totally eliminated from the mind of one who begins his study of Christology with the historical Jesus of Nazareth? The very choice of Jesus as a subject presupposes his importance, to take things at the lowest level. If the theologian so engaged is a person of faith, how can he divest himself entirely of an outlook, mental categories, modes of thought, automatic intellectual response, which Jesus causes, conditions or affects in his psyche? His mind is made up of many layers, some of which lie in his subconscious. Will ideas deep, deep within him remain totally dormant? Had he not better face such a possibility?

Fr. Pierre Benoit analyzes searchingly the philosophical presuppositions of Form-Criticism, which would surely be a technique of those approaching Christology "from below." It is argued that R. Bultmann (qv), surely a notable practitioner of the method, was in the last resort influenced by his Lutheran inheritance of *Sola fides.*

The emphasis here is on history and due respect must be shown to the progress made over the last century and a half in the historical sciences. There is everything to gain by applying the most perfect historical method to the study of the Christian origins, and to the central figure in Christianity. An offshoot of this research has been the heavy emphasis put on the Jesus of history and the Christ of faith controversy (see article History and Jesus). It would be naive, while extolling the importance of the historical sciences, to overlook the dark, even black spots in modern historiography; fallibility, falsification, fear of the popular media which have taken to history with relish; in religious history confessional prejudice, apologetic motivation, and much else besides.

The prime historical source for study of Jesus being the gospels, supported by other NT writings, the task of the advocate of Christology from below is to compose, fashion, elaborate a biblical Christology. It is an awesome task and John Bowden rightly remarks that some Catholic writers who took it up enthusiastically did not at once see its drawback.[2] One should perhaps say limitations, within which it is most valuable; there is nothing derogatory either to authors or their writings in the word limitations. We are dealing with mystery. We are dealing with the "Lord of history" (qv). He has, through the ages, stirred human inspiration to the heights of heroism, literary and artistic expression; he has unmistakably enlarged the human personality of one after another of his followers.

We meet the problem of dogma versus biblical exegesis, which has engaged giants of the age like Karl Rahner and Hans Urs von Balthasar (qqv). That there is at times tension does not mean that harmony and cooperation are unattainable. A study of recent literature on Christology will also show that biblical theology may be approached so ardently from one or other standpoint that there is a risk of distortion; one may quote, with entire respect for those engaged in difficult, at times unrewarding work, liberation and feminist theologians. They are welcome, but they, as all of us, have to realize that Jesus Christ is bigger than their concerns or projects. Jesus Christ was interested in personal freedom and liberty, not as transcendental absolutes, but as a human endowment which will dignify and enhance the person's response to the Creator's demand; he was committed to the welfare, the well-being of women (qv), but not of women in competition with men, and not merely at the level of their feminine characteristics, but far beyond these, in their spiritual being.

The statement issued by the Biblical Commission (qv) on Scripture and Christology has many points of interest to our subject. Specifically it refers to it thus: "Among the above-mentioned Christologies,

those that begin with the historical Jesus seem somewhat like Christologies that proceed 'from below.' On the contrary, those that concentrate on Jesus' relation to God the Father can rightly be called 'Christologies from above.' A number of contemporary writers try *to combine both aspects*. Beginning with a critical study of the (New Testament) texts, they show that the Christology implicit in the words of Jesus and in his human experience forms a certain continuum and is profoundly united with the different Christologies that are *explicitly* found in the New Testament. Yet this bond of union is discovered in very different ways (e.g., L. Bouyer, R. Fuller, C. F. D. Moule, I. H. Marshall, B. Rey, Chr. Duquoc, W. Kasper, M. Hengel, J. D. G. Dunn, etc.).

Although the approaches and the conclusions of these authors are far from being in agreement, the two following principal points are common to them:

1) One must distinguish, on the one hand, the way Jesus presented himself to his contemporaries and was able to be understood by them (his family, opponents, disciples); on the other, the way those who came to believe in Jesus understood his life and his person *after the manifestations of him as one raised from the dead*. Between these two periods there is, indeed, no interruption; nevertheless, an advance of no little importance is noted, consistent with the early views, and it is to be regarded as a constitutive element of Christology itself. This Christology, if it has to take into account the limits of the humanity of (Jesus of Nazareth), has to acknowledge in him at the same time 'the Christ of faith,' fully revealed by his resurrection (qv) in the light of the Holy Spirit.

2) Also to be noted are the *different* ways of understanding the mystery of Christ that already appear in the *New Testament* books themselves. This is seen, however, when an *Old Testament* mode of speaking is employed, and when Scripture is said to be fulfilled in Jesus, the Savior of the world. For the fulfillment of Scripture presupposes a certain amplification of meaning, whether it is a question of a meaning that the biblical texts originally bore, or of a meaning that Jews, rereading these texts, were attributing to them in the time of Jesus. Indeed, such an amplification of meaning should scarcely be attributed to secondary theological speculation; it has its origin in the person of Jesus himself, whose own characteristics it sets in a better light.

With such considerations (these) exegetes and theologians approach the question of *the individual personality of Jesus*.

1) This individual personality was cultivated and formed by a Jewish education, the positive values of which Jesus took fully to himself. But it was also en-

dowed with a *quite singular consciousness (qv) of himself,* as far as his relation to God was concerned as well as the mission he was to carry out for human beings. Some gospel texts (e.g., Lk 2:40-52) lead us to recognize a certain *growth* in this consciousness.

2) Nevertheless, (these) exegetes and theologians refuse to get involved in a 'psychology' of Jesus, both because of critical problems in the texts and because of the danger of speculating (in some wrong way, either by excess or defect). They prefer a reverent circumspection before the mystery of his personality. Jesus took no pains to define it precisely, even though through his sayings or his deeds he did allow one to catch a mere glimpse of the secrets of his intimate life (H. Schurmann). Various Christologies in the New Testament, as well as the definitions of councils—in which are repeated in an 'auxiliary language,' things already contained in Scripture—have indicated the *route* along which theological speculation can proceed, without exactly demasking the mystery itself.

In their studies of Jesus Christ, (these) exegetes and theologians also agree that *Christology should in no way be* separated from soteriology. The Word (qv) of God was made flesh (Jn 1:14) to play the role of Mediator between God and human beings. If he could be a human being 'fully free' and 'a man for others,' this was so because this freedom and this gift of himself flowed forth from a source none other than the intimate union of himself with God, since he was able to turn to God as Father in a special and quite unique sense. Questions, then about the knowledge and pre-existence of Christ can in no way be avoided, but each of them pertains to a later stage of Christology.''[3]

---

[1]Bibl. to article, 'Christology from above'; add E. Troeltch, "Über historische und dogmatische Methode in der Theologie," *Gesammelte Schriften,* II, Tübingen, 1913, 729–53; H. Urs von Balthasar, "Exegese und Dogmatik," *Internationale katholische Zeitschrift,* 5 (1976) 385–92; [2]*Jesus, the Unanswered Questions,* London, 1988, 153; [3]Tr. J. A. Fitzmyer, S.J., *Scripture and Christology,* London, 1966, 17–19; cf. author's commentary, 90–92.

COMMUNICATION OF IDIOMS, THE

The name given to the mental and linguistic process whereby human properties are attributed to God in Jesus Christ and divine properties to man in him.[1] The basis of the practice is the single divine Person, with two natures, united in Christ. It was accepted in the NT and taken up by the Fathers, in the east and the west, with doctrinal explanation forthcoming from St. Augustine (qv) in the west and St. Gregory of Nyssa (qv) in the east. Where two persons are affirmed, as by the Nestorians and only one nature by the Monophysites (qv) there is confusion, as there is when the divine or human properties are attributed, without the Person as the obvious reference. 'Humanity is divinity' is not justified; 'Jesus is divine' is. The teaching which vindicates the usage was promulgated at Ephesus and Chalcedon (qqv). It is part of the mystery of Christ that in him is centered the communication of idioms; through it we touch the essence of the Incarnation. Understandably then, the usage is more certain in concrete contexts, but there has to be care in affirmative and negative affirmation; theological common sense dictates the limits when the communication of idioms would not function and heresy would arise. The test is the centrality of the Person, in discourse as in reality, with the distinction of natures. An outstanding instance of the usage is the application of the term *Theotokos* to Mary at Ephesus.

---

[1]St. Thomas, *Summa Theologiae,* III, a. 16; A. Michael, *DTC* VII, 595–602; K. Forster, *LTK,* 607–09; J. F. Rigney, *NCE,* 35–37.

CONSCIOUSNESS OF JESUS, THE

An important document on this subject was issued by the International Theological Commission under date of December 8, 1985.[1] The official communique recorded the history of the text; three successive drafts were considered, and the final one, benefitting by suggestions and amendments, was voted quasi-unanimously and then approved by Cardinal Ratzinger. Preliminaries do not affect the essence of the teaching which is contained in the following section. The Commission recognizes the need to speak in the philosophical knowledge of the time. It goes on:

"Controversies on the question we are dealing with come precisely from the diversity of philosophic conceptions. The Commission does not wish, in its statement, to be bound by a fixed philosophical terminology. Its starting point is a common general assumption that as men we are present to ourselves in our 'heart,' in all our actions. We know, nevertheless, that the consciousness of Jesus partakes the singularity and the mysterious character of his Person. That is why it is beyond purely rational reflection. We can treat the question submitted to us only in the light of faith, which sees Jesus as the Christ, Son of the living God.

Four Propositions

"Our study will then be limited to certain major statements on the consciousness of Jesus in regard to his own Person and mission. The four propositions which follow are in the context of what the faith has always believed about Christ. They deliberately avoid entering into the theological developments which try to expound this datum of the faith. There will be no question then of attempts to formulate theologically *how* this consciousness was expressed in the humanity of Christ. The commentaries on the four propositions follow broadly a plan which comprises three stages. First we state what the apostolic preaching says about Christ. We seek next to discover what the synoptic gospels allow us, by the convergence of their different lines, to say about the very consciousness of Jesus. Finally we consider the testimony of St. John, who sometimes says explicitly what the synoptic gospels contain implicitly, with no mutual opposition.

First Proposition
Enunciation

"The life of Jesus bears witness to consciousness of his filial relationship with the Father. His behavior and his words, which are those of the perfect 'servant' imply an authority which far surpasses that of the ancient prophets and reverts to God alone. Jesus derived this incomparable excellence from his singular relationship with God whom he calls 'my Father.' He was conscious of being the only Son of God, and in this sense, of being himself God.

Commentary

"1.1 The post-paschal apostolic preaching, which proclaims Jesus as Son and Son of God, is not the result of a late development in the primitive Church; it is already in the core of the most ancient enunciations of the kerygma, confessions of faith or hymns (cf. Rom 1:3f; Ph 2:6f). St. Paul goes so far as to summarize his entire preaching in the phrase 'the Gospel of God concerning his Son' (Rom 1:3, 9; cf. 2 Cor 1:19; Gal 1:16). Particularly significant, from this point of view, are also the 'formulas of mission': 'God sent his Son' (Rom 8:3; Gal 4:4). The divine sonship of Jesus is therefore at the center of the apostolic preaching. This may be understood as an explanation, in the light of the Cross and resurrection, of the relationship of Jesus to his 'Abba.'

"1.2 In fact, the designation of God as 'Father,' which has become purely and simply the Christian way of naming God, goes back to Jesus himself; that is one of the surest results of historical research on Jesus. But Jesus did not only call God 'Father' or 'My Father' in general; it is in addressing him in prayer that he invokes him by the name of 'Abba' (Mk 14:36; cf. Rom 8:15; Gal 4:6). There is here something new. Jesus' way of praying (cf. Mt 11:25) and the way of praying he teaches his disciples (cf. Lk 11:2) suggest the distinction (which will be explicit

after Easter, cf. Jn 20:17) between 'My Father' and 'your Father,' and the character of the relationship which unites Jesus to God, one that is unique and untransferable. Prior to the manifestation of his mystery to men, there was in the human perception of Jesus' consciousness a singular, singularly profound certainty, that of his relationship with the Father. The invocation of God as 'Father' implies consequently the consciousness which Jesus had of his divine authority and of his mission. Not without reason does one find in this context the term 'reveal' (Mt. 11:27; and par; cf. Mt 16:17). Conscious of being the One who knows God perfectly, Jesus knows that he is at the same time the messenger of God's definitive revelation to men. He is and he is conscious of being 'the Son' (cf. Mk 12:6; 13:22).

"By reason of this consciousness Jesus speaks and acts with an authority which belongs properly to God alone. It is the attitude which men have towards him, Jesus, which decides their eternal salvation (Lk 12:8; cf. Mk 8:36; Mt 10:32). Here and now Jesus calls people to follow him (Mk 1:17); to follow him, he must be loved more than parents (Mt 10:37), considered above all earthly goods (Mk 10:29); one must be ready to 'lose one's life because of *me*' (Mk 8:35). He speaks as sovereign lawgiver (Mt 5:22, 28, etc.), putting himself above prophets and kings (Mt 12:41f). There is no other Master but him (Mt 23:8); all will pass away, save his word (Mk 13:31).

"1.3 The Gospel of St. John says more explicitly whence Jesus holds this unheard-of authority; it is because 'the Father is in me and I in the Father' (10:38); 'I and the Father are one' (10:30). The 'I' who speaks here and who legislates in sovereign manner has the same dignity as the 'I' of Yahweh (cf. Ex 3:14). Even from the historical point of view there is a sure basis for the affirmation that the primitive apostolic proclamation of Jesus, as Son and as Son of God relies on the very consciousness Jesus had of being the Son and the envoy of the Father.

Second Proposition
Enunciation

"Jesus knew the purpose of his mission: to announce the kingdom of God and to make it present already in his Person, his deeds and his words, so that the world should be reconciled with God and renewed. He freely accepted the Father's will: to give his life for the salvation of all men; he knew that he was sent by the Father to serve and to give his life 'for man' (Mk 13:24).

Commentary

"2.1. The apostolic preaching of Christ's divine sonship comprises equally and inseparably a soteriological significance. In fact, the sending, the coming of

Jesus in the flesh (Rom 8:3), under the law (Gal 4:4), his self-abasement, aims at our uplifting; to secure our righteousness (2 Cor 5:21), to enrich us (2 Cor 8:9), to make us sons through the Spirit (Rom 8:15f; Gal 4:5f; Heb 2:10). Such a participation in the divine sonship of Jesus, which is realized in faith and is expressed especially in Christians' prayer to the Father, assumes the consciousness which Jesus himself had of being Son. The whole apostolic preaching is based on the conviction and persuasion that Jesus knew that he was the Son, the One sent by the Father. Without this consciousness of Jesus, not only Christology, but also all soteriology, would lack a foundation.

"2.2. The consciousness which Jesus possesses of his singular filial relationship with the Father is the foundation and the presupposition of his mission. Conversely it is possible to argue from his mission to his consciousness. According to the synoptic gospels Jesus knows that he has been sent to announce the Good News of the kingdom of God (Lk 4:43; cf. Mt 15:24). It is for that that he came forth (Mk 1:38) and has come (cf. Mk 2:17). Through his mission on behalf of men one can at the same time discern the One whose envoy he is (cf. Lk 10:16). In gesture and in word Jesus manifested the purpose of his 'coming': to call sinners (Mk 2:17), 'to seek and save the lost' (Lk 19:10), not to abolish, but to accomplish the law (Mt 5:17), to bring the sword of separation (Mt 10:34), to cast fire upon the earth (Lk 12:49). Jesus knows that he has come not to be served, but to serve and 'to give his life as a ransom for many' (Mk 10:45).

"2.3. This 'coming' can have no other origin but God. St. John's Gospel says it clearly, making explicit, in his theology of mission (Sendung-schristologie) the more implicit testimonies of the Synoptics on the consciousness which Jesus had of his incomparable mission; he knows that he has come from the Father (Jn 5:43), came forth from him (8:42; 16:28) (issu in French). His mission, received from the Father, is not imposed on him from outside; it is his own to the point of coinciding with his whole being: it is his whole life (6:57), his food (4:34), it alone he seeks (5:30), for the will of the One who sent him is his whole will (6:38), his words are the words of his Father (3:34; 12:49), his works the works of the Father (9:4) in such wise that he can say of himself: 'He who has seen me has seen the Father' (14:9). The consciousness Jesus has of himself coincides with the consciousness of his mission.

This has much deeper significance than consciousness of a prophetic mission received at a particular moment, even were it from 'the womb of his mother' (Jeremiah, cf. Jer 1:5; the Baptist, cf. Lk 1:15; Paul, cf. Gal 1:15). This mission is rather traceable to an original 'coming forth' from God, 'For it is from God that I . . . came forth' (8:42), which presupposes, to make it possible, that he has been 'from the beginning' with God (1:1-18).

"2.4. The consciousness which Jesus has of his mission implies then the consciousness of his 'pre-existence.' In fact, the mission is its 'prolongation,' The human consciousness of his mission 'translates,' so to speak, the eternal relationship with the Father into the language of a human life.

"This relationship of the Word incarnate with the Father assumes in the first place the mediation of the Holy Spirit. The Spirit must then be in the consciousness of Jesus insofar as he is Son. His very human existence already is the result of an action by the Spirit; since the Baptism of Jesus, all his work—whether action or passion among men or communion of prayer towards the Father—is accomplished only in and through the Spirit (Lk 4:18; Acts 10:38; cf. Mk 1:12; Mt 12:28). The son knows that in the accomplishment of the good will of the Father the Spirit guides and upholds him to the Cross. There, with his earthly mission achieved, he 'hands over' (paredoken) his 'spirit' (pneuma) (Jn 19:30) in which some people read an insinuation of the gift of the Spirit. After his resurrection and ascension (qqv) he becomes a man glorified, which as God he was from all eternity, 'a vivifying Spirit' (1 Cor 14:45; 2 Cor 3:17), Lord empowered to distribute, in sovereign manner, the Spirit to raise us to the dignity of sons in himself.

"But this very relationship of the Son incarnate with the Father is, at the same time, expressed in a self-emptying manner. So as to achieve perfect obedience, Jesus freely renounces (Ph 2:6-9) whatever could be a hindrance to this attitude. For example, he does not wish to use the legions of angels which he could have (Mt 26:53), he wills to grow as a man 'in wisdom, in age and in grace' (Lk 2:52), to learn obedience (Heb 5:8), to face temptations (Mt 4:1-11 and par.), to suffer. This is not incompatible with the assertions that Jesus 'knows all things' (Jn 5:20; cf. 13:3; Mt. 11:27), if these assertions are understood in the sense that Jesus receives from his Father all that allows him to accomplish his work of revelation and of universal redemption (cf. Jn 3:11-32; 8:38-40; 15:15; 17:8).

Third Proposition
Enunciation

"To accomplish his saving mission Jesus willed to gather men with a view to the kingdom and to call them around him. With this plan in view Jesus performed specific acts, which taken together can only be interpreted as the preparation of the Church, which will be definitely established in the events of Easter and Pentecost. It must then be said that Jesus willed to found the Church.

Commentary

"3.1. According to apostolic testimony the Church is inseparable from Christ. According to a formula current with St. Paul, the Churches are 'in Christ' (1 Thess 1:1; 2:14; 2 Thess 1:1; Gal 1:22), they are 'the Churches of Christ' (Rom 16:16). To be a Christian means that 'Christ is in you' (Rom 8:10; 2 Cor 13:5), it is 'life in Christ Jesus' (Rom 8:2); 'you are all one in Christ' (Gal. 3:28). This unity is expressed especially by the analogy of the unity of the human body. It is the Holy Spirit who constitutes the unity of this body: body of Christ (1 Cor 12:27), or 'in Christ' (Rom 12:5), and even Christ (1 Cor 12:12). It is the heavenly Christ who is the principle of life and of growth of the Church (Col 2:19; Eph 4:11-16), he is the 'head of the body' (Col 1:18; 3:15), the 'fullness' (Eph 1:22f) of the Church.

"Now this infrangible unity of Christ with his Church is rooted in the supreme act of his earthly life: the gift of his life on the Cross. It was because he loved it that 'he delivered himself for it' (Eph 5:25), for he wished to 'present it to himself in splendor' (5:25; cf. Col 1:22). The Church, body of Christ, takes its origin from the body delivered on the Cross, from the 'precious blood' (qv) of Christ which is the 'price' of our ransom (cf. 1 Cor 6:20). For the apostolic preaching the Church was really the aim of the work of salvation accomplished by Christ in his earthly life.

"3.2. When Jesus preaches the kingdom of God, he does not simply announce the imminence of a great eschatological change; he first calls men to enter the Kingdom. The seed and beginning of the Kingdom is the 'little flock' (cf. Lk 12:32) of those whom Jesus came to call around him, whose shepherd he himself is (Mk 14:27 par; Jn 10:1-29; cf. Mt 10:16 par.), he who came to gather together his sheep and set them free (Mk 15:24; Lk 15:4-7). Jesus speaks of this calling together under the image of the guest at a wedding (Mk 2:19 par), God's sowing (Mt 13:24; 15:13), a fishing net (Mt 13:47; Mk 1:17). The disciples of Jesus make a city on a hill-top, visible from afar (Mt 5:14); they constitute the new family which has God for Father, in which all are brethren (Mt 23:9); they make up the true family of Jesus (Mk 3:34 par). The parables of Jesus and the images he uses to speak of those he came to call together contain an 'implicit ecclesiology.'

"There is no question of asserting that this intention of Jesus implies the express wish of founding and establishing all the institutional aspects of the Church, as these have developed through the ages. It is, on the other hand, necessary to assert that Jesus willed to endow the community which he came to call around him with a structure that will remain until the full accomplishment of the Kingdom. Here we must mention in the first place the choice of the Twelve and of Peter as their head (Mk 3:14f). This choice, most clearly intended, aims at the eschatological constitution of the People of God, which will be open to all men (cf. Mt 8:11f). The Twelve (Mk 6:7) and the other disciples (Lk 10:1) share in the mission of Christ, in his power, but also in his lot (Mt 10:25; Jn 15:20). In them, it is Jesus himself who comes and in him is present the One who sent him (Mt 10:40).

"'The Church will also have its own prayer,' that which Jesus gave it (Lk 11:2-4); she receives especially the memorial of the Supper, center of the 'New Alliance' (Lk 22:20) and of the new community gathered in the breaking of bread (Lk 22:19). Jesus also taught to those whom he gathered around him a new 'pattern of behavior,' different from that of the ancients (Mt 5:21, etc.), of the pagans (cf. Mt 5:47), of the great one of this world (Lk 22:25f). Did Jesus wish to found a Church? Yes, but this Church is the People of God which he gathers, beginning with Israel, through which he aims at the salvation of all peoples. For it is first 'towards the lost sheep of the house of Israel' (Mt 10:6; 15:24) to which Jesus knows that he is sent, and to which he sends his disciples. One of the most poignant expressions of the consciousness Jesus had of his divinity and of his mission is this complaint (the complaint of the God of Israel): 'O Jerusalem, Jerusalem . . . How often would I have gathered your children, as a hen gathers her brood under her wings, and you would not!' (Lk 13:34; cf. 19:41-44). It is God (Yahweh), in effect, who in the Old Testament seeks ceaselessly to gather the people of Israel in one people, his people. It is this 'You would not' which altered not the intention, but the way the gathering of all men around Jesus will take. It will be henceforth the 'time of the pagans' (Lk 21:24; cf. Rom 11:1-6) that will characterize the *ecclesia* of Christ. Christ had consciousness of his saving mission. This comprised the foundation of his *ecclesia,* that is to say, the calling of all men into the 'family of God.' The history of Christianity is based, in the last analysis, on the intention and will of Jesus to found his Church.

"3.3 In the light of the Spirit, the Gospel of St. John sees the whole earthly life of Christ as lit by the glory of the Risen One. Thus the gaze of the circle of Jesus' disciples opens already on all those who 'will believe in me through their word' (Jn 17:20).

Those who, during his earthly life were with him, those whom the Father had given him (17:6) and whom he had kept, and for whom he had 'consecrated' (17:19) himself by giving his life, they represent already all the faithful, all who will receive him (1:12) and will believe in him (3:36). By faith they are united to him as the branches to the vine without which they dry up (Jn 15:6). This intimate union between Jesus and believers ('You in me and I in you,' 14:20) has its origin, on the one hand, in the design of the Father who 'gives' his disciples to Jesus (6:39, 44, 65), but it is ultimately effected by the free gift of his life (10:18) 'for his friends' (15:3). The Paschal Mystery remains the source of the Church (cf. Jn 19:34); 'And I, when I am lifted up from the earth, will draw all men to me' (12:32).

Fourth Proposition
Enunciation

"The consciousness which Christ has of being sent by the Father for the salvation of the world and for the calling of all men into the people of God implies, mysteriously, love for all men, so that all of us can say: 'The Son of God has loved me and gave himself for me' (Gal 2:20; *Gaudium et Spes,* 22:3).

Commentary

"4.1. The apostolic preaching, in the first expressions given to it, carries the conviction that 'Christ died for our sins according to the Scriptures' (1 Cor 15:3), that he 'gave himself for our sins' (Gal 1:4), and this in agreement with the will of God the Father, who delivered him for our trespasses' (Rom 4:25; cf. Is 53:6) 'for us all' (Rom 8:32) 'to redeem us' (Gal 4:4). God who 'desires all men to be saved' (1 Tim 2:4) excludes no one from his plan of salvation which Christ espouses with his whole being. The whole life of Christ from his 'entry to the world' (Heb 10:5) to the giving of his life is one unique gift 'for us.' That is what the Church preached from the beginning (cf. Rom 5:8; 1 Thess 5:10; 2 Cor 5:15; 1 Pet 2:21; 3:18).

"If he died for us, it means that he loved us. 'Christ loved us and gave himself up for us a fragrant offering' (Eph 5:2). 'Us' here means all men whom he wishes to gather into his Church: 'Christ loved the Church and gave himself for her' (Eph 5:25). Now the Church has not understood this love only as a general attitude, but as a love so concrete that each one is personally intended. Thus the Church understands things when she hears St. Paul recalling respect for the 'weak.' 'Do not let what you eat cause the ruin of anyone for whom Christ died' (Rom 14:15; cf. 1 Cor 8:11; 2 Cor 5:14f). To the Christians of Corinth, divided into parties, the same Paul puts the question: 'Is Christ divided? Was Paul crucified

for you?' (1 Cor 1:13). And it is on his own account that Paul, who, however, did not know Jesus 'in the days of his flesh' (Heb 5:7) can assert: 'The life I live now in the flesh I live by faith in the Son of God' (Gal 2:20).

"4.2. The apostolic witnesses recalled above supporting the idea of a loving death of Jesus, entirely personal in manner, 'for us,' 'for me' and my 'brethren' include in one view the limitless love of the preexisting 'Son of God' (Gal 2:20), he who is, at the same time recognized as the glorified 'Lord.' The loving 'for us' of Jesus has its basis in the preexistence and is maintained up to the love of the Glorified One who now 'intercedes for us' (Rom 8:34), he who 'has loved us' (Rom 8:37) in his incarnation and in his death. The 'preexisting' love of Jesus is the continuous element which characterizes the three 'stages' (preexistence, earthly existence, glorified existence).

"This continuity of his love is expressed in *the words of Jesus.* According to Lk 22:27, Jesus grasps the whole of his earthly life and his conduct under the image of 'one who serves at table.' 'To be the servant of all' (Mk 9:35 par); that is the fundamental rule in the circle of the disciples. The serving love of Jesus reaches its peak in the farewell meal, in the course of which he sacrifices himself, giving himself as one who is to die (Lk 22:19f. par) On the cross his life of service changes completely into a death of service 'for man' (Mk 10:45; cf. 14:22-24). Jesus' service in his life and in his death was equally in the final estimate a service of the 'Kingdom of God,' in words and in deeds, to the point that he can depict his life and his action in his future glory as a 'service at table (Lk 12:37) and as an 'intercession for . . .' (Rom 8:34). This service was the service of love, associating the complete love of God with a love of the neighbor full of self-abnegation (cf. Mk 12:28-34).

"This love of which the whole life of Jesus gives proof, first appears to us as universal, in the sense that he excludes no one who comes to him. This love seeks out 'the lost one' (Lk 15:3-10, 11, 32), tax collectors, and sinners (cf. Mk 2:15; Lk 7:34-36, 50); Mt 9:1-8; Lk 15:1f), the rich (Lk 19:1-10), and the poor (Lk 16:19-31), men and women (Lk 8:2-3; 7:11-17; 13:10-17), the sick (Mk 1:29-34), the possessed (Mk 1:21-28), those who weep (Lk 6:21), and those who are heavy laden (Mt 11:28). This openness of the Heart of Jesus (qv) to all is meant to transcend the limits of his generation. This appears in the 'universalization' of his mission, of his promises. The beatitudes go beyond the limits of his immediate audience, they are meant for all the poor, all the hungry (cf. Lk 6:20f). Jesus identifies himself with the little ones and with the poor (Mk 10:13-16); he who receives one of these little ones receives Jesus himself, and in him he receives the One who sent him (Mk 9:37). Only at the last judgment will it appear openly how far this identification, now still hidden, has really gone (Mt 25:31-46).

"4.3. At the center of our faith there is this mystery: the inclusion of all men in this eternal love with which God has loved the world to the extent of giving up his own Son (Jn 3:16). 'By this we know love, that he (that is Christ) laid down his life for us' (1 Jn 3:16). In reality 'the good Shepherd gives his life for his sheep' (Jn 10:11); he knows them (Jn 10:14), and he calls each one by his name (Jn 10:3).

"4.4. It is because they have known this personal love for each one that so many Christians have committed themselves to the love of the poorest, without discrimination, and that they continue to bear witness to this love which knows how to find Jesus in each of the 'least' who are his 'brethren' (Mt 25:40). 'There is question of everyone for each one has been included in the mystery of the Redemption; Jesus Christ has united himself to each one for ever, through this mystery'" (John Paul II, *Redemptor hominis*, 13: *AAS* 1979, I, 283; cf. *Gaudium et Spes* 22).

[1]Author's tr. from *La Documentation Catholique* 83 (1986) 916–21; cf. *ibid.* for history of the text; available also Vatican City Press, English tr., *Jesus' Self-Awareness*; cf. articles Knowledge of Christ, The "I" of Christ.

COUNCILS, GENERAL

The findings and teaching of the Councils with some relevance to Christology are summarized here: Nicaea, 325 (qv), established the true divinity of Jesus Christ, pronouncing his *homoousios* with the Father; Constantinople I, 381, by the words "Lord and Giver of Life," defined the divinity of the Holy Spirit, and condemned Apollinarianism (qv) which denied the full humanity of Christ; Ephesus, 431, condemned Nestorius, and asserted that in Christ, true God and true man, there was but one Person, divine—in consequence of which Mary is rightly called *Theotokos*; Chalcedon, 451 (qv), consonant with the doctrine of Leo the Great (qv) defined the two natures, human and divine, in one divine Person; Constantinople II, 553, confessed that the divine Word in Jesus is that which constitutes his Person, in this dwelling his divine and human natures; *enhypostasia*—the two natures dwell in the Person of the Word; Constantinople III, 680/681, condemned Monothelitism (qv), stating that in Jesus two fully operating wills exist; Trent, Session XIII, 1551, defined Jesus' substantial presence in the Eucharist, and Session XXII, 1562,

clarified his role as priest and victim in the Mass; Vatican II, 1962–65 (qv), gave centrality to the mystery of Christ in its teaching on the Church, revelation, the different ministries and Christian callings—a key sentence, "Christ is the mediator and the fullness of divine revelation" (Constitution on Divine Revelation, art. 2).[1]

[1]F. Dvornik, *Emperors, Popes and Councils, DOP* 6 (1951) 1–23; *id., The Ecumenical Councils,* New York, 1961; *id., NCE* IV, 375–77; P. Hughes, *The Church in Crisis,* London, 1960; H. Jedin, *The Ecumenical Councils of the Catholic Church,* New York, 1960; V. Peri, *I Concili e le Chiese,* Rome, 1965; W. Thompson, *The Jesus Debate,* New York, 1985, 327; J. R. Murphy, *The General Councils of the Church,* New York, 1959.

CYRIL OF ALEXANDRIA, ST., DOCTOR OF THE CHURCH (d. 444)

Unrivalled in his knowledge of the Fathers who had preceded him, well equipped in the principles and subtleties of doctrine, C. was not only the Doctor of the *Theotokos,* but a sure theologian of the Incarnate Word.[1] Only the terminology is at times slightly tinged with ambiguity, from which difficulties were to arise later. It is agreed, moreover, among scholars that C.'s thinking evolved, gained depth and accuracy before the challenge of Nestorius (qv). Whereas in his earlier works on the *Thesaurus* and the *Dialogues* he was content with a formulation taken from Athanasius (qv), 'The Word was made man, but did not descend upon a man,' and used metaphors like 'temple' and 'house' to explain what he spoke of as 'inhabitation,' he later dropped this phraseology and really propounds the hypostatic union: "For we do not affirm that the nature of the Word underwent a change and became flesh, or that it was transformed into a whole or perfect man consisting of soul and body, but we say that the Word, having in an ineffable and inconceivable manner personally united to himself flesh instinct with a living soul, became man and was called the Son of Man (qv), yet not of mere will or favor, nor again by the simple taking to himself of a person (i.e., of a human person to his divine person); and that while the natures which were brought together into this true unity were diverse, there was of both one Lord and Christ and Son by their unutterable and unspeakable concurrence and unity. And thus, although he subsisted and was begotten of the Father before the worlds, he is spoken of as having been born also after the flesh of a woman; not that his divine nature had its beginning of existence in the holy Virgin, or needed of necessity on its own account a second generation after its generation from the Father, for it is foolish and absurd to say that he who subsisted before all worlds, and was co-eternal with the Father, stood in need of a second beginning of existence; but forasmuch as the Word having 'for us and for our salvation' personally united to himself human nature, came forth of a woman, for this reason he is said to have been born after the flesh. For he was not first born an ordinary man of the holy Virgin, and then the Word descended upon him, but having been made one with the flesh from the very womb itself, he is said to have submitted to a birth according to the flesh, as appropriating and making his own the birth of his own flesh."[2]

This is a central passage in the anti-Nestorian corpus, which is extensive in the whole prolific output of C.—his writings fill ten volumes of *PG*. In the *Thesaurus on the Holy and Consubstantial Trinity*, and the *Dialogues* on the same subject, he is concerned with replying to the Arian objections. From 429 he wrote constantly on the problems raised by Nestorius. The latter had challenged the unity of Christ, demonstrating this by his refusal to give Mary the title *Theotokos*. The debate has often been presented as essentially Marian in its content. It was Christological, but because "The Word was made flesh" depended intrinsically on "Let it be done unto me," Mary was perforce involved.

To the passage from Epistle IV may be added others from Epistles XVII and XXXIX to amplify his thought: "He vouchsafed to be born as we, and proceeded forth, a man from a woman, not ceasing to be what he was, but even when he became man by taking upon him flesh and blood, still continuing what he was, God in nature and truth . . . we say that the Son of God while visible to the eyes, and a babe in swaddling clothes, and still at the breast of his Virgin Mother, filled all creation as God, and was seated with his Father. For the divine nature is without quantity and without magnitude and without limit."[3] "If any one in the one Christ divides the subsistences (*hypostaseis*) after the union, connecting them only by a conjunction of dignity or authority or rule, and not rather by a union of natures (*enosis physike*), let him be anathema."[4] "If any one distributes to two Persons or Subsistences the expressions used both in the Gospels and in the Epistles, or used of Christ by the saints, or by him of himself, attributing some to a man, conceived of separately, apart from the Word which is of God, and attributing others, as befitting God, exclusively to the Word which is of God the Father, let him be anathema."[5] C. rules out anything less than real union of the natures: not mere indwelling, not juxtaposition, not a form of participation.

Quasten sums up C.'s doctrine, while pointing to the problems of faulty terminology: "To sum up, it is evident that Cyril in reality sees the union in Christ resulting from the Person, the duality from the natures. In this he has anticipated the decision of the Council of Chalcedon and prepared the theological foundation for it. However, his terminology is by no means satisfactory and was no doubt a source of great misunderstanding. He used the terms *physis* and *hypostasis* without any distinction to signify 'nature' as well as 'person.' He speaks of the one incarnate nature of the 'Word,; *mia physis theou Logou sesarkomene* (Ep 46, 2), when he intends to denote the unity of the person, thinking that St. Athanasius was responsible for this dangerous expression (*Rect. Fid. ad Reg.* 1, 9). As a matter of fact, the formula had been invented by Apollinarius of Laodicea (qv) who identified nature with person and taught that there was only one nature in Christ."[6] Similar looseness of terminology elsewhere did afterwards lead to charges of Apollinarianism and Monophysitism against C. He was trying by every means in his power to defend the traditional doctrine against both extremes, Apollinarianism and Nestorianism. His thinking was profound.

For C., the defeat of Nestorianism was vital also in the sphere of redemptive theology. Because Christ came in the flesh, this assumed by the Word, we have access through him to the Godhead and to the Holy Trinity. Thus we are also in Christ accepted as sons in the Son; the divine image is restored to us and in the Eucharist; the flesh of Christ there is a wonderful consummation of the total mystery.

[1]Cf. Quasten, III, esp. 140f for bibl.; E. Mersch, *The Whole Christ*, Milwaukee, 1938, 337–64; J. Van Den Dries, *The Formula of St. Cyril of Alexandria, mia physis tou Theou Logou sesarkomene*, Rome, 1939; H. du Manoir, S.J., *Dogme et spiritualité chez St. Cyrille d'Alexandrie*, Paris, 1944, 99–162; G. Basetti-Sani, *Il primato di Cristo in San Cirillo*, Kyrilliana, Cairo, 1947, 137–96; J. Liebart, *La doctrine christologique de saint Cyrille d'Alexandrie avant la querelle néstorienne*, Lille, 1951; P. Galtier, "L'unio secundum hypostasim 'chez saint Cyrille," *Greg* 33 (1952) 351–98; id., "Saint Cyrille et Apollinaire," *Greg* 37 (1956) 584–609; G. Jouassard, "Une intuition fondamentale de saint Cyrille d'Alexandrie en Christologie dans les premières années de son épiscopat," *REB* 11 (1953) 175–86; id., "Un problème d'anthropologie et de Christologie chez saint Cyrille d'Alexandrie, *RSR* 43 (1955) 361–78; id., "Saint Cyrille d'Alexandrie et le schema Verbe-chair," *RSR* 44 (1956) 234–42; id. "Impassibilité du Logos et impassibilité de l'âme humaine chez Cyrille d'Alexandrie," *RSR* 45 (1957) 209–44; H. M. Diepen, "La Christologie de St. Cyrille d'Alexandrie et l'anthropologie néoplatonicienne," *Euntes Docete* 9 (1956) 20–63; id., *Aux origines de l'anthropologie de St. Cyrille d'Alexandrie*, Bruges, 1957 (against Liebart and Jouassard); Kelly, *Doctrines*, 317–29; Grillmeier, 473–83; F. M. Young, *From Nicaea to Chalcedon*, London, 1983, 240–65; [2]Ep. 4; [3]Ep. 17, 3; [4]Ep. 17, 3; [5]Ep. 17, 4; [6]*Op. cit.*, 139f.

CYRIL OF JERUSALEM, ST., DOCTOR OF THE CHURCH (d. 386)

In the fourth century the word *homoousios* had become the center of so much debate, was loaded with such meaning and implications, charged with such an ecclesial content which made it a test of orthodoxy, that acceptance or rejection seemed to make a dividing line. One prominent theologian, possibly knowing the risk he was taking, still would not use the word; he has been cleared of any deviation from orthodoxy. Different explanations are put forward for his silence. The word was not scriptural and C. was quite explicit in prescribing for the candidates for Baptism a credal formula, "the principal points collected out of the whole Scripture to complete a single doctrinal formulation of the faith."[1] He did not have a profoundly speculative approach to the Person of Christ, his task was pastoral, catechetical; he may have been influenced by those who saw a Sabellian implication in *homoousios*—he was careful to condemn the Sabellian heresy frequently.

C. was also explicitly opposed to anything of Docetic (qv), Gnostic or Manichean theory, entirely convinced therefore of the true humanity of Jesus Christ. In opposition to the Arians—though he had had some contact with the semi-Arians—he insisted on the identity between the incarnate Redeemer and the *Logos* who existed from before all time with the Father. There was no time when he was not, and he was not the Son of God by adoption: "But time does not come into the begetting of the Son from the Father. Bodies are begotten in an imperfect state, but the Son of God was begotten perfect. For what he is now, that has he been timelessly begotten from the beginning. We are begotten so as to develop from childishness to rationality. Being man, your first state is imperfect and your advance is by stages. But do not imagine anything of that sort in divine generation, or charge the Begetter with lack of power. For you might charge the Begetter with lack of power if the Begotten was first imperfect and then reached perfection in time; that is if the Begetter did not fully grant from the beginning what was by supposition granted after the lapse of time. . . . For God was not at first childless, and then, after a lapse of time, became Father, but he had his Son from all eternity, not begetting him as men beget men, but as he alone knows who begat him, true God before all ages. The Father, being himself true God begat a Son like to himself, true God."[2]

C. was emphatic in his profession of faith in Christ, the Son of God (qv); "Believe also in the Son of God, who is one and sole, our Lord Jesus Christ, God begotten from God, life begotten from life, light gendered from light, like in all things to him who begat him: Who did not receive his being in time but was begotten of the Father before all ages in a manner eternal and incomprehensible. He is God's wisdom and power and his righteousness, existing hypostatically. He is enthroned at God's right hand from before all ages. For he was not, as some have supposed, crowned after his passion, as though God seated him at his right hand for his endurance of the cross, but has royal dignity from that source whence he has his being, to wit, in being eternally begotten from the Father, and shares the Father's throne, being God, and, as we said, being the wisdom and the power of God. . . . Nor must you make the Son alien from the Father nor, on the other hand put your faith in a Father-who-is-his-own-Son by making the concepts coalesce, but you must believe that there is one only-begotten Son of one God, the Word who is God before all ages."[3] C. seems to have Arianism and Sabellianism in mind in the last sentence. His orthodoxy is beyond reproach.

---

[1]Works *PG* 33, 33–11, improved by W. K. Reischl and J. Rupp, 2 vols. Munich, 1848, repr. Hildesheim, 1967; English tr., L. McCauley and A. A. Stephenson, *The Works of St. Cyril of Jerusalem,* 2 vols., Washington, 1969, 1970; *LNPF* VI: cf. J. Marquardt, *S. Cyrilli Hieros. de contionibus et placitis Arianorum sententia,* Braunsberg, 1881; B. Niederberger, *Die Logosidee des heiligen Cyrillus von Jerusalem,* Paderborn, 1923; esp. J. Lebon, "La position de St. Cyrille de Jérusalem dans les luttes provoquées par l'Arianisme," *RHE* 20 (1924) 181–210, 367–86; V. Iliev, "The Orthodoxy of St. Cyril of Jerusalem," *Duchovna Kultura* (1930) 237–48; (1932) 131–51; H. A. Wolfson, "Philosophical Implications of the Theology of Cyril of Jerusalem, *DOP* 11 (1957) 1–19; Quasten III, 369–71; Grillmeier, 256, 307; [2]*Catechetical Lecture* XI, 7, 8, *LNPF,* 66; [3]*Op. cit.,* IV, 7, 20, 21.

D

DEATH OF JESUS, THE

Reflection on the death of Jesus begins with the fact taken as indisputable that he did die by the Roman form of execution used for slaves and social outcasts, crucifixion.[1] An understanding of his death may be attempted at many levels, physical, psychological, theological and later branches into Trinitarian dogma, kenosis (qv) and soteriology (see article Redemption).

The approach is either existential or biblical: existential, for we inevitably think of any death in terms of our own experience of death in those we know, or in terms of our expectation of death. Here we know that death may complete, or establish, or reveal life. Death faced for a transcendent ideal may add so much to life as to transform it. Life which seems precarious through lack of the social and cultural supports it needs, may, in the final moment, move into an area of existence and awareness where its intrinsic quality shines over all; and it may so continue.

Above all there is the revelation which death often brings. A perspective freed from the meanness of life, the jealousy, animosity, hatred which blind people to reality, provides a full, clean view of the excellence that may have been ignored if not studiously obscured. Martyrs afford the outstanding evidence and the case of St. Maximilian Kolbe, who died in the starvation bunker in Auschwitz on August 14, 1941, is luminous in this context.

Such reflection, however, is limited by the very mystery of death. It is unknowable as a phenomenon, incommunicable as to its inner constituent, which has to be experienced and the experience is not shared; each one knows his own death in dying.

The mystery does not conceal the metaphysical frustration, the evil of death, its apparently fatal wound to the supreme gift of life, that which renders it meaningless to those without some solution to the problem of the hereafter; that which surrounds it with fear. Those who accept the truth of the Bible know that death is a consequence of sin (Rom 5:12f).

The divine paradox of Jesus' lifework is that through his own death he changed its meaning, fully for those who belong to him, potentially for all mankind. He disarms those who make death an idol, pursuing its worship through countless other lives. Each victim may find in him that which reverses totally the material power apparently crushing him. "Here" loses its significance before a completely new "hereafter" (1 Cor 15:25f; 2 Tim 1:10).

His own death embodies to the highest degree all the attributes of perfect death; and very much more. For through his death he passed to a new mode of existence, exaltation at the right hand of the Father (Phil 2:9), where he cannot be touched by death ever again (Rom 6:9). His victory is comprehensive: "Since, therefore, the children share in flesh and blood, he himself likewise partook of the same nature, that through death he might destroy him who has the power of death, that is the devil, and deliver all those who through fear of death were subject to lifelong bondage" (Heb 2:14-15).

How Christ's death is shared with the Christian, how through this sharing Christ's victory is also open to his follower is thus theologically explained by St. Paul: "Do you not know that all of us who have been baptized into Christ Jesus were baptized into his death? We were buried therefore with him by baptism into death, so that as Christ was raised from the dead by the glory of the Father, we too might walk in newness of life. For if we have been united with him in a death like his we shall certainly be united with him in a resurrection like his. . . . For if we have died with Christ, we believe that we shall also live with him. . . . For the wages of sin is death, but the free gift of God is eternal life in Christ Jesus our Lord'' (Rom 6:3-5, 8, 23).

Death for those who know not Christ may mean unbearable solitude; it may mean emptiness, as the things which gave some sentiment of fullness to life are eaten away. The mysterious cry, ''My God, my God, why hast thou forsaken me?'' (Mt 27:46; Mk 15:34) shows Jesus' acceptance of a certain solitude, which was a consequence of his kenosis (qv). That he passed this way must psychologically assist his follower. He accepted death by a mode not altogether explained, perhaps exhaustion through the draining of his blood which deprived him of the physical strength to raise his body and breathe. But he had the strength to say with a loud voice, ''Father, into thy hands I commend my spirit'' (Lk 23:46). Jn tells us that ''he bowed his head and gave up his spirit'' (19:30). One interpretation of this text by E. Hoskyns almost invites us to rethink the whole meaning of Christ's death. Did he pour out the Spirit? If so, was his acceptance of death, in its precise moment, not a voluntary act? Could it have been otherwise?

[1]L. Mathieu, ''L'Abandon du Christ sur la croix,'' *MSR* 2 (1945) 209-45; R. Schnackenburg, ''Todes-und Lebensgemeinschaft mit Christus. Neue Studien zu Rom 6:1-11,'' *Münchener Theologische Zeitschrift,* 6 (1955) 32-53; J. Carmichael, *The Death of Jesus,* London, 1963; H. W. Bartsch, ''Die Bedeutung des Sterbens Jesu nach den Synoptiker,'' *TZ* 20 (1964) 143-69; L. Malevez, ''La mort du Christ et la mort du chrétien,'' in *Problèmes actuels de Christologie,* Bruges, 1965, 317-65, 412-26; W. Schrage, ''Das Verständnis des Todes Jesu Christi im Neuen Testament,'' in E. Bizer et al., ed., *Das Kreuz Jesu Christi als Grund des Heils,* Gütersloh, 1967, 49-89; A. Strobel, ''Die Deutung des Todes Jesu im ältesten Evangelium,'' in *Das Kreuz Jesu,* Göttingen, 1969, 32-64; H. Kessler, *Die theologische Bedeutung des Todes Jesu. Eine traditionsgeschichtliche Untersuchung,* Düsseldorf, 1970; J. Jeremias, *The Theology of the New Testament,* London, 1971, 276-99; B. Vawter, *This Man Jesus,* New York, 1975, 57-89; W. Kasper, *Jesus the Christ,* London, 1976, 113-23; E. Käsemann, *Die Bedeutung des Todes Jesu. Exegetische Beiträge,* Gütersloh, 1967; A. George, ''Le sens de la mort de Jésus pour Luc,'' *RB* 80 (1973) 186-217; U. B. Mueller, ''Die Bedeutung des Kreuzestodes Jesu im Johannesevangelium,'' *Kerygma und Dogma,* 21 (1975) 49-71; K. Kettelge, ed., *Der Tod Jesu Deutungen im Neuen Testament,* Freiburg i. Brisgau, 1976; G. O'Collins, S.J., *The Calvary Christ,* London, 1977; *id., Interpreting Jesus,* London, 1982, 74-107; A. Buchele, *Der Tod Jesu im Lukasevangelium,* Frankfurt/Main, 1978; K. Stock, ''Das Bekenntnis des Centurio, Mk 13:39 im Rahmen des Markusevangeliums,'' *ZKT* 100 (1978) 289-301; J. Sobrino, *Christology at the Crossroads,* London, 1978, 179-235; X. Léon-Dufour, ''Le dernier cri de Jésus,'' *Etudes,* 348 (1978) 666-82; J. P. Mackey, *Jesus the Man and the Myth,* London, 1979, 52-85; E. Schillebeeckx, *Jesus. An Experiment in Christology,* London, 1979, 294-319; C. F. D. Moule, *The Origin of Christology,* Cambridge, 1977, 107-26; J. P. Galvin, ''Jesus' Approach to Death,'' *ThS* 41 (1980) 713-44; A. Feuillet, ''Mort du Christ, mort du chrétien d'après les épitres pauliniennes,'' *RB* 66 (1959) 481-513; C. Bourgin, ''La mort du Christ et le chrétien,'' *LV* 68 (1964) 35-58; H. Clairer, ''Le drame de la vie et de la mort dans Le Nouveau Testament,'' *Studia evangelica,* 3, *TU* 88, Berlin, 1964, 166-77; P. Hoffman, *Die Totem in Christus,* Munich, 1966; L. Chordat, *Jesus devant sa mort dans l'évangile de Marc,* Paris, 1970; A. George, ''Comment Jésus a-t-il perçu sa propre mort?'' *LV* 101 (1971) 34-59; H. Schürmann, *Comment Jésus a-t-il vécu sa mort?* Paris, 1977; Ch. Duquoc, *Christologie* II, Paris, 1971, 19-69.

DEMYTHOLOGIZING THE GOSPELS

R. Bultmann, the popularizer of this manner of presenting the message of the NT, aimed at meeting what he thought an important need: to present the essential message in terms accessible to people of today.[1] He did not intend to promote diminished respect for the sacred text, but to open its contents to the modern mind. He thought that these contents were remote because of the mythological shell to which, he thought, there had been too much adherence. Myth was not something totally false but an image or cluster of images elevated out of normal currency, given an untouchable character that in time was identified with the message itself. It was important to show that not only could the message survive when the mythology was stripped away, but that it would regain its compelling force, challenging people to a decision. He prized the kerygma (qv) and on it he wished to focus attention and vital interest. It was, he thought, obscured to modern man by the mythological framework of NT times, such as a three-tiered universe of heaven, earth and hell, and much else. All this calls for evaluation by biblical scholars, a number of whom have already refused to accept its validity. It is for them to show to what extent Bultmann's thinking was conditioned by an enclosed European mentality, and to analyze what exactly is the life-span of ''modern man'': When will he yield his place to a future man? The noble evangelizing purpose would have to be measured against the achievements of the Gospel in past ages, summoning the modern man of age after age to decision, conveying the kerygma which was welcomed despite the alleged mythological obstacle; or for that matter, in the great missionary areas contemporary with Bultmann, the new Christian churches of sub-Saharan African. Perhaps the new interest in the Jewishness of Jesus (qv) will help solve the whole problem: if it is a problem—there is a parallel here with the movement to dehellenize dogma, which does not seem to have endured very significantly.

[1]Cf. R. Bultmann, *Jesus Christ and Mythology*, New York, 1958; *id., New Testament and Mythology and other Basic Writings*, ed. S. Ogden, London, 1985, first published 1941–1961; *id., Das Verhältnis der urchristlichen Christusbotschaft zum historischen Jesus*, Heidelberg, 1960; I. Malevez, *The Christian Message and Myth*, London, 1960; J. Macquarrie, *The Scope of Demythologizing, Bultmann and his Critics*, London, 1960; S. Ogden, *Christ without Myth*, London, 1962; P. J. Cahill, "The Scope of Demythologizing," *ThS* 23 (1962) 79–92; *id., NCE* IV, 761–63; R. A. Johnson, *The Origins of Demythologizing*, Leyden, 1974.

DIDYMUS THE BLIND (c. 313–398)

Alexandrian, blind from birth, D. amassed considerable learning; he was put in charge of the Catechetical School in Alexandria by St. Athanasius (qv) and there he labored for half a century.[1] His Christology is found in his work, *De Trinitate*, long known, in his *In Zachariam* found among papyrus codices in Toura, south of Cairo in 1941; some remains of a *Commentary on the Psalms* were also in the find. A tract passing under the name of St. Gregory of Nyssa (qv) which may be his work, is directed against the Arians and Sabellius. Books IV–V of Pseudo-Basil *Contra Eunomium* are also probably from D.

D. apparently first thought in terms of a *Logos-sarx* (qv) Christology. In his controversy with the Arians and with Apollinarianism and Docetism (qqv), he was led to teach the full reality of Christ's humanity. In particular he saw the need for emphasis on the soul of Christ as things were experienced by Christ that "neither befit the Godhead nor flesh which is without a soul." If the *Commentary on the Psalms* survives the challenge to its genuineness, we have from it "the deepest recognitions of the significance and activity of Christ's soul to appear in the fourth century."[2] D. considered the soul in its role as a physical factor and reached towards an understanding of its theological aspect: its capacity to bear the original image of God and to offer complete obedience to God.

[1]Cf. L. Doutreleau, "Le 'De Trinitate' est-il de Didyme l'Aveugle? *RSR*, 45 (1957) 514–57; *id., Didyme l'Aveugle. Sur Zacharie I–III, SC* 83–85, Paris, 1962; L. Beranger, *Etudes sur la christologie du De Trinitate attribué à Didyme d'Alexandrie*, Doctoral Dissert. Lyons, 1959–60; *id.,* "Sur deux enigmes du De Trinitate de Didyme l'Aveugle," *RSR* 51 (1963) 255–67; A. Gesche, "L'âme humaine de Jésus dans la christologie du IVe siècle," *RHE* 54 (1959) 385–425; *id., La christologie du 'Commentaire sur les Psaumes' découvert à Toura*, Gembloux, 1962, on the *De Trinitate*, 353–54; Grillmeier, 271–76, 361–66; F. M. Young, *From Nicaea to Chalcedon*, London, 1983, 83–91; [2]Grillmeier, 273, 363.

DIODORE OF TARSUS (d. c. 390)

Born in Antioch, educated in Athens, D. left the monastery near Antioch, which he ruled, to resist Arianism and defend the Church against Julian the Apostate (d. 363); he later suffered banishment, was named Bishop of Tarsus in 378.[1] He was present at the Council of Constantinople (qv). Through the fragments of his extensive works, which survive largely through quotation by his opponents, scholars seek to reconstruct and evaluate his Christology. He followed the Antiochene method of exegesis, emphasizing the literal, historical meaning of the biblical text. Much of his writing disappeared when his pupil Theodore of Mopsuestia (qv) was condemned—D. seems to have been deemed guilty by association! D. was thought to be openly and constantly opposed to Apollinarianism (qv), though Grillmeier (qv) thinks that is was not so much the diminishing of the humanity in the heresy which worried him, but the endangering of the Godhead of the Logos in the Apollinarian system: "He is not concerned with the diminishing of the humanity of the Lord. But he sees the Godhead endangered by the *mia hypostasis* formula because in his opinion it makes a natural unity of Word and flesh—and as far as Apollinarius is concerned, he is right. It is therefore this special kind of union which he contests, and does so only because he is concerned about any diminishing of the Godhead. Diodore is unable to construct an effective Christology with a 'Word-man' framework, but he nevertheless prepares the ground in important ways for another Antiochene who is to carry on the task, Theodore of Mopsuestia." Grillmeier admits that his opinion—attributing a *Logos-sarx* Christology to D.—is "as yet insufficiently recognized among scholars."[2]

[1]Cf. R. Abramowshi, "Der theologische Nachlass des Diodor von Tarsus," *ZNTW* 42 (1949) 19–69; V. Ermoni, "Diodore de Tarse et son rôle doctrinal," *Mus* NS, 2 (1901) 422–44; R. Abramowski, "Untersuchungen zu Diodor von Tarsus," *ZNTW* 30 (1931) 234–62; M. Richard, "Les Traites de Cyrille d'Alexandrie contre Diodore et Theodore et les Fragments dogmatiques de Diodore de Tarse," *Mélanges Felix Grat* I, Paris (1946) 99–116; G. Brundhuber, C.Ss.R., *Diodor von Tarsus, Die Bruchstücke seines dogmatischen Schriftums, gesammelt, übersetzt und untersucht*, Gars/Inn, 1949; M. Jugie, A. A., "La doctrine christologique de Diodore de Tarse d'après les fragments de ses oeuvres," *Euntes Docete* 2 (1949) 171–91; F. A. Sullivan, *The Christology of Theodore of Mopsuestia*, Rome, 1956, 172–96; L. Abramowski, *DHGE* XIV (1960) 496–504; esp. Grillmeier, 260–70; 352–60; [2]Grillmeier, 360.

DOCETISM

A loosely coherent opinion already noted in the NT (1 Jn 4:1-3; 2 Jn 7; Col 2:8f) supported later by the Gnostics, that the body of Jesus Christ was not fully material; he had the appearances only of a man and his sufferings were not genuine.[1] 1 Jn 4:1-3 reads:

"Beloved, do not believe every spirit, but test the spirits to see whether they are of God; for many false prophets have gone out into the world. By this you know the Spirit of God: every spirit which confesses that Jesus Christ has come in the flesh is of God, and every spirit which does not confess Jesus is not of God." 2 Jn 7 reads: "For many deceivers have gone out into the world, men who will not acknowledge the coming of Jesus Christ in the flesh; such a one is a deceiver and the antichrist." Col 2:8f refers to those who make a prey of people "by philosophy and empty deceit" and v. 9 says of Christ: "For in him the whole fullness of deity dwells bodily, and you have come to fullness of life in him, who is the head of all rule and authority."

Different factors counted in the acceptance of docetic ideas: a tendency on the part of some to see material things, the flesh in particular, as inevitably evil, a reluctance to admit anything that could look like weakness in the Son of God made man. Echoes of the mentality, for it is a mentality rather than an intellectual system, are heard in some of the Apocrypha—the *Gospel of Peter,* the *Acts of Peter,* the *Ascension of Isaiah.* Support was forthcoming from Gnostic quarters; the names of Basilides and Valentinian are mentioned in this context.

The reaction against docetic opinions was strong from earliest times. Ignatius of Antioch (qv) after recalling, in Trallians IX, that "Jesus Christ, who was of the family of David, and of Mary, who was truly born, both ate and drank, was truly persecuted under Pontius Pilate, was truly crucified, and died in the sight of those in heaven and on earth and under the earth, who also was truly raised from the dead . . ." deals with the heresy in ch. X: "But if, as some affirm who are without God—that is, are unbelievers—his suffering was only a semblance (but it is they who are merely a semblance), why am I a prisoner, and why do I even long to fight with the beasts? In that case I am dying in vain. Then indeed I am lying concerning the Lord."[2]

In the letter to the Smyrnaeans, Ignatius, after recalling the Passion and Resurrection, continues: "For he suffered all these things for us that we might attain salvation, and he truly suffered even as he truly raised himself, not as some unbelievers say, that his Passion was merely in semblance—but it is they who are merely in semblance, and even according to their opinions it shall happen to them, and they shall be without bodies and phantasmal."[3] Polycarp of Smyrna states briefly: "For everyone who does not confess that Jesus Christ has come in the flesh is an anti-christ"—paraphrasing 2 Jn 7.[4]

St. Irenaeus and Tertullian (qqv) maintained the opposition, as did St. Clement of Alexandria and Origen (qqv). With Tertullian it is thought to have ended, but St. Basil the Great (qv) suspected something like it in his time.

[1]Cf. G. Bareille, *DTC* IV, 2, 1484–1501; G. Bardy, *DSp* III, 1461–1468; A. Grillmeier, S.J. (qv), *LTK* III (1959) 47f; [2]K. Lake, *The Apostolic Fathers,* I, 221; [3]*Ibid.,* 253, 255; [4]*Ibid.,* 293.

DUNN, JAMES D. G. (1939–)

The prolific biblical scholar best known perhaps for his work, *Christology in the Making,* which prompted an intense debate, as had *Baptism in the Holy Spirit* earlier, has many other published items of interest to our subject.[1] He has an article on 'Incarnation' appearing in the *Anchor Bible Dictionary,* is the author of "2 Corinthians, 3:17: The Lord is the Spirit," *JTS* 21 (1970) 309–20; "Jesus—Flesh and Spirit: An Exposition of Romans 1:3-4," *JTS* 24 (1973) 40–68; "Paul's Understanding of the Death of Jesus," in *Reconciliation and Hope: NT Essays on Atonement and Eschatology,* L. L. Morris Festschrift, ed. R. J. Banks, Paternoster, 1974, 125–41; "1 Corinthians 15:45—Last Adam, Life-giving Spirit," in *Christ and Spirit in the New Testament: Studies in Honor of C. F. D. Moule,* ed. B. Lindars and S. S. Smalley, Cambridge, 1973, 127-41; *Jesus and the Spirit, A Study of the Religious and Charismatic Experience of Jesus and the First Christians as Reflected in the New Testament,* London, 1975; *Unity and Diversity in the New Testament: An Inquiry into the Character of Earliest Christianity,* London, 1977; "Let John be John: A Gospel for its Time," in *Das Evangelium und die Evangelien,* ed. P. Stuhlmacher, Mohrsiebeck, 1983.

D.'s contribution to the theology of the Holy Spirit is treated in the author's *Veni Creator Spiritus.*[2] The articles written after the publication of *Christology in the Making* are listed in the annotation to the present article. The importance of the work and of the subsequent discussion, what D. magnanimously calls "dialogue," is that it brought methodology into sharp focus; much else is covered and, all through, D.'s enormous erudition and meticulous documentation are evident. He invited those differing from him to consider two methodological principles: 'historical context of meaning' and 'conceptuality in transition.' By the first idea he sets the task "of trying to hear the words of the text as the writer of these words intended those for whom he wrote to hear them." He adds: "That I continue to regard as the primary exegetical (though by no means the only hermeneutical) task confronting the NT scholar."[3]

On the second principle he writes: "The task of historical exegesis requires a recognition that important concepts will often be in transition. They may be on their way to becoming something else, something slightly but perhaps significantly different in the meaning they are heard to express. This will be all the more likely in the case of documents (e.g., Paul's letters) which were recognized to have more than merely occasional significance from the first, and especially where they deal with a subject (Christology) of particular and growing significance for the movement (Christianity) within which these documents first emerged. For not all concepts are in transition to the same degree; conceptuality in transition is also a relative phenomenon."[4] How these ideas are applied to the biblical texts relevant to Christology is to be investigated and evaluated in D.'s works. In the second edition of *Christology in the Making,* he deals, in a lengthy foreword (xi-xxxix) with the varied reactions to his first presentation of his findings—with ample annotation as is his custom.

---

[1]Bibl. in 2nd ed. of *Christology in the Making,* notes to Foreword; cf. D.'s replies to critics: "In Defense of a Methodology," *ExpT* 95 (1983-84) 295-99; id., "Some Clarifications on Issues of Method," *Semeia* 30 (1984), issue devoted to "Christology and Exegesis: New Approaches," ed. R. Jewett, cf. infra; the varied responses evoked, J. F. Balchin, "Paul, Wisdom and Christ," in *Christ the Lord. Studies in Christology Presented to D. Guthrie,* (1982) 204-19; D. Hagner, *Reformed Journal* 32 (1982) 19-20; A. T. Hanson, *The Image of the Invisible God,* London, 1982, 59-75, 80; L. Morris, "The Emergence of the Doctrine of the Incarnation," *Themelios* 8/1 (1982) 15-19; B. Cranfield, "Some Comments on Professor J. D. G. Dunn's 'Christology in the Making,' with Special Reference to the Epistle to the Romans," in *The Glory of Christ in the New Testament. Studies in Christology in Memory of G. B. Caird,* ed. L. D. Hurst and N. T. Wright, Clarendon, 1987, 271ff; C. Holloday, "New Testament Christology: A Consideration of Dunn's 'Christology in the Making,' *Semeia* j.c. 65-82 (=*NovT* 25, 1983, 257-78); A. Segal, *ibid.,* "Pre-existence and Incarnation: A Response to Dunn and Holloday," 83-95; further references in *Christology in the Making,* 2nd ed., p. xxxiii, n. 16, p. xxxix, n. 83; [2]*Veni Creator Spiritus,* S.V.; [3]*Christology in the Making,* 2nd ed., xiv; [4]*Ibid.,* xv, 74-76.

DUNS SCOTUS, JOANNES, BLESSED
(1265-1308)

The great Franciscan doctor, *Doctor Subtilis* as he is named, deploys all his subtlety in his exposition of the hypostatic union (qv); his view of human personality is simpler than that of St. Thomas and he refines his thinking on the relation which constitutes the union accordingly.[1] He shows how it is not irrational to hold the idea of such a union, looking at the subject from many aspects.

The originality of S. lay, as is well known, in the plenary exposition and defense of the absolute primacy of Christ (qv). His approach was through the question of Christ's predestination. In regard to this predestination three points are considered by S.: a) how the hypostatic union can fall under predestination; b) how Christ was predestined; c) what is the order of this predestination in relation to other predestinations? It is this last point that is relevant. S. writes: "It is said that the fall of man is the necessary reason for this predestination. Since God saw that man would fall, he saw that he would be redeemed in this way, and so he foresaw (Christ's) human nature to be assumed and to be glorified with so great a glory. I declare, however, that the fall was not the cause of Christ's predestination. In fact, even if no man or angel had fallen, nor any man but Christ were to be created, Christ would still have been predestined in this way. I prove this as follows: because everyone who wills in an orderly manner, wills first the end, then more immediately those things which are closer to the end; but God wills in a most orderly manner; therefore, that is the way he wills. In the first place, then, he wills himself, and immediately after him, *ad extra,* is the soul of Christ. Therefore first after willing the intrinsic things, he willed this glory for Christ. Therefore, before any merit or demerit, he foresaw that Christ would be united with him in the oneness of person.

"Again, as was declared in the First Book (*dist.* 41) on the question of predestination, the preordination and complete predestination of the elect takes place before anything is done about the reprobate *in actu secundo,* lest anyone rejoice over the damnation of another as a benefit to himself. Therefore, the entire process (of predestination) concerning Christ was foreseen before the fall and all demerit were foreseen.

"Again, if the fall were the reason for Christ's predestination, it would follow that the greatest work of God (the Incarnation) was mostly occasional (*maxime occasionatum*—entirely an afterthought), because the glory of all was not as great in intensity as was the glory of Christ; and it seems very unreasonable that God would have left so great a work (i.e., the Incarnation) undone on account of a good deed performed by Adam, for example, if he had not sinned.

"Therefore, I declare the following: *First,* God loves himself. *Secondly,* he love himself for others, and this is an ordered love. *Thirdly,* he wishes to be loved by him who can love him with the greatest love—speaking of the love of someone who is extrinsic to him. And *fourthly,* he foresees the union of that nature that must love him with the greatest love even if no one had fallen."[2]

For an understanding of the final paragraph, it must be remembered that S., in contrast with St. Thomas (qv), gave priority in this theological system to love and the will. *Deus charitas est* is the key to his doctrinal and moral theology. Subject to his overruling intention of love God decided to institute the entire supernatural economy of grace, and all that is needed to attain this divine love.

With these general premises on the Incarnation, S. deals also with other problems discussed by his contemporaries, notably St. Thomas Aquinas (qv). Since he differs from St. Thomas on the constitutive element of personality, and since he holds, also in opposition to St. Thomas, that essence (nature) and existence are not really distinct, he explains differently the meaning of the hypostatic union (qv). He adheres fully to the dogma and insists on the unity of Christ and on the unique personality; he does postulate two modes of existence, divine and human in Christ. With all theologians he holds that the human nature of Christ was totally perfect. He taught the impeccability or sinlessness of Christ, but explained it differently from St. Thomas; God's power intervened to ensure it, since S. did not think that it flowed automatically from the hypostatic union.

Again he has his own views on the threefold knowledge attributed to Christ: the vision of God, acquired knowledge and infused knowledge. He thought of a certain global character in Christ's vision of things in God, *habitualiter non tamen actualiter,* as he also refined subtly the difference between infused and acquired knowledge. His theory of redemption (qv) likewise diverged from that of St. Anselm and St. Thomas: he insisted on God's acceptance, through his infinite decree of love, as the essential element, while attributing the full merit of loving response to Christ, *a persona dilectissima et ex maxima charitate. . . . Maxima fuit misericordia, in persona offerente, sic se offerre pro inimicis Trinitatis, quam summe dilexit.* Scotus was always true to his principle that he preferred in exalting Christ to exceed in praise than to fail, if perchance his ignorance might lead to excess.

[1]Critical edition of the works by the International Scotistic Commission, 1950.; for bibl., O. Schafer, O.F.M., *Bibliographia de vita, operibus et doctrina Johannis Duns Scoti,* Saec. XIX, XX, Rome, 1955, 4, 506 entries; *id.,* "Conspectus brevis bibliographiae Scotisticae recentioris," *Annales Ordinis Fratrum Minorum,* 85 (1966) 531–50; S. Gieben, "Bibliographia Scotistica recentior," 1952–1965, *Laurentianum* 6 (1965) 492–522; cf. R. Seeberg, *Die Theologie des Johannes Duns Scotus.* Studien zur Geschichte der Theologie und der Kirche, V (1900); P. Minges, *Johannis Duns Scoti Doctrina Philosophica et Theologica quoad res praecipuas proposita et exposita,* 2 vols., Quaracchi, 1930; E. Longpré "La primauté de Jésus Christ d'après le B. Duns Scot," Texte inédit du ms. Ripoli 53, *SF* 5 (1933) 218–25; *id.,* "Le Bienheureux Duns Scot, Docteur du Verbe Incarné,' *FF* 17 (1934) 1–36; *id.,* "La primauté de Jésus Christ d'après le B. Duns Scot. Texte inédit du ms. 661 de Troyes, *Wissenschaft und Weisheit,* 2 (1935) 89–93; *id.,* "Robert Grosseteste et le B. Duns Scot. Le motif de l'Incarnation," *FF* 21 (1938); 21 (1938) supplem. docum, IV, 1–16; *id., The Kingship of Christ according to St. Bonaventure and Bl. Duns Scotus,* tr. from contribution to A. Gemelli, O.F.M., ed. *La Regalitá di Cristo,* Milan, 1926, Paterson, N.J., 1944; C. Balic, O.F.M., "Dun Skotus Lehre über Christi Pradestination im Lichte der neuersten Forschungen," *Wissenschaft und Weisheit,* 3 (1936) 19–35; *id.,* "Duns Scotus," *NCE* IV, 1102–6; *id.,* "Scotism," *NCE* XI, 1226–29; P. Hercedez, O.F.M., "La place du Christ dans le plan de la création selon le B. Jean Duns Scot," *FF* 19 (1936) 30–52; J. Bissen, O.F.M., "De praedestinatione absoluta Christi secundum Duns Scotum expositio doctrinalis," *Antonianum* 12 (1937) 3–36; A. B. Wolter, O.F.M., "Duns Scotus on the Predestination of Christ," *Cord* 5 (1955) 366–72; *id.,* "John Duns Scotus on the Primacy and Personality of Christ," in *Franciscan Christology,* ed. D. McElrath, New York, 1980, 139–82; K. Adam, *The Christ of Faith,* New York, 1957, 226–30; J. Carol, O.F.M., "Duns Scotus on the Incarnation," *Homiletic and Pastoral Review,* 83 (June, 1983) 4; esp. *id., Why Jesus Christ?* Manassas, Virginia, 1986, 120–49, 255–352; A. Kandler, O.F.M.Cap., "Die Heilsdynamik im Christusbild des Johannes Scotus," *Wissenschaft und Weisheit,* 27 (1964) 175–97; 28 (1965) 1–14;   [2]*Opus Parisiense* Lib III, d. 7, q. 4 apud J. Carol, *Why Christ?,* 126.

E

EUTYCHES (c. 378–454)

E. enters history as a first principal proponent of the Monophysite heresy, though whether he had sufficient knowledge to construct a theological system, or any such intention is not clear.[1] Things moved him in that direction. The primary factor was his deep-seated anti-Nestorianism, and his fanatical attachment to a formula of St. Cyril of Alexandria (qv) which he misunderstood, *mia physis*, one nature. Cyril had used the term and concept in regard to the Person, giving it the same meaning as *hypostasis* or *prosopon*; E. misapplied it to mean only one nature. E. was not a bishop, though as Archimandrite of a monastery in the outskirts of Constantinople he had prestige. Still more so, enabling him to aim at being a 'bishop of bishops' was his strong political position. Through his godson, Chrysaphius, all-powerful eunuch court chamberlain, he would, in a crisis, have the Emperor Theodosius on his side. The crisis came when the Bishop of Constantinople, Flavian, influenced by Theodoret of Cyrrhus, whose work *Eranistes* was a veiled attack on E., and by Bishop Eusebius of Dorylaeum, summoned the Archimandrite to a Synod of Bishops, the so-called *synodos endemousa,* of those who were in the capital. It opened on November 8, 448. After Eusebius had instituted a *libellus* against E., practically accusing him of heresy, a trial, in seven sessions, took place, November 12 to 22; E. was present in court for the last session. The central formula in the confession of faith proposed by Flavian was: "We acknowledge that Christ is from two natures after the Incarnation, in one hypostasis and one Person confessing one Christ, one Son, one Lord." It had to be made clear in the fluctuating terminology, that in the context 'from two natures' was equivalent to '*in* two natures.' E. would admit '*from* two natures' before the Incarnation, but not after—"after the union I acknowledge only 'one nature.'"

E. was deposed and when the proceedings were reported to Rome by Flavian, Leo (qv) approved. He said so in a letter to the Emperor and in a lengthy letter to Flavian (the Tome, qv). Meanwhile neither the Emperor, doubtless through the influence of Chrysaphius, or the Bishop of Alexandria, Dioscoros, successor to St. Cyril (he had been Archdeacon of Alexandria in his lifetime) agreed with the sentence. The Emperor summoned a Council to meet in Ephesus in August, excluding from it the prominent opponent of Eutyches, Theodoret of Cyrrhus. The Pope agreed and sent Legates. The first session took place on August 8, 449.

By imperial command, Dioscoros presided at the Council, which paid little attention to the papal Legates, or to the Tome, reinstated E. triumphantly; and finally degenerated into an unseemly attack on Flavian, in which physical violence from a mixed invited rabble featured. A decree condemning the Bishop of Constantinople was signed by 135 bishops, many apparently under duress. Flavian was exiled, but had managed to send an appeal to the Pope, borne by the Legates who escaped the fracas. The whole proceedings are known as the 'Robber Synod' from the word used by Leo in a letter to the Council of Chalcedon, *In illo Ephesino non judicio sed latrocinio.*

E. did not long enjoy his rehabilitation. Flavian had died on the way to exile. But within a year Theodosius died, July 28; the throne was taken by his sister Pulcheria, who married a senator Marcian, bestowing on him the title of Augustus. Chrysaphius, E.'s protector, was executed and the Archimandrite exiled to a veil of silence. But the central Christological question awaited the solution which Chalcedon (qv) would provide. The Monophysites lasting for centuries are in part E.'s legacy to Christendom.

¹E. Schwartz, *Der Prozess des Eutyches,* Bavarian Academy, Munich, 1929; R. Deveresse, "Les premières années du monophysisme," *RSPT* 19 (30) 251–65; R. Draguet, "La christologie d'Eutyches d'après les Actes du Synode de Flavien," *Byzantion* 6 (1931) 441–47; T. Camelot, O.P., in *Chalkedon* I (1951) 229–42; H. Bacht, *ibid.,* II, 1953, 197–222, 224–28; B. Emmi, O.P., "Leone ed Eutiche," *Angelicum* 29 (1952) 3–42; M. Jugie, A. A., *DTC* V, 2, 1582–1609; M. Richard, "L'introduction du mot 'hypostase'dans la théologie de l'incarnation," *MSR* 2 (1945) 5–32, 243–70; P. Hughes, *The Church in Crisis,* London, 1960, ch. IV, "The General Council of Chalcedon," 53–75; J. F. Rivera, "San Leon Magno y la herejia de Eutiques desde el sinodo de Constantinople hasta la muerte de Teodosio II," *RET* 9 (1949) 31–58; H. Chadwick, "The Exile and Death of Flavian of Constantinople: A Prologue to the Council of Chalcedon," *JTS* 6 (1955) 17–34; Grillmeier, 523–26; 520–539.

EXORCIST, JESUS AS

In the existential order, once the public ministry of Jesus had begun, Satan is never absent.¹ The life of the God-man was a challenge, a divine defiance to Satan; a duel would ensue in different phases with Christ as the ultimate Victor. Satan's rule would be overthrown; his sway, though in some respects insecure, was widespread (Mt 12:26; Mk 3:23; Lk 4:6; 11:18): he manifested his power in certain peak moments by the phenomenon of diabolical possession.

Jesus met Satan directly in three phases of his ministry: at the outset he was tempted by him (Mt 4:1; Mk 1:13; Lk 4:2); in the days of his teaching he had to deal with instances of diabolical possession; his Passion was the final struggle, wherein Satan was totally defeated, as Jesus saw beforehand (Lk 10:18). The traitor was influenced by Satan (Jn 13:2, 27; Lk 22:3); this was the hour of the power of darkness (Lk 22:53).

The gospel incidents present particular characteristics and raise many problems. The boy from whom the disciples could not cast out the demon (Mt 17:14-21; Mk 9:14-29; Lk 9:37-43) would, from the features described, be diagnosed by modern clinicians as a victim of epilepsy. There is a grey area between such medically recognizable symptoms and genuine diabolical possession. On this fragile basis a number of modern writers have erected a purely medical interpretation of the cases brought to Jesus' attention with a prayer that he relieve them. The conclusion does not follow and it overlooks the essentially supernatural core of Christ's mission, which involved a war on the powers of darkness.

It is likewise intriguing that Jesus is said to have cast out many demons (Mt 8:16; Mk 1:34; Lk 7:21), the action being described globally or in summary form. It was something he wished to do publicly, a work that he wished to be associated with his essential vocation or mission. When Pharisees came and said to him, "Get away from here, for Herod wants to kill you," he replied, "Go and tell that fox, 'Behold I cast out demons and perform cures today and tomorrow, and the third day I finish my course'" (Lk 13:32).

From the first there was a very significant element in Jesus' exorcisms: "And in the synagogue there was a man who had the spirit of an unclean demon; and he cried out with a loud voice, 'Ah! What have you to do with us, Jesus of Nazareth? Have you come to destroy us? I know who you are, the Holy One of God.' But Jesus rebuked him, saying, 'Be silent, and come out of him.' And when the demon had thrown him down in the midst, he came out of him, having done him no harm" (Lk 4:33-35). With this very first instance of his power we may take this account of a day spent at Capernaum: "And demons also came out of many, crying, 'You are the Son of God!' But he rebuked them, and would not allow them to speak, because they knew that he was the Christ" (Lk 4:41).

This fact that the demons knew Jesus' messianic identity poses problems; it is also evident in the well-known case of the possessed of Gerasa. Mk may be heard: "They came to the other side of the sea, to the country of the Gerasenes. And when he had come out of the boat, there met him out of the tombs a man with an unclean spirit, who lived among the tombs; and no one could bind him any more, even with a chain; for he had often been bound with fetters and chains, but the chains have wrenched apart, and the fetters he broke in pieces; and no one had the strength to subdue him. Night and day among the tombs and on the mountains he was always crying out, and bruising himself with stones. And when he saw Jesus from afar, he ran and worshipped him; and crying out with a loud voice, he said, 'What have you to do with me, Jesus, Son of the Most High God? I adjure you by God, do not torment me.' For he had said to him, 'Come out of the man, you unclean spirit!' And Jesus asked him 'What is your name?' He replied, 'My name is legion; for we are many.' And he begged him eagerly not to send them out of the country. Now a great herd of swine was feeding there on the hillside; and they begged him, 'Send us to the swine, let us enter them.' So he gave them leave. And the unclean spirits came out, and entered the swine; and the herd, numbering about two thousand, rushed down the steep bank into the sea, and were drowned in the sea" (Mk 5:1-13).

The sequel to this exorcism was a spreading religious fear in the neighborhood, which led to a request that Jesus leave, and his refusal to take the healed man with him. "Go home to your friends, and tell them how much the Lord has done for you, and he has had mercy on you" (Mk 5:19).

What emerges from the various episodes is that the demons recognized Jesus as Messiah, that they bowed to his power, yet would seek to plead with him for some mitigation of his expulsion order. He acts directly, not through any intermediary like an angel. The human being victim of the possession is the primary object of his concern and care. As with all his miraculous (qv) interventions he responds to a request, made by the victim or his friends. But his very presence mostly suffices to unmask the evil presence and the demon feels threatened.

---

[1] Cf. *Demoniacs in the Gospel,* in *Satan,* an issue of *Etudes Carmélitaines,* ed. Bruno de Jesu Maria, O.C.D., tr. M. Carroll, London, 1951, 163–77; S. Lyonnet, "Jésus et les demons," *DSp* III, 146–52; J. Forget, *DTC* V 1762–80; E. J. Gratsch, L. J. Elmer, *NCE* IV, 748–50.

F

FAITH OF JESUS, THE

The question of Jesus' faith has been raised in a considerable recent literature, in a number of works by Catholics, notably by Hans Urs von Balthasar (qv). It is linked with the other problems of Jesus' knowledge and his consciousness (qqv), all heavily involved in mystery. There is, as yet, no entirely comprehensive treatment of the subject, which would draw on the full resources of Scripture and Tradition to meet the demands of psychology, logic, and epistemology: all of considerable moment.[1]

Psychology: how did the truths which Jesus is thought to have accepted on faith enter his mind? What was their genesis and growth? What different channels of knowing gave him concrete, factual knowledge, and the abstract ideas related to the deity which he was to express? As an example and merely such, when twelve years old he spoke to Mary of his Father (in heaven) (Lk 2:49), how had this idea entered the stock of ideas which he shared with Jewish children of his age? What was the cognitive process? A similar query arises in regard to his Abba prayer (qv).

Logic: how was his knowledge allegedly on faith linked with his acquired knowledge? This implies the solution of the epistemological questions: what gave him certainty, in regard to his knowledge on faith? Every believer needs a motive of credibility, and this is generally provided by family or some other person (persons) capable of similar influence. But where could he obtain a motive of credibility for truths which he alone knew, which he was to express for the first time? When the act of faith has to be made by a believer, there has to be an inner power that we call the virtue, which is personal, but reinforced by corporate experience and exchange of ideas. The virtue assures the validity of the act. What assured Jesus Christ of the validity of a whole range of teaching which came from him for the first time? Men test their beliefs by critical reflection, by comparison, by consultation, gaining thus assurance. How did he test his alleged beliefs? Whom could he consult? Even those who defend a thesis on the faith of Jesus would be shocked by such questions. But they are implied in this thesis. Proponents cannot deny that they make Jesus Christ, the "Light of the world" (Jn 8:12; 9:5), the "Mediator and the fullness of all revelation" (Vatican II) less than transcendent in the vital mission he came to fulfill.

Each of the themes thus far outlined would demand enormous research and reflection. The evidence to be scientifically collected, assessed, and interpreted is as follows. Nowhere did Jesus say that he had learned any divine truth from any man; nowhere did anyone claim to have so instructed him. Nowhere did he say that he was making an act of faith, or urge his followers to imitate him in this practice; he did propose himself as a model of love, "By this all men will know that you are my disciples, if you have love for one another. . . . As the Father has loved me, so have I loved you; abide in my love. If you keep my commandments, you will abide in my love, just as I have kept my Father's commandments and abide in his love. . . . This is my commandment, that you love one another as I have loved you" (Jn 13:35; 14:9, 10, 12). Faith precedes love logically and if he lived by faith, he would first urge them to imitate him in this. But instead of saying, "Believe as I do," he said, "Believe me that I am in the Father and the Father in me; or else believe me for the sake of the works themselves. Truly, truly,

I say to you, he who believes in me will also do the works that I do; and greater works than these will he do, because I go to the Father'' (Jn 14:11, 12).

Account must be taken next of texts which seem to imply that Jesus had experience of faith. After calming the storm Jesus said to those in the boat with him: ''Why are you afraid? Have you no faith?'' (Mk 4:40 par.). Again when the disciples asked him why they could not cast out a devil, his reply was, ''Because of your little faith. For truly, I say to you, if you have faith as a grain of mustard seed, you will say to this mountain, 'Move from here to there,' and it will move; and nothing will be impossible to you'' (Mt 17:20, 21). In the first instance here mentioned, it is clear that the faith should be directed to him, with his power just made manifest. In the second it would still be pressing the evidence too far to conclude that Jesus spoke from his own experience.

There is understandably much attention given to the Pauline expressions, which bringing ''Christ'' and ''faith'' together with ''Christ'' in the genitive; they seem to refer to faith of Christ (cf. esp. Gal 2:16; Rom 3:22, 26; Phil 3:9). TOB and RSV translate ''faith in Christ.'' The genitive has been described as objective, genitive of origin, i.e., indicating that Christ is the source of faith; mystic, subjective by some. This latter is by no means a majority consensus. The mystic genitive is thus described by von Balthasar, after A. Deissmann, who thought of it: ''The faith of Christ is the faith within the reality of Christ, the faith which shares in the fullness of truth, of love, of action, of the Passion (qv) and the Resurrection (qv) of Christ, and in every aspect of his reality, which is based on it.''[2] ''It is'' says Deissmann, ''faith lived in communion with the Christ of the Spirit, that is faith in God, identical in content with the faith of Abraham in the sacred times of origins, an absolute confidence in the living God.''[3] The very error in this assertion—making faith in Christ only equal to that of Abraham—discloses the dangers inherent in theorizing about the subject.

The Letter to the Hebrews must be taken separately. Chapter XI opens with a definition of faith: ''the assurance of things hoped for, the conviction of things not seen.'' Within that frame there comes the list of heroic figures of the past. We are then encouraged to ''run with perseverance the race that is set before us looking to Jesus the pioneer and perfecter of our faith'' (Heb 12:1-2). (TOB ''celui qui est l'initiateur de la foi et qui la mène à son accomplissement''). It has been suggested that if these words are read with certain others in Heb—his learning obedience (5:8), his being made perfect through suffering (2:10), his fidelity (3:1-2), and his prayer when threatened with pain and death (5:7)—they

could bear the interpretation of Jesus being the subject of faith. But though all the texts would thus cohere, the author in question adds: ''Nevertheless, one must admit that not even Hebrews 12:2 unequivocally ascribes faith to Jesus.''

There is this added difficulty: how to distinguish clearly what Jesus could not have received by faith, that is the truths which came from him directly, and could only come from him, from truths which the proponents of his faith would contend, must, by the very terms of their thesis, contend, came to him on faith. So far this analysis has not been made. Those who write at length of the faith of Jesus pursue the story of Christ with no sharp advertence to the problems inherent in his self-revelation as God, his teaching on the Father and the Spirit, his institution of the Eucharist and his effective means of its perpetuity. It is not a question of his human faith, by which he believed, on the word of others, facts and ideas within the knowable range of the human mind; the question at issue is of divine or supernatural faith. For those who, like St. Thomas Aquinas, reject the possibility, the dividing line is firmly exclusive; the others do not seem to know where to draw it.

Hans Urs von Balthasar (qv) enlarged the meaning of faith in reference to Christ, to his fidelity, sharing in God's fidelity. But this is not what people mostly mean by faith, and it is a term calling for precision in use, as the great master so well knew. An a priori approach can easily prompt the argument that he had to have faith since he was truly human. The principle is valid provided that it does not compromise his uniqueness and his self-sufficiency. To postulate faith in Jesus Christ would compromise the plenitude of his role as unique Mediator—he himself would need a mediator— and generally lead to a reductionist Christology. It is an abuse of the ''Christology from below'' (qv).

Especially such a theory ignores the plenary gift of the Spirit and the communication of the gifts which are characteristically his (see article Spirit, the Holy). If the prophets were directly enlightened by the Spirit, owing their divine insights to none but him, who shall deny a still higher, more complete illumination of the soul of Jesus from the same divine Person. Recognition of the Spirit's role in his life, and reflection on its diverse modalities, would help lift the tension people feel between belief in the full humanity of Jesus and acceptance of his extraordinary knowledge of things divine, away beyond the restriction of faith. The Spirit achieved this unique spiritual endowment in view of the universal mission which he would himself accomplish as a result of the redemptive life and death of Jesus Christ.

[1]Article, "The Faith of Christ?" *Trinitas*, 106f; F. Prat, S.J., *The Theology of St. Paul*, London, 1945, Detached Notes, V, 'Faith' in St. Paul, 448–55; H. Urs von Balthasar, *La Foi du Christ*, Paris, 1968; J. Sobrino, S.J., *Christology at the Crossroads*, London, 1976, 79–139; P. Schoonenberg, *The Christ*, London, 1967, 175–80; G. O'Collins, *Interpreting Jesus*, 1983, 190–93; J. Guillet, *La Foi De Jésus Christ*, Paris, 1980;   [2]Apud. H. Urs von Balthasar, *La Foi du Christ*, Paris, 1968;   [3]*Ibid.*

FORM CRITICISM

The validity of this method of biblical exegesis is admitted in the Instruction on the Historical Truth of the Gospels (qv) issued by the Biblical Commission (qv) in 1964.[1] The intrinsic meaning, presuppositions, and limits are a matter for biblical experts to analyze, discuss, and decide. The great Catholic exegete, Pierre Benoit, O.P., drew attention to certain shortcomings in the published work of the masters, especially R. Bultmann (qv), and he pointed out the philosophical presuppositions from which the form-critics sometimes proceed. He was particularly skeptical about the creative capacity of the Christian community, which is an assumption of the school: in the period between the happenings or pronouncements in the life of Jesus and the composition of the gospels, there were in circulation versions of these important events and words, stories and sayings. It is contended that analysis of the gospel text can extract these items, one by one, from the finished work transmitted to us; their different literary forms are identified. It is assumed that they were retained and transmitted not primarily because of their content, often historical in kind, but because of the mentality, the desires of the Christian communities. Some of the form critics rule out history (qv) as a decisive factor in the choice and arrangement of the materials they would preserve, which they would select as particularly helpful in their situation. Another element is here to be mentioned: the first Christians, it is contended, were more conscious of the presence among them of the risen Jesus, through his Spirit, and he would be the point of reference they chose, not the earthly Jesus who died through crucifixion. So these form critics would not consider merely an oral tradition, but a collective editorial activity. This world, where scientific method has scope, but where conjecture equally operates, is beyond the competence of all but the most highly qualified biblical scholars.

[1]V. Taylor, *The Formation of the Gospel Tradition*, London, 1933; E. Florit, "La 'storia delle forme' nei vangeli in rapporto alla dottrina cattolica," *BB* 14 (1933) 212–48; F. M. Braun, O.P., *Où en est le problème de Jésus?*, Paris, 1932, 213–65; id., *DSB* III, 312–17 ("Formgeschichte, Ecole de la"); S. E. Donlan, S.J., "Form-Critics, the Gospels and St. Paul," *CBQ* 6 (1944) 159–79, 306–25; J. Muilenberg, "Form Criticism and Beyond," *JBL* 88 (1969) 1–18. B. Gerhardsson, *Memory and Manuscript, Oral Tradition and Written Transmission in Rabbinic Judaism*, Uppsala, 1961; K. Koch, *Was ist Formgeschichte? Neue Wege der Bibelexegese*, Neukirchen, ed. 2, 1967, ET 1969; E. V. McKnight, *What is Form Criticism?* Philadelphia, 1969; L. A. Schökel, *NCE* V, 1017–23; esp. P. Benoit, O.P., "Reflections on 'Formgeschichtliche Methode'" in *Jesus and the Gospel*, London, 1973, 11–45 (originally *RB* 1946, 481–512).

FRIEND, JESUS THE IDEAL

"This is my commandment, that you love one another as I have loved you.[1] Greater love has no man than this, that a man lay down his life for his friends. You are my friends if you do what I command you. No longer do I call you servants, for the servant does not know what his master is doing; but I have called you friends, for all that I have heard from my Father I have made known to you" (Jn 15:12-15). Even if we did not have this revealing statement from the Lord, the whole of his final discourse as related by the evangelist speaks eloquently of friendship. It is a consistent thread running through all the narrative of his relationship with the disciples, especially with the Twelve. Emphasis on their role in the institution, their mission and their future duties in the Church, has possibly clouded the profound Person to person relationship that was sustained with each one of them. So many of the attributes we look for in friends: tolerance, affection, trust, deep-seated concern are exemplified in Jesus. His friendship reached its climax with the readiness to die for them.

Did he have any friend among them whom he specially cherished? Clearly this was the "beloved disciple." He protected him as friends do for those they love. Can we pursue the analysis through the gospel record? Surely the woman who wept at the empty tomb, Mary of Magdala (Jn 20:11) who was addressed by Jesus "Mary" did not stand in any merely official, impersonal relationship to Jesus. How else but on the basis of profound friendship shall we explain the narrative of Jesus and the family at Bethany? Where shall we find a more touching episode than this: "Then Mary, when she came where Jesus was and saw him, fell at his feet, saying to him, 'Lord if you had been here, my brother would not have died.' When Jesus saw her weeping, and the Jews who came with her also weeping, he was deeply moved in spirit and troubled; and he said, 'Where have you laid him?' They said to him, 'Lord, come and see.' Jesus wept. So the Jews said, 'See how he loved him!'" (Jn 11:32-36). It is noteworthy that Jesus did not say to Mary as he had said to Martha, "Your brother will rise again" (Jn 11:23). He just performed the miracle and gave Mary back her brother. An act of friendship, or an apologetic and messianic sign? Both if we accept the fact that Jesus, more than all the great ones of history, enjoyed a plenitude of spirit which enabled him to act fully at different levels.

A complete study of Jesus as friend would need to trace the theme through the lives of his great saints, through those where the consummation of love known as the spiritual marriage was attained. The history of devotion to the Heart of Jesus (qv) is especially revealing on the sublime reality: the God-man, true, abiding, utterly faithful, sensitive, caring friend of men. Here as in the gospel record we see Jesus making close friends of those whom he had converted from a life of indifference, mediocrity, or sinfulness.

[1]R. E. Brown, *The Community of the Beloved Disciple,* New York, 1979; R. H. Benson, *The Friendship of Christ,* London, 1912; S. Carrals, *Jesus as Friend,* Dublin, 1981.

G

GALOT, JEAN, S.J. (1919–)

This prolific Belgian Jesuit, for long associated with the Gregorian University, has written scholarly works on Marian theology, on the Church and women, on the Catholic priesthood, and on post-conciliar themes related to the religious life.[1] He has published enlightened works of devotion, *Le Coeur du Père, Le Coeur du Christ,* and *Le Coeur de Marie,* all three widely translated. In 1965 G. turned to soteriology with *La Rédemption, Mystère d'Alliance.* Since then questions of Christology have increasingly claimed his attention. In 1969 appeared *La Personne du Christ. Recherche ontologique,* a constructive attempt to solve the problem of the hypostatic union (qv), always retaining the dogma of Chalcedon (qv), by rethinking the union in close relationship with the mystery of the Holy Trinity. In 1971 the author felt obliged to issue serious criticism of three contemporary writers, Hulsbosch, P. Schoonenberg, and E. Schillebeeckx (qv) in his work, *Vers une nouvelle Christologie.* In that year, in another work, he addressed a much debated question, *La Conscience de Jésus* (see articles Consciousness of Jesus and "I" of Jesus Christ), a subject to which he returned in the pages of *Gregorianum.* In *Le problème christologique actuel,* 1980, G. analyzed the problematic of the subject; *Le Christ. Foi et contestation,* a year later, was a wide-ranging survey of writers open to criticism. Some years earlier G. had entered the controversial area of the "suffering" God: *Dieu souffre-t-il,* 1976. *Rencontrer le Christ,* 1984, is spirituality on a high plane? With *Christ. Qui es tu?* I, *Le témoignage de l'Ecriture,* 1985, he has given the first volume of what will be an over-all synthesis.

---

[1]For assessment of works cf. annual Christology bulletin, *NRT,* by L. Renwart.

GREGORY OF NAZIANZUS (329–389)

Like his fellow Cappadocians, G. was fully committed to the defense of the Nicene faith.[1] His Christology is found in the important letters to Cledonius, a priest of Nazianzus, on Apollinarianism (qv), and in two of the Theological Orations; he finds it congenial to revert to relevant themes elsewhere in his works.

G., it has been said, partially anticipated and solved the problems that would be raised in the following century. He writes like this: "Do not let the men deceive themselves and others with the assertion that the 'Man of the Lord,' as they call him, who is rather our Lord and God, is without human mind. For we do not sever the man from the Godhead, but we lay down as a dogma the unity and identity of Person, who of old was not the man but God, and the only Son before all ages, unmingled with body or anything corporeal; but who in these last days has assumed manhood also for our salvation; passible in his flesh, impassible in his Godhead; circumscript in the body, uncircumscript in the Spirit; at once earthly and heavenly, tangible and intangible, comprehensible and incomprehensible; that by one and the same Person, who was perfect man and also God, the entire humanity fallen through sin might be created anew. If anyone does not believe that Holy Mary is the Mother of God, he is severed from the Godhead. If anyone should assert that he passed through the Virgin as through a channel, and was not at once divinely and humanly formed in her (divinely, because without the intervention of a man; humanly, because in accordance with the laws of gestation), he is in like manner godless. If any assert that the manhood was formed and afterwards was clothed with the Godhead, he too is to be condemned. For this were not a generation of God, but a shirking of generation. If any introduce the notion of two sons, one of the God the Father, the other of the Mother, and discredits the unity and identity, may he lose his part in the adoption promised to those who believe aright. For God and man are two natures, as also soul and body are; but there are not two sons or two Gods. . . . And (if I am to speak concisely) the Savior is made of elements which are distinct from one another (for the invisible is not the same with the visible, nor the timeless with that which is subject to time), yet he is not two Persons. God forbid. For both natures are one by the combination, the deity being made man, and the manhood deified or however one should express it. And I say different elements because it is the reverse of what is the case in the Trinity; for there we acknowledge different Persons so as not to confound the *hypostases*; but not different elements, for the Three are one and the same in the Godhead."[2]

G. was using the Trinitarian terminology in the area of Christology, though the full precision to be attained in the debates leading to Nicaea and Chalcedon (qqv) could not be expected of him. He is enlightening on the soul of Christ: "If anyone has put his trust in him as a man without a human mind, he is really bereft of mind, and quite unworthy of salvation. *For that which he has not assumed he has not healed*; but that which is united to his Godhead is also saved. If only half Adam fell, then that which Christ assumes and saves may be half also; but if the whole of his nature fell, it must be united to the whole nature of him that was begotten, and so be saved as a whole. Let them not, then, begrudge us our complete salvation, or clothe the Savior with bones and nerves and portraiture of humanity. For if his manhood is without soul, even the Arians admit this, that they may attribute his Passion to the Godhead, as that which gives motion to the body is also that which suffers. But if he has a soul, and yet is without a mind, how is he man, for man is not a mindless animal?"[3]

G. sees the divination of man as the goal of the Incarnation, and this influences his thinking: "For he whom you now treat with contempt was once above you. He who is now man was once the uncompounded. What he was he continued to be; what he was not he took to himself. In the beginning he was uncaused; for what is the Cause of God? But afterwards for a cause he was born. And that cause was that you might be saved, who insult him and despise his Godhead, because of this that he took upon him your denser nature, having converse with flesh by means of mind. While his inferior nature, the humanity, became God, because it was united to God, and became one (with him). In that the stronger part (i.e., the Godhead) prevailed in order that I too might be made God so far as he is made man."[4]

---

[1]Cf. J. Draseke, "Gregorios von Nazianz und sein Verhältnis zum Apollinarianismus," *ThStKr* 65 (1892) 473–512; K. Holl, *Amphilochius von Ikonium in seinem Verhältnis zu den grossen Kappadoziern*, Tübingen, 1904, 178–96; E. Weigel, *Christologie vom Tode des Athanasius bis zum Ausbruch des nestorianischen Streites*, Munich, 1925, 53–79; E. Mersch, S.J., *The Whole Christ*, Milwaukee, 1938, 303–14; J. Plagnieux, *St. Grégoire de Nazianze, Théologien*, Paris, 1952; J. Rousse, *DSp* VI, 932–71; Quasten III, esp. 252; Grillmeier, 368–70; F. M. Young, *From Niceaea to Chalcedon*, London, 1983, 113–16; [2]*Ep.*, 101, *LNPF*, VII, 439f; [3]*Ibid.*, 440; [4]*Or.* 29, 19, *ibid.*, 308.

GREGORY OF NYSSA, ST., DOCTOR OF THE CHURCH (c. 330–c. 395)

G. must, like all the Cappadocians, be seen in the context of the great debate of the century in which he lived, which had come to a climax before his time at the Council of Nicaea (qv), but which to some extent lingered.[1] He turned, too, to the precise question of the two natures in Christ: "Our contemplation, however, of the respective properties of the flesh and of the Godhead remains free from confusion, so long as each of these is contemplated by itself, as, for example, 'the Word was before the ages but the flesh came into being in the last times'; but one could not reverse this statement, and say that the latter is pretemporal, or that the Word came into being in the last times. The flesh is of a passible, the Word of an operative nature; and neither is the flesh capable of making the things that are, nor is the power possessed by the Godhead capable of suffering. The Word was in the beginning with God, the man was subject to the trial of death; and neither was the human nature from everlasting, nor the divine nature mortal; and all the rest of the attributes are contemplated in the same way. It is not the human nature that raises up Lazarus, nor is it the power that cannot suffer that weeps for him when he lies in the grave; the tear proceeds from the man, the life from the true Life. It is not the human nature that feeds the thousands, nor is it omnipotent might that hastens to the fig tree. Who is it that is weary with the journey, and who is it that by his Word made all things subsist? What is the brightness of the glory, and what is that that was pierced with the nails? What form is it that is buffeted in the Passion, and what form is it that is glorified from everlasting? So much of this is clear (even if one does not follow the argument into detail), that the blows belong to the servant in whom the Lord was, the honors to the Lord whom the servant compassed about, so that by reason of contact and the union of natures the proper attributes of each belong to both, as the Lord receives the stripes of the servant, while the servant is glorified with the honor of the Lord, for this is why the Cross is said to be the Cross of the Lord of glory, and why every tongue confesses that Jesus Christ is Lord, to the glory of the Father."[2] This is a statement of the separate natures and of the Communication of Idioms (qv). But G. insists on the singleness of the Person: "This is our doctrine, which does not, as Eunomius charges against it, preach a plurality of Christs, but the union of the man with the divinity . . ."[3]

G. draws out his Christology in several chapters of the 'Great Catechetical Oration' and in the 'Refutation of Apollinarius' (*Antirrheticus adversus Apol-*

linarem), the latter a most important document in the anti-Apollinarian dossier, in which he clarifies again the Communication of Idioms (qv). Of great importance also is Letter 38 attributed to St. Basil (qv), which scholars now think is the work of G. Here he wrestles with the concepts of nature and hypostasis. He especially shows the relationship of the Son with the Father and the Spirit: "And if any one verily receives the Son, he will hold him on both sides, the Son drawing towards him on the one his own Father, and on the other his own Spirit. For he who eternally exists in the Father can never be cut off from the Father, nor can he who worketh all things by the Spirit ever be disjoined from his own Spirit. Likewise, moreover, he who receives the Father virtually receives at the same time both the Son and the Spirit; for it is in no wise possible to entertain the idea of severance or division, in such a way as that the Son should be thought of apart from the Father, or the Spirit be disjoined from the Son. But the communion and distinction apprehended in them are, in a certain sense, ineffable and inconceivable, the continuity of nature being never rent asunder by the distinction of the hypostases, nor the notes of proper distinction confounded in the community of essence."[4]

On the evolution of doctrine on the question of Person, Grillmeier writes: "Only in the writings of Nestorius (qv), and even in some of the Fathers up to John of Damascus, will it become apparent what the Cappadocians have and have not achieved with their hypostasis-prosopon doctrine . . . they remain fast in a realm which we may describe as individuality. It is here that they make the difficulties which Nestorius and some Fathers of the sixth century are to feel when they transfer to Christology the conceptual analysis which the Cappadocians apply to the Trinity. Gregory of Nyssa, in fact, himself began this transference, though without making his readers or his hearers conscious of it. The distinction between the universal substance and the particularizing characteristics is applied to Christ's human nature so as to rob of its force the Apollinarian charge that Gregory (and all those who believe in a soul of Christ and a complete manhood of the Lord) teaches a two-fold sonship of the Lord, or two Sons. In his letter to Theophilus of Alexandria he excludes the 'two Sons' precisely by allowing a human physis in the exalted Christ while denying it the particularizing characteristics which make a hypostasis."[5]

[1]Cf. F. Diekamp, *Die Gotteslehre des hl. Gregor von Nyssa*, 1896; J. Riviere (qv), *Le dogme de la rédemption*, 2nd ed., Paris, 1905, 151–59, 384–87; J. H. Shrawley, "St. Gregory of Nyssa on the Sinlessness of Christ," *JTS* 7 (1906) 434–41; J. B. Aufhauser, *Die Heilslehre des hl. Gregor von Nyssa*, Munich, 1910; K. Holl, *Amphilochius v. Iconium in seinen Verhältnis zu den grossen Kappadoziern*, Tübingen, 1904, 196–235; J. Lenz, *Jesus Christus nach der Lehre des hl. Gregor von Nyssa*, Trier, 1925; L. Malevez,

"L'Eglise dans le Christ," *RSR* 26 (1935) 257–80; V. Koperski, *Doctrina S. Gregorii Nysseni de processione Filii Dei*, Diss., Rome, 1936; E. Meresch, S.J., *The Whole Christ*, Milwaukee, 1938, 314–22; A. Lieske, "Zur Theologie der Christusmystik Gregors von Nyssa," *Scholastik* 14 (1939) 485–514; *id.*, "Die Theologie der Christusmystik Gregors von Nyssa," *ZKT* 70 (1948) 49–93, 129–68, 315–40; G. Gonzalez, "La formula 'mia ousia treis hypostaseis' en S. Gregorio di Nisa," Rome, *AGreg* 21 (1939); J. Daniélou, *Platonisme et Théologie mystique*, Paris, 1944; *id.*, "L'état du Christ dans la mort d'après Grégoire de Nysse," *HJG* 77 (1958) 63–72; J. Plagnieux, *St. Grégoire de Nysse, Théologien*, Paris, 1952; P. Godet, *DTC* VI (1920) 1807–52; M. Canevet, *DSp*, VI (1967) 971–1011; Quasten, III, esp., 288; F. M. Young, *From Nicaea to Chalcedon*, London, 1983, 116–19; [2]*Contra Eunomium*, V, 5; *LNPF*, V, 180f; [3]*Ibid.*, 181; [4]*LNPF* VIII, 139; [5]*Christ in Christian Tradition*, 288f.

GRILLMEIER, ALOYSIUS, S.J. (1910–)

A patristic scholar, joint editor with H. Bacht of *Chalkedon,* to the first volume of which his own contribution on the early history of Christology occupied pp. 5–202.[1] It was enlarged and translated into English by J. S. Bowden, the highly meritorious religious publisher, writer, and translator. With the title *Christ in the Christian Tradition,* it appeared in English and was at once recognized as authoritative; it has become a quarry for all those studying Christology in the early centuries. The first volume brought the story to the Council of Chalcedon (qv); a further volume continued to Gregory the Great and a third will reach the iconoclastic struggles in the east and adoptionism in Spain. *Christ in the Christian Tradition,* I, has been considerably enlarged in the second edition, 1973. The author's excellence is manifold, painstaking analysis of each author's works and of the great trends, up to date bibliographies, lucid exposition. He partnered Hans Urs von Balthasar in vol. XII of *Mysterium Salutis* on the Paschal Mystery,[2] and contributed important articles to *LTK,* or collections, and theological reviews. He has been attached to the Jesuit Higher Institute of Theological Studies in Stuttgart. Recently the best of his occasional articles, all directly or indirectly related to his central theme, in past or recent times, have been reworked and assembled in a volume over 760 pp., *Mit ihm und in ihm.*[3] *Christ in the Christian Tradition,* is used throughout the present work. All are indebted to the author for reminding us, with his immense scholarship, at the present time when Christological problems are so hotly debated, that many centuries ago the Christian mind was also wrestling with problems of this kind. His principal work is widely translated. A recent German edition of his main work runs to 900 pp., in his case quantity and quality are in harmony.

[1]*Die theologische und sprachliche Vorbereitung der einer Formel von Chalkedon;* [2]*The Effect of the Saving Action of God in Christ,* pp. 279–369, French ed.; [3]Freiburg, 198.

H

HAURIETIS AQUAS, May 15, 1956

The most substantial Encyclical on the Sacred Heart of Jesus. The author, Pius XII, was deeply committed to the theology of the Hearts of Jesus and Mary.[1] On October 31, 1942, he consecrated the world to the Immaculate Heart of Mary, recalled this event, for inspirational purposes, during his pontificate, as in his Apostolic Exhortation, *Menti Nostrae,* September 23, 1950, on the priestly life. He wrote on the Sacred Heart of Jesus in his first Encyclical, *Summi Pontificatus,* October 20, 1939. He drew attention to the fact of his election in the fortieth year since *Annum Sacrum* (qv), "Forty years ago, our Predecessor of immortal memory, Leo XIII, in the dying years of the last century and upon the threshold of the Holy Year, enjoined on the whole world the consecration of the human race to the divine Heart of Jesus. It was with wholehearted assent and with keen pleasure that we welcomed, as a message from another world, that Encyclical Letter of his, *Annum Sacrum,* at the very moment when we were entering upon the priesthood, and taking upon our lips the words, *Introibo ad altare Dei,* as we made ready to perform the sacrifice of the altar. It was with burning enthusiasm that we made the guiding principles and intentions of that enactment our own; an enactment made, under the impulse of God's Providence, by a Pope whose clear insight had revealed to him all the maladies of his age, whether open or latent, and the remedies they needed." The Pope also evoked Pius XI's (qv) teaching on the Kingship of Christ (qv), which he made his own: "So yesterday the Vicar of Christ addressed himself to the unbelievers, the waverers, the doubters, all those who either refused to follow, or followed feebly and half-heartedly, that glorious Redeemer who reigns through all the ages in his Church; pleaded with them, remonstrated with them, and cried out to them, 'Behold your King.' Day by day the devotion to the Sacred Heart of Jesus had taken wider and deeper root in the minds of men. That result is due, not only to the consecration of the human race which was made at the end of the last century, but also to the institution by our immediate Predecessor of the Feast of Christ the King. It has brought countless blessings to Christendom, it has been 'a floodtide of happiness for the city of God.' And what age has ever stood in more need of such blessings than ours?"

The theme of the Heart of Christ had, then, a profound relevance to the spiritual life of Pius XII. The Encyclical stands on its intrinsic merits, irrespective of such motivation. The text falls into six parts: introduction; basis of this devotion; Sacred Heart as the symbol of love; the love of Christ manifest in his life; history and doctrine of this devotion; conclusion.

In the introduction the Pope centers everything on divine charity, stressing the essential basis, the personality of the Holy Spirit (qv); "There is according to Holy Scriptures the closest connection between divine charity which must burst into flames in the hearts of Christians, and the Holy Spirit whose very *property* it is in God to be Love. And this connection, Venerable Brethren, makes clear to us all the real meaning and nature of that cult which is to be offered to the Heart of Jesus Christ."

In the second part of the Encyclical Pius XII wishes to counter objections made to the devotion: naturalism and sentimentalism. He appeals to the authority of his predecessors, Leo XIII and Pius XI (qqv) and he examines OT texts which he thinks relevant. In the next part he expounds the love of which the Heart of Jesus is the symbol. He mentions that the evangelists do not "point to his Heart explicitly as a symbol of his boundless love," but still maintains that "they do nevertheless frequently set in their proper light his divine love and its concomitant emotions of the sense, that is to say desire, joy, sickness of heart, fear, and anger, insofar as they are betrayed by his facial expression, his words, and his gestures." The Pope had earlier fixed the principle: "Wherefore without any doubt the Heart of Jesus Christ hypostatically united to the Person of the divine Word, beat with the pulsations of love and of all the other emotions." Pius had also appealed to the authority of the Fathers, of the east and west.

The central passage in the Encyclical relates to the threefold love of Christ, of which his Heart is the symbol: "Therefore the Heart of the Word made flesh is rightly looked upon as the principal token and sign of that threefold love wherewith the divine Redeemer ceaselessly loves both his Eternal Father and all mankind. It is the sign of that divine love which he shares with the Father and with the Holy Spirit, but which in him alone, that is to say in the Word which was made flesh, is made manifest to us in a frail and corruptible human body, since 'in him dwells all the fullness of the Godhead corporeally' (Col 2:9). It is moreover the sign of that white-hot charity which was infused into Christ's human soul, and which enriches his human will. The acts of this charity are illumined and guided by Christ's twofold most perfect knowledge, and that is to say his *beatific* knowledge (qv) and his *bestowed* or *infused* knowledge. And finally, his Heart is a sign—and this in a more direct and natural way—of his emotional affection, since the body of Jesus Christ, formed by the work of the Holy Spirit in the womb of the Virgin Mary, enjoyed in the fullest degree the power of feeling and perceiving, more perfectly in fact than the bodies of all other men." This threefold love, the Pope says a little later, was openly directed by Christ to "the achievement of his purpose which was our Redemption."

In the fourth part of the Encyclical the Pope interprets, in the light of the threefold love, the phases and decisive events in the earthly life of the God-man. He delays on the threefold gift: "But who can adequately depict the throbbings of the divine Heart, tokens of his boundless love, at those moments when he bestowed his greatest gifts upon mankind? That is to say the gift of himself in the Sacrament of the Eucharist, the gift of his most Holy Mother, and the sharing with us of his priestly office." Each point is elaborated. Then the Pope turns to "the ultimate proof of (Jesus') intimate and boundless charity, the

bloody Sacrifice of the Cross." The Church, he goes on to show, was born from Christ's wounded Heart.

The Encyclical continues with an account of the Ascension and of Pentecost, when the Spirit "pours into (the Apostles') hearts an abundance of divine charity and of other heavenly gifts." "The torrent of this divine charity rises also in the Heart of our Savior 'in whom are hid all the treasures of wisdom and knowledge' (Col 2:3). For this charity is the gift both of the Heart of Jesus and of his Spirit, who is indeed the Spirit of the Father and of the Son. From this Spirit comes the origin of the Church and its marvelous spreading before the face of all those nations and peoples who were sunk in the degradation of idolatry, fraternal hatred, violence and moral corruption. This divine charity is the inestimable gift of the Heart of Christ and of his Spirit." After some further reflections the Pope gives this admirable summary: "The Heart then of our Savior is in some sense a reflection of the divine Person of the Word, and likewise of his twofold nature, divine and human: and we may see in it not only a symbol, but also a compendium or summary of the whole mystery of our redemption."

The fifth part of the Encyclical deals with history, of the devotion and of developing doctrine. The Pope mentions those who, especially in medieval times, helped propagate the ideal. He gives pride of place in later times to St. Margaret Mary (qv). But he wished to make it clear that private revelations added nothing new to Catholic doctrine: "Wherefore it is clear that the revelations to St. Margaret Mary added nothing new to Catholic doctrine. Their vital importance, however, lies in this: that Christ our Lord, by displaying his Sacred Heart, willed, in a most perfect and unheard of way, to arouse the hearts of men to contemplate and adore the mystery of God's most merciful love for the human race. In these unique revelations Christ again and again clearly indicated his Heart as the symbol by which men might be drawn to a knowledge and appreciation of his love; and at the same time he established it as a sign and pledge of mercy and grace for the Church in the needs of our times." The Pope urged the faithful "to go right back to Sacred Scripture, to Christian Tradition and to the deep limpid waters of the Sacred Liturgy if they wish to understand the true nature of devotion to the Sacred Heart of Jesus, and, by loving meditation thereon, to receive food for the nourishment and growth of their religious ardor."

Then the Pope turns to exhortation, appealing to the former teaching of his predecessors in office. He explains the basis of devotion to the Eucharistic Heart of Jesus and gives a pithy persuasive summary of the doctrine of the two Hearts, concluding thus:

"It is altogether fitting that the Christian people, who have received the divine life of grace from Christ through Mary, should, after paying rightful homage to the Sacred Heart of Jesus, also render to the loving Heart of their heavenly Mother the corresponding debt of filial loyalty, love, gratitude and reparation."

---

[1]*AAS* 48 (1956) 309-53.

HEAD OF THE BODY

At the first Vatican Council some of the Fathers found disconcerting the sentence in a draft document, "The Church is the Mystical Body of Christ."[1] The word mystical clashed with the institutional mentality prevailing, expressed in Bellarmine's classic definition of the Church, one which had passed into all popular catechisms; it also caused uneasiness through overtones of illusion and the unreal. A large number of works in the early decades of the century, ranging from the popular, like Msgr. R. H. Benson's *Christ in his Church,* to Emil Mersch's scholarly corpus clarified things. Any remaining misgivings were removed by Pius XII's masterly Encyclical, *Mystici Corporis Christi* (qv). Vatican II, though widening the range of analogy and imagery, as taught in Sacred Scripture, and despite the prominence given to an idea hitherto somewhat overlooked, that of the People of God, fully affirmed the doctrine of the Mystical Body of Christ.

St. Paul (qv), exponent of the doctrine, proclaims that Christ is the Head of the Body. "He is the Head of the Body, the Church; he is the beginning, the first-born from the dead that in everything he might be pre-eminent" (Col 1:18); "the Head from whom the whole body, nourished and knit together through its joints and ligaments, grows with a growth that is from God" (Col 2:19). Likewise the deutero-Pauline epistle to the Ephesians: "Rather, speaking the truth in love, we are to grow up in every way into him who is the Head, into Christ, from whom the whole body, joined and knit together by every joint with which it is supplied, when each part is working properly, makes bodily growth and upbuilds itself in love" (4:15, 16).

Theologians through the ages, notably St. Augustine, St. Thomas (qqv), Suarez, and Petavius, developed the Pauline idea, St. Augustine defending the concept of *Totus Christus,* the whole Christ, made up of Head and members: "Though absent from our eyes, Christ our Head is bound to us by love. Since the whole Christ (*Totus Christus*) is Head and body, let us so listen in the Psalms to the voice of the Head that we may also hear the body speak."[2] The mystical union between the Head and the body is treated by Augustine especially in his commentary on the Psalms. Scheeben chooses this fine passage: "The psalm (62) is uttered in the person of our Lord Jesus Christ, both Head and members. For that one Person, who was born of Mary, and suffered, and was buried, and rose from the dead, and ascended into heaven, and now sits at the right hand of the Father and intercedes for us, is our Head. If he is the Head, we are the members; his entire Church, which is spread throughout the world, is his body, of which he himself is the Head. Not only the faithful who are now on earth, but also those who preceded us, and those who are to come after us until the end of time, pertain one and all to his body; and of this body he is the Head, who has ascended into heaven. We now know the Head and the body, he being the Head, we the body. When we hear his voice, we ought to hear it as proceeding both from the Head and from the body; for whatever he has suffered in the body, we too have suffered, just as whatever we suffer in ourselves, he too suffers. . . . When one of our members suffers, all the other members hurry to aid the ailing member. Therefore if, when he has suffered, we too have suffered in him, and if he has already ascended into heaven, and sits at the Father's right hand, whatever his Church suffers in the troubles of this world, in temptations, in trials, in tribulations (for thus the Church must be proved, as gold is purified by fire), he suffers. We prove this truth, that we have suffered in him, from words of the Apostle: 'If then you be dead with Christ . . . why do you live as if you still belonged to the world?' (Col 2:20). And again he said: 'Our old self was crucified with him, so that the sinful body might be destroyed' (Rom 6:6). If then we have died in him, we have also risen with him. For the same Apostle states: 'Therefore if you be risen with Christ, seek the things that are above, where Christ is seated at the right hand of God' (Col 3:1). Accordingly if we are dead in him, and are risen in him, and he died in us and rises in us (for he is the unity of the Head and the body), rightly we may say that his voice is our voice, and also that our voice is his. Let us, therefore, listen to the psalm, and let us understand that Christ is speaking in it."[3]

St. Thomas Aquinas (qv) devotes a whole question (with 8 articles) of his treatise on the Incarnation to Christ's headship, his grace as Head, of the body. The problems he raises illustrate his approach: Is Christ the Head of the Church? Is Christ the Head of men, as to their bodies, or only as to their souls? Is Christ the Head of all men? Is Christ the Head of the angels? Is the grace of Christ, as he is Head of the Church, the same as his habitual grace, as an individual man? Does it belong to Christ only to be Head of the Church? Is the devil the head of all evil ones? Can Antichrist also be called head of all evil ones? The biblical basis of the saint's theses is understandably largely Pauline.

St. Thomas' key passage is in the first article, wherein to expound the metaphor he speaks of three attributes of the head in the human body: order, perfection, power. "These three," he continues, "belong to Christ spiritually. First, through his nearness to God, his grace is higher and first, though not in time; because all others have received grace in relationship to his grace, as it is said: 'For those whom he foreknew he also predestined to be conformed to the image of his Son, in order that he might be the first-born among many brethren' (Rom 8:29). Secondly, he enjoys perfection, in point of the fullness of all graces, as it is said: 'We saw him full of grace and truth' (Jn 1:14). As has already been shown (q VII, a.9, he has the power of bestowing grace on all the members of the Church, as it is said: 'Of his fullness we have all received' (Jn 1:16). And thus it is clear that Christ is rightly called Head of the Church.''[4]

The doctrine of the Church as the Mystical Body of Christ did not always hold the prominence given it by the Scholastics; it was certainly maintained, and inspired great spiritual writers, but at times the emphasis was on the Church as institution; this view given its pithy form in Bellarmine's definition. Already in the nineteenth century a renewal was under way, thanks to J. A. Möhler and M. J. Scheeben (qv).

Pius XII (qv) in the present century clarified things by *Mystici Corporis Christi* (qv). The Pope considers Christ's headship under these separate headings: his pre-eminence; Christ as one who rules the Church (by invisible and extraordinary government, by visible and ordinary government, in the universal Church through the Roman Pontiffs, in each diocese through the bishops); Christ and his body need each other; the likeness between Christ and his members; the fullness of Christ; his dynamic influence; Christ, the source of light; Christ, the source of holiness.

Christ's pre-eminence and his rule of the Church, which entitle him to headship, are fully demonstrated by the traditional arguments. How Christ and his body need each other prompts a comment like this: "That Christians stand in absolute need of the divine Redeemer's help is clear enough, since he himself has said: 'Without me, you can do nothing,' and the Apostle tells us that all increase of this mystical Body for the building up of itself is from Christ the Head. And yet it is also certain, surprising though it may seem, that Christ needs his members. The first

reason is because Jesus Christ is personally represented by the Sovereign Pontiff who, in order not to be overwhelmed by the weight of his pastoral office, must call many others to share his responsibility, and also needs daily to have his burden eased by the prayers of the whole Church."

"But also," the Pope goes on, "our Savior, in his capacity of direct and invisible ruler of the Church, wants to be helped by the members of his Mystical Body in carrying out the work of Redemption. This is not due to any need or insufficiency in him, but rather because he has so ordained it for the greater honor of his Immaculate Spouse. Dying on the Cross he bestowed upon his Church the boundless treasure of the Redemption without any cooperation on her part; but in the distribution of that treasure he not only shares this work of sanctification with his spotless Bride, but wills it to arise in a certain manner out of her labor. This is truly a tremendous mystery, upon which we can never meditate enough, that the salvation of many souls depends upon the prayers and voluntary mortifications offered for that intention by the members of the Mystical Body of Jesus Christ, and upon the cooperation which pastors and faithful, and especially parents, must afford to our divine Savior.''[5]

As to likeness between Head and members, the Pope recalls Christ's *kenosis* "that his brethren according to the flesh might be made partakers of the divine nature, both during this earthly exile by sanctifying grace and in their heavenly home by the possession of eternal beatitude." Pius immediately invokes the important idea of the image: "For this cause did the Only-begotten of the Eternal Father vouchsafe to become a Son of man, that we might be made conformable to the image of the Son of God and be renewed according to the likeness of him who created us.''[6]

There is a corporate aspect to the likeness with Christ: "But Christ intends the whole Body of the Church, as well as each of its members, to be like himself.''[7] This likeness is seen when the Church "in the footsteps of her divine Founder, teaches, governs and offers the divine sacrifice." The practice of the evangelical counsels and the example of the Orders and institutions in the Church further manifest the resemblance between Christ and his Body.

"A further reason," said the Pope, "why Christ is to be regarded as the Head of the Church lies in the surpassing plenitude and perfection of his supernatural gifts, in consequence of which his Mystical Body draws upon that fullness.''[8] Finally, the Pope sees in Christ's dynamic influence a reason "which shows in a very particular way that Christ is the Head of his Mystical Body." As the nerves are diffused from the head to all the members of our body, giving them the power to feel and move, so our Savior pours forth into the Church his power and virtue, giving to the faithful a clearer understanding and a more ardent desire of the things of God. From him flows into the body of the Church all the light which divinely illumines those who believe, and all the grace which makes them holy, as he himself is holy.'"[9] The two themes, Christ the source of light, and Christ the source of holiness, are developed so as to carry complete conviction.

Vatican II expounding the reality of the Church as a body in which the "life of Christ is communicated to those who believe, and who, through the Sacraments, are united in a hidden and real way to Christ in his passion (qv) and glorification," goes on to treat of aspects of Church's life, emphasizing the role of the Eucharist and of the Spirit. Then come the words:

"The Head of this Body is Christ. He is the image of the invisible God and in him all things came into being. He is before all creatures, and in him all things hold together. He is the Head of the Body which is the Church. He is the beginning, the first-born from the dead, that in all things he might hold the primacy (cf. Col 1:15-18). By the greatness of his power he rules heaven and earth, and with his all-surpassing perfection and activity he fills the whole body with the riches of his glory (cf. Eph 1:18-23). All the members must be formed in his likeness, until Christ be formed in them (cf. Gal 4:19). For this reason, we who have been made like to him, who have died with him and risen with him, are taken up into the mysteries of his life, until we reign together with him (cf. Phil 3:21; 2 Tim 2:11; Eph 2:6; Col 2:12, etc.). On earth, still as pilgrims in a strange land, following in trial and oppression the paths he trod, we are associated with the sufferings as the body with its Head, suffering with him, that with him we may be glorified (cf. Rom 8:17)."[10]

Christ's headship raises problems, opens perspectives affecting his universal primacy (qv), his work as Redeemer (qv), the coalition of angels and men in the scheme of salvation and glory. It helps solve a problem much discussed latterly, the social dimension of sin and virtue, Christocentric spirituality, informing the lay apostolate; here is a preparation for the final judgment of mankind (cf. Mt 25:31-46). Here is the foundation for an ethical system based on the doctrine of the Mystical Body.

[1]Cf. esp. E. Mersch, S.J., *Le Corps mystique du Christ. Etudes de théologie historique,* Louvain, 1933, English tr., *The Whole Christ,* Milwaukee, 1938, London, 1949; *id., La théologie du Corps mystique,* 2 vols. ed. J. Levie, Brussels, 1954, English tr. earlier ed., St. Louis, 1951, *The Theology of the Mystical Body*; F. Jür-

gensmeister, *The Mystical Body of Christ,* Milwaukee, 1939, 66-79; P. Benoit, O.P., "Corps, Tête et Plérôme dans les épitres de la captivité," *RB* 63 (1956) 5-44; *Exégèse et théologie* (1961), 107-53; S. Tromp, S.J., *Corpus Christi quod est ecclesia,* II, *De Christo capite Mystici Corporis,* Rome, 1960; esp. Y. Congar, O.P., *Le Christ, Chef invisible de l'Eglise visible en Jésus Christ,* Paris, 1965, 145-85; [2]In Ps 56, *PL* 36, 662; [3]*Enarr. in Psalm.,* 62, 2, *PL* 36, 748f; cf. M. J. Scheeben, *The Mysteries of Christianity,* tr. C. Vollert, S.J., St. Louis, 1951, 371, n. 14; [4]III, q. VIII, a. 1; [5]Text of the Encyclical, *AAS* 35 (1943) 193-248; *CTS* tr. here used; [6]*Ibid.*; [7]*Ibid.*; [8]*Ibid.*; [9]*Ibid.*; [10]Constitution on the Church, a.7.

HILARY OF POITIERS, ST., DOCTOR OF THE CHURCH (c. 315–367)

The great Latin champion of orthodoxy in the Arian dispute deals with Christology in his magnum opus, *De Trinitate,* in his *Commentary on Matthew,* and in his commentaries on the Psalms.[1] The mystery of Christ is central to his thinking and he returns to it again and again. H. was convinced that there was unity between the Old and New Testaments, and throughout his work biblical allusions and quotations are frequent. The elaboration of his Christology was within the framework of his treatise on the Trinity. It was the traditional Christology of the Church, clear affirmation of the full manhood of Christ and of the true Godhead.

H. could not, with the development yet to be achieved in regard to terminology and concepts, formulate his doctrine with the clarity of the following century. But the basic truths he made quite clear. On the unity in Christ he wrote: "Being, then, man with this body, Jesus Christ is both the Son of God (qv) and Son of Man (qv) who emptied himself of the form of God, and received the form of a servant. There is not one Son of Man and another Son of God; nor one in the form of God, and another born perfect man in the form of a servant; so that, as by the nature determined for us by God, the Author of our being, man is born with body and soul, so likewise Jesus Christ, by his own power is God and man with flesh and soul, possessing in himself whole and perfect manhood, and whole and perfect Godhead."[2]

H. separates three aspects of Christ: pre-existence, kenosis (qv), and exaltation. In the course of a lengthy exposition of the relationship between the Father and Christ, H. can write: "His works testify of him that he was sent by the Father; but the testimony of these works is the Father's testimony; since, therefore, the working of the Son is the Father's testimony, it follows of necessity that the same nature was operative in Christ, by which the Father testifies to him. So Christ, who does the works, and the Father who testifies through them, are revealed as possessing one inseparable nature through the birth, for the operation of Christ is signified to be itself the testimony of God concerning him. . . . By the mystery of the divine nature we are forbidden to separate the birth of the living Son from his living Father. The Son of God suffers no such change of kind, that the truth of his Father's nature does not abide in him. For even where, by the confession of one God only, he seems to disclaim for himself the nature of God by the term 'only,' nevertheless, without destroying the belief in one God, he places himself in the unity of the Father's nature. . . . God Unbegotten brought God Only-begotten to a perfect birth of divine blessedness; it is, then, the mystery of the Father to be the author of the birth, but it is no degradation to the Son to be made the perfect image of his author by a real birth. The giving of power over all flesh, and this, in order that to all flesh might be given eternal life, postulates the Fatherhood of the giver and the divinity of the Receiver; for by giving is signified that the one is the Father, and in receiving the power to give eternal life, the other remains God the Son. . . . He teaches that he is come out from the Father, proclaims that the Father is with him, and testifies that he has conquered the world."[3]

Such strong statements and others similar make it clear that H. considered that Christ remained in his divine nature. This view must be remembered when he is quoted on the *kenosis* (qv). The theme certainly fascinated him, as it has others like Hans Urs von Balthasar; he often reverts directly or indirectly to the Pauline text in 2 Phil. Commenting on it, he writes: "As regards his being in the form of God, by virtue of God's seal upon him, he still remained God. But inasmuch as he was to take the form of a servant and become obedient unto death, not grasping at his equality with God, he emptied himself through obedience to take the form of a slave. And he emptied himself of the form of God, that is, of that wherein he was equal with God—not that he regarded his equality with God as any encroachment—although he was in the form of God and equal with God and sealed by God as God."[4] Not only here, but in many other passages H. is so explicit on the divinity that he cannot be invoked in support of modern (Anglican and Russian) kenotic theories; this has been shown in the deservedly famous article by P. Henry on kenosis in *DBS* (see article Kenosis).

Again he writes: "Yet through the mystery of the gospel dispensation the same Person is in the form of a servant and in the form of God, though it is not the same thing to take the form of a servant and to be abiding in the form of God; nor could he who was abiding in the form of God, take the form of a servant without emptying himself, since the combination of the two forms would be incongruous. Yet it was not another and a different Person who emptied himself and who took the form of a servant. To take anything cannot be predicated of some one who is not, for he only can take who exists. The emptying of the form does not then imply the abolition of the nature; he emptied himself, but he did not lose his self; he took a new form, but remained what he was. Again, whether emptying or taking, he was the same Person; there is, therefore, a mystery, in that he emptied himself, and took the form of a servant, but he does not come to an end, so as to cease to exist in emptying himself, and to be non-existent when he took."[5] Elsewhere he writes: "For the Son of God possesses, in virtue of his birth, everything that is God's; and therefore the Son's work is the Father's work because his birth has not excluded him from that nature which is his source and wherein he abides, and because he has in himself that nature to which he owes it that he exists eternally. And so the Son, who does the Father's works and demands of us that, if we believe not him, at least we believe his works, is bound to tell us what the point is as to which we are to believe the works. And he does tell us in the words which follow."[6] Then follows a quotation from Jn.

H. had a clear idea on the existence of Christ's soul. But he had a problem with Christ's sufferings. In the *Commentary on Matthew* he wrestles with it in the Agony (qv); Christ feared that his suffering and death might prove a stumbling block for his disciples; he prayed that that cup might be given to his disciples, so that they should drink it as fearlessly.[7]

In the *De Trinitate* he was explicit in a comprehensive way: "So the man Jesus Christ, Only-begotten God, as flesh and as Word, at the same time Son of Man (qv) and Son of God, without ceasing to be himself, that is God, took true humanity after the likeness of our humanity. But when, in this humanity, he was struck with blows, or smitten with wounds, or bound with ropes, or lifted on high, he felt the force of suffering without its pain. (H. uses the image of a dart piercing water, flame, or the air without making a hole, for such things do not admit this.) So our Lord Jesus Christ suffered blows, hanging crucifixion, and death. But the suffering which attacked the body of the Lord, without ceasing to be suffering, had not the natural effect of suffering. It exercised its function of punishment with all its violence; but the body of Christ by its virtue suffered the violence of the punishment, without its consciousness. That flesh, that is that Bread, is from heaven; that humanity is from God. He had a body to suffer, and he suffered: but he had not a nature which could feel pain. For his body possessed a unique nature of its own; it was transformed into heavenly glory on the Mount, it put fevers to flight by its touch, it gave new eyesight by its spittle."[8]

H. completes his theology of Christ with an affirmation of the exaltation, "the Word was made flesh in order that the flesh might begin to be what the Word is."[9] The *forma servi* is taken up into the *forma Dei*. But the humanity is not abolished as Arians maintained, relying on 1 Cor 15:24-28. "It is therefore for the promotion of us that he assumed humanity, that God shall be all in all. He who was found in the form of a servant, though he was in the form of God, is now again to be confessed in the glory of God the Father; that is, without doubt he dwells in the form of God, in whose glory he is to be confessed. All is therefore a dispensation only, and not a change of his nature; for he abides still in him, in whom he ever was."[10] As Christ enters thus into immutable glory, we gain by his exaltation. "We shall be promoted to a glory conformable to that of him who became man for us, being renewed unto the knowledge of God, and created again in the image of the Creator, as the Apostle says (he quotes Col 3:9, 10). Thus is man made the perfect image of God. For being conformed to the glory of the body of God, he is exalted to the image of the Creator, after the pattern assigned to the first man."[11]

[1]Works *PL* 9, 10, *CSEL* 22, 65; English tr. de Trinitate, *LNPF* IX, S. McKenna, Fathers of the Church, Washington, 1954; exhaustive bibl., C. Kannengiesser, *DSp* VII, 466–99; for Christology, cf. J. P. Baltzer, *Die Christologie des hl. Hilarius* (Festschrift Karl von Würtemberg), Rottweil, 1889; R. Favre, "La communication des idiomes dans les oeuvres de saint Hilaire," *Greg* 17 (1936) 481–514; P. Smulders, *La doctrine trinitaire de Saint Hilaire de Poitiers*, Rome, 1944, 195–206; F. Raifer, *Die Soteriologie des Hl. Hilarius*, Rome, 1946; J. J. MacMahon, *De Christo Mediatore Doctrina Sancti Hilarii Pictaviensis*, Mundelein, 1947; G. Giamberardini, O.F.M., "De Incarnatione Verbi secundum S. Hilarium Pictaviensem," *Divus Thomas*, Piacenza 50 (1947) 35–56, 194–205; 51 (1948) 3–18; *id.*, "S. Hil. Pict. De Praedestinatione Verbi Incarnati," *MiscFr* 49 (1949) 266–300, 514–33; J. F. McHugh, *The Exaltation of Christ in the Arian Controversy. The Teaching of St. Hilary*, Shrewsburg–Gregorian, 1959; P. Galtier, *St. Hilaire de Poitiers*, Paris, 1960, 108–58, bibl. 122; *id.*, "La forma Dei et la forma servi selon St. Hilaire," *RSR* 48 (1960), 101–18; H. A. Orazzo, S.J., *La salvezza in Ilario di Poitiers. Cristo Salvatore del'uomo nei Tractatus super Psalmos*, Naples, 1986; Patrology IV, M. Simonetti, 36–61; [2]*De. Trinitate*, X, 19, *LNPF* 186; [3]*Op. cit.*, IX, 20, 24, 31; *LNPF* 161, 163, 165; [4]*Op. cit.*, VIII, *LNPF* 150f; [5]*Op. cit.*, IV, 14, *LNPF* 159; [6]*Op. cit.*, VII, 27, *LNPF* 130; [7]*In evang. Mt* 31, 4–7, *PL* 9, 1067B–1069A; [8]*Op. cit.*, X, 23, *LNPF* 187; [9]*De synodis*, 48, *LNPF* 17; [10]XI, 49, *LNPF* 217; [11]*Op. cit.*, ibid.

HISTORY AND JESUS

"The compelling personality which emerges from the Gospels is one and vividly real, but little effort is made to delineate him fully. We can believe that the atmosphere of mystery in which he appears reflects the atmosphere of his historic presence; those who knew him and related the anecdotes from which the Gospels were written knew that there were depths in him which they never comprehended. The modern historian will do well to respect their reserve."[1] The words of J. L. McKenzie may serve as an introduction to the subject of Jesus and history. He suggests one perspective. We should consider one still wider: the impact made on the course of human history by Jesus Christ.

A mass of evidence from every sector of human life, social organization, ethical codes, literature of every kind, art in every medium, churches in every department of their existence, mysticism varied in types and signs, theologies and Christian philosophies, all combine to proclaim the unchallenged uniqueness of Jesus Christ within the frame of history. He is the only one of whom it can be said that he has been making history recognizably and with continuing advertence to him since he emerged from the obscurity of Nazareth into the public life of his people. It is tenable that on any day before it merges into the accumulated past Jesus Christ, directly or indirectly, has a meaning unrivalled by any other figure in that past. For those who accept his absolute, universal primacy, he is the Lord of history (qv). Others must still agree that he has brought and brings a dignity to the human species, without which its fortunes would be dark and deprived.

One who surveys this immense, multiple impact of Jesus Christ in history, who knows how much history has been, is being, made by him, in his name, may be taken aback by the debate on the Jesus of history. It was opened by Hermann Samuel Reimarus in the Age of Enlightenment. His thesis broadly was that the real life and teaching of Jesus had to be distinguished from the misleading portrait of him put into circulation by the Church. In the present century the idea was taken up by Albert Schweitzer, in a book known in English as *The Quest of the Historical Jesus*. Schweitzer thought that the lives of Jesus provided an inescapable temptation to project oneself onto the empty areas in the Gospel accounts. Then the attitude must be one of historical pessimism? The argument favoring such a position would be the acknowledged fact that the gospels do not provide the data for a complete biography. But they have a value as historical records, though their primary purpose is to publish faith.

It is rather daring, too daring, to write off all the lives of Christ written over the last century and a half, written from many diverse viewpoints, with different evaluations, more or less reliable in their evocation of the past, their fulfillment of the historian's task, which Michelet described as "the resurrection of the flesh." The list of authors is not composed of intellectual or scholarly mediocrities: Strauss, Renan, Edersheim, Goguel, Klausner, De Grandmaison, Fouard, Fillion, Prat, Riccioti, Cadoux, to mention only the best known or those widely translated.

It was, of course, Form Criticism (qv) that changed the approach and for many, froze the hope of writing scientific history. But not everyone agreed. Vincent Taylor published in 1954 a work entitled *The Life and Ministry of Jesus*. With the opening sentence of his first chapter he faces the problem: "Many scholars believe that the attempt to write a Life of Christ is so difficult as to be almost impossible."[2] With a review of recent studies on the question and careful analysis of the opinions expressed, he justifies his own work. C. H. Dodd, a very great scholar, writes by way of preface to the section of his book, *The Founder of Christianity,* entitled "The Story," as follows: "I have essayed an outline, and an interpretation, of the course of events, so far as this may be inferred from data in the four gospels. Inevitably this is to some extent conjectural. Informed conjecture, a legitimate tool of the historian, is often an indispensable tool to the historian of antiquity. For the result I do not claim more than a degree—as it seems to me a high degree—of probability."[3]

Taylor and Dodd (qqv) thus reacted against the effect of R. Bultmann's (qv) ideas in this particular area. Bultmann appeared to solidify the view that the Jesus of history was out of reach. What counted for the early Church was the Christ of faith proclaimed in the kerygma. The historical Jesus held no interest for the early Christians, from whom had come the gospels. The theory was not cast-iron to Bultmann himself, for in his two works, *The History of the Synoptic Tradition* and *Jesus and the Word,* he pursued the quest of the words and deeds of Jesus. The post-Bultmannians thought to follow him here and thus came the new quest for the historical Jesus. In 1956 came M. Kähler's *The So-Called Historical Jesus and the Historic Biblical Christ,* English tr., 1964: an anticipation of the post-Bultmannian dissent. The turning-point is taken as Ernst Käsemann's article, "The Problem of the Historical Jesus," 1953.

Käsemann's case was stated with lucidity and power. If there is no intrinsic relationship between the earthly Jesus of history and the exalted Lord of Christian faith, Christianity is a myth without historical foundation; if the first Christians had no interest in the Jesus of history, why were the gospels written? Though the gospels came out of the Easter faith and it may be difficult to reach the historical Jesus,

Christian faith must necessarily assume identity between the earthly Jesus and the exalted Lord. Käsemann offered guidelines to the new quest: rules to facilitate identifying authentic words and deeds of Jesus. Everything with a kerygmatic ring must be eliminated (though) not thereby classified as unauthentic); whatever is paralleled from contemporary Judaism is to be discarded as dubious; a genuine saying of Jesus should have an Aramaic character. Käsemann applied these rules and considered that he had established certain elements as unquestionably originating in Jesus himself. E. Fuchs, another post-Bultmannian, in an article on "The Quest of the Historical Jesus," 1956, put forward his criteria for this research. He concluded that the deeds of Jesus were more easily established than his words; they were less susceptible of change in Church tradition.

In the whole debate there are lacunae which surprise. Why should the early disciples and converts, Jews, seek to depart from the historical origins of their religion, when their intellectual and religious inheritance and training taught them that revelation and history are inseparably intertwined? A Jew thought of God in terms of history; he could not do otherwise. The new search for the Jewishness of Jesus (qv) will demonstrate this convincingly; it will set a question mark after one of Käsemann's criteria.

To suggest that those who framed the kerygma overlooked, forgot, or were just indifferent to Jesus Christ is to make two enormous assumptions: 1) that his impact on them was practically nil in what was the heart of their lives, religious belief; and 2) that they were capable on their own of fashioning, almost creating, a core of religious ideas so credible that it would command the assent of the mightiest minds and most heroic spirits in two thousand years of history. The first Christians have been elevated into an innovative role of cosmic dimensions, something they themselves never for a moment contemplated. How can we affirm this? Because they ensured full publication of the relevant essential facts about the One who had chosen them from a background utterly inadequate to shape creative religious leaders. On him, as the first proclamations in Acts make abundantly clear, they depended. His personality and his teaching are dominant as we learn not only from the canonical writings, but from the Apostolic Fathers.

That everything was changed in the moment of the Easter faith is taken as lessening the disciples' appreciation of Jesus, whom they had previously known; he seems, in some accounts, almost to have vanished before the risen Christ. But surely it was the exact opposite that happened. The risen Christ gave a powerful new clarity to everything they had seen in him, heard from him, known about him. How could it be otherwise? He was the same Jesus Christ, separated from them in time only by a few days, his identity emphasized by his triumph from the grave. This may be taken as psychologizing. In fact it is the proponents of a dichotomy between the Jesus of history and the Christ of faith who do the psychologizing. There is no evidence to adduce. No one ever said explicitly or implicitly: This is someone else. No one ever thought the risen Christ different from the crucified Jesus—witness the marks of the nails, spoken of, seen, narrated.

Continuity was needed for the exercise of faith. Faith could not have been given to a fabrication, no matter how well meant. Its ultimate foundation was Jesus Christ, risen indeed, but totally himself, Author especially of the gift that made the new life possible, the Holy Spirit. Here is where proponents of the division between the Jesus of history and the Christ of faith have not been sufficiently heard. Jesus promised the Spirit, the exalted Christ sent him; he assures the continuity which supported faith: in the crucified, apparently defeated, humiliated, abandoned Jesus, the disciples' faith had floundered; it must be revived in the same Jesus, now the risen Christ.

The antithesis between the 'Jesus of history' and the 'Christ of faith' has been artificially and unjustifiably enlarged. The French biblical scholar, Xavier Léon-Dufour, noting the changed attitude of some of Bultmann's (qv) disciples, writes: "By using those literary methods of Form Criticism which Bultmann has developed so splendidly, they seek to advance from a knowledge of the religion of the early Christians to a knowledge of Jesus himself, because he must surely have been a greater figure than anyone in the early Church. This development cannot but be welcomed by all who believe in traditional Christianity, but it should also make people ask whether there has not been a fundamental error in drawing a distinction between the 'historical Jesus' and the 'Christ of faith.' Does not the risen Christ belong in some way to history? And did the disciples have no kind of faith in Jesus until after the Resurrection? The continuity of the disciples' faith before and after the Resurrection and the identity of the Risen Christ with Jesus of Nazareth can be denied only on a priori grounds, because of philosophical or theological presuppositions, not because there is historical evidence to the contrary."[4]

Reimarus zu Wrede, 1906, English tr., The Quest of the Historical Jesus, London, 2nd ed., 1911; later German ed., Die Geschichte der Leben-Jesu-Forschung, 1913; W. Sanday, The Life of Christ in Recent Research, London, 1908; G. Baldensperger, "Un demi-siécle de recherches sur l'historicité de Jésus," RTP 12 (1924) 161–210; C. C. McCown, The Search for the Real Jesus. A Century of Historical Study, New York, 1940; J. G. H. Hoffmann, Les Vies de Jésus et le Jésus de l'histoire, Paris, 1947; V. Taylor, The Life and Ministry of Jesus, London, 1954; id., The Person of Christ in the New Testament Teaching, London, 1958; E. Käsemann, "Das Problem des historischen Jesus," ZTK 51 (1954) 125–43; N. A. Dahl, "Der historische Jesus als geschichtswissenschaftliches und theologisches Problem," KD 1 (1955) 104–06; H. Diem, Der irdische Jesus und der Christus des Glaubens, Tübingen, 1957; W. Grundmann, Die Geschichte Jesu Christi, Berlin, 1957; B. Rigaux, O.F.M., "L'historicité de Jésus devant l'exégèse récente," RB 65 (1958) 481–522; J. Jeremias, "The Present Position in the Controversy Concerning the Problem of the Historical Jesus," ExT 69 (1958) 333–39; id., Das Problem des historischen Jesus, Stuttgart, 1964; G. Ebeling, "Jesus und der Glaube," ZTK 55 (1968) 64–110; id., Die Frage nach dem historischen Jesus und das Problem der Christologie, I, 1959, 14–30; J. M. Robinson, A New Quest of the Historical Jesus, London, 1959; G. Bornkamm, Jesus of Nazareth, New York, 1960; M. Kähler, Der sogennante historische Jesus und der geschichtliche Christus, Munich, 1961; B. Gerhardsson, Memory and Manuscript. Oral Tradition in Rabbinic Judaism and Early Christianity, Uppsala, 1961; id., The Gospel Tradition, Lund, 1986; E. Lohse, "Die Frage nach dem historischen Jesus in der gegenwärtigen ntl. Forschung," TLZ 87 (1962) 162–74; H. Ristow and K. Matthiae, Der historische Jesus und der kerygmatische Christus, Berlin, 1962; K. Schubert, ed., Der historische Jesus und der Christus unseres Glaubens, Vienna, 1962; C. Braaten and R. Harrisville, ed., The Historical Jesus and the Kerygmatic Christ, Nashville, 1964, 47 contributors, Catholic and Protestant; E. Fuchs, Studies of the Historical Jesus, London, 1964; A. Dulles, S.J., "Jesus as the Christ," Thought 39 (1964) 359–79; J. Peter, Finding the Historical Jesus, London, 1965; J. R. Geiselmann, Jesus der Christus, Munich, 1965; X. Léon-Dufour, S.J., The Gospels and the Jesus of History, London, 1968; O. Borchert, The Original Jesus, 1968; C. Anderson, Critical Quests of Jesus, Grand Rapids, 1969; id., The Historical Jesus. A Continuing Quest, Grand Rapids, 1972; J. Roloff, Das Kerygma und der irdische Jesus, Göttingen, 1970; L. Keck, A Future for the Historical Jesus, Nashville, 1971; C. H. Dodd, The Founder of Christianity, London, 1971; P. Grech, "Recent Developments in the Jesus of History Controversy," BTB 1 (1971) 190–213; K. Ketelge, ed., Rückfrage nach Jesus, Freiburg i. B., 1974; G. Aulen, Jesus in Contemporary Historical Research, Philadelphia, 1976; I. H. Marshall, I Believe in the Historical Jesus, Grand Rapids, 1977; J. Mackey, Jesus the Man and the Myth, New York, 1979; E. Schweizer, Jesus, London, 1971; R. Feneberg and W. Feneberg, Das Leben Jesu im Evangelium, Freiburg i. B., 1980; M. Cook, The Jesus of Faith, New York, 1981; G. Vermes, Jesus the Jew, Philadelphia, 1982; I. Wilson, Jesus, the Evidence, SE (1984); W. M. Thompson, The Jesus Debate. A Survey and a Synthesis, New York, 1985; J. D. G. Dunn, The Evidence for Jesus, Philadelphia, 1985; L. Boff, O.F.M., Jesus Christ, Liberator, London, 1985; A. E. McGrath, The New Quest of the Historical Jesus from Käsemann to Pannenberg, Oxford, 1986; J. H. Charlesworth, Jesus within Judaism, London, 1987; H. U. von Balthasar, "The Biblical Picture of Jesus and Modern Exegesis," The von Balthasar Reader, 1980, 127–32; S. Kealy, Gospel Studies Since 1970, ITQ 56 (1990) 3, 161–69; 57 (1991) 2, 93–104; [2]Op. cit., p. 3; [3]Op. cit., London, 1971, 179; [4]The Gospels and the Jesus of History, London, 1970, 274.

[1]J. L. McKenzie, Jesus Christ, Dictionary of the Bible, Milwaukee, 1966, 432; W. Wrede, Das Messiasgeheimnis in den Evangelien, Göttingen, 1901, 2nd ed., 1913; A. Schweitzer, Von

HUMILITY OF JESUS, THE

"Take my yoke upon you and learn from me, for I am meek and humble of heart, and you will find rest for your souls. For my yoke is easy and my burden is light" (Mt 11:29-30). "Whoever humbles himself like this child, he is the greatest in the kingdom of heaven" (Mt 18:4). "For everyone who exalts himself will be humbled, and he who humbles himself will be exalted" (Lk 14:11). There is a whole mentality conveyed by the Bible, with which these remarks are in harmony.[1] It is nonetheless true that this is a unique instance of a religious founder, committed by this very role and duty to leadership on a vast scale, eventually seen to be universal, offering himself as a model of humility. In the most profound sense a model, for it is not only the practice of this virtue, but understanding of it which must come from him to his follower.

The Christian must embody humility in his person. The body of Christians, of those really united with Christ, must be structured on humility. Part of the misunderstanding which the word arouses, part of its depressing, almost demoralizing effect on some disciples, is due to failure to comprehend its creative, liberating aspect. A possible source of misunderstanding is the use of the word "Heart." Jesus, faithful to biblical usage, expresses in the word the very core of his being, the dynamic thrust of his entire self, involving his total identity. Humility of heart was integral to the structure of his being. It is to be understood in the light of the self-emptying (kenosis qv) of which St. Paul speaks in the hymn in Phil 2:6-8: "Christ Jesus who, though he was in the form of God, did not count equality with God a thing to be grasped, but emptied himself taking the form of a servant, being born in the likeness of men. And being found in human form he humbled himself and became obedient unto death, even death on a cross."

[1]A. Schlatter, *Jesu Demut, ihre Missdeutung und ihr Grund,* Gutersloh, 1904; K. Thieme, *Die christliche Demut: Wortgeschiechte und die Demut bei Jesus,* Glessen, 1906; W. B. Ullathorne, *The Groundwork of the Christian Virtues,* London, 1885; Columba Marmion, O.S.B. (qv), *Christ, the Ideal of the Monk,* London, 1926, 209-50; id., *Christ, the Ideal of the Priest,* London, 1952, 114-27; E. Schweizer, *Erniedrigung und Erhohung bei Jesus und seinen Nachfolgern,* Zurich, 1955; P. Adnes, *L'humilité d'après St. Augustin,* RAM 28 (1952) 208-33; id., *DSp* VII, 1, 1134-87, esp. *Le Christ, modèle de l'humilité,* 1154; R. Arbesmann, Christ the *Medicus humilis* in St. Augustine, *Augustinus Magister,* II, Paris, 1955, 623-29; B. Haering, *The Law of Christ,* I, London, 1961, 546-57; A. Gelin, *The Poor of Yahweh,* Collegeville, 1953; A. Stoger, Bauer III, 385-90.

HYPOSTATIC UNION, THE

The theological term used to express the doctrine which explains how Jesus Christ is true God and true man.[1] As a result of the controversies of the first five centuries the solution finally adopted to the problem was that in Christ there were two natures, divine and human, but only one Person, divine, the Word, second Person of the Blessed Trinity. This is the solemnly defined doctrine of the Church. To explain how it originated is relatively easy; to explain it in language accessible to modern man may not be so easy, though this task should not be abandoned.

The early centuries were seized by the important word of St. John: "The Word became flesh" (1:14). As the meaning imposed itself, that there were in this being, someone who could be called divine and someone who was patently human, with an equally evident unity binding both, the intelligence of those who had this faith was powerfully challenged: What terms to use? What formulation was allowed? What were the pitfalls in speculation?

The Church starting out from the Jewish community, with its sharply defined ethos and religious concepts, made, within a few centuries, large intellectual gains in a very different world, Graeco-Roman civilization, within which the Greek mind was dominant. The Greek mind provided the intellectual framework, the key concepts for continuing reflection on the primal truths embedded in the divine message, available to man, inviting his scrutiny. The adoption of the Greek word *hypostasis* (person) was decisive. There had been attempts made to formulate doctrine which were deemed heretical: Christ did not have a truly human body, but merely a corporeal appearance—Docetism (qv); he did not have a soul, the Logos being thought to supply its functions—Apollinarianism and also Arius (qqv); he was fully two beings, divine and human, being a human person, as well as retaining his inalienable divine personality—Nestorius condemned at the Council of Ephesus; he had only one nature (*physis*), the divine, into which the human nature was absorbed—Eutyches, and monophysitism (qqv) which ultimately was his teaching. This latter view brought things to a head in the pontificate of St. Leo the Great (qv) whose Tome (qv) decisively influenced the events that reached a climax in the Council of Chalcedon, and its definition (qqv).

There are vast ontological implications in this definition. In God nature and personality are one, inseparable. When a divine Person became man, he did not change (see Suffering of God?, The). The word "assume" is used to convey the mysterious event, that at a given moment, at the Annunciation, without losing his divine personal identity, he was also truly man. In that moment man was God without losing his human dignity; by being substantially united to a divine Person, he had the incalculable benefit of sharing in the personal existence of the

Word, of losing his own human personality only to have it replaced by one infinitely superior. Nothing is lost to human nature, which with all its powers intact, thinks, acts, and feels autonomously: all this through the power of a divine Person.

What is a person? St. Thomas Aquinas (qv) defined it as *distinctum subsistens in intellectuali natura*. The key word here is *subsistens*. A person implies subsistence, which may be defined as self-existence. But when used of God and men the word is analogous. Man is not self-existent as is God, nor is his self-existence limitless, that is infinite. It is limited by his nature, which being created, has a beginning and end, though the spirit which is also created, will not end. In Christ the ultimate root of self-existence is divine. Here is one aspect of the awesome mystery.

Another is the fully established power of Jesus Christ to live an authentic human life, in the active and passive aspects of this existence. As man he is fully within the world of human beings, and since he is also God he is a perfect Mediator between God and man (1 Tim 2:5), uniquely endowed to achieve the redemption (qv) of mankind (1 Tim 2:6). As man Jesus Christ has full human equipment of thought, consciousness, freedom, feeling. No one, in the course of his life, expressed the slightest doubt on his genuine human quality, attributes, response. When we seek, with the limited historical resources available to us, to describe his character (qv) and evaluate his distinctive characteristics, we may be arrested by a sentiment of mystery, of the enigmatic, much more so than in studying other remarkable human beings, but never so much as to doubt his essential humanity. His contemporaries were often astounded by what he did, but their reading of him was in the light of their previous religious history, never skepticism about his human reality.

As a man he offered religious homage to God, choosing the modalities congenial to his religious inheritance and upbringing: adoration, obedience to divine law, prayer (qv). In all this he manifested in human religious discourse his specific divine personality, addressing the eternal Father, conforming to his will, accepting from him entirely and answering the ultimate demand, the free sacrifice of his life. The mystery lies in the fact that he did not act as less a man because he was God. Nor did his sense of mission, a dominant idea in his earthly career, as related by St. John (qv), in any sense clash with his distinctive property within the eternal Trinity, as the Only-

begotten of the Father. This brings us back again to ontology. The human nature of Christ cannot be considered a distinct ontological subject, that is possessed of a personality of its own. But in excluding every use of the word personality in relation to it, one may easily give the impression of unreality. St. Thomas himself says: "The human nature does not constitute the divine Person strictly speaking, but it constitutes it insofar as the divine Person is designated by the human nature."[2]

The full explanation is given by J.-H. Nicolas, O.P.: "A person who has a human nature, who subsists in it, or in whom this nature has subsistence, is a human person. What must be absolutely avoided is the idea that it would be a human person distinct from the Word. It is the Word who has become a human person, without ceasing to be a divine Person. This seems a valid and necessary expression of the mystery of the Incarnation. It allows us besides to refute a fundamental objection which we have already met: how would Jesus be a real man, fully a man if he were deprived of the most precious human value, personality? If we reply that he has the divine personality, what does this mean? Has the man Jesus a divine personality? That can be understood only in the way it has been said: a personality which a man has is a human personality; we must then say: the divine Person in becoming incarnate, became a human person, without ceasing, on that account, to be a divine Person, the second Person of the Trinity."[3]

Is the definition of Chalcedon, because of its antiquity and Greek mental categories, out of date, not to be presented in a serious modern work of Christology? The International Theological Commission does not think so, nor does Karl Rahner (qqv), nor the writer just quoted, nor another systematic theologian, Jean Galot, S.J., of the Gregorian University (qv), nor Bernard Lonergan. One must also note that no important successful attempt to explain the theology of the Incarnation otherwise has so far appeared.

[1]Cf. standard theological works, esp., L. Billot, *De Verbo Incarnato,* Rome, 1928; B. Lonergan, *De Verbo incarnato,* 3rd ed., Rome, 1964; *id., De constitutione Christi ontologica et psychologica,* 3rd ed., Rome, 1961; H. Diepen, *La théologie de l'Emmanuel,* Bruges, 1960; J. Knox, *The Humanity and Divinity of Christ,* Cambridge, 1967; W. Kasper, *Jesus the Christ,* London, 1976; 240–42; D. Lane, "The Incarnation of God in Jesus," *ITQ* 46 (1979) 158–69; G. O'Collins, *Interpreting Jesus,* London, 1983, 171–83; J. Sobrino, *Christology at the Crossroads,* 311–45; K. Rahner, "On the Theology of the Incarnation," *Theological Investigations,* IV 105–20; J.-H. Nicolas, *Synthèse Dogmatique,* Fribourg, 1986, 301–58; [2]*Summa Theologica,* III, q. 20, a.2; [3]*Op. cit.,* 341f.

I

"I" OF JESUS CHRIST, THE

When Jesus said "Before Abraham was, I am" (Jn 8:58) he was speaking from a very special consciousness, that of a human being who knew he was God.[1] How is the consciousness explained? It is a question much debated by theologians, subject of a whole book by Jean Galot (qv). Some have thought that Jesus had this certainty, this intuition, at the point where the hypostatic union (qv) is achieved. K. Rahner thought that the vision enjoyed by Jesus gave him this consciousness of being who he was, as we have a consciousness of being who we are, though we do not give it objective character; Jesus could give his consciousness objective character as he gave thematic form to knowledge acquired by experience or reflection on experience. J. Mouroux thought Jesus attained the conviction at the fine point of the soul, where he escaped the existential condition of other men. J. Maritain thought that the vision given to Jesus was precisely objective knowledge of the Word. Jean Galot thought that "The structure of the act of consciousness of Christ requires no other extraordinary element but the hypostatic union itself." "We touch here," he writes, "the mystery of the hypostatic unity. The Incarnation is nothing other than the crossing by the Person of the Word of the distance which separates God from man. The disproportion has thus been covered. It seems that one should say that the Incarnation has entailed, for the human nature that was assumed, a supernatural ontological elevation, which harmonizes his activity with the divine 'I' of the Word. This elevation allows the human activity of consciousness to be set in motion by a divine 'I' and to perceive the divine 'I' reflexively."[2]

This position has been subjected to grave criticism by J.-H. Nicolas.[3] He cannot accept that human nature would be elevated by the fact of the hypostatic union. Jean Galot is aware of the danger of a monophysite temptation to think of the human nature penetrated by the divine, but Nicolas thinks it real. He himself thinks that the solution is to think of inter-action or synthesis between vision and active or reflective consciousness, neither of which by itself would suffice.

Catholic theologians do not see any difficulty in speaking of the awakening of consciousness, or progress in Jesus' consciousness. Nicolas thinks that his theory is easily integrated into a fully Chalcedonian Christology.

The same theologian considers the question of the 'unconscious' in Jesus. If by unconscious is meant what in organic life is not normally perceived, this was part of Jesus' psycho-physical make-up, part of the assumed humanity. But if we speak of the subconscious, in the manner of Sigmund Freud, then some distinctions are in order. If the implications are pathological, then we must affirm the wholeness and integrity of the sacred humanity. If we refer to a normal element in the mind without implying defect or failure of any kind, we are faced with the kind of mystery we meet in studying the lives of all others. Even with the cooperation of the one involved, entry to the subconscious is better reserved to specialists. These theses can be suggested without directly invoking the kenosis (qv). But the kenosis must be borne in mind throughout the entire study of the consciousness of Christ, especially in regard to his consciousness of the Word. This also means that much that is advanced as informative or enlightening is tentative. Is this an admission of failure in most important research? It is an admission of mystery, which does not necessarily impede research, but warns us of its limits.

[1]Cf. J. Galot, S.J., *La Conscience de Jesus,* Paris, 1971; *id.,* "La conscience humaine du Christ. A propos de quelques publications récentes," *Greg* 32 (1951) 525–68; *id.,* "La conscience humaine du Christ," *Greg* 35 (1954) 335–46; *id.,* "Science et conscience de Jésus," *NRT* 82 (1960) 113–131; *id., Esprit et Vie,* 92 (82) 145–152; *id.,* "Le Christ terrestre et la vision," *Greg* 67, 3 (1986) 442–59; P. Parente, *L'Io di Cristo,* 2nd ed., Brescia, 1955; K. Rahner, S.J. (qv) "Dogmatic Considerations on Knowledge and Consciousness in Christ," in *Dogmatic vs Biblical Theology,* ed. H. Vorgrimler, Baltimore, 1964, 241–67; *id.,* "Dogmatic Reflections on the Knowledge and Self-consciousness of Christ," in *Theological Investigations,* V (1966) 193–215; P. Galtier, *L'Unité du Christ. Etre, Personne, Conscience,* Paris, 1939; B. de Margerie, S.J., "De la science du Christ, Science, préscience, conscience même prépascales du Christ Rédempteur," in *Doctor Communis,* 36 (1983) 123–57; M. Nédoncelle, "Le moi du Christ et le moi des hommes à la lumière de la réciprocité des consciences" in *Problèmes actuels de Christologie,* Paris, 1965; J.-H. Nicolas, *Synthèse Dogmatique,* Fribourg, 1986, 375–403, esp. 397–403; J. Ashton, "The Consciousness of Christ," *The Way* 10 (1970) 59–71, 147–57, 250–59; [2]*Op. Cit.,* 179; [3]*Op. cit.*

ICONOGRAPHY OF JESUS CHRIST

There are different problems which arise when there is question of artistically depicting Jesus Christ. There have not been uniform answers through the ages.[1] Nor are we intellectually equipped to evaluate the solutions which in successive centuries emerged. Attempts were made from early times to give visual representation to the God-man, despite sharp discouragement from some Fathers of the Church. Performance in this task led to a fierce controversy in the eastern Church, in the eighth and early ninth centuries, the iconoclastic crisis. When peace was restored, the making of images was resumed: icons with all their mystery in the east, representations determined by the successive varying cultures in the west. The west did excel in stained glass and sculpture as well as painting. The note of austere spirituality characteristic of medieval Christian art gradually, with the Renaissance, gave way to more naturalist products in keeping with the whole Renaissance ethos. It is for historians of art to analyze the different elements in this complex reality.

The theologian is interested in the preference of early generations, even in the catacombs, for the Good Shepherd image; the reluctance, for centuries, to depict the crucified One, possibly through fear of a bad reaction from those imbued with Roman ideas, even prejudice. There is too the problem of excessive emphasis on the humanity of Jesus at the expense of belief in his divinity—the iconoclasts pushed this

objection to intransigent extremes. And there is the relationship of religious imagery to faith, especially faith that is dynamic, issuing in good works.

Mass-produced religious art, sometimes not notably beautiful, open to commercial exploitation, for which it may have been made, can scarcely always effect the union between the spiritual impulse and the aesthetic intuition which should be the ideal. Beauty in what is made to represent sacred figures should raise the mind to their essential beauty, to the reality of divine beauty which is shared with those divinized.

An entirely different perception is called for and generally given to images which are miraculous in origin, such as that of Our Lady of Guadalupe and, in the case of Jesus himself, the Shroud of Turin. So too there is a different reaction to images directly related to a devotion spread by an apostle with charismatic power. Such is the image of the Sacred Heart (qv), multiform in design but always related to the revelations to St. Margaret Mary (qv); such is the imagery associated with the devotion to divine mercy, propagated by Sister Faustina.

The human spirit can triumph over all shortcomings in what is offered to it; and the human spirit works within every kind of cultural, social, economic limitation. That is why spiritual intensity which is ultimately essentially personal may arise out of contact with utterly mediocre religious imagery, imagery that appeared hopelessly tainted by the profit motive. What was so often derided as cheap, almost vulgar repository religious art has sometimes helped saints in their ascension to God through Jesus Christ.

[1]Cf. G. E. Meille, *Christ's Likeness in the History of Art,* London, 1924; H. Priebe, *Das Christusbild in der Kunst des 19 und 20 Jahrhundert,* Berlin, 1932; H. Preuss, *Das Bild Christi im Wandel der Zeiten,* Leipzig, 1932; C. C. Dobson, *The Face of Christ,* Milwaukee, 1933; G. de Jerphanion, "L'image de Jésus Christ dans l'art Chrétien," *NRT* 65 (1938); P. Morand, *Visage du Christ,* Paris, 1938; F. Mader and R. Hoffmann, *Christus in der Kunst,* Munich, 1947; Propagation of the Gospel, Westminster, Maryland, *The Son of Man* (Chinese, Indian, African art), 1946; A. Grabar, *Christian Iconography: A Study of Its Origins,* 1969; Gertrud Schiller, *Ikonographie der christlichen Kunst,* 3 vols., English tr. 1971; D. Talbot Rice, *The Beginnings of Christian Art,* 1957; L. Réau, *Iconographie de l'art Chrétien,* 3 vols.; E. Mâle, *Religious Art from the Twelfth to the Eighteenth Centuries,* 1949; E. Kirschbaum and others (eds.) *Lexikon der christlichen Ikonographie,* 8 vols., 1968–1976; H. Leclercq, O.S.B., *DACL* VII, 2, 2393–2468; esp., L. P. Siger and L. A. Leite, *NCE* VII, 956–969.

IGNATIUS OF ANTIOCH, ST. (c. 35–c. 107)

If ever there was an existential theology of Jesus Christ, I. is its author.[1] Christ was the immediate, irreplaceable focus of his life and of his thinking;

both were entwined within the mystery of Christ. A keynote to this total thrust is in such a sentence as this from the Epistle to the Romans: "It is better for me to die in Christ Jesus than to be king over the ends of the earth. I seek him who died for our sake. I desire him who rose for us."[2] Christ is the revelation of God. I. was resolutely opposed to Docetism (qv): "For our God, Jesus the Christ, was conceived by Mary by the dispensation of God, 'as well of the seed of David' as of the Holy Spirit: he was born and was baptized, that by himself submitting he might purify the water."[3] "If Jesus Christ permit me through your prayers, and if it be his will, in the second book, which I propose to write to you, I will show you concerning the dispensation of the new man Jesus Christ, which I have begun to discuss, dealing with his faith and his love, his suffering and his resurrection."[4] "For the divine prophets lived according to Jesus Christ. Therefore they were also persecuted, being inspired by his grace, to convince the disobedient that there is one God, who manifested himself through Jesus Christ his son, who is his Word proceeding from silence, who in all respects was well-pleasing to him that sent him."[5] God who is invisible made himself visible for us in Jesus Christ: "Wait for him who is above seasons, timeless, invisible, who for our sakes became visible, who cannot be touched, who cannot suffer, who for our sakes accepted suffering, who in every way endured for our sakes."[6]

A sentence of I. could have been incorporated in Vatican II's Constitution on Divine Revelation (qv): "But why are we not all prudent seeing that we have received knowledge of God, that is Jesus Christ? Why are we perishing in our folly, ignoring the gift which the Lord has truly sent?"[7]

Christ's coming was mysterious and miraculously manifested: "And the virginity of Mary, and her giving birth were hidden from the Prince of this world, as was also the death of the Lord. Three mysteries of a cry which were wrought in the stillness of God." But "a star shone in heaven beyond all the stars, and its light was unspeakable, and its newness caused astonishment, and all the other stars, with the sun and moon, gathered in chorus round the star, and it far exceeded them all in its light." The perplexity arising vanished, wondrous effects ensured "for God was manifest as man for the 'newness' of eternal life, and that which had been prepared by God received its beginning." Then comes the soteriological conclusion: "Hence all things were disturbed, because the abolition of death was being planned."[8]

Christ is one with the Father: "Jesus Christ, who was from eternity with the Father, and was made manifest at the end of time."[9] "Hasten all to come together as to one temple of God, as to one altar, to one Jesus Christ, who came forth from one Father and is with one and departed to one."[10] "As then the Lord was united to the Father and did nothing without him, neither by himself nor through the Apostles, so you do nothing without the bishop and the presbyters."[11]

I. knows of the Spirit and of his guidance,[12] but his emphasis in spirituality is on Christ the life of the Christian: "There is one Physician, who is both flesh and spirit, born and yet not born, who is God in man, true life in death, both of Mary and of God, first passible and then impassible, Jesus Christ our Lord."[13] "For Jesus Christ, our inseparable life, is by the will of the Father, even as the bishops, who have been appointed throughout the world are by the will of Jesus Christ."[14] "Nothing is hid from the Lord, but even our secret things are near him. Let us, therefore, do all things as though he were dwelling in us, that we may be his temples, and that he may be our God in us. This indeed is so, and will appear clearly before our face by the love which we justly have to him."[15] "You are then all fellow travelers, and carry with you God, and the Temple, and Christ, and holiness, and are in all ways adorned by commandments of Jesus Christ."[16]

Jesus Christ was with this singular witness, a divine obsession: "It is therefore seemly in every way to glorify Jesus Christ, who has glorified you." "Therefore by your concord and harmonious love Jesus Christ is being sung." "Remember me, as Jesus Christ also remembers you." ". . . believers bear the stamp of God the Father in love through Jesus Christ." ". . . in everything love one another in Jesus Christ." "Jesus Christ, our hope, from which God grant that none of you be turned aside." "I have faith in the grace of Jesus Christ, and he shall loose every bond from you." "May nothing of things seen or unseen envy me my attaining to Jesus Christ." Such words culled at random show the texture of the wholly doctrinal, wholly existential Christocentrism of I.

[1]Works, J. B. Lightfoot, *The Apostolic Fathers,* with English tr., London, 1883; P. T. Camelot, *SC* 10, second ed., 1951; K. Lake, *The Apostolic Fathers,* I, London, 1912, here used; cf. M. Rackl, *Die Christologie des Hl. Ignatius von Antiochien,* Freiburg i. B., 1914; J. Lebreton, S.J., "La théologie de la Trinité dans saint Ignace d'Antioche," *RSR* 15 (1925) 97–126, 393–419; *id., Histoire du dogme de la Trinité,* II, Paris, 1928, 326–31; L. Cristiani, "Saint Ignace d'Antioche. Sa vie d'intimité avec Jésus-Christ," *RAM* 25 (1949) 109–16; Th. Rusch, *Die Entstehung der Lehre vom Hl. Geist bei Ignatius,* Zurich, 1952; K. Hormann, *Leben in Christus. Zusammenhänge zwischen Dogma und Sitte bei den Apostolischen Vätern,* Vienna, 1952, Ignatius, 21–82; C. Tomic, "L'intima natura della vita cristiana secondo S. Ignazio martire," *Miscellanea francescana,* 54 (1954) 49–89; G. F. Snyder, "The Historical Jesus in the Letters of Ignatius of Antioch," *Biblical Researches* 8 (1963)

3–12; G. Bareille, *DTC* VII, 1, 1922, 685–713; P. T. Camelot, *DSp* VII, 2, 1972, 1250–66; ²Rom VI, 2, p. 233; ³Eph XVIII, 2, p. 191f; ⁴Eph XX, 1, p. 195; ⁵Mag VIII, 2, p. 205; ⁶Poly III, 2, p. 271; ⁷Eph XVII, 2, p. 191; ⁸Eph XIX, p. 193; ⁹Mag VI, 2, p. 203; ¹⁰Mag VII, 2, p. 203; ¹¹Mag VII, 1, p. 203; ¹²Eph IX, 1, p. 183; XVIII, 2, p. 193; Mag XIII, 1, p. 209; Philad VII, 2, p. 247; ¹³Eph VII, 2, p. 181; ¹⁴Eph III,, 2, p. 177; ¹⁵Eph XV, 2, p. 189; ¹⁶Eph IX, 2, p. 183.

IMAGE OF THE INVISIBLE GOD, CHRIST

"So God created man in his image; in the image of God he created him; male and female he created them" (Gen 1:27).[1] When St. Paul speaks of Christ as the "image of the invisible God, the first-born of all creation" (Col 1:15), his words evoke the first divine project. By those redeemed by Christ it will be restored despite the initial catastrophe, which erased it. Christ realized the divine plan for a human being perfectly. An immeasurably new dimension is added to his redemptive work, since he stands as the splendid Icon of the deity, with power to share this treasured intrinsic characteristic with his fellow-men. Image has especially a spiritual connotation, not superficially reflecting the deity, but inviting attention to the interior constituents of Christ's humano-divine being, to the entire array of natural gifts and supernatural endowment which are guaranteed by his essence as God and his integral human nature.

Christ is the image of the invisible God not merely statically but dynamically, for, as Vatican II teaches, he is the "Mediator (qv) and fullness of all revelation."[2] Thus the Council abandoned the propositional theory of revelation, prevalent in the schools, in favor of a personalist view centered on Christ. "Jesus Christ, therefore, the Word made flesh, sent as a man to men, speaks 'the words of God' (Jn 3:34) and completes the work of salvation which his Father gave him to do (cf. Jn 5:36; 17:4). To see Jesus is to see his Father (Jn 14:9). For this reason Jesus perfected revelation by fulfilling it through his whole work of making himself present and manifesting himself through his words and deeds, his signs and wonders, but especially through his death and glorious resurrection from the dead, and final sending of the Spirit of truth."[3]

Christ is the revealer of God, the "writing of God" to use von Balthasar's happy metaphor. He is not the image of humankind collectively and then, at a second stage, to each individual. He is the image to each one first and then, as a consequence, to all. Hence the personal character of faith which is the response, the recognition of the invisible God in his most perfect image, Jesus Christ.

¹S. V. McClasland, "The 'Image of God' according to Paul," *JBL* 69 (1950) 85–100; J. Alfaro, *Cristo Glorioso, Revelador del Padre,*

Christus Victor Mortis (-Gregorianum, vol. 39), Rome, 1958, 222–70; R. Latourette, "L'idée de révélation chez les Pères de l'Eglise," *Sciences Ecclésiastiques* 11 (1959) 297–344; E. Larsson, *Christus als Vorbild: Eine Untersuchung zu den paulinischen Tauf und Eikontexten,* Uppsala, 1962; J. J. Latour, *Imago Dei invisibilis.* "Esquisses sur les relations de l'anthropologie chrétienne et de la psychologie du Christ," in *Problèmes actuels de Christologie,* Brussels-Paris, 1965, 227–64; Y. M.-J. Congar, *Jésus Christ,* Paris, 1965, "Le Christ, image du Dieu invisible," 9–50; L. Cerfaux, *Christ in the Theology of St. Paul,* London, 1966, 432–38; U. Mauser, "Image of God and Incarnation," *Interpretation* 24 (1970) 336–56; *id., Gottesbild und Menschwerdung: eine Untersuchung zur Einheit des Alten und Neuen Testaments,* Tübingen, 1971; F. Refoulé, *Le Christ, visage de dieu,* Paris, 1975; A. Heron, "Logos, Image, Son; Some Models and Paradigms in Early Christology," in *Creation, Christ and Culture: Studies in Honor of T. F. Torrance,* ed. R. W. A. McKinney, Edinburgh, 1976, 43–62; A. T. Hanson, *The Image of the Invisible God,* London, 1982; P. Lamarche, *Dictionary of Biblical Theology,* ed. X. Léon-Dufour, London, 1967, 224f.; ²Constitution on Divine Revelation; ³*Ibid.*

INSTRUCTION ON THE HISTORICAL TRUTH OF THE GOSPELS, April 21, 1964

This official document emanating from the Biblical Commission (qv) appeared in the *Osservatore Romano* on May 14, 1964, the Latin text accompanied by an Italian translation. The Biblical Commission sent out soon after, its own English translation, which is here reproduced.[1] J. A. Fitzmyer's pithy judgment is apposite: "The document will go down in history as the first official statement which openly countenances the method (Form Criticism) itself and frankly admits the distinction of the three stages of tradition in the Gospel material which has emerged from a Form-Critical study of the Gospels."[2]

"Our Holy Mother the Church, which is 'the pillar and ground of the truth' (1 Tim 3:35) has invariably made use of Sacred Scripture in her work of ministering eternal salvation to souls, safeguarding it always from every sort of false interpretation. Problems there will always be, and the Catholic exegete, engaged in expounding the word of God and answering the difficulties brought forward against it, should not lose heart. He must keep on vigorously at his work of bringing out ever more clearly the genuine sense of the Scriptures, not relying merely on his own capabilities, but putting his trust chiefly and unshakably in the help of God and the light shed by the Church.

"It is highly gratifying that the Church today can number so many faithful sons possessed of the proficiency in matters biblical which is required at the present time, who have responded to the call of the Supreme Pontiffs and are devoting themselves wholeheartedly and with unflagging energy to their weighty and exacting task. 'And all other children of the Church should bear in mind that the efforts of these valiant laborers in the vineyard of the Lord are to be judged not only with fairness and justice, but also with the greatest charity' (*Divino afflante Spiritu,* EB 564), for even interpreters of the highest reputation such as Jerome himself, in their endeavors to clear up certain more difficult points, have on occasion arrived at results which were far from happy (cf. *Spiritus Paraclitus,* EB 451). All should be on their guard 'lest in the heat of debate the limits laid down by mutual charity be transgressed; and lest, in debate, the impression be given that it is the revealed truths and the divine traditions themselves that are being controverted. For unless the various studies of many different scholars are pursued by them together in a spirit of harmony and with the principles themselves placed beyond dispute, we cannot well expect them to accomplish any great progress in this branch of learning' (Litt. Apost. *Vigilantiae,* EB 143).

"Today the labors of exegetes are all the more called for by reason of the fact that in many publications, circulated far and wide, the truth of the events and sayings recorded in the Gospels is being challenged. In view of this the Pontifical Biblical Commission, in the discharge of the duty entrusted to it by the Supreme Pontiffs, has thought it opportune to set forth and to insist on the following points:

"1. The Catholic exegete, under the guidance of the Church, must turn to account all the resources for the understanding of the sacred text which have been put at his disposal by previous interpreters, especially the holy Fathers and Doctors of the Church, whose labors it is for him to take up and to carry. In order to bring out with fullest clarity the enduring truth and authority of the Gospels, he must, while carefully observing the rules of rational and Catholic hermeneutics, make skillful use of the new aids to exegesis, especially those which the historical method, taken in its widest sense, has provided; that method, namely, which minutely investigates sources, determining their nature and bearing, and availing itself of the findings of textual criticism, literary criticism, and linguistic studies. The interpreter must be alert to the reminder given him by Pope Pius XII of happy memory when he charged him 'to make judicious inquiry as to how far the form of expression or the type of literature adopted by the sacred writer may help towards the true and genuine interpretation, and to remain convinced that this part of his task cannot be neglected without great detriment to Catholic exegesis' (*Divino afflante Spiritu,* EB 560). In this reminder Pius XII of happy memory is laying down a general rule of hermeneutics, one by whose help the books of the Old Testament and of the New are to be explained, since the sacred writers when composing them followed the way of writing and of thinking current among their contemporaries.

In a word, the exegete must make use of every means which will help him to reach a deeper understanding of the character of the gospel testimony, of the religious life of the first churches, and of the significance and force of the apostolic tradition.

"In appropriate cases the interpreter is free to seek out what sound elements there are in 'the Method of Form-History,' and these he can duly make use of to gain a fuller understanding of the Gospels. He must be circumspect in doing so, however, because the method in question is often found allied with principles of a philosophical or theological nature which are quite inadmissible, and which not infrequently vitiate both the method itself and the conclusions arrived at regarding literary questions. For certain exponents of this method, led astray by rationalistic prejudices, refuse to admit that there exists a supernatural order, or that a personal God intervenes in the world by revelation properly so called, or that miracles and prophecies are possible and have actually occurred. There are others who have as their starting-point a wrong notion of faith, taking it that faith is indifferent to historical truth, and is indeed incompatible with it. Others practically deny a priori the historical value and character of the documents of revelation. Others finally there are who on the one hand underestimate the authority which the Apostles had as witnesses of Christ, and the office and influence which they wielded in the primitive community, whilst on the other hand they overestimate the creative capacity of the community itself. All these aberrations are not only opposed to Catholic doctrine, but are also devoid of any scientific foundation, and are foreign to the genuine principles of the historical method.

"2. In order to determine correctly the trustworthiness of what is transmitted in the Gospels, the interpreter must take careful note of the three stages of tradition by which the teaching and life of Jesus have come down to us.

"*Christ our Lord* attached to himself certain chosen disciples (cf. Mk 3:14; Lk 6:13) who had followed him from the beginning (cf. Lk 1:2; Acts 1:21-22), who had seen his works and had heard his words (cf. Lk 24:48; Jn 15:27; Acts 1:8; 10:39; 13:31) and were thus qualified to become witnesses of his life and teaching. Our Lord, when expounding his teaching by word of mouth, observed the methods of reasoning and of exposition which were in common use at the time; in this way he accommodated himself to the mentality of his hearers, and ensured that his teachings would be deeply impressed on their minds and would be easily retained in memory by his disciples. These latter grasped correctly the idea that the miracles and other events of the life of Jesus were things purposely performed or arranged by him in such a way that men would thereby be led to believe in Christ and to accept by faith the doctrine of salvation.

"The *Apostles,* bearing testimony to Jesus (cf. Lk 24:44-48; Acts 2:32; 3:15; 5:30-32), proclaimed first and foremost the death and resurrection of the Lord, faithfully recounting his life and words (cf. Acts 10:36-41), and, as regards the manner of their preaching, taking into account the circumstances of their hearers (Cf. Acts 13:16-41, with Acts 17:22-31). After Jesus had risen from the dead and when his divinity was clearly perceived (Acts 2:36; Jn 20-28), the faith of the disciples, far from blotting out the remembrance of the events that had happened, rather consolidated it, since their faith was based on what Jesus had done and taught (Acts 2:22; 10:37-39). Nor was Jesus transformed into a 'mythical' personage, and his teaching distorted, by reason of the worship which the disciples now paid him, revering him as Lord and Son of God. Yet it need not be denied that the Apostles, when handing on to their hearers the things which in actual fact the Lord had said and done, did so in the light of that fuller understanding which they enjoyed as a result of being schooled by the glorious things accomplished in Christ (Jn 2:22; 11:51-52; 12:16; cf. 14:26; 16:12-13; 7:39), and of being illumined by the Spirit of truth (cf. Jn 14:26; 16:13). Thus it came about that, just as Jesus himself after his resurrection had 'interpreted to them' (Lk 24:27) both the words of the Old Testament and the words which he himself had spoken (cf. Lk 24:44-45; Acts 1:3), so now they in their turn interpreted his words and deeds according to the needs of their hearers. 'Devoting themselves to the ministry of the word' (Acts 6:4), they made use, as they preached, of such various forms of speech as were adapted to their own purposes, and to the mentality of their hearers; for it was to 'Greek and barbarian, to learned and simple' (Rom 1:14) that they had a duty to discharge (1 Cor 9:19-23). These varied ways of speaking which the heralds of Christ made use of in proclaiming him must be distinguished one from the other and carefully appraised: catecheses, narratives, testimonies, hymns, doxologies, prayers and any other such literary forms as were customarily employed in Sacred Scripture and by people of that time.

"*The sacred authors,* for the benefit of the churches, took this earliest body of instruction, which had been handed on orally at first and then in writing—for many soon set their hands to 'drawing up a narrative' (cf. Lk 1:1) of matters concerning the Lord Jesus—and set it down in the four Gospels. In doing this each of them followed a method suitable to the special purpose which he had in view. They selected certain things out of the many which had been handed on; some they synthesized, some they explained with an eye to the situation of the churches, painstakingly using every means of bringing home to their readers the solid truth of the things in which they had been instructed (cf. Lk 1:4). For, out of the material which they had received, the sacred authors selected especially those items which were adapted to the varied circumstances of the faithful as well as to the end which they themselves wished to attain; these they recounted in a manner consonant with those circumstances and with that end. And since the meaning of a statement depends, amongst other things, on the place which it has in a given sequence, the Evangelists, in handing on the words or the deeds of our Savior, explained them for the advantage of their readers by respectively setting them, one Evangelist in one context, another in another. For this reason the exegete must ask himself what the Evangelist intended by recounting a saying or a fact in a certain way, or by placing it in a certain context. For the truth of the narrative is not affected in the slightest by the fact that the Evangelists report the sayings or the doings of our Lord in a different order (cf. St. John Chrys., *In Mat. Hom* I, 3; PG 57, 16-17) and that they use different words to express what he said, not keeping to the very letter, but nevertheless preserving the sense. (cf. St. Augustine, *De consunsu Evang* 2, 12, 28, PL 34, 1090f). For as St. Augustine says: 'Where there is question only of those matters whose order in the narrative may be indifferently this or that without in any way taking from the truth and authority of the Gospel, it is probably enough that each Evangelist believed that he should narrate them in that same order in which God was pleased to suggest them to his recollection. The Holy Spirit distributes his Gifts to each one according as he wills (1 Cor 12:11); therefore, too, for the sake of those Books which were to be set so high at the very summit of authority, he undoubtedly guided and controlled the minds of the holy writers in their recollection of what they were to write; but as to why, in doing so, he should have permitted them, one to follow this order in his narrative, another to follow that—that is a question whose answer may be found with God's help, if one seeks it out with reverent care' (*De consensu Evang.* 2, 12, 28, PL 34, 1090–1091).

"Unless the exegete, then, pays attention to all those factors which have a bearing on the origin and the composition of the Gospels, and makes due use of the acceptable findings of modern research, he will fail in his duty of ascertaining what the intentions of the sacred writers were, and what it is that they actually said. The results of recent study have made it clear that the teachings and the life of Jesus were not simply recounted for the mere purpose of being kept in remembrance, but were 'preached' in such a way as to furnish the Church with the foundation on which to build up faith and morals. It follows that the interpreter who subjects the testimony of the Evangelists to persevering scrutiny will be in a position to shed further light on the enduring theological value of the Gospels, and to throw into clearer relief the vital importance of the Church's interpretation.

"There remain many questions, and these of the gravest moment, in the discussion and elucidation of which the Catholic exegete can and should freely exercise his intelligence and skill. In this way each can contribute individually to the advantage of all, to the constant advancement of sacred learning, to preparing the ground and providing further support for the decisions of the Church's teaching authority, and to the defense and honor of the Church herself. But at all times the interpreter must cherish a spirit of ready obedience to the Church's teaching authority, and must also bear in mind that when the Apostles proclaimed the Good Tidings they were filled with the Holy Spirit, that the Gospels were written under the inspiration of the Holy Spirit, and that it was he who preserved the authors immune from all error. 'For we received our knowledge of the economy of our salvation by means of no others than those same by whose means the Gospel came to us: that the Gospel which they first proclaimed as heralds and afterwards, by the will of God, passed on to us in the Scriptures to be the ground and pillar of our faith. Thus no one has any right to say that they preached before they had the perfect knowledge, as some venture to assert, boasting that they are correctors of the Apostles. For after our Lord had risen from the dead and they were invested with power from on high by the descent of the Holy Spirit upon them, they were filled with all the gifts and had the perfect knowledge; they went forth to the ends of the earth spreading the good tidings of the blessings we have from God and announcing heavenly peace to man, all of them and each of them equally possessing the Gospel of God' (St. Iren., *Adv. Haer.*, III, 1, 1, Harvey II, 2: PG 7, 844).

"3. *Those charged with the duty of teaching in Seminaries and similar establishments* 'must make it their first care to see . . . that the teaching of Holy Writ is carried out in a manner thoroughly in keeping with the importance of the subject itself, and with the requirements of the present day' (Litt. Apost. *Quoniam in re biblica*, EB 162). Professors should make theological doctrine the main subject-matter of their exposition, so that the Sacred Scriptures 'may become for the future priests of the Church a pure and never-failing source of spiritual life for themselves, and of nourishment and vigor for the office of sacred preaching which they are to undertake' (*Divino afflante Spiritu*, EB 567). Professors, when they make use of critical methods, especially of what is called literary criticism, should not do so for the mere sake of criticism, but with a view to gaining by means of it a deeper insight into the sense intended by God speaking through the sacred writer. They should not stop halfway, therefore, resting on the discoveries they have made from the literary point of view, but should go on to show how such findings make a real contribution towards the better understanding of revealed doctrine, or, if occasion arises, towards the refutation of misleading views. By following these guiding principles, teachers will ensure that their pupils find in Sacred Scripture themes of a nature 'to raise their minds to God, nourish their souls, and foster their interior life' (*Divino afflante Spiritu*, EB 552).

"4. But it is *those who instruct the Christian people by sacred preaching* who need the greatest prudence. It is doctrine above all that they must impart, mindful of the admonition of St. Paul: 'Pay attention to yourself and to the doctrine which you teach; be persistent in these things. For by doing so, you will bring salvation to yourself and to your hearers' (1 Tim 4:16). They must altogether shun what is merely newfangled or what is insufficiently proved. New views for which there is solid support they may when necessary put forward, using discretion and taking into account the qualifications of their audience. When they narrate biblical events they are not to introduce imaginary additions at variance with the truth.

"This same virtue of prudence should be especially practiced by *those who write for the Christian public at popular level.* They should make it their study to bring out the treasures of the word of God 'in order that the faithful may be moved and spurred on to shape their lives in conformity with it' (*Divino afflante Spiritu*, EB 566). Let them regard themselves as in duty bound never to depart in the slightest from the common doctrine and tradition of the Church. And whilst undoubtedly they should lay under contribution whatever real advances in biblical knowledge the labors of modern scholars have brought about, they should keep altogether clear of the precarious fancies of innovators' (Cf. Litt. Apost. *Quoniam in re biblica*, EB 175). They are strictly charged not to yield to a mischievous itch for novelty by recklessly giving wide publicity, indiscriminately and without any previous sifting, to each and every tentative solution of difficulties that happens to be proposed; this way of acting disquiets the faith of many people.

"Already on a previous occasion this Pontifical Biblical Commission thought it opportune to recall to mind that books, and also magazine and newspaper articles, dealing with biblical matters, are subject to the authority and jurisdiction of Ordinaries, since they are concerned with religious topics and with the religious instruction of the faithful (Instruction to Ordinaries, EB 626). Ordinaries are requested, therefore, to be particularly vigilant where such popular publications are concerned.

"5. *Those in charge of biblical associations* must observe inviolably the laws already laid down by the Pontifical Biblical Commission (EB 622–633).

"If all these instructions are kept, the study of the Sacred Scriptures will redound to the advantage of the faithful. All without exception will experience even today the truth of what St. Paul wrote: that the Sacred Scriptures 'can make wise unto salvation, which is had by faith in Christ Jesus. All scripture inspired by God is profitable for teaching, for reproving, for correcting, for training in right conduct: so that the man of God may be complete, equipped for every good' (2 Tim 3:15-17).

"Our Most Holy Lord, Pope, Paul VI, in an audience graciously granted to the undersigned Right Reverend Consultor-Secretary on April 21, 1964, approved this Instruction and ordered its publication.

Benjamin N. Wambacq., O.Praem., Consultor-Secretary Rome, April 21, 1964.

---

[1]Cf. J. Fitzmyer, S.J., "The Biblical Commission's (qv) Instruction on the Historical Truth of the Gospels," *ThS* 25 (1964) 386–408; *id., A Christological Catechism: New Testament Answers,* New York, 1982, 97–130; extensive list of the commentaries on the Instruction, p. 129f, n. 49; text of the Instruction, 131–140; [2]*Ibid.,* 287.

INTERNATIONAL THEOLOGICAL COMMISSION, THE

This body is remarkable from several points of view.[1] Founded by Pope Paul VI in 1969, it assembled a number of highly qualified theologians. It has issued a series of important papers on subjects at the heart of theological interest at the present time. The historian of theology will probably agree that seventy or a hundred, or a hundred and fifty years ago any such body named even on an international level within the Catholic Church would not have equalled the Commission in the quality and achievement of its members or the value of its published work. Still more in contrast with such times is the singular attention given to Christology. Fr. Y. M. J. Congar, O.P., in his very important article in *DTC* on theology, history, nature, divisions, problems, rightly

gives attention to the renewal in the nineteenth century.[2] It was set in the pattern required by the errors of the day, by the requirements of the papacy and the dominant personalities of the time, the popes and the great academics like Franzelin, Scheeben, and Kleutgen, especially the great pathfinder, Möhler. None of these had to cope with any meaningful renewal, which so often carries the risk of deviation, in the theology of the Incarnate Word. Yet in the twenty-one years since Paul VI launched the International Theological Commission the members have felt called on to issue statements on Christology three times—with a promise to continue still further reflection on one particular subject, the consciousness of Christ (qv). This paper is so important that it is reproduced in full in the present work. Appearing in 1986, it had been preceded by two valuable commentaries, correctives, on the vast debates of our time.

The first paper had reached its final stage in 1979, was issued in 1981. It was the work of some of the greatest theologians of the age. The responsible subcommission, under the presidency of Msgr. K. Lehmann, was composed of these members: Hans Urs von Balthasar, Y. M. J. Congar, O.P., R. Cantalamessa, O. Gonzalez de Cardenal, J. H. Walgrave. The aspects of Christology dealt with were: I. How to attain to knowledge of the Person and the work of Jesus Christ; II. The Christological faith of the first Councils; III. The actual meaning of the Christological dogma; IV. Christology and Soteriology; V. Christological dimensions which should be restored— these are: The Anointing of Christ by the Holy Spirit (qv), and The Primacy of Christ over the Cosmos (qv). What is said on these live questions is enlightened, balanced, succinct.

In 1983 the Commission issued a paper on *Theology, Christology, Anthropology.* It had been voted affirmatively with one dissenting voice in October, 1982. The whole text falls into two parts: I. The foundation and context of Christology; II. Some more important points of present day Christology. Part I is thus subdivided: A. The economy of Jesus Christ and the revelation of God; B. The relation between Theocentrism and Christocentrism; C. Christology and the revelation of the Trinity; D. The relation between Christology and anthropology; E. The image of God in man or the Christian meaning of the divinization of man. Part II is thus subdivided: A. The problem of the pre-existence of Jesus Christ; B. The Trinitarian aspect of the Cross of Jesus or the problem of the suffering of God.

The Commission, in its report on the consciousness of Christ, dealt with the *quid,* the content, not the *quo modo,* the manner, which will presumably be the subject of its next report. It is fulfilling a unique role in such work, providing authoritative surveys and answers to problems, with the authoritative note inherent in the contents, not in any official status.

---

[1]1981 report, *DCath,* 1981, 222–31; 1983 report, *DCath,* (1983) 119–26; for the section dealing with the 'Pre-existence of Christ,' cf. *Trinitas,* s.v., 183f. where it is fully reproduced; [2]*DTC* XIII, full article, 341–502, on the nineteenth century, 435–43.

IRENAEUS, ST., (c. 130–c. 200)

Like all those of the first centuries who sought to reflect on the essentials of the faith, guided by the *regula fidei* and searching the Scriptures, I., the father of Christian theology, the first intentionally biblical theologian, was seized by the *Logos* (qv).[1] In his admirable summary of the faith in the *Proof of the Apostolic Preaching,* he writes: "But the second article is the Word of God, the Son of God, Christ Jesus our Lord, who was shown forth by the prophets according to the design of their prophecy and according to the manner in which the Father disposed; and through him were made all things whatsoever. He also, in the end of time, for the recapitulation of all things, is become a man among men, visible and tangible, in order to abolish death and bring to light life, and bring about the communion of God and man."[2]

I. was very conscious of the profound meaning of Baptism, the rebirth "unto God the Father, through his Son, by the Holy Spirit," and he saw the interrelation of the Persons in the life of the baptized: "For those who are bearers of the Spirit of God are led to the Word, that is to the Son, but the Son takes them and presents them to the Father; and the Father confers incorruptibility. So without the Spirit there is no seeing the Word of God, and without the Son there is no approaching the Father; for the Son is knowledge of the Father, and knowledge of the Son is through the Holy Spirit. But the Son, according to the Father's good-pleasure, administers the Spirit charismatically as the Father will, to those to whom he will."[3]

I. goes deep into the question of the Son's eternal origin: "If someone asks us: 'How then has the Son been uttered by the Father?' we shall answer him that this utterance, or generation or speaking, or revelation, or finally this ineffable generation, by whatever name one wishes to call it, no one knows it, neither Valentinus, nor Marcion nor Saturninus nor Basilides, neither angels nor archangels, neither principalities nor powers, no one but the Father who has begotten and the Son who has been born. Since then his generation is ineffable, all those who claim to explain generations and utterances do not know that they are saying, when they promise or explain what is ineffable."[4]

The Son is eternal, like the Father: "The Son, who always coexists with the Father from the beginning, reveals the Father to angels, archangels, powers, virtues, to all those to whom God wishes to reveal himself."[5] "The Word of God did not seek the friendship of Abraham through want, he who was perfect from the beginning: 'before Abraham was, I am,' he says; but it was to give Abraham eternal life."[6]

I. worked on the strong belief in the unity of the OT and the NT, in the prefiguration of Christ in the OT. But the NT brings the new reality, his coming. All this is thought out by I. in the context of his refutation of the Gnostics. His central idea is the 'recapitulation' of all things in Christ. "For there is but one God the Father, as we have shown, and one Christ Jesus our Lord, coming throughout the whole of the universal plan of salvation and recapitulating all in himself. In this 'all,' man also is included, fashioned by God. Therefore he recapitulates man in himself, he who is invisible becoming visible, he who is incomprehensible becoming comprehensible, he who is impassible becoming passible, he who is the Word now man, recapitulating all in himself, so that as the Word of God is at the head of the supracelestial, spiritual, invisible world, so he also has sovereignty over things visible and corporeal, assuming to himself the primacy; and while he takes his place as 'Head of the Church,' he draws all to himself at the right time."[7]

I. was wholly convinced of the unity of the *Logos* and the flesh in Christ. With his doctrine on the recapitulation of Mary as the new Eve, he fashioned a synthesis at the core of salvation history which has held out promise of development and potential of biblical theology to all the ages down to the promulgated text of Vatican II (qv).

---

[1]Works, *Adversus Haereses, SC* 100, 151,153, 213, 214, 210, 211; *The Proof of the Apostolic Preaching,* tr., J. P. Smith, *ACW*; French tr., L. M. Froidevaux, *SC* 62; cf. A. Benoit, *Sainte Irénée. Introduction à l'étude de sa théologie,* Paris, 1961; G. Jouassard, "Le 'premier-né' de la Vierge chez St. Irénée," *RevSR* 12 (1932) 509–32; G. N. Bonwetsch, *Die Theologie des Irenaeus,* Gütersloh, 1925; A. Houssiau, *La christologie de St. Irénée,* Louvain, 1955; M. Widmann, "Irenäus und sein theologischen Vater," *ZTK* 54 (1957) 156–73; A. Bengsch, *Heilsgeschichte und Heilswissen. Eine Untersuchung zur Struktur und Entfaltung des theologischen Denkens im Werk 'Adversus Haereses' des hl. Irenäus von Lyon,* Leipzig, 1957; A. Orbe, *Hacia la primera teologia de la procesión del Verbo,* Rome, 1958; G. Wingren, *Man and the Incarnation,* London, 1959; Quasten, I, 287–313; F. Vernet, *DTC,* VII, 1923, 2194–2533; L. Doutreleau, S.J., - L. Regnault, O.S.B., *DSp* VII, 1971, 1923–69; *Theotokos,* 189f; *Trinitas,* 136f; Grillmeier, 114–22; [2]*ACW* 6, p. 51; [3]*Ibid.,* 52; [4]*Adv. Haer.,* II, *SC* 294, 282; [5]*Ibid.,* 322; [6]*Ibid.;* [7]*Adv. Haer.,* III, 16, 6, *SC* 34, F. Sagnard, O.P., 202.

J

JESUS PRAYER, THE

The blind beggar, Bartimaeus, outside Jericho, addressed Jesus thus: "Jesus, Son of David, have mercy on me!" (Mk 10:47; cf. Lk 18:38). This is probably the origin of a very important prayer formula used in the Orthodox Church.[1] It is phrased thus: "Lord Jesus Christ, Son of God, have mercy on me." Sometimes the word "sinner" is added at the end, which recalls the prayer of the publican (Lk 18:13). Minor variations are found and the plural "us" may replace "me." A bodily technique has at times—from the time of St. Nicephorus the Hesychast, thirteenth century—accompanied the use of the words: the head is bowed, the eyes (if open) are fixed on the place of the heart, the rhythm of the breathing is carefully controlled and correlated with the prayer. This bodily accompaniment was justified on the grounds that human beings are psychosomatic and prayer should be of the whole being. It is, however, not now encouraged.

The prayer is in widespread use in the Orthodox communities and in the diaspora. It is also adopted by an increasing number in the West. The formula is first found in its full wording in the *Life of Abba Philemon* (sixth and seventh centuries). Without the words, "Son of God," it is found in St. Barsanuphius and St. John of Gaza (early sixth century), and a little later in St. Dorotheus of Gaza, *The Life of Dositheus.* St. John Climacus (d. 649) and his followers, St. Hesychius and St. Philotheus of Sinai (eighth to tenth centuries). Coptic sources testify to the use of the prayer. It was known to Evagrius Ponticus, Macarius the Egyptian, surnamed "The Great" and Theodoret of Cyrrhus. But powerful figures in eastern theology and spirituality like Maximus the Confessor (qv) and Symeon the New Theologian seem to know nothing of it.

The influence of the Indian Chakras technique in the origins and the similarity with Yoga have been discussed. Association with Hesychasm is a matter for historical evaluation. This has been in its simple form a mode of prayer which stresses interiority, in its sophisticated development a whole theology of the spiritual life, principally due to St. Gregory Palamas, emphasizing the gift of divine light. Only in recent times, thanks to Valdimir Lossky, has the importance of St. Gregory been fully seen.

---

[1]J. Hausherr, S.J., "La Méthode d'oraison hesychaste," *Orientalia Christiana Analecta* 9 (1927) 101–209; *Id.,* "Noms du Christ et voies d'oraison," *Orientalia Christiana Analecta* 157, Rome, 1960; H. Bacht, "Das 'Jesus-Gebet,' seine Geschichte und seine Problematik," *Geist und Leben* 24 (1951) 326–38; A. Recheis, "Das Jesus-Gebet," *Una Sancta* 9 (1954) 1–25; E. J. Ryan, "The Invocation of the Divine Name in Sinaite Spirituality," *Eastern Christian Quarterly* 14 (1962) 291–99; L. Bouyer, *The Origins of Hesychasm and the Jesus Prayer, A History of Christian Spirituality,* II, London, 1968, 576–79; P Adnès, *DSp,* VIII, 1126–50; K. Ware. *A Dictionary of Christian Spirituality,* London, 1983, 223f.

JEWISHNESS OF JESUS, THE

Forty-five years ago the Anglican Benedictine monk, Gregory Dix, in his work on *The Shape of the Liturgy,* gave some attention to the fact that Jesus, in the celebration of the Last Supper, was a Jew. The fact and what it implied did not affect two valuable collections of Eucharistic texts of early and patristic times, by Johannes Quasten and Fr. Jesus Solano, S.J.[1] Some time previously the Louvain biblical scholar, Fr. J. Coppens, was off-hand in his dismissal of "the so-called Jewish analogies with the Eucharist," and the great Père Lagrange, some time later, though sensitive in his approach, rejected a similar thesis.[2]

Things have changed, dramatically almost. Two collections of early Eucharistic texts, one by the French liturgist and hymnographer, Fr. Lucien Deiss, C.S.Sp., the other exhaustively edited by two Fribourg professors, Fr. Anton Hanggi and Fr. Irmgard Pahl, with notable collaborators, reflect the change. In the latter collection Jewish liturgical texts occupy one tenth of the whole volume; the first chapter of Fr. Deiss' book is given to Jewish sources of prayer. Fr. Louis Bouyer of the French Oratory was the first, in his doctrinal work on the Eucharist, to make a profound theological analysis of the Jewish liturgical prayers as a helpful, constructive insight.

Vatican II (qv), while drawing attention to the "common spiritual heritage" of Christians and Jews, encouraged further mutual understanding and appreciation. This can be obtained "especially by way of biblical and theological enquiry and through friendly discussion." Guidelines issued on December 1, 1974, on "Religious Relations with the Jews" by the committee charged with this subject emphasized the Jewish aspects of Jesus' life and lifework—"although his teaching had a profoundly new character, Christ nevertheless, in many instances, took his stand on the teaching of the Old Testament . . . Jesus also used teaching methods similar to those employed by the Rabbis of his time."[3]

In 1984 the Biblical Commission (qv), revamped under Paul VI, and composed of some of the outstanding biblical scholars in the Catholic Church, issued a statement on Biblical Christology very different in approach and content from the kind of document that emanated from the body in the early days of the century. It was an attempt to classify and assess the multiplicity of writings on its theme. One section of the document dealt with the approach to Jesus from Judaism. It opened with these words: "The *Jewish religion* (original italics) is obviously the first to be studied so that the personality of Jesus may be understood. The Gospels depict him as one deeply rooted in his own land and in the tradition of his people."

As the Biblical Commission reminds us, recovery of ancient targums and the literature of Qumran have spurred research into these areas. The literature grows all the time. One has the feeling of release from previous constraints, themselves the result of a whole complex of ideas not favorable to the Jewishness of anyone, not even of the greatest Jew of all time. The Jews themselves took the initiative. "After the First World War," says the Biblical Commission, "some

Jewish historians, abandoning a centuries-old animosity—of which Christian preachers were themselves not innocent—devoted studies directly to the person of Jesus and to Christian origins." Then follow the names of Jewish scholars, like Joseph Klausner, who published works on Jesus Christ, and they are characterized thus: "They sought to bring out the Jewishness of Jesus (e.g., P. Lapide), the relation between his teaching and rabbinical traditions, and the unusual character, prophetic or sapiential, of his message that was so closely tied up with the religious life of the synagogue and the temple. Certain borrowings were investigated either in Qumran literature— by Jewish historians (Y. Yadin, etc.) or by persons quite alien to Christian faith (Allegro)—or in the liturgical paraphrases of Scripture (targums)—by Jewish authors (e.g., E. I. Kutscher, etc.) or Christians (R. Le Déaut, M. McNamara, etc.)."[4]

The Commission sketches the results of research and reflection by some Jewish historians interested in "brother Jesus" (a phrase used by S. ben Chorim): "They have found in him a teacher like the Pharisees of old (D. Flusser) or a wonder-worker similar to those whose memory Jewish tradition has preserved (G. Vermes).[5] Some have hesitated to compare the Passion of Jesus with the Suffering Servant mentioned in the book of Isaiah (M. Buber)." Then the Commission gives a directive: "All these attempts (at interpretation) are to be accorded serious attention by Christian theologians engaged in the study of Christology." Stronger language is used later when a final assessment is offered: "*The diligent study of Judaism* (italics in original) is of the utmost importance for the correct understanding of the person of Jesus, as well as of the early Church and its distinctive faith." With this endorsement there goes a caveat: Jesus is not to be reduced to one of the characteristic types, teachers, prophets, wonder-workers; least of all is he to be considered a political instigator. The overall guiding principle must be that Jesus brought a new way of understanding one's relation to God and 'the fulfillment of Scripture.' This uniqueness must not be lost sight of in a study of Jesus' Jewish character.

We are then fully encouraged to pursue studies of Jesus the Jew. Much work has already been done in the field; literature suited to every taste, popular, professional, academic, specialized will not be wanting. Some years ago Fr. D. J. Harrington, S.J., for his presidential address to the Catholic Biblical Association, took the theme *The Jewishness of Jesus. Facing Some Problems.*[6] The scholars will take care of the problems. Meanwhile we may ponder some aspects of the subject which are of universal moment, capable of appealing widely.

To focus attention on Jesus' ethnic origins and characteristics, background emphasizes his historical existence. This may appear a naive thing to say. To those acquainted with the long debate on the Jesus of history and the Christ of faith, it will not appear so. It began with Reimarus in the Age of the Enlightenment—J. Jeremias called it a "Child of the Enlightenment"—was stirred to life by Albert Schweitzer in the present century, was intensified by R. Bultmann and the Form-Critics, given a new, more optimistic lease of life by a disciple of Bultmann's, E. Käsemann, who parted company with him and publicized the fact in a famous lecture: this was the "new quest" for the Jesus of history.

One can scarcely say that this debate recedes into the purely academic with full awareness of Jesus' Jewish life and world; but it seems to lose much of its sharpness, if not relevance.

Such a reversal of an intellectual trend would be facilitated also by recent documentary and archaeological finds. We think especially of the Qumran documents. One New Testament figure near to Jesus, John the Baptist, accomplished his ministry at a spot from which, if the local tradition is correct, the site of the monastic settlement of Qumran is visible. It is scarcely possible that he was ignorant of the sectaries, the Essenes who composed the community. Had he been one of them? Scholars are divided, some thinking that he may have been so for a while. The historian Josephus states that the monks had the custom of adopting orphans; John born in his parents' old age may have been so adopted. But when John assumed his mission as the precursor of Christ, his message was singular, so different from their beliefs that it would imply a clean break.

John thus serves to show a living detailed background for Jesus at a turning-point in the Savior's career. But there is the large question which, until the present state of thinking, would not have been imagined: Was Jesus for some time in Qumran? Or did he have more than passing contact with the community? Scholars have argued for and against positive influence. James H. Charlesworth, in one of the most readable books on the general subject we are considering, *Jesus within Judaism*,[7] suggests a negative influence: Jesus may have been disturbed by an aspect of Essene life or thought and reacted against it, their rigid rules for the Sabbath, for example. The whole subject is opened up and there is much research yet to be done.

To help locate Jesus more clearly in Jewish history, Charlesworth would also invoke documents from another great find in recent times, the Coptic papyrus codices discovered near Nag Hammadi in Upper Egypt in 1945. It was a gnostic library, but hasty assessments of all the items as gnostic have had to be revised. One writing on which our present interest centers, the *Gospel of Thomas,* is not accepted as gnostic by all scholars. It has stirred phenomenal interest; Charlesworth has counted 397 publications on it alone. He deems it significant in the search for the historical Jesus for these reasons: it is a document of Jesus sayings reminiscent of the lost source (Q) apparently used independently by both Matthew and Luke; it contains sayings of Jesus, at least in some passages, that are independent of the so-called canonical gospels; it is now becoming well recognized that it is improper to discard the *Gospel of Thomas* as late, derivative, and gnostic.

To pursue all these topics would be beyond the scope of this article. Another important source of knowledge on the Jesus of history, that is on Jesus the Jew, rightly emphasized by Charlesworth, is archaeology. He contrasts the series of German scholars who have written on the problem of Jesus in history without any reference to archaeology with Americans, English, and French who have excelled in the use of this particular discipline. What the finds, the results of the scientific "digs" in different areas, notably Capernaum, the Judean desert, above all in Jerusalem, do achieve is a powerful sense of the concrete, of time and space in the story of the incarnate God; this is a spur to still more thorough investigation of the background, revealed or implied, in the gospel narratives.

What we have been considering is a new approach to Jesus Christ, the one that would have been deemed essential, a first choice, but for so many strange things that have happened in the history of Christian thought, Christian thought about Jesus and about his people. It is not an exclusive approach which will allow us to dispense with others. It should be retained, the reflection it prompts should be preserved to act as a corrective to excesses we might easily otherwise commit, a stimulus to seek new insights.

We should not expect too much in any such approach. Suppose we think for a moment of all that has been written in recent times by people like Karl Rahner on the consciousness (qv), the self-understanding, of Jesus. There is in that sacred area a depth of mystery, but theologians see it as their duty to come as near to the mystery as possible, to show the reality of the mystery by examining closely that which surrounds it. But in these essays, so often compelling and thought-provoking, one does not always see advertence to the distinctive quality of the Jewish mind.

Now there are manifest limits to the usefulness of such advertence. There were realities that entered the soul of Christ which would not be directly affected by his ethnic character. Whether it is a German or a Frenchman or a Nigerian or Indian who is at grips with the deep problems of the human spirit, these problems do not change with geography. But would the modality of judgment, the phrasing of thought, the global activity of the mind, the manner of expression, not vary from one race or nation to another? St. Thomas Aquinas and St. Theresa of Avila have spoken of the same divine reality. But one did it with the intellectual equipment of an Aristotelian philosopher, the other with a piercing mystical intuition unequalled by any woman in history outside the Bible.

How was a Jew motivated? How did a Jew respond to a unique tradition? What were the mental categories of a Jew through which he sifted the words and deeds that made up his experience? What was the Jewish cast of mind? What were the sacred verities woven into the very fabric of the Jewish mind, molding thought, dictating reactions and reflexes?

God became man; he became a Jew. The mere assertion of the fact must evoke Auschwitz for anyone who has seen the prison, even in its "museum" condition; or read the proceedings of the Nuremberg trial at the relevant section; or again, read the confessions of the camp commandant, Rudolf Hess. It may appear irreverent to ask the question: If God had not become a Jew, would so many innocent millions of this race have died so cruelly? For their racial characteristics and their racial identity are bound up with the unique destiny which decreed that one of their number would be God. One of the recurring enigmas of history is that they arouse, by these very characteristics, a hatred which seeks its outlet in a "final solution." The question is frightening in its implications.

So to proclaim the Jewishness of Jesus is no mere polite compliment. And perhaps it is understandable that full attention has not been given to the reality until now. It is so awesome a reality that the human spirit must be especially braced to cope with it. Theologians, biblical scholars, and the faithful have been latterly wrestling with all the intricate relationships between the Old and New Testaments: the New is latent in the Old and the Old is patent in the New.

A comforting formula. But applied to the life and lifework of Jesus himself, what vistas it opens. There is an immense field to explore in his use of Old Testament concepts and idioms in the proclamation of his totally new, distinctive message. The miracle of the Old and New Testament mutual enrichment is this, that the language used in the Old Testament conveyed a satisfying meaning to its audience, and yet could express new ideas which would both fulfill and transcend the earlier revelation: the same language would embrace the new divine communication without frag-menting or betraying its earlier function. One striking example is the word *Ruah,* Spirit.

In thinking or talking of the Jewishness of Jesus we are not engaged in dilettante dialogue. We are touching the theology of history at the very roots of all becoming, under divine power. The theme brings into sharp focus two ideas of cosmic dimension, the destiny of the Jews and the salvation of the human race.

The two ideas are brought together by an Apostle of the Master, a Jew like the other Apostles and so many of the early Christians. Introducing the theme of the final conversion of the Jewish people, St. Paul offers this hope: "Now if their trespass means riches for the world, and if their failure means riches for the Gentiles, how much more will their full inclusion mean!" (Rom 11:12). Then using the image of the olive tree, Paul later continues: "And even the others, if they do not persist in their unbelief, will be grafted in, for God has the power to graft them in again. For if you have been cut from what is by nature a wild olive tree, and grafted, contrary to nature, into a cultivated olive tree, how much more will these natural branches be grafted back into their own olive tree" (11:24). Paul announced that "all Israel will be saved," appealing to Old Testament promises. Then comes the basic tenet so often quoted: "As regards the gospel they are enemies of God for your sake; but as regards election they are beloved for the sake of their forefathers. For the gifts and the call of God are irrevocable" (Rom 11:28-29).

In this final consummation of salvation history the full meaning of the Jewishness of Jesus Christ will be made manifest. The divine choice of his race will achieve concrete glory in him, highest exemplar of the perfection to which all Jews are called, the bearer of divine gifts which fulfill all the ancient promises, at once the guarantor, the treasurer, and the artisan of the glory of Israel and of its saving mission to all mankind.

---

[1] J. Quasten, *Monumenta eucharistica et liturgica vetustissima,* Bonn, 1935–37; J. Solano, S.J., *Textos Eucaristicos Primitivos,* I, II, 2nd ed., Madrid, 1979; L. Deiss, C.S.Sp., ed., *Springtime of the Liturgy, Liturgical Texts of the First Four Centuries,* Collegeville, 1979; A. Hanggi-I. Pahl, *Prex Eucharistica,* Fribourg, 1968; cf. L. Bouyer, *Eucharist, Theology and Spirituality of the Eucharistic Prayer,* London, 1968, 70–115; [2] Cf. *Ephemerides Theologicae Lovanienses* 8 (1931) 238–48; id., *Dictionnaire de la Bible, Supplément,* II 1192–93; M. J. Lagrange, *Evangile selon St. Marc,* Paris, 1947, 357f.; [3] *Vatican II and Post-conciliar Documents,* ed. A. Flannery, O.P., I, 747; [4] This and subsequent quotations are taken from *Scripture and Christology,* English translation of the text with commentary by J. A. Fitzmyer, S.J., New York, London, 1986; [5] His book, *Jesus the Jew,* London, 1973, is one of the best known of the crop that has arisen; cf. also *The Gospel of Jesus the Jew,* Riddell Memorial Lectures, New-

castle on Tyne, 1981; [6]Repr. *Catholic Biblical Quarterly,* 49 (1987) 1-13; [7]London, SPCK, 1989. Bibliographies growing all the time are given in this book, 223-43, and E. P. Sanders, *Jesus and Judaism,* London, 1985, 341-54; J. Neusner, *Judaism in the Beginning of Christianity,* London, 1984; B. J. Lee, *The Galilean Jewishness of Jesus,* New York, 1988; B. H. Young, *Jesus and His Jewish Parables,* London, 1989; I. M. Zeitlin, *Jesus and the Judaism of His Time,* Oxford, 1988; D. A. Hagner, *The Jewish Reclamation of Jesus,* Grand Rapids, 1984.

JOHN OF DAMASCUS, ST., DOCTOR OF THE CHURCH (c. 675–c. 749)

The last and greatest of the eastern Fathers, J., strong defender of orthodoxy in the iconoclastic controversy, summed up the Greek traditions in his principal work, *De fide orthodoxa.*[1] He gives the classic exposition of the doctrine of the hypostatic union with some interesting additional views found in a less acceptable sense elsewhere. He develops his ideas throughout the third book and into the fourth. A preliminary summary runs thus: "For the divine Word was not made one with flesh that had its own person existing, but taking up his abode in the womb of the holy Virgin he unreservedly by his own person, took upon himself, through the pure blood of the perpetual Virgin, a body of flesh animated with the spirit of reason and thought, thus assuming to himself the first-fruits of man's compound nature, himself the Word having become a person in the flesh. So that he is at once flesh, and at the same time flesh of God the Word, and likewise flesh animated, possessing both reason and thought. Wherefore we speak not of man as having become God, but of God as having become man. For being by nature perfect God, he naturally became likewise perfect man: and did not change his nature nor make the dispensation (*oikonomia,* the plan of salvation) an empty show, but became, without confusion or change or division, one in substance with the flesh, which was conceived of the holy Virgin, and animated with reason and thought, and had found existence in him, while he did not change the nature of his divinity into the essence of flesh, nor the essence of flesh into the nature of his divinity, and did not make one compound nature out of his divine nature and the human nature he had assumed."[2]

J. dismissed opponents sharply: "But this is what led the heretics astray, that they look upon nature and person (*hypostasis*) as the same thing . . . there is no predicable form of 'Christhood,' so to speak, that he possesses. And therefore we hold that there has been a union of two perfect natures, one divine and one human; not with disorder or confusion, or intermixture, or commingling, as is said by the God-accursed Dioscorus and by Eutyches and Severus, and all that impious company; and not in a personal

or relative manner, or as a matter of dignity or agreement in will, or equality in honor, or identity in name, or good pleasure, as Nestorius, hated of God, said, and Diodorus and Theodorus of Mopsuestia, and their diabolical tribe; but by synthesis, that is, according to person (*hypostasis*) without change or confusion or alteration or difference or separation, and we confess that in two perfect natures there is but one person of the Son of God incarnate; holding that there is one and the same person belonging to his divinity and his humanity, and granting that the two natures are preserved in him after the union, but we do not hold that each is separate and by itself, but that they are united to each other in one compound person. For we look upon the union as substantial, that is as true and not imaginary. We say that it is substantial, moreover, not in the sense of two natures resulting in one compound nature, but in the sense of a true union of them in one compound person of the Son of God, and we hold that their substantial difference is preserved."[3]

J. is clear on the communication of idioms (qv).[4] He did adopt the view of Leontinus of Byzantium on *enhypostasia,* but refined it to fit the Chalcedonian dogma—the essence of the theory is that the humanity shares in the divine personality, so that there would be nothing lacking in its integrity within the hypostatic union.[5] Similarly, J. speaks of the theandric energy of Christ, but this he does while safeguarding the orthodox dogmatic position.[6] He also considers certain of the features of Christ's life, such as his prayer[7] and the great mysteries like the Resurrection (qv).[8] His exposition is generally fairly elaborate.

[1]Works, *PG* 94-96; cf. J. Bilz, *Die Trinitätslehre des Johannes von Damaskus,* Paderborn, 1909; J. Gregoire, "La relation éternelle de l'Esprit au Fils d'après les écrits de Jean de Damas," *RHE* 64 (1969) 713-55; K. Rozemond, "La Christologie de Saint Jean Damascene," *Studia Patristica et Byzantina,* VIII, 1959; J. J. Meany, *The Image of God in Man according to the Doctrine of St. John Damascene,* Dissert., Manila, 1954; J. Meyendorff, *Le Christ dans la théologie byzantine,* Paris, 1969; M. O'Rourke, "Christ the Eikon in the Apologies for the Holy Images of John of Damascus," *Greek Orthodox Theological Review,* 15 (1979) 175-86; C. Georgehescu, "The Doctrine of the Hypostatic Union in St. John Damascene," *Orthodoxia* 23 (1971) (in Greek), 181-93; A. Kallis, "Handapparat zum Johannes Damaskenos Studium," *Ostkirchliche Studien* 16 (1967) 200-13; [2]Bk III, ch 2, *LNPF* IX, 46; [3]*Ibid.,* ch 3, 47; [4]*Ibid.,* ch 4, 48f; [5]*Ibid.,* ch 7, 51f; [6]*Ibid.,* ch 19, 67f; [7]*Ibid.,* ch 24, 70; [8]*Ibid.,* Bk IV, ch 1, 2; 75.

JOHN OF THE CROSS (1542-1591)

A poet's poet, prince of mystics, J. made a unique contribution to the renewal and expansion of the order of Carmel in an age of crisis, assuring thereby sinews of youth and power to Catholicism;

thoroughly instructed in Thomist theology, well read in the mystics preceding him in the West, through his own eminent mystical genius and intuitive familiarity with the Bible, he fashioned a synthesis of mystical theology, monumental in its excellence.

J.'s Christocentric ideal, theologically expounded, is integral to that monument: mountain were we to borrow his own venerable image. He saw Christ as the plenitude of divine revelation. With Heb 1:1 as a starting point he expresses his thought in this wonderful passage: "Wherefore he that would inquire of God, or seek any vision or revelation, would not only be acting foolishly, but would be committing an offense against God, by not setting his eyes altogether upon Christ, and seeking no new thing or aught beside. And God might answer him after this manner, saying: If I have spoken all things to thee in my Word, which is my Son, and I have no other word, what answer can I now make to thee, or what can I reveal to thee which is greater than this? Set thine eyes on him alone, for in him I have spoken and revealed to thee all things, and in him thou shalt find yet more than that which thou askest and desirest. For thou askest locutions and revelations, which are the part; but if thou set thine eyes upon him, thou shalt find the whole; for he is my complete locution and answer, and he is all my vision and all my revelation; so that I have spoken to thee, answered thee, declared to thee and revealed to thee, in giving him to thee as thy brother, companion and master, as ransom and as reward. For since that day when I descended upon him with my Spirit on Mount Tabor, saying: *Hic est filius meus dilectus, in quo mihi bene complacui, ipsum audite* (Mt 17:5) (which is to say: This is my beloved Son, in whom I am well pleased; hear you him), I have left all these manners of teaching and answering, and I have entrusted this to him. Hear him for I have no more faith to reveal, neither have I any more things to declare. For if I spoke aforetime, it was to promise Christ; and if they inquired of me, their inquiries (their hopes) were directed to petitions for Christ and expectancy concerning him, in whom they should find every good thing (as is now set forth in all the teaching of the Evangelists and the Apostles); but now any who would inquire of me after that manner, and desire me to speak to him or reveal aught to him, would in a sense be asking me for Christ again, and asking me for more faith, and be lacking in faith, which has already been given in Christ."[2]

J. goes on to cite Pauline texts: Col 2:3; 2:9; 1 Cor 2:2, to emphasize his doctrine of the revelation made in Christ. With this passage from *The Ascent of Mount Carmel* may be compared another from *The Spiritual Canticle*. The saint had been dealing shortly

before with the soul's search for the beauty of God: "Let us so act that, by means of this exercise of love aforementioned, we may even come to see ourselves in thy beauty in life eternal; that is that I may be so transformed in thy beauty that, being alike in beauty, we may see ourselves in thy beauty, since I shall have thy own beauty; so that, when one of us looks at the other, each may see in the other his beauty, the beauty of both being thy beauty alone, and I being absorbed in thy beauty; and thus I shall see thee in thy beauty and thou wilt see me in thy beauty."[3]

In the next stanza J. writes thus: "The rock of which she here speaks, according to St. Paul, is Christ. The lofty caverns of this rock are high and deep mysteries of the wisdom of God which are in Christ, concerning the hypostatic union of human nature with the divine Word, and the correspondence to this which is in the union of men in God, and in the agreement which there is between the justice and mercy of God as to the salvation of the human race in the manifestation of God." Speaking a little later of the "great depths to be fathomed in Christ," J. goes on, "for he is like an abundant mine with many recesses containing treasures, of which, for all that men try to fathom them, the end and bottom is never reached; rather in each recess men continue to find new veins of new riches everywhere, as St. Paul said of Christ himself in these words: In Christ dwell hidden all treasures and wisdom, whereunto the soul cannot enter and whereto it cannot attain unless first, as we have said, it pass through the straight place of exterior and interior suffering into the divine Wisdom. For even that degree of these mysteries of Christ to which a soul may attain in this life cannot be reached save through great suffering and until it has received from God many favors, both in the intellect and the senses, and until many spiritual exercises have been first performed by it. For all these favors are inferior to the wisdom of the mysteries of Christ, for all are, as it were, preparations for coming thereto."[4]

This is an existential approach to the theology of Jesus Christ but it comes from a world not often thought of as real, mystical experience. Through this God is directly the object of the soul's knowledge. Therein J. was a supreme practitioner. His testimony is for this reason most precious; doubly so, as he had theological competence to discern its reality and appraise its validity.

[1]Works ET A. Peers, *Collected Works,* 3 vols., London, 1943; 1 vol. K. Kavanaugh, O.D.C. and O. Rodriguez, O.D.C., London, 1966; *Lives,* G. de Santa Maddalena, O.D.C., Westminster, Maryland, 1946; Crisogono de Jesús Sacramentado, O.D.C., New York, 1959; bibl. P. P. Ottonello, "Bibliografia di S. Juan de la Cruz," *Archivum Bibliographicum Carmelitanum,* Rome, 9–10,

67-68, 1-194; cf. G. Moel, *Le sens de l'existence selon St. Jean de la Croix,* 3 vols., Théologie 45-47, Paris, 1961; Giovanni de la Croce, "Christus in der Mystik des hl. Johannes vom Kreuz," *Jahrbuch für Mystiche Theologie* 10, 1964; Jean de la Croix Peters, "Función de Christo en la mistica," *Revista de espiritualidad* 17 (1958) 507-32; P. Varga, *Schöpfung in Christus nach Johannes vom Kreuz,* thesis, Vienna, 1968; Jose V. de la Eucaristia, "Christus in economia salutis secundum Sanctum Joannem a Cruce," Ephemerides Carmeliticae 16 (1965) 313-51; K. Wojtyla (now John Paul II), *Faith in the Doctrine of St. John of the Cross,* Dissertation, Angelico University, available in ET; the following articles in *DSp,* IV, "Expérience mystique," 1591-92; VII, "Humanité du Christ," VII, 1099-1104; VIII, 408-47, "Jean de la Croix, St.," Lucien Marie de Saint Joseph, esp., 431-32 on Christology; [2]*Ascent of Mount Carmel,* Bk II, ch 22, 5, ed. A. Peers, vol. 1, 174f; [3]*Spiritual Canticle,* Stanza XXXV, 3, vol. 2, 164; [4]Stanza XXXVI, 2, 3, 168f. (tr. slightly adjusted).

JOHN THE EVANGELIST, ST.

The focus of Jn's gospel is Jesus Christ.[1] The prologue contains the unique summary of the Incarnation, "And the Word became flesh and dwelt among us, full of grace and truth and we have beheld his glory, glory as of the only Son from the Father" (1:14). The gospel culminates in this profession of faith: "Now Jesus did many other signs in the presence of the disciples, which are not written in this book; but these are written that you may believe that Jesus is the Christ, the Son of God, and that believing you may have life in you" (20:30-31). We are reminded of the centrality of Jesus by the great "I" sayings: "I am the bread of life" (6:36, 48); "I am the light of the world" (8:12; 9:5); "I am the door of the sheep" (10:7); "I am the Good Shepherd" (10:11); "I and the Father are one" (10:30); "I am the resurrection and the life" (11:25); "I am the way and the truth and the life" (14:6); "I am the true vine" (15:1).

The relationship of Jesus with the Father is given overwhelming importance. Jesus speaks of the Father over sixty times, a frequency unparalleled in the other gospels. This is a unique revelation of the Father, consonant with the role of Jesus as revealer. But there is an emphasis, again very remarkable by comparison with the other gospels, on the mission of the Son by the Father: "For God sent the Son into the world, not to condemn the world, but that the world might be saved by him" (3:17; cf 3:34; 5:23; 5:37; 6:39; 7:16).

Jesus is, in Jn, the sacrament of the Father: "He who has seen me has seen the Father" (14:9). He comprehends his followers in a mysterious union with the Father: "In that day you will know that I am in my Father, and you in me, and I in you" (14:20). And the one who speaks thus is uniquely glorified by the Father. As mission so glory is wondrously taught by Jn: "If I glorify myself, my glory is noth-ing; it is my Father who glorifies me, of whom you say that he is your God" (8:54). "The hour has come for the Son of man to be glorified" (12:23). "Now is the Son of man glorified, and in him God is glorified; if God is glorified in him, God will also glorify him in himself, and glorify him at once" (13:31-32). The solemn prayer in Jn 17 has these marvelous words summarizing Jesus' and John's outlook: "And this is eternal life, that they know thee the only true God, and Jesus Christ whom thou has sent. I glorified thee on earth, having accomplished the work which thou gavest me to do; and now, Father, glorify thou me in thy own presence with the glory which I had with thee before the world was made" (17:4-5).

All the time Jesus makes himself the focus of attention, true to his indispensable role as the unique and totally satisfactory revealer. All the time he is the one who holds all the treasures sought and needed by the truly enlightened. He is manifold and quintessentially unique, reflecting light which varies from an invariable center; to the disciples, the Mother at Cana, the traders in the Temple, Nicodemus, the Samaritan woman, the sick who sought healing, the enemies who passed from verbal harassment to hard plotting, to the family at Bethany, in the table fellowship sharing with his intimate friends, to Pilate, to the fellow crucified and the faithful few on Calvary; He is the same source of light, with the same sensitivity to his objects in his risen status. Historicity and links with Qumran naturally occupy experts.

---

[1]Cf. modern commentaries, esp. R. E. Brown, in the Anchor Bible, dictionary articles, esp. J. L. McKenzie, *John, Gospel of,* 446-50; C. H. Dodd, *The Interpretation of the Fourth Gospel,* Cambridge, 1953; J. Dupont, *Essais sur la Christologie de St. Jean: Le Christ, Parole, Lumière et Vie, La Gloire du Christ,* Bruges, 1951; J. Macquarrie, "The Witness of John" in *Jesus Christ in Modern Thought,* London, 1990, 97-122; I. de La Potterie, *La Vérité dans St. Jean,* Rome, 1977; J. L. Martyn, *History and Theology in the Fourth Gospel,* New York, 1968; J. Sidebottom, *The Christ of the Fourth Gospel,* London, 1961.

JUDGE, CHRIST AS

Especially in Jn where the theme of judgment is frequently met, where the idea seems to imply a series of paradoxes, all judgment is centered on Jesus. 1 Pet 4:5 says Christ "is ready to judge the living and the dead."[1] The various texts so often quoted and discussed find their unity in this truth: Jesus is judge for decision on him, or failure to make it, constitutes the very essence of the judgment of each individual person. This is the profound meaning of the texts: "The Father judges no one, but has given all judgment to the Son, that all may honor the Son, even as they honor the Father" (Jn 5:22). "Now is the judgment of this world, now shall the ruler of this world be cast out; and I, when I am lifted up from the earth will draw all men to myself'' (Jn 12:31-32). "He who rejects me and does not receive my sayings has a judge; the word that I have spoken will be his judge on the last day'' (Jn 12:48). The judgment is portrayed in apocalyptic colors in Rev: "Then I saw heaven opened, and behold, a white horse! He who sat upon it is called Faithful and True, and in righteousness he judges and makes war. His eyes are like a flame of fire, and on his head are many diadems; and he has a name inscribed which no one knows but himself. He is clad in a robe dipped in blood, and the name by which he is called is The Word of God'' (Rev 19:11-13). (See article King, Christ the.)

---

[1] J. Dupont, "Vie et jugement," *Essais sur la Christologie de S. Jean,* Bruges, 1951, 171–80; S. Cipriani, "San Giovanni," *Il giudizio in San Giovanni,* 17th Biblical Week, Brescia, 1964, 164–83; L. Sabourin, "Le Juge," *Les noms et les titres de Jésus,* Paris/ Bruges, 1962, 221–32; J. L. McKenzie, "The Judge of All the Earth," *The Way* 2 (1962) 209–18; J. Winandy, "La scène du jugement dernier, Mt 25:31-46," *ScEccl* 18 (1966) 160–86; M. du Duit, "Les paraboles du jugement," *Evangelium* 68 (1967) 5–59; P. Adnès, *DSp,* VIII, 1571–91, W. Pesch, *Bauer* II, 448f.; J. H. Wright, *NCE* VIII, 37–40; articles in Biblical dictionaries.

JUSTIN MARTYR, ST. (c. 100–c. 165)

Like those of his time, J., in the *Apologies* and the *Dialogue* with Trypho, centered a great deal of his thinking on the Logos—Adolf von Harnack thought that J.'s Christology could be summed up in the formula, "Christ is the Logos and Nomos."[1] He gave much more thought to the Logos. Ultimately J. developed a first outline of a theology of history. He did so with the help of some original ideas on the meaning of the Logos. He dignified it with the title *Logos spermatikos,* and spoke of *spermata tou Logou.* Revelation was mediated by the Logos, and this happened in a historical context of revelation.

J. was a Platonist, interested in a Platonic theory of knowledge adjusted to Christian truth. He saw the *spermata* as the means whereby the human spirit participates in the Logos; thus the Logos distributed knowledge. It is not a full communication, merely partial; but though open to all in its action, through the divine seed, it varies in different categories: pagans especially philosophers like Heraclius or Socrates, OT prophets in a very privileged way, Christians, in whom the Logos dwells in the freedom of grace, wholly, personally. Foremost of all is the case of Christ, Logos and man united uniquely. In a controverted passage J. states: "Our religion is clearly more sublime than any teaching of man for this reason, that the Christ who has appeared for us

men represents the Logos principle in its totality (*to logikon to holon*) that is both body and Logos and soul. For all that the philosophers and legislators at any time declared or discovered aright they accomplished by investigation in accordance with that portion of the Logos which fell to their lot. But because they did not know the whole of the Logos, who is Christ, they often contradicted each other."[2]

In the *Dialogue with Trypho,* J. also pursues the Logos theme. He attempts to convince his Jewish opponent that the Old Law and Covenant are abrogated, that Jesus is the promised Messiah and that Christians are the new Israel. There is much discussion, at times with an impression of talking at cross-purposes, of OT messianic texts. It is in the *Dialogue* that the much-quoted passage on the New Eve occurs. Preceding it are these words: "For also one of his disciples called Simon aforetime, when he recognized him as Son of God, even Christ, according to the revelation of his Father, he surnamed Peter. And finding him written down in the Memoirs of his Apostles (i.e., the Gospels) as Son of God and calling him Son, we have understood that he is so, and also that he came forth before all things that were made of the Father by his power and will. He also is termed both Wisdom and Day and Dayspring and Sword and Stone and Rod and Jacob and Israel in this fashion or in that, in the words of the prophets, and has become man by the Virgin, in order that by the same way in which the disobedience caused by the serpent took its beginning, by this way it also should take its destruction."[3]

In view of the mentality of the time there is a dimension of direct, almost harsh, confrontation in the *Dialogue* that would not appeal nowadays in similar encounters (see article Jewishness of Jesus, The).

---

[1] Cf. A. Feder, *Justins des Märtyrers Lehre von Jesus Christus,* Freiburg, 1906; E. R. Goodenough, *The Theology of Justin Martyr,* Jena, 1923; G. Bardy, "Saint Justin et la philosophie stoicienne," *RSR* 13 (1923) 491–510; 14 (1934) 33–45; id., *DTC* VIII, 2, 2228–2277; B. Seeberg, "Die Geschichtstheologie Justins des Märtyrers," *ZKG* 58 (1939) 1–81; id., *Logos und Nomos,* Berlin, 1955; G. Aeby, *Les missions divines de Saint Justin à Origène,* Fribourg, 1958, 6–15; J. Leclercq, "L'idée de la royauté de Christ dans l'oeuvre de Saint Justin," *L'Année théologique* 7 (1946); E. Bellini, "Dio nel pensiero di S. Giustino," *La Scuola Cattolica* 9 (1982) 387–406; R. Holte, "Logos spermatikos, Christianity and Ancient Philosophy according to St. Justin's Apologies," *Studia Theologica* 12, Lund, 1958, 109–68; W. Pannenberg, "Die Aufnahme des philosophischen Gottesbegriffs als dogmatisches Problem der frühchristlichen Theologie," *ZKG* 70 (1959) 1–45; G. T. Armstrong, *Die Genesis in der Alten Kirche,* Tübingen, 1962, 18–51; N. Pycke, *Connaissance rationelle et connaissance de grâce chez saint Justin,* ETL 37 (1961) 52–85; Grillmeier, 105–111; [2] *Apol.* II, 10, 1; [3] *Dialogue* tr. A. L. Williams, London, 1930, ch. 100, 3, 4, p. 209.

K

KENOSIS, SELF-EMPTYING OF CHRIST, THE

"Have this mind among yourselves, which was in Christ Jesus, who though he was in the form of God, did not count equality with God a thing to be grasped, but emptied himself, taking the form of a servant, being born in the likeness of men.[1] And being found in human form he humbled himself and became obedient unto death, even death on a cross. Therefore God has highly exalted him and bestowed on him the name which is above every name, that at the name of Jesus every knee should bow, in heaven and on earth and under the earth, and every tongue confess that Jesus Christ is Lord, to the glory of God the Father'' (Phil 2:4-11).

The passage has been described as a summary of the whole of Pauline Christology, even of all NT Christology. All the phases of Christ's existence are successively evoked: the pre-existence, the Incarnation with the Servant (qv) theme, the program of life based on obedience, the crucifixion, the exaltation, marked by the mysterious name (qv), the right to adoration and universal sovereignty, the conferring of the essential divine title, Lord, the resumption of glory. The key word is "he emptied himself." It cannot mean, what some modern theologians have sought to establish, that he renounced his very divine nature. But he could forego any overt manifestation of the glory which went with it. That he could still receive this glory was shown in the mystery of the Transfiguration (qv). He was a fitting subject for full divine glory. In renouncing it, he showed another dimension of his title, the New Adam. Where Adam overreached himself without warrant, he did not call on the sure warrant he possessed.

The self-emptying covered his entire existence, from the moment of the Annunciation to the entombment: it reveals in each phase something new, hitherto unthought-of, facilitating the act of faith in his divinity, and also challenging it radically. There is a whole study of the phases, events, words, gestures, situations of Christ's life which will fulfill some spiritual genius: the bare, little known setting for the Annunciation, the haphazard place of the birth, the village life, with the duty of a tradesman, the Baptism among sinners—but here, as in the Transfiguration, a momentary break in the bleakness, the public ministry where he had no place to lay his head, and the grim finale; where the kenosis reached bewildering depths, permitted to enhance the imminent exaltation: Resurrection and Ascension (qqv). He was buried in another man's grave.

This may appear homiletic rhetoric. The basis is utterly factual. "He emptied himself" is the most comprehensive statement about the Word made flesh, apart from this revelation itself of his identity. It affects in one way or another every aspect of the human earthly existence of Jesus Christ and should be remembered in considering many of the apparently insoluble problems which theologians or biblical scholars raise. When we attempt to penetrate the consciousness of Christ (qv) we are of necessity hampered by the immense barrier raised by the kenosis: all the wonders which would follow the assumption by the Word of God of a human nature are muted. The theophanies of the Baptism and the Transfiguration (qqv) are momentary; the kenosis is a vast curtain or canopy covering so much that we should wish to see unveiled. The difficulty is that many searchers for the truth about Jesus Christ forget that the kenosis implies this veil.

The contrast in the passage quoted between the "form of a servant" and the assertion that "Jesus

Christ is Lord" restates the whole mystery of human history. It must be borne in mind when we speak of Jesus as the "Lord of History" (qv). For his lordship too is covered by the kenosis: what he is, at the heart of human affairs, what he accomplishes, is hidden, unrecognizable save to his intimates.

As the kenosis extends to his life in the Church, apart from the contrast between the natural and the supernatural, with all that this entails of puzzlement for those who have not the faith, there is the continuity between the life of Christ on earth and his life in his Church. As he willed to withhold his glory while on earth, so in his mystical life in the Church, his body, he does not always reveal the wonders of his grace in the souls of his saints. How often they have died without much recognition of their sanctity, in some instances completely unrecognized.

Thereby they showed, perhaps, how a code of conduct fashioned on the kenosis comes naturally from identification with Christ: "Take my yoke upon you and learn from me, for I am meek and humble of heart, and you will find rest for your souls. For my yoke is easy and my burden is light" (Mt 11:29-30). "Whoever humbles himself like this child, he is the greatest in the kingdom of heaven" (Mt 18:4). "For everyone who exalts himself will be humbled and he who humbles himself will be exalted" (Lk 14:11). This is the kenosis in practice, supremely exemplified by Jesus himself.

¹Cf. H. Schumacher, *Christus in seiner Präexistenz und Kenose,* 2 vols., Rome, 1914, 1921; R. A. Knox, *The Kenotic Theory,* Cambridge Summer School *The Incarnation,* London, 1926, 211–28; L. Cerfaux, "L'Hymne au Christ-Serviteur de Dieu," *Miscellanea Alberti de Meyer,* I, Louvain, 1946, 117–30; id., *Christ in the Theology of St. Paul,* London, 1966, 374–97; A. Feuillet, "L'hymne christologique de l'épitre aux Philippiens (2:6-11)," *RB* 72 (1965) 352–80, 481–507; E. Käsemann, "A Critical Analysis of Philippians 2:5-11," *Journal for Theology and Church,* 5 (1968) 45–88; T. F. Glasson, "Two Notes on the Philippians Hymn (2:6-11) *NTS* 21 (1974–75) 133–39; R. P. Martin, *Carmen Christi: Philippians 2:5-11 in Recent Interpretation and in the Setting of Early Christian Worship,* Cambridge, 1967; I. H. Marshall, "The Christ-hymn in Philippians 2:5-11, *Tyndale Bulletin* 19 (1968) 104–27; J. A. Sanders, "Dissenting Deities and Philippians 2:1-11," *JBL* 88 (1969) 279–90; J. T. Sanders, *The New Testament Christological Hymns: Their Historical Religious Background,* Cambridge, 1971, 58–74; J. Murphy-O'Connor, O.P., "Christological Anthropology in Phil 2:6-11," *RB* 83 (1976) 25–50; esp., P. Henry, S.J., "Kénose," in *DBS* V (1937) 7–161; D. Georgi, "Der vorpaulinische Hymnus Phil 2:6-11," *Zeit und Geschichte. Dankesgabe an R. Bultmann,* ed. E. Dinkler, Tübingen, 1964, 263–93; J. Dupont, O.S.B., "Jésus Christ dans son abaissement et son exaltation d'après Phil 2:6-11," *RSR* 37 (1950) 500–14; D. G. Dawe, "A Fresh Look at the Kenotic Christologies," *SJT* 15 (1962) 337–49; id., *The Form of a Servant. A Historical Analysis of the Kenotic Motif,* Philadelphia, 1963; D. F. Hudson, "A Further Note on Philippians 2:6-11," *ExpT* 77 (1965–66) 29; J. M. Furness, "Behind the Philippian Hymn," *ExpT* 79 (1967–1968) 178–82; C. F. D. Moule, "Further Reflections on Philippians 2:5-11," in *Apostolic History and the Gospel,* Essays ed. for F. F. Bruce by W. W. Gasque and R. P. Martin, Paternoster, 1970, 264–76; E. Käsemann, "A Critical Analysis of Philippians 2:5-11," *JTh* 5 (1968) 45–88; J. Richard, "La kénose de Dieu dans le Christ d'après T. J. J. Altizer," *Eglise et Théologie* 22 (1971) 207–28; P. Grelot, "La tradition et l'intérpretation, de Phil 2:6-7. Quelques éléments d'enquête patristique," *NRT* 93 (1971) 897–922; F. Varillon, *L'humilité de Dieu,* Paris, 1974; M. D. Hooker, "Philippians 2:6-11," *Festschrift W. G. Kümmel: Jesus und Paulus,* Göttingen 1975, 151–56; O. Hofius, *Der Christushymnus: Philipper 2:6-11,* Tübingen, 1976; G. Howard, "Phil. 2:6-11 and the Human Christ," *CBQ* 40 (1978), 368–84.

KING, CHRIST THE

St. Pius X took as the motto of his pontificate "To restore all things in Christ." It was a logical step from this for Pius XI (qv) to give prominence to the doctrine of Christ's universal kingship. This he did within four years of his election as Pope, when by the Encyclical Letter *Quas Primas,* December 11, 1925 (qv) he taught the doctrine and instituted the feast, decreeing that it should be celebrated on the last Sunday of October, that is the Sunday nearest to the feast of All Saints. The same Pope gave a new impulse to the Church's missionary apostolate and was also conspicuous for his active promotion of the lay apostolate. The ideal of Christ the King as he saw and published it was closely attuned to such a program. His initiative met a response which in places was notably enthusiastic. Apostles like Cardinal Cardijn, founder of the Young Christian Workers, directors of Catholic Scouts willingly made the feast the focus of commitment or renewal.

The enthusiasm has waned and in places doubt has been expressed on the Pope's teaching, especially certain modes of its application.¹ Was this then a passing form of piety, destined to fade out slowly? Not if the theological foundation is carefully examined. It is central to the whole Judaeo-Christian message that the Messiah would be prophet, priest, and king. The OT testimony to the idea and ideal of kingship is very strong and a principal work on the Messiah, Sigmund Mowinckel's *He That Cometh* devotes considerable space to elaboration and analysis of the idea as it took shape in concrete reality and gave rise to a very specific hope.

First as kingship, an idea taken from the surrounding cultures, evolved it took an increasingly Yahwistic meaning: "Considered from one point of view, then, the king is more than human. He is a divine being, possessing this superhuman quality because Yahweh has 'called' and 'chosen' him to be the shepherd of his people, and has made him his son, has anointed him and endowed him with his spirit. He performs the will of Yahweh, and transmits his blessing to land and people. He represents Yahweh before the people. But as a human being, a man from among the people (i.e., a representative man from the chosen people of Yahweh), he also represents the people before Yahweh; and gradually the main stress comes to be put on this aspect of his vocation." "When the idea of the spirit is transferred to the king, this means that the king is not one with Yahweh, or an incarnation of him, but endowed by the spirit of Yahweh with supernatural powers."[2]

There was a transference of ideas from the king to the Messiah, and out of this would evolve eventually the concept of Christ as King: "Secondly, we have seen that those ideas which were associated in Israel with the king share all their essential elements with the concept of the Messiah. This will be still more evident when we come to describe the Messiah concept itself. The only essential difference is that the ideal of kingship belongs to the present (though it clearly also looks to the future), whereas the Messiah is a purely future, eschatological figure. Clearly there is a historical connection between these two complexes of ideas. Either the content of the kingly ideal was derived from the concept of the Messiah, or vice versa, the content of the Messianic concept was derived from the kingly ideal. The latter alternative is manifestly the right one. 'Messiah' is the ideal king entirely transferred to the future, no longer identified with the specific historical king, but with one who, one day, will come."[3]

The theme rings through the Bible: "Of the increase of his government and of peace there will be no end upon the throne of David, and over his kingdom, to establish it, and to uphold it with justice and with righteousness from this time forth and for evermore. The zeal of the Lord of hosts will do this." Again in Jer 23:5: "Behold, the days are coming, says the Lord, when I will raise up for David a righteous Branch, and he shall reign as king and deal wisely, and shall execute justice and righteousness in the land."

Pss 2, 45, and 72 are generally invoked to illustrate the kingly theme in OT mentality: "Ask of me and I will make the nations your heritage, and the ends of the earth your possession" (2:8); "Your divine throne endures for ever and ever. Your royal scepter is a scepter of equity; you love righteousness and hate wickedness" (45[44]:6-7); "In his days may righteousness flourish, and peace abound, till the moon be no more! May he have dominion from sea to sea, and from the River to the ends of the earth!" (72[71]:7-8).

The theme is also found in Daniel, bound up in one chapter with the title preferred by Jesus to describe his mission, the 'Son of Man.' "And in the days of those kings the God of heaven will set up a kingdom which shall never be destroyed, nor shall its sovereignty be left to another people. It shall break to pieces all these kingdoms and bring them to an end, and it shall stand forever" (2:44); "I saw in the night visions, and behold, with the clouds of heaven there came one like a son of man, and he came to the Ancient of Days and was presented before him. And to him was given dominion and the glory and kingdom, that all peoples, nations, and languages should serve him; his dominion is an everlasting dominion, which shall not pass away, and his kingdom one that shall not be destroyed" (7:13-14). One OT text, Zech 9:9 will be applied to Christ in a dramatic moment of his life.

The theme of messianic royalty occurs in the infancy gospels, at the outset of Jesus' life. The Magi inquire: "Where is he who has been born King of the Jews?" (Mt 2:2). It is more fully and explicitly expressed in the capital Annunciation dialogue: "And behold, you will conceive in your womb and bear a Son, and you shall call his name Jesus. He will be great, and will be called the Son of the Most High; and the Lord God will give to him the throne of his father David, and he will reign over the house of Jacob for ever; and of his kingdom there will be no end" (Lk 1:31-33).

Jesus preached the kingdom of God. It was the core of his teaching. How then did the Church come into existence? St. Luke, in two volumes, and St. Matthew in one, show how the development or evolution was consistent in concept and ideal. "The Church is the way to the kingdom; to reject the Church is to refuse God's kingdom; the coming of the kingdom on earth was effected by the apostolic organization of the Church among the Gentiles. In Christ's earthly life, as Luke has shown in his first volume, the preaching of the kingdom was greeted with incredulity on the part of his fellow countrymen. When it ripened into hatred for his message, this incredulity compassed his death. But it was by the death of Christ and his resurrection that the coming of the kingdom into this world was definitively inaugurated."[4]

As Luke shows in Acts, Paul lived through the evolving divine plan for the establishment of the kingdom. Israel's exclusion through lack of faith would lead to the entry of the Gentiles; thus the universal kingdom of God was inaugurated.

We now face the important question: Did Jesus Christ think of himself as king? His answer to Pilate who put him this question was clear: "Pilate said to him, 'So you are a king?' Jesus answered, 'You say that I am a king. For this was I born, and for this I have come into the world, to bear witness to the truth. Everyone who is of the truth hears my voice'" (Jn 18:37). Luke gives the impression that the Jews had got the idea before. "Then the whole company of them arose, and brought him to Pilate. And they began to accuse him, saying, 'We found this man perverting our nation, and forbidding us to give tribute to Caesar, and saying that he himself is Christ the king.' And Pilate asked him, 'Are you the king of the Jews?' And he answered him, 'You have said so'" (Lk 23:1-3).

The ideas of the kingdom of God and of the Messianic kingship have then come very close together in the NT. The Messiah-King is the Son of God himself and in the manifold mystery of his being he inaugurates the kingdom and he is the kingdom. Biblical scholars trace three stages in Christ's manifestation of his kingship.

During his earthly life Christ avoided any bold, emphatic declaration of his royal office. He did not reject Nathanael's act of faith, "Rabbi, you are the Son of God! You are the King of Israel!" (Jn 1:49). But he seized the occasion to speak of the Parousia. After the multiplication of the loaves and fishes the people wished to take him by force and make him king (Jn 6:15). He withdrew to the mountain by himself.

He clearly wished to emphasize that "his kingship was not of this world" (Jn 18:36); he wanted to avoid political interpretation of his office, that is in the political world of his time. He did not oppose the tetrarch Herod who feared that he might be a rival (Lk 13:31); he taught no opposition to Caesar, confounding his enemies with an immortal saying, "Render to Caesar the things that are Caesar's and to God the things that are God's" (Mk 12:17). As his Passion approached he defended those who acclaimed him on his triumphal entry to Jerusalem: "Blessed is the king who comes in the name of the Lord. Peace in heaven and glory in the highest" (Lk 19:38; cf. Jn 12:13). Zech 9:9 is invoked by Mt 21:5 and Jn 12:15: "Tell the daughter of Zion, Behold, your king is coming to you, humble and mounted on an ass, and on a colt, the foal of an ass."

All this hastened the Passion, and at this ending of his earthly life his kingship was a point raised: not in the religious trial but in the civil trial before the Roman procurator. The power of Caesar was invoked by his enemies. But a strange irony put his title into prominence in the very events leading to his death. The soldiers, after his scourging, "clothed him in a purple cloak, and plaiting a crown of thorns they put it on him. And they began to salute him, 'Hail, King of the Jews'" (Mk 15:17-18). Mk says briefly, "And the inscription of the charge against him read, 'The King of the Jews'" (15:26). Jn is slightly more

elaborate: "Pilate also wrote a title and put it on the cross; it read, 'Jesus of Nazareth, the King of the Jews.' Many of the Jews read this title, for the place where Jesus was crucified was near the city; and it was written in Hebrew, in Latin and in Greek. The chief priests of the Jews then said to Pilate, 'Do not write, "The King of the Jews," but "This man said, I am King of the Jews."'" Pilate answered, 'What I have written, I have written'" (19:19-22). His royal title was used to mock him on the cross. Lk says it was the soldiers. Mt reads thus: "So also the chief priests, with the scribes and elders, mocked him saying, 'He saved others, he cannot save himself. He is the King of Israel; let him come down now from the cross and we will believe in him'" (27:41-42).

Significantly the confession of faith of the Good Thief on the cross was in the context of Christ's kingship: "Jesus, remember me, when you come into your kingdom" (Lk 23:42). Christ's promise of salvation there and then leads into the moment when after the Resurrection he can manifest his kingship fully: "All authority in heaven and on earth has been given to me. Go, therefore, and make disciples of all nations, baptizing them in the name of the Father and of the Son and of the Holy Spirit" (Mt 28:18-19). When his glorification is completed by the Ascension, and when the Spirit has come, the kingship of Christ enters into its second phase, that of the Church, from Pentecost to the Parousia: "Being therefore exalted at the right hand of God and having received from the Father the promise of the Holy Spirit, he has poured out that which you see and hear" (Acts 2:33). "He who conquers I will grant him to sit with me on my throne, as I myself conquered and sat down with my Father on his throne" (Rev 3:21). Salvation is now explicitly referred to his kingship: "He has delivered us from the dominion of darkness and transferred us to the kingdom of his beloved Son" (Col 1:13).

Rev 1:5 styles Jesus Christ "the faithful witness, the first-born of the dead, and the ruler of the kings on earth." The figure of glory in Rev 19 who is called "Faithful and True" and "the Word of God" bears kingly symbols and is thus finally described: "On his robe and on his thigh he has a name inscribed, King of kings and Lord of lords" (19:16).

There is one clear link between the first two phases of Christ's manifestation of his kingship: he fully exercised during his earthly life one specifically kingly power and its effect must be dominant in the second, the period of the Church. This was his legislative function. The Sermon on the Mount is the comprehensive law of his kingdom. He lays down imperatives of conduct, spiritual, but nonetheless binding: "teaching them to observe all that I have commanded you'' (Mt 28:20); "If you keep my commandments you will abide in my love, just as I have kept my Father's commandments and abide in his love" (Jn 15:10). He gave a new commandment, the essential law of his followers: "A new commandment I give to you, that you love one another; even as I have loved you, that you also love one another" (Jn 13:34). "This is my commandment that you love one another as I have loved you. Greater love has no man than this, that a man lay down his life for his friends. You are my friends if you do what I command you" (Jn 15:12-14). Christ also decides with authority, points concerning the Mosaic law.

Kingship implies not only legislative but judicial power. To Christ preeminently belongs this power: "The Father judges no one, but has given all judgment to the Son, that all may honor the Son, even as they honor the Father" (Jn 5:22-23). How this judgment will be exercised is vividly described, and in terms of Christ's royal office: "When the Son of man comes in his glory, and all the angels with him, then he will sit on his glorious throne. . . . Then the King will say to those at his right hand, 'Come, O blessed of my Father, inherit the kingdom prepared for you from the foundation of the world' . . . . Then he will say to those at his left hand, 'Depart from me, you cursed, into the eternal fire prepared for the devil and his angels' " (Mt 25: 31, 34, 41).

The final phase then of Christ's kingship is the parousia. He will annihilate the Antichrist by the manifestation of his coming (Is 11:4; 2 Th 2:9); now the identity of his kingship with the kingdom of God is fully revealed: "The kingdom of the world has become the kingdom of our Lord and Christ" (Rev 11:15). "Now the salvation and the power and the kingdom of our God and the authority of his Christ have come, for the accuser of our brethren has been thrown down, who accuses them day and night before our God" (Rev 12:10).

Christ, conqueror of all his enemies will hand over the kingdom to God the Father: "Then comes the end when he delivers the kingdom to God the Father after destroying every rule and every authority and power. For he must reign until he has put all his enemies under his feet" (1 Cor 15:24-25). Very significantly this fulfillment is promised in the passages where Christ is shown as the new Adam (qv)—"For as in Adam all die, so also in Christ shall all be made alive. But each in his own order: Christ the first fruits, then at his coming those who belong to Christ" (1 Cor 15:22-23). Christ realizing the plenitude of his vocation to supplant and surpass the first head of the race does so as king.

As king he fulfills the important promises. It is the faithful who have an "inheritance in the kingdom of Christ and of God" (Eph 5:5). "He who conquers, I will grant him to sit with me on my throne, as I myself conquered and sat down with my Father on his throne" (Rev 3:21). The glory of the kingdom will come to those whom he has here below made "a kingdom of priests for their God and Father" (Rev 1:6; 5:10; 1 Pet 2:9) echoing Ex 19:6: "and you shall be to me a kingdom of priests and a holy nation."

Especially the destiny of the Apostles is now fulfilled: "You are those who have continued with me in my trials; and I assign to you, as my Father assigned to me, a kingdom, that you may eat and drink at my table in my kingdom, and sit on thrones judging the twelve tribes of Israel" (Lk 22:28-30).

The doctrine of Christ's kingship is thus seen to be thoroughly biblical. It is intrinsic to biblical eschatology. It is an indisputable element of the eternal communion with Christ for which the Christian hopes and strives. As a king he will gather us to him to share his unalterable happiness. Debates on the origin and use of the title *Kyrios* in primitive Christianity serve but to confirm that thus Christ was portrayed and accepted: "the title," says the great Pauline scholar, Msgr. Lucien Cerfaux, "represents a basic intuition in Christianity and one of its most essential doctrines. We would be inclined to insist even more than Cullmann, Foerster, Prümm, and others do on the royal nuance in Christ's sovereignty. The Aramaic *Marana,* which corresponds to *Kyrios,* has a technical sense of royal prerogative, and Jesus is a true king in virtue of the enthronement that came about through his resurrection. . . . There is normally a connection between *Kyrios* and the resurrection and parousia. The resurrection is the Messiah's enthronement as Christ or messianic king. Christ is exalted to God's right hand; he is the sovereign whose solemn entrance we are awaiting. *Kyrios* in this connection denotes the royal dignity which belongs henceforth to Christ, 'Jesus whom you have crucified has been made Lord and Christ by God' " (Acts 2:36).[5]

For Professor Cullmann, the title 'King' (*Basileus*) is a variant of the *Kyrios* title. "In order to distinguish between *Basileus* and *Kyrios* we could perhaps say that the title King emphasizes more strongly Jesus' lordship over the Church that takes the place of Israel and he fulfills the kingship of Israel. The title *Kyrios* on the other hand emphasizes more strongly Jesus' lordship over the whole world, over the visible and invisible creation. Despite the subtle distinction one may make in principle between the application of the two titles to Jesus, they are interchangeable. On the one hand, the lordship of the *Kyrios* includes also Jesus' kingship over Israel and thus over his Church. On the other hand the title King visualizes also Jesus' lordship over all creation. *Kyrios* is thus equivalent to *Basileus* in all passages which especially emphasize opposition to the claims of the Roman emperor.'' Cullmann concludes his analysis of the two concepts and their identity by pointing out that Mt which from the first chapter emphasizes Jesus' dignity as King of Israel ends with the statement of his absolute lordship, ''All authority in heaven and on earth has been given to me'' (28:18).[6]

The same author draws attention to the immense importance in all NT thinking of Ps 110:1: ''Sit at my right hand till I make your enemies your footstool.'' Almost no other OT text is quoted so often. And it is found in the Apostolic Fathers, 1 *Clement* 36, 5 and *Barnabas* 12, 10. But whereas the ''enemies'' in the Ps are earthly, the first Christians think of the unseen powers; in 1 Pet 3:22 it is ''angels, authorities and powers.'' The idea was central and vital for the early Christians, is found in the oldest formulas of faith. It is probable that the early Christians used the title *Kyrios* in their prayer as did Paul.

The formal title King is used in *The Martyrdom of Polycarp*: ''But when the Pro-Consul pressed him and said: 'Take the oath and I let you go, revile Christ,' Polycarp said: 'For eighty and six years have I been his servant, and he has done me no wrong and how can I blaspheme my King who saved me?' '' Later the martyrs are praised for their ''unsurpassable affection toward their own King and Master.''[7]

An interpolation to Ps 96:10, ''Say among the nations, 'The Lord reigns,' '' applies the saying to Christ; ''the kingdom of Jesus is on the wood,'' *Letter to Barnabas,* 8, 3; ''the Lord reigned from the tree,'' St. Justin Martyr, *Dialogue,* 73. Tertullian and other Latin Fathers would repeat this and it is found in the hymn *Vexilla Regis, Regnavit a ligno Deus.*

St. Augustine spoke occasionally of Christ as king, linking the title with priest. ''Thus since through him (the Father) made the ages, he is rightly called 'King of the ages' by the Apostle, as the one superior to the inferior beings, and powerful to rule, ruling those who have need of rule.''[8] Here it is more explicit. Many of the Fathers quote the phrase applied to Christ, ''judge of the living and the dead.'' ''Seated at the right hand of the Father Almighty'' is in the Apostles' Creed, and the Nicene Creed says ''his'' kingdom will have no end.

Thought out theology of the kingship is not ample. St. Thomas (qv) dealt with the glorification of Christ at the right hand of the Father, and with his judicial power.[9] Pius XI's Encyclical *Quas Primas* should have opened a period of reflection and research, but there is no substantial literature from the systematic theologians on the subject. Most of what can be assembled to form a synthesis comes from the biblical theologians, as the present article shows.

Pius XI gave indications of how the subject should be studied theologically. Christ's kingship is founded on the hypostatic union. ''From this it follows not only that Christ is to be adored by angels and men, but that to him angels and men are subject, and must recognize his empire; by reason of the hypostatic union Christ has power over all creatures.''

The Pope made it clear in the Encyclical that he wished to combat secularism; he pointed to the Kingship of Christ as an ideal to counter what he saw ''as the plague of secularism, its errors and impious activities.'' He went on thus: ''This evil spirit, as you are aware, Venerable Brethren, has not come into being in one day; it has long lurked beneath the surface. The empire of Christ over all nations was rejected. The right which the Church has from Christ himself, to teach mankind, to make laws, to govern people in all that pertains to their eternal salvation, that right was denied. Then gradually the religion of Christ came to be likened to false religions and to be placed ignominiously on the same level with them.'' ''We firmly hope however,'' said Pius, ''that the feast of the Kingship of Christ, which in future will be yearly observed, may hasten the return of society to our loving Savior.'' The Pope thought that it ''would be the duty of Catholics to do all they can to bring about this happy result.''[10]

With this directive Vatican II (qv) links up with Pius XI. First we should consider the teaching of the Council on Christ's kingship: ''Christ obeyed even at the cost of death, and was therefore raised by the Father (cf. Phil 2:8-9). Thus he entered into the glory of his kingdom. To him all things are made subject until he subjects himself and all created things to the Father that God may be all in all (cf. 1 Cor 15:27-28). Now, Christ has communicated this power of subjection to his disciples that they might be established in royal freedom and that by self-denial and by a holy life they might conquer the reign of sin in themselves (cf. Rom 6:12). Further, he has shared this power so that by serving him in their fellow men they might through humility and patience lead their brother men to that King whom to serve is to reign.'' Then comes a special lesson for the laity: ''For the Lord wishes to spread his kingdom by means of the laity also, a kingdom of truth and life, a kingdom of holiness and grace, a kingdom of justice, love and peace. In this kingdom creation itself will be delivered out of its slavery to corruption and into the freedom of the glory of the sons of God (cf. Rom 8:21). Clearly then a great promise and a great mandate are committed to the disciples: 'For all are yours, and you are Christ's, and Christ is God's' '' (1 Cor 3:23).

The Council teaching at this point is further developed to show that the laity participate in the royal office of Christ for the advance of mankind in culture and civilization. They must further progress in secular things seeing that this progress is imbued with the grace of Christ; they must promote fair distribution of this world's goods and see that this leads to general progress in Christian liberty. "In this manner through the members of his Church, Christ will progressively illumine the whole of human society with his saving light."[11]

Such practical directives complete and illumine the doctrine of the Kingship of Christ. The Kingship must be seen in relation to his function as prophet and as priest. But especially it cannot be fully understood without close attention to the basic idea of *kenosis* or self-emptying to which the Incarnate Word submitted during his earthly life. The profound effect it can have in personal prayer is well illustrated in the life of one of the supreme mystics, St. Teresa of Avila—one title came frequently to her: "his Majesty."

Not only by his "essence and by nature" as the Pope quotes from St. Cyril of Alexandria, but by virtue of the Redemption Christ is our King: "But a though that must give us even greater joy and consolation is this, that Christ is our King by acquired, as well as by natural right, for he is our Redeemer. Would that those who forget what they have cost their Savior might recall the words 'You were not redeemed with corruptible things, but with the precious blood of Christ, as of a lamb unspotted and unstained (1 Pet 1:18-19). We are no longer our own, for Christ has purchased us 'with a great price' (1 Cor 6:20); our very bodies are the 'members of Christ.' "

Pius XI attributes the threefold kingly power to Christ, legislative, judicial, executive. He teaches that his kingdom is "primarily spiritual and concerned with spiritual things," recalling that the Savior would not countenance assumption of kingly power during his earthly life. The kingship is allied to the offices of Redeemer and Priest.

Where the Pope was more explicit than his predecessors was in asserting the authority of Christ the King in civil affairs. But the whole passage must be read, both by those who maximize its content and those who think his teaching outdated: "It would be a grave error, on the other hand, to say that Christ has no authority whatever in civil affairs, since, by virtue of the absolute empire over all creatures committed to him by the Father all things are in his power. Nevertheless, during his life on earth he refrained from the exercise of such authority, and although he himself disdained to possess or to care for earthly goods, he did not, nor does he today, interfere with those who possess them. 'No earthly crown comes he to take, who heavenly kingdoms doth bestow.' " (See article Judge, Christ as.)

[1]Text of the Encyclical, *AAS* 17 (1925) 593–610; cf. Chamblat, *La Royauté du Christ selon la doctrine catholique,* Paris, 1931; D. Fahey, C.SS.R., *The Kingship of Christ according to the Principles of St. Thomas Aquinas,* Dublin, 1931; *id., The Social Rights of our Divine Lord Jesus Christ,* adapted from French of A. Philippe, C.SS.R., Dublin, 1932; *id., The Kingship of Christ and Organized Naturalism,* 3rd ed., Dublin, 1968; L. Ott, *Fundamentals of Catholic Dogma,* Cork 1955, 180–81; S. Mowinckel, *He that Cometh,* Oxford, 1956; O. Cullmann, "The Kingship of Christ and the Church in the New Testament," in *The Early Church,* London, 1956, 105ff; *id., The Christology of the New Testament,* London, 1959, 220–32; D. M. Stanley, "Kingdom to Church" in *The Apostolic Church in the New Testament,* New York, 1963, 5–37; L. Cerfaux, *Christ in the Theology of St. Paul,* 4th impression, New York, 1966, 464–69; *id.,* "Le titre 'Kyrios' et la dignité royale de Jésus, *RSPT,* 11 (1922) 40–71; 125–53; W. Pannenberg, *Jesus God and Man,* 3rd impression, London, 1973, "Jesus' Kingship," 365–78; A. Michel, *DTC* VIII, 1355–59; M. Lefebvre, *Ils l'ont découronné;* [2]*Op. cit.,* 69, 79; [3]*Op. cit.,* 123; [4]D. M. Stanley, *op. cit.,* 28; [5]*Op. cit.,* 464, 65; [6]*Op. cit.,* 221; [7]IX, 3, ed. K. Lake, 324; ibid., XVII, 3, 336; [8]*Contra secundum Manicheum,* III, *PL* 42, 579; [9]*Summa Theologica,* III, 58, 59; qq.; [10]Tr. Msgr. G. Smith, CTS; [11]*Constitution on the Church,* art. 36.

KNOWLEDGE OF CHRIST, THE

There are certain truths to be taken as established when the question of Christ's knowledge is being considered.[1] He was God and man and cognition appropriate to his divinity and humanity was his. Some writing on his knowledge gives the impression that his divinity was entirely in abeyance when his human cognitive powers were being exercised. As God he was omniscient, so that there are really three aspects to the problem: one immediately settled on is divine knowledge, another on the modes and content of his human knowledge, a third on the inter-relationship between the two. This third point is so perplexing that it is generally avoided.

Until recently the scholastic distinction of threefold knowledge in Christ, acquired, infused, and beatific, was not challenged. As is stated in the article on the Faith of Jesus in the present work, there are three different approaches to the material available in the NT: psychological, logical, and epistemological. These will be used in regard to his human knowledge, which will follow broadly the power of human nature and the life he lived, determined by his time and place and culture, culture in its role as a vehicle of hitherto acquired and transmitted knowledge in every domain then knowable, and in its function of receiving and assimilating new ideas and facts newly happening. This would include, with so much else, the immense religious patrimony of his people (see article Jewishness of Jesus). Even within these clearly ascertainable parameters there is another mysterious element to ponder: the capacity of Jesus, by the sheer force of his individual intellect, to transcend the frontiers of knowledge limiting his contemporaries. Men of genius have often done this. Who will say that he had anything less than genius?

Immediately there may be protest that such a theory bypasses NT testimony. But as this is sometimes interpreted one is left with the impression of an individual intellectually passive and not endowed with very notable mental dynamism: consider the sheer intellectual power of St. Paul, who was privileged to be his disciple and apostle. As R. E. Brown (qv) says: "Scholastics posited special aids to the human nature of Jesus, so that he would know more than other people, e.g., beatific vision, infused knowledge. Current systematic theologians of various tendencies (K. Rahner, B. Lonergan, H. U. von Balthasar, J. Galot) deny the presence of such aids and/or recognize that Jesus did not have unlimited knowledge. Appeal may be made to the teaching of Chalcedon (qv) (*DS* 301 based on Heb 4:15) which made Jesus consubstantial with human beings in all things except sin—note that the exception to his human limitations was sin, not ignorance."[2] Brown quotes St. Cyril of Alexandria (qv): "We have admired his goodness in that for love of us he has not refused to descend to such a low position as to bear all that belongs to our nature, included in which is ignorance."[3] Just what the great Doctor, the "orthodox arch-foe of Nestorianism" (qv) meant by "ignorance" may very well take considerable study of his writings. That Jesus Christ did not have the mental categories, say of Graeco-Roman philosophy, or need to possess mentally all the findings of modern science and technology is "ignorance" of a kind, but not of the kind that would lessen his intellectual stature in the world of his time.

J. Galot (qv), named by Brown, a frequent writer on this theme, did say "faced with the witness of Scripture, the scholastic doctrine of a threefold knowledge, beatific, infused, and acquired in Christ does not appear as arbitrary as it might appear at first sight."[4] Brown, in a reverent study, evaluates the biblical evidence, taking care to insist that the evaluation "does not predetermine the theological interpretation to be drawn from it."[5] He claims that "accepting a limited human knowledge for Jesus does not deny that he was God," which should satisfy systematic theologians, while, for biblical students it would mean "doing justice to passages like Mk 5:30-32; 10:17-18; 13:32; Lk 2:40, 52; Heb 4:15; 5:8-9."[6]

There are very many other problems in this highly sensitive area. Jesus' knowledge of persons would demand a lengthy study. It was marked by compassion, unrivalled in religious founders; but it was utterly penetrating, whether in one to one situations, as with those who sought his healing power, like the centurion, or whom he instructed as the Samaritan woman and Nicodemus, or those who were to condemn him as Pilate; or again with the chosen group of the disciples, notably the Twelve, or the faction that surrounded him as critics.

Above all there is Jesus' knowledge as the bearer and embodiment of divine revelation (qv). He was the "Mediator and the fullness of all revelation." One may approach this most testing of all questions about his knowledge in a general way, insofar as the Christian religion, with its distinctive message, came from him; or one may essay an explanation of how particular truths taken singly, essential to Christian belief, came to him. He spoke with authority, he invoked none but that of God. How came he to such knowledge and such certainty in his possession of it? Among many items that may be taken as tests are the centerpiece of Christian belief, the doctrine of three Persons in God, the reality of the third Person, not only as existing, but as God's self-communication to the followers of Christ, the whole sanctifying system of the Sacraments, with at its center the summit and sublime mystery of the Eucharist. Those who talk of Jesus' knowledge do not enter into this detailed analysis. But this is what must be explained by any theory claiming attention. If this knowledge was not infused, then how is it explainable?

[1]F. Vigue, "Quelques précisions concernant l'objet de la science acquise du Christ," *RSR* 10 (1920) 1–27; J. Lebreton, *Histoire du dogme de la Trinité*, I., Paris, 1927, 559–90; A. Durand, "La science du Christ," *NRT* 71 (1949) 497–503; J. Ternus, "Das Seelenbewustseinleben Jesu," *Chalkedon* III, 81–237; J. Galot, "Science et conscience de Jésus, *NRT* 82 (1960) 113–31; E. Gutwenger, *Bewusstein und Wissen Christi. Eine dogmatische Studie*, Innsbruck, 1960: *id.*, "The Problem of Christ's Knowledge," *Concilium* 11 (1966) 91–105; A. Michel, "Science du Christ," *Ami du Clergé*, 1960, 641–49; *id.*, *DTC* "Science du Christ," XV, 1626–65; K. Rahner, "Dogmatic Considerations on Knowledge and Consciousness in Christ," in *Dogmatic vs Biblical Theology*, ed. H. Vorgrimler, London, 1964, 241–67; H. Riesenfeld, "Observations on the Question of the Self-Consciousness of Jesus, *Svensk Exegetisk Arsbok* 25 (1960) 23–36; Y. Congar, *Jésus-Christ*, Paris, 1965, "Ce que Jésus a appris," 53–70; R. E. Brown, "How Much did Jesus Know?" in *Jesus God and Man*, London, 1967, 39–105; B. Lonergan, *De Verbo Incarnato*, 3rd ed., Rome, 1964, 332–416; articles in a special issue of *Doctor Communis* 38 (1983) 123–411, listed with pagination in "Knowledge of Christ, The," in M. O'Carroll, *Corpus Christi*, Wilmington, 1988, 116f; cf. *ibid.*, 117 for bibl.; G. O'Collins, *Interpreting Jesus*, London, 1983, 190; see articles on Consciousness of Christ, The, "I" of Christ; [2]*NJBC*, 1356; [3]*PG* 75, 369; [4]*Op. cit.*, 131; [5]*Jesus God and Man*, 99; [6]*NJBC*, 1356.

KÜNG, HANS (1928–)

A theologians who from the beginning of his writing career has been given very great publicity, K. came increasingly to the fore with the preliminaries to Vatican II and its history and aftermath.[1] His early intellectual concerns—with the exception of the well-known university dissertation on Barth's (qv) theory of justification—were in the domain of ecclesiology. During the seventies he was mostly interested in Christology, theism, eternal life. His theology of Jesus Christ is found principally in: *The Incarnation of God: An Introduction to Hegel's Theological Thought as Prologomena to a Future Christology,* his most difficult book in his own opinion, first published in Germany in 1970; *On Being a Christian,* 1976; the section on "The God of Jesus Christ," in *Does God Exist? An Answer for Today,* 1978; the section on the Resurrection of Jesus in *Eternal Life,* 1984; some passages in the later works, *Christianity and the World Religions: Paths of Dialogue with Islam, Hinduism, and Buddhism,* 1985; and *Theology for the Third Millennium: An Ecumenical View,* 1990.

K.'s fellow-countryman, Hans Urs von Balthasar (qv) refused offers of university chairs, choosing to remain independent of the academic establishment. K. is firmly attached to Tübingen University, though deprived of his *missio canonica,* after publication of his book on infallibility. K. is a guiding force in *Concilium*; Balthasar, dissatisfied with this review, with others founded the successful rival, *Communio.* K., in his book on Incarnation, expressed admiration for Balthasar's Christology; Balthasar regretted K.'s theological stance.

The Biblical Commission speaks thus of K.: "H. Küng, concerned about the present-day conflict between the Christian religion and other word religions and various forms of humanism, concentrates his study on the *historical existence of the Jew that was Jesus.* He examines the way in which Jesus took upon himself the cause of God and that of humanity; then the sad events that brought him to his death; and finally the mode of life of which he was the promotor and initiator and which does not cease to flow in the Church, thanks to the Holy Spirit. Hence, Christian conduct is seen as a 'radical humanism' that gives human beings real freedom."[2]

K.'s synthesis is contained in *On Being a Christian.* Whether one agrees or disagrees with every constituent part or detail of the system he so skillfully organizes, one must admire the industry that has given such vast research, and the literary skill that has made the results so readable. The Biblical Commission classifies K.'s Christology as "anthropological"; it is "a historical Christology from below" (qv) (see article Methodology) but he is very comprehensive and ranges over a very wide selection of topics which he wants to relate to the historical Jesus and to modern man, for whom he wishes to make faith in him accessible; K. assumes expert knowledge of the contemporary religious situation and the mentality of modern man. In his treatment of every topic he aims at total realism, is the enemy of everything spurious, and is ruthless in exposing what he considers sham reading of Christianity, for example, in the history of Jewish-Christian relations.

K. bases his theses on the older, earlier NT writers, thinking them closer to the historical Jesus; he will not accept the NT data about Jesus linked with reflection on him and on his relation to the OT. In this way his interpretation of the NT may prove to be erroneous. One striking instance is his misleading affirmation that "The Jesus of history was not a priest." "He was an ordinary 'layman' and a priori suspect to the priests as the ringleader of a lay movement from which they dissociated themselves."[3] K. dismisses the teaching of Heb as "post-paschal interpretation." (See article High Priest, Christ the.)

Overall K. is influenced by a methodological principle, that second to the Bible the wealth of human experience in the world in which we live today is a source for Christian theology. There are some references to the Fathers of the Church in his work, but there is nothing like the patristic sustenance which nourished the work of Hans Urs von Balthasar. This leaves the reader at times with the impression that thinking of a serious kind about Christ is of our time solely—"our time" being a dangerous point of reference, for it is a moving entity. Names of recent philosophers like Hegel, of popular figures like Che Guevarra are frequent. So are allusions to the world religions, and to the Reformers, Calvin and Luther; the work is generally amply allusive.

K., in his search for the real Christ, discusses some stereotypes: the Christ of piety, the Christ of dogma, the Christ of the enthusiasts, the Christ of literature, the Christ of myth. These images are his summary formulas of the manifold action of Christ on those who believe in him. It is a restricted list and each item is hastily dealt with. There is, for example, no Christ of the mystics, no Christ of the missionaries, no Christ of the martyrs, and so on. When one seeks to relate great disciples of Christ to the scheme, one is at a loss. How does one classify St. Thomas Aquinas, St. Bernard, St. Teresa of Avila, St. Thomas More? The list is indefinite. Christ in the Eucharist does not draw his interest.

But K., even when not convincing, is stimulating. This is so too with his analysis of the organized forces or dominant thought patterns with which Christ had to contend. As he moves to the conclusion of his lengthy enterprise, having passed in review the mysteries of Christ and given his ideas about the Church, K. interprets Christianity as radical humanism. Though he has considerations on the Holy Spirit, he does not in the decisive events in Christ's life, or in the call to his followers to imitate him in deciding for God and for men, allow any place for the action of the Holy Spirit, as a guide and force in every Christian life. K. set out to propose an answer to secular humanism which has to be Christian humanism. In this age it is truly surprising that he has not a word about charisms.

K. thinks that the teaching of Chalcedon (qv) on the two natures does not meet today's intellectual need. With the increasing attention to history in many disciplines, it may be that those so oriented will seek study and analysis of Chalcedonian thinking, derive help from it. Karl Rahner (qv), who has shown originality in his Christology, found Chalcedon acceptable. "For me the Chalcedon dogma is of an absolute binding dimension."[4] Rahner did not see an "absolute defiance" on K.'s part on the question of whether Jesus was one in essence with the Son of God. He went on: "I have read K.'s book *On Being a Christian* from cover to cover—perhaps there are not so terribly many people who have done that—and I have to confess that I could not discover any absolute defiance against a defined dogma in this Christology. Whether K.'s Christology completely 'includes' all the official teachings of the Church is another question."[5]

Rahner wondered why K. did not state his position thus: " 'Of course I affirm my obligation to the Christological dogmas of Ephesus and Chalcedon. I am just reflecting to the best of my knowledge and in good conscience how to make Christology understandable and express it in a modern perspective.' Then the magisterium could not find fault with him in the Christological question. I do not understand why K. did not simply—if I may say it this way—'parry the thrust' of the Roman congregation."[6]

[1]W. G. Jeanrond, *The Modern Theologians*, I, 164–80; H. Häring and K. J. Kuschel, ed., *Hans Küng: His Work and his Way,* London, 1979; *The Küng Dialogue. Facts. Documents,* United States Catholic Conference, Washington, 1980, esp. 78–143; L. Swidler, ed., *Küng in Conflict,* New York, 1981; R. Nowell, *A Passion for Truth. Hans Küng: A Biography,* London, 1981; Catherine LaCugna, *The Theological Methodology of Hans Küng,* Atlanta, 1982; J. Kiwiet, "Hans Küng," in *Makers of the Modern Theological Mind,* B. L. Patterson, ed., Waco, Texas, 1985; *New Dictionary of Theology,* R. J. Bauckham, 373f; (with reservation) L. Jammarone, *Hans Küng Eretico. Eresie christologiche dell'opera 'Christ Sein,'* Brescia, 1977; cf. *Jésus en débat. Dialogue entre Hans Küng et Pinhas Lapide,* Paris, 1979; cf. L. Renwart, S. J., *NRT* 102 (1980) 747–55; *Contemporary Theologies,* 59–68; [2]Text tr. J. Fitzmyer, S.J., *Scripture and Christology,* London, 1986, 1.1.7.3., p. 12 and cf. commentary by editor, 79, 80; [3]*On Being a Christian,* 178; [4]*Karl Rahner in Dialogue,* Ed. P. Imhof, H. Biallowons, 1986, 249; [5]*Ibid.;* [6]*Ibid.*

L

LAMB OF GOD

Christians are mostly accustomed to think of this title as liturgical, since it figures in the *Gloria* of the Mass, in the pre-Communion prayer and exhortation, and in the Easter Preface,[1] yet the biblical basis of the title is not immediately linked with the liturgy. NT designation of Jesus as Lamb of God is as follows: John the Baptist (qv) so names him, Jn 1:29, 36; 1 Peter does so, 1:19; the title occurs 28 times in Rev; St. Paul comes nearest to a liturgical meaning when he speaks of "Christ, our paschal lamb" (1 Cor 5:7).

Explanation takes account of diverse elements. John the Baptist echoes Is 53:12, "yet he bore the sin of many, and made intercession for the transgressors." The words apply to the Servant of Yahweh. John says: "Behold the Lamb of God who takes away the sin of the world." The Servant is "like a lamb that is led to the slaughter, and like a sheep that before his shearers is dumb." J. Jeremias suggests an explanation: the original Aramaic word, *talya,* means both lamb and slave, and there has been a mistranslation in Jn 1:29, 36.

The other OT theme is one rooted in the mighty saving act of God for his people. Here too we meet an echo of OT language in the NT. "You know," says 1 Pet 1:19, "that you were ransomed from the futile ways inherited from your fathers, not with perishable things like silver and gold but with the precious blood of Christ like that of a *lamb without blemish* or spot." Ex 12:5 reads: "Your lamb shall be *without blemish,* a male a year old." This was part of the prescription which made the blood of the lamb the saving sign for the Jews, as they were about to be delivered from the bondage of Egypt. In time Jewish tradition gave a quasi-redemptive power to the blood of the lamb. As the Passover meal each year commemorated the initial saving event, the Jews experienced a kind of *anamnesis,* an act of divine power in being recalled comes to life in a certain way. The blood marked a moment of destiny, the beginning of their identity as a consecrated people, God's chosen, subject to the Torah.

R. E. Brown agrees that Jn intended the 'Lamb of God' to refer to the Suffering Servant and to the Paschal Lamb. He also thinks that though 1 Pet gives prominence to the theme of the Paschal Lamb, the author of the letter is also conscious of the other idea: "He committed no sin, no guile was found on his lips. When he was reviled, he did not revile in return; when he suffered, he did not threaten; but he trusted to him who judges justly. He himself bore our sins in his body on the tree, that we might die to sin and live to righteousness. By his wounds you have been healed. For you were straying like sheep" (2:22-25). The similarity with Is 53:5-6 is striking: "But he was wounded for our transgressions, he was bruised for our iniquities; upon him was the chastisement that made us whole, and with his stripes we are healed. All we like sheep have gone astray."

Each interpretation, the Servant or the Paschal Lamb, leads us directly to the idea of redemption (see article Redeemer, Christ the). 1 Pet has the notion of ransom, and Is 53: 6 continues from the words quoted to declare: "We have turned every one to his own way; and the Lord has laid on him the iniquity of us all." There is a subtle interplay of the ideas of ransom and substitution or vicarious acceptance; each aspect—and they are not mutually exclusive, on the contrary—will be developed with the passage of time.

[1]Cf. J. Jeremias, "Lamb of God—Servant of God" (original German) *ZNW* 34 (1935) 115–23; *id., TDNT* I, 338–41; V, 702; E. E. May, *"Ecce Agnus Dei." A Philological and Exegetical Approach to Jn 1:29, 36,* Washington, 1947; C. K. Barrett, "The Lamb of God," *NTS* 1 (1954, 55) 210–18; J. Leal, "Exegesis catholica de Agno Dei in ultimis 25 annis, *Verbum Domini* 28 (1950) 98–109; M. E. Boismard, O.P., *Du baptême à Cana,* Paris, 1956, 43–60; I. de la Potterie, S.J., "Ecco l'Agnello di Dio," *BibOr* 1 (1959) 161–69; R. E. Brown, *The Gospel According to John,* Anchor Bible, Garden City, New York, 1966, I, 58–63.

LEO THE GREAT, ST., DOCTOR OF THE CHURCH (d. 461)

With St. Gregory the Great, L. is one of the mighty figures in the early Papacy.[1] He is a capital force in the history of the office, in the establishment of the Roman Petrine claim. Significantly this achievement is intimately linked with his principal doctrinal intervention, his teaching on the essential meaning of the Incarnation, substantially accepted by the Council of Chalcedon (qv) and since then the foundation of Christian theology. The 'Tome' (qv) constitutes L.'s major theological work. The precise composition, the part played by Prosper of Aquitaine in the textual drafting has its interest, but the sources are in L.'s previous writings, principally in the sermons. L. had dealt with the theology of Christ in fifty-four sermons and in four of the great letters.[2] In the edition of the 'Tome' made by C. Silva-Tarouca, the text is numbered in 205 verses. The doctrinal core is contained in verses 54-176, which can be shown to borrow considerably from sermons 21 to 25, *De Nativitate.*

The 'Tome,' which is reproduced in full in the present work, falls into the following sections: Introduction (Eutyches' (qv) disregard of Scripture and Creed in which he shows himself to be *multum imprudens et nimis imperitus*), the origin of the two natures in Christ shown in Creed and Scripture, the co-existence of the two natures of Christ in the unity of Person, the mod of operation of the two natures, the *Communicatio idiomatum* (qv), conclusion (the *imprudentia hominis imperiti,* Eutyches, who was insufficiently censured at the synod of 448).

Here is the charter document of the hypostatic union (qv). L. had his main opponent in mind, Eutyches. In his other writings he defends the divinity of Christ against the Arians, his complete humanity against the Apollinarians and Eutychians. Against those who "fashion for themselves a Christ of false body, who presented in himself nothing solid nor true to the eyes and touch of men; but showed the empty semblance of simulated flesh," that is, the Docetists (qv), he was explicit: "He who is true God is also true man; and there is no deceit in either substance."[3]

L.'s teaching on the two natures, as he applied it, was misunderstood and critics tried to see in his account of the two activities (human and divine) two subjects, practically accusing him of Nestorianism. His words leave no doubt: "He who was made in the form of a slave did not cease to be the form of God, neither is he one (Person) and another, but a single (Person) in both . . . whether in the miracle of power, or in the insults of suffering we believe that both he who is man is God, and he who is God is man."[4] "Let Nestorius (qv) therefore be condemned, who believed that the Blessed Virgin Mary was only the Mother of a man, so that he made one Person of the flesh and another of the Godhead, and did not suppose that there was one Christ in the Word of God and the flesh, but taught that there was one Son of God and one Son of Man, separately and apart from one another."[5]

The human origins of Jesus Christ involved the virginal conception, *virginitas in partu* and perpetual virginity of his Mother: "Sustained by divine power, she conceived as a virgin, brought forth as a virgin and remained a virgin"[6] (see article Birth of Christ). L. thought that the birth of Christ, in comparison with others which he mentions, those of Isaac, Samuel, John the Baptist "surpasses our understanding and exceeds all other instances; nor can it be compared to any other, being unique among them all."[7]

The soteriological aspect, never far from his thought, is apparent in his explanation of the miraculous birth: "For when our Lord Jesus Christ was born as true man, he who never ceased to be true God, he made unto himself the beginning of a new creation, and in the character of his birth gave to the human race a spiritual origin, so that for the sake of removing the contagion of carnal generation, there might be for those who were to be reborn a beginning without the seed of sin."[8]

L. emphasizes the sinlessness of Christ. He goes through the phases of the Passion (qv) with enlightening comments. He saw a certain link between the Nativity and the Resurrection. To this he attached immense importance. The *triumphus victoriae* celebrated at Easter is the Lord's *transitus ad gloriam* and for us the beginning and the pledge of glorification. The Ascension in particular manifests the full splendor of the paschal mystery. Christ's exaltation is the *provectio nostra* and his headship; the *assumptio totius generis humani,* is irreversibly established. L. works out the beneficial effects of Christ's presence in the Church most profoundly; the doctrine of the Church vitalized by Christ is central to his thinking and this he sees in the teaching—the Church as *mater et schola veritatis*—and in Christ's priestly action through the Sacraments: priesthood and sacrifice come from Christ in the Church. In the theory of the papal primacy and even of Church and State, L. saw a Christological aspect.

[1]Sermons and Letters *PL* 54, 55, 56; sermons, *SC* 22, 49, 74, ed., tr. R. Dolle, O.S.B., 1947–73; letters, critical ed., E. Schwartz, *ACO*, II, 4 (1932); cf. P. Kuhn, *Die Christologie Leos des Grossen in systematischer Darstellung,* Wurzburg, 1894; J. Riviere, "La rédemption chez St. Léon le Grand," *RevSR* 9 (1929) 17–42; C. Burgio, Le ragioni dell'incarnazione secondo S. Leone Magno," *Studi Francescani* 37 (1940) 81–94; D. Mozeris, *Doctrina S. Leonis Magni de Christo Restitutore et Sacerdote,* Mundelein, Illinois, 1940; T. Jalland, "Leo as a Theologian, the Doctrine of the Incarnation," *The Life and Times of St. Leo the Great,* ch. 20, 451–68; M. J. Nicolas, "La doctrine christologique de saint Léon le Grand," *RT* 51 (1951) 609–70; C. Lepelley, *Les mystères chrétiens chez St. Léon le Grand,* Diss., Paris, 1955; H. Denis, *La théologie de l'ascension d'après St. Léon le Grand,* Diss., Lyons, 1959; B. Studer, "Consubstantialis Patri—consubstantialis matri. Une antithèse christologique chez Léon le Grand," *REA* 18 (1972) 87–115; J. P. Jossua, *Le Salut, Incarnation ou mystère pascal chez les Pères de l'Eglise de St. Irénée à St. Léon le Grand,* Paris, 1968; P. Galtier, "Saint Cyrille d'Alexandrie et Saint Léon le Grand à Calcédoine," *Chalkedon* I, 345–87; Pius XII, *Sempiternus Rex* (qv); P. Battifol, *DTC* X, 1 (1926) 214–301; Grillmeier, 460–77; [2]*Serm.* 21–38, 52–77; *Epp.* 51, 59, 124, 165; [3]*Serm.* 24, 3; [4]*Serm.* 91, 2; [5]*Epp.* 124, 2; [6]*Serm.* 22, 2; [7]*Serm.* 30, 4.; [8]*Serm.* 27, 2.

LIBERATOR, CHRIST THE

The vast, intense debate which is occasioned by the lively literature on the theology of liberation will probably achieve its proper result when there is full agreement on a Christology of liberation.[1] Towards that end already substantial, impressive effort has been made by theologians of liberation such as Leonardo Boff, Jon Sobrino, and J. L. Segundo. The call of the theologians to the Church asking it to free itself of social and political ties which cramp or even nullify its evangelizing mission has sometimes been misunderstood by those who fail to recognize that liberation theology raises a problem of methodology (qv). Freedom is a Christian and a biblical concept: Moses was God's instrument to set his people free. He was a type of the Savior who proclaimed a charter of freedom: "If you adhere to my teaching, you will truly be my disciples; you will know the truth and the truth will set you free" (Jn 8:31–32). "So if the Son liberates you, then you are truly free" (Jn 8:36). What liberation theology advocates is often political, social, economic freedom, including reform of ecclesiastical structures which seem to compromise the Church in Latin America. Here is the birthplace of the movement; theologians like Gustavo Gutierrez, a founding father, rightly contend that without the experience which is theirs in that area, their problem, methodology, and theory cannot be fully understood.

What is the relation between political, social, economic reform guaranteeing liberation and personal salvation which is essentially religious? It would be imprudent to expect a totally satisfactory answer at once; there is much development of doctrine to take place. Tentatively it may be suggested that the cry of the deprived and oppressed has a theological value. The fact is that the socio-economic world of Latin America was so tightly organized that locked within it Christian ideals declined or perished—while all the time Christian names and symbols were by the proponents of the tyrannical regimes, mostly military, openly, brazenly advertised.

Does the Word of God speak to us out of this social agony? Do the poor, for which liberation theologians advocate a "preferential option," teach us something about Jesus Christ, who defended the poor and exalted the poor in spirit? When the poor are organized in base communities and fully open to the Christian spirit, do we not have an instance of the "sensus fidelium," which Newman championed in his time, which Vatican II endorsed amply? If the "signs of the times" that John XXIII brought back on the theological agenda, point the way to Christ's action in the world, here they must be highly relevant, albeit demanding uncommon discernment. Among the gains to be noted from writers on Christology is the rejection of tension between the Jesus of history and the Christ of faith (see article History and Jesus). The Jesus of history must be studied resolutely as he enlightens us on the actual circumstances of contemporary suffering in his faithful. Vast problems, fully recognized in the ferment of thinking and writing, the occasion of two important Roman documents, the second more sympathetic than the first: *Instruction on Certain Aspects of the Theology of Liberation,* Vatican City, 1984; *Instruction on Christian Freedom and Liberation,* 1986. The theses of a Christology of liberation must stand the criticism, which can be sympathetic, though utterly objective, on, for instance the limits of orthopraxis as norm, the too close assimilation of Christ to our faith, our prayer, our death: his uniqueness must be proclaimed. It existed in a village carpenter's shop and can do so in the depths of the Latin-American agony and splendor.

[1]For bibl., F. P. Vanderhoff, *Bibliography, Latin-American Theology of Liberation,* CIDOC, Doc. I/1 73/398, 838 entries; R. Vekemans, *Bibliography: Church and Liberation, Development and Revolution,* CIDOC, Doc. I/1 73/399; *Bibliografia de la Teologia de la Liberaciòn, Boletin Bibliografico Iberoamericano,* OCSHA, Ciudad Universitaria, Madrid; N. Ormerod, *Contemporary Theologies,* 11 and 12, Gustavo Gutierrez and Leonardo Boff, 129–151 with bibl.; *The Theology of Liberation,* The Ladoc 'Keyhole' Series, Washington; L. Boff, *Jesus Christ, Liberator,*

London, 1985; J. Sobrino, *Christology at the Crossroads,* New York, 1978; J. L. Segundo, *Jesus of Nazareth, Yesterday, Today,* 5 vols., 1984–1987; J. Macquarrie, *Jesus Christ in Modern Thought,* London, 1990, 316–20; M. L. Cook, S.J., "Jesus from the Other Side of History: Christology in Latin America," *ThSt* 44 (1983) 2258–87.

LORD, JESUS AS

The authors of the Septuagint version of the OT used *Kyrios,* Lord, to translate the divine name Yahweh. Scholars have problems in this matter. Probably from within the Hellenistic churches in the early years of Christianity, the title and significance of *Kyrios* was transferred from its secular meaning in Hellenistic civilization—the possessor of power and authority especially over persons and things with the right to dispose of them—and given to Jesus (Rom 10:9; 1 Cor 12:3, esp. Phl 2:11). In Acts 2:36 Peter concludes his account of the resurrection (qv) and exaltation of Jesus with the words, "Let all the house of Israel therefore know assuredly that God has made him both Lord and Christ, this Jesus whom you crucified."

With St. Paul there appears a whole range of functions and activities of Christ directly related to his Lordship: in regard to the apostles (2 Cor 4:5; 1 Cor 3:5; 2 Cor 20:8, 13; 1 Cor 16:7); in regard to his followers and their commitment to him (1 Cor 4:19; 14:37; 2 Cor 8:5; 10:8; Rom 14:8-9). Through his Lordship he is Savior to all, "for everyone who calls on the name (qv) of the Lord will be saved" (Rom 10:13). Paul has subtle variations in his use of the title, the fullness being eventually manifest: in his exalted state Christ is equal to Yahweh, the Eucharist announced his death and anticipates the Parousia (qv); as Lord he has dominion over all who become his *douloi.*

The concept continued in the tradition, though it did not figure centrally in the early Christological controversies, nor in the great scholastic syntheses. It was retained in the liturgy. In the dogmatic definition of the Council of Constantinople, 381, the phrase "Lord and Giver of Life" was applied to the Holy Spirit to signify his divinity. In recent times Fr. Y. Congar entitles a section of his work on Jesus Christ *Le Christ Seigneur;* therein his attention is taken largely by the Church, Christ's headship and effective rule. His summary is in these theses: "The Lordship of Christ is total and absolute; his plenary exercise of it is eschatological; its conclusion is the realization of perfect Monotheism; its economic exercise (i.e., the earthly regime of the Redemption) comprises a duality of domains, the Church and the world, a struggle (resistance of the Powers and the

flesh) and in Christ himself, a priestly manner of the Suffering Servant."[2]

The first formula used as a basis for membership of the World Council of Churches was "a fellowship of churches which accept the Lord Jesus Christ as God and Savior." At the New Delhi meeting in 1961 this was altered to "a fellowship of churches which confess the Lord Jesus Christ as God and Savior, according to the Scriptures, and which seek to fulfill together their common calling to the glory of the One God, Father, Son and Holy Spirit."

[1]W. Bousset, *Kyrios Christos,* Göttingen, 1913, ET recent ed., 1970; E. Lohmeyer, *Christuskult und Kaiserkult,* Tübingen, 1919; id., "Kyrios Jesus, Eine Untersuchung zu Phil 2:5-11," *Sitzungsberichte der Heidelberger Akademie der Wissenschaften,* Philos.-histor. Kl, 1927-28, 4, Heidelberg, 1928; W. Förster, *Herr ist Jesus,* Gütersloh, 1924; id., article "Kyrios," *TDNT,* III, 1038-56; 1081-98; K. Prumm, "Herrscherkult und N.T.," *BB* 9 (1928) 3-25, 129-42, 289-301; E. Peterson, "Die Einholung des Kyrios," *Zeitschrift fur systematische Theologie,* 7 (1929) 682-702; L. Cerfaux, "The Lord," in *Christ in the Theology of St. Paul,* 461-79; id., "Le titre Kyrios et la dignité royale de Jésus," *RSPT* 11 (1922) 40-71; *ibid.,* 12 (1923) 125-53; id., "Kyrios dans les citations pauliniennes de l'Ancien Testament," *ETL* 20 (1943) 5-17; id., "L'Hymne au Christ-Serviteur de Dieu (Phil 2:6-11—Is 52:13 à 53:12) *Miscellanea historica Alberti De Meyer,* Louvain, 1946; id., "Le nom divin Kyrios dans la Bible grecque" and "Adonai Kyrios" in *Recueil Lucien Cerfaux,* I, Louvain, 1954, 113ff; id., "Kyrios," *DBS* V, 200-28; O. Cullmann, *The Christology of the New Testament,* London, 1973, 195-237; id., *The Earlist Christian Confessions,* London, 1966; F. Hahn, *The Titles of Jesus in Christology,* London, 1969, 68-135; D. Murray, *Jesus is Lord,* Dublin, 1973; [2]*Jésus Christ,* Paris, 1965, 191.

LORD OF HISTORY

To those who do not believe in the divinity of Jesus Christ and to those who do not believe in God, it may appear excessive, if not irrelevant, to claim that Jesus is the Lord of History.[1] The thesis has to be set forth with due attention to the variations in religious or non-religious mentality. In its simplest form the title may be presented thus: this man must be considered one of the greatest of all time, by reason of his sublime teaching and his utterly heroic conduct. This uniqueness and excellence give him a lordship of influence, achieved by example, by the intrinsic power of his message to inspire others, especially those cast in a heroic mold.

Of a more particular kind is his relationship with those who give him religious allegiance. They are found broadly in three traditions: Catholic, Orthodox, Protestant. History has been made by all these bodies: Christian civilization, in its different phases, is their achievement, the glory of Byzantium from the fifth to the fifteenth centuries, the High Middle Ages and the Renaissance, the seventeenth century

Spanish Renaissance and the Grand siècle in France contemporaneous with it, the Christian revival after the French Revolution, the twentieth century missionary expansion.

The evidence in these differing ages is to be found in all that comes from human genius, literature, science, the arts, social and political organization. At other times the Lordship of Jesus Christ is manifest in another kind of testimony: the witness of blood. From the victims of the Roman persecutions in the Age of the Catacombs, to those who suffered in the two tyrannies of our century, Marxist (Russia and China and their dependencies) and Nazi (three thousand priests of Polish origin alone), the inner fabric of history has been sustained and strengthened by followers of Christ. The elements which raise history to the heights, heroism, unbreakable human dignity, the splendor and inexhaustible resource of the human person, proclaim the majesty of Jesus Christ.

With so much achieved so far, he may now be entitled the "norm of history." He challenges, through the continuing years, men to match what he has made of man. Where there is unyielding corporate faith in him he bestows on the believers an unrivalled capacity for survival. He exerts his potent influence through mighty personalities like Ambrose of Milan, Bernard of Clairvaux, Francis of Assisi, Ignatius Loyola, Francis Xavier, Teresa of Avila; or again he pervades by his creative power whole communities.

Jesus, Lord of history, has one irreplaceable lever of power: he is master of time, transcendent, capable of carrying forward the central impulse of a great life, beyond the moment of death, not only oriented surely and successfully to the eschatological future, but actively involved in the day to day lives of his faithful. A young Carmelite dies unknown in a remote Normandy town; soon she is intervening in a myriad human lives, from soldiers in the First World trenches to the highest prelate in the Catholic world; and as she comes more and more to the consciousness of the Catholic world, officially sponsored as a teacher and exemplar of true Christian virtue, the Master molds lives at the deepest level. God in history will be dealt with more fully in the author's forthcoming *Gloria Deo*.

[1]Cf. J. (Cardinal) Daniélou, *The Lord of History*, London, 1958; W. Pannenberg, "The Lordship of Jesus Christ," in *Jesus, God and Man*, London, 1968.

LUKE, ST.

What are often called the distinctive characteristics of Lk's gospel relate to Christ.[1] There is more about the Holy Spirit than in either of the other two synoptic gospels (1:15, 35, 41, 67; 2:25, 26, 27; 3:16, 22; 4:1, 14, 18; 10:21; 11:13, 20—where Finger of God means the Spirit; 12:10, 12). The most important instance here is the descent of the Spirit on Mary at the moment of the Incarnation; the relationship with Jesus is plenary, unparalleled. The first mention is about John the Baptist, who also speaks of Jesus baptizing with the Holy Spirit and with fire and, of course, John's whole career is integrated with that of Christ. Simeon receives the Spirit to identify the Lord Christ and give his special message to the parents. Jesus himself is the recipient of the Spirit at his Baptism; he is full of the Holy Spirit, returning to Galilee in the power of the Spirit, claiming that the prophecy of Isaiah on the Spirit is fulfilled in him. He teaches the disciples about the Spirit. The Spirit is then a dominant reality in the consciousness of Christ. (See article Spirit, the Holy.)

Not unconnected with this theme surely is the evangelist's insistence on prayer in the life of Jesus. Like Mt and Mk, he speaks of Jesus praying in Gethsemane (22:41) (see article Agony). But Lk is the only one who tells us that the Lord was praying at the descent of the Spirit after the Baptism (3:21), before he called the Twelve (6:12), before he questioned the disciples and evoked Peter's confession of faith (9:18), as he ascended the mountain of the Transfiguration (9:28), and before he answered the disciples' request to teach them to pray (11:1).

Jesus is, in his social concerns, portrayed by Lk as a friend of the deprived, the marginalized. Lk also emphasizes the prominent place given to women (qv) in the years of Jesus' public ministry. The tenderness of Jesus towards the wayward is a recurring theme: the Son of Man has come to seek and save what is lost (19:10). Jesus is also portrayed as one compassionate towards those who suffer (7:11-17; 13:11-17; 14:1-6; 17:11-19).

Lk seems to depict the events and sayings in the life of Jesus in the light of the Passion and Resurrection (qv). He is the only one of the evangelists who applies to Jesus the prestigious title Lord in its full post-Easter meaning; and he sees Jesus as the Savior. Not only the Savior of his people, but of all mankind, for universalism is a marked feature of Lk's record; the gospel is for all mankind. Among many signs of this all-embracing role for Christ, in the evangelist's view, is the genealogy which begins with Adam, "the Son of God" (3:38); Lk at times sees God and Jesus acting identically.

[1]Cf. biblical commentaries, esp. J. Fitzmyer, S.J., Anchor Bible; R. F. O'Toole, *The Unity of Luke's Theology*, Wilmington, 1984; H. Conzelman, *The Theology of St. Luke*, London, 1960; G. W. H. Lampe, "The Lukan Portrait of Christ," *NTS* 2 (1955–56) 160–75; I. H. Marshall, *Luke, Historian and Theologian*, Exeter,

1970; L. Cerfaux and J. Cambier, *DBS* V, 545–94; S. Kealy, *The Gospel of Luke,* New Jersey, 1979, 86f.

LUX VERITATIS, December 25, 1931

The Encyclical Letter of Pius XI issued to commemorate the fifteenth centenary of the Council of Ephesus.[1] The Pope thus outlines the teaching he proposed to base on the Council: "In the process which the Council of Ephesus followed, in opposing the Nestorian heresy and conducting the Council, three dogmas of the Catholic religion, which we shall treat principally, shine forth with brilliance in the eyes of all; namely, that the person of Jesus Christ is one and divine; that the Blessed Virgin Mary should be acknowledged and venerated by everyone as really and truly the Mother of God; and that when matters of faith or morals are concerned, the Roman Pontiff has from on high an authority which is supreme, above all others and subject to none."

After a rather derogatory sketch of the career of Nestorius (qv) the Pope puts "the principal points of the Nestorian heresy" thus: "This highly elated man, claiming that there were two hypostases, the human of Jesus and the divine of the Word, meeting in one common 'prosopo,' as he termed it, denied the marvelous union of the two natures, which we call hypostatic, and asserted that the only-begotten Word of God was not made man, but was in human flesh only by indwelling, by good pleasure and by virtue of operating in it: that therefore he should be called not God but 'Theophoron' or god-bearer, in much the same manner as prophets or other holy men, owing to the divine grace imparted to them, might be called god-bearing. From these perverse fabrications of Nestorius it was easy to recognize in Christ two persons, one divine, the other human. It followed necessarily that the Blessed Virgin Mary is not truly the Mother of God, *Theotokos,* but Mother rather of the man Christ, *Christotokos,* or at most *Theodoctos,* that is, the recipient of God."

The Pope deals with the relative roles of the Pope of the day, Celestine I (d. 432) and Cyril of Alexandria, and he cites those who subsequently supported the conciliar decrees. He then goes on to "investigate further those points of doctrine which the Ecumenical Council of Ephesus openly professed and sanctioned with its authority by the condemnation of Nestorius." What he rejected is certain "that there is one person in Christ and that divine." Pius quotes the words of Cyril adopted by the Council: "On no account is it lawful to divide our one Lord Jesus Christ into two sons. . . . For Scripture does not say that the Word associated with himself the person of man, but was made flesh. That the Word was made flesh means it communicated like us with flesh and blood. It made our body its own and came forth as man from a woman not losing divinity nor origin from the Father, but in assuming flesh it remained what it was."

Then the Pope gives his own exposition of the doctrine: "We are taught by Sacred Scripture and by divine tradition that the Word of God united himself not to any individual man, already in existence, but that the one and the same Christ is the Word of God dwelling in the bosom of God before all ages, and made man in time. Divinity and humanity in Jesus Christ, Redeemer of the human race, are bound together in the wonderful union which is justly styled hypostatic, and this is proved most clearly in the Holy Writ wherein the one Christ is called not only God and man, but distinctly held also as God and likewise as man, and finally, as man to die, and as God to rise from the dead." The Pope goes on to illustrate how Christ acted through each nature. He shows the harmony of the teaching with the dogma of the Redemption.

"For how could Christ, said to be 'First born of many brethren,' wounded on account of our iniquities, redeem us from the servitude of sin unless, like ourselves, he possessed human nature? In like manner, by what right could he be said to satisfy the justice of the Heavenly Father, outraged by the human race, unless by his divine Person he was able to do so by his immense and infinite dignity?"

The Pope faces a problem sometimes raised about the theology of the Incarnation: if Christ did not have a human personality is he not lacking some perfection of human nature, is he not therefore as man inferior to us? He replies in the words of St. Thomas Aquinas: "Personality belongs to the dignity and perfection of any being insofar as the dignity and perfection of any being require that it should have its own existence as is understood by the term person. It is, however, a greater dignity for anyone to exist in someone of greater dignity than to have one's own existence. Therefore human nature is more dignified in Christ than in us, because in us with our own existence it has its own personality, whereas in Christ it exists in the person of the Word."

The Pope remarks that "with the abandonment of the doctrine of the hypostatic union, on which the dogma of the Incarnation and human Redemption rests and depends, the whole foundation of the Catholic religion falls away in ruin." He also teaches that with the dogma safely established "the entire fabric of mundane things has by the mystery of the Incarnation been invested with a dignity greater than can be imagined, far greater than that to which the work of creation was raised." The Pope speaks of those separated from Rome, recalling his Encyclical *Mortalium animos*. Then he turns to consideration of the other great dogma of Ephesus, the divine motherhood of Mary, adding some considerations on Marian piety and announcing the feast he was instituting, of the divine motherhood.

[1]*AAS* 23 (1931) 493–517.

M

MARGARET MARY ALACOQUE, ST.
(1647–1690)

The life of this Visitandine nun has immense interest for students of religious psychology and of mysticism.[1] We are concerned with her role in stimulating and helping to spread devotion to the Sacred Heart of Jesus Christ. Independently of the results of critical historical research this influence is discernible in a vast literature of popular piety, in the works of theologians, in papal pronouncements such as the Encyclical *Miserentissimus Deus* (qv) of Pius XI and, more nuanced admittedly, in *Haurietis Aquas* (qv) of Pius XII. One overwhelming effect of the saint's charism has been the primacy given in teaching, at every level, to the Heart of Jesus as the symbol of his love. Here the much quoted text is her report of the communication made to her by the Lord in 1675, on a day within the Octave of Corpus Christi, probably June 16: "Behold this Heart which has so love men, that it has spared nothing, to exhausting and consuming itself to testify to this love for them, and in return I receive from most ingratitude, by their irreverence and sacrileges, and by the disregard and coldness they have for me in the sacrament of love. What wounds me still more is that it is hearts consecrated to me who behave like this."[2]

In her letters the saint shows a comprehensive outlook: "I believe that the reason behind our Lord's great desire that especial honor should be paid to his Sacred Heart is his wish to renew in our souls the effects of our redemption. For his Sacred Heart is an inexhaustible spring which has no other purposes than to overflow into hearts which are humble, so that they may be ready and willing to devote their lives to his good will and pleasure. Out of this divine heart three streams gush forth uninterruptedly.

The first stream is one of mercy for sinners to whom it brings in its flow the spirit of contrition and penance. The second stream is one of charity which flows to bring help to all those who are laboring under difficulties and especially to those who are aspiring after perfection, that all may find support in overcoming difficulties. But the third stream flows with love and light to those who are Christ's perfect friends, whom he wishes to bring to complete union with himself, to share with them his own knowledge and commandments, so that they may give themselves up entirely, each in his own way, to enhancing Christ's glory. This divine heart is an ocean full of good things wherein poor souls can cast all their needs; it is an ocean full of joy to drown all our sadness, an ocean of humility to overwhelm our folly, an ocean of mercy for those in distress, an ocean of love in which to submerge our poverty."[3]

The saint was fortunate in her spiritual guide, Blessed Claude de la Colombière of the Society of Jesus. He supported her, having the required spiritual discernment. With such a backing she was able to put forward the special requests made of her by the Sacred Heart: that a feast in honor of his Heart should be instituted, that there should be certain practices of reparation, the Holy Hour and Communion on the first Friday of each month. In 1689 there took place a singular event. Probably on June 17, a date which sound research favors, St. Margaret Mary received an important message for the king of France, Louis XIV. In 1638 his father had consecrated the realm to the Blessed Virgin Mary. Now he was invited to consecrate himself and his court to the divine Heart of Christ, "King of kings and Lord of lords" (Rev 19:16). The king refused the request. Indeed the saint, though supported by Blessed

Claude, did not have much success in her lifetime. The feast was not granted until long after her death; only a few Visitandine monasteries accepted the cult at the time. Blessed Claude was sent elsewhere and the author of the first book on the devotion, a work inspired by St. Margaret Mary's experience, Père Croiset, S.J., a professor in Lyons, suffered the same fate; his book was put on the Index. Rigorists, later Jansenists and Rome, for a long time, distrusted this eminently theological devotion. The Polish hierarchy obtained the feast in 1765; Pius IX in 1856 extended it to the universal Church. Images of the Sacred Heart frowned on for long, were now universally displayed.

With the impetus of the approved feast, and the zeal of the members of the Society of Jesus, named as special promoters of the devotion, a vast new current of spirituality opened. It would profoundly influence the life of the faithful and inspire remarkable personalities. The devotion went into a decline after Vatican II, for no justifiable reason. The tercentenary of the saint's death, and the strong impulse of John Paul II, already felt on his visit to Paray-le-Monial in 1986 will, hopefully, see the revival.

[1]St. Margaret Mary Alacoque, *Letters,* tr. C. H. Herbert, Chicago, 1954; *The Autobiography,* tr. V. Kerns, Westminster, Maryland, 1961; L. Gauthey, *Vie et oeuvres de la Bienheureuse Marguerite Marie Alacoque,* 3rd ed., Paris, 1915, 3 vols.; J. Bainvel, *La dévotion au Sacré Coeur de Jésus, Doctrine, Histoire,* Paris, 1906; *id., DTC* III, 1, 320–351; P. Blanchard, *Ste. Marguerite-Marie. Expérience et doctrine,* Paris, 1961; A. Hamon, *Histoire de la dévotion au Sacré Coeur,* Paris, 1923, I, *Vie de Sainte Marguerite Marie,* also published separately; [2]*Autobiography,* ed. L. Gauthey, II, 103; [3]Repr. for the saint's feast, *The Divine Office,* III, London, 336f.

MARK, ST.

There is a debate, ever since G. Volkmar in the last century, on whether Mark is indebted substantially to Paul (qv); it has been contended that in the gospel we have a narrative rendering of the main Pauline themes. Loisy and Bacon defend the view in more recent times, while A. Schweitzer, P. Wernle and M. Werner stoutly deny it. From a close study of the vocabulary, V. Taylor concludes: "From this list it would be hazardous to infer more than that Mark may have lived in a Pauline environment and possibly knew Romans and 1 Thessalonians." But he goes on: "Mark has doctrinal affinities with Pauline teaching in respect of Christology, soteriology, the universality of salvation, the hardening reprobation of the Jews, and the Law. In Christology the most notable agreement is in the use of the terms Son of God and the Son. This usage, however, is characteristic of primitive Christianity as a whole."[2] The

author points out the differences between Mark's Son of Man (qv) Christology and the Wisdom-Logos Christology of Paul. Mark does not have the Pauline idea of "the image of the invisible God" or show knowledge of pre-existence or kenosis. But Taylor admits: "As regards soteriology the affinities are greater, but Paul uses analogies other than that of a ransom, and is not influenced to the same degree by sacrificial ideas and the idea of the Suffering Servant, while his emphasis on the death of Christ 'for our sins,' and as the commendation of the love of God himself, is less apparent in Mark."[3]

The idea of a "messianic secret" in Mk was propounded in 1901 by W. Wrede. On this theory which has faded considerably, at least from the author's blunt assertion, Jesus did not claim to be the Messiah (qv); he forbade publication of the title. It was the early Jewish Christians who put the idea in circulation. Thus was explained the failure of the Jews of his time to recognize him as Messiah. Certain texts are invoked in support of a certain reticence on the matter (1:34, 44; 3:12; 5:43; 7:36; 8:26, 30; 9:9). The valid explanation is that the idea of Messiah had been altered and there would have been confusion if Jesus accepted the current interpretation of the title.

Taylor's conclusion on the general value of Mk is relevant to our study: "Without this Gospel, which is not only invaluable in itself, but is also one of the most important sources upon which all the Gospels depend, it is impossible to account for the history of primitive Christianity, or to imagine the perils from which it was preserved; for it sets at the center the personality of Jesus himself and his redemptive work for men."[4]

[1]Cf. commentaries on the Gospel, esp. V. Taylor, *The Gospel according to St. Mark,* London, 1952 and subsequent repr., M. J. Lagrange, O.P., *Evangile selon Saint Marc,* Paris, 5th ed., 1929; S. Kealy, *Who Is Jesus of Nazareth* (Mark). New Jersey, 1977; [2]V. Taylor, *op. cit.,* 127; [3]*Ibid.;* [4]*Ibid.,* 149.

MARMION, COLUMBA, O.S.B. (1858–1923)

The significance of Dom Marmion's writings was threefold: this was spirituality with a thoroughly doctrinal core; it was Christocentric, basing the spiritual life immediately on the Person of the Savior, eliminating secondary ideals, programs, and practices which could delay, perhaps indefinitely, response to his direct call; and it was drawn from the pure sources, essentially Sacred Scripture, with noted advertence—for that age—to the Liturgy as an incentive to Christian perfection.[1] Born and educated in Dublin, he first thought God wished him in the secular clergy and after studies in Rome, he was ordained on April 15, 1881. Within a few years he decided to seek entry to the Benedictine Order in Maredsous. After some years in Louvain, and experience in teaching and direction he was elected Abbot of Maredsous. His spiritual lectures were taken down by Dom Raymond Thibaut and signed for publication by himself. The first basic work, *Le Christ, Vie de l'âme* (*Christ the Life of the Soul*), was very widely distributed: by 1974 over 200,000 copies of the French edition were printed, with translations in Italian, Spanish, Portuguese, Dutch, German, Polish, Hungarian, Croatian, Japanese, Arabic, as well as English.

This work was followed by *Christ in his Mysteries* (*Le Christ dans ses mystères*), 1919; *Christ, the Ideal of the Monk* (*Le Christ, idéal du moine*), 1922; *Sponsa Verbi*, 1923. After his death *L'Union à Dieu d'après les lettres de Dom Marmion* appeared, 1941; *Christ, Ideal of the Priest* was based on notes which he had compiled on this subject; *English Letters of Abbot Marmion* appeared in 1962.

---

[1]Cf. R. Thibaut, O.S.B., *Un Maître de la Vie spirituelle, Dom Columba Marmion,* Maredsous, 5th ed., 1953, ET, London, 1932; E. Caronti, "Un grande mistico contemporaneo," *La Scuola Cattolica* 51 (1923) 913-34; P. Nyssens-Braun, *Dom Columba Marmion intime,* Tournai, 1939; B. M. Morineau, *Dom Marmion, Maître de Sagesse,* Paris, 1944; *La Vie Spirituelle,* special issue, January, 1948: *Dom Marmion. Un maître de la vie spirituelle,* contributors: O. Rousseau, D. Buzy, L. Beauduin, O.S.B., E. Boularand, S.J., M. M. Philipon, O.P., I. Ryelandt, O.S.B., B. Capelle, O.S.B.; Monks of Glenstal, ed., *Abbot Marmion. An Irish Tribute,* Cork, 1948; M. M. Philipon, O.P., *La doctrine spirituelle de Dom Marmion,* Paris, 1954, English tr. Westminster, Maryland, 1956; T. Delforge, *Columba Marmion, Serviteur de Dieu,* Maredsous, 1963; *id., DSp* X, 627-30.

MATTHEW, ST.

For Mt, Jesus is the one who fulfills the hope of Israel as formally known in the sacred writings; of his 41 citations from the OT, 21 are shared with Mk and Lk, 20 are proper to his own gospel; "that it might be fulfilled," or some such formula introduces 37 of the citations, and some of these citations have a Matthean reflective application, the work of the writer himself.[1] The whole point is that Jesus brings to a triumphant conclusion all the saving initiate embodied in the old covenant.

Mt is therefore the evangelist of the Messiah. The messianic secret so notable in Mk is not absent but it is not stressed. Jesus from the infancy narrative is presented as a descendent of David, and Joseph, his virginal mother's husband, is a "son of David" (1:20). The messianic credentials were valid and recognizable to the Jews, who, in Mt's opinion, rejected Jesus. They were excluded from the kingdom.

The kingdom is another dominant theme in the gospel: Jn the Baptist announced, "Repent, for the kingdom of heaven is at hand" (3:2). Jesus' words opening his preaching career were identical (4:17). Yet Mt makes it clear that Jesus had a mission exclusively to Israel (10:5, 23; 15:22, 24, 26). But the kingdom was given to the Gentiles because of the Jewish rejection (3:8f; 21:43-46; 23). In the adoration of the Infant Jesus by the Magi, Gentiles, his first worshippers, there is already a strong hint of this opening, for the humble circumstances of his birth seemed to anticipate the future alienation. Jesus respects the law, he fulfills it, he is its fulfillment, and therefore above it, free of any restricting tie.

Jesus is the new and eminently greater Moses. His charter was proclaimed on the mountain, which evokes Sinai—thus Mt in contrast to Lk who puts the meeting taught "on a level place" (Lk 6:17). The "six antitheses" of the Sermon on the Mount (Mt 5:21-48) illustrate the role of new and creative lawgiver, but promulgating his code with the same authority as of old.

---

[1]Cf. commentaries, dictionary articles s.v. Matthew, esp. M. J. Lagrange, *Evangile selon Saint Matthieu,* 7th ed., Paris, 1948; K. Stendahl, *The School of Matthew,* Uppsala, 1954; E. Massaux, *Influence de l'évangile de saint Matthieu sur la littérature chrétienne avant St. Irénée,* Louvain, 1950; R. Stendahl, *The School of St. Matthew,* 2nd ed., Ramsey, NJ, 1990.

MAXIMUS THE CONFESSOR (c. 580-662)

M., from an aristocratic background, with experience in imperial administration, turned to monasticism, eventually became abbot of the monastery of Chrysopolis.[1] Fleeing to Africa to escape from the Persian invasion, he became involved in the opposition to the Monothelite (qv) heresy. He was influential in securing its condemnation by African synods and took part in the Lateran Council in Rome, 649, where he worked to the same end. He was brought to Constantinople to enlist his support for the Typos of Constans II. Refusing to collaborate, he was exiled. Again he was summoned to the imperial city and again refused his assent to what he considered heresy. He was tortured, resisted, was driven into exile to the Caucasus, where his death occurred soon after. His heroic conduct was the outward witness to a powerful theological synthesis.

M. thought that the Incarnation was the purpose of all history, and its inseparable adjunct was *theiosis,* the divinization of man. There is much debate on what he owed to Dionysius the Pseudo-Areopagite, and Dom Polycarp Sherwood has aligned lists of borrowings but they prove to be essentially verbal.[2] The influence of Gregory of Nazianzus (qv) is marked. But M. took up the Alexandrine and Cappadocian traditions and brought to bear on them his own reflection. The idea of divinization was intrinsic to Greek thinking about the Redemption (qv). M., who espoused to thorough-going Christocentrism, saw Jesus Christ as the center, foundation, scope, and synthesis of creation, the goal of all preceding him, and logically for him it followed that the divinization of all others would be through and in Jesus Christ. "This is that great and hidden mystery. This is the blessed Christ." "The Incarnation," says M., "is the great plan of God, mystery manifesting the super-infinite, pre-existing in a manner infinite before the ages (Eph 1:10-11). A plan of which the Word of God himself in his essence, made man, became the messenger (Is 9:6); having himself, if one may so express it, the most interior foundation of the Father's loving-kindness, and having shown in him the purpose through which creatures clearly had a beginning in view of existence. Really through Christ, that is, the mystery of Christ, all the ages and the things in the ages, have taken their beginning of existence and end in Christ. In reality before the ages there had been conceived this union of that which has limit and that which has none, of that subject to measure and that free of it, of that which ends and that without end, of Creator and creation, of stability and movement."[3]

M. was deeply faithful to Chalcedon: "It was in the setting of the economy and not by natural law that the Word came to men in the flesh. Thus Christ is not a compound nature, against the new theory of those who empty the gospel for he exists hypostatically in a way totally independent of the law of compound nature. But he is a compound person who does not comprise a conjoint nature attributed to him by essence. This is truly a paradox: to contemplate a compound person without the nature being attributed to him by its essence."[4]

It is through the Incarnation that the theologian can seize the sense of the entire divine plan. He devotes a whole question (60 of the *Queastiones ad Thalassium*) to an exposition of the truths underlying or flowing from the Petrine text in 1 Pet 20: "He was destined before the foundation of the world but was made manifest at the end of the times for your sake."

M. showed that Christ, by his Incarnation, he who is our Lord and our God, honored our threefold birth: our birth to existence, to well-being, and to eternal being, the first bodily, the second by baptism, the third from the resurrection in which we will be transformed by grace. Each moment has its parallel in the life and glorious existence of Christ.

M. developed two themes of interest: the free consent of Christ's will to the filial attitude which marks the hypostatic character of the Word makes him the Mediator which Adam failed to be; and by recapitulating in himself all the ages, he realizes the unity of all orders of beings. He thus opens the way to filial adoption for those who, renouncing their own wills, decide to follow him and thus is made possible divinization. The image of God according to which man was formed from the beginning, is restored. M. brings the Word nearer to us by adopting the idea of Leontinus of Byzantium on the *enhypostasis*. Like St. John of Damascus (qv), he does so in complete orthodoxy and fidelity to Chalcedon.

[1]Works, *PG* 90, 91; cf P. Sherwood, *An annotated Date-List of the Works of Maximus the Confessor*, Rome, 1952; bibl. *DSp* X 835-47, I. *Dalmais*; critical ed. *Quaestiones ad Thalassium*, CCSG, J. Declerck, with Latin tr. of John Scotus Eriugena, 1982; for newly discovered "Life of Mary," *Maxime le Confesseur, Vie de la Vierge,* tr. M.-J. van Esbroeck, S.J., *CSCO* 479, *Scriptores Iberici* 22; cf. M. O'Carroll, C.S.Sp., "The Life of Mary," *ITQ* 53 (1987) 235-36; Hans Urs von Balthasar, *Kosmische Liturgie,* 2 ed., Einsiedeln, 1961, French tr., 1947; F. M. Lethel, *Théologie de l'agonie du Christ chez saint Maxime,* Institut Catholique, Paris, 1976; J. M. Garrigues, *La charité, avenir divin de l'homme, Maxime le Confesseur,* Paris, 1976; id., "La personne composée du Christ d'après Maxime le Confesseur," *RT* 74 (1974) 181-204; L. Thunberg, *Microcosm and Mediator. The Theological Anthropology of Maximus the Confessor,* Lund, 1965; esp. P. Piret, *Le Christ et la Trinité selon Maxime le Confesseur,* Paris, 1983; esp. F. Heinzer and C. Schönborn (ed.), *Maximus Confessor* (symposium), Fribourg, 1982; M. O'Carroll, *Trinitas*, 160f; id., *Veni Creator Spiritus,* 149f; [2]*DSp* III, 298-300; [3]*Quaestiones ad Thalassium,* 60, *PG* 90, 621 BC; [4]*Ibid.,* 681.

MEDIATOR, CHRIST THE ONE

"For there is one God, and one mediator between God and men, the man Christ Jesus, who gave himself a ransom for all, which was attested in due time (1 Tim 2:5-6)."[1] The idea of mediation is implicit or explicit in most thinking about religion. In practice human beings need to attain the deity or deities in whom they believe, as they hope that benefaction will reach them from on high. It is the function of mediators to answer one need and the other. In many religions priests are the mediators: this would be the raison d'être of the office. The Christian religion rejoices in the perfect fulfillment and exemplar of the mediatorial function. Jesus Christ, true God and true man, by his being and activity, assures the union between God and men. He is the totally proper representative of the deity to humankind, for he is God himself; equally acceptable on behalf of human persons to God since he is fully, perfectly human. His mediatorial office was exercised in his teaching (see article Prophet) as spokesman of the Father, in his priesthood (see article High Priest) which saw its fulfillment in his work as Redeemer (qv), in his prayer (qv), as it will be shown in his function as judge, as it is also in his kingly (qv) prerogative. He shares his power to mediate with his Church, and this is seen especially in the priests of the Church. Vatican II teaches thus: "Partakers of the function of Christ, the sole Mediator (1 Tim 2:5) on their level of ministry, they announce the divine word to all. They exercise this sacred function of Christ most of all in the Eucharistic liturgy or synaxis. There, acting in the person of Christ, and proclaiming his mystery, they join the offering of the faithful to the sacrifice of the Head."[2]

The Pauline text seems exclusive, as do the words of Christ, "no one comes to the Father, but by me" (Jn 14:6), and of Peter, "And there is salvation in no one else, for there is no other name under heaven given among men by which we must be saved" (Acts 4:12).

How then is Christ's mediation shared? As a man he achieved the work of mediation, finally, principally, indispensably. But through divine generosity there is a possible participation in the ongoing working of this mediation, solidarity with Christ which conforms to the law of participation written into the order of nature and of grace. Vatican II, explaining this participation by Our Lady, the one who excelled therein, teaches thus: "For no creature could ever be classed with the Incarnate Word and Redeemer. But, just as the priesthood of Christ is shared in various ways, both by ministers and by the faithful people, and as the one goodness of God is in reality communicated diversely to his creatures, so also the unique mediation of the Redeemer does not exclude but rather gives rise among creatures to a manifold cooperation which is but a sharing in this unique source."[3] This concept harmonizes admirably with the thesis of the absolute universal primacy (qv) of Christ, defended in the present work. The universe was planned and designed to be the glowing home, temple, setting of the God-man; embedded in every important sector was a power, and a capacity to share in his existence, in the mode and degree commensurate with its place in the hierarchy of creation. His mediation was not to be enclosed within his own human nature and existence. All would share in it, benefit by it, its richness thus made manifest and dynamic. Each would see in it an irreplaceable reality, wherein it would be one and self-sufficient and yet open and available to all.

---

[1]Cf. M. J. Scheeben (qv), "Mystical Position and Significance of the God-man as Mediator between the Trinitarian God and the World," in *The Mysteries of Christianity,* English tr., C. Vollert,

St. Louis, London, 1951, Ch. XV, 405-30; Y. Congar, O.P., "Notre Médiateur," in *Jésus Christ,* Paris, 1965, 53-142; M. P. Nilsson, "The High God and the Mediator," *HTR* (1963) 101-20; C. Spicq, *Bauer* II, 569-73; E. Brunner, *The Mediator,* London, 1937; M. Schulze, "Der Mittler," Festschrift, R. Seeberg, Leipzig, 1929, 225-38; J.-H. Nicolas, O.P., "Le Médiateur," *Synthèse Dogmatique,* 1986, 546-58; J. Smith and C. Spicq, *DBS* V, 997-1083.

MERCY OF JESUS, THE

Jesus chose to be publicly associated with sinners: "Now the tax collectors and sinners were all drawing near to hear him. And the Pharisees and the scribes murmured, saying: 'This man receives sinners and eats with them'" (Lk 15:1-2; cp 5:29-30; 7:34; 19:7; Mt 9:10-13; Mk 2:15-17).[1] Jesus went further; he proclaimed it a priority in his mission to seek out and save sinners: "Go and learn what this means, 'I desire mercy and not sacrifice'—Hos 6:6. For I came not to call the righteous, but sinners" (Mt 9:13; Mk 2:17; Lk 5:32, with addition 'to repentance.'). "Just so, I tell you, there will be more joy in heaven over one sinner who repents than over ninety-nine righteous persons who need no repentance" (Lk 15:7). These general principles were amplified pedagogically by the parables of the lost sheep, the lost coin, and the prodigal son.

Jesus showed by his action towards certain individuals that his ideas were to be operative in his lifetime. It was not a policy of deferred absolution after the Paschal Mystery (qv). Whereas the Sacraments would be entrusted to the Church to be administered in the era of the Spirit, with the exception of the Eucharist, which he celebrated so as to institute it, forgiveness of sinners was available during the days of his own life. He used the formula "Your sins are forgiven" in working his miracles (Mt 9:2; Mk 2:5; Lk 5:20). He demonstrated his power of reform in clearcut cases like the Samaritan woman (Jn 4:7-26), and the woman taken in adultery (Jn 8:3-11); sensationally in the rehabilitation of Peter, who had denied him (Jn 21:15-19). For the Samaritan he made the first clear affirmation of his Messiahship (qv) (Jn 4:26); for the woman taken in adultery he made an exception to his general mode of communication, which was oral: he wrote on the ground, in her defense obviously. What did he write? In delicacy towards her accusers he wrote on a surface blown away before long. We do not know what he did write, may conjecture that in some way it embarrassed them. St. Augustine's succinct summary could stand for Jesus and all humankind: *Manent duo, miseria et misericordia.* The Redemption (see article Redeemer) opened divine mercy to sinful humankind. It expanded, made available to the entire human race what he bestowed on needy individuals. Mercy has a cosmic dimension as it achieves a total penetration of the human person. It does not damage freedom, for its effect, which is cleansing and renewal with release of spiritual power restricted by sin, follows only a free act of repentance. Jesus, in exercising mercy set in motion, in each case where his condition was met, an inter-action of divine grace and human aspiration. Vast theological perspectives are opened by acceptance of this divine attribute in Jesus. Through his humanity he channeled the power from the infinitely holy God to souls soiled, infected by sin. But the divine physician is capable of healing and of sharing his healing power. Those who benefit by his compassion and forgiveness with true awareness which is, too, an effect of his mercy, become instruments of his healing power. His headship of the Body (see article Head of the Body) ensures this participation in his power by the members.

Pope John Paul, in the Encyclical, *Dives in misericordia,* November 30, 1980, deals with Christ, the doer and teacher of mercy in part II, 3, with the parable of the Prodigal Son in part IV, 5, with the Paschal Mystery in part V, which ends with reflections on the Mother of Mercy. In the entire Encyclical, the Pope, in keeping with custom in such matters, does not refer to the Polish visionary, the Servant of God, Faustina Kowalska (1905–1938). She is known worldwide as the apostle of divine mercy and she was a religious in the Pope's own diocese of Cracow. The revelations which she received and which have been rigorously examined and approved in the process for her beatification, unfold the inexhaustible depths of the mercy of Jesus Christ.

¹J. Haas, *Die Stellung Jesu zu Sünde und Sünder nach der vier Evangelien,* Fribourg, 1953; Y. Congar, O.P., "La miséricorde, attribut souverain de Dieu," *VS* 196 (1962) 380–95; A. Gouhier, *Pour une métaphysique du pardon,* Paris, 1969; U. Wilckens, "Vergebung für die Sünderin (Lk 7:36-50)," 394–424, K. Ketelge, "Die Vollmacht des Menschensohnes zur SünderVergebung (Mk 2:10)," 205–13, in Paul Hoffmann, ed., *Orientierung an Jesus. Zur Theologie der Synoptiker,* Festschrift Josef Schmid, Freiburg i. B., 1973; P. Fiedler, *Jesus und die Sünder,* Berne, 1976; F. Asensio, *Misericordia et Veritas,* Rome, 1949; V. Tascon, "Jesucristo, sacerdote misericordioso e fiel," *Ciencia Tomista* 100 (1973) 139–90; T. Koehler, S. M., "Miséricorde," *DSp* X, 1313–28, esp. 1319–21; J. Guillet, "Pardon," *DSp* XII, 207–14, esp. 210–14.

MESSIAH, JESUS THE

The word is almost proverbially part of the Jewish ethos. Its meaning, through the passage of generations, is complex.¹ A Jewish scholar, aware of the changes, felt justified in so defining the idea: "The Jewish Messiah is a redeemer strong in physical power and in spirit, who in the final days will bring complete redemption, economic and spiritual, to the Jewish people—and along with this, eternal peace, material prosperity, and ethical perfection to the whole human race. The Jewish Messiah is truly human in origin, of flesh and blood like all mortals. . . . What in essence is the task of the King-Messiah? He redeems Israel from exile and servitude, and he redeems the whole world from oppression, suffering, war, and above all from heathenism and everything which it involves: man's sins both against God and against his fellow man, and particularly the sins of nation against nation."²

The author, Joseph Klausner, in his opinion invites comparison with a recent Jewish scholar, Geza Vermes, who gives more attention to the Dead Sea Scrolls, in which his expertise is recognized. Vermes takes account of the fact that "modern research has tended to blur the traditional Jewish view of the Messiah, as King Messiah, Messiah son of David." He quotes opinions such as that "the word Messiah has no fixed content," or that though the word was connected especially with the expected Son of David, "there still remained a wide variety in details." How then to reach a clear idea of the Messiah as the Jews looked for him? Vermes, by study of the Prayers of Solomon, the *Tefillah,* the Eighteen Benedictions with the Psalms of Solomon, their content compared with a Qumran liturgical blessing and with rabbinic interpretation of the classic Messianic texts like Is 11:1-3, concludes that in the inter-testamental period a man claiming to be 'the Messiah' would have been understood to refer to a divine Redeemer with extraordinary qualities. Vermes shows how speculation in different religious circles in Palestinian Jewry had added to this basic concept, fantastic additions as another author maintains. It remains true that messianic hope was intrinsic to the mental fabric of Judaism, like the covenant notion, and closely linked with it. The earliest phase of Christian belief clung to Jesus as not only a Messiah, but as *the* Messiah, and this attitude persists down to the Second Vatican Council, which speaks of "that messianic people which had for its Head Christ."³ The whole NT supports the view that with the completion of his mission (qv) Jesus appeared as the concentration in reality of the hope on which the generations had lived (cf. Lk 24:25-27; 2 Cor 3:14, 15).

When people enter into this mysterious reality of Jesus as the satisfying epitome and the living fulfillment of a unique history, they meet problems. We hear of the messianic secret, of messianic temptation. He rejects a messianism that would degenerate into mere eating food miraculously provided (Mt 4:4; Lk 4:4), use of the marvelous for its own sake (Mt 4:7; Lk 4:12), world domination (Mt 4:10; Lk 4:8).

In dealing with his attitude toward, even his awareness of his messianic character, we must, as scholars remind us in different ways, bear in mind the contemporary mentality with which he had to contend. His contemporaries would have thought sonship of David central to Messiahship. But this entailed much which he would ultimately have to abandon, especially a political movement to free the country and revive the kingship and a mission bounded by such earthly considerations.

But the particular instances where the title was at issue must be considered. The outstanding incident is Peter's confession, in answer to the question put to the disciples, "But who do you say that I am?," "You are the Christ, the Son of the living God" (Mt 16:16; cp. Mk 8:29; Lk 9:20). In each synoptic report of the incident, those of Mk and Lk shorter than in Mt, the same ending occurs. Mt puts it thus: "Then he strictly charged the disciples to tell no one that he was the Christ" (16:20; Mk 8:30; Lk 9:21). Faced with similar statements implying knowledge of his identity, or people otherwise aware of this knowledge, he imposed silence: on those from whom he cast out demons (Mk 1:25, 34; 3:12); on those whom he healed (Mk 1:44; 5:43; 7:36; 8:26).

Instances of direct appeal to him as "Son of David" are in the context of miracles. The title is known to have a clear messianic connotation from the *Psalms of Solomon,* dated first-century BC, reflecting Jewish mentality of the time: "Behold, O Lord, and raise up unto them their king, the son of David" (cf. Mt 9:27-31; 15:21-28; 20:29-34).[4]

This title, too, is a feature of the popular acclamation he received on his entry to Jerusalem before the Passion (qv): "And the crowds that went before him and that followed him shouted, 'Hosanna to the Son of David! Blessed is he who comes in the name of the Lord! Hosanna in the highest!' " (Mt 21:9; cf. Mk 11:10; Lk 19:38). The author of the gospel has prefaced the whole narrative by the quotation from Zech 9:9, "Tell the daughter of Zion, Behold, your king is coming to you, humble and mounted on an ass, and on a colt, the foal of an ass." Jesus may have meant the messianic prophecy to remind his followers that the kingship to which he looked was one of meekness and humility. Previously when the title "Son of David" was given to him, he did not show signs of positive approval, any more than he accepted an initiative of enthronement during the Galilean ministry (Jn 6:15). Echoes of the acclamation by the crowd are found in the accusation before Pilate (Mk 15:2, 9, 12), and in the words in the *titulus crucis* (Mk 15:26) as in the mockery during the Passion (Mt 27:29, 42). Throughout his career, in glory or humiliation, he retained a certain reserve.

Jesus' discussion with the Pharisees about the Messiah as reported in Mt 22:41-46, is highly enigmatic; in the technical sense the debate took place in Jerusalem, a classic spot for messianic hope: " 'What do you think of the Christ? Whose son is he?' They (the Pharisees) said to him, 'The Son of David.' He said to them, 'How is it then that David, inspired by the Spirit, calls him Lord, saying: "The Lord said to my Lord, sit at my right hand, till I put thy enemies under thy feet"'? If David thus calls him Lord, how is he the son?' And no one was able to answer his word, nor from that day did any one dare to ask him any more questions." Here Jesus was using a literary form, *kidah,* which did not oblige him to reveal his innermost conviction. He was conveying the idea expressed by Paul, in Rom 1:3-4, that the real Messiah is greater than the expected one.

The dialogue with Caiaphas shows how Jesus, in a different way, diverts attention from the Messiah concept to the Son of Man, his preferred title: "And the high priest said to him, 'I adjure you by the living God, tell us if you are the Christ, the Son of God.' Jesus said to him, 'You have said so. But I tell you, hereafter you will see the Son of man seated at the right hand of Power, and coming on the clouds of heaven' " (Mt 26:63-64). Scholars debate the precise meaning of Jesus' reply to the question (cf. Mk 14:61-62; Lk 22:67-70).

Jn presents us with clearer affirmation of Jesus' messianic identity than do the synoptic gospels. Already in chapter 1 we read: "One of the two who had heard John speak, and followed him, was Andrew, Simon Peter's brother. He first found his brother Simon, and said to him, 'We have found the Messiah' (which means Christ)" (Jn 1:40-41). Jesus himself says that he is the Messiah. The Samaritan woman by Jacob's well said to him, "I know that the Messiah is coming (he who is called Christ); when he comes he will show us all things. Jesus said to her, 'I who speak to you am he' " (Jn 4:25-26). Jesus, praying in the presence of the Apostles, said: "This is eternal life: to know thee the one true God and Jesus Christ whom thou hast sent" (Jn 17:3). But Jn has no outright *public* proclamation by Jesus that he is the Messiah.

Things change dramatically with the first generation of Christians, of whom we read in Acts. More striking still is the fact that Peter was the first spokesman on the theme: "Let all the house of Israel therefore know assuredly that God has made him both Lord and Christ, this Jesus whom you crucified" (2:36). This same Peter though complimented during the public ministry, when he confessed that Jesus was the Messiah, was still bound to secrecy and brought back to harsh reality by a forecast of the Passion (Mt 16:17, 20); he was chastised verbally, "Get behind me, Satan," when he tried to deflect Jesus from his Passion (16:23).

That Jesus was the Messiah was a principal theme in the first preaching (Acts 8:5, 9:22; 18:5, 28). Jesus had, during his life, taken to himself the prophecy of the suffering Servant of God (qv). In Acts this is explicitly linked with his Messiahship: "And now, brethren, I know that you acted in ignorance, as also did your rulers. But what God foretold by the mouth of all the prophets, that his Christ should suffer, he thus fulfilled" (3:17-18). Of Paul in the synagogue at Thessalonica, we read: "And Paul went in, as was his custom, and for three weeks he argued with them from the scriptures, explaining and proving that it was necessary for the Christ to suffer and to rise from the dead, and saying, 'This Jesus whom I proclaim to you, is the Christ' " (Acts 17:2-3); to King Agrippa he spoke thus: "To this day I have had the help that comes from God, and so I stand here, testifying both to small and great, saying nothing but what the prophets and Moses said would come to pass: that the Christ must suffer, and that, by being the first to rise from the dead, he would proclaim light both to the people and to the Gentiles" (Acts 26:22-23). In these texts, too, there is a close link between Messiahship and the Resurrection (qv).

"Messiah" cannot be taken in isolation from the other titles which Jesus assumed or accepted, Son of Man, Servant of God, Prophet. If we seek to enter the mysterious manifold world of Jesus' consciousness, we must recognize our own severe limitations, and not overlook any great theme, notably that of the Kingdom of God. By emphasis on this he raised the thoughts of the disciples from earthly kingship (qv) to royalty that is celestial, to which a key is apocalyptic: "The Son of Man will send his angels, and they will gather out of his kingdom all causes of sin and all evildoers, and throw them into the furnace of fire; there men will weep and gnash their teeth" (Mt 13:41; cf. 16:28; 25:31-46). Jesus, as the fulfillment of messianic prophecy and hope, shows that no human language, even inspired, could match or adequately express his sublime power, splendor, and glorious creative mystery. His Messiahship ultimately is unintelligible apart from his eternal divine sonship of the Father in the Holy Spirit.

[1]Cf. J. Drummond, *The Jewish Messiah*, 1877; V. H. Stanton, *The Jewish and Christian Messiah*, 1886; W. Wrede, *Das Messiasgeheimnis in den Evangelien*, 1901; A. Schweitzer, *Das Messianitäts—und Leidensgeheimmis. Eine Skizze des Lebens Jesu*, 1901; E. F. Scott, *The Kingdom of the Messiah*, 1911; W. Bousset, *Kyrios Christos*, ed. 2, 1921; A. Lukyn Williams, *The Hebrew Christian Messiah*, 1916; A. E. J. Rawlinson, *The New Testament Doctrine of the Christ*, 1926; H. J. Ebeling, *Das Messiasgeheimnis und die Botschaft des Marcus-Evangelisten*, 1939; A. G. Herbert, S.S.M., *The Throne of David. A Study of the Fulfillment of the Old Testament in Jesus Christ and his Church*, 1941; H. Gressman, *Der Messias*, 1929; W. Manson, *Jesus the Messiah*, 1943; J. Coppens, ed., *L'attente du Messie*, Bruges, 1954; id., *Le messianisme royal. Son origine. Son développement. Son accomplissement*, Paris, 1968; A. Bentzen, *Messias, Moses Redivivus* (Abhandlungen zur Theologie des Alten und Neuen Testaments, 17, 1948); J. Klausner, *The Messianic Idea in Israel*, London, 1956; S. Mowinckel, *He That Cometh*, London, 1956; V. Taylor, *The Gospel According to St. Mark*, London, 1959, 122-24; id., *The Names of Jesus*, F. Hahn, *The Titles of Jesus in Christology*, London, 1959, 136-239; L. Cerfaux, *Christ in the Theology of St. Paul*, London, 1966, 484-92; C. Duquoc, *Christologie, essai dogmatique*, vol. II, 1972, *Le Messie*; G. Vermes, *Jesus the Jew*, 1973, 129-56; U. B. Muller, *Messias und Menschensohn in Jüdischen Apokalypsen und in der Offenbarung des Johannes*, Gütersloh, 1972; N. A. Dahl, *The Crucified Messiah and Other Essays*, Minneapolis, 1974; H. Cazelles, *Le Messie de la Bible. Christologie de l'Ancien Testament*, Paris, 1978; B. Laurent and F. Refoulé, eds., *Initiation à la pratique de la théologie, Messianisme et Rédemption. Dieu Sauve*, B. Dupuy, 83-127, bibl.; M. G. Cordero, O.P., "El mesianismo dinastico-davidico e el concepto de realeza sacra en el antiguo Oriente," in *De la Torah au Messie, Mélanges H. Cazelles*, Paris, 1981, 263-73; B. Vawter, C.M., *ibid.*, "Realized Messianism," 275-80; esp. A. Gelin, *DBS* V (1957), 1165-1212; [2]J. Klausner, *The Messianic Idea in Israel*, London, 1956, 9; [3]*Constitution on the Church*, art. 9; [4]Cf. O. Cullmann, *The Christology of the NT*,[2] London, 1963, 115.

METHODOLOGY

The one seeking knowledge of Jesus Christ must fix the precise scope of his study, the materials available, and the proper approach to these and adequate use of them. In every element of the program thus outlined there has been much rethinking in recent times. Many factors caused the change. There has been a loosening of the rigidly exclusive confessional compartments, with free movement of ideas between theologians of all the churches; ecumenism was in practice at this level before it was espoused by those in official positions. One result is that Catholic theologians are more sensitive towards the biblical theology of Christ which Protestants investigate and towards the role of the Holy Spirit in Christ and in the Church which is in the focus of Orthodox thought. Another stimulus to rethinking and renewal is the immense advance in the historical sciences, recognition of the need to see doctrinal statements in their true historical setting, not in that of our own time. We live in a historicized world, are conscious of the dynamics of history, obliged to evaluate the legacy of the past objectively.

In searching for a satisfactory, coherent methodology the student is fortunately amply supplied. A great contribution is undoubtedly Walter (now Bishop) Kasper's *Jesus the Christ*, wherein the whole explosion of Christological literature is accurately assessed.[1] The reader will find in the first part of this admirable work, *Jesus Christ Today,* indications of the need for change and the attempted modes of change. Thinking has been influenced by the debate on the Jesus of history and the Christ of faith (see article History and Jesus), by the intellectual revolution inside the Catholic Church since the Second Vatican Council (see article Vatican II), prepared by the epoch-making Encyclical of Pius XII (qv), *Divino Afflante Spiritu.*

Liberation theology (see article Liberator, Jesus as) has prompted much radical reflection. Not only on this movement of thought but on all else in recent times that is relevant to Christology, the reader has a competent guide in John Macquarrie's *Jesus Christ in Modern Thought.*[2] All that is offered by the different schools of thought, by important theologians, is there reported and judged. But in the overall view the way ahead is seen.

The theological giants of our time, Karl Barth and Hans Urs von Balthasar (qqv), saw the necessity to maintain the centrality of Christ in theology. Christ must not become an ideology. It is the Person who must dominate thinking. At certain times effort has been wasted in ideas, theses, and speculation *about* Christ, but not directly related to him. In addition, improved methodology not only in regard to Sacred Scripture, but also Patrology must be rigorously obeyed. The old method of aligning theses supported by biblical texts and patristic quotations, all of which were selected on a priori grounds, is no longer valid or acceptable. What Scripture says must be judged by proper hermeneutics; what the Fathers say must be interpreted by adequate historical scholarship.

The basic statement is that Jesus is the Christ and Christology, no matter how much it may be enriched by a world view, by anthropology, mysticism, or metaphysics, must be founded in Jesus Christ. He is the norm of all that is thought of him, as he is the norm of time and eternity, since he is God. Through his divine nature and the operation of his Spirit he transforms "us" into "me" and "thee." He begins with "me" and "thee" and then comprehends "us," whereas we in our attitudes begin with "us" and painfully reach "me" and "thee." And thus it is too for the theologian of Christ.

When we seek an appropriate methodology we need not discard all that past thinkers have achieved, not all the classical doctrine put together by the Fathers, the Palamite theologians, the great scholastic doctors. It is the best in modern thinking that must be preserved. Certain antinomies have been exaggerated: between the existential and the transcendental, "Christology from above" and "Christology from below" (qqv), between the Jesus of history and the Christ of faith, between kerygma and dogma. The

best Christology will accomplish a higher synthesis from apparently irreducible opposites. This is the unique value and power of Jesus Christ as a subject of intuitive thought and rational process, that he makes this endeavor possible. The theologian must not fail in the sense of mystery. No single individual, no school of thought will exhaust this subject. Christology can assimilate soteriology without dissolution of its identity, as the Church can commit itself to the world's misery without losing its identity. Jesus Christ did so; he still does so through those truly representative of him. The great thinkers, ancient and modern, who guide us, whose thinking stands the test of Vatican II, on Sacred Scripture, Sacred Tradition, and the Teaching Authority as a triple enriching source, will prove either valuably seminal or validly instructive. As W. Kasper says, an important landmark in modern Christology was K. Rahner's (qv) reflection on Chalcedon as end or beginning:[3] a capital moment in dogma challenging a great theologian of our time.

---

[1]1985 ed., 15–61; [2]l.c.; [3]W. Kasper, *op. cit.,* 17, K. Rahner, *Chalkedon,* III, 3–49, ET *Theological Investigations* I, London, 1966; cf. also J. Guitton, *Jesus, The Eternal Dilemma,* London, 1959; D. Lane, ch. VIII, "Reshaping the Christological Dogma," ch. IX, "Relocating the Dogma of the Incarnation," in *The Reality of Jesus,* Dublin, 1975; J. Macquarrie, "Problems of Christology," and "The Prehistory of Christology," in *Jesus Christ in Modern Thought,* London, 1990, 3–47; J. Galot (qv), *Vers une nouvelle Christologie,* Gembloux and Paris, 1971; G. O'Collins, "Preliminaries," *Interpreting Jesus,* London, 1983, 1–34; C. F. D. Moule, *The Origin of Christology,* Cambridge, 1977 (see article Dunn, J. D. G.); J. Bowden, *Jesus, the Unanswerd Questions,* London, 1988.

MIRACLES OF JESUS, THE

Jesus Christ is the greatest miracle in the course of human history.[1] What he was, what he did, how he lived, died, and came back to a new, glorious existence is a totality which strikes a response of wonder that is proper to the miraculous. Whether miracle be understood as an event beyond ordinary laws or as a sign of divine revelation, he preeminently meets the definition. Within the framework of an ordinary, authentic human existence he manifested a transcendental dimension never equalled by another human being. He is more than a sign of God, he is the language, the sacrament of God.

That the miraculous would emanate from him during the years when he assumed and fulfilled his public vocation has in it an inescapable logic. Like produces like. Miraculous beings manifest miraculous phenomena about them. How often this happened we do not know for certain. But the reliable record presents the fact incontrovertibly. First we think of the gospels, which have been subjected to examination bordering on vivisection in modern times, for the most part faithfully, honorably. For very many decades one layer after another in the composition of the sacred texts has been detached and scrutinized. Miracle stories are never missing. Almost one half of Mk's gospel is taken up with such narratives. On the basis of detailed analysis of every item claiming attention, general syntheses are available to guide the curious reader through the intricacies of New Testament scholarship. As with the Resurrection (qv), there has been a massive intellectual concentration on the miracles, for which we must be grateful; multiple challenge has been met. Aggression, scholarly and less so, has been expended on the miracle stories, at times possibly with a hidden agenda: to discredit the miraculous stories would at least serve to raise doubt about the miraculous being, from whom they derive.

From the viewpoint of biblical exegesis and theology the question of miracles has been admirably treated by D. Senior in the *NJBC*. The overall problems, with detailed analysis of the NT miracles of Jesus, are fully considered in R. Latourelle's *The Miracles of Jesus and the Theology of Miracles*. Nineteenth century rationalists assailed the reality of miracles either by attributing the works to the possession by Jesus of natural powers in advance of his time, or by questioning the reality of the special wonderful work accomplished, or again by accusing the NT writers of creating fictional tales to buttress a divine hero image.

More subtly, Form Criticism worked to show the influence of Judaism and Hellenism: these, each in its own way, spoke of wonder-working rabbis or professionals in the Hellenistic world. Pressure was on the first Christian generation to match such performance and they, it is alleged, invented a wonder-working Jesus. R. Bultmann (qv) hardened the rejection, with plausible argument. He distinguished pronouncement miracle stories and miracle stories proper. In the first the miracles were an appendage used solely to give emphasis to the pronouncement and were not to be considered historical. In the miracle stories proper, Bultmann saw a close parallel with similar narratives of achievements by Greek wonderworkers. It has been pointed out that this resemblance was to be expected and proves nothing. The material Bultmann worked on was not sufficiently ample.

If form-critics start from the presupposition that miracles are impossible, their approach is not scientific; it inevitably leads to argument in vicious circles. They show lack of appreciation for a supremely religious body of writing: perhaps, too, an unjustifia-

bly patronizing or condescending attitude towards an alien, antique culture.

We benefit by relaxing the rigid apologetic approach that Catholic theologians used towards miracles. We have to take account of the different view of the world and the forces and laws within it presupposed in the Bible, very different from our conceptions, our certainties about scientific law, though we also do well to remember that what we sometimes call law is but an empirical generalization, statistically established, not yet entirely valid. Miracles in the gospel are called either *dynameis* (things of power) or *erga* (works), or *semeia* (signs). Everything was seen to come from God and the distinction between incidents causing wonder through an unusual concentration of personal magnetism and acts needing a divine intervention may not always be clear in biblical narrative; nor need we classify all miracles as equally important in value, scale of divine power, or social effect. But with such allowance made, we have no right to assume that the great, immediately plainly discernible acts of Jesus Christ in healing, in multiplication of loaves and fishes, in changing water into wine, in bringing the dead back to life, in casting out devils, in mastering the forces of nature, can all be written off because they happened in the first century and we live in the twentieth. Our sense of superiority does not mean that in discerning sickness and health, in identifying the moment of death, these first century historians were ignorant, or the people about whom they were writing backward and deficient in response to life's phases and problems: in some ways they may have been superior to us. R. Latourelle offers the reader a painstaking analysis of every miracle in the gospels, with full scholarly documentation; in face of such erudition and judgment, skepticism has little justification.

There is, with the miracles of Christ, which we learn about centuries after he worked them, and contemporary miracles, analyzed and evaluated with the help of modern science, still a problem of faith. When faith is lacking, people sometimes take refuge in spurious argument, allegedly scientific: invoking the possibility of psychosomatic disease, an area by no means fully explored, but high-sounding, plausibly sophisticated. Better simply to face the challenge to faith and admit incapacity.

This is not to confuse the different kinds of recognition, nor the essential meaning of miracle as a sign of God's power oriented to the life of grace through recognition of Christ as unique Mediator, and commitment to him as Savior. Where the miracles of Christ had a plenary effect, there was an irresistible attraction towards him, and readiness to enter into discipleship. R. Latourelle offers the following definition of a miracle, which he considers based on the essential data of the Scriptures, tradition and the magisterium: "A miracle is a religious wonder that expresses, in the cosmic order (human beings and the universe), a special and utterly free intervention of the God of power and love, who thereby gives human beings a sign of the uninterrupted presence of his word of salvation in the world." If one were to suggest amendment it would perhaps be to add "compassion" to power and love, since miracles so often touch human misery and suffering, and to replace "special" with either "exceptional" or "singular."

[1]Bibl. on miracles: L. Sabourin, *The Divine Miracles Discussed and Defended,* Rome, 1977, 237–71; X. Léon-Dufour, S.J., ed., *Les miracles de Jésus,* Paris, 1977, 375–78; R. Latourelle, S.J., "Miracle," *DSp* X (1979), 1284–86; J. E. Martins Terra, *O Milagre,* Sao Paulo, 1981, 230–51; cf. esp. D. Senior, "The Miracles of Jesus," *NJBC,* 1369–73; esp. R. Latourelle, *The Miracles of Jesus and the Theology of Miracles,* New York, 1988; id., "Miracles," *DSp* X, 1274–86; A. Lefevre, *DBS* V (1957) 1299–1308; J. P. Charlier, "La notion de signe dans le 4e evangile," *RSPT* 49 (1959) 434–448; R. H. Fuller, *Interpreting the Miracles,* London, 1963; C. F. D. Moule, ed., *Miracles,* London, 1965; H. Van der Loos, *The Miracles of Jesus,* Leiden, 1965; L. Sabourin, "The Miracles of Jesus," I, II, III, *BTB* 1 (1971) 59–80; 4 (1974) 115–73; 5 (1975) 146–200; A. Friedrichsen, *The Problem of Miracle in Primitive Christianity,* Minneapolis, 1972; J. Galot, S.J., "Il miracolo, segno di Gesù," *Civiltà Cattolica,* 125 (1974) 131–42; A. George, "Paroles de Jésus sur les miracles (Mt 11:5, 21; 12:27-28)" in *Jésus aux origines de la Christologie,* Gembloux, 1975, 283–301; P. E. Langevin, "La signification du miracle dans le message du Christ," *Science et Esprit* 27 (1975), 161–86; J. Martorell, *Los milagros de Jesus,* Valencia, 1980; G. Blandino, "Miracolo e leggi della natura," *Civiltà Cattolica,* 1982, 224–238; F. J. I. Gonzalez, *Clamor del Reino, Estudio sobre los milagros de Jesus,* Salamanca, 1982; id., "Que pensar de los milagros de Jesus?" *Razon y Fe,* 205 (1982) 479–94; G. Theissen, *Miracle Stories of the Early Christian Tradition,* Edinburgh, 1983; H. C. Kee, *Miracle in the Early Christian World,* London, 1983; T. Penndu, *Les miracles de Jésus, signes du monde nouveau,* Paris, 1985; A. Richardson, *The Miracle Stories of the Gospels,* London, 1941; H. J. Richards, *The Miracles of Jesus: What Really Happened?,* London, 1986; H. C. Kee, *Medicine, Miracle and Magic in New Testament Times,* Cambridge, 1986; H. Hendrickx, *The Miracle Stories: Studies in the Synoptic Gospels,* San Francisco, 1987; [2]*The Miracles,* 276.

MISERENTISSIMUS REDEMPTOR, May 8, 1928
Pius XI's Encyclical on "the duty of honorable reparation, as it is styled, which we all owe to the Most Sacred Heart of Jesus."[1] The Pope attaches very much importance to the revelations of St. Margaret Mary (qv); "when the Jansenist heresy, the most crafty of all heresies, hostile to love and piety towards God, was creeping in and proclaiming that God was not to be loved as a father, but rather to be feared as an implacable judge, the most bountiful Jesus displayed his Most Sacred Heart to the nations as a standard of peace and charity raised aloft, and portending certain victory in the conflict." When he comes to speak of "the act of pious consecration" as "prominent and worthy of mention among the things which specially pertain to the worship of the Most Sacred Heart," he writes: "When our Savior moved not so much by his own rights as by his boundless love for us had taught that most pure disciple of his Heart, Margaret Mary, how much he desired that this duty of devotion should be rendered to him by men, she, herself, with her spiritual director, Claude de la Colombière, was the first of all to render it; as time went on, her example was followed by individuals, then by private families and associations, and finally, even by public officials, States and Kingdoms." Again Pius quoted the memorable words of the Savior to the saint on the subject of his unrequited love, "Behold this Heart which has so loved men . . ." All this contrasts with *Annum Sacrum* (qv) and *Haurietis Aquas* (qv): the first does not mention the already beatified saint; the second is sparing in reference.

The central theme of the Encyclical is reparation to the Sacred Heart, which explains the Pope's reliance on the saint. There is a biblical content in his letter, but little from the Fathers of the Church—just two allusions, one to St. Augustine (qv), the other to St. Cyprian (qv). The duty of reparation for sin, of expiation—the Pope deals at length with the latter—is possible of fulfillment through the condescension of God: "Moreover, this duty of expiation is incumbent on the whole human race, since, as we learn from the Christian faith, after Adam's miserable fall, infected with hereditary guilt, subject to concupiscence, and most wretchedly depraved, it was destined to be thrust into eternal perdition. . . . Indeed, even from the earliest times, men have in a manner recognized the obligation of this common expiation, and led by some natural instinct, have labored to appease God even by public sacrifices. But no created power would have sufficed to expiate the sins of men, had not the son of God assumed human nature in order to redeem it. . . . Yet, though the copious redemption of Christ had abundantly 'forgiven us all offenses,' nevertheless, because of that wonderful dispensation of divine Wisdom, by which what is lacking in the sufferings of Christ for his body, which is the Church, is to be filled up in our flesh, we can add, nay even we are bound to add, our own praises and satisfactions to the praises and satisfactions 'which Christ rendered unto God in the name of sinners.' But we must always remember that the whole virtue of the expiation depends on the one blood sacrifice of Christ, which is renewed without intermission on our altars in an unbloody manner. . . . The more perfectly our oblation and sacrifice correspond with the Lord's sacrifice, that is to say, the more perfectly we immolate our self-love and our desires, and crucify our flesh with that mystic crucifixion, of which the Apostle speaks, the more abundant fruits of the propitiation and expiation shall we reap for ourselves and for others.''

The Pope appeals to the doctrine of the Mystical Body to justify his teaching. Later he emphasizes the importance of the practice he is commending: "And in truth the spirit of expiation or reparation in particular has ever held the foremost place in the worship to be rendered to the Most Sacred Heart of Jesus, and nothing is more in harmony with the origin, character, power, and distinctive practices of this form of devotion, as is proved from the records of history and from custom, as well as from the sacred liturgy, and the acts of the Sovereign Pontiffs.'' The Pope contrasts consecration with expiation thus: "Wherefore, just as consecration professes and strengthens union with Christ, so does expiation begin the same union by wiping away faults, accomplish it by sharing in the sufferings of Christ, consummate it by offering victims for the brethren.''

Pius XI recalls the words of Christ to St. Margaret Mary on his love for men and their ingratitude; he mentions the two forms of piety commended by the Savior, the "Communion of Reparation,'' and the Holy Hour. He speaks of the sins of the world and of the faithful as a reason for increase in reparation; he announced that he was raising the Feast of the Sacred Heart to the rank of a double of the first class, and he prescribed that annually, on this feast, a special, newly drafted 'Act of Reparation to the Most Sacred Heart of Jesus' be recited "in all churches throughout the world.''

---

[1]*AAS* 20 (1928) 165–78.

MISSION OF CHRIST, THE

"But when the fullness of time had come, God sent forth his Son, born of woman, born under the law, to redeem those who were under the law, so that we might receive adoption as sons. And because you are sons, God has sent the Spirit of his Son into our hearts, crying, 'Abba, Father!' '' (Gal 4:4-6). This pithy summary of the plan of salvation and its principal benefit, adoptive divine sonship, reveals that the initiative lies entirely with God. This initiative is seen in the mission of the Son.[1] The mission is occasionally a theme in the synoptics (Mt 15:24; Mk 12:6-11; Lk 4:18; 9:48; 10:16). It is above all in Jn that it is fully developed, related to the very meaning of Christ's human existence, and lifework; it comprehends his teaching and his relationship with his followers. "For God sent his Son into the world, not to condemn the world, but that the world might be saved through him'' (Jn 3:17). "My food is to do the will of him who sent me, and to accomplish his work'' (Jn 4:14). "My teaching is not mine, but his who sent me'' (Jn 7:16). "For I have not spoken on my own authority; the Father who sent me has himself commanded me what to say and what to speak'' (Jn 12:49; cp. 14:24). Our response to Christ, our faith in him is bound up with his mission. "This is the work of God, that you believe in him whom he has sent'' (Jn 6:29; cp. 12:44). The meaning of eternal life is this, "that they know thee the one true God and Jesus Christ whom thou has sent'' (Jn 17:3). The perfect consummation of union between Christ and his disciples will be a proof to the world of his mission.

Just as Christ's mediation (qv) is shared with others, so is his mission: "As the Father has sent me, even so I send you'' (Jn 20:21). We enter into the vast subject of divine missions for a full explanation of the reality. But the understanding of Jesus is powerfully advanced by constant reference to his mission. Hans Urs von Balthasar (qv) has brought this idea forward as is necessary: "Where God says to a spiritual subject who that subject is for him, the eternally abiding and true God; where God says to it in the same breath why it exists—this bestowing on it its divinely attested mission—at that point it can be said of a spiritual subject that it is a person. But that has taken place once, archetypically, in Jesus Christ, who was given his eternal 'definition'—'You are my beloved Son'—when his unique and universal mission was bestowed on him from time immemorial, and with it the most precise knowledge of who he is not only for God, but also from the beginning, with God (Jn 1:1). Yes, it must be said that the combination of an exact definition of the personal uniqueness and the universal meaning of this uniqueness which lies in the mission of Jesus is the incontrovertible expression of his divinity. It is this way because it is a matter of mission, a received divinity, but which then is no contradiction in itself only if it is not merely God's sharing with a creature, but the giving over of divinity to one who is God (*Deum de Deo*). Everything which, beside Jesus, still merits a claim on the title 'person' can raise it only on the basis of a relation to him and derivation from him. There can be no talk about the identity between I and mission, as it exists in Jesus, in regard to any other person; but only of the endowing of their spiritual subjectivity with a part or aspect of his universal mission.''[2]

---

[1]Bibl. for articles on Primacy of Christ, and Redeemer, Christ as; J. Jeremias, "The Mission of Jesus,'' in *New Testament Theol-*

ogy, I, 11, 42–75; see articles, Consciousness of Jesus, "I" of Christ, The; J. Kahl, *Die Sendung Jesu und der Kirche nach dem Johannesevangelium,* St. Augustin-Siedburg, 1967; J. McPolin, S.J, "Mission in the Fourth Gospel," *ITQ* 36 (1969) 113–22; [2]*Theodramatik,* II, 2, 190, tr. *The von Balthasar Reader,* eds., M. Kehland, W. Loser, tr., R. J. Daly, F. Lawrence, 132.

MOLTMANN, JÜRGEN (1926–)

A very powerful force in contemporary theological reflection, M., schooled in personal suffering as a prisoner of war, smarting under the memory of Auschwitz, has followed a path of bright personal illumination which his intelligence and learning have enabled him to discern, and his fluency helped him to share with a very diverse audience.[1] His reputation was first made by the trilogy, *Theology of Hope,* 1967, *The Crucified God,* 1972, *The Church in the Power of the Spirit,* 1975. What he has to say of importance for us in the present work is mostly contained in *The Crucified God,* and in his recently published *The Way of Jesus Christ—Christology in Messianic Dimensions,* 1989, ET, 1990. The latter volume is the third in a new series of what M. calls "contributions" to theological discussion; it was preceded by *The Trinity and the Kingdom of God,* 1980, and *God in Creation,* 1985.

M.'s theology is not easily summarized and the reader is advised to consult M.'s own works. *The Crucified God* was acclaimed as a powerful study of the crucifixion. M.'s position as to methodology is very clearly and emphatically asserted: "The death of Jesus on the cross is the *center* (author's emphasis) of all Christian theology. It is not the only theme of theology, but it is in effect the entry to its problems and answers on earth. All Christian statements about God, about creation, about sin and death have their focal point in the crucified Christ. All Christian statements about history, about the Church, about faith and sanctification, about the future and about hope stem from the crucified Christ. The multiplicity of the New Testament comes together in the event of the crucifixion and resurrection of Jesus and flows out again from it."[2] He goes on to relate the resurrection to his thesis, having apparently realized that it must have an important place. But with a curious reservation: "For cross and resurrection are not facts on the same level; the first expression denotes a historical happening to Jesus, the second an eschatological event. Thus the center is occupied, not by 'cross and resurrection,' but by *the resurrection of the crucified Christ,* which qualifies his death as something that has happened for us, and *the cross of the risen Christ,* which reveals and makes acces-

sible to those who are dying his resurrection from the dead." M. goes on to set forth the anti-Scotist thesis in the narrowest possible fashion (see article on Primacy of Christ): "The incarnation of the Logos is completed on the cross. Jesus is born to face his passion."[3] He labors this point, which is mentioned here because of the importance it has in his thinking.

M. analyzes with great subtlety the Trinitarian involvement in Christ's passion, an insight which deserves consideration. But he links it with his idea, not universally acceptable of a suffering (qv) God. He quotes from *Night* by E. Wiesel, the story of a young Jew hanged in Auschwitz: "As the youth still hung in the noose after a long time, I heard the man call again, 'Where is God now?' And I heard a voice in myself answer, 'Where is he? He is here. He is hanging there on the gallows. . . .' " M.'s comment: "Any other answer would be blasphemy. There cannot be any other Christian answer to this torment. To speak here of a God who could not suffer would make God a demon. To speak here of an absolute God would make God an annihilating nothingness. To speak here of an indifferent God would condemn men to indifference."[4] M.'s conclusions are not cogent, to put it gently. If God cannot suffer because of his impassibility, it is far-fetched to speak of a "demon." There is also a much more damaging question raised: If God is suffering with the victim, why does he, in his infinite mercy, not relieve the sufferer? This is not to deny divine compassion, but to point to an unjustified simplification of the problem of evil. Though M. adheres to his view in his latest work, *The Way of Jesus Christ,* the book is much more comprehensive and links Christology with the great themes of the preceding work, *God in Creation;* he has an enlightening treatment of *The Cosmic Christ.*[5] He can still write: "The theology of surrender is misunderstood and perverted into its very opposite unless it is grasped as being the theology of the pain of God, which means the theology of *the divine co-suffering* or *compassion.*"[6] (Author's italics). He uses the word compassion in a very strict sense to imply actual suffering. The work, as also *The Crucified God,* abounds in passages which combine penetrating insights with immense erudition.

[1]*The Modern Theologians,* I, 293–310, R. Bauckham; *id., Messianic Theology in the Making,* Basingstoke, 1987; M. D. Meeks, *Origins of the Theology of Hope,* Philadelphia, 1974; B. Fernandez Garcia, *Cristo de esperanza, la cristologia escatologica de J. Moltmann,* Salamanca, 1988; H. F. Bergin, O.P., "The Death of Jesus and its Impact on God: Jürgen Moltmann and Edward Schillebeeckx," *ITQ* 52 (1986) 193–211; [2]London, 1974, 204; [3]*Ibid.;* [4]*Op. cit.,* 274; [5]London, 1990, 46–55; [6]*Ibid.,* 178.

MONOPHYSITISM

In the context of Christology, Monophysitism was the denial of two natures in Christ—the human nature was absorbed in the divine.[1] There have been varying forms of it in the history of theology, semantics playing a part. An extreme form was condemned in the person of Eutyches (qv) by the Tome (qv) of St. Leo the Great (qv) and the Council of Chalcedon (qv). A great Father of the eastern Church, St. Severus of Antioch (c. 465–538) has been largely cleared of the charge by a great modern patristic scholar, J. Lebon of Louvain. The attempts to win back Monophysites to orthodoxy, the establishment of churches with the doctrinal allegiance—the Copts and Abyssinians, the Syrian Jacobites and the Armenians—are all matters of church history.

[1]Cf. J. Lebon, *Le Monophysisme Sévérien,* Louvain, 1909; A. A. Luce, *Monophysitism Past and Present. A Study in Christology,* London, 1920; W. A. Wigram, *The Separation of the Monophysites,* London, 1923; W. H. C. Frend, *The Rise of the Monophysite Movement,* Cambridge, 1972; M. Jugie, A. A., *DTC* X, 2 (1929) 2216–51.

MONOTHELITISM

Severus of Antioch (512–518) proposed a very subtle theory about the will and action of Christ: the divine and human natures worked so harmoniously that it was possible to assume that there was one will and one action.[1] A Patriarch of Alexandria, Eulogius (580–607), taught that in Christ there were two wills and two activities. Followers of Severus opposed him, but without the necessary safeguards of orthodoxy. They advocated one sole will in Christ. Thus arose the heresy of Monothelitism, but the origins were complicated by political factors enmeshed with religion. The eastern empire was threatened by Persian and then Mohammedan invasion. Union of all forces was eminently desirable, and in the prevailing situation that meant a coalition of Monophysite adherents with those who had accepted the Chalcedonian dogma.

The important personalities in the ensuing sequence of events were the emperor Heraclius (575–641), who exercised all the powers allowed to emperors in that epoch: Sergius I, Patriarch of Constantinople (610–638), St. Sophronius of Jerusalem (c. 560–638), Pope Honorius I (Pope 625–638), and his successors, and St. Maximus the Confessor (qv). Sergius thought that the Monophysites of Syria and Egypt could be won over by conceding to them that there was but one energy or operation in Christ; results of the first overtures were meager. Heraclius approached Cyrus, Metropolitan of Sebastopolis, who was favorable to the idea of Sergius, and he found Theodore of Pharan in Arabia amenable to the suggestion. Five years later, in 631, Heraclius appointed Cyrus to the influential patriarchate of Alexandria; he was to effect the return of the Monophysites to the Church. The Act of Union (June 3, 633) professed "one Christ and Son, performing things attributable to God and man in one theandric operation."[2] Heraclius also made a treaty of union with the Armenian Church. The basis of the agreements was, therefore, one mode of activity (*mia energia*) in Christ. This could be read in an orthodox sense, meaning that the human and divine wills in Christ acted in total harmony; but it could also be interpreted to signify only one will in Christ.

Sophronius of Jerusalem was the sharp spearhead of opposition. First as monk and then as Patriarch, he argued that the Fathers had spoken of two operations in Christ. He had urged Cyrus not to speak of operations. Sergius, faced with such an opponent, wrote to Honorius. He affirmed his acceptance of the Catholic faith as set forth by Leo I (qv); he had advised Cyrus not to speak of operations; he thought that the problem was to avoid conflict between two wills in Christ, in the moment of the Passion especially. He asked for the Pope's opinion.

With the Pope's reply we enter a thorny area, for in the debate about papal infallibility he became something of a *cause célèbre.* We are concerned with what he said about the problem put to him by Sergius. Honorius did write: "Hence we confess one will of our Lord Jesus Christ also, because surely our nature, not our guilt was assumed by the Godhead, that certainly which was created before sin, not that which was vitiated after the transgression."[3] Use of the words *hen thelema,* "one will" was unfortunate. So was the fact that Honorius lent his authority to a ban on discussion of one or two operations, thus appearing to put truth and error on the same level. It can be argued that the letter was a private communication to a brother bishop and did not have the formulation, nor the solemn phrases that would signify that it was universally binding on the faithful; to realize this, one has but to compare the whole letter with either *Ineffabilis Deus,* December 8, 1854, by which Pius IX defined the dogma of the Immaculate Conception, or *Munificentissimus Deus,* November 1, 1950, by which Pius XII defined the dogma of the Assumption of Our Lady. Honorius, moreover, professed his adherence to the dogmatic statement of Chalcedon (qv); the context within which he saw the whole problem, the possibility of a clash between the divine and human wills, must not be forgotten, though it is deeply regrettable that he could not break out of this narrow context, as it is regrettable that he did not see that, in the evolving situation, a judgment from him on the use of language was, if not imperative, at least highly desirable.

Things did not improve with a second letter sent by Honorius to Sergius. Sophronius had written to the Pope a synodical letter; in it he argued from the difference of the divine and human natures to the existence of distinct operations, though he did not speak of two wills. The reply sent by Honorius to Sophronius has been lost, but we have his missive to Sergius. These words are important: "So far as pertains to ecclesiastical doctrine, what we ought to hold or to preach on account of the simplicity of men and the inextricable ambiguities of questions (which) must be removed . . . is to define not one or two operations in the Mediator of God and of men, but both natures united in one Christ by a natural union, when we should confess those operating (each) with the participation of the other and the operators, both the divine indeed, performing what is of God and the human performing what is of the flesh. . . . Therefore, doing away with the scandal of the new invention, we, when we are explaining should not preach one or two operations, but instead of one operation, which some affirm, we should confess one operator, Christ the Lord, in both natures; and instead of two operations—when the expression of two operations has been done away with—rather of the two natures themselves, that is of divinity and of the flesh assumed, in one Person, the Only-begotten of God the Father unconfusedly, inseparably, and unchangeably performing their proper (works) with us"[4]

The *Ecthesis* of Heraclius, the formulary of belief basic to Monothelitism, hardened this thinking; the document was drafted early in 638 by Sergius, was issued later in the year by the emperor. It forbade talk or teaching "about one or two operations in the divine incarnation of the Lord." It also contained this explicit statement: "Hence, following in all things and in this the Holy Fathers, we confess one will of our Lord Jesus Christ, true God, for never at any time did his body, rationally animated, separately and from its own impulse, perform a natural movement in opposition to the direction of the Word of God personally united to it, but acted when and how and as much as God the Word willed."[5] The *Ecthesis* was accepted by two Councils held at Constantinople in 638 and 639. It was replaced by an imperial edict, issued by Constans II, in 647 or 648, the *Typos*. This forbade any defense of either Monothelite or Dyothelite (i.e, the presence of two wills in Christ) doctrines.

Popes after Honorius affirmed orthodoxy. John IV (640-642) condemned the *Ecthesis*: he regretted the use made of the Honorius letters by Pyrrhus, the new patriarch of Constantinople to support Monothelitism. He explained Honorius' teaching thus: "So, my aforementioned predecessor said concerning the mystery of the incarnation of Christ, that there were not in him, as in us sinners, contrary wills of mind and flesh; and certain ones converting this to their own meaning, suspected that he taught one will of his divinity and humanity which is altogether contrary to the truth . . ."[6] St. Maximus, a formidable opponent of Monothelitism, on the grounds of its repercussion on the dogma of the Redemption (qv), still defended Honorius in a disputation with Pyrrhus, now expatriarch, in July, 645.[7] John IV's successor, Theodore I, excommunicated Paul of Constantinople, because he refused to condemn Monothelitism. The next Pope, St. Martin I (649-653/5) convened a synod in Rome in 649. Present and influential was St. Maximus the Confessor. Canons 10 to 15 were a comprehensive condemnation of Monthelitism; for example 13, "If anyone according to the wicked heretics, contrary to the doctrine of the Fathers, confesses both one will and one operation, although two wills and two operations, divine and human, have been substantially preserved in union in Christ God, and have been piously preached by our holy Fathers, let him be condemned."[8] Martin I and Maximus were seized, taken to Constantinople; when they refused to accept the *Typos* they were horribly tortured and banished to exile. Constans II was assassinated in 668; thereafter the *Typos* lapsed. His successor, Constantine IV (668-685), approved the calling of a Council, Constantinople III (680-681), by Pope Agatho. This council thoroughly condemned Monothelitism: "And so we proclaim two natural wills in him, and two natural operations indivisibly, inconvertibly, inseparably, unfusedly according to the doctrine of the Holy Father, and two natural wills not contrary, God forbid, according as impious heretics have asserted, but the human will following and not resisting or hesitating, but rather even submitting to his divine and omnipotent will. For, it is necessary that the will of the flesh act, but that it be subject to the divine will according to the most wise Athanasius."[9] "(Christ's) human will deified has not been destroyed but, on the contrary, it has been saved."[10] "We confess two natural wills and operations concurring mutually in him for the salvation of the human race."[11]

[1]Cf. J. Chapman, O.S.B., "The Condemnation of Pope Honorius," *Dublin Review* 139 (1906) 129–154; 140 (1907) 42–72; V. Grumel, A. A., "Recherches sur l'histoire du monothélisme," *Echos d'Orient,* 27 (1928) 6–16, 257–77; 28 (1929) 19–34, 158–66, 272–82; 29 (1930) 16–28; E. Caspar, "Lateran Synode," *Zeitschrift für Kirchengeschichte* 51 (1932) 75–137; P. Galtier, S.J., "La

première lettre du Pape Honorius," *Greg* 29 (1948) 42–61; G. Kreuzer, *Die Honoriusfrage im Mittelalter und in der Neuzeit,* Stuttgart, 1975; E. Amann, "Honorius I," *DTC* VII, 1 (1926) 92–132; M. Jugie, "Monothélisme," *DTC* X, 2 (1929) 2307–23; [2]Mansi, 11, 565; [3]*DS* 487; [4]*DS* 488; [5]C. Kirch, *Enchiridion Fontium Historiae Ecclesiasticae Antiquae,* 1947, 1073; [6]*DS* 498; [7]*PG* 91, 327f; [8]*DS* 513; [9]*DS* 556; [10]*Ibid.;* [11]*Ibid.*

MORALITY AND CHRIST

Moral theology as a fixed, self-contained compartment of the whole science has been reviewed and revised in recent times, under pressure from powerful new trends: the search for a positive ideal rather than enumeration of negative precepts; awareness of the claims of personalism and existentialism; revelation of the new dimensions of the human psyche with progress in depth psychology; in Christian theology emphasis on the importance of the biblical approach and attention to the kerygma.

Since the overwhelming meaning of the Christian vocation is a call to live the new life of Christ, an admirable compound of the Johannine and Pauline Christology: "I am the way, the truth and the life" (Jn 14:6); "For me to live is Christ" (Phil 1:21), the challenge to moral theologians was to achieve a synthesis which would keep Christ unmistakably in the focus of thought, and fully meet the demands of rigorous analysis of the moral imperative. Bernard Häring's *The Law of Christ* has met with widespread approval, which may be noted while allowing for further developments. He thus explains his whole three-volume project: "We seek a more complete synthesis in the doctrine of the life in and with Christ (I), in the dialogue of love with God and with our neighbor (II). This dialogue of love with its superabundant endowment and its total commitment continues in the realization of the all-embracing dominion of God's love, a realization of loving dominion in all our spiritual and psycho-physical powers and potentialities in all spheres of life" (III).[1]

The practical problem in every Christian life is to combine in one decision and act maximum response to the call of duty and identification of Christ with duty, thus transforming free act into wholehearted gift. With the grace of Christ which is essentially directed to this achievement, it is for all in substance attainable. For the refinements the individual needs special divine helps available in the gifts of Christ's Spirits. Faith in the primacy (qv) of Christ, in his perfect moral example, is indispensable. A full theory on the subject calls for a study of the mutual harmony of nature and grace, of the Word of God at the origin of all creation, of the Word Incarnate as the Mediator between God and men.

[1]*The Law of Christ,* 3 vols., Westminster, Maryland, 1961; F Bourdeau and A. Danet, *Introduction to the Law of Christ,* Preface by B. Häring, Cork, 1966; G. Gillemain, S.J., *The Primacy of Charity in Moral Theology,* London, 1959; J. C. Ford and G. Kelly, *Contemporary Moral Theology,* 2 vols., Westminster, Maryland, 1958, 1963; B. Häring, C.SS.R., *Towards a Christian Moral Theology,* Notre Dame, Indiana, 1966; *id.,* with Trilhaas, *Sacramentum Mundi* IV (1969) 122–133; G. Grisez, *The Way of the Lord Jesus,* Chicago, 1983, esp. XIX, XXII, XXXV; R. Schackenburg, *The Moral Theology of the New Testament,* London, 1969.

MYSTICI CORPORIS CHRISTI, June 29, 1943

In this Encyclical Pius XII (qv) gives us a Christology in terms of the Church, as Christ's Mystical Body.[1] Briefly recalling the corporate fall in Adam (qv) and corporate redemption (qv) in Christ, he goes on to deal, in part one of the Encyclical, with Christ as the founder of the Body, the Head of the Body (qv), the upholder of the Body, and the Savior of the Body. Part two is devoted to the union of the faithful in and with Christ; and part three is an exhortation to love the Church. Pius XII thus ratified an important work of doctrinal revival, reinstating the Pauline and patristic concept of the Church, which had been a little obscured by emphasis on the institution. He set the seal on an abundant literature, to which great theologians had contributed, notably Emile Mersch, S.J.

On Christ as founder of the Church, Pius first quotes Leo XIII: "The Church, already conceived, was born from the side of the second Adam on the Cross; and it was first clearly manifested to the eyes of men on the solemn day of Pentecost" (*Divinum illud*). The Pope then continues: "The divine Redeemer began to build the mystical temple of his Church when he was preaching and giving his commandments; he completed it when he hung in glory on the Cross; he manifested and promulgated it by the visible mission of the Paraclete, the Holy Spirit, upon his disciples." The different ideas in this statement are then developed, and the Pope is particularly ample on the theme of Redemption.

Pius develops a number of arguments to show why Christ is the Head of the Body: because of his preeminence; because he rules the Church—a) by invisible and extraordinary government, b) by visible and ordinary government, in the universal Church through the Roman Pontiff, in each diocese through the bishops; because Christ and his Body need each other; by reason of the likeness between Christ and his members; by reason of his fullness; by reason of his dynamic influence, as the source of light and of holiness.

Treating of Christ as upholder of the Body, the Pope shows how the Church is under Christ by reason of her juridical mission, and of her supernatural life. The Church, he further teaches, is animated by the Spirit of Christ, who is the soul of the Body; here, too, the Pope quotes his predecessor, Leo XIII, and during his pontificate the idea had been very much expounded by the Jesuit professor in the Gregorian University, Fr. Sebastian Tromp who is thought to have prepared a draft of the Encyclical. After dealing with Christ as Savior of the Body, the Pope gives some general considerations on the meaning of the Mystical Body, on certain conclusions which follow therefrom and on errors occasionally found on the matter.

On the theme of the union of the faithful with Christ, Pius expounds sensitively the nature of Christ's indwelling in us through the Spirit, relating thereto the indwelling of the Holy Trinity and the Eucharist. He recalls certain errors on this subject and goes on to the exhortation to love the Church in a meaningful way, to see Christ in the Church; forced conversion is condemned and there are words of encouragement for Christian reunion and for the rulers of states in their relations with the Church. The epilogue is a concise summary of Pius XII's teaching on Mary, Mother of all the members of Christ "to whose Immaculate Heart he had trustingly consecrated all men."

[1]Text of the Encyclical, *AAS* 35 (1943), 193–248, text used *CTS*; cf. R. Brunet, L'Enseignement de *Mystici Corporis*, *DSp* 11, 2398–2403.

MYSTICS, CHRIST OF THE

Jesus Christ is known to us, as he lived on earth, from the works of the NT, and the immediate reliable tradition stemming from the first Christian community.[1] On the data thus available the reflection of great Christian minds, spurred by strong faith and ardent love for Christ and for his members, has gone on incessantly in age after age, each theologian working with his own mental categories. The methodology (qv) seems to prescind entirely from study of Christ as he is at present. There is, of course, recognition of all that his resurrection means, consciousness of a vague enough reality at times. Is there no means of knowing how Jesus Christ lives, acts, thinks, feels, decides, endures, waits, chooses, punishes, rewards, rejects, welcomes, postpones, advances, in all the centuries between Pentecost and the Parousia? Must all, faithful, theologians, teachers, face a blank curtain stretching indefinitely on and on?

The obvious answer is that, through faith, Christ's members know him in his Church; they meet him in the Body of which he is the Head, in its sacramental life. Is there no other medium by which he communicates himself? The great mystics have the answer; but how sure can we be of their accuracy in receiving knowledge from him and in transmitting it to us? There is an immense field here to be studied scientifically. Theologians recognized as Doctors of the Church, such as St. Gregory of Nyssa and St. Bonaventure (qqv), the two women Doctors, Catherine of Siena and Teresa of Avila, are outstanding among a vast company admitted to special intimacy with the Lord. In many cases we are dealing with strong personalities, individuals endowed with gifts of mind and heart which won recognition from their contemporaries, and had in the life of the Church a profound and enduring impact.

The phenomenon of mysticism, studied by people as far apart as Evelyn Underhill and Joseph Maréchal, will persist in the Church of Christ. The spiritual literature, especially the spiritual biography, of the present age is ample evidence of the fact. When Hans Urs von Balthasar (qv) insists that his work, especially his writing, must never be dissociated from the influence of Adrienne von Speyr, he is indirectly informing us of what Catholic thought owes to this great mystic. Her own writings, as his, afford a striking example, yet to be fully explored, of how the authentic mystic sense operates, not in any way to the detriment of true scholarship, but rather as a stimulus to its expansion and accuracy.

Certain aspects of the mystery of Christ have been brought to the forefront of theological inquiry by mystics. The starting-point was with them; biblical, patristic, and systematic theologians entered the field later. The highly gifted, cultured mystics of Helfta and St. Margaret Mary Alacoque had this role in the theological development of the doctrine of the Sacred Heart of Jesus. When Marian theology was at its lowest ebb, with Marian piety thereby impoverished, in the early decades of the nineteenth century, the revival did not come from the schools of theology; it was set in motion by a charismatic event in the life of St. Catherine Labouré, the hidden apostle of the Miraculous Medal.

Great mystics have marked turning-points in the life of the Church. Witness the role of Blessed Mary of the Incarnation, Mme. Acarie (1566–1618) in seventeenth-century France, or her namesake, Blessed Mary of the Incarnation, Mme. Guyard in Quebec (1599–1672), a lifetime later. When these privileged souls, advancing to perfection by the help of God's special grace, reach the summit, they are given a degree of intimacy with the Lord which has been designated Spiritual Marriage. St. John of the Cross speaks thus of this state: "It has remained now, for the said Spiritual Marriage to be made between the soul aforementioned and the Son of God. This is without comparison far greater than the Spiritual Betrothal because it is a total transformation in the Beloved, wherein on either side there is made surrender by total possession of the one to the other with a certain consummation of the union of love, wherein the soul is made divine and becomes God by participation, insofar as may be in this life."[2] Blessed Mary of the Incarnation (of Canada) writes thus of the same reality: "Divine matrimony is the most sublime of all states, God takes possession of the soul in such a way that he becomes the very basis of its substance, and what transpires there is so subtle and divine that it is impossible to describe it. It is a permanent state in which the soul lives peacefully and tranquilly in perfect union with God. Its sighs and longings are for the Beloved, in a state free from every admixture as far as possible in this life. In these sighs the soul speaks to him without effort of his mysteries and of all that it desires."[3]

St. John of the Cross, again on the divine communication: "In this high state of the Spiritual Marriage the Spouse reveals his wondrous secrets to the soul, as to his faithful consort, with great readiness and frequency, for true and perfect love can keep nothing hidden from the loved person. He communicates principally to it sweet mysteries concerning his Incarnation and the ways and manners of human redemption, which is one of the highest works of God, and is thus most delectable to the soul."[4]

We have not to analyze the phases and fruits of this mystical union, the access of souls so privileged to the inner Trinitarian life of God. We have to focus on the added dimension of life which seems their proper endowment. "The activity which such souls manifest is infinite and truly divine," says the Spanish authority on mysticism. One such soul is sometimes able in a few years' time to effect a general reform, as we see in the case of St. Bernard, St. Dominic, St. Francis, St. Hyacinth, St. Anthony of Padua, St. Vincent Ferrer. The author gives still more

attention to St. Catherine of Siena and St. Teresa of Avila, and their achievements in the life of the Church. We have here something of the robustness which Henri Bergson was surprised and cheered to find in the great mystics.

We still await a full satisfactory account of the mystical endowment of one of the greatest mystics of all time, St. Paul. A more perfect, succinct definition of the Spiritual Marriage could not be given than Paul's words: "I have been crucified with Christ; it is no longer I who live, but Christ who lives in me; and the life I now live in the flesh I live by faith in the Son of God who loved me and gave himself for me" (Gal 2:20). Paul and all the great known mystics are so identified with Christ that through them Christ speaks to us. It is something more than Christ's voice and action through the Church, his Mystical Body. He lives in the Body, acts through it, influences thus the life of mankind. But that is corporate, mediated, influenced, delayed, diminished, or flawed, possibly by the weakness of the institutional Church at one time or place. Through the mystics he seems to act almost directly, unfettered by any personal defect, the Christ of the gospels come to life, charismatic in some instances, sheer compassion in others, unpredictable, boundless in the scope of his beneficence, sensitively caring and always respectful in his dealings with persons, forgiving the repentant; one who encourages, heals wounded spirits and stricken bodies, clearly opens the path to faith and hope and love.

[1]Cf. J. Maréchal, S.J., *Etudes sur la psychologie des mystiques,* 2 vol., Louvain, 1924, 1937; English tr. I, 1924; esp. J. G. Arintero, O.P., *The Mystical Evolution in the Development and Vitality of the Church,* 2 vol., tr. from Spanish by J. Aumann, O.P., Rockford, Illinois, 1949, 1951, reissue, Tan Books, 1978; A. Fonck, "Mystique (Théologie)," *DTC* X, 2, 1929, 2559–2674; T. Corbishley, S.J., *NCE,* X (1967) 175–79; esp. *DSp,* X, 1889–1984, A. Solignac, J. Lopez Gay, A. Delbarre, P. Adnès, P. Agaesse, M. Sales; E. Underhill, "Mysticism and Christology," in *The Mystic Way,* London, 1913, 73–156; see articles on Origen; Marmion, Columba; de Bérulle, Pierre; de John of the Cross; Von Speyr, Adrienne, Vassula Ryden; [2]Apud J. G. Arintero, O.P., *The Mystical Evolution,* Rockford, Illinois, 1978, 220; [3]*Ibid.,* 222f.; [4]*Ibid.,* 223, n. 68; [5]*Ibid.,* 230.

N

NAME OF JESUS, THE HOLY

There are over a hundred direct or indirect references in the NT to the name of Jesus.[1] This impressive fact must be understood in the light of biblical usage. A name had deep significance, evoked the mystery of the one who bore it, could stand for him, enshrined his identity, was, in the case of Yahweh, the key to his power. All this was uniquely realized in Jesus. His name was declared by divine revelation: "She (Mary) will bear a son and you shall call his name Jesus, for he will save his people from their sins" (Mt 1:21). "And behold, you will conceive in your womb and bear a son, and you shall call his name Jesus" (Lk 1:31).

This name he bore through the hidden years, with no public advertence to it that we know of. When he entered public life his name, for many reasons, became a focus of interest, a source of power, a total innovation in nomenclature; it has remained a continuing creative factor in personal and collective human thought; it seems to have meaning in depth upon depth, enshrines not only the human earthly and the heavenly life of its original bearer, but the destinies of countless individuals who have taken it into their lives, invested it with unique motivation and dynamism. In a profound way Jesus, by his name, adds a mysterious dimension to every name borne by one who is given to him.

Its mysterious power was manifest from the beginning. It had supernatural force. When the seventy-two disciples returned to Jesus, after the mission entrusted to them, they said with joy, "Lord, even the demons are subject to us in your name" (Lk 10:17). The deutero-canonical appendix to Mk reports the word of Jesus: "In my name they will cast out demons" (16:17). Among the rejected of whom the Master speaks in Mt 7:22, we note those who will say to him: "Lord, Lord, did we not prophesy in your name, and cast out demons in your name, and do many mighty works in your name?" We read of an exorcist using the name of Jesus to cast out demons: "Teacher, we saw a man casting out demons in your name, and we forbade him, because he was not following us." Jesus' reply was "Do not forbid him; for no one who does a mighty work in my name will be able soon after to speak evil of me" (Mt 9:38-39).

Acts, on the other hand, narrated an incident wherein Jewish exorcists used a formula, "I adjure you by the Jesus whom Paul preaches," but with no effect: the demon answered sulkily and overpowered "the seven sons of a Jewish high priest named Sceva," who fled in terror. The coda is revealing: "And this became known to all residents of Ephesus, both Jews and Greeks; and fear fell upon them all and the name of the Lord Jesus was extolled" (Acts 19:13, 17). Authorized used of the name worked miracles. Peter, at the Beautiful Gate of the Temple, healed the lame man with these words: "I have no silver and gold, but I give you what I have; in the name of Jesus Christ of Nazareth, walk" (Acts 3:6). Paul cast out a demon from the slave girl with a spirit of divination: "I charge you in the name of Jesus Christ to come out of her" (Acts 16:18). Or again the name may be mentioned, with the desired result: "Aeneas," said Peter to a man who had been bedridden for eight years, "Jesus Christ heals you; rise and make your bed" (Acts 9:34).

The Apostles summoned to account for their action were asked: "By what power or by what name did you do this?" "Then Peter, filled with the Holy Spirit, said to them, 'Rulers of the people and elders, if we are being examined today concerning a good deed done to a cripple, by what means this man has been healed, be it known to you all, and to all the people of Israel, that by the name of Jesus Christ of Nazareth, whom you crucified, whom God raised from the dead, by him this man is standing before you all' " (Acts 4:8-10). The rulers and elders decided "to warn them to speak no more to anyone in this name." "So they called them and charged them not to speak or teach at all in the name of Jesus" (4:17-18). The Apostles and their friends prayed, ending "while thou stretchest out thy hand to heal, and signs and wonders are performed through the name of thy holy servant Jesus" (4:30). Their meeting place was shaken "and they were all filled with the Holy Spirit and spoke the word of God with boldness" (4:31). The Spirit was especially with those who invoked the name of Jesus.

The NT hymns deal with the praise of Jesus remarkably. But first Heb should be noted: "When he had made purification for sins, he sat down at the right hand of the Majesty on high, having become as much superior to angels as the name he had obtained is more excellent than theirs" (Heb 1:3-4); and Rev: "Then I saw the heaven opened, and behold, a white horse! He who sat upon it is called Faithful and True, and in righteousness he judges and makes war. His eyes are like a flame of fire, and on his head are many diadems; and he has a name inscribed which no one knows but himself" (Rev 19:11-12).

The hymn, Phil 2:6-11, has this passage on the name of Jesus: "Therefore God has highly exalted him and bestowed on him the name which is above every name, that at the name of Jesus every knee should bow, in heaven and on earth and under the earth, and every tongue confess that Jesus Christ is Lord, to the glory of God the Father" (Phil 2:9-11). L. Cerfaux comments that to interpret this mysterious attribution one must bear in mind that the name is a kind of personification, summing up the whole nature of a being with its powers and functions, and the name above all names means the mysterious name that denotes the essence of the divine being. His interpretation: "Here we have acclamation, with *kyrios* as the principal word indicating Christ's special dignity. But the construction of the sentence makes it unlikely that *Kyrios* is the name above every other name. If the final acclamation is not to be a mere tautology, the name of Jesus must denote some dignity which provides the reason for adoring him and confessing his sovereignty. The name above every name is the basis of this sovereignty, and it cannot be *Kyrios* because *Kyrios* expresses precisely the lordship of Christ. One has to look further than the title *Kyrios* to a deeper reality, an inaccessible, unspeakable name. We may say that *Kyrios,* if used as a

proper name, corresponds to it, in that it denotes Christ's domination."[2]

St. Peter proclaimed salvation in the name of Jesus: "And there is salvation in no one else, for there is no other name under heaven given among men by which we must be saved" (Acts 4:12). This echoes the word of Jesus on the evening of Easter Sunday: "Thus it is written that the Christ should suffer and on the third day rise from the dead, and repentance and forgiveness of sins should be preached in his name to all nations, beginning from Jerusalem" (Lk 24:46-47). An echo, too, of Mt's quotation of Is 42:1-4, with this ending, "And in his name will the Gentiles hope . . ." (Mt 12:21). Hence the Apostles preached the name of Jesus: "To him all the prophets bear witness that every one who believes in him receives forgiveness of sins through his name" (Acts 10:43). The custom was to add that Jesus was the Christ or the Son of God: "And in the synagogues immediately he (Paul) proclaimed Jesus, saying, 'He is the Son of God' " (Acts 9:20). This goes before "how at Damascus he had preached boldly in the name of Jesus" (9:28). Acts also speaks thus of Paul: "But the Lord said to him (Ananias), 'Go, for he is a chosen instrument of mine to carry my name before the Gentiles and kings and the sons of Israel; for I will show him how much he must suffer for the sake of my name" (Acts 9:15-16). Paul himself, in his Epistle to the Romans, speaks thus, "Jesus Christ our Lord, through whom we have received grace and apostleship to bring about the obedience of faith for the sake of his name among all the nations" (Rom 1:5). Likewise, Philip led the Samaritans to baptism "as he preached good news about the kingdom and the name of Jesus Christ" (Acts 8:12).

Belief is to be in the name of Jesus with all it comprises, his resurrection, his elevation to the post of Lord. This is already clear in Jn: "He who does not believe is condemned already, because he has not believed in the name of the only Son of God" (3:18). "And this is his commandment, that we should believe in the name of his Son Jesus Christ and love one another, just as he has commanded us" (1 Jn 3:23). "I write this to you who believe in the name of the Son of God, that you may know that you have eternal life" (1 Jn 5:13). "Now Jesus did many other signs in the presence of the disciples, which are not written in this book; but these are written that you may believe that Jesus is the Christ, the Son of God, and that believing you may have life in his name" (Jn 20:30-31). The prologue to the gospel says: "But to all who received him, who believed in his name, he gave power to become children of God" (1:12). There is here a textual problem about the final pertinent words, which several of the Fathers omit, an omission variously explained, one commentator suggesting that the words were added under the influence of 1 Jn 5:13.

The theme of suffering for the name is an interesting sequel to belief. Jesus urges his disciples to surrender everything for his name's sake: "And everyone who has left houses or brothers or sisters or father or mother or children or lands, for my name's sake, will receive a hundred-fold, and inherit eternal life" (Mt 19:29). Mk 10:29 has "for my sake and for the gospel" instead of "for my name's sake," which indicates that the name is identified with the individual and his life work. Rev also abounds in use of the name in the sense of endurance, or suffering for it, a lesson inculcated in such texts as these: "and you will be hated by all for my name's sake" (Mk 13:13 par, cf. also Lk 21:12; Mt 24:9).

There are finally exhortations concerning the name, which are of immense importance. Reunion in the name of Jesus will be especially blessed: "For where two or three are gathered in my name, there I am in the midst of them" (Mt 18:20). Such a gathering must be fully meaningful in terms of Jesus, preferably of his Lordship, which is confessed in the manner of the early Christians. One can imagine so many cells animated by faith in Jesus, strengthened by his presence, as the fabric of the whole Mystical Body. Again there is the unique guarantee about the "little ones": "Whoever receives one such child in my name receives me" (Mt 18:5). The promise has a twofold thrust: it translates lofty ideals into the language and situation of realism; and it assures motivation.

There is also the question of prayer "in the name." Paul, who has an intriguing text on the treatment to be meted out to a public sinner, "I have already pronounced judgment in the name of the Lord Jesus on the man who has done such a thing," and goes on to prescribe appropriate treatment (1 Cor 5:3-5), elsewhere says: "And whatever you do, in word or deed, do everything in the name of the Lord Jesus, giving thanks to God the Father through him" (Col 3:17). In the deutero-Pauline Eph 5:20, we read "always and for everything giving thanks in the name of our Lord Jesus Christ to God the Father." Paul himself prays for the Thessalonians "that God may make you worthy of his call, and may fulfill every good resolve and work of faith by his power, so that the name of the Lord Jesus may be glorified in you, and you in him, according to the grace of our God and the Lord Jesus Christ" (2 Thess 1:11-12).

Prayer in the name is quite special in Jn: "Whatever you ask in my name, I will do it that the Father may be glorified in the Son; if you ask any-

thing in my name, I will do it" (Jn 14:13-14). "Hitherto you have asked nothing in my name; ask and you shall receive that your joy may be full" (16:24). These recommendations are to be seen in the overwhelming emphasis on the Father as the source of all in the farewell discourse of Jesus: the word "Father" occurs 49 times from ch. 14 to ch. 17. Hence this assurance from the Lord: "I have said this to you in figures; the hour is coming when I shall no longer speak to you in figures but tell you plainly of the Father. In that day you will ask in my name; and I do not say to you that I shall pray to the Father for you; for the Father loves you, because you have loved me and have believed that I came from the Father" (16:26-28). And in the wonderful finale Jesus brings into the brightest focus, thus illuminating all else, the name of the Father: "I have manifested thy name to the men whom thou gavest me out of the world . . . Holy Father, keep them in thy name, whom thou hast given me, that they may be one, even as we are one. While I was with them, I kept them in thy name, whom thou hast given me. . . . O righteous Father, the world has not known thee, but I have known thee; and these know that thou has sent me. I made known to them thy name and I will make it known, that the love with which thou hast loved me may be in them, and I in them" (17:6, 11-12, 25-26).

With the growth of the Church, two trends of interest in the name of Jesus were evident, explanation of its meaning and perception of its power. References to the name of Jesus in patristic times were manifestly influenced by Sacred Scripture. Western piety found the devotion congenial and great names like St. Anselm, St. Bernard, and especially St. Bonaventure gave validity and encouragement. The Franciscan, St. Bernardine of Siena (1380-1444), fully espoused the cause of promoting the devotion; his role as a popular preacher was suited to the task, and he won support in dealing with critics and opponents. First attempts to secure a Mass and Office, undertaken by Bernardine of Busti (1440-1513) did not succeed. A first official step had been taken by the Second Council of Lyons, July 17, 1274, which ordered genuflection at the mention of the name of Jesus (cf. Phil 2:10); Mass and Office appeared in the sixteenth century and Innocent XIII, at the request of Charles VI, extended these to the universal Church in 1721. It was reduced to the rank of a Votive Mass in the reformed Missal of 1970. From the sixteenth century Litanies and Confraternities were also approved. One of the most influential of the latter exists since the nineteenth century in the United States.

[1]Cf. C. Mariotti, *Il Nome di Gesù ed i Francescani*, Rome, 1898; W. Heitmuller, *Im Namen Jesu,* 1903; C. A. Kneller, "Aus der Geschichte der Namen-Jesu-Verehrung," *Zeitschrift fur Ascese und Mystik,* 1 (1926) 288–94; M. de Jonghe, "Le baptême au nom de Jésus d'après les Actes des Apôtres," *ETL* 10 (1933) 647–53; S. New, "The Name, Baptism and Laying on of Hands," in eds. F. J. Foakes Jackson and K. Lake, *The Beginnings of Christianity,* I, *The Acts of the Apostles,* V, London, 1933, 121–40; E. Longpre, O.F.M., "St. Bernardin et le Nom de Jésus," *Archivum Franciscanum Historicum* 28 (1935) 443–76; 29 (1936) 142–68, 443–77; 30 (1937) 170–92; A. Cabasut, "La dévotion au Nom de Jésus dans l'Eglise d'Occident, Le Nom de Jésus," *VS* 86 (1952) 45–69; V. Taylor, *The Names of Jesus,* London, 1953; A. Montanaro, *Il culto al SS Nome di Gesù, Teologia, Storia, Liturgia,* Naples, 1958; A. M. Besnard, *Le Mystère du Nom,* Paris, 1962; J. E. Menard, "Les elucubrationes de l'Evangelium veritatis sur le nom," *Studia Montis Regii* 5 (1962) 185–214; esp. P. R. Biassotto, *History of the Development of Devotion to the Holy Name,* New York, 1963; L. Sabourin, *Les noms et les titres de Jésus,* Bruges/Paris, 1963; W. Repges, "Die Namen Christi in der Literatur der Patristik und des Mittelalters," *Trierer Theologische Zeitschrift* 73 (1964) 161–77; among dictionary articles, cf. esp. H. Bietenhard, "Onoma," *TDNT* V (1954) 242–83; C. Biber, *Vocabulaire biblique,* ed. J. J. von Allmen, Neuchâtel/Paris, 1954, 191–93; W. Bauer, *Griechisch-deutches Wörterbuch zu den Schriften des N.T. und der übrigen urchristlichen Literatur,* Berlin, 1957, "Onoma," fasc. VI, 1130–37; J. Dupont, O.S.B., "Nom de Jésus," *DBS* VI (1961) 514–41; I. Noye, *DSp* VIII, 1109–26; for etymology, cf. J. A. Fitzmyer, *The Gospel According to Luke, I–IX,* New York, 1981, 347; [2]L. Cerfaux, *Christ in the Theology of St. Paul,* London, 1966, 397.

in agreement with the teaching of Nicaea. The pertinent words: "For we do not say that the nature of the Word was changed and made flesh, nor yet that it was changed into the whole man (composed) of soul and body, but rather (we say) that the Word uniting with himself according to person a body animated by a rational soul, marvelously and incomprehensibly was made man, and was the Son of man, not according to the will alone or by the assumption of a person alone, and that the different natures were brought together in a real union, but that out of both in one Christ and Son, not because the distinction of natures was destroyed by the union, but rather because the divine nature and the human nature formed one Lord and Christ and Son for us, through a marvelous and mystical concurrence in unity. . . . For in the first place no common man was born of the holy Virgin; then the Word thus descended upon him; but being united from the womb itself he is said to have endured a generation in the flesh in order to appropriate the producing of his own body. Thus (the holy Fathers) did not hesitate to speak of the holy Virgin as the Mother of God."[2]

[1]Cf. M. Jugie, A. A., *Nestorius et la controverse nestorienne,* Paris, 1912; F. Loofs, *Nestorius and his Place in the History of Christian Doctrine,* London, 1914; L. I. Scipioni, O.P., *Nestorio e il consilio di Efeso,* Milan, 1974; F. M. Young, *From Nicaea to Chalcedon,* London, 1983, 229–40; Grillmeier, 560–68; [2]DS, 250, 251.

NESTORIUS (d. c. 451)

N. is of interest to the theology of Jesus Christ because as Bishop of Constantinople, to which he had been appointed by Theodosius II, he lent his authority to those who rejected the title *Theotokos* for the Blessed Virgin Mary.[1] He had been a monk in Antioch, probably taught by Theodore of Mopsuestia (qv) and generally favored Antiochene theology; this emphasized the manhood of Christ. N. seems to have had difficulty with the communication of idioms (qv), and thought that the Word of God was conjoined rather than united to him who was born of the Virgin Mary; hence, his preference for the title *Christotokos* for Mary. The ensuing controversy between him and Cyril of Alexandria (qv) focussed at times on Mariology, but the real problem was Christological; the name signifying Mary's relationship depended for its validity on the ontological constitution of her Son. The matter was settled in its first active stage at Ephesus, thanks to the phenomenal energy and drive of Cyril. The Nicene Creed (qv) was read out, and so was his second letter to N., *Kataphluarousi*; the assembly voted that Cyril's missive was

NICAEA, COUNCIL OF (325 A.D.)

The first Council of the Universal Church met at Nicaea (modern Iznik), according to tradition, on May 20, 325.[1] It was called by the emperor Constantine to deal with the theological dispute between Arius (qv) and the Bishop of Alexandria. As to the number of bishops present, we have the word of St. Ambrose and of St. Hilary (qqv) on 318, symbolic, some thought, from the number of Abraham's servants (Gen 14:14); 220 signed and possibly 250 attended. The majority were from the east: 100 from Asia Minor, 30 Syro-Phoenicians, and less than 20 from Palestine and Egypt. Besides the two priests, Vitus and Vincentius, who represented Pope Sylvester, there were few from the west, six bishops in all. Among them, however, was the man with the most influence on the emperor, Hosius (Ossius) of Cordova. There were participants whose names would recur in the subsequent history: Eustathius of Antioch, Eusebius of Caesarea, Marcellus of Ancyra. Alexander of Alexandria, who was principally involved, was accompanied by his powerful secretary, Athanasius. Others of some note at the time were

Leontius of Caesarea in Cappadocia, Caecilianus of Carthage, and Macarius of Jerusalem.

The historian, Eusebius of Caesarea, narrates the opening of the Council by the emperor; he describes in rich detail the apparel of Constantine and reproduces his opening speech. One passage reads thus: "Accordingly, when, by the will and with the cooperation of God, I had been victorious over my enemies, I thought that nothing more remained but to render thanks to him and sympathize in the joy of those whom he had restored to freedom through my instrumentality; as soon as I heard that intelligence which I least expected to receive, I mean the news of your dissension, I judged it to be of no secondary importance, but with the earnest desire that a remedy for this evil also might be found through my means, I immediately sent to require your presence. And now I rejoice in beholding your assembly; but I feel that my desires will be most completely fulfilled when I can see you all united in one judgment and that common spirit of peace and concord prevailing amongst you all, which it becomes you, as consecrated to the service of God, to commend to others. Delay not then, dear friends; delay not, you ministers of God, and faithful servants of him who is our common Lord and Savior; begin from this moment to discard the causes of that disunion which has existed among you, and remove the perplexities of controversy by embracing the principles of peace. For by such conduct you will at the same time be acting in a manner most pleasing to the supreme God, and you will confer an exceeding favor on me who am your fellowservant."[2]

We are here at the beginning of the Constantinian era and a comparison of this speech with that of John XXIII to the Fathers of the Second Vatican Council, October 11, 1962, will reveal the different world in which we now live. At issue centrally was the Arian question, the solution being a clear statement of the full divinity of the Son. What took place is known to us only by patient attempts at reconstruction from different partial accounts, for the minutes of the Council, if they ever existed, have perished. There were three groups distinguishable: one between 17 and 22 led by Eusebius of Nicomedia, supported Arius; a second, at the other extreme, wished for a forthright affirmation of the divinity of the Son, preferring the word *Homoousios,* once it had been suggested; a third held the middle ground, wishing to reject Arianism, but shrinking from the word *Homoousios,* because it was not found in Sacred Scripture and had an ambiguous pre-history. When Denis (c. 262) of Alexandria (d. c. 264) was denounced to his namesake, Pope St. Denis (d. 268), he explained that he did not use the word as he had not found it in Scripture—he did profess his belief in the common nature of the Father and the Son. Interestingly the Pope in his reply did not himself use the word, even in passages where it would have been appropriate to do so. The attack on Denis of Alexandria came from those whom he had quite rightly condemned for Sabellianism. The great Athanasius (qv) wrote a special work in defense of Denis.

It is not clear who introduced the word to the discussions at Nicaea. Eusebius of Caesarea, in his letter to the people of his diocese, related the emperor's reaction to this reading of his own creed, implying that *homoousios* had imperial origin: "He advised all present to agree to it, and to subscribe its articles and to assent to them, with the insertion of the single word *homoousios.*"[3] Others think that Hosius of Cordova, then the emperor's chief advisor, suggested the word; he may have done so through Constantine. The historian Philostorgius thought that Hosius and Athanasius had come to an agreement, at a meeting in Nicomedia, before the Council. The Nicene formula is: "We believe in one God, the Father almighty, maker of all things, visible and invisible.

"And in one Lord Jesus Christ, the Son of God, begotten from the Father, only-begotten, that is, from the substance of the Father, God from God, light from light, true God from true God, begotten not made, consubstantial with the Father (*homoousion toi patri*), through whom all things came into being, things in heaven and things on earth, who because of us men and because of our salvation came down and became incarnate, becoming man, suffered and rose again on the third day, ascended to the heavens, and will come to judge the living and the dead.

"And in the Holy Spirit.

"But as for those who say, 'There was when he was not' and 'Before being born he was not,' and that he came into existence out of nothing, or who assert that the Son of God is from a different hypostasis or substance, or is created, or is subject to alteration or change—these the Catholic Church anathematizes."[4]

[1]Articles in *Trinitas,* Nicaea, 167f, Nicene Creed, The, bibl., 168f; Consubstantial, bibl., 76–78; P. Hughes, *The Church in Crisis,* London, 1961, 11–24; Fliche-Martin, III, G. Bardy, 69–176; Ortiz de Urbina, *Is Simbolo niceno,* Consejo Superior de Investigaciones Cientificas, 1947; G. L. Dossetti, *Il simbolo di Nicea edi Constantinopoli,* critical ed., 1967; E. Boularand, *L'Hérésie d'Arius et la foi de Nicée,* Paris, I, 1972; B. Lonergan, S.J., *The Way to Nicaea,* London, 1976; J. N. D. Kelly, *Creeds,* 205–62; F. M. Young, *From Nicaea to Chalcedon,* London, 1983; [2]Eusebius of Caesarea, *Life of Constantine the Great, LNPF* I, III, 12, p. 523; [3]*Letter of Eusebius to the People of Caesarea, LNPF,* IV, 75; [4]Tr. Kelly, *op. cit.*

O

ORIGEN (c. 185–254)

The greatest scholar of Christian antiquity, one of the most prolific writers of all time, reputedly the author of 800 works, O. does not furnish us with an extended treatise on Jesus Christ.[1] He is, among the Fathers, the principal exponent of the mystical (qv) approach to Christ. For him Christ is the mediator of the mystical union of the soul with the invisible God, of the Church with God. The ultimate aim is union in knowledge and love with the self-communicating God, who returns to self-communion. Like all the great minds of the Hellenistic world, O. was seized by the revelation contained in the Logos, though he thought the Gnostics exaggerated its importance; but he still integrated the concept, with all the essential elements of traditional Christology, the Godhead and the true humanity of Christ, into his mystical synthesis.

On this assemblage of ideas he set the impress of his mystical insights and thought-patterns. His favorite intellectual technique was study of the *epinoiai,* whereby Christ's manifold being is expressed—*epinoiai* being a title, an expression, and yet an objective reality. We are reminded of the modern search for a theology of Jesus Christ by study of his titles (qv). He sought out the names which Scripture records—one commentator on O. enumerates 34. Some of the names are partly independent of Adam's sin: Wisdom, Logos, Life, Truth; some partly dependent on it: Light of men, Firstborn of the dead, Shepherd, Physician, Priest, etc. The titles are sometimes absolute, sometimes relative, possessed "for us." Three classes of names are elsewhere distinguished by O.: 1) those which are given to Christ alone; 2) those which are proper to Christ and others; 3) those which describe Christ only in relation to others, such as Shepherd, Way, etc.

Such *epinoiai* are not applied to the Father, because of his simplicity and transcendence. The Father is revealed through the Logos, who is his Mediator towards the world. In this mediation there is a certain multiplication of Christ, in different forms, which O. can hold without compromising belief in the divinity. The Logos is the image of God, but the soul of Christ is the image of the Logos. O. believes strongly in the soul's immortality, influenced by his Platonist tendency to look backward as well as forward: Platonism, after the Bible, was the great influence on his thinking. His interpretation of the OT theophanies in terms of the Logos does not diminish his appreciation of the Incarnation, which he regards as the really new element in the New Testament. With the Incarnation the Logos has come in the plenary sense. It is understandable that O.'s views on the manifold manifestation of the Logos would lead some to think of him as an advocate of the cosmic Christ; in this respect he has been compared to Teilhard de Chardin (qv).

In an age when the danger of a Logos-sarx (Logos-flesh) Christology threatened, O. was emphatic on the reality of the soul in Christ. But when that is said it remains true that, though faithful to the true biblical traditions, he does mix with his opinion some dubious anthropological elements. Unity of Christ is achieved through the mediacy of the soul of Christ between sarx and Logos. The soul has—here we are in Platonism, surely—already been united with the eternal Logos through understanding and love of God. Grillmeier sums up a lengthy analysis thus: "When all is said and done, Christ is in danger of being still only a 'quantitatively' different exceptional case of the universal relationship of the 'perfect' to the Logos, however mystically deep O. may wish to make the relationship between Logos and soul in the God-man. Incidentally, it is interesting to see that the problem of unity in Christ is stated quite explicitly as such, and is described as being a mystery. John the Baptist is not worthy to loose the thong of Jesus' sandal, because the loosing of the sandal signifies the mystery of how the Logos had assumed human nature. Even as a Platonist, O. is nonetheless conscious of the Christian 'Mysterium.' "[2]

There are other points of interest to the unfolding theology of Christ in O.'s work. There are admittedly elements from Stoic philosophy intermingled with his theories. He lacked the concept of 'person.' There was no place in his synthesis for a full recognition of Christ's humanity. Hence, it has been alleged that the redemptive death of Christ is deprived of its full value. But a recently discovered work, the *Dialektos* enlarges our knowledge of his Christological anthropology.[3] He distinguishes in Christ body, soul, spirit, and divine pneuma. He formulates a principle which would have capital importance: "The whole man would not have been redeemed had he not assumed the whole man."[4]

[1]Works *PG* 11–17 and critical ed. *GCS,* 1899, 1913, 1930; *SC* 71, 87, 120, 147, 222, 132, 136, 147, 227, etc.; cf. A. Wintersig, *Die Heilsbedeuting der Menscheit Jesu in der vornicänischen griechischen Theologie,* Tübingen, 1932, 73–85; A. Lieske, S.J., *Die Theologie der Logos-Mystik bei Origenes,* Münster, 1938; F. Bertrand, *Mystique de Jésus chez Origène,* Paris, 1951; H. Crouzel, *Théologie de l'image de Dieu chez Origène,* Paris, 1956; *id.,* esp., *Origène et la connaissance mystique,* Paris, 1961; H. (Cardinal) de Lubac, S.J., *Histoire et Esprit,* Paris, 1950; H. Crouzel, "Origène devant l'Incarnation et devant l'histoire," *BLE* (1960) 81–110; G. Aeby, *Les Missions divines de saint Justin à Origène,* Fribourg, 1958, 146–83; M. Harl, *Origène et la fonction révélatrice du Verbe Incarné,* Paris, 1958, bibl.: R. P. C. Hanson, *Allegory and Event. 'A Study of the Sources and Significance of Origen's Interpretation of Scripture,'* London, 1959; F. Refoulé, "La christologie d'Evagre et l'origénisme," *OCP* 27 (1961) 221–66; R. Gogler, "Die christologische und heilstheologische Grundlage der Bibelexegese des Origenes," *TQS* 136 (1956) 1–13; G. Gruber, *Wesen, Stufen und Mitteilung des wahren Lebens bei Origenes,* Munich, 1962; J. A. Lyons, *The Cosmic Christ in Origen and Teilhard de Chardin,* Oxford, 1982;   [2]Grillmeier, 169f.;   [3]*Ibid.,* 171; [4]*Ibid.,* n. 6.

P

PARABLES, THE

The description, analysis, and interpretation of the Parables must call for biblical expertise.[1] Those acquainted with the work of scholars know the immense achievement due to patience, erudition, and exegetical skill thus far registered; the names of those marking phases and fresh insights are deservedly respected: A. Jülicher, C. H. Dodd, Joachim Jeremias. The student of Christology finds his research, necessarily of a different kind, enriched by such studies. He has to note a dimension in the lifework of the God-man which stimulates reflection on his social consciousness, his pedagogic genius, his Jewishness (qqv), all that we try to express when we think of his human character (qv). Great themes of his teaching are convincingly conveyed, and the transcendent Word of God allows his mental powers, his selective memory, his imagination, to move with easy familiarity among concrete details of everyday life. The mystic power which Jesus possessed to the highest degree did not close his attention to what is matter of fact, under the attention of ordinary sense observations, capable, through the Master's spiritual genius, of illuminating lofty ideals.

[1]A. Jülicher, *Die Gleichnisreden Jesu*, 2 vols., 1888, 1889; esp. C. H. Dodd, *The Parables of the Kingdom*, 1935; esp. J. Jeremias, *The Parables of Jesus*, 1954; D. O. Via, *The Parables, Their Literary and Existential Dimension*, Philadelphia, 1967; J. C. Little, "Parable Research in the Twentieth Century," *ExT* 87 (1975–76) 356–60; 88 (1976–77) 40–43, 71–75; N. Perrin, "The Modern Interpretation of the Parables of Jesus and the Problems of Hermeneutics," *Interpretation* 25 (1971) 131–148; J. D. Crossan, "A Basic Bibliography for Parable Research," *Semeia* 1974 (1) 236–74; W. J. Harrington, "The Parables in Recent Study," *BTB* 2 (1972) 219–41; J. Lambrecht, *Once More Astonished. The Parables of Jesus*, 1988; J. D. Crossan, *In Parables: The Challenge of the Historical Jesus*, San Francisco, 1973; P. Perkins, *Hearing the Parables of Jesus*, New York, 1981; R. W. Funk, *Parables and Presence: Forms of the New Testament Tradition*, Philadelphia, 1982; J. Drury, *The Parables of the Gospels: History and Allegory*, New York, 1985; J. R. Donahue, *The Gospel in Parable*, Philadelphia, 1988; N. F. Fisher, *The Parables of Jesus: Glimpses of God's Reign*, New York, 1990.

PAROUSIA

The second and therefore final definitive coming of Jesus Christ.[1] How this future, utterly decisive event is portrayed in Sacred Scripture, that is in the NT, is a matter of considerable interest to biblical scholars. The one solid certain element in all this thinking is that human history (qv) will reach its final moment; there will be a judgment, universal in scope, of all mankind; evil will be finally and irretrievably vanquished and all the claims of God completely established. That diverse imagery, varying notions of chronology, are woven into the whole story does not alter this sure, reliable prediction. That the precise moment is uncertain, that the scene is presented in imagery borrowed from Dan 7:13ff need not in the slightest affect belief in the revelation. It centers on the glorious triumph of Jesus Christ, the effective proclamation of his universal kingship (qv) and sovereignty, the realization of all the promises of the Book of Revelation.

How will the "new heavens and the new earth in which righteousness dwells" (2 Pet 3:13) be established? What is the meaning of the text preceding these words? "Since all these things are thus to be dissolved, what sort of persons ought you to be in lives of holiness and godliness, waiting for and hastening the coming of the day of God, because of which the heavens will be kindled and dissolved, and the elements will melt with fire!'' (2 Pet 3:11-12).

Will the new heavens and the new earth, fitting abode for God's elect, be set in our world, purified, renewed, confirmed in splendor that will never fail or diminish? If such is the divine plan, how must the words "melt with fire" be understood?

History as a sequence of good things mingled with evil, or of evil things apparently triumphant, will be brought to an end.

---

¹A Janssens, "La signification sotériologique de la Parousie," *Divus Thomas,* Piacenza 36 (1933) 25–38; O. Cullmann, *Le retour du Christ,* Neuchâtel, 1943; id., *Christ and Time,* London, 1964; P. Humbert et al., "La fin du monde," *LumVie* 11 (1953) September issue; J. A. T. Robinson, *Jesus and His Coming,* London, 1957; G. R. Beasley-Murray, *Jesus and the Future,* New York, 1954; W. G. Kummel, *Promise and Fulfillment,* Naperville, Illinois, 1957; E. Grasser, *Das Problem der Parusie verzugerung in den Synopt. EV.,* Berlin, 1957; T. F. Glasson, *The Second Advent,* London, 1963; J. Wright, "The Consummation of the Universe in Christ," *Greg* 39 (1958) 285–94; A. Michel, "La doctrine de la parousie et son incidence dans le dogme et la théologie," *Divinitas* 3 (1959) 397–437; A. M. Henry, "The Return of Christ," in *The Historical and Mystical Christ,* Chicago, 1958; A. Winkelhofer, *The Coming of His Kingdom,* New York, 1963; R. Schnackenberg, *God's Rule and Kingdom,* New York, 1961; A. L. Moore, *The Parousia in the New Testament,* Supplement to *Novum Testamentum,* 8, 1966; J. Daniélou, S.J., *Chalkedon,* III, 269–86; J. Galot, S.J., "Eschatologie," *DSp* IV, 1020–59; A. Feuillet, *DBS* VI, 1331–1419; E. Pax and K. Rahner, *LTK* VIII, 120–24; E. Pax, *Bauer* II, 633–38; A. Ströbel, *Untersuchungen zum eschatologischen Verzogerungsproblem,* Leiden, 1961.

PASSION OF JESUS CHRIST, THE

The Passion of Jesus Christ comprises a unique series of events in history.¹ The details on which attention is much concentrated must not obscure the essential reality: God entered human history (qv), becoming a member of the human race, and those around him so resented this that they took the means available to them to end his life. The Incarnation took place in a historical situation within which the different factors or decisive elements were determined; one such element was the centuries-old anticipation of his coming, however this may be interpreted, which was linked with the particular people in which he chose to be born and to live; another was the fact that, due to the time factor of his coming, the Jewish people, those of his choice, were included within the empire fashioned by a super-power of the times, the Romans. God could have chosen another time and political setting; he could have chosen any time or place. This was his choice and in this historical situation his whole human existence, totally strange, for one who was God, and his death, which brought the pattern of strangeness to a paroxysm, were enacted.

Analysis of the historical sequence of events preceding his death relies on documentary evidence which has a sacred character for those whose religion derives from him; this evidence is handled by scientific historians with their professional methodology, and herein there is already much controversy, and some divergent opinions. Very many Christians have a fixed set of ideas and images about the Passion; these are nourished on popular tradition, iconography, annually emphasized by liturgical acts. A vast literature of piety consolidates the main points of the story, while the special product of mysticism (qv) adds its own kind of vividness.

Certain things are beyond doubt in this drama. On the research side there is the assurance that the documents narrating the Passion were the first consigned to writing of any narrating events of the life of Jesus. On the side of historical content there is equal certainty that the Passion and death of Christ were inflicted on one totally innocent. His execution by public authority was a monstrous act of injustice.

Since in first-century Palestine public authority in regard to a Jew demanded the exercise of an established legal mechanism, a man to be executed could appear before two judicial bodies, the Jewish Council tolerated by the Roman occupying power and the Roman Prefect of the area. In fact, Jesus was brought before both, but in regard to the Jewish Council the record is open to different interpretations.

First he was seized and deprived of his liberty, for no justifiable reason that was put to him: an armed band set upon him at a favorite haunt which had been divulged by one of his followers who was venal and disloyal; he collected a fee. The armed band had been organized by the Temple authorities, ancillary to the Jewish Council, and Jesus was kept in detention during the short time they took to secure his death, probably not more than two days. Roman soldiers may have been involved in the arrest. The initiative had been taken at night and the judicial proceedings seem to have been rushed at the first tribunal, the Jewish. There was either a night trial which lasted until dawn, or was followed by a brief session at dawn, or just an early morning interrogation; or again it may have been an informal questioning by some Jewish official, possibly, Annas, father-in-law of Caiaphas, the high priest at the time. Caiaphas himself may have been the first to suggest the killing of Jesus (Jn 11:49ff), and crucial events took place in his house— it was there the plans for the arrest were made and there an interrogation before the court was held (Mt 26:3ff; 26:57ff; Mk 14:53ff; Lk 22:54ff).

On what grounds could Jesus have been charged and condemned? How can anyone reading the record of his activity among his people, activity of a noble didactic or humanitarian kind, think of a valid case against him? What could his opponents find to substantiate a criminal charge? They made their case from diverse items which they alleged to be criminal, such as threats against the Temple, acting contrary to the religious regulations of the Jews, behaving as a false prophet, claiming transcendent status. They summed it up as blasphemy and on that they condemned him. It was the questioning of Caiaphas on Jesus' messiahship which was the occasion of this decision (Mt 27:62ff; Mk 14:61ff).

The Jewish leaders referred the matter to the Roman Prefect, so that they could press for execution (Mt 27:1-2; Jn 18:31). They translated the religious charge into political terms, making it amount to a threat against the Roman authority. All four Passion narratives state that Pilate found Jesus innocent (Mt 27:24; Mk 12:14; Lk 23:13-16, 22; Jn 18:38; 19:6). The Roman official even made a public symbolic gesture to emphasize his judgment (Mt 27:24); he tried to elude the pressure on him by use of the Passover amnesty, offering a choice between Jesus and a notorious criminal, Barabbas. To no avail.

To the unlawful incarceration and unjust trial there was now added Roman flagellation, the first phase in the physical Passion. Contemporary descriptions show its frightful cruelty—tough Roman soldiers hacked at a man's body with leather thongs tipped with sharp pieces of iron. To this physical assault was added mockery and a painful new form of torture, pressure on Jesus' head of a mass of thorns, long and sharp. Then there was the Via Dolorosa, the forced march through the jostling crowds, in the narrow streets, with the cross beams on the victim's shoulder; not only through exhaustion induced by hunger, bleeding, and the rough beating, but for lack of a free path he must stumble.

Death (qv) was by crucifixion, a combination of torture and killing; it could last for hours. When the body was drained of blood through the nail wounds, the crucified had no energy to raise himself in order to breathe and he died. The evangelists, in the case of Jesus, add accompanying details which show a certain significance in the event: the cosmic repercussions to follow are symbolized in the darkness over the whole land (Mt 27:45; Mk 15:33; Lk 23:44), the earthquake (Mt 27:51) and the rending of the veil of the Temple (Mt 27:51; Mk 15:38) that marked the ending of the Old Law and the cult which matched it, the inauguration of the new age: "the tombs also were opened, and many bodies of the saints who had fallen asleep were raised, and coming out of the tombs after his resurrection they went into the holy city and appeared to many" (Mt 27:52-53). Here is the sign of salvation henceforth available through the death and resurrection of Christ. Finally the confession of the centurion, a Roman, showed that Pilate's moral collapse would not mean closure of salvation to the non-Jewish world. "Truly this was the Son of God!" (Mt 27:54; Mk 15:39) echoes another Roman confession of faith, "Lord, I am not worthy to have you come under my roof; but only say the word, and my servant will be healed" (Mt 8:8; Lk 7:6).

[1]Cf., J. Blinzler, *The Trial of Jesus*, Westminster, Maryland, 1959; E. Linnemann, *Studien zur Passionsgeschichte*, Göttingen, 1970; V. Taylor, *The Passion Narrative According to St. Luke*, Cambridge, 1972; D. Catchpole, *The Trial of Jesus*, Leiden, 1971; A. Dauer, *Die Passionsgeschichte im Johannesevangelium*, Munich, 1972; H. Schlier, *Der Markuspassion*, Einsiedeln, 1974; P. Winter, *On the Trail of Jesus*, Berlin, 1974; W. Schenk, *Der Passionsbericht nach Markus. Untersuchungen zur Ueberlieferungsgeschichte der Passionstradition*, Gütersloh, 1974; L. Schenke, *Der gekreuzigte Christus. Versuch einer literarkritischen und traditionsgeschichtlichen Bestimmung der vormarkinischen Passionsgeschichte*, Stuttgart, 1974; D. Senior, *The Passion Narrative According to Matthew. A Redactional Study*, Louvain, 1975; W. H. Kelber, ed., *The Passion in Mark*, Philadelphia, 1976; M. Hengel, *Crucifixion*, Philadelphia, 1977; M. Bastin, *Jésus devant sa Passion*, Paris, 1976; C. Mateos, *Los relatos evangelicios de la passión de Jesus*, Valladolid, 1978; A. Vanhoye, Ch. Duquoc, I. de la Potterie, *La Passion selon les quatre évangiles*, Paris, 1981; J. P. Lemonon, *Pilate et le gouvernement de la Judée*, Paris, 1981; E. Rivkin, *What Crucified Jesus?*, Nashville, 1984; A. O. Rahilly, *The Crucified*, Dublin, 1985; P. Benoit, O.P., *The Passion and Resurrection of Jesus Christ*, London, 1969; id., "The Trial of Jesus" and "Jesus Before the Sanhedrin," in *Jesus and the Gospel*, I, London, 1973, 123-46, 147-66; id., "Les outrages à Jésus prophète" in *Exégèse et Théologie*, III, Paris, 1968, 262–68; E. Lohse, *Die Geschichte des Leidens und Sterbens Jesu Christi*, Gütersloh, 1964; A. Vanhoye, "Structure et théologie des récits de la Passion chez les synoptiques," *NRT* 89 (ET, Collegeville, 1967); D. Senior, *The Passion of Jesus in the Gospel of Mark*, Wilmington, 1984;, id., *The Passion of Jesus in the Gospel of Matthew*, Wilmington, 1985; id., *The Passion of Jesus in the Gospel of Luke*, Wilmington, 1989; id., *The Passion According to John*, Collegeville, 1990; G. Lohfink, *The Last Day of Jesus*, Notre Dame, Indiana, 1984; J. D. Crossan, *The Cross that Spoke: The Origins of the Passion Narrative*, San Francisco, 1988; S. G. F. Brandon, *The Trial of Jesus of Nazareth*, New York, 1968; R. E. Brown, *A Crucified Christ in Holy Week*, Collegeville, 1986; F. J. Matera, *Passion Narratives and Gospel Theologies: Interpreting the Synoptics Through Their Passion Stories*, New York, 1986; R. J. Karris, *Luke, Artist and Theologian: Luke's Passion Account as Literature*, New York, 1985; J. Neyrey, *The Passion According to Luke: A Redaction Study of Luke's Soteriology*, New York, 1985; M. L. Soards, *The Passion According to Luke: The Special Material of Luke 22*, Sheffield, 1987; J. de la Potterie, S.J., *The Hour of Jesus*, St. Paul, 1984.

PAUL, ST.

" 'Saul, Saul, why do you persecute me?' And he said, 'Who are you, Lord?' And he said, 'I am Jesus, whom you are persecuting; but rise, enter the city, and you will be told what to do' " (Acts 9:4-5). "For I through the law died to the law, that I might live to God. I have been crucified with Christ; it is no longer I who live, but Christ who lives in me; and the life I now live in the flesh I live by faith in the Son of God, who loved me and gave himself for me" (Gal 2:19-20). "When we cry 'Abba! Father!' it is the Spirit himself bearing witness with our spirit that we are children of God, and if children then heirs, heirs of God and fellow heirs with Christ, provided we suffer with him in order that we may also be glorified with him" (Rom 8:15-17). "He is the image of the invisible God, the first-born of all creation; for in him all things were created, in heaven and on earth, visible and invisible, whether thrones or dominions or principalities or authorities—all things were created through him and for himself before all things and in him all things hold together. He is the Head of the body, the Church; he is the beginning, the first-born from the dead, that in everything he might be pre-eminent" (Col 1:15-18). "Have this mind among yourselves, which is yours in Christ Jesus, who though he was in the form of God, did not count equality with God a thing to be grasped, but emptied himself, taking the form of a servant, being born in the likeness of men" (Phil 2:5-7).

Such basic statements by Paul reveal the vastness of his Christology.[1] His outlook was intrinsically Christocentric. He exemplified uniquely with the exception of the Master, a doctrine at one and the same time totally personalized and completely objective. How he acquired it, since he was not a companion of the Master, and was not present at Pentecost, is a matter for detailed investigation by biblical experts. He exhibits an originality, within the Christian revelation, never equalled. Whatever he touched in regard to Jesus, especially such a prime mystery as the Resurrection, acquires in his words new illumination. The texts here quoted have been studied to illustrate Christ's primacy (qv) in all creation, his pre-existence, his status as unique example of perfection, his continuing existence as a norm of human conduct, and source of the most sublime ethical code, his power to act as guarantor of the entire eschatological future.

[1]C. H. Dodd, *The Meaning of Paul for Today*, London, 1920; F. Prat, S.J., *The Theology of St. Paul*, 2 vols., London, 1945; A. Deissmann, *The Religion of Jesus and the Faith of Paul*, London, 1923; L. Cerfaux, *Christ in the Theology of St. Paul*, London, 1958; M. E. Boismard, "La divinité du Christ d'après St. Paul," *Lumière et Vie* 9 (1953) 75-100; H. N. Ridderlos, *Paul and Jesus: Origin and General Character of Paul's Preaching*, Philadelphia, 1958; id., *Paul. An Outline of His Theology*, Grand Rapids, 1975; D. M. Stanley, "Pauline Allusions to the Sayings of Jesus, *CBQ* 23 (1961) 26-39; G. Bornkamm, *Paul*, New York, 1969; F. F. Bruce, "Paul and the Historical Jesus," *BJRL* 56 (1973/74) 317-33; D. E. H. Whiteley, *The Theology of St. Paul*, 2nd ed., Oxford, 1974; L. Grollenberg, *Paul*, Philadelphia, 1978; G. Leudemann, *Paul, Apostle to the Gentiles: Studies in Chronology*, Philadelphia, 1984; J. A. Fitzmyer, "The Gospel in the Theology of St. Paul," in *To Advance the Gospel: New Testament Studies*, New York, 1981; id., *NJBC*, 1329-37, 1382-1402; id., rep. *Paul and His Theology: A Brief Sketch*, 2nd ed., Englewood Cliffs, New Jersey, 1986; H. Maccoby, *The Mythmaker: Paul and the Invention of Christianity*, San Francisco, 1986; W. Harrington, O.P., *Jesus and Paul: Signs of Contradiction*, Wilmington, 1987; W. Trilling, *Conversations with Paul*, New York, 1987; E. E. Ellis, *Pauline Theology: Ministry and Society*, Grand Rapids, 1989; id., *Jesus: God's Emptiness, God's Fullness: The Christology of St. Paul*, New York, 1990; *IDBSup* 648-51; *DBS* VII, 278-387; J. Macquarrie, *The Witness of Paul* in *Jesus Christ in Modern Thought*, London, 1990, 48-68.

PERICHORESIS

In Trinitarian theology the word, as also circumincession, denotes the mutual immanence of the three divine Persons, their reciprocal interiority, their ceaseless, vital presence to each other, interpenetration with total independence.[1] *Circuminsession* emphasizes the abiding reality; *circumincession* the dynamic circulation of Trinitarian life from each to the other. In like manner the word has a possible application to the mystery of the hypostatic union (qv): to express the mutual, mysteriously close presence of the divine and human nature to each other in the Logos. The difference between the idea thus expressed and its application to Trinitarian theology is profound. In the Holy Trinity the interaction and mutual participation is between divine Persons sharing the same nature, all infinite, whereas the reality in Christ is a finite human nature, assumed by the Logos, who is eternally one with the Father and the Spirit in the deity. Christ as the Logos is consubstantial with the Father; in his human nature he is consubstantial with his Mother. It is through his status as assumed by the Logos, made one in him with the eternal Son of God, who he is, that Christ as man has a guarantee of perfect holiness, cannot possibly sin, enjoys impeccability. It is through this intrinsic harmony in being that Christ can act simultaneously with his two wills, human and divine, is capable of theandric acts (qv). That it is not a fusion of one nature with another, but a most perfect union, which while making each totally present to the other, maintains in each distinct identity, is the effect of the Logos as unifying principle. He is divine in nature, the source of all that the human nature of Christ has of the divine. He makes Jesus Christ as man the Son of God.

[1]E. G. Kaiser, *NCE* XI, 128-29; F. Malmberg, *Über den Gottmenschen*, Basel, 1960; E. H. Schillebeeckx, O.P., *Christ, the Sacrament of God*, London, 1963; K. Rahner, "Current Problems in Christology," in *Theological Investigations*, I, 1965, 149-200.

PETER LOMBARD (d. 1160)

Author of the *Sententiarum libri quattuor,* 1155–1158, for a long time an established theological textbook in the schools, until it was supplanted by the *Summa* of St. Thomas (qv).[1] Book III deals with the Incarnation, and from there leads on to the virtues and gifts. The method throughout is that followed in the whole work, very much quotation from previous writers, especially the Latin Fathers, foremost St. Augustine (qv); St. John of Damascus (qv), then known in the west, is also pressed into service. Since most of the great Scholastics, notably St. Bonaventure, St. Thomas, and Duns Scotus (qqv) expounded their doctrine in commentaries on P.'s work, it is useful to know of it; but there was no originality. Many of the questions dealt with in the treatises on the Incarnate Word come up and P. provides quotations. He was attacked for a defective presentation of the hypostatic union (qv), but was insistent on his orthodoxy. He did write an unguarded passage like this: *"Ex his manifeste ostenditur quod natura divina incarnata est. Unde et eadem vere dicitur suscepisse humanam naturam."*[2] But he also wrote thus: *"Dei Filius dicitur factus homo, vel esse homo not solum quod hominem assumpsit set quia ipsum in unitatem et singularitatem sui, id est personae accepit."*[3] He was also accused of Christological nihilism, *Quod Christus ut homo nihil est,* but merely quoted this opinion, did not adhere to it. What he does is to ask the question, *An Christus, secundum quod homo, sit persona vel aliquid,* to which his answer, after much discussion, is orthodox.[4]

[1]Works *PL* 190, 191; *Sentences* ed here used Quaracchi, 1916; cf. J. de Ghellinck, S.J., *Le mouvement théologique au XIIe siècle,* Louvain, 1948; *id., DTC* XII, 2 (1935) 1941–2019; A. Emmen, *NCE* XI, 221–22; I. Brady, *LTK* VIII, 367–69; I. Brady, A. Emmen, *DSp* XII 1604–12; M. O'Carroll, *Veni Creatur Spiritus,* 138f; [2]Bk III, Dist. V, ch. 1, Quaracchi ed., 570; [3]*Ibid.,* ch. 2, 571; [4]Bk III, Dist. X, ch. 1, 593f.

PIUS XII (1876–1958, Pope, 1939)

Vatican II (qv) proclaimed an admirable Christocentrism.[1] Such was a growing trend in spirituality for some decades previously. Thereto the contribution of Dom Columba Marmion (qv) must be considered. Pius XII, who influenced the thinking of the Council more than any modern writer—as over 200 references to his writings manifest, was in this area also most explicit and ample. His doctrinal and devotional intention was made clear in the first Encyclical of his pontificate, *Summi Pontificatus* (October 20, 1939). In its opening passages he dealt with two events which had had special significance in his life, the publication of Leo XIII's *Annum Sacrum* (qv), and the institution by his immediate predecessor of the feast of Christ the King (qv). "There is no duty more urgent, Worshipful Brethren, than 'to make known the unfathomable riches of Christ' to the men of our time. There is no nobler ambition than to unfurl the standards of our divine King and let them take the wind, in the sight of men who have enrolled themselves under false colors; than to rally, in the joyful service of the triumphant Cross, those who have had the unhappiness to desert from it." Speaking of the coming feast he wrote, "The dedication of the human race to the Sacred Heart of Jesus Christ, which will be made on that day with solemn observance and with special devotion, ought to rally the faithful of all nations to the altar of their Eternal King."[2]

The Christology developed by the Pope in the years after this initial declaration was intuitive, erudite, dynamic. It is found in the substantial section of *Mystici Corporis* in which he treats of Christ as founder, head, support, and savior of the Body (see article Head of the Body). It is found in two Encyclicals explicitly Christological, *Sempiternus Rex* (qv) and *Haurietis Aquas* (qv). In the doctrinal Encyclical, *Divino afflante Spiritu,* Pius recalled the words of St. Jerome that ignorance of the Bible is ignorance of Christ. In the third major Encyclical, *Mediator Dei,* on the liturgy, he centered celebration on the person of Christ: "The sacred Liturgy, then, is the public worship which our Redeemer, the Head of the Church, offers to the heavenly Father, and which the community of Christ's faithful pays to its Founder, and through him to the eternal Father; briefly it is the whole public worship of the Mystical Body of Jesus Christ, Head and members."[3] This definition is abbreviated by Vatican II as follows: "Rightly then the Liturgy is considered as an exercise of the priestly office of Jesus Christ.[4]

Elsewhere in the Encyclical, Pius deals with the presence of Christ in the Liturgy: "Therefore in the whole conduct of the Liturgy the Church has her divine Founder present with her. Christ is present in the august Sacrifice of the altar, in the person of his minister and especially under the Eucharistic species; he is present in the Sacraments by his power which he infuses into them as instruments of sanctification; he is present, finally, in the prayer and praise that are offered to God, in accordance with his promise, 'When two or three are gathered together in my name, I am there in the midst of them.' "[5]

The passage is written into the Council Constitution on the Liturgy with some alterations: the words "so that when a man baptizes, it is really Christ himself who baptizes" are added to the clause on the Sacraments and interestingly, these very words are found in *Mystici Corporis*: "It is indeed he who baptizes through the Church." The words "prayer and praise" become "when the Church prays and sings" in the Council text. The latter has, moreover, this significant addition: "He is present in his word, since it is he himself who speaks when the Holy Scriptures are read in the Church."[6]

All of this is in harmony with the *Mysterienlehre* of Dom Odo Casel, whose disciples welcomed *Mediator Dei*. A further passage gave them comfort: "In thus reminding the faithful of the mysteries of Jesus Christ the Sacred Liturgy seeks to make them share them in such a way that the divine Head of the Mystical Body lives by his perfect holiness in each of his members."[7]

Pius integrated his idea of the priesthood with Christ: "It has been taught by our predecessors, especially by Pius X and Pius XI, and mentioned by us in the Encyclicals *Mystici Corporis* and *Mediator Dei,* that the priesthood is indeed a great gift of the divine Redeemer, who in order to perpetuate until the end of the world the work of human redemption which he consummated on the Cross, committed his power to the Church and decreed that she should share in his one eternal priesthood. The priest is a 'second Christ.' Sealed with an indelible character, he becomes, as it were, a living image of the Savior. The priest assumes the person of Jesus Christ, who said: 'As the Father has sent me, I also send you' (Jn 20:21); 'he that heareth you, heareth me' " (Lk 10:16).[8]

In one of his great Christmas addresses the Pope dwelt at length on the theme of Christ and the world: Christ as the comfort of those who lament disharmony and despair of any harmony in the world; as the pledge of harmony in the world; as the light and way for every effort by men to establish harmony in the world. He shows that pessimism is not justified. "The ultimate motive of this hope is based on the mystery of Christmas: Christ the Man-God, author of all harmony, visits his work. How could the creature despair of the world, if God himself does not despair? if the divine Word, through whom all things were made, became flesh and dwelt amongst us, so that finally his glory as the Only-begotten of the Father should shine forth? And how could the glory of the Creator and Restorer of all things shine forth in a world necessarily founded on contradictions and disharmonies?" Pius opposed to social existence in which anonymity and the iron disciple of collectivism pervade, the community based on Christ's relationship with the world and with man: fraternal cooperation, mutual respect, "a life worthy of the first principle and final end of every human creature." The world adhering to Christ can return

to its primitive harmony. "The coming of Christ indicates, in fact, that he intended to set himself as a guide for men, as their support in history and society. The fact that man has won, in the present technical and industrial age, a marvelous power over both the organic and inorganic materials of the world, does not establish a right to be free from the duty of submission to Christ, the Lord of history, nor does it diminish the need that man has to be sustained by him. And indeed the uneasy search for security has become more urgent."[9]

Before becoming Pope, Cardinal Pacelli had preached on the universal primacy of Christ: "This is God's masterpiece, the most excellent of his works; whatever may be the date and circumstances of his manifestation in time, this was assuredly what he willed first, and in view of which he made all the rest. But wishing that this unique object of his complacency be born of a woman, he cast on thee, O Mary, a very gentle glance and predestined thee to be his Mother."[10] As Pope Pius XII, in a public pronouncement in 1952, he gave further evidence of his opinion on the primacy of Christ: "The (Catholic man) knows that Christ, the God made man, is the center of human history; he knows that all things have been made in him and for him."[11] The great authority on the primacy of Christ (qv), Fr. Juniper Carol, O.F.M. (qv), concluded from these texts that his view had support in the Pope's teaching. He thought that as Cardinal he had come under the influence of the French Franciscan, who was also a champion of this Christocentric view, Fr. J. F. Bonnefoy.

[1]Cf. G. R. Pilote, *Guide de consultation des discours du Pape Pie XII,* Ottawa, 1963; M. O'Carroll, C.S.Sp., "The Mystery of Christ," in *Pius XII. Greatness Dishonored,* Dublin, 1980, 192–94; *id.,* "Pie XII," *DSp* XII, 1438–42; J. F. Bonnefoy, O.F.M., "Sa Sainteté Pie XII et la primauté du Christ et de la Trés Sainte Vierge," *SF* 12 (1940) 2–6; D. J. Unger, O.F.M. Cap., "The Absolute Primacy of Christ and Mary according to Pope Pius XII," *FS* 8 (1948) 417–20; J. Carol, *Why Christ,* 202–12; [2]*CTS* tr.; [3]*CTS* tr.; [4]Constitution on the Liturgy, 7; [5]*CTS* tr.; [6]Art. 7; [7]*CTS* tr.; [8]Apostolic Exhortation *Menti nostrae, CTS* tr.; [9]*AAS* 48 (1956) 8–18; [10]Sermon on 70th anniversary of the Association of Our Lady of a Happy Death, November 28, 1937, *Discorsi e Panegirici,* 2nd ed., Milan, 1939, 633f; [11]Address to Catholic men, October 12, 1952, *AAS* 44 (1952) 833.

PRAYER OF JESUS, THE

The prayer of Jesus, as we may attempt to reconstruct its forms and its motivation, is unique in human record.[1] It was founded on a unique *Abba* (qv) relationship. It was motivated by the intention to praise, to give thanks, and to petition, but never to seek forgiveness, save for others: "Father, forgive them for they know not what they do" (Lk 23:34).

There are certain gospel incidents which show a special intensity in prayer and an incomparable formulation. The summit of this prayerful expression is reached in Gethsemane (see article Agony of Jesus): "Abba, Father, all things are possible to thee; remove this cup from me; yet not what I will, but what thou wilt" (Mk 14:36 par.).

Jesus urged his followers to pray in secret and he gave this example: "In those days he went out to the mountain to pray; and all night he continued in prayer to God" (Lk 6:12). "And in the morning, a great while before day, he rose and went out to a lonely place, and there he prayed" (Mk 1:35). "But he withdrew to the wilderness and prayed" (Lk 5:16). "And after he had dismissed the crowds, he went up on the mountain by himself to pray. When evening came he was there alone" (Mt 14:23).

Lk is the evangelist of Jesus' prayer. He tells us that at great moments of Jesus' public life, prayer was a marked element: at the Baptism (3:21-22); before the choice of the Twelve (6:12-13); before he asked the disciples, "Who do the people say that I am?", eliciting Peter's confession of faith (9:18-20); before the Transfiguration (9:28-29); before the institution of the Eucharist, as the other evangelists (22:19); in the moment of the agony, as the others (22:41-43); and in the moment before his death (24:46): "Father, into thy hands I commit my spirit."

Jesus warned his disciples against the defects in prayer noticeable in those of his time (Lk 18:11; Mt 6:5-8; 7:21; Mk 12:38). His prayer of thanksgiving is exemplary: "In that same hour he rejoiced in the Holy Spirit and said, 'I thank thee, Father, Lord of heaven and earth, that thou hast hidden these things from the wise and understanding, and revealed them to babes; yea, Father, for such was thy gracious will' " (Lk 10:21).

The prayer of Jesus needs to be studied and understood in many contexts. It reveals his living, practical conception of God, ultimately, as in the Lucan text quoted, leading to a Trinitarian outlook. It shows how prayer can and must be integrated with life—notably he would turn aside from his activities and pray, giving the impression that the two aspects of his life fused into unity.

The prayer of Jesus was a determining factor in his historical role. By prayer he altered the course of history. Sufficient attention has not been given to the redemptive aspect of his prayer. Through his prayer he brought God into human life and lifted men to the life of God. When the final fabric of human existence will be seen in its totality, the ardent, powerfully intuitive prayer of Jesus will appear as wholly efficacious, giving pattern and permanence to all that has been salvific.

Prayer stamps the humanity of Christ as utterly authentic. He prayed because, though the eternal Word through whom all things were made, he did become flesh, one of us, taking on himself everything truly human. He prayed because he was a normal man. This meant too that he entered wholeheartedly into the liturgical prayer of his people. He prayed as a devout Jew and this prayer will never be lost to his own people (see article Jewishness of Jesus).

---

[1]Cf. besides dictionary articles on prayer, "Jesus and Prayer," in K. Adam, *Christ our Brother,* London, 1932, 17–37; J. Jeremias, *New Testament Theology,* London, 1971, 184–303; *id., The Prayers of Jesus,* Naperville, Illinois, 1967; G. Bornkamm, *Jesus of Nazareth,* New York, 1960; J. Gnilka, "Jesus und das Gebet," *Bibel und Leben,* Heft 2, Düsseldorf, 1965, 79–91; J. Sobrino, S.J., *Christology at the Crossroads,* London, 1978, 146–78; Y. Congar, *Jesus Christ,* Paris, 1965, 95–118.

PRE-EXISTENCE OF CHRIST

Exponents of a Christology from below (qv) question the possibility of knowing certainly the reality of Christ's pre-existence. The subject was treated in masterly fashion by the International Theological Commission in its 1981 plenary session. On the precise meaning the Commission had this to say: "We are speaking of a systematic concept which synthesizes many theological meanings. In many statements it rather furnishes a background (*l'arrière-plan, Hintergrund*) or a presupposition of the reason for the other aims. Therefore, just as we cannot be satisfied with a purely formal use of the term, neither must we use it in an univocal fashion but rather analogically, carefully and according to the content and the richness of the various doctrinal elements already mentioned. Although it is subject to multiple interpretations, the concept of pre-existence does not signify only an 'interpretation' which would in the end be purely subjective, but in fact the real ontological origin of Jesus Christ, his origin outside of time of which he is also consciously aware, as we have already said."[1]

The Commission traces the evolution of the original datum within the limits of the New Testament, as "the full meaning of the pre-existence of Jesus becomes clear." This is the sequence: "the eternal election and predestination of Jesus Christ (cf. Eph 13:7, 10f; 1 Pet 1:20); "the sending of the Son of God into the world and into the flesh (cf. Gal 4:4; Rom 8:3; 1 Tim 3:16; Jn 3:16f); "'kenosis,' incarnation, death on the cross, and glorious resurrection of Jesus Christ, as steps on the way from the Father, all of which show the soteriological and salvific meaning of the event of Jesus Christ (cf. esp. Phil 2:6-11); "Jesus Christ was already present and active in the history of the people of Israel in a hidden way (cf. 1 Cor 10:1-4; Jn 1:30; 8:14, 58); "Jesus Christ, as the intermediary in the creation of the world, now also keeps the world in being. He is head of the body of the Church and the reconciler of all things. All mediators or acts of mediation which seemed to have significance for salvation, are taken away or must be understood in a subordinate fashion. Jesus Christ himself has an absolute pre-eminence over against all other acts of mediation, and in his work and in his person is God's final action and event; "Jesus Christ obtains the lordship of the universe and gives redemption to all, a process which is understood as a new creation (cf. Col 1:15f; 1 Cor 8:6; Heb 1:2f; Jn 1:2); "in the exaltation of Jesus Christ the process of vanquishing evil powers has begun (cf. Phil 2:10; Col 1:16-20).

[1]Text *ITQ* 49 (1982) 293–96; *DCath* 1983, 123–24; P. Benoit, O.P., "Pauline and Johannine Theology: A Contrast." *Cross-Currents* 16 (1965) 339–53; R. E. Brown, S.S., *Jesus, God and Man*, 1968, 1–38; O. Cullmann, *The Christology of the New Testament*, London, 1957, 270–305; M. O'Carroll, *Trinitas*, Wilmington, 1987, 183–85; W. Kasper, *Jesus the Christ*, 1977 ed., 172f.

PRESENCE OF CHRIST

The answer to the question, Where is Christ? is given in the Constitution on the Sacred Liturgy issued by Vatican II:[1] "To accomplish so great a work (the paschal mystery) Christ is always present in his Church, especially in her liturgical celebrations. He is present in the sacrifice of the Mass, not only in the person of the minister, 'the same one now offering, through the ministry of priests, who formerly offered himself on the Cross' (Council of Trent, Session 22, September 17, 1562), but especially under the Eucharistic species. By his power he is present in the Sacraments, so that when a man baptizes it is really Christ himself who baptizes. He is present in his word, since it is he himself who speaks when the holy Scriptures are read in the church. He is present, finally, when the Church prays and sings, for he promised, 'Where two or three are gathered together for my sake (in my name), there I am in the midst of them' (Mt 18:20). Christ indeed always associates the Church with himself in the truly great work of giving perfect praise to God and making men holy. The Church is his dearly beloved Bride who calls to her Lord, and through him offers worship to the Eternal Father." To give completion to this teaching it is necessary to see the Holy Spirit in union with Christ throughout his life, and in the Church (see article Holy Spirit), for it is through his Spirit that Christ effects his presence. This enhances the very human presence of Christ, enriching the bene-

ficiary with a more vivid realization of it, giving the most profound dimension to the Christian experience.

[1]Article 7; [2]St. Augustine, *In Jo.* tract VI, 1, vii, *PL* 35, 1428; cf. J. L. Cypriano, *NCE* VII, 943, 44; J. A. Miller, *Signs of Transformation in Christ,* Englewood Cliffs, New Jersey, 1963; J. Mouroux, *The Christian Experience,* New York, 1954; M. Dupuy, *DSp* XII, 2107–36; J. Guillet, *DSp* VIII, 1065–1110.

PRIEST, CHRIST THE HIGH

This is a title consecrated by tradition, intrinsically, as to its meaning, related to the lifework of Jesus Christ.[1] His redemptive death was sacrificial, an act of his priesthood; he sanctifies his Church through his priests who act *in persona Christi*; his priesthood is at times said to be shared with the Church, which thought comprehends the ministerial priesthood as well as the priesthood of the laity.

Christ was priest from the moment of his Incarnation. The formal constituent of his office was therefore the anointing of his sacred humanity by the *gratia unionis,* not the bestowal on his soul of the *gratia capitis,* which makes him Head (qv) of the Mystical Body. Christ was the High Priest because he was the God-man. St. Thomas says: *Unus tamen et idem fuit sacerdos et Deus.*[2] We have to ask ourselves how this schematic summary, capable of expansion in the great thinking preserved in the literature on Christ's priesthood, finds its initial validity in Sacred Scripture. It is well known that Jesus does not give himself the title priest; in no book of the NT, save Heb, does he receive it explicitly. The title is applied to the Christian community in 1 Pet 2:5; Rev 1:6; 5:10. The wording is borrowed from Ex 19:6; Is 61:6. What of Christ himself?

O. Cullmann concludes a survey of the evidence thus: "Thus we see that, contrary to the usual assumption, the High Priest concept is not only present in Hebrews, but lies behind the Christological statements of other New Testament passages. It is of course true that no other writing has so concentrated all the Christological assertions in the high Priest concept as has Hebrews. Also in subsequent times it has never again been made the center of a whole Christology. On the other hand, the concept has never completely disappeared and has in any case played a much larger role in the history of doctrine than the ancient *ebed Yahweh* Christology."[3]

The other NT passages which Cullmann has in mind are Mk 12:35ff par. and Mk 14:62, where Jesus applies the important Ps 110 to himself. Cullmann agrees that "Jesus' interpretation of the meaning of the psalm clearly suggests that he speaks of himself. If so, it is very important for an understanding of his self-consciousness that he applied to himself this psalm in which the messianic king appears as High Priest after the order of Melchizedek. Then we would have to reckon with the probability that the idea was not foreign to Jesus that he had also to fulfill the office of the true high priesthood.''[4] As the author says, the idea derives support from the words of Jesus to the high priest: ''You will see the Son of Man seated at the right hand of Power, and coming with the clouds of heaven'' (Mk 14:62). The reference to Ps 110 is combined with an evocation of Dan 7. ''Sitting at the right hand'' is inseparably linked with the idea of the priest-king, after the order of Melchizedek. Ps 110 is so important that it is cited in the NT more often than any other OT passage.

There is, too, the Gospel of John, in which ch. 17 is often described as ''the high priestly prayer.'' C. Spicq maintained that the author of Heb took over the idea of Jesus as the High Priest from the Johannine writings. St. Cyril of Alexandria (qv) commented that in ch. 17, Jesus appears as High Priest. Yet it was Chytraeus, a Protestant writer of the sixteenth century, who first used the description ''high priestly prayer.'' It is in common usage since then. The terms of the prayer are ideally priestly, suited to the oblation forthcoming. There are also items elsewhere in John's gospel easily integrated into a synthesis on the priestly office. Cullmann would see the concept of Paraclete in this light.

Heb remains the *locus classicus* for a theology of Christ's priesthood. Ch. V first defines priesthood: ''For every high priest chosen from among men is appointed to act on behalf of men in relation to God, to offer gifts and sacrifices for sins. He can deal gently with the ignorant and the wayward, since he himself is beset with weakness'' (5:12). The call must come from God. Thus the call of Christ is explained: ''So also Christ did not exalt himself to be made a high priest, but was appointed by him who said to him, 'Thou art my Son, today I have begotten thee' '' as he says also in another place, 'Thou art a priest forever after the order of Melchizedek' '' (5:5-6). The superiority of Jesus' priesthood to that of the OT is made clear (7:11-17; 8:6); his priesthood is forever (7:23), and he intercedes for us always: ''Consequently he is able for all time to save those who draw near to God through him, since he always lives to make intercession for him'' (7:27). Christ offered up himself; he mediates a new and better covenant.

The priesthood of Christ transcends any relationship of blood, as the symbolic figure of Melchizedek emphasizes: ''He (Melchizedek) is without father or mother or genealogy, and has neither beginning of days nor end of life, but resembling the Son of God he continues a priest for ever'' (Heb 7:3). The singularity of Christ's priesthood is underlined by the use, in his regard, of ''great priest'' (10:21) and ''high priest'' (2:17, etc., ten times in all), even ''great high priest'' (4:14), whereas ''priest'' is used of Melchizedek (7:1, 3, 11, 15), and of the Levitical priesthood (7:14-23; 8:4; 9:6; 10:11).

The idea has occasionally been expressed that Christ was a priest before the Incarnation. It must be abandoned in the light of Heb 5:1 and 5:5. But there is an intriguing question as to why it was the Eternal Son becoming man who so fittingly brought to his humanity this unique endowment. What was in his filial personality, in his relationship to the Father as his Only-begotten, that founded the priesthood once he became man? How were the essence and modalities of his priesthood specifically determined by his Sonship, and by the reality of his relationship with the Spirit, who proceeds eternally from him and the Father?

The Trinitarian reality within which his priesthood mysteriously originated and operated was especially manifested at the Baptism (qv): ''Now when all the people were baptized and when Jesus also had been baptized and was praying, the heaven was opened, and the Holy Spirit descended upon him in bodily form, as a dove, and a voice came from heaven, 'Thou art my beloved Son; with thee I am well pleased' '' (Lk 3:21-22; cp. Mk 1:10-11; Mt 3:16-17; Jn 1:32-34). From the event came the public manifestation of the office. St. Peter spoke thus of this change, ''You know . . . how God anointed Jesus of Nazareth with the Holy Spirit and with power; how he went about doing good and healing all that were oppressed by the devil, for God was with him'' (Acts 10:38). Jesus himself announced the program which would give expression to his priesthood. In the synagogue of Nazareth he read out the words of Is 61:1-2: ''The Spirit of the Lord is upon me, because he has anointed me to preach good news to the poor. He has sent me to proclaim release to the captives, and recovering of sight to the blind, to set at liberty those who are oppressed, to proclaim the acceptable year of the Lord!'' Jesus then added ''Today this scripture has been fulfilled in your hearing'' (Lk 4:21).

Priesthood implies, is correlative with sacrifice, whether one understands this as oblation or immolation. Christ's priesthood was pre-eminently exercised in the sacrifice of the Last Supper and the Cross. Here a new feature of the office, as he possessed it, is revealed: the intrinsic power within it to share it, communicate with others. ''Christ,'' says St. Thomas, ''is the source of all priesthood.''[5] Is this dimension to the priestly office related to his divine Sonship? As he redeemed us by making us adopted sons of God, sharing with us his intimate bond with the Father, so, as a consequence, we enter into his priesthood, to the degree that he wishes for the life of his Church.

Heb addresses Christ thus, "Thou, Lord, didst found the earth at the beginning, and the heavens are the work of thy hands" (1:10). With such outright assertion of the divinity, the author also emphasizes the humanity of Christ. "Therefore he had to be made like his brethren in every respect, so that he might become a merciful and faithful high priest in the service of God, to make expiation for the sins of the people. For because he himself has suffered and been tempted, he is able to help those who are tempted" (2:17-18). "Although he was a Son, he learned obedience through what he suffered" (5:8). By this humanity Jesus is linked with all of us, but this physical solidarity does not explain the sharing of his priesthood, which is the work of the Spirit. There is a difference of opinion here between Catholics and Protestants. How reconcile the shared priesthood, its central act the Mass, with the uniqueness of Christ's priestly act on Calvary, on Friday and Sunday? "But when Christ appeared as a high priest of the good things that have come, then through the greater and more perfect tent (not made with hands, that is, not of this creation) he entered once for all into the Holy Place, taking not the blood of goats and of calves but his own blood, thus securing an eternal redemption." "Nor was it to offer himself repeatedly, as the high priest enters the Holy Place yearly with blood not his own; for then he would have to suffer repeatedly since the foundation of the world." "Every priest stands daily at this service, offering repeatedly the same sacrifices, which can never take away sins. But when Christ had offered for all time a single sacrifice for sins, he sat down at the right hand of God, then to wait until his enemies should be made a stool for his feet" (9:11-12; 25-26; 10:11-12).

The apostles and first disciples of Christ affirmed the continuity of his priestly action by preaching and the "breaking of bread" (Acts 2:46). Through the centuries the truth has been accepted as integral to the synthesis of Christian worship. It was articulated fully by the Council of Trent: "He, therefore, our God and Lord, though he was about to offer himself once to God the Father upon the altar of the Cross by the mediation of death, so that he might accomplish an eternal redemption for them, nevertheless, that his sacerdotal office might not come to an end with his death (Heb 7:24, 27) at the Last Supper, on the night he was betrayed, so that he might leave to his beloved spouse, the Church, a visible sacrifice (as the nature of man demands), whereby

the bloody sacrifice once to be completed on the Cross might be represented, and the memory of it remain even to the end of the world (1 Cor 11:23ff.) and its saving grace be applied to the remission of those sins which we daily commit, declaring himself constituted 'a priest forever according to the order of Melchizedek' (Ps 110:4), offered to God the Father his own body and blood under the species of bread and wine, and under the symbols of those same things to the apostles (whom he was then constituting priests of the New Testament), so that they might partake, and he commanded them and their successors in the priesthood in these words to make offering: 'Do this in commemoration of me,' etc. (Lk 22:19; 1 Cor 11:24), as the Catholic Church has always understood and taught."[6] Vatican II says: "The Liturgy is then rightly seen as an exercise of the priestly office of Christ" (SC 7).

[1]H. Bouesse, "Le mystère de l'Incarnation,' in Le Sauveur du monde, II, Paris, 1953; M. J. Scheeben, The Mysteries of Christianity, London, 1951, 411f, 436, 585; H. M. Esteve, De coelesti mediatione sacerdotali Christi juxta Heb 8:3-4, Madrid, 1949; J. Lécuyer, Le sacerdoce dans le mystère du Christ, Paris, 1957; A. Gelin, "Le sacerdoce du Christ d'après l'Epitre aux Hébreux," in Etudes sur le Sacrament de l'ordre, Paris, 1957, 43–76; J. Roloff, "Die mitleidende Hohenpriester: Zur Frage nach der Bedeutung des irdischen Jesus fur die Christologie des Hebraerbriefes," in Jesus in Historie und Theologie, Tübingen, 1973, 143–66; O. Cullmann, "Jesus the High Priest," in The Christology of the New Testament, London, 1959, 83–107; G. Gaide, "Jésus, le prêtre unique, (Heb 4:10-14, 25), Evangile 53 (1964) 5–73; A. J. B. Higgins, "The Priestly Messiah," NTS 13 (1967) 211–39; J. R. Schaefer, "The Relationship between Priestly and Servant Messianism in the Epistle to the Hebrews, CBQ 30 (1968) 359–85; V. Tascon, "Jesucristo sacerdote misericordioso y fiel," Ciencia tomista 100 (1973) 139–90; A. Vanhoye, "Le Christ, grand-prêtre selon Heb 2:17, 18," NRT 91 (1969) 449–74; A. M. Javière, "Réalité et transcendence du sacerdoce du Christ, Heb 5:1-6," Assemblées du Seigneur 61 (1972) 36–43; J. Galot, Theology of the Priesthood, San Francisco, 1985, 31-69; [2]Summa Theologiae, III q. 22, art. iii, ad 1; cf. L. Billot, De Verbo incarnato, ed. 7a, Rome 1925, 147; [3]Op. cit., 107; [4]Op. cit., 88; [5]Summa Theologiae, III, q. 50, art. iv ad 3; [6]DS 1739-41.

PRIMACY OF JESUS CHRIST, THE

There are subjects on which one author has, because of his exhaustive scholarship, said the last word. Of such is Fr. Juniper Carol (qv) in regard to the Primacy of Christ. The research of a lifetime is displayed in scientific order in his Opus Magnum, Why Jesus Christ?[1] It has rightly been written of his book: "As a result of his lengthy and diligent investigation, he is now in possession of what may be regarded as the most complete collection of texts (mostly in photostatic copies) bearing on the subject, both pro and con, from ancient times to the present day. The author's primary purpose in writing this book is precisely to make this massive documentation available to a discerning public in the hope that it may serve to set the record straight. One of the valuable features of the book is that, by giving the pertinent texts of Duns Scotus in full, both in Latin and in English, it lays to rest a good deal of the rampant misinformation concerning the authentic teaching of the Subtle Doctor on the question of Christ's primacy and predestination."[2]

The author is scrupulously fair to both sides. He sets forth first in considerable textual detail the opinion of St. Thomas Aquinas (qv), and his followers, and only then at page 120 begins his exposition of the Scotistic thesis, prefacing it with these words: "The discerning reader who has seriously pondered the wealth of material presented in *Part One* of the present treatise, has undoubtedly been impressed by the weight of reasoning favoring the Thomistic thesis. Indeed, he may well wonder if *Part Two* will turn out to be an exercise in futility." Pleading for consideration of every aspect of the question, he outlines his treatment as follows: "In *Part Two* of our book we will endeavor to set forth as accurately as possible the teaching of Blessed Duns Scotus (d. 1308) on the question at issue, and the various interpretations of that teaching within the circle of his followers (Ch. One). This will be followed by a brief exposition of the grounds on which the Scotistic thesis is said to rest, biblical, patristic, ecclesiastical, liturgical (Chs. Two to Four). Then follows a discussion of the plausibility of the Scotistic position from the viewpoint of reason (Ch. Five). Finally, we shall offer an extensive dossier of favorable witnesses from the period of early Scholasticism up to the present time (Chs. Six to Eleven)."[3]

This entire plan from the beginning of the book to the end comprises as part of the text an immense dossier; the names listed in the index run to 22 pages, and in practically every case throughout the book there is an exact description of the relevant work, with page reference where necessary. Books and articles are included, reviews of books, if helpful towards clarification.

The first service the author renders is to clarify the problem. As he says, the word "primacy" is used indiscriminately; and the hypothetical form of the question does not help: If Adam had not sinned, would God have become incarnate. The essential point is in the question: "Whether in the present world order (the only one willed by God) the Word's Incarnation depended or not on the sin of our first parent. Or, rephrased somewhat differently: Whether or not Christ and his Blessed Mother were efficaciously predestined to existence with a logical priority to all others."[3a]

But in the time of St. Thomas, as the broader question was not discussed, it was in terms of the hypothetical question about Adam's sin. The Angelic Doctor is restrained, as his principal passage on the question shows. He takes note of two answers current to the hypothetical question. He concludes with the negative answer. The whole text reads: "I answer that people think differently on this matter. For some say that even if man had not sinned, the Son of God would have become incarnate. Others state the opposite; and it seems that to this assertion assent should be given. For such things as come from God's will alone, beyond all that is due to the creature cannot be made known to us save insofar as they are transmitted in sacred Scripture, through which the divine will is made known to us. Since therefore the reason of the Incarnation is attributed to the sin of the first man everywhere in sacred Scripture, it is more appropriate to say that the work of the Incarnation was ordained by God as a remedy for sin, so that if there were no sin the Incarnation would not have taken place. Although God's power is not limited to this; God could also have become incarnate, if no sin existed."[4]

In the earlier Commentary on the Sentences of Peter Lombard, he did not take a view even as restrained as this; he almost left the question open: "On this question the truth can be known only by him who, because he himself willed it, was born and offered in sacrifice." Influenced by Scripture, as he understood it and the Fathers, he opts for the opinion of those who think that God would not have become man if Adam had not sinned. He adds: "Others, however, say that since not only redemption from sin, but also the exaltation of human nature and the consummation of the entire universe was accomplished by the Incarnation, therefore even if there had been no sin, he would have become incarnate for these reasons, and this opinion can also be called probable."[5] In the commentary on the *First Epistle to Timothy,* he just briefly notes the divergent opinions and makes his own choice: "This is not a very important question, because God ordained things to be accomplished as they have been accomplished. And we do not know what he would have ordained if he had not foreseen sin. Nevertheless, authoritative writers seem to state expressly that he would not have become incarnate if man had not sinned; I am inclined to accept this view."[6]

Commentators and theological heirs of St. Thomas tended to harden his position. It was supported by arguments from Scripture, from the Fathers of the Church, and from the Teaching Authority and the Liturgy. The array of biblical texts which speak of Christ's coming as related to the sin of mankind is, on first reading, impressive (Mt 1:21; 18:11, 20:28; Mk 10:45; Lk 5:32; 19:10; Jn 3:17; Rom 8:3; Gal 4:4-5; 1 Tim 1:15; Heb 2:16-17; 10:3-12; 1 Jn 3:5; 4:10). Closer examination will show, however, that the combined meaning is not conclusive as to the initial divine plan or design; it is rather limited to the factual, almost the empirical order. The context is historical, not theological, in the most profound sense.

An impressive list of patristic quotations in the same sense can be set forth. Not all are as explicit as that from St. Irenaeus (qv): "If man had not been in need of salvation, the Word would in no way have become man."[7] One who does speak similarly is St. Athanasius (qv): "Even if nothing had been created, nevertheless the Word of God existed and God was the Word. But the Word himself would in no way have become man unless caused by man's need."[8]

Texts are taken from the corpus of the Church's public teaching to support the Thomist thesis. But they are better studied independently. From the Liturgy it is especially the words from the *Exultet* of Easter Saturday that are invoked: "O certainly necessary sin of Adam which was destroyed by the death of Christ. O happy fault that merited for us so great and so distinctive a Redeemer."

Opposed to the whole position here exposed and defended is the theory which stems from John Duns Scotus. Again there have been developments and refinements of thought as his teaching was transmitted and interpreted by his intellectual disciples and heirs. This theological history is for specialists. Some basic texts give his view and show his originality. He raised the debate to a different level, that of Christ's predestination (qv). He believed that "the predestination of anyone to glory is prior by nature to the prevision of anyone's sin or damnation . . . this is true *a fortiori* of the predestination of the soul which was predestined to the greatest glory."[9] God, who predestines, wills in an orderly manner: "For it seems to be universally true that he who wills in an orderly manner, intends first that which is nearer the end; and just as he first intends one to have glory before grace, so among those predestined to glory, he who wills in an orderly manner would seem to intend first the glory of the one he wishes to be near the end, and thus he wills glory for this soul before he wills glory for any other soul, and for every soul he wills glory and grace before he foresees those things which are the opposite of these habits (i.e., sin and damnation)."

Scotus develops his ideas, then, keeping an eye on opponents: "All the authorities (to the contrary) may

be explained in the sense that if man had not sinned, Christ would not have come as redeemer, nor perhaps as passible, since there would have been no need for a union with a passible body for this soul glorified from the beginning, to which God chose to give not only the highest glory, but also willed that it be always present. If man had not sinned, there would have been no need for a redemption; but it does not seem to be only on account of that (redemption) that God predestined this soul to so great a glory, since the redemption or the glory of the soul to be redeemed is not comparable to the glory of Christ's soul. Neither is it likely that the highest good in creation is something that was merely occasioned only because of some lesser good; nor is it likely that he predestined Adam to such good before he predestined Christ; and yet this would follow. In fact if the predestination of Christ's soul was for the sole purpose of redeeming others, something even more absurd would follow, namely, that in predestining Adam to glory he (God) would have foreseen him as having fallen into sin before he predestined Christ to glory. It can be said, therefore, that with a priority of nature God chose for his heavenly court all the angels and men he wished to have with their various degrees of perfection before he foresaw either sin or the punishment for sinners; and no one has been predestined only because somebody else's sin was foreseen, lest anyone have reason to rejoice over the fall of another."[10]

This text from the *Ordinatio* or *Opus Oxoniense* may be supplemented by a further passage in the same work, but in this case there is a question of textual authenticity.[11] The Subtle Doctor develops his thought on similar lines in the different *Reportationes,* all of which are now available in the critical editions of the great Scotist scholar, Fr. Charles Balic, O.F.M. The basic position is summed up in the idea of predestination and in the rejection of the incarnation as *occasionatum,* an afterthought. Scotus does add refinements to his theory. Thus in the *Reportatio Parisiensis* (also known as the *Opus Parisiense*), having stated the order in which God's love acts, he proceeds: "How, then, are we to understand holy and authoritative writers (*auctoritates sanctorum*) who say that God would not have been a mediator unless someone had been a sinner, and many other authorities who seem to hold the opposite? I state that glory is ordained to the soul of Christ, and to his body in a way suitable to the flesh, and as it was granted to his soul when it was assumed (by the Godhead); and so, it (the glory) would have been granted to his body immediately, but this was delayed on account of a greater good, namely, so that the people could be redeemed from the power of the devil through the mediator who could and should do so, because the glory of the blessed to be redeemed through the passion of his body was greater than the glory of Christ's body. For this reason, in the fifth instant God saw the mediator coming, suffering and redeeming his people. And he would not have come as a suffering and redeeming mediator unless someone had first sinned; nor would the glory of the body have been delayed unless there were people to be redeemed, but immediately the whole Christ would have been glorified."[12]

In the *Reportatio Barcinonensis* he refers to Christ's predestination as "Head of the heavenly court," which could not be occasioned by the fall or demerit of the reprobate. "Therefore," he continues, "God first loves himself, and the nearest thing to this is to love the soul of Christ to have the greatest glory in the world. And this was the first thing willed among all the created things that were willed—a subsistence which was foreseen prior to all merit and hence prior to all demerit."[13]

From these texts has been formed the Scotist, one may say the Franciscan, tradition in regard to the primacy of Christ. There have been differences of opinion within the followers. The theory has been fleshed out by some to the absolute and universal primacy. A primacy of excellence all must accept. The Franciscan school does not limit the attribute even to this particular kind. The position has been well expressed by St. Lawrence of Brindisi: "Christ is the foundation of all creation, all grace, all glory since he is the end of all things, because of whom all things were created."[14]

The question then is how much support does this view have in Scripture and Tradition. The approach to Sacred Scripture is very different from that of the Thomists. Instead of looking for texts directly related to the fact of the Incarnation, texts which explain his coming, Scotists seek illumination on Christ's relationship to the universe. Without pressing the terms too closely it would, perhaps, be rather the difference between an Aristotelian approach on the Thomists' side, and a Platonic on the Scotists'. The latter look for something which will disclose the preexisting plan, the overall design which in some way included Christ. Does Scripture tell us what place Christ has in the entire scheme of creation? Are we given an insight into the comprehensive harmony of the universe, a view which would relate to Christ independently of the chronology of his life, the sequence of events including his Passion and death, which would therefore enlighten us on the totality of the Christ event?

The Scotists find such enlightenment in the Christological hymns contained in the epistles to the Colossians and to the Ephesians, and in another Pauline text, Rom 8:29-30. They are here reproduced: Col 1:13-20: "He (the Father) has delivered us from the dominion of darkness and transferred us to the kingdom of his beloved Son, in whom we have redemption, the forgiveness of sins. He is the image of the invisible God, the first-born of all creation for in him all things were created, in heaven and on earth, visible and invisible, whether thrones or dominions or principalities or authorities—all things were created through him and for him. He is before all things, and in him all things hold together. He is the Head of the body, the church; he is the beginning, the first-born from the dead, that in everything he might be pre-eminent. For in him all the fullness of God was pleased to dwell, and through him to reconcile to himself all things, whether on earth or in heaven, making peace by the blood of his cross."

There has been discussion as to St. Paul's precise subject in this passage: Christ exclusively as God? Christ as man? Christ as God and man, that is, as he entered human history? We may confidently follow those who interpret the verses as referring to Christ as both God and man. The references to Christ as our Redeemer, as the first-born from the dead, as the one who makes peace by the blood of his cross, clearly are to the man. That Christ is the one through whom all things were created, and in whom dwells the fullness of God must be taken in the context of his divinity solely. It is arguable and successfully so, that Christ as the "image of the invisible God" is Christ as man; a similar interpretation is justifiable of "the first-born of all creation"; "in him all things hold together" points to the cosmic role of Christ. He is the center of all, towards whom all things must intrinsically turn for support; mainstay of the universe.

The passage from Eph 1:3-10 reads thus: "Blessed be the God and Father of our Lord Jesus Christ, who has blessed us in Christ with every spiritual blessing in the heavenly places, even as he chose us in him before the foundation of the world, that we should be holy and blameless before him. He destined us in love to be his sons through Jesus Christ, according to the purpose of his will, to the praise of his glorious grace which he freely bestowed on us in the Beloved. In him we have redemption through his blood, the forgiveness of our trespasses, according to the riches of his grace, which he lavished upon us. For he has made known to us in all wisdom and insight the mystery of his will, according to the purpose which he set forth in Christ as a plan for the fullness of time, to unite all things in him, things in heaven and things on earth."

It may be said, by way of interpretation, that the dominant theme in this passage is utterly Christocentric, in the sense that man's sinful condition is marginal, mentioned after the full destiny of Christ had been affirmed. Christ's central position in the whole universe is equally affirmed. There is a cosmic sweep in the words "the purpose which he set forth in Christ as a plan for the fullness of time, to unite all things in him, things in heaven and things on earth." Certainly when the whole passage is read along with that from Col, the idea is of Christ thought of, planned, willed on a scale, in a universal context, which by no means at all can be restricted to the task, a most important one clearly, of dealing with men and women who have sought to foil the initial beneficent design, a design of incomparable splendor precisely because Christ is its centerpiece, its shining glory, its indispensable key and its necessary foundation.

All this is confirmed by Paul's words in Rom 8:29-30: "For those whom he foreknew he also predestined to be conformed to the image of his Son, in order that he might be the first-born among many brethren. And those whom he predestined he also called; and those whom he called he also justified; and those whom he justified he also glorified." The central idea here, explaining the destiny of all whom God "foreknew" is "conformed to the image of his Son." Again we hear nothing about sin, or its need for atonement. We get the original grandiose concept; the "image" promised from the first moment of man's creation (Gen 1:26) was seen as realizable in Christ. The call to divine sonship, God's astonishing gift to men, is dependent on there being one before all others, "the first-born among many brethren."

The expert who is here followed, Fr. Juniper Carol, sets forth a lengthy series of quotations from the Fathers favorable to the Franciscan thesis. Some of the Fathers appear to have expressed opinions both for and against, notably St. Irenaeus and St. Athanasius (qqv). It can scarcely be maintained that they were conscious of the problem as it has been formulated in successive refinements since medieval times. The same author appeals to important texts from the Teaching Authority and he studies liturgical evidence. He has no poverty of material when it comes to the teaching of the Franciscans subsequent to Scotus. With some interesting variations or nuances, the entire written tradition of this great order supports the doctrine of Christ's primacy.

What should determine the stance of those not bound by any ties to one school or the other? The anthropological approach, with some emphasis on the existential dimension, must surely raise the question: If Christ was not intended from all eternity, if the rest of creation was not in so many different ways seen in relation to him, prepared for his coming, how were things so readily accommodated or adjusted to such a stupendous new element, innovation? Why was there no apparent disruption in the many relationships which, of necessity, he must make? Why was communication with those around him so smooth? How could he, a God in the flesh, use ordinary human language, enter into the complex of ideas transmitted through generations to a particular people, use the thought symbols and modes of expression proper to that people, convey and in reality become a divine revelation to all mankind if all the mechanisms of thought and communication were not planned deliberately to match his manifold gifts? To maintain that mankind and its future was organized without any thought of him and that his entry and unique achievement within this world just took place with no executive and detailed forethought, no profound change in the very structure of the universe, is to contend that a vast, highly specialized, sophisticated machine which has taken generations to invent and make, could suddenly take on a new addition going deep into its structure and functioning, an addition which had never featured in the innumerable drawings that such machinery requires: the result would be disruption, destruction.

It is not only the Pauline texts which have been considered that tell us of the cosmic Christ. In a certain sense, many of the great Johannine sayings of Christ presuppose a pre-existing pattern that was not intrinsically affected by the sins of men, because God is not changed by what men do: "all things were made through him, and without him was not made anything that was made" (Jn 1:3). Christ came into his own universe. He could say within this, his own world, that all that the eternal Father gave him to say and do he accomplished, for so they had foreseen. He could take very human images to exemplify his varied role in regard to men—the vine, the shepherd—for all belonged to him, could be related to him. Above all, he could raise human, inanimate elements to an incomparable dignity, when he instituted the Eucharist (qv) and gave it abiding reality by the Paschal Mystery (qv). How could such a sublime reality be dependent on an after-thought? Is it even conceivable that the Eucharist was dependent on the sin of Adam?

In this connection no mention is ever made of the Holy Spirit (qv). But possession of the Spirit in a uniquely exemplary way, sending of the Spirit as a living, infinite Gift, everlasting, destined to universalize the lifework of Christ, all presupposed so much that it is unbearable to think of him as a late dispensation. The sacramental system to which he gives life presupposes the same infinite care in modeling human things capable of symbolizing divine realities, and of effecting them.

Every moment in the life of Christ, especially those in its culminating phase of his glorification (see article Ascension), seems to point to a preordained harmony between the event and the social, spiritual environment. This harmony, once realized, in turn presupposes an overruling primordial decision. Christ was first willed, all things else were willed in dependence on him. He is the final end of all things created.

This general thesis is reinforced by consideration of the special privileges granted to his Mother; it is not surprising that great Marian doctors have tended to proclaim the primacy of Christ. The Immaculate Conception in particular arrests the attention as does the Assumption. But each relates to what is fundamental and unique, the divine motherhood. This singular destiny is inexplicable without reference to the "one and the same decree" which the Popes have told us comprised Jesus Christ, the incarnate Word and Mary, his Mother.

[1]The most exhaustive treatment and bibl., in J. B. Carol, O.F.M. (qv), *Why Jesus Christ?*, Trinity Communications, Manassas, Virginia, 1986; cf. F. M. Risi, *Sul motivo dell'Incarnazione del Verbo . . . libri IV*, Brescia, 1897–98, encyclopaedic, 1, 5552 pp.; Jean-Baptiste du Petit Bornand, O.F.M.Cap., *Essai sur la primauté de Jésus Christ et sur le motif de l'Incarnation*, Paris, 1900; Chrysostom Urrutibehetyi, O.F.M., *Christus Alpha et Omega, seu de Christi regno, auctore Fratre Minore Provinciae Franciae*, Lille, 1910; *id.*, many other articles on the motive of the Incarnation, listed in Carol, *op. cit.*, 429ff; U. Lattanzi, *Il primato universale di Christo secondo le S. Scritture*, Rome, 1937; J. M. Bissen, O.F.M., "De primatu Christi absoluto apud Col 1:13-20," *Antonianum* 11 (1936) 3–26; V. Kelly, O.F.M.Cap., "Three Franciscans and the Primacy of Christ," *Round Table of Franciscan Research* 4 (1938, 39) 296–301; 392–99; 464–72; J. F. Bonnefoy, O.F.M. (qv), "La primauté absolue et universelle de N.S. Jésus Christ et de la T. S. Vierge," *Etudes Mariales* 4 (1938) 43–60; *id.*, "Raison de l'Incarnation et primauté du Christ," *Divus Thomas* (Piacenza) 46 (1943) 103–20; *id.*, "La place du Christ dans le plan de la création," *MSR* 4 (1947) 257–84; 5 (1948) 39–62; *id.*, "Il primato di Christo nella teologia contemporanea," in *Problemi e Orientamenti di Teologia Dommatica*, Milan, 1957, 123–236; *id.*, esp. *La primauté du Christ selon l'Ecriture et la Tradition*, Rome, 1959, English tr. ed., M. D. Meilach, O.F.M., *Christ and the Cosmos*, Paterson, N.J., 1965; D. Unger, O.F.M.Cap., "Franciscan Christology. Absolute and Universal Primacy of Christ," *FS* 2 (1942) 428–48; for other studies by *id.*, cf. Carol, *op. cit.*, 427, 28; B. Aperribay, O.F.M., "Primado de Jesucristo en la Escuela Franciscana," *Verdad y Vida* 5 (1947) 401–17; E. Rabbitte, O.F.M., "The Primacy of Christ. A Study in Speculative Theology," *IER* 70 (1948) 878–89; M. D. Meilach, O.F.M., *The Primacy of Christ in Doctrine and Life*, Chicago, 1964; *id.*, *NCE* V (1944–45); A. Martini, O.F.M., "Primato assoluto di Cristo e della Vergine," *SF* 61 (1964) 455–512; G. Giamberardini, O.F.M., "La predestinazione assoluta di Christo nella cultura orientale prescolastica e in Giovanni Scoto," *Antonianum* 59 (1979) 596–621; F. X. Pancheri, O.F.M. Conv., *The Universal Primacy of Christ*, Front Royal, Christendom Publications, 1984; A. D. Galloway, *The Cosmic Christ*, London, 1951; G. Strachan, *Christ and the Cosmos*, Dunbar, 1985; J. Moltmann (qv), "The Cosmic Christ," ch. VI, in *The Way of Christ*, London, 1990, 274–312, bibl. 374ff; [2]Publisher's editorial comment, *Why Christ?*; [3]*Why Christ?*, 120; [3a]*Ibid.* 4; [4]*Summa theol.* III, q. 1, a.3; [5]*In III Sent.*, d. 1, ql, a. 3 (ed. Parma) VIII, 12; [6]*In 1 Tim*, c. 1, lect 4: *In omnes S. Pauli Apostoli Epistolas commentaria*, 9 ed. 4, (Taurini, 1912) II, 189–90; cf. *De Veritate*, q. 29, a. 4. ad 3; [7]*Adv. haer.*, lib 5, c. 14; *PG* 6, 1087; [8]*Orat 22 contra Arianos*, 56, *LNPF* IV, 179; [9]*Ordinatio*, III d. 7. q 3; ed. C. Balič, *Joannis Duns Scoti doctoris Mariani, theologiae Marianae elementa*, Sibenici, 1933, 4f; [10]*Ibid.*; [11]J. Carol, *op. cit.*, 125; [12]*Opus Parisiense*, Lib III, d. 7, q. 4, ed. Balič, 15; [13]Ed. Balič 184; *Reportatio Barcinonensis*, II, d. 7. q 3; [14]"Sermo primus super Missus est," in *Mariale*, ed. Padua 1928, 80.

PROPHET, JESUS AS

Jesus is traditionally given three titles deemed fundamental among so many others which he has received: Prophet, Priest, and King (qqv).[1] In recent times the Teaching Authority has spoken of all three. Vatican II (qv) has this to say about Christ as prophet: "Christ is the great prophet who proclaimed the kingdom of the Father both by the testimony of his life and by the power of his word. Until the full manifestation of his glory he fulfills this prophetic office, not only by the hierarchy who teach in his name and by his power, but also by the laity." This statement is in the chapter on the laity in the Constitution on the Church, art. 35. In the chapter on the People of God, the phrasing is: "The Holy People of God shares also in Christ's prophetic office; it spreads abroad a living witness to him, especially by a life of faith and love and by offering to God a sacrifice of praise, the fruit of lips praising his name (cf. Heb 13:15)" (art. 12).

The precise significance of the word prophet and the way in which it is applied to Jesus have been much investigated in recent times. The OT prophet gave a message from God with authority. His message is not the product of deep religious thinking on the part of the prophet, nor is it to be confused with ecstatic utterance. There must be a commission from God, a vocation and with this is granted a direct experience of divine things with the certainty that God wills the knowledge so acquired to be given in his name, to the people or to individuals. The Spirit has a role in the bestowal of the gift of prophecy.

This is the broad picture in the OT. The general sense of the NT is of bringing the ancient prophecies to fulfillment. Occasionally we receive insight into the very meaning of prophecy in a particular context: "The prophets who prophesied of the grace that was to be yours searched and inquired about this salvation; they inquired what person or time was indicated by the Spirit of Christ within them when predicting the sufferings of Christ and the subsequent glory'' (1 Pet 1:11); ''First of all you must understand this, that no prophecy of scripture is a matter of one's own interpretation because no prophecy ever came by the impulse of man, but men moved by the Holy Spirit spoke from God (2 Pet 1:20-21).

How Jesus is shown to be a prophet in the NT is indicative of his entirely singular character as a religious teacher. His infancy is surrounded by prophetic figures. And when John the Baptist undertakes his mission, appearing as the last of the OT prophets, he points to Jesus as his superior (Mk 1:7 par): part of John's prophetic vocation was to identify the greater one. In Jesus' public life his behavior was reminiscent of the prophets: he denounced hypocrisy, quoting Is (Mt 15:7; Is 29:13); he rebuked the Jews for not behaving as Abraham did, those who claimed to be Abraham's sons; he cleansed the Temple (Mk 11:15f par.; cp. Is 56:7; Jer 7:11).

Jesus was called a prophet and did not object: by the Samaritan woman to whom he revealed her lifestyle (Jn 4:19); when he raised the widow of Nain's son from the dead he was called ''a great prophet'' (Lk 7:16); the man to whom he restored his sight said he was a prophet (Jn 9:17); the disciples told him that some thought him ''one of the prophets'' (Mk 8:28); the people hearing him speak of the Spirit said, ''This is really the prophet'' (Jn 7:40); when he fed the multitude, they said, ''This is indeed the prophet who is to come into the world'' (Jn 6:14); again the crowd proclaimed him ''the prophet Jesus from Nazareth of Galilee'' (Mt 21:11); the chief priests and the Pharisees would have arrested him, but ''they feared the multitudes, because they held him to be a prophet'' (Mt 21:46); Cleopas, one of the disciples on the road to Emmaus, spoke of him as ''a prophet mighty in deed and word before God and all the people'' (Lk 24:19).

Jesus himself did not assume the title prophet, as he did Son of Man. He claimed it obliquely as when he said to those who took ''offense at him, 'A prophet is not without honor, except in his own country, and among his own kind, and in his own house' '' (Mk 6:4 par). He was alive to the impact of his words, as he warned against ''false prophets'' (Mt 24:11). As the moment of destiny drew near, Jesus spoke the ominous words, ''for it cannot be that a prophet should perish away from Jerusalem. O Jerusalem, Jerusalem, killing the prophets and stoning those who are sent to you'' (Lk 13:33f).

Account must be taken of the widespread expectation in inter-testamental Judaism of a ''heavenly messenger who, at the end of time, would deliver God's final words to Israel. This so-called eschato-logical prophet assumes two different forms in the sources, one dependent on the figure of Elijah, and the other on that of Moses, both of them drawn from classic scriptural proof-texts'' (Mal 4:5; Deut 18:15). John the Baptist rejected any claim to be this eschatological messenger; Jn underlines the fact in his gospel. Was he answering the pretensions of a Baptist sect?

Yet Jesus did attribute the title, ''Elijah who is to come'' to John the Baptist: ''For all the prophets and the law prophesied until the time of John; and if you are willing to accept it, he is Elijah who is to come'' (Mt 11:13f). ''And the disciples asked him, 'Then why do the scribes say that first Elijah must come?' He replied, 'Elijah does come, and he is to restore all things; but I tell you that Elijah has already come, and they did not know him, but did to him whatever they pleased. So also the Son of man will suffer at their hands.' And the disciples understood that he was speaking to them of John the Baptist'' (Mt 17:10-15).

¹Cf. C. H. Dodd, ''Jesus as Teacher and Prophet,'' *Mysterium Christi: Christological Studies,* London, 1930, 53–66; R. Meyer, *Der Prophet aus Galiäa,* Leipzig, 1940, repr., Darmstadt, 1970; P. E. Davies, ''Jesus and the Role of Prophet,'' *JBL* 64 (1945) 241–54; J. (Cardinal) Daniélou, ''Jésus Prophète,'' *VS* 78 (1948) 154–70; F. W. Young, ''Jesus the Prophet. A Re-examination,'' *JBL* 68 (1949) 285–99; H. Duesberg, *Jésus, Prophète et Docteur de la loi,* Paris/Tournai, 1955; F. Gils, *Jésus Prophète d'après les évangiles synoptiques,* Louvain, 1957; H. Riesenfeld, ''Jesus als Prophet,'' *Spiritus et Veritas,* Festschrift für Karl Kundzini, Eutin, 1953, 135–48; A. J. B. Higgins, ''Jesus as Prophet,'' *ExT* 45/46 (1957) 292–94; J. A. T. Robinson, ''Elijah, John, Jesus. An Essay in Detection,'' *NTS* 4 (1957/58) 263–81; O. Cullmann, *The Christology of the New Testament,* London, 1959, 13–50; A. Hastings, *Prophet and Witness in Jerusalem, A Study of the Teaching of St. Luke,* London, 1958; R. Swaeles, ''Jésus nouvel Elie dans St. Luc, Assemblées du Seigneur,'' *Bruges,* 69 (1964) 41–66; R. H. Fuller, *The Foundations of New Testament Christology,* London, 1965, 125–31; F. van Segbroeck, ''Jésus rejété par sa patrie (Mt 13:54-55),'' *BB* 49 (1968) 167–98; F. Hahn, *The Titles of Jesus in Christology,* 1969, Appendix: ''The Eschatological Prophet,'' 352–406; F. Schneider, *Jesus der Prophet,* Göttingen/Fribourg (Switzerland), 1973; G. Vermes, *Jesus the Jew,* London, 1973, 86–102; E. Boismard, *Jésus le prophète par excellence d'après Jean 10:24-39, Neues Testament und Kirche für R. Schnackenburg,* Freiburg i. Briesgau, 1974, 160–71; H. Cousin, *Le prophète assassiné,* Paris, 1976; J. Coppens, *Le messianisme et sa relève prophétique. Les anticipations vétero-testamentaires et leur accomplissement en Jésus,* Gembloux, 1974; H. Mussner, ''Vom 'Prophetes' Jesus zum 'Sohn' Jesus,'' in A. Falaturi, J. J. Pituchowski, W. Strolz, eds., *Drei wege zu dem einen Gott,* Freiburg i. Briesgau, 1976, 103–16; J. D. G. Dunn, ''Prophetic 'I' Sayings and the Jesus Tradition. The Importance of Testing Prophetic Utterances in Early Christianity,'' *NTS* 24 (1977–78) 175–98; U. B. Muller, ''Vision und Botschaft; Erwägungen zur prophetischen Stuktur der Verkündigung Jesu,'' *ZTK* 74 (1977) 416–48; P. Grelot, *L'espérance juive à l'heure de Jésus,* Paris, 1978; M. Hengel, *The Charismatic Leader and his Followers,* Edinburgh, 1981; M. E. Boring, ''Christian Prophecy and the Sayings of Jesus: The State of the Question,'' *NTS* 29 (1983) 104–12.

Q

QUAS PRIMAS, December 11, 1925

The Encyclical Letter of Pius XI announcing his institution of the Feast of Christ the King, and giving the theological justification for this title (see article Kingship of Christ, The).[1] There are sections of the Encyclical on the OT origins of the idea, on the use in the NT. Among the OT texts, Is 9:6-7 and the Son of Man (qv) text from Dan 7:13-14, are given prominence. In regard to the NT, the Pope says that "on several occasions (Jesus) called himself King (Mt 25:31-40). He confirmed the title publicly (Jn 18:37). He solemnly proclaimed that all power was given him in heaven and on earth (Mt 28:18). These last words, especially, show the greatness of his power, the infinite extent of his kingdom." The Pope adds to these references texts from Rev 1:5; 19:16; Heb 1:2; 1 Cor 15:25.

Citing a text from St. Cyril of Alexandria (qv), the Pope states that "by reason of the hypostatic union Christ has power over all creatures." "But," he continues, "a thought that must give us even greater joy and consolation is this, that Christ is our King by acquired, as well as by natural right, for he is our Redeemer." The Petrine text, 1 Pet 1:18-19, is cited, as are 1 Cor 6:20 and 6:15. Though Christ's kingdom is primarily spiritual, opposed "to none other than that of Satan," Pius defends the threefold kingly power of Christ: legislative, judicial, executive.

Christ's kingship is universal. With Leo XIII, Pius proclaims that "the whole of mankind is subject to the power of Jesus Christ." With secularism especially in mind the Pope proclaims that "all men, whether individually or collectively, are under the dominion of Christ." He quotes what he had said in his first Encyclical, *Ubi Arcano,* December 23, 1922, on what has followed from "excluding God and Christ from political life, with authority derived not from God but from man." "The result is that human society is tottering to its fall, because it has no longer a secure and solid foundation." We are given a sketch of a better world: "If princes and magistrates duly elected are filled with the persuasion that they rule, not by their own right, but by the mandate and in the place of the divine King, they will exercise their authority piously and wisely, they will make laws and administer them having in view the common good and also the human dignity of their subjects. The result will be order, peace, and tranquillity, for there will no longer be any cause of discontent. Men will see in their king or in their rulers men like themselves, perhaps unworthy or open to criticism, but they will not on that account refuse obedience if they see reflected in them the authority of Christ, God and man."

The Pope went on to explain that the institution of the special feast would have a pedagogic effect—he illustrates this law from past liturgical history in different sectors, the cult of the saints, the feast of Corpus Christi, that of the Sacred Heart. He links his initiative with the consecration of the human race to the Sacred Heart of Jesus (qv) by Leo XIII (qv) and points to the opportuneness of his decision in the Holy Year. The feast will be celebrated on the last Sunday of October, each year, and on that day the Act of Consecration to the Sacred Heart of Jesus, to be renewed annually by the command of St. Pius X, will be reenacted.

---

[1]*AAS* 17 (1925) 593–610.

R

RAHNER, KARL, S.J. (1904–1984)

The great German theologian thought and wrote much on Jesus Christ.[1] He was concerned to elaborate a Christology which would be modern in the valid and creative sense. He gathered together in the section on Christology in his work entitled *The Foundations of Christian Faith* much of what he had expressed in different works. His approach is characterized thus by the Biblical Commission: "According to K. Rahner the starting point of Christological reflection is to be sought in *human existence,* in what he calls its 'transcendental' aspect; this consists basically in knowledge, love, and freedom. These aspects of existence, however, find their full perfection in the person of Jesus, in the course of his earthly life: by his resurrection, by his life in the Church, and by the gift of faith granted by the Holy Spirit to those who believe. Christ makes it possible that the perfect image and goal of humanity are realized, which without him could never be brought to realization."

The Commission comments thus on this approach: "Speculative attempts dealing with *the philosophical analysis of human existence* (italics in original) run the risk of being rejected by those who do not grant the philosophical premises involved. Certainly the biblical data (regarding Jesus Christ) are not disregarded (in this approach); but they ought often to be scrutinized anew in order that the demands of biblical criticism and the multiplicity of the New Testament Christologies be better met. Only in this way can a philosophical anthropology be rightly applied, on the one hand, to the personal existence of Jesus in the world, and, on the other, to the role that the glorified Christ plays in Christian existence."[2]

R. was committed in all his theological speculation to the "transcendental method." This methodology was adopted by him as a reaction against certain defects which he noticed in neoscholastic theology, often manualistic. There are different aspects to the method. It implies a special approach to philosophical theology, a special metaphysics of knowledge, a use of the ontology of the symbol. This was used by R. in his Trinitarian theology. The Father expresses himself in the Son in order to possess himself in the Spirit. The processions of the Son and the Spirit are thus processions of self-expression and self possession. R. went on to apply these concepts to the Incarnation; this for him was the highest example of the ontology of the symbol. "As the Word is the real, symbolic expression of the Father within the Trinity, so the human nature in Christ is the real, symbolic expression of the divine Word in time and space."[4]

He was led by his ontology of the symbol to defend the view that only the second Person of the Trinity could become man, an idea which raises too many problems and has not gained support—as his earlier view on the "anonymous Christian." The view is put tentatively: "Since the time of St. Augustine it has undoubtedly been customary in the schools to take it for granted that any one of the non-numerical three, whom we call the persons of the one God, could become man, presuming he willed to. On this supposition, the Word of God in the statement made above does not mean much more than any divine subject, a divine *hypostasis*: 'one of the Trinity became man.' On this supposition, therefore, one needs to know only what is proper to the divine 'Word' himself. Nothing more is needed to understand the sentence. But if one follows the pre-Augustinian tradition and has doubts about the pre-supposition in question, it will no longer be so easy to give up trying to understand the predicate in the light of the subject of the sentence. For it is the essence and meaning of the Word of God that he and he alone is the one who begins and can begin a human history; if indeed God's way of owning the world is that the world is not only his work, a work distinct from him, but becomes his own reality (as the 'nature' which he has assumed or the 'milieu' necessarily adjoined to that nature): then it could well be that one only understands incarnation when one knows what precisely *Word* of God is. And perhaps one only understands well enough what Word of God is when one knows what incarnation is.''[3]

R. pursues a profound reflection on the depths of meaning in the sentence, ''God became man.'' He fuses his characteristic anthropology with Christology: ''We could now define man, within the framework of his supreme and darkest mystery, as that which ensures when God's self-utterance, his Word, is given out lovingly into the void of god-less nothing. Indeed the Logos made man has been called the abbreviated Word of God. This abbreviation, this code word for God is man, that is the Son of Man and men, who exist ultimately because the Son of Man was to exist. . . . We do not think that we could see what is behind man except by seeing through him into the blessed darkness of God himself and then really understanding that this finite being is the finitude of the infinite Word of God himself. Christology is the end and beginning of anthropology. And this anthropology, when most thoroughly realized in Christology, is eternally theology. It is the theology which God himself has taught, when speaking out his Word, as our flesh, into the void of the non-divine and sinful. It is also the theology which we pursue in faith, unless we think that we could find God without the man Christ, and so without man at all.''[4]

Discussing with an interviewer the Christology of Hans Küng (qv), R. made some points in his theology quite clear: ''The matter is, as you see, as follows. Since the Councils of Ephesus and Chalcedon (qqv), we have dogmatically binding Christological pronouncements. It is, of course, self-evident that these pronouncements, which in the last analysis, represent an inexpressible mystery of God in his relationship to the world, must be constantly thought out anew in terms of their understandability and assimilatability. . . . For me the Chalcedon dogma is of an absolutely binding dimension. This fact, however, does not prevent me in any way from thinking through this dogma anew from different viewpoints. It does

not prevent me from offering my contemporaries—as far as it is possible—reflections, formulations, and aids to understanding, which would not have been offered through the pure repetition of the dogma. As a Catholic theologian, I must search for these aids today for my fellow believers.''[5]

R. recalls that at the Würzburg synod he protested against a statement made by Cardinal Höffner. The Cardinal had said: Jesus of Nazareth is God. ''Of course, that is a Christian, irreversible, finally binding truth, but one can misunderstand the sentence too. While other sentences with the verb *to be* express an identity of a simple type with the content of the predicate, such an identity between the humanity of Jesus and God's eternal Logos just does not exist. A unity exists here, not an identity. I only say that to make clear the fact that there are questions remaining and even differences of opinion regarding Christological dogma within the Church and its orthodoxy.''[6]

R. has also stimulating insights in regard to Jesus' redemptive role,[7] the theology of the Cross,[8] and on subjects such as Jesus' self-consciousness,[9] and on the Sacred Heart of Jesus.[10] A mighty intellect at the service of the Incarnate Word.

---

[1]*Gott in Welt, Festgabe für Karl Rahner,* ed. J. B. Metz and others, 2 vols. Freiburg i. Breisgau, 1964, bibl. II, 900–36; *Bibliographie Karl Rahner,* ed. R. Bleistein and E. Klinger, I, 1924–1969; II, 1969–1974, ed. R. Bleistein, Freiburg i. Breisgau; 1974–1979, ed. P. Imhof and H. Treziak, *Wagnis Theologie,* ed. H. Vorgrimler, *ibid.,* 579–97; 1979–1984, *Glaube im Prozess,* ed. E. Klinger, 854–71; C. J. Pedley, ''An English Bibliographical Aid to Karl Rahner,'' *Heythrop Journal* 24 (1984) 319–65; G. A. McCool, *A Rahner Reader,* New York, 1975; esp. *Karl Rahner in Dialogue,* ed. P. Imhof and H. Biallowons, New York, 1986, Part I, 11, ''What do I mean when I say: Jesus is God?'' pp. 78–85; *I Remember: An Autobiographical Interview,* with M. Kraus, tr. H. D. Egan, New York, 1985; cf. esp. *Foundations of Christian Faith. An Introduction to the Idea of Christianity,* London, 1978, 176–321; L. Roberts, *The Achievement of Karl Rahner,* London, 1967; H. Vorgrimler, *Karl Rahner, His Life, Thought and Works,* New York, 1966; id., *Karl Rahner, An Introduction to his Life and Thought,* London, 1986; K. H. Neufeld, ''UnterBrudern: zur Frühgeschichte der Theologie K. Rahners aus der Zusammenarbeit mit H. Rahner,'' *Wagnis Theologie,* 341–54; K. H. Weger, *Karl Rahner. An Introduction to his Theology,* London, 1980; C. Annice Callahan, R.S.C.J., *Karl Rahner's Spirituality of the Pierced Heart: A Reinterpretation of Devotion to the Sacred Heart,* Lanham, MD, University Press of America, 1985; L. J. O'Donovan, ''A Journey into Time: The Legacy of Karl Rahner's Last Years,'' *ThS* 46 (1985) 621–46; B. Marshall, *Christology in Conflict: The Identity of a Savior in Rahner and Barth,* Oxford, 1987; *Contemporary Theologies,* 93–104; J.A. DiNoia, O.P., in *The Modern Theologians* I, 183–204; [2]Text tr., J. Fitzmyer, S.J., *Scripture and Christology,* London, 1986, 1.1.7.2; 1.2.7.2; cf. editor's comment, 77, 78; [3]J. Fitzmyer, *op. cit.,* 78; [4]*Foundations of Christian Faith,* 214f; [5]*Ibid.,* 224f; [6]*Karl Rahner in Dialogue,* 249f; [7]*Ibid.,* 250.

REDEEMER, JESUS CHRIST THE

Redeemer comprehends or evokes all that Jesus Christ accomplished for men. Other words are used, each with its own nuance: salvation, liberation, atonement or satisfaction, reconciliation, expiation.[1] The human race and indirectly the world, was estranged from God. How this came about implies a theology of original sin and of Adam's (qv) headship of the human family. Restoration of man to God's friendship was the lifework undertaken by Jesus Christ. The idea of such a recovery was already foretold, in different ways, in the OT. The very idea of a Messiah (qv), a deliverer, is woven into the thought contained in these books, the promises held out by the covenant, Yahweh's lordship expressing itself in love and mercy, form a powerful collective testimony: "I have swept away your transgressions like a cloud, and your sins like a mist; return to me for I have redeemed you" (Is 44:22). "You will have your creator as your husband, and his name is the Lord of hosts; and the Holy One of Israel is your Redeemer, the God of the whole earth he is called. For the Lord has called you like a wife forsaken and grieved in spirit, like a wife of youth when she is cast off, says your God. For a brief moment I forsook you, but with great compassion I will gather you. In overflowing wrath for a moment I hid my face from you, but with everlasting love I will have compassion on you, says the Lord, your Redeemer" (Is 54:5-8).

The Servant (qv) oracles portray the ideal of the perceptive, docile servant through whom Yahweh will establish his kingdom in Israel and among the nations (Is 42:1-7; 49:1-6; 50:4-9; 52:13–53:12). Through an eternal covenant with Israel Yahweh wished to inaugurate the reign of God which would be extended through Israel to all peoples: "Incline your ear and come to me; hear that your soul may live. I will make you an everlasting covenant, my steadfast, sure love for David. Behold, I made him a witness to the peoples, a leader and commander for the peoples. Behold, you shall call nations that you know not, and nations that knew you not shall run to you, because of the Lord your God, and of the Holy One of Israel, for he has glorified you" (Is 55:3-5).

The NT binds redemption and salvation inseparably to the person of Jesus. God's saving action reaches its definitive character in him. It is in the future lordship of God that salvation consists according to Jesus. Once this has been proclaimed, inaugurated, Jesus is singled out as its irreplaceable author (Lk 10:23f par., Lk 11:20 par.). It consists in the merciful, saving benevolence of God towards all. God sets no condition except repentance and holds out the hope of liberation from self-righteousness (Lk 18:9-14), and from all inhibiting social taboos (Mk 12:31 par.; Mt 5:38-48 par.)

Conscious of the universal burden of sin (Lk 19:10; Mt 9:13), fully committed to the proclamation of the kingdom (Mt 12:28), which was "the pearl of great price," "the hidden treasure" (Mt 13:44-46), Jesus, foreseeing his death, knew that it would be vicarious in fulfillment of his role as the Servant of Yahweh (Is 52:13–53:12). In Mt 16:21 we read, "From that time Jesus began to show his disciples that he must go to Jerusalem and suffer many things from the elders and chief priests and scribes, and be killed, and on the third day be raised." At the institution of the Eucharist he spoke of the "blood of the covenant ("new" in Lk and Paul) which is poured out for many for the forgiveness of sins" (Mt 26:26-28; Mk 14:22-24; Lk 22:19-20; 1 Cor 11:23-25). He was explicit on the idea of ransom, "even as the Son of Man came not to be served but to serve, and to give his life as a ransom for many" (Mt 20:28; Mk 10:45).

St. Paul's soteriology certainly comprises the idea of ransom, expressed in his famous *Unus Mediator* text (1 Tim 2:6). Paul enlarged the theme of redemption by his teaching on the universality of sin, in consequence of Adam's fault (Rom 5:12; cp. 1 Cor 15:21-22). Paul also identified the mission of Christ as redeemer: "But when the time had fully come, God sent forth his Son, born of a woman, born under the law, to redeem those who were under the law, so that we might receive adoption as sons" (Gal 4:4-5).

St. Paul emphasizes the importance of the death of Christ as a redeeming act, the death as a revelation of the love of God and of Jesus: "But God shows his love for us in that while we were yet sinners Christ died for us" (Rom 5:8). "He who did not spare his own Son but gave him up for us all, will he not also give us all things with him?" (Rom 8:32). "I have been crucified with Christ; it is no longer I who live, but Christ who lives in me; and the life I now live in the flesh I live by faith in the Son of God, who loved me, and gave himself up for me" (Gal 2:20).

There is for Paul a necessary complement to this idea of the redemptive death of Christ: his resurrection (qv): "And he died for all, that those who live might live no longer for themselves but for him who for their sake died and was raised" (2 Cor 5:15). "Christ died for us sinners and rose again for our justification" (Rom 4:25). At his resurrection Christ became "a life-giving spirit" (1 Cor 15:45). The redemptive theology of the resurrection has been well developed in recent times, with important monographs by F. Durrwell, C.SS.R. and D. M. Stanley, S.J.

How is a synthesis effected of the various strands of thought centering on the redemption through the ages? The easterners focused their speculation mostly on the divinization of man, restoration of the divine image which had been implanted in the moment of creation. To give some kind of systematic unity to the ideas developed in the eastern and the western traditions, we should perhaps take questions that would serve as a guide:

Why did Christ have to be a Redeemer? Mankind was estranged from its Creator, who had endowed men with supernatural life; this had been rejected by the First Parents, whose sin, Original, was a universal inheritance, through the Creator's design of human solidarity. This state of sinfulness may be described as bondage or proneness to fail morally; it would imply influence but not dominion by the Evil One.

Did Christ come primarily as a Redeemer? On the view sustained in this work, no. Christ came to give glory to his heavenly Father; this entailed the work of redemption, which he undertook as the Father's will, but in a manner subordinate to his first intention.

What was the work of redemption? It was essentially a reconciliation of estranged mankind to their munificent Creator; it was the possibility of restoring the divine image lost by sin; it was liberation from sinful bondage, total triumph over the powers of evil by the Redeemer, an impress of splendid human perfection on a whole human life, which reflecting the divine attributes accurately, was efficacious by its very existence, as this included the entire span of life and afterlife.

How was this work achieved? Jesus Christ, true God and true man, was accepted in the place of all men, making his central act of love of the Father vicarious for others. Thus, in the mysterious plan of God, it was decreed. The act of love demanded of him was—again we are at the point of mystery—the surrender of his life, in the particular circumstances in which it was cast (see articles Passion of Christ, The; Death of Christ, The). Since his life was taken by the shedding of his blood (qv), this has been considered symbolic, richly so, of the whole saving event. Since he was a free man he merited fully, and since he was God his merit was infinite.

Who provided the unalterable driving force and moral endurance in the ordeal of suffering and death unjustly inflicted, compounded by betrayal, treachery, collapse of close associates? The Spirit of God who dwelt in the soul of Jesus Christ in plenitude.

He saw him through every phase of his saving task to its total accomplishment.

Was it by his death alone that Jesus Christ redeemed us? Yes as to efficacy, no as to availability. It was his resurrection (qv), rightly considered with his death as one Paschal Mystery, which opened to us the treasure completely and certainly acquired.

Does this end the drama of Redemption? No. The Spirit who filled the soul of Jesus was given to construct the organic system which would ensure the benefits of the Redemption to all men until the end of time, long after the events which achieved it were, in their historical character, past. This divine Spirit created a living organism, the Church, wherein and from which the essential element of supernatural life, source of redemption applied and received, divine grace would be distributed as his intrinsic, personal gift.

Why is the Redemption spoken of as a sacrifice? Because the Redeemer was a priest (qv) and linked his exercise of this calling with his final act of love. By a supreme act of divine generosity he brought those who would benefit by his redemptive act into a unique solidarity with him, through the essential sacrifice to be offered by his Church, the Eucharist.

Was the work of Redemption an isolated event in his life? In its capital and conclusive sense, by his Paschal Mystery, it had to be so. Insofar as this was a culmination, a completion of his whole life, he was our Redeemer from the outset, from the first moment of the Incarnation. All the lineaments of his prodigious existence, some more strikingly than others, were together in his redemptive purpose. This originated in his love of the Father and his love for us. One strand shining very brightly in his life was mercy, on which he spoke some of his most moving words.

---

[1]Cf J. Rivière (qv), *The Doctrine of the Atonement. A Historical Essay,* St. Louis, 1909; *id., Le dogme de la Rédemption. Etude théologique.* 3rd ed., bibl., Paris, 1931; *id.,* "Rédemption," *DTC* XII, 1912–2004, bibl.; *id.,* esp. *Le dogme de la Rédemption dans la théologie contemporaine,* bibl., Albi, 1948; L. Richard, "La Rédemption, mystère d'amour," *RSR* 13 (1923) 193–217, 397–418; esp., *id., The Mystery of the Redemption,* Baltimore/Dublin, 1965; Summer School of Catholic Studies, July 31–August 9, 1926, *The Atonement,* London, 1928; E. Masure, "Le Rédempteur" in *Le Christ,* eds. G. Bardy and A. Tricot, Paris, 1932, 518–551; V. Taylor, *Jesus and his Sacrifice. A Study of the Passion Sayings in the Gospel,* London, 1937, repr., 1955; *id., The Atonement in New Testament Teaching,* London, 1941; *id., Forgiveness and Reconciliation. A Study in New Testament Theology,* 2nd ed., 1946, repr. 1956; A. Vonier, O.S.B., *The Victory of Christ,* London, 1934; A. Hennessy, *Victory of Christ over Satan,* Washington, 1946; T. H. Hughes, *The Atonement,* London, 1949; H. E. W. Turner, *The Patristic Doctrine of the Redemption. A Study of the Development of Doctrine during the First Five Centuries,*

London, 1952; J. Dupont, O.S.B., *La Réconciliation dans la Théologie de Saint Paul*, Louvain, 1953; Philippe de la Trinité, *What is Redemption?*, New York, 1961; R. S. Franks, *The Work of Christ*, New York, 1962; F. X. Durrwell, C.SS.R., *The Resurrection. A Biblical Study*, London, 1960; id., *In the Redeeming Christ*, London, 1963; D. M. Stanley, S.J., *Christ's Resurrection in Pauline Soteriology*, Rome, 1961; S. Lyonnet, S.J., *De peccato et Redemptione*, Rome, 1956; B. Sesboué, S.J., *Jésus Christ, l'unique Médiateur. Essai sur la rédemption et le salut*, I, *Problématique et relecture doctrinale*, Paris, 1988.

REDEMPTOR HOMINIS, March 4, 1979

The first Encyclical of John Paul II (qv) which contains substantial passages on the redemption in the mystery of Christ.[1] After recalling important themes and concerns of the age which is the eve of the third millennium, and paying tribute to his predecessor, Paul VI (qv), the Pope, speaking within the context of his office, its imperatives in the light of Vatican II (qv), and the first Encyclical of his predecessor, evokes Christ in these terms: "Our spirit is set in one direction; the only direction for our intellect, will and heart is towards Christ our Redeemer, towards Christ, the Redeemer of man. We wish to look towards him—because there is salvation in no one else but him, the Son of God—repeating what Peter said: 'Lord, to whom shall we go? You have the words of eternal life' (Jn 6:68; cf. Acts 4:8-12). Through the Church's consciousness, which the Council considerably developed, through all levels of this self-awareness, and through all the fields of activity in which the Church expresses, finds, and confirms herself, we must constantly aim at him 'who is the Head' (cf. Eph 1:10, 22; 4:25; Col 1:18), 'through whom are all things and through whom we exist' (1 Cor 8:6; cf. Col 1:17), who is both 'the way and the truth' (Jn 14:6) and 'the resurrection and the life' (Jn 11:25), seeing whom we see, the Father (cf. Jn 14:9), and who had to go away from us (cf. Jn 16:7)—that is, by his death on the Cross and then by his ascension into heaven—in order that the Counsellor should come to us and should keep coming to us as the Spirit of truth (cf. Jn 16:7, 13). In him are 'all the treasures of wisdom and knowledge' (Col 2:3) and the Church is his Body (cf. Rom 12:5; 1 Cor 6:15; 10:17; 12:12, 27; Eph 1:23; 2:16; 4:4; Col 1:24; 3:15). 'By her relationship with Christ the Church is a kind of sacrament or sign and means of intimate union with God, and of the unity of all mankind' (*LG* 1) and the source of this is he, he himself, he the Redeemer."

The Pope speaks of the appeal of Christ, the man, to those who do not believe in his divinity: "The life of Christ speaks, also, to many who are not capable of repeating with Peter: 'You are the Christ, the Son of the living God' (Mt 16:16). He, the Son of the living God, speaks to people also as Man: it is his life that speaks, his humanity, his fidelity to the truth, his all-embracing love. Furthermore, his death on the Cross speaks—that is to say the inscrutable depth of his suffering and abandonment."

The Pope considers the divine and human dimensions of the Redemption, recalling the Council's brief summary of anthropology: "The truth is that only in the mystery of the incarnate Word does the mystery of man take on light. For Adam, the first man, was a type of him who was to come (Rom 5:14). Christ the Lord, the new Adam, in the very revelation of the mystery of the Father and of his love, *fully reveals man to himself* and brings to light his most high calling" (*GS* 22). The Pope quotes again: "He who is the 'image of the invisible God' (Col 1:15) is himself the perfect man who has restored in the children of Adam that likeness to God which had been disfigured ever since the first sin. Human nature, by the very fact that it was assumed, not absorbed in him, has been raised in us also to a dignity beyond compare. For by his Incarnation, he, the Son of God, *in a certain way united himself with each man*. He thought with a human mind, he acted with a human will, and with a human heart he loved. Born of the Virgin Mary, he has truly been made one of us, like to us in all things except sin."

The Pope expounds the divine dimensions of the Redemption: "The Redemption of the world—this tremendous mystery of love in which creation is renewed (*GS* 37; *LG* 53-54)—is, at its deepest root, the fullness of justice in a human heart—the heart of the firstborn Son—in order that it may become justice in the hearts of many human beings, predestined from eternity in the firstborn Son to be children of God" (cf. Rom 8:29-30; Eph 1:8). The line of thought then takes up the theme of divine love, to conclude thus: "This revelation of love is also described as mercy; and in man's history this revelation of love and mercy has taken a name: that of Jesus Christ."

Dealing then with the human dimension, the Pope considers the new creation which Christ effects: "The man who wishes to understand himself thoroughly—and not just in accordance with immediate, partial, often superficial, and even illusory standards and measures of his being—he must with his unrest, uncertainty and even his weakness and sinfulness, with his life and death, draw near to Christ. He must, so to speak, enter into him with all his own self, he must 'appropriate' and assimilate the whole of the reality of the Incarnation and Redemption in order to find himself." As the Pope then shows how the mystery of Christ is the basis of the Church's mission and of Christianity, he can enunciate a central truth like this: "Jesus Christ is the stable principle and fixed center of the mission that God has entrusted to man." Different aspects of the truth are treated, and throughout the Encyclical the centrality and the universal call of Christ recur. All this is not remote from the doctrine of the primacy of Christ (qv).

---

[1]AAS 71 (1979) 257–324.

RESURRECTION, THE

This event in the life of Christ has been the subject of immense research and reflection in recent times.[1] All the relevant scriptural texts have been scrutinized with expert methodology. The content of the mystery has been analyzed. It has been taken from the domain of apologetics, where it was used as an argument for the divinity of Christ, always valid, to the more profound far-reaching area of soteriology and salvation history. Here its mighty significance stimulates theological speculation. Meanwhile, in the liturgy the Resurrection is englobed in the Paschal Mystery (qv), with gains increasingly appreciated. Such rethinking has arguably a deepening effect on the whole Catholic ethos, eliminating any danger of intrinsic pessimism, defeatism in the Christian approach to life.

Popular interest in the historicity of the Resurrection has been occasionally stimulated by a technique that is not new: someone socially, professionally, or clerically prominent challenges the traditional belief. What of the historicity then? There was no witness to the event, no one who could have seen Jesus Christ take up his dead body and leave the tomb. The nearest to that requisite is the finding of the empty tomb (Mk 16:1-8; Mt 28: 1-20; Lk 16:9-20; Jn 20:2).

In our labors to sift the evidence and strengthen our faith, we may benefit by hearing the opinion of a highly intelligent man of equal integrity, who lived and worked in a key church center in the age immediately after the apostles. St. Ignatius of Antioch (qv) was St. Peter's immediate or second successor in the see of Antioch. Antioch had been privileged to have Paul (qv) and Barnabas to evangelize it for a whole year. "And in Antioch the disciples were for the first time called Christians" (Acts 11:26). Here, with the impress of Peter and Paul, the essential facts of the Christian story were firmly delineated and retained. Ignatius gathered them carefully, for his life was at issue in the matter. Here are his words, and the circumstance which validates them: "(He was) truly nailed to a tree in the flesh for our sake under Pontius Pilate and Herod the Tetrarch (and of its fruit we are from his divinely blessed Passion) that 'he might set up an ensign' for all ages through his Resurrection, for his saints and believers, whether among the Jews, or among the heathens, in one body of his Church. For he suffered all these things for us that we might attain salvation, and he truly suffered even as he also truly raised himself, not as some unbelievers say, that his Passion was merely in semblance, but it is they who are merely in semblance, and even according to their opinions it shall happen to them, and they shall be without bodies and phantasmal. For I know and believe that he was in the flesh even after the resurrection. And when he came to those with Peter he said to them: 'Take, handle me and see that I am not a phantom without a body.' And they immediately touched him and believed, being mingled both with his flesh and spirit. Therefore they despised even death, and were proved to be above death. And after his Resurrection he ate and drank with them as a being of flesh, although he was united in spirit to the Father. . . . For if it is merely in semblance that these things were done by our Lord, I also am a prisoner in semblance. And why have I given myself up to death, to fire, to the sword, to wild beasts?'"[2]

Ignatius had the Docetists in mind. But his sense of concrete historical reality which turns on the Resurrection is undeniable. Perhaps we have another lesson to learn from him: the whole story of the Passion, Death (qqv) and Resurrection is a totality, the whole story of the Public Life which so terminated, is a totality, which needs more than Form Criticism, valuable as this method is, to seize its dominant characteristics. The Passion, the trial, the torture, the manner of killing, were enacted with the full physical presence of Jesus, with his physique made more prominent in the last phase; it was all exposed to public observation, open to witness and the ensuing testimony. The inner thought and literary dynamic of the story was thus irresistibly set and could not be reversed by the writers; they also, in consequence so narrated the remainder, one of glory and splendor, but its fabric consistent. They could not talk of one Jesus in the Passion and another in the Resurrection appearances.

The Resurrection is also part of the totality of the gospels, but in a less tightly bound manner. The predictions (Mk 8:31; 9:30; 10:34, allusions, 9:9; 14:28; Mt 12:40; 16:4, 21; 17:9; 20:19; Lk 9:22; 18:33) may be shown to be adapted by each evangelist to his general outlook and plan, but all through, the conceptual structure, the categories of thought, the realistic language match the literary character of the text, comply with its implications. The disciples may not have understood the Master in the sense of knowing how he would rise from the dead. But the writers knew what they were writing: a consecutive story, its elements and modes consistent because referable to the same Person.

Though part of the same history as that of the public ministry, the risen Jesus was not enclosed within it. His resurrection was an eschatalogical event, his body, though still retaining its identity, imbued with a new mysterious mode of existence. Identity is the word which explains and answers the objections based on the variant accounts of the Resurrection appearances. The reader who will study the charts on *The Variant Accounts of Resurrection Appearances,* made by R. E. Brown, will see all the differences as to persons and places: the notable prominence given to the women visiting the tomb, their purpose, either for anointing (which creates a problem since some days had passed), or just to see, their discovery of the empty tomb, encounter with a youth, or with men, or with an angel or angels, the message received and discharged, Jesus himself seen, who also gives a message (Mk 16:1-8; Mt 28; Lk 24; Jn 20); the specific details about appearances to the women (first to Mary Magdalene [Mk 16:19-20]; to women returning from the tomb [Mt 28:9-10]; at the tomb to Mary Magdalene [Jn 20:16]); to the disciples on the road to Emmaus (Lk 24:13-31), in the country (Mk 16:12); to the eleven in Jerusalem, at a meal (Mk 16:14), Easter night (Lk 24:36-50), to disciples, Thomas being absent, Easter night (Jn 20:19-23), to disciples, with Thomas present, a week later (Jn 20:26-29), to seven disciples by the Sea of Tiberias (Jn 21:4-21).

Biblical scholars who approach the narratives of these events without presuppositions have to analyze the different traditions behind them. Catholic scholars have shown freedom in applying modern techniques to the relevant material, a number of them like A. Descamps, R. E. Brown, J. A. Fitzmyer named members of the Biblical Commission (qv). The language has to be chosen carefully to express the unique aspect of Christ's rising, not a mere revivification of a corpse, but a total transformation, though still bodily (cf. 1 Cor 15); a mystery, but one brought adequately to our faith. As an object of faith it was proposed to the first Christians, who were capable of assimilating it: "If Christ has not been raised then our preaching is in vain, and your faith is in vain" (1 Cor 15:14). Faith in divine truth, faith likewise in the embodiment of this truth in factual concrete reality. It is this very emphasis on faith and its capacity to enlighten that the Resurrection should prompt. Sadly in an age when the theology of the mystery has been so fruitfully developed, very many have allowed themselves to delay unduly on the historicity. Did it take place? Was it bodily? These questions have distracted attention from: How is it related to the Eucharist? How does it fit into the whole scheme of our salvation? How is it related to the exaltation of Christ and the sending of the Spirit?

Newman, in the *Lectures on Justification,* one of the great theological works of the nineteenth century, anticipated much of the thinking expressed and further stimulated by a seminal work of the present century, Fr. F. X. Durrwell's *La résurrection, mystère du salut;* it was followed soon after by Fr. D. M. Stanley's monograph, *Christ's Resurrection in Pauline Soteriology.* First Newman outlines the role of the Spirit: "Whatever then is done in the Christian Church is done by the Spirit; Christ's mission ended when he left the world; he was to come again, but by his Spirit. The Holy Spirit realizes and completes the redemption which Christ has wrought in essence and virtue. If the justification, then, of a sinner be a continual work, a work under the new Covenant, it must be the Spirit's work and not simply Christ's. The atonement for sin took place during his own mission, and he was the chief Agent; the application of that Atonement takes place during the mission of his Spirit, who accordingly is the chief Agent in it."[2]

Newman then speaks of the meaning of Christ's words that unless he went the Spirit would not come to us. "And thus his rising again was the necessary antecedent of his applying to his elect the virtue of the Atonement which his dying wrought for all men.

With the completion of the Passion, Newman says "the treasure existed, the precious gift was perfected, but it was not yet diffused, communicated, shared in, enjoyed." He explains further: "Thus he died to purchase what he rose again to apply. 'He died for our sins; he rose again for our justification; he died in the flesh; he rose again 'according to the Spirit of holiness,' which, when risen, he also sent forth from him, dispensing to others that life whereby he rose himself. He atoned, I repeat, in his own Person; he justifies through his Spirit. For he himself was raised again and 'justified' by the Spirit; and what was wrought in him is repeated in us who are his brethren, and the complement and ratification of his work."[3]

The mysteries of Christ's death, exaltation, and sending of Spirit are therefore closely related. "If Christ has not risen," says St. Paul, "your faith is futile and you are still in your sins" (1 Cor 15:17). The whole cosmic plan moves around the Resurrection: "But in fact Christ has been raised from the dead, the first fruits of those who have fallen asleep. For as by a man came death, by a man has come also the resurrection of the dead. For as in Adam all die, so also in Christ shall all be made alive" (1 Cor 15:20-22).

St. Paul, the great mystic (qv) derived his spirituality, his personal ethic, from the Resurrection: "that I may know him and the power of his resurrection, and may share his sufferings, becoming like him in his death, that if possible I may attain the resurrection from the dead" (Phil 3:10-11). Here Newman meets him: "But if, as we have seen, the Resurrection be the means by which the Atonement is applied to each of us, if it be our justification, if in it are conveyed all the gifts of grace and glory which Christ has purchased for us, if it be the commencement of his giving himself to us for our spiritual sustenance, of his feeding us with the Bread which has already been perfected on the Cross, and is now a medicine of immortality, it is that very doctrine which is most immediate to us, in which Christ most closely approaches us, from which we gain life, and out of which issue our hopes and our duties. Christ is God from everlasting; he became man under Caesar Augustus; he was an Atonement for the world on the Cross; but he became a Savior on his resurrection. He was then 'exalted to be a Prince and a Savior; 'to come to us in the power of the Spirit, as God, as man, and as atoning sacrifice.' "[5]

[1]H. B. Swete, The Appearances of Our Lord after the Passion, London, 1907; J. H. (Cardinal) Newman, "Righteousness, the Fruit of Our Lord's Resurrection," in Lectures on the Doctrine of Justification, ed., 1874, 202-22; A. M. Ramsey, The Resurrection of Christ, Philadelphia, 1946, rev. ed., London, 1961; F. X. Durrwell, La résurrection de Jésus, mystère de salut, 1950, English tr., London, 1960, The Resurrection of Jesus, A Biblical Study; W. Kunneth, Theologie der Auferstehung, 4th ed., Munich, 1951; K. H. Rengstorf, Die Auferstehung Jesu: Form, Art und Sinn der urchristlichen Osterbotschaft, Witten, 1952; Christus Victor Mortis, Papers of the Third Theological Week, Gregorian University, Greg 39 (1958) 201-524; A. Descamps, "La structure des récits évangeliques de la résurrection," BB 40 (1959) 726-41; C. M. Martini, Il problema storico della risurrezione negli studi recenti, Rome, 1959; D. M. Stanley, Christ's Resurrection in Pauline Soteriology, Rome, 1961; N. Fuglister, Die Heilsbedeutung des Pascha, Munich, 1963; J. Kremer, Das älteste Zeugnis von der Auferstehung Christi, Stuttgart, 1966; id., Die Osterevangelien, Stuttgart, 1977; C. H. Dodd, "The Appearances of the Risen Christ. An Essay in Form-Criticism of the Gospels," in More New Testament Studies, Grand Rapids, 1968, 102-33; W. Pannenberg, "Did Jesus Really Rise from the Dead?" Dialog 4 (1965) 128-35; id., Jesus, God and Man, London, 1968, 53-114; H. W. Bartsch, Die Auferstehungzeugnis, Hamburg, 1965; C. F. D. Moule, ed., The Significance of the Message of the Resurrection for Faith in Jesus Christ, London, 1968; W. Marxsen, The Resurrection of Jesus of Nazareth, London, Philadelphia, 1970; G. Koch, Die Auferstehung Jesu-Christi, Tübingen, 1959; J. Comblin, La résurrection de Jésus Christ, Paris, 1959; esp. R. E. Brown, The Virginal Conception and Bodily Resurrection of Jesus, London, 1973, 69-129; B. Rigaux, O.F.M., Dieu l'a réssucité, Gembloux, 1973; E. Dhanis, ed., Resurrexit, Vatican City, 1974, bibl., 1920-1973; X. Léon-Dufour, Resurrection and the Message of Easter, London, New York, 1975; C. F. Evans, Resurrection and the New Testament, London, 1970; P. Benoit, O.P., The Passion and Resurrection of Jesus Christ, London, 1969; R. C. Ware, "The Resurrection of Jesus," Heythrop Journal 16 (1975) 22-35, 174-94; G. O'Collins, S.J., The Resurrection of Jesus Christ, Valley Forge, 1974, new ed., The Easter Jesus, 1980; id., Jesus Risen, New York, 1987; J. D. G. Dunn, Jesus and the Spirit, London, 1975, 95-134; W. Kasper, Jesus the Christ, London, 1976, 134-60; C. Duquocq, Christologie, Paris, 95-162; Russell, "Modern Exegesis and the Fact of the Resurrection," Downside Review 76 (1958) 251-64, 329-43; H. Wansbrough, Risen from the Dead, Slough, 1978; J. Sobrino, Christology at the Crossroads, London, 1978, 236-72; esp. R. H. Fuller, The Formation of the Resurrection Narratives, 1980; P. Grelot, "La résurrection de Jésus et l'histoire," Quatre Fleuves 15-16 (1982) 145-79; P. Perkins, Resurrection, New York, 1984; G. R. Osborne, The Resurrection Narratives. A Redactional Study, Grand Rapids, 1984; H. H. Hendrickx, The Resurrection Narratives of the Synoptic Gospels, 2nd ed., London, 1984; W. L. Craig, The Historical Argument for the Resurrection of Jesus during the Deist Controversy, Lewiston, New York, 1985; H. Kessler, Sucht den Lebenden nicht bei den Toten. Die Auferstehung Jesu Christi, Düsseldorf, 1985; G. Greshake and J. Kremer, Resurrectio Mortuorum . . . Leibliche Auferstehung, Darmstadt, 1986; J. Schmitt and K. Rahner (qv), LTK I, 1028-35, 1038-41; J. Schmitt, DBS X 487-582; R. E. Brown, NJBC, 1373-77; L. Coenen, C. Brown, TDNT 250-309; A. Oepke, TDNT I, anistemi, 368-72; TDNT II, egeiro, 333-39; D. Geels, NCE X, The Bible, 402-10; F. X. Durrwell, NCE X, Theology, 410-19; see articles on Bultmann, R., Paul, St., Schillebeeckx, E., Shroud of Turin; [2]Ad Smyrnaeos III, IV, tr. K. Lake, The Apostolic Fathers I, London, 1912, 255f.; [3]Newman, op. cit., 204; [4]Ibid., 206; [5]Ibid., 222.

RIVIÈRE, JEAN (1878-1946)

Author of "the most extensive and complete modern Catholic work on the redemption,"[1] R. was for years a professor on the Catholic Theology Faculty of Strasbourg. After the publication of his first two books, he became engaged in controversy with the Modernist, J. Turmel, who wrote under pseudonyms (H. Gallerand, etc.). R.'s articles were published in subsequent volumes. R.'s thinking was most amply and cogently expressed in Le dogme de la Redémption, which first appeared in 1915 in Paris, and which came out in a third edition in 1931, enlarged by 16 pages of bibliographical notes. The text was also revised throughout, over 600 pp. The list of R.'s works is: Le dogme de la Rédemption. Essai d'étude historique, Paris, 1905, English tr. L. Cappadella, The Doctrine of the Atonement, A Historical Essay, St. Louis, 1909; Le dogme de la Rédemption chez Saint Augustin, Paris, 1928, 3rd much enlarged edition, 1933; Le dogme de la Rédemption après Saint Augustin, 1930; Le dogme de la Rédemption. Etudes critiques et documents, Louvain, 1931; Le dogme de la Rédemption au début du Moyen Age, Paris, 1934; "Rédemption," in DTC XIII, 2 (1937) 1912-2004, bibl. 1992-2004, repr. in the posthumous Le dogme de la Rédemption dans la théologie contemporaine, Albi, 1948. Recent theologians approach the subject of the Redemption (qv) from different viewpoints.

R. was perhaps unduly preoccupied with the idea of satisfaction, and with the contrast between Protestant and Catholic theologies of the subject. His immense historical research, and his concentration over forty years on the theme explain the esteem in which he was held and give his work value as exemplifying the theology of his time.

[1] L. Richard, *The Mystery of the Redemption*, Baltimore, Dublin, 1965, 353f; for R. cf. *Jean Rivière, Bibliographie et souvenirs,* Albi, Secrétariat de l'Archevêché, 1952, bibl., 7–21.

RUETHER, ROSEMARY RADFORD (1936–)

This American writer has sought to think the feminist ideal deep down to its religious roots, to analyze basic themes in Christian theology which are relevant, all theology being so to some extent.[1] She has given much thought to Christology and has sought to present her insights and syntheses with a thoroughly thought-out methodology. Her approach to the subject is comprehensive and she delays on the OT basic concepts. She has sought to trace the seeds of anti-semitism to certain positions in Christology. In a wider context she wishes to recall the priority of the poor in the original project of Jesus; she is concerned to release, liberate, promote all those marginalized or depressed for whatever reason. Her published work so far has aroused enthusiasm among those imbued with the same ideals and ideas. In one in particular, her analysis of the theological (?) roots of anti-semitism, she has met sharp dissent and radical criticism. She is engaged in an ongoing project of deep import and her contribution to the literature will be examined with sharpness and, it is hoped, sympathy and compassion. She is the author of many articles and of the following works which reflect her thinking: *Messiah of Israel, and the Cosmic Christ: A Study of the Development of Christology in Judaism and early Christianity,* Unpublished, Washington, 1971; *Faith and Fratricide: The Theological Roots of Anti-Semitism,* New York, 1979; ed., *Religion and Sexism. Images of Women in the Jewish and Christian Traditions,* New York, 1979; *To Change the World. Christology and Cultural Criticism,* London, 1981; *Disputed Questions. On Being a Christian,* Nashville, 1982; *Sexism and God-talk,* Boston, 1983; *Womanguides. Readings Towards a Feminist Theology,* Boston, 1985; *Contemporary Roman Catholicism, Crisis and Challenges,* Kansas City, 1987. Among her many articles is "The Liberation of Christology from Patriarchy," in *Religion and Intellectual Life,* 2, Spring 1985, 116–128.

[1] Cf. M. H. Snyder, *The Christology of Rosemary Radford Ruether: A Critical Introduction,* Mystic, Connecticut, 1988; *Contemporary Theologies,* 165–75.

S

SACRED HEART, THE

Mention of the Sacred Heart raises two separate problems: Is this a meaningful devotion at the present time? Has the theology of the heart a valid, and profound place in the entire Christian synthesis?[1] In other words, has the individual Christian here a true means of growing in spiritual stature and has he certainty that his ideal has a hard doctrinal core?

History has its lessons here as elsewhere. The Sacred Heart was the object of Christian reflection and of mystical insights in medieval times, in the writings of St. Bonaventure and notably in the monastery of Helfta in the thirteenth century. But this movement was within the limits of private piety and did not seek expression in any liturgical service. This change would come in the seventeenth century to the extent that liturgical services could depend on local initiative. St. John Eudes is the best known name, though the inspiration in the domain of purely personal piety came from St. Margaret Mary Alacoque (qv).

There then followed a period of discussion, controversy on the validity and meaning of devotion to the Sacred Heart and on the possibility of Roman approval for a feast. Inside the Congregation of Rites, the official body in the Curia, there was for a while firm opposition to any such approval. As late as 1704 a book on the Sacred Heart, by Fr. Croiset, was put on the Index. But requests were increasingly made to Rome, notably from Poland and by the Sisters of the Visitation, the religious order to which St. Margaret Mary had belonged.

A memorandum was submitted to Clement XIII by the Polish hierarchy and he was impressed by its contents as by the fact that there existed more than a thousand confraternities throughout the world. The memorandum was one third indebted to a book by Fr. Joseph de Gallifet, S.J., *The Adorable Heart of Jesus.* On January 25, 1765, the Pope granted the feast to the Polish bishops and to the Archconfraternity of the Sacred Heart. On July 10 the Sisters of the Visitation obtained the same privilege. A number of other requests were received and favorably met. By 1865 the practice was fairly general. The French bishops, meeting in Paris for the baptism of the Prince Imperial, asked Pius IX (qv) to grant the feast to the universal Church. On August 23 he did so, specifying the rite as double major. The beatification of Margaret Mary in 1864 gave a certain confirmation to the devotion. On June 28, 1889, Leo XIII (qv) raised the feast to the rite of double of the first class. On May 8, in the Encyclical *Miserentissimus Redemptor,* Pius XI raised it still higher to double of the first class with octave.

By now the Papacy was overtly involved with the cult and spiritual ideal of the Heart of Jesus. On May 25, 1899, Leo XIII published the Encyclical *Annum Sacrum* (qv), announcing his intention to consecrate the world to the Sacred Heart on June 11 following. The suggestion that he do so had been very strongly put to him in a personal message from a Good Shepherd nun, Sister Droesch-Vichering. Popes sanctioned the practice of consecration by granting indulgences to particular formulas. On May 8, 1928, Pius XI issued his Encyclical on reparation to the Sacred Heart, *Miserentissimus Redemptor.* He had instituted the feast of Christ the King (qv) in 1925 with the publication of the Encyclical *Quas Primas.* He directed that annually there should be a renewal of the consecration to the Sacred Heart on the feast of the Kingship, and an act of reparation publicly read on the feast of the Sacred Heart.

Pius XII chose the centenary of the extension of the feast to the universal Church as the occasion for his Encyclical *Haurietis Aquas* (qv), a more substantial contribution to theology than either of the previous papal documents. The theme also figures in John Paul II's Encyclical *Dives in Misericordia,* 1980.

The cursory listing of the papal texts does, however, obscure the fact that the devotion, the theology of the Heart, suffered something of an eclipse in the aftermath of Vatican II. Different explanations may be proposed for this decline, as different explanations have been proposed for the decline in Marian piety at the same time—each was a source of anxiety, possibly suffering, to Catholics, though the number affected is clearly difficult to ascertain. Was it the success of the liturgical movement and the change from forms of piety centered on persons but persons symbolized? Was it general loss of nerve among Catholics in regard to things distinctively Catholic? Was it the biblical movement?

There is no incompatibility between the Liturgy fully valued and lived and a concentration of thought and volition on the Person of the Savior accessible through this symbol, which is part of him, bound to the very center of his being. While divine revelation in itself is complete, every generation has to exercise on its content the maximum of research, understanding, clarification in teaching and exposition. New insights will complement, correct, or serve to deepen those already perceived and formulated. The inherent truth of genuine tradition is not thus endangered or compromised.

In such a context we can contrast what Pius XII said in his magisterial Encyclical and what John Paul II (qv) teaches. Pius XII spoke principally of the Heart of Jesus as the symbol of his love: "Therefore the Heart of the Word made flesh is rightly looked upon as the principal token and sign of that threefold love wherewith the divine Redeemer ceaselessly loves both his eternal Father and all mankind. It is the sign of that divine love which he shares with the Father and with the Holy Spirit, but which in him only, that is to say in the Word which was made flesh, is made manifest to us in a frail and corruptible human body, since 'in him the whole fullness of deity dwells bodily' " (Col 2:9). It is, moreover, the sign of that white-hot charity that was infused into Christ's human soul, and that enriches his human will. The *acts* of this charity are illumined and guided by Christ's twofold most perfect knowledge, and that is to say his beatific knowledge and his *bestowed* or *infused* knowledge. And finally, his Heart is a sign— and this in a more direct and natural way—of his

emotional affection, since the body of Jesus Christ, formed by the work of the Holy Spirit in the womb of the Virgin Mary, enjoyed in the fullest degree the power of feeling and perceiving, more perfectly in fact than the bodies of all other men."[2]

John Paul II brought to the subject a different set of ideas. Whereas Pius XII admirably summarized and clarified the doctrine accepted in countries of Latin tradition, giving ample development to the Savior's word to St. Margaret Mary, 'Behold this Heart which has so loved men,' John Paul shows the influence of his training in phenomenology; he was before election as Pope author of "The Acting Person," which appeared in the *Analecta Husserliana* and was written as a contribution to phenomenological anthropology.[3]

With such an outlook the Pope can speak thus to Canadian Catholics (September 15, 1984, Toronto): "The mystery of the Cross on Golgotha and the mystery of the Cross in the Heart of the Mother of the Crucified One cannot be read in any other way: only in the perspective of eternal Wisdom is this mystery clarified for our faith. Indeed it becomes the beam of a special light in human history, in the midst of a people's destiny on earth. This light is, first of all, in the Heart of Christ lifted on the Cross. This light, reflected by the power of a special love, shines forth in the Heart of the Sorrowful Mother at the foot of the Cross."[4]

Later he dealt with another aspect of the same theme: "This cry of the Son's Heart and of his Mother's Heart—a cry which from the human standpoint would reject the Cross—is expressed in the Psalm of today's liturgy. This Psalm is a cry for salvation, for help, for deliverance from the snare of evil (Ps 31:3, 5, 16). Since these words of the Psalm reflect 'human' truth of the Hearts of the Son and of the Mother, they also express an act of absolute entrusting to God—dedication to God. This dedication is even stronger than the cry for deliverance (Ps 31:15). This awareness—'You are my God. Into your hands I commend my spirit'—prevails absolutely in the Heart of the Son 'lifted up' on the Cross, and in the Mother's Heart humanly emptied by the Son's crucifixion."[5] For the Pope the heart is the very center of the individual's being, a sanctuary of self-awareness in which is summarized and condensed the concrete essence of man.

We have in this contrast the scholastic approach of Pius and the modern phenomenological interpretation of John Paul II. Pluralism is to be welcomed here as in other areas of theology. The touchstone is Sacred Scripture, which John Paul II has invoked. Pius XII prefaced his review of biblical evidence with the words: "It cannot be denied that nowhere in the

Sacred Scriptures is there clear mention of any veneration or love for the physical heart of the Word Incarnate, considered precisely as the symbol of his ardent charity."[6] Having said that, the Pope goes on to trace the idea of God's love through the OT, in such passages as Hos 11:1, 3-4; Is 49:14-15; Song 2:2; 6:2; 8:6, ending with the promise of the covenant in Jer 31, a promise which includes the word "I will put my law within them, and I will write it upon their hearts; and I will be their God and they shall by my people" (Jer 31:33).

Turning to the NT, the Pope points out the contrast between the Old Covenant and that of Christ, "the law was given by Moses (recipient of the former Covenant); grace and truth came by Jesus Christ" (Jn 1:16-17). He is next led to the text of Eph 3:17-19, "and that Christ may dwell in your hearts through faith; that you being rooted and grounded in love, may have power to comprehend with all the saints what is the breadth and length and height and depth, and to know the love of Christ which surpasses knowledge, and that you may be filled with all the fullness of God." The Pope speaks of "the love which breathes in the Gospels, in the Epistles and in the pages of the Apocalypse, wherein the love of the Heart of Jesus is depicted," and he insists with the words of 2 Jn 7 that this must have the human sentiments proper to Christ, "For many seducers are gone out into the world who confess not that Jesus Christ is come in the flesh. This is a seducer and an antichrist." Pius also refers to and quotes Heb 2:11-14, 17-18.

The Pope is not content with generalities. He returns to the Gospels to consider the sequence of events wherein one can discern the love of the Heart of Jesus: in the hidden life at Nazareth, in the journeyings, the miracles and the preaching, the prayer vigils; there are moments especially revealing as when he had "compassion on the multitude, cried out with love for Jerusalem, cleansed the Temple. He delays on the Passion and reflects on the generosity of Christ, "But who can adequately depict the throbbings of the divine Heart, tokens of his boundless love, at those precious moments when he bestowed his greatest gifts upon mankind? That is to say the gift of himself in the Sacrament of the Eucharist, the gift of his most holy Mother, and the sharing with us of his priestly office."[7]

Interestingly, the Pope speaks of the Church born from the side of the dead Christ and goes on to see a significance in the wounding for understanding of the Sacred Heart. He goes on to expound the meaning for our lives of Pentecost, with its outpouring of charity: "For this charity is the gift both of the Heart of Jesus and of his Spirit, who is indeed the Spirit of the Father and of the Son. From this Spirit comes the origin of the Church and its marvelous spreading before the face of those nations and peoples who were sunk in the degradation of idolatry, fraternal hatred, violence and moral corruption."[8]

Pius lists the categories of Christian heroes and achievers, concluding thus: "This divine charity flows from the Heart of the Word made flesh, and is poured out by the Holy Spirit in the hearts of all believers."[9] The climax to his thought is the Pauline text in Rom 8 which begins, "Who shall separate us from the love of Christ?"

That is one approach to the biblical witness. In his remarkable contribution to *Mysterium Salutis* on the Paschal Mystery, Hans Urs von Balthasar takes up the idea of the open side of the dead Christ, considering the "open heart." A man who takes a very different view, Ignace de la Potterie, S.J., comments thus: "Like other recent theologians, Balthasar seems to assume that the text of Jn 19:31-37 is the most important biblical passage on which devotion to the Sacred Heart is based. These authors give us theological examinations of the importance of the heart in biblical anthropology or of the symbolism of blood and water. It must be noted, however, that the word 'heart' is not even mentioned in this text. To be sure, the open side of Jesus, or the blood and water which flow from it, are extremely rich symbols, but even so they are no more than symbols or signs. Moreover, they are associated with the moment immediately following Jesus' death on the cross. We are told nothing of the living heart of the earthly Jesus, of the interior life of Jesus the man, in the course of his public life. This is where new developments in Christology can make their precious contribution."[10]

Fr. de la Potterie proposed that the subject be approached from two viewpoints arising from contemporary Christology: the attempt to base Christology on the historical Jesus, recovering the entire dimension of his actual life—while avoiding the snares of historicism, and the attempt of scholars to reinterpret Chalcedon (qv), without rejecting its essential meaning. As he says, the first approach brings us straight into the question of the consciousness of Jesus (see article Knowledge of Jesus). "To talk of a person's deep consciousness amounts to the same as speaking of what he has in his heart, and this also holds true for the Heart of Jesus. This reminds us that we are dealing with Jesus' consciousness and hence also invites us to be less exclusively concerned with the anatomical reality of his physical heart, about which it would be remembered that the New Testament says nothing, whereas, as we shall see, it provides quite a number of pointers which make it possible for us to glimpse at Jesus' interior life."[11] As he adds, this approach may help ecumenism and it meets the contemporary renewed interest in Christ's consciousness, a "formidable problem," as he says, quoting Maurice Blondel, but one that must be faced.

The attempt to carry forward—rather than contradict—the teaching of Chalcedon (qv) converges with this approach. For now the Church, while accepting the ontological finding on the mystery of Christ, seeks to reflect on it in a principally historical perspective. As an author quoted by Fr. de la Potterie says, "This historical interpretation of Christology presupposes the ontological one, for the history of Jesus would lose all its theological meaning if it were not the human history of a divine Person. Our texts show that the Chalcedonian dogma is in no way being called into question again, but is, on the contrary, perfectly incorporated into the proposed interpretation. The Word's human freedom considered within actual history belongs in point of fact to the nature taken on by him, and is even its innermost center. This is truly the 'heart' of Christ's holy humanity. It is possible to build an authentic spirituality of the 'Sacred Heart' on a dogmatic foundation as solid as this."[12]

Much of what Fr. de la Potterie has to say will concern us in the article on Christ's consciousness. In the context of the Heart of Christ he looks closely at certain aspects of the historical Jesus' life which are inescapably documented: his proclamation of the kingdom of God, his obedience to the Father and his filial consciousness of the Father and intimacy with him. He thinks that "these three dimensions contain the entire interior space of the mystery of Christ." He suggests that "read within the faith of the Church, the Gospels in fact make it possible for us to discover these three aspects of the mystery in the human Heart of Jesus."[12]

Is the essential question resolved? From where in the New Testament does the Heart of Jesus speak to us? Does it speak directly at all? If indirectly, with what language? That of the OT? And is this to be given a fuller sense and wider relevance now that we speak of a man who was God? If we are to attempt a final synthesis, should it not incorporate the diverse elements here reviewed?

The heart related to the whole being is rich in symbolism and meaning. It speaks of the spirit that sustains a man, as when we say of someone "he will never give in, he is lion-hearted," or in the opposite case, "he failed because he lost heart." Christ was, in this sense, a man of great heart, the "Lion of the Fold of Juda." He radiated power; he was dynamic in the noblest sense. He never faltered or retreated on the path of duty.

Even in the case of ordinary mortals, the heart speaks of mystery, "the thoughts that are in the heart of man." Where is there more subtle, manifold, profound mystery than in the heart of one where human mystery opened on a world of sheer unknowable transcendence? What thoughts does the Son of God translate and express through this medium which vibrates and echoes in the incalculable depths of omnipotence and eternity?

The heart loves and responds to love. Love is essentially of the will, source of freedom, initiative and endurance. But the intimacy of mighty love needs the heart for its excellence. What love Jesus Christ has poured out on us, pours out daily on his intimate friends!

[1]Cf J. Croiset, S.J., *La dévotion au Sacré Coeur de Notre Seigneur Jésus Christ,* Lyons, 1691; 3rd ed., 1694, placed on Index, 1704, removed at request of Bishop Stadler of Sarajevo, August 29, 1887, with no textual change; English tr., P. O'Connell, Dublin, 1959; J. B. Terrien, *La Dévotion au Sacré Coeur de Jésus d'après les documents authenticques et la théologie,* 1893; J. de Gallifet, S.J., *De Cultu Sacrosancti Dei et Domini nostri Jesu,* Rome, 1726; French tr., 1732; English tr., *The Adorable Heart of Jesus;* A. Hamon, *Histoire de la dévotion au Sacré Coeur,* 5 vols., 1923–41; id., *DSp,* II, 1, 1023–46; J. V. Bainvel, *Devotion to the Sacred Heart, The Doctrine and its History,* 1924; id., *DTC* III (1908) 271–351; E. Agostini, *Il Cuore di Gesù,* Bologna, 1950; J. Stierli, ed., *The Heart of the Savior,* 1957; id., J. Stierli and A. van Rijen, *LTK* V, 289–94; A. J. Daschauer, *The Sacred Heart,* Milwaukee, 1959; H. Marin, ed., *El Sagrado Corazon de Jesus,* Bilbao, 1961; A. Feuillet, "Le Nouveau Testament et le Coeur de Jésus," *L'Ami du Clergé,* 74 (1964) 321–33; K. Rahner, *Theological Investigations,* III (1967) 321–52; L. Verheylezoon, S.J., *Devotion to the Sacred Heart: Object, Ends, Practice, Motives,* tr. from Flemish, 1954; *Towards a Civilization of Love: Proceedings of the International Congress on the Heart of Jesus,* Toulouse, July 24–28, 1981, English tr., San Francisco, Milwaukee, 1985; [2]*CTS* tr., 21f; [3]Tr. and revised from 1969 Polish ed. in collaboration with the author by Anna Teresa Tymieniecka, *Analecta Husserliana,* X, Dordrecht, Boston, London, 1979; [4]*AAS* 77 (1985) 411; [5]*Ibid.,* 413; [6]*CTS* tr., 11; [7]*Ibid.,* 25; [8]*Ibid.,* 29; [9]*Ibid.;* [10]In *Towards a Civilization of Love,* 46; [11]*Op. cit.,* 48; [12]*Op. cit.,* 50; author quoted, F.-M. Lethel, "Théologie de l'Agonie du Christ. La liberté humaine du Fils de Dieu et son importance sotériologique mises en lumière par saint Maxime le Confesseur," *Théologie historique,* 52, Paris, 1979, 109.

SCHEEBEN, MATTHIAS JOSEPH (1835–1888)

In his presentation of dogmatic theology, S. followed the traditional theses, adding his distinctive erudition.[1] In *The Mysteries of Christianity,* he devotes 150 pages to "The Mystery of the God-man and his Economy." True to the deep orientation of the whole work, the mystery is considered in a Trinitarian context. The leading themes with their subdivisions are as follows: *The God-man*—Nature and Constitution of the God-man; The Attributes of the God-man. *Our Knowledge of the God-man*—The Incarnation not Knowable from the External Appearance of the God-man; The Objective Motivation of the Incarnation not Discoverable within the Sphere of Reason; The true Motivation for the Incarnation found in the Supernatural Sphere. *The God-man in his Relations with the Trinity, the Human Race and the World*— Relations of the God-man with the Trinity; The Mysterious Position Occupied by the God-man with Reference to the Human Race; First Significance of the God-man as Head of the Race: Communication of Divine Nobility; Foundation and Consummation of the Divine Sonship; Second Significance of the God-man as Head of the Race: Communication of Divine Life; Third Significance of the God-man as Head of the Race: Vocation to the Infinite Glorification of God; Summary View of the Elevating Influence Exercised by the God-man as Head of the Race: Relation of this Influence to his Restorative Function; Mystical Position and Significance of the God-man as Head of the Entire Universe. *Mystical Position and Significance of the God-man as Mediator between the Trinitarian God and the World*— The Mediatory Function of the God-man; Subjective Significance, for God and Man, of the Incarnation and its Economy; Justification and Further Development of the Doctrine about the Meaning and Motivation of the Incarnation; The God-man in Every Respect the Focal Point and Center of Gravity of the World. *Activity of the God-man in the Execution of his Divine Plan*—Nature and Latreutic Character of Christ's Mystical Sacrifice; The Mystery of Free Will in the Sacrifice and Merits of Christ; The Mystery in the Propitiatory and Meritorious Value of Christ's Sacrifice, or in his Moral Causality; Physical or Dynamic Character of the Causality Exercised on the Race by the God-man.

These pages (313–465) are replete with illumination on the great themes of classical Christology and soteriology. The author's patristic erudition is not as often evident as in other sections of his work, but it is always assumed. He invested the Scotist thesis on the Incarnation with a special freshness and power (see article Primacy of Christ): the main purpose of God was the glory of God and Christ and this would have been fulfilled even if Adam had not sinned. Christ's sufferings and death did not have as their primary purpose atonement for our sins, but to offer an infinite act of love and worship to the Father. "The infinite dignity of the God-man makes it impossible for him to play a subordinate, secondary role in God's plan. All that he is and does cannot exist exclusively for the sake of man or on account of sin. In everything he is willed essentially for his own sake and for God's sake. If he is given to men and delivered up for men, men at the same time belong to him more than he belongs to them, and as his surrender conduces to their advantage, so it redounds to his own honor and the glorification of his Father. As he and his activity are ordained to the salvation of men and of the whole world, so men and the whole word are ordained to him as their Head and King (qqv) who, in freeing them from the servitude of evil, makes of them his kingdom, and along with himself lays them at the feet of his heavenly Father, that God may be all in all (cf. 1 Cor 3:22f). . . . The answer to the question *Cur Deus homo?* is then also an answer to the question *Cur mundus?* or *Ad quid mundus?* What direction is given to the world by the Incarnation? This question, although ordinarily too little noted in theological science, is as much in place as the first question."[2] These intuitions are developed with a logical splendor; rarely has the absolute universal primacy of Christ over the world, men and angels been so magnificently expounded. So it is with the other themes addressed by the author.

[1]*Gesammelte Schriften*, ed., J. Hofer, 8 vols., Freiburg in Breisgau, 1941–1967; *The Mysteries of Christianity*, tr., C. Vollert, S.J., St. Louis, 1946; cf. K. Feckes and others, *M. J. Scheeben*, Mainz, 1935; F. S. Pancheri, O.F.M., *The Universal Primacy of Christ*, Front Royal, Virginia, 1984, 90–93; *id., Il pensiero teologico di M. J. Scheeben e S. Tommaso*, Rome, 1956; E. Paul, *Denkweg und Denkform der Theologie von Matthias Joseph Scheeben*, Munich, 1970, bibl., esp. *M. J. Scheeben. Teologio cattolico nel centenario della morte*, 32 contributors, Rome, *Divinitas*, 1988; G. Fritz, *DTC* XIV, 1 (1939) 1270–74; J. Hofer, *LTK* IX (1964) 376–79; J. Carol, O.F.M., *Why Christ?* 387f; M. O'Carroll, *Theotokos*, 318–19; *id., Veni Creator Spiritus*, 206–10;   [2]*The Mysteries of Christianity*, 428f.

SCHILLEBEECKX, EDWARD, O.P. (1914–)

One of the theologians to come to worldwide prominence since Vatican II, S. has made a very considerable contribution to Christology.[1] It is contained in *Christ, the Sacrament of the Encounter with God*, 1960–1963; in the two massive works, *Jesus: An Experiment in Christology*, 1974–1979, and *Christ: The Experience of Jesus as Lord*, 1977–1980; and *Interim Report on the Books Jesus and Christ*, 1978–1980. The first book was concerned chiefly with the Sacraments, aiming at giving them a personalist dimension in regard to Christ; but the introductory chapters which deal with Christ, Sacrament of God, and The Church, Sacrament of the Risen Christ contain many enlightening insights. S.'s training in existentialist and personalist philosophy, his pedagogic role for so many at different levels in the Church in Holland in the testing days after the Council, his attention to the historical dimension of divine revelation give his thinking and his expression of it a quality which challenges some readers excessively; the effort to follow him is very worthwhile. The two large works are part of a trilogy, which is to be completed. The *Interim Report* provides what may for many be a useful introduction to the whole corpus, while fulfilling its author's purpose which was to deal with the varied reactions to the large volumes.

S.'s academic background is Le Saulchoir in Paris, the Dominican center which has produced many of the active theologians of recent times, Y. M. Congar, best known of them, Louvain University and his intellectual home for 26 years until he retired from his professorship in 1983, Nijmegen. Since the Council, he has been a regular contributor to *Concilium,* which he helped to found.

S.'s erudition is massive; over 800 authors are cited or referred to in the two volumes on Christology. The Biblical Commission (qv) summarized his approach to Christology thus: "E. Schillebeeckx so studies *Jesus' personal experience* that he sets up a connection and a link between Jesus' experience and the common human experience, and first of all that of the people who were his companions in his lifetime. The death that Jesus underwent as an 'eschatological prophet' did in no way put an end to their faith in him. The announcement of his resurrection, understood as a divine ratification of his life, shows that the same people recognized in Christ a sign of God's victory over death and a pledge of the salvation promised for all those who would follow him in his Church."[2]

The Biblical Commission commented thus: "Legitimate, indeed, is the attempt *to establish continuity between Jesus' experience and that of Christians.* But then it must also be established, without reliance on hypotheses that are too minimal, how and in what sense Jesus, the 'eschatological prophet,' came to be acknowledged in faith as the Son of God; how the inchoative faith and hope of the disciples could come to be transformed into a firm certitude about his triumph over death; how among the conflicts that affected the churches of the apostolic period, one was able finally to come to recognize the true 'praxis' that Christ desired—that which was the basis of the authentic 'sequel of Jesus'; how, finally, the different interpretations of his person and mission as Mediator of God and human beings, which are found in the New Testament, could at length be considered as presenting the true picture of Jesus, as he really was, and of the revelation that took place in him and through him. Only on such conditions will ambiguity be avoided in proposing a Christology."[3]

[1]Cf. *God is New Each Moment, Edward Schillebeeckx, Conversation with H. Oosterhuis and P. Hoogeven,* New York, 1983, esp. on Christology, 19–33; J. Bowden, *Edward Schillebeeckx, In Search of the Kingdom of God: Portrait of a Theologian,* London, 1983; J. Owen, "Today's Word for Today," VII *ExT* 93, 1 (1981) 4–6; J. Ramisch, "The Debate Concerning the 'Historical Jesus' in the Christology of Schillebeeckx," *Semeia* 29 (1984) 29–48; R. Schreiber and M. Catherine Hilkert, eds., *The Praxis of Christian Experience: An Orientation to Edward Schillebeeckx,* San Francisco, 1989; R. J. Schreiter, *The Schillebeeckx Reader,* Edinburgh, 1988, complete bibliography of E. S. to 1983; for S.'s discussion with Roman authorities, cf. *DCath,* 1980, p. 16, and for his correspondence with them, *DCath,* 1981, 667–70; H. F. Bergin, O.P., "The Death of Jesus and its Impact on God: Jürgen Moltmann and Edward Schillebeeckx," *ITQ* 52 (1986) 193–211; R. J. Bauckham, *New Dictionary of Theology,* 617–18; Ted Schoof, O.P., ed., *The Schillebeeckx Case, Letters and Documents between E.S. and the Congregation for the Doctrine of the Faith,* New York, 1984; F. G. Brambilla, *La Cristologia di Schillebeeckx. La singolarità di Gesù come problema d'ermeneutica teologica,* Brescia, 1989, 620pp; *Contemporary Theologies,* 81–93; R. I. Schreiber in *The Modern Theologians* I, 154–63;   [2]Text tr., J. Fitzmyer, S.J., *Scripture and Christology,* London, 1986, 1.1.7.4., p. 12f;   [3]1.2.7.4., p. 26f; cf. editor's comment, 80–82.

SEMPITERNUS REX, September 8, 1951

The Encyclical Letter of Pius XII (qv) on the fifteenth centenary of the Council of Chalcedon (qv).[1] It is largely an account of the historical preliminaries to the event, with a good deal about the role of Leo the Great (qv). The two truths which the Pope sought to emphasize were: "the primacy of the Roman Pontiff, which emerges very clearly from the very serious Christological controversy, and the extreme importance of Chalcedon with regard to dogmatic definition." The insistence on the papal role may be connected with the fact that little less than a month before, Pius had published the Encyclical *Humani Generis* (qv), correcting what he considered dangerous theological tendencies.

The Encyclical deals succinctly with the heresy of Eutyches, tells of the particular Council held at Constantinople under Flavian which condemned him, and his letters of protest, including that sent to Leo. Thereon comes an account of the *Latrocinium* (qv), the appeals to Leo and the sequel, his intervention, the change of imperial policy after the death of Theodosius, and the Council itself. Before dealing with it, Pius XII dwells at length on the Tome of Leo (qv). The text of the Chalcedonian definition is reproduced at length. There is an explanation of the terms used, and reference to the need for proper understanding of the terms used. The Pope traced dissident groups to misunderstanding of the terms. He referred briefly to supporters of the kenotic theory (qv), and made a very moving plea for Christian unity, recalling all that he had done to secure understanding of the separated, spoke of his relief work, with no discrimination, on behalf of the suffering during World War

II. He knew the difficulties, and also believed in the power of prayer. Finally, Pius appealed for faithful adherence to the dogma of Chalcedon, in the face of "the fallacies of human reasoning" and "the ambiguities of human language."

¹*AAS* 43 (1951) 625–44.

SERVANT OF GOD, THE

This is one of the oldest titles (qv) given to Jesus and it goes back to himself.¹ Like that of prophet (qv), it did not last in prominence for very long, which poses a number of problems. The title *ebed Yahweh* is rooted in OT, in the Servant poems in Is 40–55; the title "Servant" is widely used in the OT, applied to Moses, David, Zerubbabel, Elijah, Ahijah, and other prophets. Much discussion has taken place, with as yet no satisfactory solution, of the problems related to the poems in Is 40–55: what is their origin? who is the Servant? The Servant has been interpreted individually and collectively. There are passages which seem to identify the Servant with Israel, or with the "remnant," or again with a single individual, one personality. Closely connected with such problems is that of the relation of the *ebed Yahweh* to the Messiah. There is much research and reflection on his relation to the Teacher of Righteousness, portrayed in the Qumran (qv) documents. O. Cullmann thinks that official expectation did not include the concept of a suffering Messiah, certainly not atoning suffering; any thoughts of this kind he would hold were on the periphery of Judaism. The Servant as portrayed in Is 53 was a man of suffering. J. Jeremias differs from Cullmann: "For Is 42:1ff and 52:13ff, messianic interpretation is constant from pre-Christian times. Is 52:13 is in this connection regarded as a last judgment scene. As far as the messianic interpretation of the passages about suffering in Is 53:1-12 is concerned, this can be traced back with great probability to pre-Christian times. Here the suffering of the Messiah is thought of without exception up to the talmudic period as taking place before the final victorious establishment of his rule. When the meaning of messianic suffering is considered, the answer is that the Messiah suffers vicariously to expiate the sins of Israel."²

The title is found eight times in the NT (Mt 12:18; Lk 1:54, 69; Acts 3:13, 26; 4:25, 27, 30). One of these texts refers to Israel (Lk 1:54), two to David (Lk 1:69; Acts 4:25), the remaining five to Jesus. This usage, in scholarly opinion, goes back to an ancient tradition. The description of Jesus as the servant of God is presumed to lie behind the voice at the Baptism of Jesus (qv) (Mk 1:11 par), and the voice at the Transfiguration (qv) (Mk 9:7 par). The OT text echoed is Is 42:1, "Behold my servant, whom I uphold, my chosen, in whom my soul delights." The assumption in NT echoes of this promise is that it has been fulfilled. Account must also be taken of Jn 1:29, 36, where "the Lamb of God" is understandable in reference to an Aramaic origin, equivalently lamb or boy, servant; this overcomes the difficulty that in late Judaism the Savior is never described as a lamb. J. Jeremias suggests that with this and other considerations one may conclude that "the predication *pais Theou* of Jesus must spring from an Aramaic-speaking primitive church."³ He insists also that the title was treated with reserve by the gentile church, "a reserve which can only be due to the offense caused by its lowly character." In the Apostolic Fathers (qv), the title is found in eleven places and only in three writings:⁴ it is never found in Paul. It survived chiefly as a liturgical formula, or in solemn sacral speech, not as a stimulating concept in doctrinal exposition or development. From the fifth century it disappears entirely as a description of Christ.

Due consideration of all the evidence supports the view that the theology of the suffering Servant—*ebed* Christology—is integral to the revelation of Jesus Christ in the NT. Direct application of the deutero-Isaian texts, from 42 and especially 53 may be rare (Mt 8:17/Is 53:4; Mt 12:18-21/Is 42:1-4; Lk 22:37/Is 53:12; Jn 12:38/Is 53:1; Acts 8:32f/Is 53:7; Rom 15:21/Is 52:15). But indirect or implied reference strengthens this testimony, 1 Cor 15:3-5 interpreted as an allusion to Is 53; the Eucharistic words of 1 Cor 11:23-25; the Christological formula of Rom 4:25; the confessional formula of Rom 8:34; the Christ hymn in Phil 2:6-11; the word about ransom in 1 Tim 2:6 with many other texts from the synoptics, Acts, the Johannine writings, 1 Pet all susceptible of interpretation in the sense of deutero-Isaian servant hymns. The mentality of the early Church was instinctively oriented towards interpretation of the death of Christ and its value as universal vicarious sacrifice in the light of Is 53: this molded the entire Christian mentality and marked a clear line of development of early Christology. This was expressed in the liturgy.

Jesus had full consciousness (qv) of himself as the *ebed Yahweh*. He knew that in him the prophetic utterance of Is 53:3-12 would be fulfilled: "He was despised and rejected by men; a man of sorrows, and acquainted with grief; and as one from whom men hide their faces he was despised and we esteemed him not. Surely he has borne our griefs and carried our sorrows; yet we esteemed him stricken, smitten by God, and afflicted. But he was wounded for our transgressions, he was bruised for our iniquities;

upon him was the chastisement that made us whole, and with his stripes we are healed. All we like sheep have gone astray; we have turned everyone to his own way; and the Lord laid on him the iniquity of us all. He was oppressed, and he was afflicted, yet he opened not his mouth; like a lamb that was led to the slaughter, and like a sheep that before its shearers is dumb, so he opened not his mouth. By oppression and judgment he was taken away; and as for his generation, who considered that he was cut off out of the land of the living, stricken for the transgression of my people? And they made his grave with the wicked and with a rich man in his death, although he had done no violence, and there was no deceit in his mouth. Yet it was the will of the Lord to bruise him; he has put him to grief; when he makes himself an offering for sin, he shall see his offspring, he shall prolong his days; the will of the Lord shall prosper in his hand; he shall see the fruit of the travail of his soul and be satisfied; by his knowledge shall the righteous one, my servant, make many to be accounted righteous; and he shall bear their iniquities. Therefore I will divide him a portion with the great, and he shall divide the spoil with the strong; because he poured out his soul to death, and was numbered with the transgressors; yet he bore the sins of many, and made intercession for the transgressors."

The texts which show Jesus applying one or other phrase from this chapter to himself, or being, in the course of his passion (qv) described in terms equivalent to those here used, for example, in regard to his silence before his accusers during the passion, are: Mk 2:20 par; 9:12; Lk 11:22; Mk 10:45 par; Mt 20:28; Mk 14:8—on his burial without anointing; Mk 14:24 par—his blood "poured out for many" fulfilling deutero-Isaiah "poured out his soul to death . . . yet he bore the sins of many": Lk 22:37; Mk 14:61, par; Mt 26:63; Mk 15:5 par; Mt 27:12, 14; Jn 19:9; Lk 23:9, 34; Jn 10:11, 15, 17.

The concept of Jesus as *ebed-Yahweh* has stirred controversies among recent biblical scholars. Bultmann (qv) dismisses the predictions of the passion as *vaticinia ex eventu*; they were invented by the early Church to explain Jesus' death after it had occurred. Cullmann rightly replies that, on Bultmann's own admission, the *ebed*-Christology was not widespread in the early Church. The retort is acceptable even by those who do not agree with either Cullmann or Bultmann on the prevalence of the *ebed*-Christology.

The idea of an atoning death, central to *ebed*-Christology, came from Jesus himself; it was not invented by Paul, as liberal theologians like to maintain. Did Jesus become fully conscious of the *ebed*-vocation at his baptism, as Cullmann contends? "There can be no doubt," he writes, "that the fourth evangelist understood the voice from heaven as a summons for Jesus to take on himself the task of the *ebed Yahweh*. This is the only way we can understand the witness of the Baptist when he says, 'Behold the Lamb of God, who takes away the sin of the world.' The words clearly relate Jesus' baptism and his vicarious suffering. The connection lies in the words of the voice from heaven. As we have seen, it is even clearer in the Gospel of John than in the Synoptics that this voice uses the words of Is 42:1, addressed to the *ebed-Yahweh*, because the original reading of this account of Jesus' baptism depends more closely on the Old Testament text."[5] The opinion is challenged.

It is noteworthy that Jesus united the two concepts central to Jewish faith, the Son of Man (qv) and *ebed Yahweh*. This is very clear in Mk 10:45: "For the Son of Man also came not to be served but to serve, and to give his life as a ransom for many." Perhaps one of the effects of the new understanding of the Jewishness of Jesus (qv) will be a proper appreciation of the Savior as the suffering Servant of God.

[1]A. V. Harnack, "Die Bezeichnung Jesu als 'Knecht Gottes' und ihre Geschichte in der alten Kirche," Berlin, *Sitzungberichte der Pruss. Akad.* 28 (1926) 212–38; L. L. Carpenter, *Primitive Christian Application of the Doctrine of the Servant,* 1929; H. J. Cadbury, "The Titles of Jesus in Acts," in Jackson-Lake, *Beginnings of Christianity,* I, 5, 1933, 364–70; G. Kittel, "Jesu Worte über sein Sterben," *Deutsche Theologie,* III, 1936, 166–89; O. Procksch, "Jesus der Gottesknecht" in *In piam memoriam Alexander von Bulmerincq,* Riga, *Abhan. der Herder-Gesellschaft zu Riga,* VI, 3, 1938, 146–65; G. Sass, "Zur Bedeutung von doulos bei Paulus," *ZNW* 40 (1941) 24–33; E. Lohmeyer, *Gottesknecht und Davidsohn* (Symbolae Biblicae Upsalienses, 5) 1945; L. Cerfaux, "L'hymne au Christ-Serviteur de Dieu (Phil 2:6-11 et Is 52:13–53:12)," *Miscellanea Historica in honorem A. de Meyer,* Louvain, 1946, 117–30; J. Jeremias, "Das Lösegeld für Viele," *Judaica* 3 (1948) 249–64; id., *The Eucharistic Words of Jesus,* London, 1955; id., esp., ch. IV, "Pais Theou in the New Testament," in W. Zimmerli and J. Jeremias, *The Servant of God,* London, 1957, repr. from *TDNT* V, 654–717; K. H. Schelkle, *Die Passion Jesu in der Verkündigung des N.T.,* 1949, 60–194; O. Cullmann, "Gesù, servo di Dio," *Protestantesimo* 3 (1948) 49–58; id., esp. *The Christology of the New Testament,* London, 1959, 51–82; C. Maurer, "Knecht Gottes und Sohn Gottes im Passionsbericht des Markusevangeliums," *ZTK* 50 (1953) 1ff; T. W. Manson, *The Servant-Messiah. A Study of the Public Ministry of Jesus,* 1953; H. H. Rowley, "The Servant of the Lord in the Light of Three Decades of Criticism," in *The Servant of the Lord and Other Essays on the Old Testament,* 1954, 1–58; [2]*TDNT* V, 699 (tr. slight variant from separate issue); [3]*Ibid.,* 702; [4]*Ibid.*; [5]*Christology of the New Testament,* 67.

SHROUD OF TURIN, THE

In a special chapel in the Italian city of Turin, there is kept under heavy guard a piece of old linen about fifteen feet by three and a half feet.[1] It has been alleged that this cloth is the burial shroud of Jesus Christ. As such it has been honored for centuries, until the present century almost exclusively by Catholics; this was due to the fact that it was in the possession of the Catholic House of Savoy. Officially the Church was reserved in its attitude. Beyond a remark made by Pius XI—"this is not the work of human hands"—and Paul VI, there was no papal pronouncement binding the faithful, no prescribed liturgical honors. When the shroud became known and was exposed to the faithful, a bishop dubbed it a forgery.

Reflection on the subject must take account of certain facts of history. First, in 1357, the existence of the shroud was made known in the French town of Lirey, about one hundred miles southeast of Paris. In that year Jeanne de Vergy, widow of Geoffrey de Charny, killed the previous year by the English at the battle of Poitiers, exhibited the cloth in a small wooden church in the town. Its history before that date is uncertain. Church authorities locally were not sympathetic. They were less hostile when the relic came into the possession of the powerful house of Savoy. In 1532 it was partially damaged when a fire broke out in the special chapel constructed for it in Chambéry; in 1578 it was brought to the new Savoy capital in Turin.

The next important date is May 28, 1898. On that day an Italian lawyer who also did some photography, Secondo Pia, was given permission to photograph the shroud. It was a dramatic moment. When Pia removed the glass negative from the developing solution, he saw a positive image—it is the only occasion such a thing has happened. Moreover, the image was far more living and detailed than what has been visible to the naked eye on the cloth. Technically more perfect photographs were taken in 1931 by Giuseppe Enrie.

In the twentieth century scientists began to show increasing interest in the shroud. A French agnostic, Yves Delage, professor of comparative anatomy at the Sorbonne, shocked his colleagues in the French Academy of Sciences by a report, in which he concluded on purely medical grounds, that the shroud had been used as the burial cloth of Jesus Christ. His colleagues were incensed and refused to issue the report under their aegis. The reaction did not deter other scientists from study of the cloth: well known among them were Paul Vignon, a biologist, and Pierre Barbey, a surgeon. In 1976 Max Frei, a Zurich criminologist, Zwinglian Protestant, reported after prolonged examination, that he had found on the shroud pollen of six species of exclusively Palestinian plants and from a significant number of plants from Turkey, mostly from the Anatolian steppe.

The next event in the research of the shroud took place in 1976 when Dr. John Jackson, a scientific expert with the rank of captain in the United States Air Force, and Bill Mottern, an image enhancement specialist at the Sandia Laboratories in Albuquerque, New Mexico, used a laboratory machine called an Interpretation Systems VP-8 Image Analyzer, which plots shades of image brightness as adjustable levels of vertical relief, on a three by five inch transparency of the shroud. When Mottern set the machine in action, both men had an experience similar to that of Secondo Pia. What they saw on the television screen with which the image analyzer was linked, was a three dimensional image; the image has been seen widely since they first obtained it.

It was thought that science would have the last word with the application to the shroud of the carbon 14 dating technique. The following statement issued by Anastasio Cardinal Ballestrero, Archbishop of Turin, on October 13, 1988, covers the event and result: "Through the mediation of Dr. Tite of the British Museum, coordinator of the project, the laboratories of the University of Arizona, the University of Oxford, and the Polytechnical Institute of Zurich, which effected the dating process of the tissue of the Holy Shroud, by means of radioactive carbon, finally communicated on September 28 the results of their operations to the pontifical guardian of the Holy Shroud. This document makes clear that the dating interval of Shroud tissue, reached with a reliability rate of the order of 95 per cent, lies between 1260 and 1390 of our era. I have first given this information to the Holy See, the proprietor of the Holy Shroud. The Church reaffirms its respect for this venerable icon of Christ, which remains the object of homage from the faithful, consistently with the attitude always expressed about the Holy Shroud, whereby the value of the image is more important than its eventual value as a historical document; this attitude nullifies gratuitous suppositions, theological in tendency, which have been put forward in the context of research, which aimed at being solely and rigorously scientific.

"At the same time, problems of the origin and preservation of the image still remain largely unresolved; they will demand further research and study, for which the Church will show the same openness, inspired by the same love of truth, of which she gave evidence in allowing the dating (of the Shroud) by the method of radioactive carbon, when a reasonable work program was submitted to her."[2]

What are the problems? If the image was painted in the thirteenth century, who was the artist? How did he succeed in achieving a double, full-length portrait, anatomically so perfect and totally unlike any other given us through the ages, totally superior to all? Why did he compose this masterpiece and no other? By what unimaginable means did he conceal his real picture beneath a rather dull mass of marks on the cloth, so that it had to be "extracted" (Msgr. O'Rahilly's word) by modern photography? How, in addition, did he make his image of the Savior of a kind that, with ultra-modern twentieth century computer techniques, is shown to be three-dimensional?

Scientific research will seek answers to these problems. Specialized groups fostering interest in the shroud are non-denominational as are individual experts. Dr. John H. Heller, who collaborated in the most ambitious scientific project launched from the U.S., and reported its proceedings, is a Southern Baptist. For years those cooperating in study of the shroud in England had the support of two Bishops of the Anglican Church, Hugh Montefiore and John A. T. Robinson, the latter a biblical scholar. Scientific congresses continue their work.

One such meeting was the *Symposium de Paris sur le Linceul de Turin,* which took place in the Chaillot-Galiera Center on September 7-8, 1989. The speakers included Gino Zaninotto, a specialist in the history of Roman crucifixion; Ian Wilson, author of an important work on the shroud; M. J. Dubois, an expert in specialized photography; Dr. Marie Claire Van Oosterwick-Gastruche, a specialist in Carbon 14 dating; Dr. Balma Bollone, professor of legal medicine; Dr. John Jackson of NASA; M. Rinaudo of the laboratory of nuclear medicine in Montpelier; M. Tite of Oxford; especially Professor Jerome Lejeune of the French *Académie de Médecine.* The lectures and discussions made abundantly clear that with so many essential questions unanswered, the need is for continued research.

---

[1]Cf. P. Vignon, *Le Saint Suaire de Turin devant la science, l'archéologie, l'histoire, l'iconographie, la logique,* 2nd ed., Paris, 1939; L. Barbey, *A Doctor at Calvary,* New York, London, 1953; L. Fossati, *La Santa Sindone,* Turin, 1961; eds. J. A. Gaughan, A. O'Rahilly, *The Crucified,* Dublin, 1985 (completed 20 years earlier); esp. I. Wilson, *The Turin Shroud,* London, 1978; esp., J. H. Heller, *Report on the Shroud of Turin,* Boston, 1983—results of investigation by 40 scientists, with bibl. of expert studies on the Shroud in learned periodicals by 21 members, p. 223-25; M. S. Tite and 20 others, physicists, "Radiocarbon Dating of the Shroud of Turin," in *Nature,* vol. 337, February 16, 1989, 611–15; Dossiers in *The Catholic Counter-Reformation of the 20th Century,* ed. R. P. Georges de Nantes, English tr., Morden Surrey (D. R. Boyce, 38 Greenwood Close, SM4 4HZ), March, April, May, June issues, 1989; H. M. Decher-Hauff, *RGG*[3] VI, 1087–89; H. Leclercq, O.S.B., *DACL* XV, 2, 1718-24; for recent developments, cf. R. Laurentin on the Paris symposium, *Chrétiens Magazine,* October, 1989, 10–11; M. Haigh, O.S.B., *The Tablet,* December 5, 1988, 1392–93; R. E. Brown, *Biblical Exegesis and Church Doctrine,* New York, 1985, 147–55; id., "Brief Observations on the Shroud of Turin," *BTB* 14 (1984) 145–48; M. T. Casey, O.P.,

"The Holy Shroud of Turin," *ITQ* 56 (1990) 60–62;   [2]*Osservatore Romano,* October 14, 1988; *DCath,* 1988, 1110.

SINLESSNESS OF JESUS

There are many great religious leaders whose lives have been marked by a moment of conversion, a crisis which revealed to them the error of their ways, or their positive misdeeds, from which they emerged profoundly changed.[1] It may have been a new consciousness of sinfulness, of personal unworthiness; it may have been rejection of sinful habits, even of grave sin; it may have been a realization of the reality of the evil one and a desire to avoid him.

Any such moment is totally absent from the life of Jesus. He was tempted overtly at the opening of his public ministry and triumphed over the tempter. "For we have not a high priest who is unable to sympathize with our weaknesses, but one who in every respect has been tempted as we are, yet without sin" (Heb 4:15). "Which of you convicts me of sin?" (Jn 8:46) "You know that he appeared to take away sins, and in him there is no sin" (1 Jn 3:5).

In the Synoptics, Jesus is preeminently the one who conquers sin (see article Mercy of Jesus, The). He associated freely with sinners without condoning sin. He freed the thinking of his disciples from mere conformism or legalism, teaching where the essence of sin lies; he knew the nature of sin and the psychology of the sinner: "For out of the heart come evil thoughts, murder, adultery, fornication, theft, false witness, slander. These are what defile a man; but to eat with unwashed hands does not defile a man" (Mt 15:19-20).

Jesus, as Jn reports him, points to the devil as the origin of sin, and emphasizes the slavery of sin. But as the Synoptics insist on Jesus as conqueror of sin, the one who expels it, so Jn proclaims that Jesus is the Lamb (qv) who takes away our sins, the sins of the world (1 Jn 2:2; 3:5; 4:10; Jn 1:29). In Rom where Paul elaborates the theology of sin, the summit of his thinking is reached in the doctrine of the new Adam (qv).

---

[1]L. Ott, *Fundamentals of Catholic Dogma,* Cork, 2nd ed., 1958, 168f; G. O'Collins, S.J., *Interpreting Jesus,* London, 1983, 193f.; I. Solano, *Sacrae Theologiae Summa,* BAC, 3.1, 329–69; L. Scheffczyk, "Undsündlichkeit Christi," *LTK* X, 527f; E. A. Weis, *NCE* VII, 395f.

SON OF DAVID

The title is given to Joseph in the infancy narrative of Mt.[1] It is given to Jesus especially by those begging for his healing power. Jesus is spoken of as "descended from David" in Rom 1:3 and 2 Tim 2:8, a reflection of belief in the early Church that Jesus as the Messiah was of this royal descent. The Jewish belief that the Messiah would be of this lineage is conveyed in the Gospels (Mt 22:45; Mk 12:35; Lk 20:41; Jn 7:42). The crowds who welcomed and acclaimed Jesus on Palm Sunday cried out, "Hosanna to the Son of David! Blessed is he who comes in the name of the Lord! Hosanna in the highest!" (Mt 21:9); later when the chief priests and the scribes protested to Jesus as the children took up the cry in the temple, his reply was "Yes, you have never read 'Out of the mouth of babes and sucklings thou hast perfected praise' " (Mt 21:16). Earlier, when the city "was stirred, saying, 'Who is this?' the crowds said 'This is the prophet Jesus from Galilee' " (vv. 10-11). Jesus' messianic and prophetic character was manifest under the sign of this title. It was not a strictly historical identification with David, not as if he had, through personal achievement and merit, established a spiritual dynasty, not even as a religious founder in the Catholic Church: Jesus was not a Davidite in the sense of a Benedictine, Dominican, or Franciscan. The family was the vehicle of God's choice; the direct link was with God, the family was part of a historic process.

---

[1]O. Cullmann, *The Christology of the New Testament,* London, 1963, 117–33; L. R. Fisher, "Can This Be the Son of David?" in *Jesus and the Historian,* ed., E. T. Trotter (in honor of E. Calwell), Philadelphia, 1968, 82–97; F. Hahn, *The Titles of Jesus in Christology,* London, 1969, 240–78; J. A. Fitzmyer, *The Son of David Tradition and Mt 22:41-46 and Parallels: Essays on the Semitic Background of the New Testament,* London, 1971, 113–26; J. D. Kingsbury, "The Title 'Son of David' in Matthew's Gospel," *JBL* 95 (1976) 591–602; esp. R. E. Brown, *The Birth of the Messiah,* New York, 1977, 505–12; J. P. Meier, *NJBC,* 1319; D. J. Haughton, "Jesus, Son of David, the Son of Abraham," *ITQ,* 1991, 185–95; W. R. G. Loader, "Son of David," *CBQ* 44 (1982) 570–85.

SON OF GOD

"And in one Lord Jesus Christ, the Son of God, begotten from the Father, only-begotten, that is, from the substance of the Father, God from God, light from light, true God from true God, begotten not made, of one substance with the Father, through whom all things came into being, things in heaven and things on earth, who because of us men and because of our salvation came down and became incarnate, becoming man, suffered and rose again on the third day, ascended to the heavens, and will come to judge the living and the dead."[1]

Thus was the faith of the Church expressed at the Council of Nicaea (qv). Christ is proclaimed the Son of God in the fullest, most exact sense. Divine transcendence and all divine attributes are his, omniscience, omnipotence, eternity. That is the approach of "Christology from above" (qv). How does "Christology from below" interpret the title? We have to consult the biblical witness. Jesus does not in the synoptic Gospels call himself the Son of God; he does call himself the Son of Man (qv). Others call him the Son of God (9 times in Mt, 5 times in Mk, 5 times in Lk). It is very probable that his own conviction on the subject was the source of this belief. This conviction is insinuated strongly in the contrast between the servants and the son, the heir in the parable of the vinedressers (Mk 12:1-12), in the use of "my Father" to point to the different relationship he enjoyed with God from that of the disciples, marked by use of "your Father" (Mt 7:21; 10:32-33; 11:27; 12:50; Lk 2:49; 10:22). He never refers to God as "our Father," though he taught the disciples this mode of address. A passage in Mt which is important as enclosing a truth later perceived fully, is 11:27: "All things have been delivered to me by my Father, and no one knows the Son except the Father; nor does anyone know the Father except the Son, and him to whom the Son chooses to reveal him."

There are other texts to be considered: Mt 16:16, Peter's confession, the words spoken from on high in the Baptism and the Transfiguration (qqv), the dialogue in the trial as related by Mk 14:61-64 and Lk 22:67-71. To all these must be added the Johannine and Pauline texts, the epistle to the Hebrews, in which the 'Son of God' concept is dominant.

Fr. P. Benoit thinks that the Son of Man (qv) title so frequently used by Jesus leads into the mystery of his self-revelation as divine, the Son: "The populace were not acquainted with it (the title, 'Son of Man') and could ask 'who is this Son of Man?' (Jn 12:34; cf Mt 16:13-14 and par). The leaders of the Jews being better informed, were well aware what was at stake and sensed that Jesus would claim to be that heavenly person, the expectation of whom they themselves rejected. When he declared this to them formally, the members of the Sanhedrin accused him of blasphemy, and from their own point of view they were right. . . . By identifying himself with the 'Son of Man' of Daniel, he gave the title "Son of God" itself a meaning that was no longer metaphorical, but proper and transcendent, and that was unacceptable to their strict monotheism (cf Lk 22:70; Jn 19:7; Mt 27:40, 43). This was why they decided on his death."[2] As Fr. Benoit makes clear, the title 'Son of God' is often found in a moral or metaphorical sense. Overall there is the difficulty Jesus faced of speaking a Trinitarian language to those who had not yet had the illumination which would enable them to reconcile the Trinity with their inherited monotheism. All would be made clear after Pentecost.

---

[1]Cf. esp. article "Son of God," in M. O'Carroll, *Trinitas,* 202–04, bibl.; cf. R. E. Brown, *Jesus, God and Man,* London, 1968; O. Cullmann, "Jesus the Son of God," *The Christology of the New Testament,* London, 1959, 10, 270–305; W. Pannenberg, "The Dialectic of Jesus' Sonship," *Jesus, God and Man,* London, 1968, 344–49; P. Benoit, O.P., "The Divinity of Jesus in the Synoptic Gospels," *Jesus and the Gospel,* 3, London, 1973, 42–70; C. P. Ceroke, "The Divinity of Christ in the Gospels," *CBQ* 24 (1962) 125–39; W. Kramer, *Christ, Lord, Son of God,* London, 1966; E. G. Jay, *Son of Man, Son of God,* London, 1963; I. H. Marshall, "The Divine Sonship of Jesus," *Interpretation* 21 (1967) 87–103; P. Pokorny, *Der Gottessohn,* Zurich, 1971; L. Bouyer, C. Orat., *Le Fils éternel. Théologie de la Parole de Dieu et Christologie,* Paris, 1974 (ET, *The Eternal Son*); W. Kasper, "Jesus, Son of God," *Jesus, the Christ,* III, 1, 163–196; [2]*Op. cit.,* 69.

SON OF MAN, THE

Anyone who approaches study of this subject in Sacred Scripture, especially in the NT, will quickly learn how complex it has become in the work of biblical scholars.[1] J. P. Meier, in *NJBC* introduces it thus: "The most widely debated and confusing title (or designation) applied to Jesus is Son of Man (in Aramaic *bar ('e) n*āsā). The questions whether the historical Jesus used the title and, if so, in what sense he used it have received every answer imaginable."[2] P. Winter said some time before his death that the literature on the Son of Man was becoming more and more impenetrable, with no two people agreeing on anything. G. Vermes summed it up in these words: "Contemporary New Testament scholarship has expended much effort, erudition and ink, to agree in the end on almost nothing, except that the *son of man* is a vitally important title."[3]

Two authors, F. Hahn and O. Cullmann, who have taken as their methodology in the study of Jesus Christ, analysis of his titles, and have given substantial works on this subject were certainly convinced of the importance of the title. F. Hahn wrote: "Of all the Christological titles, that of the Son of Man has been most thoroughly investigated. The reason for this is that it has been hoped, by means of this predicate of dignity, to penetrate most deeply to the preaching of Jesus himself. Moreover, the outlook of the early Palestinian community on the person and work of Jesus is discernible in a relatively exclusive context. Hence the consideration of the title of the Son of Man is an appropriate starting-point for an investigation of the oldest Christological traditions."[4] Hahn was aware of "many problems," and the lack of "firm conclusions."

O. Cullmann made a still larger claim: "Alone with the concept *ebed Yahweh,* the Son of Man is the most important concept we have to investigate. Its Christological use also goes back to Jesus himself. Surprisingly, systematic theologians have never treated it as exhaustively, with its important Christological implications, as it deserves." Cullmann thought that the absence of a Christology founded on the Son of Man was due to preoccupation with the Logos concept. "We have seen that the *ebed Yahweh* concept explains the Christological work of the incarnate Jesus in an exhaustive way. Above all, it explains the central act of salvation, his death. We shall see that the idea of the Son of Man is even more comprehensive; it embraces the total work of Jesus as does almost no other idea."[5] Cullmann devotes maximum space to the formula, more than to any other he studies.

In the face of such diverse judgments and hopes we can take comfort in certainties. The formula is found over sixty times in the Synoptic Gospels and thirteen times in Jn; outside the gospels there is one reference in Acts 7:56, two in Rev: 1:13; 14:14. In the gospels usage is exclusively by Jesus himself; he is never addressed by anyone with this title. Moreover, according to the gospels, it is the only title Jesus applied to himself.

Jesus did not invent the title. There is a well-known text in Daniel which runs thus: "I saw in the night visions, and behold, with the clouds of heaven there came one like a son of man, and he came to the Ancient of days and was presented before him. And to him was given dominion and glory and kingdom, that all peoples, nations, and languages should serve him; his dominion is an everlasting dominion, which shall not pass away, and his kingdom one that shall not be destroyed" (7:13-14). Further on the prophet receives an interpretation of the vision and of that seen previously of four great beasts: "These four great beasts are four kings who shall arise out of the earth. But the saints of the Most High shall receive the kingdom, and possess the kingdom for ever, for ever and ever" (7:17-18).

There are problems in the early Jewish exegesis of this text. There is difficulty also in any attempt to seek illumination on the Son of Man formula in chapter XIII of the Fourth Book of Ezra;[6] it is likewise with the chapters (XLVI to LXXI) of the Book of Parables of the Ethiopic Book of Enoch, where Son of Man occurs sixteen times.[7]

What of the usage in the NT? J. L. McKenzie identifies these five groups in the Synoptics: a context wherein Jesus speaks of his human condition (Mt 8;20; Lk 9:58; Mt 11:19; Lk 7:34); a context wherein superhuman powers are attributed to Jesus—to forgive sins (Mt 9:6; Mk 2:10; Lk 5:24), lordship over the Sabbath (Mt 12:8; Mk 2:28; Lk 6:5); contexts which describe the messianic mission of Jesus: sower of the word of God (Mt 13:37), he for whom the disciples must suffer (Lk 6:22; Mt par. 5:11 has "on my account"), he who seeks and saves the lost (Lk 19:10), he whom men must identify (Mt 16:13), the sin of speaking against the Son of Man (Mt 12:32; Lk 12:10); context of the Passion and death (Mt 12:40; 17:12, 22; 20:18; Mk 9:31; 10:33; Lk 9:44; 11:30; 18:31), he serves and gives his life for many (Mt 20:28; 26:2, 24, 45; Mk 8:31; 9:12; 10:45; 14:21, 41; Lk 9:22; 22:22, 48; 24:7); context of the apocalyptic-eschatological coming of the Son of Man at the end of time, as outlined by Daniel 7:13 (Mt 10:23; 13:41; 16:28; Lk 9:26), the resurrection (Mt 17:9; 24:27, 30, 37, 39, 44; 25:31; Mk 9:9; 13:26; Lk 17:24, 26; 21:27), the second coming (Mt 26:64; Mk 14:62; Lk 12:8; 22:69; 17:22; 18:8), enthroned with judicial power (Mt 13:41; 16:27; 19:28; 25:31ff; 26:64; Mk 14:62; Lk 22:69).

The Johannine passages emphasize the pre-existence of the Son of Man; he is a heavenly figure, with angels about him (1:51); he has descended from heaven (3:13); his suffering is linked with his being "lifted up," which will be beneficial to others (3:14; 8:28; 12:34); the concept of glory is associated with the formula—he must be glorified, and when he is glorified, God is glorified in him (12:23; 13:31).

Jn has new dimensions in regard to the theme. Jesus demands faith in the Son of Man (9:35), which prompts the question of his identity (9:35), also put elsewhere (12:34)—we may add, with respect, that the enormous mass of recent writing shows that the question is painfully still being asked! Still more significantly, Jn, who did not give the institution narrative of the Eucharist (qv), relates the mystery specifically to the Son of Man status, linking this with the Father, and framing the obligation to receive the Eucharist directly in terms of the formula (6:27, 53). Outside the gospels, the formula occurs only once (Acts 7:56) in reference to Jesus (cf. Rev 1:13; 14:14).

Such is the data of the NT. Scholars have worked on it to extricate textual origin, whether the formula is traceable to Jesus himself or was thought of by the Christian community, whether it always echoed Daniel 7:13, especially on the lips of Jesus, whether it had a messianic content, whether it was a title or a circumlocution. On this last point, solely by way of illustration, these contradictory judgments are expressed by two very erudite scholars. G. Vermes: "To sum up, there is no evidence whatever, either inside or outside the Gospels, to imply, let alone demonstrate, that the *son of man* was used as a title."[8] J. D. G. Dunn: "There is no question that in the

Gospels as they now stand the Son of Man is a title, and for a particular individual Jesus."[9]

Investigation of the gospel passages has stimulated interest in the exegesis of Daniel 7:13; the phrase "son of man" therein is generally interpreted down to Christian times collectively. Attention has also been given to the absence of the Son of Man theology from the writings of St. Paul, with a suggestion that the Last Adam has taken its place. And the question of implied pre-existence has been debated with conflicting views. H. E. Tödt thinks that the Son of Man sayings in the Synoptic tradition do not "link up with the concept of pre-existence from apocalyptic literature." J. D. G. Dunn thinks that the "pre-existence element in the Johannine Son of Man sayings is a distinctively Johannine redaction or development of the Christian Son of Man tradition."[10] Hamerton-Kelly, quoted by Dunn, asserts: "In using this self-designation ('Son of Man') Jesus implied his own pre-existence."[11] And there are scholars who deny that Jesus used the title himself; because of its messianic meaning, an accretion, with the passage of time, to Daniel's original meaning, it would have been given to Jesus by the early Church.

If the idea was not part of Jesus' self-consciousness (qv), why was it thus given to him alone? Why does no one else address him with the title? Why is it found in so many different strata of gospel tradition? If the Johannine use, clearly implying pre-existence, is the result of redaction, does this also apply to the Eucharistic context? Above all, why the massive use of the title? Why was it linked with the most crucial events in the life of Jesus? What prompted such a vast series of interpolations in the very language of Jesus Christ? Did the early Church think so little of Jesus Christ's own outlook and intuitive power, that they would pick up an OT phrase and tack it on, almost meaninglessly on the conjecture, to his most moving utterances on the deeply poignant, epoch-making events in his life? Could they do such a thing without demeaning him and themselves? If this was midrashic procedure, was the procedure not irresponsible? Even pointless, as it would be ultimately unmasked?

Is O. Cullmann's request entirely unrealistic? "It would be still more important if a modern theologian would undertake to build a Christology entirely on the New Testament idea of the Son of Man. Not only would such a Christology be entirely oriented toward the New Testament and go back to Jesus' self-designation; it would also have the advantage of putting the logically insoluble problem of the two natures of Christ on a level where the solution becomes visible: the pre-existent Son of Man, who is with God already at the very beginning and exists with him as his image is *by his very nature* (author's italics) divine Man. From this point of view the whole toilsome discussion which dominated the earlier Christological controversies actually becomes superfluous."[12] The last sentence clearly implies a simplification of the history of theology.

We are left with the multiplicity of Jesus' use of the title, as we now read the NT as literature, respecting the canonical texts, urged to see what they convey. Perhaps the new interest in the Jewishness (qv) of Jesus will prove enlightening, showing us the unequalled comprehensive span of this mysterious idea so cherished by him. When it is closely linked with the title Servant of the Lord (qv), it assumes a new dimension. A vista is opened of human potential responding to divine action in its plenitude when it is offered to him in service.

---

[1]Cf. H. Lietzmann, *Der Menschensohn*, Freiburg, 1896; P. Fiebig, *Der Menschensohn*, Tübingen, 1901; P. Billerbeck, "Hat die Synagoge einen praexistenten Messias gekannt?" *Nathanael* 21 (1905) 89–150; D. Volter, *Die Menschensohn-Frage, neu untersucht*, Leiden, 1916; M. Messel, *Der Menschensohn in den Bilderreden des Henoch*, Giessen, 1922; J. M. Creed, "The Heavenly Man," *JTS* 26 (1924–25) 113–36; G. Dupont, *Le Fils de l'homme*, Bruges, 1927; C. H. Kraeling, *Anthropos and the Son of Man, A Study in the Religious Syncretism of the Hellenistic Orient*, New York, 1927; R. Otto, *The Kingdom of God and the Son of Man*, ET, Lutterworth, 1938; E. Sjoberg, *Der Menschensohn im äthiopischen Henochbuch*, Lund, 1946; *id.*, *Der verbogene Mehschensohn in den Evangelien*, Lund 1955; V. Taylor, "The Son of Man Sayings Relating to the Parousia," *ExT*, 58 (1946–47) 12–15; *Id., The Names of Jesus*, London, 1953, 25–35; J. Y. Campbell, "The Origin and Meaning of the Term Son of Man," *JTS* 48 (1947) 145–55; M. Black, "The 'Son of Man' in the Teaching of Jesus," *ibid.*, 32–36; *id.*, "The Eschatology of the Similitudes of Enoch," *JTS* 3 (1952) 1–10; *id.*, "Servant of the Lord and Son of Man," *SJT* 6 (1953) 1–11; *id.*, "The Son of Man Problem in Recent Research and Debate," *BJRL* 45 (1962–63) 305–18; *id.*, "The 'Son of Man' Passion Sayings in the Gospel Tradition," *ZNW* 60 (1969) 1–8; *id.*, "Die Apotheose Israels: eine neue Interpretation des danielischen Menschensohns," in *Jesus und der Menschensohn, Für Anton Vögtle*, ed. R. Pesch and R. Schnackenburg, Freiburg, 1975, 92–99; and, "The Throne-Theophany Prophetic Commission and the 'Son of Man': A Study in Tradition History," in *Jews, Greeks and Christians*, Essays for W. D. Davies, ed. R. Hamerton-Kelly and R. Scroggs, Leiden, 1976, 57–73; *id.*, "The Parables of Enoch (1 Enoch 37-71) and the 'Son of Man,' " *ExpT* 88 (1976–77) 5–8; *id.*, "Jesus and the Son of Man," *JSNT* 1 (1978) 4–18; C. C. McCown, "Jesus, Son of Man: A Survey of Recent Discussion," *Journal of Religion* 28 (1948) 1–12; A. Vögtle, "Die Adam-Christustypologie und 'der Menschensohn,' " *TTZ* 60 (1951) 308–28; *id.*, "Der Menschensohn und die paulinische Christologie," *SPCIC*, I, 199–218; T. Preiss, *Le fils de l'homme*, Montpelier, 1953; A. Feuillet, P.S.S., "Le fils d'homme de Daniel et la tradition biblique," *RB* 60 (1953) 170–202, 321–46; S. Schulz, *Untersuchungen zur Menschensohn-Christologie im Johannesevangelium*, Göttingen, 1957; E. M. Sidebottom, "The Son of Man as Man in the Fourth Gospel," *ExpT* 68 (1956–57) 231–35; 280–83; L. Bouyer, "La notion christologique du Fils de l'homme a-t-elle disparu dans la patristique grecque," in *Mélanges bibliques . . . André Robert*, Paris, 1957, 519–30; P. Vielhauer, "Gottesreich und Menschensohn in der Verkündigung Jesu," *Festschrift G. Dehn*, Neukirchen, 1957, 51–79; *id.*, "Jesus und der Menschensohn. Zur Diskussion mit H. E. Tödt und E. Schweizer," *ZTK* 60 (1963) 133–77; J. A. Emerton, "The Origin of the Son of Man Imagery," *JTS* 9 (1958) 225–42; C. H. Dodd, *According to the Scriptures*, London, 1953, 116–19; *id.*, *The Interpretation of the Fourth Gospel*, Cambridge, 1953, 241–49; O. Cullmann, *The Christology of the New Testament*, 137–92; A. J. B. Higgins, "The Son of Man *Forschung* since the Teaching of Jesus," *New Testament Essays in Memory of T. W. Manson*, ed. A. J. B. Higgins, Manchester, 1959, 119–35; *id.*, *Jesus and the Son of Man*, Lutterworth, 1964; *id.*, "Is the Son of Man Problem Insoluble?" *Neotestamentica et Semitica, Studies in Honor of Matthew Black*, ed. E. E. Ellis, M. Wilcox, Edinburgh, 1969, 70–87; *id.*, " 'Menschensohn' oder 'Ich' in Q, Luke, 12:8-9, Mt 10:32, 33," in *Jesus und der Menschensohn, Für Anton Vögtle*, Freiburg, 1975, 117–23; *id.*, *The Son of Man in the Teaching of Jesus*, Cambridge, 1980, bibl., 159–68; O. Moe, "Der Menschensohn und der Urmensch," *StTh* 14 (1960) 199–29; J. Muilenburg, "The Son of Man in Daniel and the Ethiopic Apocalypse of Enoch," *JBL* 79 (1960) 197–209; J. Morgenstern, "The 'Son of Man' of Daniel 7:13f," *JBL* 80 (1961) 65–77; T. W. Manson, "The Son of Man in Daniel, Enoch and the Gospels," *Studies in the Gospels and Epistles*, Manchester, 1962, 123–45; H. E. Tödt, *The Son of Man in the Synoptic Tradition*, London, 1963; E. G. Jay, *Son of Man, Son of God*, London, 1965; I. H. Marshall, "The Synoptic Son of Man Sayings in Recent Discussion," *NTS* 12 (1965–66) 327–51; R. E. C. Formesyn, "Was there a Pronominal Connection for the Bar Nasha Self-designation?" *NovT* 8 (1966) 1–35; G. Haufe, "Das Menschensohn-Problem in der gegenwärtigen wissenschaftlichen Diskussion," *EvTh* 26 (1966) 130–41; R. Marlow, "The Son of Man in Recent Journal Literature," *CBQ* 28 (1966) 20–30; N. Perrin, "The Son of Man in Ancient Judaism and Primitive Christianity: A Suggestion," *BR* 11 (1966) 17–28; J. Jeremias, "Die älteste Schicht der Menschensohn-Logien," *ZNW* 58 (1967) 159–72; *id.*, *New Testament Theology*, I, London, 1971, 257–76; J. Bowman, "The Background of the Term 'Son of Man,' " *ExpT* 59 (1947–48) 283–88; F. H. Borsch, *The Son of Man in Myth and History*, London, 1967; *id.*, "Mark 14:62 and 1 Enoch 62:5," *NTS* 14 (1967–68) 565–67; E. D. Freed, "The Son of Man in the Fourth Gospel," *JBL* 86 (1967) 402–09; M. D. Hooker, *The Son of Man in Mark*, London, 1967; *id.*, "Is the Son of Man problem really insoluble?", *Text and Interpretation Studies*, Matthew Black, ed., E. Best and R. McL. Wilson, Cambridge, 1959, 155–68; R. Leivestad, "An Interpretation of Mt 11:19," *JBL* 72 (1953) 179–81; *id.*, "Der apokalyptische Menschensohn ein theologisches Phantom," *Annual of the Swedish Theological Institute*, VI, 1968, 49–105; *id.*, "Exit the Apocalyptic Son of Man," *NTS* 18 (1971–72) 243–67; J. M. Ford, " 'The Son of Man'—A Euphemism," *JBL* 87 (1968) 257–66; G. Lindeskog, "Das Rätsel des Menschensohnes," *StTh* 22 (1968) 149–76; R. Maddox, "The Function of the Son of Man according to the Synoptic Gospels," *NTS* 15 (1968, 69) 45–74; *id.*, "The Quest for Valid Methods in 'Son of Man' Research," *Australian Biblical Review* 19 (1971), in German "Methodenfragen in der Menschensohnsforschung," *EvTh* 32 (1972) 143–60; *id.*, "The Function of the Son of Man in the Gospel of John," *Reconciliation and Hope*, L. L. Morris, Festschrift, London, 1974, 186–204; A. Gelston, "A Sidelight on the Son of Man," *SJT* 22 (1969) 189–96; F. Hahn, *The Titles of Jesus in Christology: Their History in Early Christianity*, London, 1969, 15–67; J. Coppens, "La vision danielique du Fils d'Homme," *VT* 19 (1969) 171–82; *id.*, *De Menschenzoon-logia in het Markus evangelie. Avec un résumé des notes et une bibliographie en français*,

Meded. Kon. Acad. Wet Lett. en Belgie 85, Fasc. 3, Brussels, 1973—bibl. 220 items; *id.*, "Le Fils de l'homme dans l'évangile johannique, *ETL* 52 (1976) 28–81; *id.*, "Le Fils de l'homme dans le dossier paulinien," *ibid.*, 309–327; *id.*, "Où en est le problème de Jésus, Fils de l'homme," *ETL* 56 (1980) 282–302, bibl. since 1973, 283–87; *id.*, "La relève apocalyptique du messianisme royal," III. "Le Fils de l'homme néotestamentaire," *BETL* 55, Louvain, 1981; E. Schweizer, *Jesus,* London, 1971; O. Michel, "Der Menschensohn: die eschatologische Hinweisung; die apokalyptische Aussage; Bemerkungen zum Menschensohn-Verständnis des Neuen Testaments," *TZ* 27 (1971) 81–104; U. B. Müller, *Messias und Menschensohn in jüdischen Apokalypsen und in der Offenbarungdes Johannes,* Gütersloh, 1972; W. O. Walker, "The Origin of the Son of Man Concept as Applied to Jesus," *JBL* 91 (1972) 482–90; *id.*, "The Son of Man: Some Recent Developments," *CBQ* 45 (1983) 584–607; G. Vermes, *Jesus the Jew,* London, 1973, 160–91; *id.*, "The Present State of the 'Son of Man' Debate," *JJS* 29 (1978); "The 'Son of Man' Debate," *JSNT* 1 (1978) 19–32; *Jesus in the World of Judaism,* Philadelphia, 1984, 89–99; R. G. Hamerton-Kelly, *Pre-existence, Wisdom and the Son of Man: A Study of the Idea of Pre-existence in the New Testament,* Cambridge, 1973; B. Lindars, "The Son of Man in the Johannine Christology," *Christ and Spirit in the New Testament,* Festschrift, C. F. D. Moule, ed. B. Lindars, S. S. Smalley, Cambridge, 1973, 43–60; *id.*, "Re-enter the Apocalyptic Son of Man," *NTS* 22 (1975, 76) 52–72; *id., Jesus, Son of Man,* London, 1983, bibl., 223–235; *id.*, "Response to Richard Bauckham, The Idiomatic Use of Bar Enasha," *JSNT* 23 (1985) 35–41; K. Müller, "Menschensohn und Messias," *Biblische Zeitschrift* 16 (1972) 161–87; 17 (1973) 52–66; *id.*, "Der 'Menschensohn' im Danielzyklus," *Jesus und der Menschensohn. Für Anton Vögtle,* Festschrift, 1975, 37–80; J. J. Collins, "The Son of Man and the Saints of the Most High in the Book of Daniel," *JBL* 93 (1974) 50–66; F. Neugebauer, "Die Davidsohnfrage (Mark 12:35-7 par.) und der Menschensohn," *NTS* 21 (1974, 75) 81–108; E. Lohse, "Der Menschensohn in der Johannesapokalypse," *Jesus und der Menschensohn,* 1975, 415–20; H. Schürmann, "Beobachtungen zum Menschensohn—Titel in der Redequelle," *Jesus und der Menschensohn,* 124–47; W. G. Kümmel, "Das Verhalten Jesus gegenüber und das Verhalten des Menschensohn," *Jesus und der Menschensohn,* 210–14; *id., Jesus der Menschensohn,* Wiesbaden-Stuttgart, 1984; T. F. Glasson, "The Son of Man Imagery, Enoch 14 and Daniel 7, *NTS* 23 (1976–77) 82–90; P. M. Casey, "The Use of the Term 'Son of Man' in the Similitudes of Enoch," *JSJ* 7 (1976) 11–29; *id.*, "The Corporate Interpretation of 'One like a Son of Man' (Dan 7:13) at the Time of Jesus," *NovT* 18 (1976) 167–80; *id.*, "The Son of Man Problem," *ZNW* 67 (1976) 147–54; *id., The Son of Man: The Interpretation and Influence of Daniel 7,* London, 1980, bibl. 41–59; *id.*, "Aramaic Idiom and the Son of Man Sayings," *ExT* 96 (1984–85) 233–36; *id.*, "General, Generic and Infinite. The Use of the Term 'Son of Man' in Aramaic Sources and in the Teaching of Jesus," *JSNT* 29 (1987) 21–56; R. Bauckham, "The Son of Man. 'A Man in my Position,' or 'Someone,' " *JSNT* 23 (1985) 23–33; D. R. Jackson, "The Priority of the Son of Man Sayings," *The Westminster Theological Journal* 47 (1985) 83–96; J. Bowker, "The Son of Man," *JTS* 28 (1977) 19–48; A. A. di Lella, "The One in Human Likeness and the Holy Ones of the Most High in Daniel 7," *CBQ* 39 (1977) 1–19; M. Müller, "Über den Ausdruck 'Menschensohn' in den Evangelien," *StTh* 31 (1977) 65–82; F. J. Moloney, *The Johannine Son of Man,* Rome, 2nd ed., 1978; J. A. Fitzmyer, S.J., "The New Testament Title 'Son of Man' Philologically Considered," in *A Wandering Aramean,* Scholars Press, 1979, 143–60; *id.*, "Another View of the 'Son of Man' Debate," *JSNT* 4 (1979) 58–68; B. McNeil, "The Son of Man and the Messiah: A Footnote," *NTS* 26 (1979–80) 419–21; S. Kim, *The "Son of Man" as the Son of God,* Tübin-

gen, 1983; M. Müller, *Der Ausdruck "Menschensohn" in den Evangelien. Voraussetzungen und Bedeutung,* Leiden, 1984; O. Betz, *Jesus und das Danielbuch II. Die Menschensohn-Worte Jesu und die Zukunftser wartung des Paulus (Daniel 7:13-14),* Frankfurt, 1985; C. Mearns, "The Son of Man Trajectory and Eschatological Development," *ExT* 97 (1985–86) 8–12; C. C. Caragounis, *The Son of Man. Vision and Interpretation,* Tübingen, 1986; J. R.Donahue, "Recent Studies on the Origin of the 'Son of Man' in the Gospels," *CBQ* 48 (1986) 484–98; R. Kearns, *Das Traditionsfüge um den Menschensohn Ursprünglicher Gehalt und älteste Verändereung im Urchristentum,* Tübingen, 1986; Y. Collins, "The Origin of the Designation of Jesus as 'Son of Man,' " *HTR* 80 (1987) 391–407; J. D. G. Dunn, *Christology in the Making,* 2nd ed., London, 1989, 65–97; [2]p. 1324; [3]*Jesus the Jew;* [4]*The Titles of Jesus in Christology,* 15; [5]*The Christology of the New Testament,* 137; [6]*Old Testament Pseudepigrapha,* ed. J. H. Charlesworth, 1983, vol. I, 551–53, B. M. Metzger; [7]*Op. cit.,* 34–50, cf. esp. XLVIII, p. 35; cf. also M. A. Knibb, *The Ethiopic Book of Enoch,* Oxford, 1978, vol. II, 131–67; [8]*Jesus the Jew,* 185; [9]*Christology in the Making,* 82, cf. also 66; [10]*Op. cit.,* 90; [11]*Op. cit.,* 88; R. G. Hamerton-Kelly, *Pre-existence, Wisdom and the Son of Man: A Study of the Idea of Pre-existence in the New Testament,* Cambridge, 1973, 100; [12]*Op. cit.,* 192.

SPIRIT, THE HOLY AND JESUS

The relationship between the Spirit and Jesus has been brought into focus in recent theological writings, notably by Y. M.-J. Congar, O.P.[1] It is a theme taken up with remarkable insights by John Paul II in the course of the catechetical series which he has devoted to the Holy Spirit in recent times. Some lengthy passages will represent not only the Pope's thinking, but very recent theological progress: "Jesus himself illustrates the role of the Spirit when he explains to the disciples that only with the Spirit's help will they be able to penetrate the depths of the mystery of his person and mission. 'When the Spirit of truth comes, the Spirit will guide you into all the truth' (Jn 16:13-14). Therefore, it is the Holy Spirit who lets people grasp the greatness of Christ and thus 'glorifies' the Savior. But it is also the same Spirit who reveals his role in Jesus' life and mission.

"This is a point of great interest, to which I wish to direct your attention with this new series of religious instruction.

"If previously we have shown the wonders of the Holy Spirit announced by Jesus and experienced at Pentecost and during the initial journey of the Church in history, the time has come to emphasize the fact that the first and greatest wonder accomplished by the Holy Spirit is Christ himself. It is towards this wonder that we want to direct your attention.

"In fact we have already reflected on the person, life and mission of Christ in the Christological series: but now we can return briefly to that topic under the heading of pneumatology, that is in the light of the action accomplished by the Holy Spirit within the Son of God made man.

"Treating of the topic of the 'Son of God' in catechetical instruction one speaks about him after having considered 'God the Father' and before speaking of the Holy Spirit, who 'proceeds from the Father and the Son.' For this reason Christology precedes pneumatology. And it is right that it is so, because even seen from a chronological standpoint, Christ's revelation in our world happened before the outpouring of the Holy Spirit who formed the Church on the day of Pentecost. Furthermore, that outpouring was the fruit of Christ's redemptive offering and the manifestation of the power acquired by the Son now seated at the Father's right hand.

"Still a pneumatological integration with Christology seems to be inevitable—as the Orientals observe—by the fact that the Holy Spirit is found at the very origin of Christ as Word Incarnate come into the world 'by the power of the Holy Spirit,' as the Creed says.

"In accomplishing the mystery of the Incarnation, there was a decisive presence of the Spirit, to the degree that, if we want to grasp and enunciate this mystery more fully, it is not enough for us to say that the Word was made flesh; we must also underline—as happens in the Creed—the Spirit's role in forming the humanity of the Son of God in the virginal womb of Mary. We will speak about this later. And we will attempt to follow the Holy Spirit in the life and mission of Christ: in his childhood, in the inauguration of his public life through his Baptism, in his sojourn in the desert, in prayer, in preaching, in sacrifice, and finally, in resurrection.

"A basic truth emerged from examination of the Gospel texts: what Christ was, and what he is for us, cannot be understood apart from the Holy Spirit. That means that not only is the Holy Spirit's light necessary for penetrating Christ's mystery, but the influence of the Holy Spirit in the Incarnation of the Word and in the entire life of Christ must be taken into account to explain the Jesus of the Gospel. The Holy Spirit left the mark of his own personality on the face of Christ.

"Therefore, arriving at a deeper awareness of Christ demands also a deeper awareness of the Holy Spirit. 'To know who Christ is' and 'to know who the Spirit is' are two indissolubly linked requirements, the one implying the other.

"We can add that even the Christian's relationship with Christ is integrally joined to his or her relationship with the Spirit. The Letter to the Ephesians helps us to understand this when it expressed the hope that believers may be 'strengthened with power' by the Spirit of the Father in the inner man, in order to be able to 'know Christ's love which surpasses knowledge' (cf. Eph 3:16-19). That means that in order to reach Christ with our knowledge and love—as happens in true Christian wisdom—we need the inspiration and the guidance of the Holy Spirit, the interior master of truth and life.'"[2]

To this splendid statement of the theological reality here under consideration we may perhaps add another passage from the teaching of John Paul II; he is speaking of the holiness of Jesus: "The union of divinity and humanity in the one Person of the Word-Son, that is the 'hypostatic union' (hypostasis: 'person') is the Holy Spirit's greatest accomplishment in the history of creation and in salvation history. Even though the entire Trinity is its cause, still it is attributed by the Gospel and by the Fathers to the Holy Spirit, because it is the highest work wrought by divine Love, wrought with the absolute gratuitousness of grace, in order to communicate to humanity the fullness of holiness in Christ: all these effects are attributed to the Holy Spirit (Cf. St. Thomas, *Summa Theol.*, III, q. 32, a. 1).

"The words addressed to Mary during the Annunciation indicate that the Holy Spirit is the source of holiness for the Son who is to be born of her. At the instant in which the Eternal Word becomes man, a unique fullness of human holiness is accomplished in the assumed nature, a fullness which goes beyond that of any other saint, not only of the Old but also of the New Covenant. This holiness of the Son of God as man, as Son of Mary, a holiness from the source, rooted in the hypostatic union—is the work of the Holy Spirit, who will continue to act in Christ to the point of crowning his masterpiece in the Easter mystery."[3]

The Pope goes on to show how this type of holiness is a result of the unique consecration effected in Christ by the Spirit, how he is the unique exemplar of the "law of the Spirit" (Rom 8:2), how his "consecration" is made known at the level of mission at the start of his messianic activity: "The Spirit of the Lord is upon me: because he has anointed me; he has sent me" (Lk 4:18). "The mystery-reality of the Incarnation, therefore, signals the entrance into the world of a new holiness. It is the holiness of the divine Person of the Son-Word who, in hypostatic union with humanity, permeates and consecrates the entire reality of the Son of Mary: soul and body. By the power of the Holy Spirit, the holiness of the Son of Man constitutes the principle and lasting source of holiness in human and world history."[4]

The Pope elsewhere reflects on the anthropological dimension of the mystery: "We can say, therefore, that in the Incarnation the Holy Spirit lays the foundations for a new anthropology which sheds light on the greatness of human nature as reflected in Christ. In him, in fact, human nature reaches its highest point of union with God, 'having been conceived by the power of the Holy Spirit in such a way that one and the same subject can be Son of God and son of man' (St. Thomas, *Summa Theol.*, III, q. 2, a. 12, ad 3). It was not possible for man to rise up higher than this high point, nor is it possible for human thought to conceive of a closer union with the divinity.''[5]

The Pope's general ideas offer a valid schema wherein the details of the Spirit's intervention in Christ's life can be fully studied. This is done in *Veni Creator Spiritus.*[6]

---

[1]Cf. with bibl. in *Veni Creator Spiritus*, 46, J. D. G. Dunn, *Jesus and the Spirit,* London, 1875; *Christ and Spirit in the New Testament: Studies in Honor of C. F. D. Moule,* eds, B. Lindars and S. S. Smalley, Cambridge, 1973; [2]General audience, March 28, 1990, *L'Osservatore Romano,* English ed., April 2, 1990; [3]General audience, June 6, 1990, *L'Osservatore Romano,* English ed., June 11, 1990; [4]*Ibid.;* [5]General audience, May 23, 1990, *L'Osservatore Romano,* English ed., May 28, 1990; [6]*Op. cit.,* 44–46.

SUFFERING OF GOD?, THE

The question has been discussed and given much prominence by the writings of Jürgen Moltmann. It ramifies into theology and raises the question of the immutability of God. The mystery of the Incarnation when fully thought out confronts us with the problem. God becoming man enters human history, which consists of constant change. The humanity of Christ is a creature, and a creature begins to exist, goes through different phases of existence before its end. But God does not change in himself. He is the eternal one, without beginning or end. How then do we explain the way in which God seems to modify his action in his dealing with creatures, whom he brought into being, as these go through certain phases? We touch the very essence of the Incarnation: to maintain divine immutability may well appear to make the Incarnation unreal; to abandon this immutability may from another angle nullify its meaning and importance, for if the Word, who became flesh, is not immutable, he is not God.

Certain truths remain absolute: God is transcendent, beyond any direct influence by the creature, which he himself does not control; the entire reality of the creature has come from God, remains totally dependent on him, was in every element foreseen by him; in every relationship between the creature and God the initiative is from God; the human mystery of free will is no mystery to God who composed all its elements, fixed its inner springs, laid down the scope of its movement, made it from nothing, as he made everything.

Those who say that God is not immutable, that he can in his very being change, are faced with a problem akin to that of the theologians who hold that Jesus Christ had faith: a problem of delimitation? Up to what point did Christ possess faith? Here it is: How much can God change? What are the limits? Who decides? If God decides, who, except God, can know? If God decides, how do we know even that he has taken such a decision? Is it revealed in the communication of idioms (qv)? In Scripture, validly interpreted? Do the reversals of punitive measures promised in the OT indicate change? Do they not indicate rather divine resource which has many modes of action available in dealing with man, all foreseen in the original constitution of the created universe and of man? That God forgives and withdraws sentence of punishment is an exercise of divine mercy, a theme rarely discussed by modern theologians.

Did God suffer in Jesus Christ? An affirmative answer here may maximize the power of sinful men intolerably. Suffering is caused by sin, often directly by sinners. Is God subject to his rebellious creatures? Since they are often prompted to inflict suffering by the demon, is it even remotely thinkable that he should have the power to touch God?

Since the question is raised in the context of God's entry to history in the Incarnation, the time factor must be considered. When did God suffer? Who fixed the time span? Has his suffering continued or is it intermittent? How are the moments caused?

More seriously, is there not a danger of reducing the dignity of Christ as a man at the very moment people think they are glorifying him? It would follow that as a man he was inadequate to the work of redeeming us, if the Word of God who had assumed his humanity had to share in his sufferings. It may be urged that the hymn quoted in Phil 2:5-11 on the kenosis (qv) or self-emptying implies that the God who became man did suffer. Close examination will show that it does nothing of the kind: "He emptied himself, taking the form of a servant, being born in the likeness of men." Then comes the lucid statement of the Passion (qv); it is made quite clear that as a man he suffered, "And being found in human form he humbled himself and became obedient unto death, even death on a Cross" (2:8).

The world is full of suffering, mostly wasted suffering. St. Paul showed how it can be made fruitful: "I have been crucified with Christ; it is no longer I who live, but Christ who lives in me; and the life I now live in the flesh I live by faith in the Son of God, who loved me and gave himself for me" (Gal 2:20). Hence he could speak of "making up in his flesh those things lacking in the Passion of Christ.'' This he could not do if the suffering were in God.

Much has been written on the subject and the bibl. is taken from J. H. Nicolas, *Synthèse Dogmatique*.[1] One fundamental aspect has not been at all considered, the Trinitarian repercussion of any theory about the mutability of God. Which of the divine Persons is subject to change? All three? How is the change reconcilable with the relations, from which originates the distinction of Persons? If only one divine Person is subject to change, there is no longer equality between the three Persons. In a word, there are so many difficulties inherent in any thesis of a change in God that the idea has to be abandoned. This is not written with any lack of respect for the theologians listed in the bibl. as favoring the theory.

---

[1]On the question of divine immutability, *FOR*: C. Carlo, ''Dio in divenire, una nuova gnosi,'' *Sal* 37 (1975) 69–91; M. Gervais, ''Incarnation et immutabilité divine, *RSR* 50 (1976) 215–43; L. Iammarone, ''Il 'divenire di Dio e Giovanni Duns Scoto,'' *Miscellanea Francescana* 77 (1977) I–II, 45–94; J. L. Leuba, ''Temps et Trinité. Esquisse d'herméneutique doctrinale,'' in *Temporalité et Aliénation*, Actes du Colloque . . . le Centre International d'Etudes humanistes. et l'Institut d'Etudes philosophiques de Rome, January 3–8, 1975, Paris, 1975, 365–75; A. Milano, ''Il 'divenire di Dio' in Hegel, Kierkegaard e san Tommaso d'Aquino,'' *Studi Tomistici*, 3, Rome, 1974, 284–94; J.-H. Nicolas, ''L'acte pur de St. Thomas et le Dieu vivant de l'Evangile,'' *Angelicum* 51 (1974) 511–32; *id.*, ''Aimante et bienheureuse Trinité,'' *RT* 78 (1978), 271–91 (= 138–87 in *Contemplation et vie contemplative en Christianisme*, Fribourg, 1980); E. H. Evert, ''La temporalité de Dieu dans la théologie du devenir,'' in *Temporalité et Aliénation*, j.c. 139–59. *AGAINST*, with differing nuances, and referring to the God of Christians: H. Urs von Balthasar, ''The Paschal Mystery,'' in *Mysterium Salutis*, XII, 13–275; H. Küng, *The Incarnation: An Introduction to Hegel's Theological Thought as Prolegomena to a Future Christology*, Edinburgh, 1987; H. Mühlen, *Die Veränderlichkeit Gottes als Horizont einer zukunftigen Christologie. Auf dem Wege zu einer Kreuzestheologie in Auseinandersetszung mit der altkirchlichen Theologie*, Münster, 1969; J. Moltmann (qv), *The Crucified God*, London, 1974; J. Galot, S.J. (qv), *Dieu souffre-t-il?* Paris, 1976; P. J. Schoonenberg, *Il est le Dieu des hommes?*, Paris, 1973.

T

TAYLOR, VINCENT (1887–1968)

With E. Hoskyns and C. H. Dodd, T. was in the wake of the Bultmann (qv) revolution a stabilizing force, ready to accept valid methods without panic.[1] His magnum opus was *The Gospel According to St. Mark,* revised edition, 1966, the most important contribution to this subject in English since H. B. Swete's work. He remained steadfast on the historicity in Mark's account, allowing for proper use of modern method. His interest for our work lies in his concentration on Christological themes, again with a sense of balance and moderation. *The Formation of the Gospel Tradition,* 1933, was an important essay in the Form Criticism (qv) debate. Important, too, are *The Names of Jesus, The Life and Ministry of Jesus,* 1954, a reaction, like C. H. Dodd's *The Founder of Christianity,* against the sweeping rejection of lives of Christ, and *The Person of Christ in the New Testament,* 1958. He allowed for the role of the apostolic preaching, but was also clear that at the origin of the preaching was the Jesus of History.

---

[1]Cf. *New Testament Essays,* by Vincent Taylor, Grand Rapids, 1972, 5–30; *NJBC,* 70, 61.

TEILHARD DE CHARDIN, PIERRE (1881–1955)

Largely unknown until the aftermath of Vatican II (qv) which may have been influenced by his optimistic spirit in face of worldly conditions and trends, T. became, in no time, a best seller, passing the million mark in sales: a striking example of posthumous success, a surprising instance of popular interest in works blending science, Christian theology, and mysticism (qv).[1] The wide readership was in part due to the conjunction in one life and literary endeavor of religion and ultra-modern science; it was a challenge to the widespread assumption that they must be opposed.

T. reflected on Christ within his whole cosmic theory, in which evolution was given a determining role. He had satisfied himself that he could think of Christ as *Evolutor,* evolver, as well as *Redemptor.* It is a delicate matter and because he had not the benefit of constructive criticism during his life—not being allowed to publish his works—we are the poorer for the restriction placed on him. He must be given the credit of opening a whole new perspective on the primacy of Christ (qv). He writes thus: "The earthly undertaking which is beyond all parallel is the physical incorporation of the faithful into Christ and therefore into God. And this supreme work is carried out with the *exactitude and the harmony of a natural process of evolution.* At the inception of the undertaking there had to be a transcendent act which, in accordance with mysterious but physically regulated conditions, should graft the person of a God into the human cosmos. This was the Incarnation: *Et Verbum caro factum est. . . .* The Incarnation means the renewal, the restoration, of all the energies and powers of the universe; Christ is the instrument, the Center and End of all creation, animate *and* material; through him everything is created, hallowed, quickened. This is the constant, *general* teaching of St. John and St. Paul (that most 'cosmic' of sacred writers), a teaching which has passed into the most solemn phrases of the liturgy, but which we repeat and which future generations will go on repeating to the end without ever being able to master or to measure its profound and mysterious meaning, bound up as it is with the comprehension of the universe."[2] He summed up his view perhaps a little too hastily thus: "Evolution preserves

Christ (by making him possible) and at the same time Christ preserves evolution (by making it specific and desirable)."[3]

How the whole concept was reconcilable with T.'s theory of the 'omega point' must be studied in his writings. How his idea of the cosmic Christ was linked with his theology of the Eucharist is enlightening: "When Christ, extending the process of his Incarnation, descends into the bread in order to replace it, his action is not limited to the material morsel which his presence will, for a brief moment volatilize: this transubstantiation is aureoled with a real though attenuated divinizing of the entire universe. From the particular cosmic element into which he has entered, the activity of the Word goes forth to subdue and draw into himself all the rest."[4]

---

[1]Works relevant to Christology: for general synthesis, *The Phenomenon of Man*, London, 1959; *The Divine Milieu*, 1960; *The Future of Man*, 1964; *Hymn of the Universe*, 1970; cf. C. Cuénot, *Pierre Teilhard de Chardin*, Paris, 1958 (ET 1965); C. Tresmontant, *Introduction à la pensée de Teilhard de Chardin*, Paris, 1956 (ET 1959); "Systema Teilhard de Chardin ad trutinam revocatum," *Divinitas* 3 (1959), 219–364; H. (Cardinal) de Lubac, S.J., *La pensée religieuse du P. Teilhard de Chardin*, Paris, 1962; id., *La prière du P. Teilhard de Chardin*, Paris, 1964; G. Crespy, *La pensée théologique de Teilhard de Chardin*, Paris, 1961; C. d'Armagnac, "La pensée du P. Teilhard de Chardin comme apologétique moderne," *NRT* 94 (1962) 598–621; J. Moltmann, *The Way of Christ*, London, 1990, 292–97; J. Macquarrie, *Christ in Modern Thought*, London, 1990, 313–15; B. de Margerie, S.J., "Teilhard de Chardin, A Cosmic Christ. Consecrator of the Cosmos," in *Christ for the World. The Heart of the Lamb*, 68–120; D. G. Jones in *New Dictionary of Theology*, 673–74;   [2]*Hymn of the Universe*, 144f.;   [3]*Christianity and Evolution*, 155;   [4]*Hymn of the Universe*, 14.

TEMPTATION OF JESUS, THE

"One who in every respect has been tempted as we are yet without sin" (Heb 4:15). "For because he himself has suffered and been tempted, he is able to help those who are tempted" (Heb 2:15).[1] The synoptic gospels narrate the three temptations, Mk merely saying that he "was in the wilderness forty days, tempted by Satan" (1:13), Mt and Lk giving the details. Mt reads: "Then Jesus was led up by the Spirit into the wilderness to be tempted by the devil. And he fasted forty days and forty nights, and afterwards he was hungry. And the tempter came and said to him, 'If you are the Son of God, command these stones to become loaves of bread.' But he answered, 'It is written, "Man shall not live by bread alone, but by every word that proceeds from the mouth of God." ' Then the devil took him to the holy city, and set him on the pinnacle of the temple, and said to him, 'If you are the Son of God, throw yourself down; for it is written, "He will give his angels charge

of you" and "On their hands they will bear you up, lest you strike your foot against a stone." ' Jesus said to him, 'Again it is written, "You shall not tempt the Lord your God." ' Again the devil took him up to a very high mountain, and showed him all the kingdoms of the world and the glory of them; and he said to him, 'All these I will give you, if you will fall down and worship me.' Then Jesus said to him, 'Begone, Satan! for it is written, "You shall worship the Lord your God and him only shall you serve." ' Then the devil left him and behold, angels came and ministered to him" (4:1-11).

Lk has the same details with a change in order: he places the mountain top before the pinnacle of the temple. A modern interpretation of the whole episode puts the emphasis on symbolism. We are shown the real meaning of Jesus' messianic identity and mission, given a preview of the society he intended to establish.

Temptation in the life of Jesus, the God-man, poses many problems. That he was tempted "in every respect as we are" cannot mean disordered concupiscence, since that would imply a sinful element in his psychological constitution. Jesus' kenosis (qv) meant that he would find himself in situations wherein Satan could mount an offensive against him. That, from outside, is comprehensible, and happened. But the inner citadel could not be touched.

That he was tempted is factual. That he could succumb to temptation is unthinkable, because of his intrinsic sinlessness (qv), impeccability. This has been the unchangeable tradition of the Church and for those who accept the dogma of the hypostatic union, it (qv) makes sense.

Why did God allow him to be tempted? One may hazard the answer that it helped people to see him as authentically and fully human; it certainly removed all notions of Docetism or Apollinarianism (qqv).

The phenomonology of temptation has been adequately studied; we need an analysis of its metaphysics. It is the meeting of evil and good at a point of tension, seeking full expression and triumph of evil in a response of the free will of man. This interaction is, in our case, confused by a proclivity towards evil already part of us. In the case of Christ it was a total, clean contrast, and the evil one had to mass his power to seek conquest. Eventually in the Passion, through the alliance made with weak men he seemed about to obtain the victory, only to be completely and forever defeated; our redemption (qv) seeks to make this triumph entirely available to us.

---

[1]Cf. biblical commentaries, e.g., M.-J. Lagrange, O.P., *Evangile selon St. Marc*, 2nd ed., Paris, 1947, 15; *Evangile selon St. Luc*,

8th ed., Paris, 1948, 127–36; *Evangile selon St. Matthieu*, 8th ed., Paris, 1948, 58–66; P. Ketter, *Die versuchung Jesu nach dem Berichte der Synoptiker, Neutestamentliche Abhandlungen*, vi, Hft 3, 1918; H. Riesenfeld, "Le caractère messianique de la tentation au désert," in *La venue du Messie Tournai*, 1960, 51–63; H. J. Vogels, "Die Versuchungen Jesu," *Biblische Zeitschrift* 17 (1926) 238–55; J. M. Vosté, *De baptismo, tentatione et transfiguratione Jesu*, Rome, 1934; A. Ranic, "Monumentum messianicum tentationum Christi," *Verbum Domini* 18 (1938) 93–96, 126–28, 151–60; E. Fascher, *Jesus und der Satan*. Eine Studie zur Auslegung der Versuchungsgeschichte (Hallische Monographien herausgegeben O. Eissfeldt x, 1949); M. Steiser, O.F.M., *La tentation de Jésus dans l'interprétation patristique de St. Justin à Origène*, Paris, 1962; K. P. Kopper, *Die Auslegung der Versuchungsgeschichte unter besonderer Berucksichtigung der alten Kirche*, Tübingen, 1961; B. Gerhardsson, *The Testing of God's Son*, Lund, 1966; R. Schackenberg, "Der Sinn der Versuchung Jesu bei den Synoptikern," *Theologische Quartalschrift* 132 (1952) 297–326; E. Best, *The Temptation and the Passion. The Markan Soteriology*, Cambridge, 1965; J. Dupont, *La tentation de Jésus*, Tournai, 1967; J. A. Fitzmyer, *The Gospel According to Luke I-IX*, Anchor Bible, New York, 1981, 519–20 bibl.

TERESA OF AVILA, ST., DOCTOR OF THE CHURCH (1515–1582)

No one who has not followed the spiritual itinerary of prayer with this astonishingly gifted woman can have an idea of the mysterious dimensions of the human spirit expanding under the influence of divine grace. T. was carried through all that and through her equally phenomenal work of founding new Carmels by her absorption in Christ. She had attained the high degree of union with him and her actions were, as closely as could be possible, equally his. She is the ideal model for contemplation and action coalescing, to mutual profit, in one individual. She is so because of Christ acting and thinking in her. With St. Paul she could have exclaimed, "For me to live is Christ" (Phil 1:21). Hence the spontaneous references all through her writings to Christ under many different titles, especially "His Majesty"; this designation, by no means merely honorary, revealed the depth of her intuition on Christ, revealed also her faculty to combine profound reverence with the intimate familiarity with the Lord which so many anecdotes have endeared to her admirers. For the student of Christology in all its facets, T. embodies an intrusion of Christ, through a human being totally adapted to the role of his instrument, into the flow of human affairs. On her then center vast questions of the Christology of history, as well as equally testing queries on the adjustment to a valid, profound, subtle theory of the Church, of a factor hitherto practically unexplored, mystical anthropology. At any stage in the inquiry, remove Christ and the personality and career of this extraordinary woman dissolve into meaningless bits and pieces.

T.'s theology of Christ was utterly orthodox. Because of the very keen interest in contemplative prayer in her world, she met and had to refute an opinion which would minimize the importance of Christ's humanity in prayer. "How much more is it necessary," she wrote, "not to withdraw through one's own efforts from all our good and help which is the most sacred humanity of dear Lord Jesus Christ."[1] Thus in the *Interior Castle*. In her *Life* she is more expansive in dealing with what looks like a prayer version of an ancient heresy. She is dealing with those who, having reached a certain degree of prayer, "advise us much to withdraw from all bodily imagination, and draw near to the contemplation of the divinity; for they say that those who have advanced so far would be embarrassed or hindered in their way to the highest contemplation, if they regarded even the Sacred Humanity itself."

Through the influence of a certain literature, T., for a moment, had lapsed into this practice: "No one could have brought me back to the contemplation of the Sacred Humanity; for that seemed to me to be a real hindrance to prayer." Thus she announces her change of mind: "O Lord of my soul, and my God! Jesus Christ crucified! I never think of this opinion, which I then held, without pain; I believe it was an act of high treason, though done in ignorance. Hitherto, I had been all my life long so devout to the Sacred Humanity—for this happened but lately; I mean by lately that it was before our Lord gave me the grace of raptures and visions. I did not continue long of this opinion, and I returned to my habit of delighting in our Lord, particularly at Communion."

Chapter XXII develops the rationale for the true opinion: the soul lacks humility somewhat and it mistakes its own condition, behaving as if it were angelic, not human. She expresses the kernel of her thought: "With so good a Friend and Captain ever present, himself the first to suffer, everything can be borne. He helps, he strengthens, he never fails, he is the true Friend. I see clearly, and since then have always seen, that if we are to please God, and if he is to give us his great graces, everything must pass through the hands of his most Sacred Humanity, in whom his Majesty said that he is well pleased. I know this by repeated experience: our Lord has told it to me. I have seen clearly that this is the door by which we are to enter, if we would have his supreme Majesty reveal to us his secrets."[2] This is the mediation of Christ as the basis of contemplative prayer. T. not only countered thus the heresy of her contemporary, Servetus, but eliminated the danger of Illuminism.

[1] *The Interior Castle,* VI, 7, Collected Works, tr. K. Kavanaugh and O. Rodriguez, Washington, 1980, 399; cf. R. Hoornaert, *St. Teresa in her Writings,* London, 1931, 206ff; Fr. Thomas, O.C.D. and Fr. Gabriel, O.C.D., (eds), *St. Teresa of Avila. Studies in her Life, Doctrine and Times,* 1963; *Ephemerides Carmeliticae*: 21, 1–2 (1970), *Sancta Teresia a Jesu: Doctor Ecclesiae.* Historia. Documenta, Doctrina; M. Jimenez Salas, *Santa Teresia de Jesus.* Bibliografia fundamental (Cuadernos bibliograficos, VI); *DTC* XV, 1 (1946) 552–73; *DSp*, XV (1991), s.v.;   [2] *Life,* ch. 22, *passim,* English tr. David Lewis, London, 1962, 156–67.

TERTULLIAN (c. 160–c. 225)

T.'s subsequent lapse into Montanism may be used to call in question his title 'Father of Latin Theology.'[1] In Christology he had to do battle on many fronts, left in different works a sum of teaching which remarkably anticipates later, substantive teaching; the anticipation was in terminology which does not mean that meaning and connotation were in each case clear and fully developed. Patrologists do not agree on appraisement of his views. Thus Quasten can comment on a passage to be quoted presently: "We recognize in these statements the formula of the Council of Chalcedon (qv) of the two substances in one person." Grillmeier (qv) feels that detailed investigation is required.

The theological background was complex and in places frenzied. Adoptionists denied the divinity of Christ; he was, they held, a man like others, richly endowed with grace and adopted somehow by God because of his sanctity. Monarchians of unorthodox allegiance identified Father and Son, satisfied to distinguish them as different aspects of the deity or distinguishable by their names; they claimed that God was incarnate in Jesus, that the Father had suffered in the passion (qv) of Jesus. Docetists (qv) of every kind denied the reality of Christ's body, or misinterpreted its nature. For Marcion Christ's body was but an appearance; he manifested himself in the fifteenth year of Tiberius, and disappears suddenly. Apelles thought that Christ had an astral body; Valentinus believed it was a psychic and spiritual body. Gnostics were thinking of a purely artificial, transitory union of the divine and human in Christ; others were talking of a transformation of the Word into flesh, both natures fused in one. And there was pagan polytheism.

T. must first affirm the reality of Christ's body. To those who say that when the angels appear to men they take on sidereal bodies, he answers that they had not to die. To deny the reality of Christ's body is to deny the suffering and death of the Savior. The whole economy of the Redemption (qv) is endangered. Since Christ came to give his life to redeem men, he had to be born in a mortal body (*De carne Christi,* 6). T. was so keen on emphasizing the full humanity of Christ that he denied the *virginitas in partu* (see article Birth of Christ) thinking that his view was supported by OT prophetic texts (*De carne Christi,* 23). He thought that Christ had all the weaknesses of humanity except sin. But though man, he is God at the same time. The Word did not change into man or into flesh. In becoming incarnate he remains what he was. The expressions used frequently by T. to express this reality are *suscepit hominem, assumpsit carnem, substantiam hominis induit.*

T. probes further: *"Igitur Sermo in carne, dum et de hoc quaerendum quomodo Sermo caro sit factus, utrumne quasi transfiguratus in carne an indutus carnem? Immo indutus. Ceterum Deum immutabilem et informabilem credi necesse est, ut aeterum. Transfiguratio autem interemptio est pristini. Omne enim quodcumque transfiguratur in aliud, desinit esse quod fuerat et incipit esse quod non erat. Deus autem neque desinit esse, neque aliud potest esse. Sermo autem Deus.*[2] There is therefore not transformation of God, *transfiguratio,* into man. God and man remain what they are. It is Christ taken in his plenitude who is the Son of God, the sonship being, as it were, lent to the man; he is not the adoptive Son of God, but Son of God through the union. Analysis of the relationship would take us back to T.'s doctrine of the Trinity, his use of the word *substantia,* and his valid concept of the *monarchia.*

T. gave currency to the word *persona*; he uses it thirty times in all and its history before him is not without interest.[3] The classic passage is a matter of some controversy, both as to translation and even punctuation: "We see plainly the twofold state of being, which is not confounded but conjoined in one person (*persona*), Jesus, God and man—I put off what is about Christ—and this so that the property of each substance (*substantiae*) is so wholly preserved that the Spirit on the one hand did all his own things in Jesus such as miracles, and mighty deeds and wonders; and the flesh, on the other hand, exhibited the affections which belong to it. It was hungry under the devil's temptation, thirsty with the Samaritan woman, wept over Lazarus, was troubled even unto death, and at last actually died. If, however, it was only some third thing, some composite essence formed out of the two substances, like the electrum, there would be no distinct proofs apparent of either nature. But by a transfer of functions, the Spirit would have done things to be done by the flesh, and the flesh such as are effected by the Spirit; or else such things as are suited neither to the flesh nor to the Spirit, but confusedly of some third character. Nay more, on this supposition, either the Word underwent death, or the flesh did not die, if the Word had been converted into flesh; because either the flesh was immortal or the Word was mortal. Forasmuch, however, as the two substances acted distinctly, each in its own character, there necessarily accrued to them severally their own operations and their own issues."[4]

T. puts it also this way: "Learn therefore with Nicodemus that what is born in the flesh is flesh and what is born of the Spirit is spirit (Jn 3:6). Flesh does not become spirit nor spirit flesh. Evidently they can (both) be in one (person) (*in uno plane esse possunt*). Of these Jesus is composed, of flesh as man and of spirit as God: and on that occasion the angel, reserving for the flesh the designation Son of Man, pronounced him the Son of God in respect of that part in which he was spirit."[5]

Grillmeier sums up the achievement of T.: "By this it is clear that Tertullian has not grasped the full depth of the Christological problem of how the unity and the distinction in Christ are to be envisaged. He drew some basic lines for the solution, which could be enlarged in later tradition. Whether his first beginnings here were really appreciated is, however, another question. The most striking thing in his writings seemed to be the formula of the *'una persona'* in Christ. But tradition up to Augustine is silent about it. Augustine himself seems to have discovered it independently of Tertullian. . . . Despite the way in which individual concepts of Tertullian's—not his formula—already seem to point towards Chalcedon, his speculative understanding is still far removed from it. But in that he regards the unity of subject in Christ along with tradition, in the light of the Logos (*Sermo*) and holds to the *communicatio idiomatum,* his Christology is preserved from the crisis to which his speculation would have had to lead him."[6]

---

[1]Works *CCSL* i, 2; *CSEL* 20, 47, 70, 76; *PL* 2; Cf. A. d'Alès, S.J., *La théologie de Tertullien,* Paris, 1905, 162–200; R. Braun, *Deus Christianorum, Recherches sur le vocabulaire doctrinal de Tertullien,* Paris, 1962, 207–336, bibl. 158f; S. Otto, *'Natura' und 'dispositio.' Untersuchung zum Naturbegriff und zur Denkform Tertullians,* Munich, 1960; K. Wolfl, *Das Heilswirken Gottes durch den Sohn nach Tertullian,* Rome, 1960, 35–117; R. Cantalamessa, O.F.M.Cap., *La Christologia di Tertulliano,* Fribourg, 1962; G. Bardy, *DTC* XV, 1, 130–71, esp. 154–56; Quasten II, 246–340, esp. 328f.; Grillmeier, 140–57; [2]*Adversus Praxeam, XXVII,* 7, *CCSL* 2, 1199; [3]Grillmeier, 146–56; [4]*Adversus Praxeam, XXVII* 11, *CCSL* 2, 1199f.; [5]*Adversus Praxeam, XXVII,* 14, *CCSL* 2, 1200; [6]*Op. cit.*

THEANDRIC ACTS OF CHRIST

Dionysius the Pseudo-Areopagite first used the phrase, but erroneously, using it to signify all acts of the God-man.[1] It was used in an orthodox sense by St. Maximus the Confessor (qv) and St. John of Damascus (qv). The Monophysite and Monothelite (qv) heresies tempted similar abuse of the term, which has, rightly understood, validity. Christ acted with his divine will, and with his human will. In certain circumstances, as when he worked miracles, the two wills were simultaneously involved. The result was a theandric act, an act of God and man at once.

---

[1]A. Michael, *DTC* XVm, 205–17; L. Billot, S.J., *De Verbo Incarnato,* 1927, thesis, 31; P. Galtier, *De Incarnatione ac Redemptione,* 1947, 136–41; C. J. Moell, *NCE* XIV, 4.

THEODORE OF MOPSUESTIA (c. 350–428)

Antiochene, a pupil of Diodore of Tarsus (qv), fellow student of St. John Chrysostom, T., as Bishop of Mopsuestia, was active in preaching and teaching, involved in the theological debates of his time. He is a conundrum of patristic textual analysis,[1] one of those who died in doctrinal peace with the Church, was later condemned and still later rehabilitated— or almost. More than once the second Council of Constantinople, 553, speaks of him disparagingly, using in one instance these words, "the impious Theodore of Mopsuestia, who said that one was God the Word (qv), and another the Christ,"[2] elsewhere speaking of "Theodore and Nestorius" and "their godlessness."[3] Centuries later the Council of Florence, in the Decree for the Jacobites, added its voice thus: "It also anathematizes Theodore of Mopsuestia and Nestorius who assert that humanity was united with the Son of God (qv) through grace, and hence there are two persons in Christ, just as they confess that there are two natures, since they are unable to understand that the union of humanity with the Word was hypostatic, and so refused to accept the subsistence of God."[4]

The great patristic scholar Otto Bardenhewer (1851–1935) branded T. "a Nestorius before Nestorius"; he accepted the genuineness of lengthy extracts from T.'s *De Incarnatione* collected by Leontius of Byzantium and presented to Constantinople II, as well as fragments from the *Contra Apollinarem*: it must be emphasized, as an element in the controversy, that T. was a firm opponent of the heresies of his time, Arianism and Apollinarianism (qqv). He was unlucky to have had Nestorius (qv) as a pupil, a fact of which St. Cyril of Alexandria was particularly mindful, "For Theodore was not a disciple of Nestorius, but rather the other way around, and both speak as from one mouth, emitting one and the same poison of heterodoxy from their hearts."

The evidence of the newly discovered homilies must now be taken into account. The eighth homily is especially invoked in the task of rehabilitating T.

Thus on the two natures he writes: "The one who assumed is not the same as the one who was assumed, nor is the one who was assumed the same as the one who assumed, but the one who assumed is God while the one who was assumed is man. The one who assumed is by nature that which God the Father is by nature, as he is God with God, and he is that which the one with whom he was, is, while the one who was assumed is by nature that which David and Abraham, whose son and from whose seed he is, are by nature. This is the reason why he is both Lord and Son of David: Son of David because of his nature, and Lord because of the honor that came to him. And he is high above David his father because of the nature that assumed him."[5]

This is the distinction of natures, but T. does not think that it means two persons: "In their profession of faith our blessed Fathers (at Nicaea) wrote . . . they followed the Sacred Books which speak differently of natures while referring (them) to one prosopon (person) on account of the close union that took place between them, so that they might not be believed that they were separating the perfect union between the one who was assumed and the one who assumed. If this union were destroyed the one who was assumed would not be seen as more than a mere man like ourselves."[6]

T. insists on the inseparable character of the union: "The one who assumed is the divine nature that does everything for us, and the other is the human nature which was assumed on behalf of all of us by the one who is the cause of everything, and is united to it in an ineffable union which will never be separated."[7] "We should also be mindful of that inseparable union through which that form of man can never and under no circumstances be separated from the divine nature which put it on. The distinction between the natures does not annul the close union nor does the close union destroy the distinction between the natures, but the natures remain in their respective existence which separated, and the union remains intact, because the one who was assumed is united in honor and glory with the one who assumed according to the will of the one who assumed him. From the fact that we say two natures we are not constrained to say two Lords or two sons; this would be extreme folly. All things that in one respect are two and in another respect one, their union through which they are one does not annul the distinction between the natures, and the distinction between the natures impedes them from being one."[8]

Historians of theology concede that T. occasionally lacked precision and restraint when, for instance, he had to deal with the impeccability and immutability of Christ. A. Grillmeier thought that no one

helped the development of theology, between Constantinople I, 381, and Ephesus, 431, more than T. Especially he clarified the doctrine of Christ's possession of a human soul. Opposing those who held that the nature of the Godhead took the place of the soul, he wrote: "If, therefore, the Godhead was performing the acts of the soul, it would also by necessity have performed the acts of the body. Only in this way could he right the opinion of the misleading heretics who deny that he assumed a body and was only in the same way as the angels and was a man in appearance only while he did not possess any qualities of human nature. Therefore it was necessary that he should assume not only the body but also the immortal and rational soul; and not only the death of the body had to cease but also that of the soul which is sin. . . . It was, therefore, necessary that sin should have first been abolished, as after its abolition there would be no entry for death. It is indeed clear that the strength of the sin has its origin in the will of the soul. . . . It is therefore great madness not to believe that Christ assumed the soul; and he would be even madder who would say that he did not assume a human mind, because such a one would imply that he either did not assume the soul or that he did assume the soul, not of man but an irrational one akin to that of animals and beasts."[9] This is Logos man Christology, not Logos sarx.

[1]Conflicting opinions are expressed in the various studies; cf. E. Amann, "La doctrine christologique de Théodore de Mopsueste," *RevSR* 14 (1934) 160–90; *id., DTC* XV (1946) 235–79; M. Jugie, A.A., "Le 'Liber ad baptizandos' de Théodore de Mopsueste, *EO* 34 (1935) 259–71; (against Amann); *id., Theologia dogmatica Christianorum orientalium ab ecclesia catholica dissidentium,* V, Paris, 1935, 99–110; W. de Vries, "Der 'Nestorianismus' Theodors von Mopsuestia in seiner Sakramentlehre," *OCP* 7 (1941) 91–148; *id.,* "Das eschatologische Heil bei Theodor von Mopsuestia, *OCP* 24 (1958) 309–38; M. Richard, "La tradition des fragments du 'Traité Peri tes enanthropeseos' de Theódore de Mopsueste," *Mus* 46 (1943) 55–75; *id.,* "L'introduction du mot hypostase dans la théologie de l'Incarnation," *MSR* 2 (1945) 21–29; R. Devresse, *Essai sur Théodore de Mopsueste,* ST 141, Vatican City, 1948; R. Tonneau, *Les homélies catéchetiques de Théodore de Mopsueste,* ST 145, Vatican City, 1949; M. V. Anastos, "The Immutability of Christ and Justinian's Condemnation of Theodore of Mopsuestia," *DOP* 6 (1951) 123–60; K. MacNamara, "Theodore of Mopsuestia and the Nestorian Heresy," *ITQ* 19 (1952) 254–78; 20 (1953) 172–91; G. H. M. Posthumus Meyjes, "De Christologie van Theodorus van Mopsuestia," *Vox Theologica,* Assen (Netherlands), 25 (1954–55); I. Onatibia, "La vida cristiana tipo de las realidades celestes," *Scriptorium Victoriense* 1 (1954) 100–33; F. A. Sullivan, *The Christology of Theodore of Mopsuestia,* Rome, 1956; P. Galtier, "Théodore de Mopsueste. Sa vraie pensée sur l'Incarnation," *RSR* 45 (1957) 161–86, 338–60; L. Abramowski, "Zur Theologie Theodors von Mopsuestia," *ZKG* 72 (1961) 263–93 (with L. Onotibia challenges W. de Vries); J. L. McKenzie, "Annotations on the Christology of Theodore of Mopsuestia," *ThS* 19 (1958) 345–73; F. A. Sullivan, "Further Notes on Theodore of Mopsuestia," *ThS* 20 (1959) 264–79; R. A. Greer, *Theodore*

of Mopsuestia. Exegete and Theologian, London, 1961; U. Wickert, *Studien zu den Pauluskommentaren Theodors von Mopsuestia,* Berlin, 1962; G. Koch, *Die Heilsverwirklichung bei Theodor von Mopsuestia,* Diss., Würzburg, 1963 (also opposed to W. de Vries); R. A. Norris, *Manhood and Christ. A Study in the Christology of Theodore of Mopsuestia,* Oxford, 1963; Quasten, III, 415–18; Kelly, *Doctrines,* 303–09; Grillmeier, 421–39; F. M. Young, *From Nicaea to Chalcedon,* London, 1983, 199–213, bibl., 352f; 393f.; [2]*DS* 434; [3]*DS* 436; [4]*DS* 1341; [5]*Cat. Hom.* 8, 1, Quasten, 415f; [6]*Cat. Hom.* 6, 3, Quasten, 416; [7]*Cat. Hom.* 8, 10, Quasten, 416; [8]*Cat Hom.* 8, 13, Quasten, 416f; [9]*Cat. Hom.* 5, 55f, Quasten, 418.

THOMAS AQUINAS, ST., DOCTOR OF THE CHURCH (1225–1274)

The Angelic Doctor composed the supreme scholastic synthesis on the Incarnation, bringing together the revelation of Scripture, the conciliar dogmatic statements, and the teaching of the Fathers under the overall logical control of Aristotelian philosophy.[1] T. expressed his mature doctrine in the first 59 questions of Part III of the *Summa Theologica*; he dealt with the subject in other works, notably the Commentary on Peter Lombard's (qv) Book of Sentences, and in the *Summa Contra Gentiles,* and elsewhere. Because of T.'s gigantic stature as a theologian, his special status as a doctor uniquely honored by Church authority, and his immense influence on the thinking of subsequent ages, it is thought better to list entirely, in their order fixed by him, the titles of the questions which he considers. Many articles in the present work are directly related to these questions: the fittingness of the incarnation; the kind of union the incarnation is in itself; the mode of union on the part of the person assuming; the union on the part of the nature assumed; the assumption of the parts of human nature; the order of assumption; the grace of Christ as an individual man; the grace of Christ as head of the church; Christ's knowledge; beatific knowledge in the soul of Christ; endowed or infused knowledge in the soul of Christ; acquired, experimental knowledge in the soul of Christ; the power of Christ's soul; the physical disabilities undertaken by Christ in his human nature; the disabilities of soul undertaken by Christ in his human nature; statements relating to Christ as existing and coming into existence (communication of idioms, qv); the unity of Christ's existence; the unity of Christ's will; the unity of Christ's activity; Christ's subjection to the Father; Christ's prayer; the priesthood of Christ; is Christ an adopted son of God?; the predestination of Christ; the reverence due to Christ; Christ, the mediator of God and men; the sanctification of the Blessed Virgin; the virginity of the mother of God; the betrothal of the mother of God; the announcement to the Blessed Virgin; bodily matter in our savior's conception; activating principle in Christ's conception; mode and order of Christ's conception; perfection of the child conceived; birth of Christ; manifestation of the new-born Christ; the child Jesus and old law observances; the baptism of John; the baptizing of Christ; Christ's manner of life; the temptation of Christ; Christ's teaching; Christ's miracles in general; the different kinds of miracles; Christ's transfiguration; Christ's passion; the cause of Christ's passion; the efficacy of Christ's passion; the results of Christ's passion; the death of Christ; Christ's burial; Christ's descent into hell; the resurrection of Christ; the qualities of the risen Christ; the manifestation of the resurrection; the causality of Christ's resurrection; the ascension of Christ; Christ's sitting at the right hand of the Father; Christ's power as judge.[2]

It is clear from the very sequence of topics chosen by T. to compose this magisterial treatise that along with the essential philosophical framework there is continuous advertence to the facts of history.

[1]Cf. W. A. Wallace, -J. A. Weisheipl, *NCE* XIV, 102–15; P. A. Walz and others, *DTC* XV, 618–761; bibl. also in F. L. Cross, *Oxford Dictionary of the Christian Church,* 2nd ed., E. A. Livingstone, 1372f; for Christology, the great commentators, Cajetan and others; more recently, L. Billot, *De Verbo Incarnato,* Rome, 1928, and Ed. H. Weber, *Le Christ selon St. Thomas d'Aquin,* Paris, 1988; [2]Titles of questions as in Blackfriars edition of *Summa Theologiae,* New York, 1965.

TOME OF LEO, THE, June 13, 449

It has been described as "the most important Christological document of its kind which the Latin Church produced."[1] It was borne to the synod held in Ephesus in August, 449, by a Roman legation. It was addressed to Flavian, Patriarch of Constantinople, and is also called *Tomus ad Flavianum.* It was not received at the synod which because of its decisions was branded a *Latrocinium* by Leo in a later letter, 495, to the Empress Pulcheria. Eventually the Tome would influence the Chalcedonian definition (qv and article Chalcedon).

As to authorship of the Tome, it is generally agreed that Leo's secretary, Prosper of Aquitaine, played an important part in the textual drafting. But he drew on the letters and sermons of Leo and in one particular case was able to avert confusion by avoiding a word which in Greek translation would have spelled difficulty.

The complete text is as follows: "Having read your affection's letter, noting with surprise its late arrival, and having taken account of the bishops' actions, we have now, at last recognized the scandal which has risen up among you, against the integrity of the faith; and what previously appeared obscure now was clarified and brought into the open. Through these means Eutyches, who with the name of presbyter seemed worthy of honor, is now shown to be very thoughtless and sadly inexperienced, so that the prophet could have said of him, 'He has ceased to act wisely and to do good; he plots mischief while in his bed' (Ps 35:3-4). What indeed is more unrighteous than to entertain ungodly thoughts and not to yield to those wiser and more learned? But they fall into this folly who impeded by some darkness in seeking to know the truth do not have recourse to prophetic voices, nor to the letters of the apostles, nor to the authority of the Gospels, but to themselves. They become teachers of error, because they have not been disciples of the truth. For what learning has he acquired from the sacred pages of the New and of the Old Testament who does not so much as understand the beginning of the creed? And that which is vocally expressed throughout the world by those still to be regenerated is not grasped by the mind of this old man. Ignorant therefore of what he should think about the incarnation of the Word of God, and unwilling to work over the extent of Sacred Scripture so that he might obtain the light of intelligence, he should at least have received with careful attention that general confession common to all, whereby the whole body of the faithful profess that they believe 'in God the Father Almighty, and in Jesus Christ, his only Son our Lord, who was born of the Holy Spirit and the Virgin Mary.' By these three causes the engines of almost all heretics are destroyed. For when God is believed to be both 'almighty' and 'Father,' the Son is shown to be everlasting with him, differing in no way from the Father, because he was born God from God, Almighty from Almighty, Co-eternal from Eternal; not later in time, not inferior in power, not unlike him in glory, not divided from him in essence. But the same everlasting and Only-begotten Son of an eternal parent *was born of the Holy Spirit and of the Virgin Mary.* This birth in time in no way lessened, in no way added to, that divine and everlasting birth, but spent itself wholly in restoring man who had been deceived, so that it might both conquer death, and by its power destroy the devil, who had the power of death. For we could not have overcome the author of sin and death unless he, whom sin could not contaminate or death detain, took on our nature and made it his own. Truly he was conceived of the Holy Spirit within the womb of a virgin Mother, who brought him forth as she conceived him with her virginity intact. But if he (Eutyches) could not draw true understanding from this pure fountain of Christian faith, because by his own blindness he had darkened for himself the brightness of truth that was clear, he should have

submitted to the teaching of the gospels, to Matthew who says: 'The book of the generation of Jesus Christ, the Son of David, the Son of Abraham'; he should also have sought the instruction of the apostolic preaching, and having read in the epistle to the Romans: 'Paul, a servant of Jesus Christ, called to be an apostle, set apart for the gospel of God, which he promised beforehand through his prophets in the holy scriptures, the gospel concerning his Son, who was descended from David according to the flesh'; he should have given devout attention to the pages of the prophets, and finding the promise of God who said to Abraham, 'And in your seed shall all the nations of the earth bless themselves', in order to have no doubt as to the proper meaning of (the word) 'seed' he should have followed the Apostle who said: 'Now the promises were made to Abraham and to his seed. It does not say "and to seeds," referring to many; but, referring to one "and to your seed," which is Christ.' With interior attention he should also have grasped the declaration of Isaiah, 'Behold a virgin will conceive in the womb and bring forth a son and they will call his name Emmanuel, which is interpreted "God with us."' And he should have read the words of the same prophet: 'For to us a child is born, to us a son is given, and the government is upon his shoulder and his name will be called Angel of great counsel, wonderful, Mighty God, counselor, Prince of peace, Father of the age to come.' Nor speaking idle words should he have said that the Word so became flesh that Christ brought forth from the womb of the virgin had a human form but not a body really derived from his mother's body.

"It is possible that he thought that our Lord Jesus Christ was not of our nature because the angel sent to blessed and ever-virgin Mary said: 'The Holy Spirit will come upon you, and the power of the Most High will overshadow you; therefore the Child to be born of you will be called holy, the Son of God'; as if because the Virgin's conception was a work of God, the flesh of the one conceived was not of the nature of her who conceived. But that generation, uniquely wonderful and wonderfully unique, is not to be understood as though the newness of the mode of production did away with the proper character of the kind. The Holy Spirit gave fruitfulness to the Virgin but it was from a body that a real body was derived; and 'when Wisdom was building herself a house,' 'the Word was made flesh and dwelt among us.' That is in that flesh which he assumed from a human being and which he animated with the spirit of rational life. Accordingly, while the distinctness of both natures and substances is preserved and both meet in one Person, lowliness was assumed by majesty, weakness by power and mortality by eternity, and in order to pay the debt arising out of our condition, an inviolable nature has been united to a nature that was passible, so that, as befitted the remedies we needed, one and the same Mediator of God and men, the man Christ Jesus, could, from one constituent (of his being) die, and from the other could not die. Therefore in the entire and perfect nature of true man, true God was born, whole in what was his, whole in what was ours—by 'ours' we mean what from the beginning the Creator established in us, and what he assumed so that he should restore it. Those things which the deceiver introduced and which man, who was deceived, admitted, had no trace in the Savior. Nor did the fact that he bore solidarity in our human infirmities mean that he shared our transgressions. He took the 'form of a servant' without the defilement of sin, increasing what was human, not lessening what was divine, because that self-emptying by which he, who was invisible, made himself visible, and, the Creator and Lord of all things, willed to be one of those mortal, was a bending down of compassion, not a lack of power. Accordingly, the one who, existing in the form of God, was made man in the form of a slave. For each nature retains its proper character without defect; and as the form of God does not take away the form of a slave, so the form of a slave does not lessen the form of God. For since the devil was glorying in the fact that man misled by his deceitfulness was deprived of divine gifts, and being stripped of the endowment of immortality, was subject to a harsh sentence of death, and that he himself, in the midst of his evils, had found some comfort in the company of a wrongdoer, and that God, in accordance with what the principle of justice required, had changed his own intention in regard to man, whom he had established with such high honor, there was need for a plan taken in secret deliberation, so that the unchangeable God, whose will cannot be deprived of its own benignity, should fulfill, by a more secret mystery, his original design of loving kindness towards us, and that man driven to fault by the subtlety of diabolical wickedness, should not perish contrary to God's purpose.

Accordingly, the Son of God descended from his heavenly seat yet not withdrawing from the glory of the Father, enters these weak things of the world, born after a new order, by a new kind of birth. After a new order because he who in his own existence is invisible, became visible in ours, he who could not be enclosed, wished to be so, abiding before all time, he began to exist in time; the Lord of the universe, the immensity of his majesty overshadowed, took on the form of a slave; the impassible God did not disdain to become a passible man, and he who is im-

mortal to be subject to laws of death. But born of a new kind of birth, because intact virginity, knowing nothing of concupiscence, supplied the matter of his flesh. Nature was assumed from the Lord's Mother, not fault, and the fact that in our Lord Jesus Christ, brought forth from a virgin's womb there was a wonderful birth, does not mean that his nature is unlike ours. For the same one who is true God is true man, and in this union there is no falsity, while the lowliness of man and the loftiness of divinity come together. For as God is not changed by compassion shown, so man is not absorbed by the dignity accepted. For each form does the acts which are proper to it in communion with the other; the Word, that is, performing what belongs to the Word, and the flesh carrying out what is proper to the flesh. One of these glows with miracles; the other succumbs to injuries.

"And as the Word does not withdraw from equality with the Father's glory, so the flesh does not give up the nature of our race. For one and the same is truly the Son of God and truly the Son of man: God through that by which 'in the beginning was the Word and the Word was with God and the Word was God,' man through that by which 'the Word was made flesh and dwelt among us,' God through that by which 'all things were made by him and without him nothing was made,' man through that by which 'he was born of a woman, born under the law.' The birth of the flesh is a manifestation of human nature; the Virgin's child-bearing is a sign of divine power. The infancy of the baby is shown by the lowliness of swaddling clothes; the greatness of the Most High is proclaimed by the voices of angels. He whom Herod impiously schemes to kill is like men in their beginnings, but he whom the Magi rejoice to adore on their knees is the Lord of all. Now when he came to the baptism of John his precursor, lest the fact that the divinity covered with a veil of flesh should be hidden, the voice of the Father spoke in thunder from heaven: 'This is my beloved Son, in whom I am well pleased.' He, therefore, whom the cunning of the devil tempted as man, is the same one to whom, as God, angels pay dutiful service. It is manifestly human to hunger, to thirst, to be weary and to sleep, but it is without possible doubt divine to provide the sufficiency of five thousand men with five loaves, to bestow on the Samaritan woman living water which being consumed preserves the one who drinks it from further thirst, to walk on the surface of the sea, with feet that do not sink, and to reduce the mounting of the waves by rebuking the storm. Just as, if I may pass over many things, it does not belong to the same nature to weep with pity for a dead friend, and by the command of a word to call him back to life, when the boulder had been removed from the grave which had had him for four days; or to hang on the wood and, after daylight had been turned into night, to cause all the elements to tremble; or to be pierced with nails and open the gates of paradise to the believing (good) thief. Thus it is not of the same nature to say, 'I and the Father are one,' and to say, 'The Father is greater than I.' For although in the Lord Jesus Christ there is one Person of God and of man, yet how contumely may be something common to both is one thing, and how glory may be common to both is another; for, from our side, he has the humanity which is inferior to the Father, from the Father he has divinity equal to the Father. Therefore, on account of this unity of the Person to be understood as being in both natures, both the Son of man, it is read, came down from heaven, since the Son of God assumed flesh from the Virgin, of whom he was born, and again the Son of God is said to have been crucified and buried, since he underwent these things not in the very divinity by which, as the Only-begotten he is coeternal and consubstantial with the Father, but in the weakness of human nature. Wherefore, we all in the very creed confess 'that the Only-begotten Son of God was crucified and buried,' mindful of the word of the apostle, 'For if they had known, they would never have crucified the Lord of Glory.' But when our Lord and Savior was by his questions informing the faith of the disciples, he said 'Who do men say that I am?' And when they had mentioned different opinions of others, he said, 'But who do you say that I am?', that is, 'I who am the Son of Man and whom you see in the form of a servant, and in the reality of the flesh, who do you say that I am?' When blessed Peter, inspired by God, and about to benefit all nations, said 'You are the Christ, the Son of the living God,' not undeservedly was he proclaimed blessed by the Lord, and he derived from the original Rock that steadfastness in virtue and in his name, for through revelation from the Father he confessed the same One to be the Son of God and the Christ; because one of these accepted without the other would not have profited to salvation, and it is equally dangerous to have believed that the Lord Jesus Christ was merely God, without being man, or merely man without being God.

"But after the resurrection of the Lord—which certainly was of a real body, for none other was of a real body, for none other was raised than the one who had been crucified and had died—what else was achieved in the interval of forty days than that the integrity of our faith should be cleased of all darkness? For conversing with his disciples, dwelling and eating with them, and allowing himself to be handled with careful and inquisitive touch by those who were under the influence of doubt, to this end he came into the disciples through closed doors, and by his breath gave them the Holy Spirit, and bestowing the light of understanding on them, he opened to them the secrets of the Sacred Scriptures, and again, he himself showed the wound in his side, the prints of the nails, and all the signs of his most recent passion, saying, 'See my hands and my feet, for it is I; touch me and see that a spirit has not flesh and bones, as you see that I have'; this that it should be acknowledged that what was proper to divine and to human nature remained in him as one, that we should thus know that the Word is not the same as flesh, so as to confess that the one Son of God is both Word and flesh.

"In regard to this mystery of the faith Eutyches must be deemed exceedingly wanting; for he has not acknowledged our nature in the Only-begotten Son of God, neither through the lowliness of mortality nor through the glory of the resurrection. Nor has he been overawed at the pronouncement of the blessed Apostle and Evangelist John saying: 'Every spirit which confesses that Jesus Christ has come in the flesh is of God, and every spirit which does not confess Jesus is not of God, and this is the spirit of antichrist' (1 Jn 4:2-3).

"But what is to 'dissolve' Jesus but to separate the human nature from him, and to empty by shameless inventions the mystery by which alone we have been saved? But being blind in regard to the nature of Christ's body, he must need be involved in the like senseless blindness also about his Passion. For if he does not think that the Lord's Cross was unreal, and does not doubt that he accepted real suffering for the salvation of the world, let him acknowledge the flesh of the one in whose death he believes, and not doubt that he whom he knows to have been capable of suffering is a man with a body like ours, since denial of his real flesh is also denial of his bodily suffering.

"Therefore if he has accepted the Christian faith and not turned away his ear from the preaching of the gospel, let him see what nature was pierced by nails and hung on the wood of the Cross; and let him understand whence it was that after the side of the Crucified One had been opened by the soldier's spear, blood and water flowed out that the Church of God might be refreshed both with the Laver and the Cup. Let him hear blessed Peter the Apostle preaching that sanctification by the Spirit is done by the sprinkling of the blood of Christ. Let him not read the words of the same Apostle cursorily, when he says: 'You know that you were ransomed from the future ways inherited from your fathers, not with perishable things such as silver and gold, but with the precious blood of Christ like that of a lamb without blemish or spot' (1 Pet 1:18). Let him also not resist the testimony of the blessed Apostle John saying: 'and the blood of Jesus, the Son (of God), cleanses us from all sin' (1 Jn 1:7). And again: 'This is the victory that overcomes the world, our faith.' And: 'Who is it that overcomes the world but he who believes that Jesus is the Son of God? This is he who came by water and blood, Jesus Christ, not with the water only but with the water and the blood. And the Spirit is the witness, because the Spirit is the truth. There are three witnesses, the Spirit, the water and the blood; these three agree (are one)' (1 Jn 5:4-8). That is, the Spirit of sanctification, and the blood of redemption and the water of baptism; which three are one and remain undivided, and therefrom none is disjoined, because the Catholic Church lives and advances by this faith, whereby it must be believed that in Christ Jesus there is neither humanity without the true divinity, nor divinity without the true humanity.

"But when Eutyches, on being questioned in your examination of him, answered, 'I confess that our Lord, before the union, was of two natures, but I confess one nature after the union,' I am surprised that such an absurd and perverse profession was not censured by any castigation of the judges, and that a statement exceedingly foolish and exceedingly blasphemous should be passed over as if nothing had been heard which could give offense: since it is as impious to say that the Only-begotten Son of God was of two natures before the incarnation as it is wicked to assert that, since the Word became flesh, there has been in him one nature only. But lest Eutyches should think that what he said was correct, or was tolerable, because it was not refuted by any statement of yours, we exhort your loving solicitude, dearly beloved brother, to see that, if by an inspiration of God's mercy, the case is brought to a satisfactory outcome, the rashness of this inexperienced man should also be cleansed of the pestilence of his notion. As the record of the proceedings made clear, he had begun well to give up his own opinion; when hedged in by the judgment of yours, he professed himself ready to say what he had not said before, and to adhere to the faith, from which he had previously stood apart. But when he refused his consent to anathematize the impious dogma, you understood, brother, that he continued in his misbelief and deserved to receive sentence of condemnation.

"If he grieves for this sincerely and to good purpose, and recognizes, even though too late, how properly the episcopal authority has been set in motion, and if with a view to full satisfaction, he shall condemn orally or under his own hand, all that he has erroneously held, no compassion, to whatever extent, shown will be blameworthy; for our Lord, the true and good Shepherd, who laid down his life for his sheep, and who came to save men's souls not to lose them, wills that we be imitators of his own loving kindness, so that justice should indeed constrain those who sin, but mercy should not reject those who are converted. For then indeed is true faith defended with the best results when a false opinion is condemned even by those who have followed it. That the whole matter may be piously and faithfully carried out, we have appointed our brethren, Julius, bishop, and Renatus, presbyter, and also my son, Hilarius, deacon, to represent us. With these we have associated as notary Dulcitius, whose faith is proven to us, confident that the help of God will be forthcoming, that he who has strayed, condemning the wickedness of his opinion, may be saved (God keep you safe, dearest brother). Given on the Ides of June, in the consulship of Asturius and Protogenes, illustrious men."

---

[1]Author's tr. of text of C. Silva-Tarouca in *Textus et Documenta*, Series Theologica 9, Rome; see article 'Leo the Great'; cf. Grillmeier, Part Three, Section II, ch. 2, 3, *Leo the Great and his Tomus ad Flavianum* with bibliography.

TRANSFIGURATION, THE

"And after six days Jesus took with him Peter and James and John, his brother, and led them up to a high mountain apart. And he was transfigured before them, and his face shone like the sun, and his garments became white as light. And behold, there appeared to them Moses and Elijah, talking with him. And Peter said to Jesus, 'Lord, it is well that we are here; if you wish, I will make three booths here; one for you and one for Moses and one for Elijah.' He was still speaking, when lo, a bright cloud overshadowed them, and a voice from the cloud said, 'This is my beloved Son, with whom I am well pleased, listen to him.' When the disciples heard this, they fell on their faces, and were filled with awe. But Jesus came and touched them, saying, 'Rise and have no fear.' And when they lifted up their eyes, they saw no one but Jesus only" (Mt 17:1-8).

"And after six days Jesus took with him Peter and James and John, and led them up a high mountain apart by themselves; and he was transfigured before them, and his garments became glistening, intensely white, as no fuller on earth could bleach them. And there appeared to them Elijah and Moses; and they were talking to Jesus. And Peter said to Jesus, 'Master, it is well that we are here; let us make three booths, one for you and one for Moses and one for

Elijah.' For he did not know what to say, for they were exceedingly afraid. And a cloud overshadowed them, and a voice came out of the cloud, 'This is my beloved Son; listen to him.' And suddenly, looking around, they no longer saw anyone with them but Jesus only'' (Mk 9:2-8).

"Now about eight days after these sayings he took with him Peter and John and James, and went up on the mountain to pray. And as he was praying, the appearance of his countenance was altered, and his raiment became dazzling white. And behold two men were talking with him, Moses and Elijah, who appeared in glory and spoke of his departure, which he was to accomplish at Jerusalem. Now Peter and those who were with him were heavy with sleep but kept awake, and they saw his glory and the two men who stood with him. And as the men were parting from him, Peter said to Jesus, 'Master, it is well that we are here; let us make three booths, one for you and one for Moses and one for Elijah'—not knowing what he said. And as he said this, a cloud came and overshadowed them; and they were afraid, as they entered the cloud. And a voice came out of the cloud, saying, 'This is my Son, my Chosen, listen to him.' And when the voice had spoken Jesus was found alone'' (Lk 9:28-36).

An isolated event in the public life of Jesus, unique in its constituent elements in the whole Bible.[1] There is no other instance of a man suddenly adopting an appearance of superhuman splendor, his very clothes thereby affected, with two personalities long since dead accompanying him, recognized by the onlookers despite a time gap of centuries. Can we believe that this really happened? Can we penetrate its mysterious meaning and purpose? Can we descend to particulars and ask why it happened only once? Why was it witnessed by only three of Jesus' disciples? How is it related to the pattern of his life, as this is discernible in the capital moments? Has it a significance in the redemptive work of Christ? What is its place in the revelation of God in Christ?

Testimony to the happening is based exclusively on the accounts in the synoptic gospels; the reference in 2 Pet 1:17-18 can scarcely be considered because of the doubtful authorship. Mt is thought to depend on Mk; Lk has additional elements: Jesus went up on the mountain to pray, and while he was praying, the "appearance of his countenance altered"—he does not say "he was transfigured," as do Mt and Mk; he spoke of "his departure, which he was to accomplish at Jerusalem"; the disciples "were heavy with sleep, but kept awake"; "they saw his glory." Lk also mentions that Jesus was praying when the Spirit descended on him after the Baptism (3:21). It has been suggested that Lk got his additional mate-

rial from Johannine circles: a conjecture not easy to establish. Where did the fact that Jesus was speaking of his "departure" with Moses and Elijah come from? Only Peter, James, or John could have transmitted such information. By what channel?

Certain OT passages are recalled by the commentators. God shows himself on a mountain: Ex 19:20-24; Dt 4:10-11; 1 Kgs 19:8-18. The divine presence is accompanied by a cloud: Ex 19:16-18; 24:15-16; 1 Kgs 8:10-11. In the OT, however, it is Israel who receives the eulogy, "first-born son." The parallel with "my beloved Son" is, in fact, in the NT, at the moment of the Baptism (qv).

The literary setting in the gospel texts is thought-provoking. The event is narrated after Peter's confession of faith (Mt 16:16; Mk 8:29; Lk 9:20); this profession was in turn followed by the words of Christ foretelling his Passion (Mt 16:21; Mk 8:31; Lk 9:22), stating too that he would be raised on the third day. The Transfiguration could then be seen as a reward to Peter, and to all, reassurance. A facile reading of things possibly. It has been suggested that the episode is a retrojection of the Resurrection appearances; it would then be held that these were luminous—the thesis is untenable. Nor is it easy to establish a close parallel between the episode and the agony in Gethsemane (qv). The suggestion made by Peter about three booths has been associated with the Feast of Booths, or Tabernacles, during which time the Temple was brightly illuminated. But these features scarcely touch the heart of the mystery.

The three apostles chosen were a privileged group: they were fishing partners when Jesus worked the miracle of the miraculous catch of fish (Lk 5:4-7) and they heard the words, "Do not be afraid, henceforth you will be fishers of men" (Lk 5:10); they witnessed the raising of the daughter of Jairus from the dead (Mk 5:21-43; Lk 8:40-46); they would be companions of Jesus in Gethsemane (qv). Why these three? Why not the Twelve? Is there a discernible relationship between the different episodes in which they figure? If their presence at the miracles and at this theophany was a preparation for Gethsemane, did they fail? Only to be fully restored after the Resurrection, with which some commentators link the Transfiguration?

Some illumination on the episode and its message is reached by comparison with Phil 2:6-11 (see article Kenosis). The Transfiguration was a momentary anticipation of what the hymn describes: "Therefore God has highly exalted him . . ."; but he had "emptied himself, taking the form of a servant, being born in the likeness of men." This was a fleeting, but remembered, glimpse of the glorified Christ. Was it also, as St. Lawrence of Brindisi maintained, a manifestation of the kind of existence the Incarnate Word would have had in a sinless world? The Franciscan Doctor held that in such a world free of sin the Incarnation would still have taken place. To a present-day mystic, Vassula Ryden (qv), the Lord has said that his Transfiguration has not yet been fully understood.[2]

[1]Cf. E. Lohmeyer, "Die Verklärung Jesu nach den Markusevangelium, *ZNW* 21 (1922) 185–215; U. Holzmeister, "Einzeluntersuchungen über das Geheimnis der Verklärung Christi," *BB* 21 (1940) 200–10; E. Boobyer, *St. Mark and the Transfiguration,* 1942; J. M. Vosté, "De baptismo, tentatione et transfiguratione Jesu Christi," II, in *Studia Theologiae biblicae Novi Testamenti,* 3 vols., Rome, 1933, 1937; E. Dabrowski, *La Transfiguration de Jésus,* Rome, 1939; T. F. Torrance, "The Transfiguration of Jesus," *Evangelical Quarterly* 14 (1942) 214–29; A. M. Ramsey, *The Glory of God and the Transfiguration of Christ,* London, 1949; A. Kenny, "The Transfiguration and the Agony in the Garden," *CBQ* 19 (1957) 444–52; G. B. Caird, "The Transfiguration," *Expository Times* 67 (1955–56) 291–94; A. Feuillet, "Les perspectives propres à chaque évangéliste dans les récits de la Transfiguration," *BB* 39 (1958) 281–301; H. Baltrensweiler, *Die Verklärung Jesu,* Zurich, 1959; H. P. Müller, "Die Verklärung Jesu," *ZNW* 51 (1960) 56–64; C. E. Carlston, "Transfiguration and Resurrection," *JBL* 80 (1961) 194–223; P. Miquel, "Le Mystère de la Transfiguration," *Questions Liturgiques Paroissiales* 42 (1963) 194–223; M. Sabbe, "La rédaction du récit de la Transfiguration," in *La Venue du Messie,* Paris, Louvain, 1963, 63–100; J. M. Nutzel, *Die Verklärungs-erzählung im Markusevangelium,* Würzburg, 1973, Forschung zur Bibel, 61; F. Hahn, *Titles of Jesus in Christology,* Excursus V, "Analysis of the Transfiguration and Baptism Narratives," 334–46, Lutterworth, 1969; E. Nardoni, *La transfiguracion de Jesu y el dialogo sobre Elias,* Buenos Aires, 1977; B. D. Chilton, "The Transfiguration," *NTS* 27 (1980–81) 115–24; A. A. Trites, "The Transfiguration of Jesus," *Evangelical Quarterly* 51 (1979) 70–78; id., esp., "The Transfiguration in the Theology (The Gospel in Microcosm) of Luke," in *The Glory of Christ in the New Testament, Studies in Christology in Memory of G. B. Caird,* eds., L. D. Hurst and N. T. Wright, Oxford, 1987, 71–82; G. O'Collins, "Luminous Appearances of the Risen Christ," *CBQ* 46 (1984) 246–54; University Dissertations: P. R. Baldacci, *The Significance of the Transfiguration Narrative in the Gospel of Luke,* Ph.D., Marquette, 1974; R. H. Gause, *The Lukan Transfiguration Account, Luke's Pre-Crucifixion Presentation of the Exalted Lord in the Glory of the Kingdom of God,* Ph.D., Emory, Atlanta, 1975; N. L. Liefeld, "Theological Motifs in the Transfiguration Narratives," in *New Dimensions in Theology,* eds., R. N. Longenecker and M. C. Tierney, Grand Rapids, 1975; J. A. Fitzmyer, *The Gospel According to Luke, I-IX,* New York, 1981, bibl. 804; J. Murphy-O'Connor, "What Really Happened at the Transfiguration?" *Bible Review* 3, June 1987, 8–21; [2]Personal communication.

V

VALTORTA, MARIA (1897–1961)

The large work written by this Italian mystic, *The Poem of the Man-God*, has had a wide international appeal in recent times.[1] The author was born in Caserta; her father was a military man, her mother a domineering woman, indifferent to religion, who successfully excluded two suitors from her daughter's life. Maria, because of her father's profession, lived in different Italian regions, but for most of her life in Viareggio. Grievously ill, she was bed-ridden from 1934. She had no theological training, had no reading matter save the Bible and the catechism of St. Pius X. Her writing was mostly done before 1953, was at its most productive between 1943 and 1947. From about 1956 she was increasingly withdrawn, in a kind of psychological isolation. Twelve years after her death her body was transferred from Viareggio to Florence, to the Capitular Chapel in the Grand Cloister of the Most Holy Annunciation; here her tomb is venerated.

Maria's literary legacy is contained in notebooks which run to almost fifteen thousand pages. Urged by a spiritual director, she had written an autobiography; she had also composed commentaries on biblical texts, hagiographical and pious works. Her correspondence is not without interest, for though absorbed in the spiritual life to the extent of offering herself as a victim not only to divine merciful Love (January 28, 1925), but to divine justice (July 1, 1931), she had a common-sense interest in the lives of her friends.

But almost two thirds of her manuscripts deal with the life of Jesus, *The Poem of the Man-God*. She said that she had no human source for what she so abundantly wrote, did not at times quite understand what she was writing. The content is what she saw in visions, what the Lord told her in explanation, insights which he shared with her. As the narrative unfolds, unexpected elements occur. There is throughout a sense of wholeness in the life narrated and described, with a mass of details which prove interesting to the faithful reader. Incidents related in the canonical gospels in skeleton form are here fleshed out to harmonize with our sense of concrete reality. No violence whatever is done to the truth of the canonical gospels, or the genuine traditions of the Church. The widespread appeal of the work is due to the fact that whereas the inspiration is genuinely mystical, the product is acceptable to those who see in Jesus Christ "the way, the truth and the life." The span of the work is from the parents and the infancy of Mary, and it ends, having traversed the hidden life, the public life, and the Passion with the glorification of Jesus. A great Marian theologian has discovered treasures in these pages. He ranks her with the greatest Marian mystics of the ages.

---

[1] English translation in five volumes: N. Picozzi, revised by P. McLaughlin, Isola del Liri, Centro Editoriale Valtortiano, 1986; cf. G. M. Roschini, O.S.M., *La Madonna negli scritti di Maria Valtorta*, Isola del Liri, Edizioni Pisani, 1973, 324pp.; id, *La Madonna negli scritti di Maria Valtorta*. Schemi di lezioni, Isola del Liri, 1973; English translation, Sherbrooke, Quebec, 1989.

VASSULA RYDEN (1942–)

The work of this author, *True Life in God*, has had, within a few years an impact little less than sensational: translations in French, Italian, German, Greek, Russian, Japanese, with others to follow. Vassula, known by this name, is Egyptian, born of Greek parents, married to a Swedish citizen, who has held high-ranking posts in the UNO and other international agencies, and is currently with I.U.C.N.[1] V. spent eighteen years in Africa, was then for some time in Bangladesh. Baptized in the Orthodox Church and favored with a mystical grace when she was ten years and another in the following year, she gave up attending church for thirty years (1955–1985), save for wedding and funeral ceremonies, and this less than a dozen times.

Everything changed in 1985 when she began to receive supernatural communications. First it was her angel who named himself Daniel, then God the Father, and as the constant source of revelation daily thereafter, Jesus: Jesus especially giving V. messages from his Sacred Heart, something unique in the Orthodox Church; so is her devotion to the Rosary.

She benefits by inner locution of a very distinctive kind. She speaks of a light, which is given, which gives an understanding of what was symbolic, or told in a parable. This light gives a deeper perception to understand clearly what God wants. She sometimes takes dictation, word by word, or she may receive a whole passage and put it in writing as perfectly as possible. When Jesus is communicating with her, she distinctly hears his voice, can distinguish if the voice is sad or full of joy. She has the sentiment of seeing the Lord interiorly, she feels him, his heart especially, knows if he is sad, happy, upset.

While V. hears the voice of Jesus, another phenomenon takes place: "While still maintaining my full freedom and with the action of the Spirit of God at work, my handwriting is transformed into a more perfect handwriting. This is while I am in dictation with the Lord. My own way of writing remains inactive, and the other perfect style comes in. As soon as I want to comment or ask, in writing, of the Lord, my own handwriting comes out again in a split second."

V.'s handwriting has been analyzed by an expert in graphology, J. A. Munier, attached to the Paris Court of Appeals. Unaware of the writer's identity, he wrote of her in terms like these: "Extraordinary telluric force. A controlled enthusiasm with a touch of delight, i.e., it seems to be the source of some kind of well-being. She is filled with a force that goes beyond herself. She is filled with invisible forces to which she reacts with a kind of primitive simplicity, whereas there is also in other areas a refined element. She is convinced of this invisible power which she perceives with intensity. She is an intermediary, like a center of transmission and amplification. She has the faith of a mystic. She is very redoubled, nourished by an invisible force that seems indestructible."

V.'s message is manifold but essentially a recall to love, love symbolized by the Sacred Heart, mirrored in the Immaculate Heart of Mary; she has also seen the two united. This devotion, this profound revelation of the Man-God, formerly so creative of holiness among Catholics, lapsed for a while, has not been an Orthodox form of piety. V. is unique as a pioneer in this regard; as an Orthodox she is also an exception in her belief in purgatory and in her attachment to the Pope. Jesus speaks to her especially of the unity he will one day effect among all his children. There will be a moment of purification, but this is said more as a warning than a threat; thereafter love will reign, there will be unity seen as essentially his work.

Extracts can scarcely give an idea of the rich flow of thought: "I am preparing you from Heaven to acknowledge the truth. I am encouraging you by displaying portents in heaven and on earth; I am giving to the poor and the small, visions. I am sending you my Mother to instruct you as a teacher in different nations; I am displaying in Infinite Mercy like a banner above your heads, generation, to educate you and bring you back to divinity. . . . I have come to you and showed you my Sacred Heart. I went in all directions seeking by what means I could make you mine. I showered blessing upon blessing on you to raise you from death and form you since you lacked Wisdom. I courted you and in my Tenderness I myself have chosen you to become a witness to a people not your own and of whom many are far from understanding why Wisdom has chosen a foreigner among them. I, the Sacred Heart, am determined to show them that I have taken you, a foreigner to them, to share the Riches of My Sacred Heart, and share its delights and sorrows. Yes, I have come to teach foreigners too, of My Sacred Heart's Riches; today I have made a new song for them for I am one and the same! Peace be with you; I have come to your very doors, it is I, the Sacred Heart who speaks to you; I come to offer you my Heart . . . but My Soul is grieving beyond your understanding to see from above dissensions like never before in the heart of my Sanctuary; my Body is bleeding and My Heart is one big wound; the shepherd's staff, which I had given you whole, lies now broken in splinters; but I mean to visit you soon to put together the shepherd's staff I had left behind me . . ."[2]

There are many other perspectives of deep doctrinal import opened in the writings of V. True to the Orthodox tradition she is particularly sensitive to all that touches belief in the Holy Spirit, his presence in the life of the Christian and in the Church. There are noteworthy passages for inclusion in an anthology of the ages where Jesus instructs her at length on the Spirit's indispensable role in the Church, in the distribution of his gifts. The theme of the Spirit is a recurring leit-motif, and there is an overwhelming sense of the identity of Jesus and his Spirit in their sanctifying action.

---

[1]International Union for the Conservation of Nature; English edition of *True Life in God,* Manchester, Belfast, Independence, Mo., 1991; French, 5 vols., Paris, 1991;   [2]Extracts from MSS provided by the author.

VATICAN II

The Council Fathers of Vatican II through their own studies or through the information accessible to them from some 200 theological experts had cognizance of powerful intellectual trends centering on Jesus Christ:[1] Catholic biblical scholars encouraged by Pius XII's epoch-making Encyclical, *Divino afflante Spiritu* (qv) were facing the problems raised by the Form-critics, notably R. Bultmann (qv); liturgists were influenced by the *Mysterienlehre* of Dom Odo Casel, which focused worship on Christ re-enacting his mysteries, especially the Paschal Mystery; spirituality had been brought back to the Person of Christ by writers like Dom Columba Marmion (qv); and theorizing on divine revelation was accentuating the personalist approach, which would break the existing mold and center God's self-communication on the Son "through whom he has spoken to us in these last days" (Heb 1:2).

There is no full treatise of the Incarnate Word in the conciliar documents; what we get are passages where the subject is particularly relevant. These amount to a compendium which would justify the opinion that the mystery of Christ is central to the teaching of Vatican II. A key sentence would be: "The most intimate truth which this revelation gives us about God and the salvation of man shines forth in Christ, who is himself both the Mediator and the fullness of all revelation."[2] Though borrowed from Pius XI's Encyclical *Mit brennender Sorge,* the words have a resonance not found in many of the classic treatises on divine revelation.

It seems better to follow the conciliar teaching chronologically. The first lines of the first Constitution promulgated, on the Liturgy, have these words: "For it is the liturgy through which, especially in the divine sacrifice of the Eucharist, 'the work of our redemption is accomplished,'[3] and it is through the liturgy especially, that the faithful are enabled to express in their lives and manifest to others the mystery of Christ and the real nature of the true Church. . . . The liturgy daily builds up those who are in the Church, making of them a holy temple of the Lord, a dwelling-place for God in the Spirit, to the mature of the fullness of Christ."[4]

These words in the introduction are followed in ch. I with this synopsis: "God who 'wills that all men be saved and come to the knowledge of the truth' (1 Tim 2:4), 'who in many times and various ways spoke of old to the fathers through the prophets' (Heb 1:1), when the fullness of time had come sent his Son, the Word made flesh, anointed by the Holy Spirit, to preach the gospel to the poor, to heal the contrite of heart (cf. Is 61:1; Lk 4:18), to be a bodily and spiritual medicine, (cf. Ignatius of Antioch: Eph 7:2), the Mediator between God and man (1 Tim 2:5). For his humanity united with the Person of the Word was the instrument of our salvation. Therefore, 'in Christ the perfect achievement of our reconciliation came forth and the fullness of divine worship was given to us' (*Sacramentarium Veronese* - Leonianum). The wonderful works of God among the people of the Old Testament were but a prelude to the work of Christ our Lord in redeeming mankind and giving perfect glory to God. He achieved his task principally by the paschal mystery of his blessed Passion (qv), Resurrection (qv) from the dead, and glorious Ascension, whereby 'dying he destroyed our death, and rising, restored our life' (Easter Preface of the Roman Missal). For it was from the side of Christ as he slept the sleep of death upon the Cross that there came forth 'the wondrous sacrament of the whole Church' " (Prayer before Second Lesson of Holy Saturday [Roman Missal, before restoration]).

The Constitution then shows how the Lord assured the continuation of his mission. His presence in the Church is vital: "To accomplish so great a work Christ is always present in his Church, especially in her liturgical celebrations. He is present in the Sacrifice of the Mass not only in the person of his minister, 'the same now offering, through the ministry of priests, who formerly offered himself on the cross' (Council of Trent, Session 22; Doctrine on the Holy Sacrifice of the Mass, ch. 2), but especially in the Eucharistic species. By his power he is present in the sacraments so that when anybody baptizes it is really Christ himself who baptizes (cf. St. Augustine, *Tract. in Joan.* VI, ch. 1, n. 7). He is present in his word since it is he himself who speaks when the holy scriptures are read in the Church. Lastly, he is present when the Church prays and sings, for he has promised 'where two or three are gathered together in my name there I am in the midst of them' (Mt 18:20)."[6]

Then comes the capital text on Christ the priest and the liturgy: "Christ, indeed, always associates the Church with himself in this great work in which God is perfectly glorified and men are sanctified. The Church is his beloved Bride who calls to her Lord, and through him offers worship to the eternal Father. The liturgy, then, is rightly seen as an exercise of the priestly office of Jesus Christ. It involves the presentation of man's sanctification under the guise of signs perceptible by the senses and its accomplishment in ways appropriate to each of these signs. In it full public worship is performed by the Mystical Body of Jesus Christ, that is, by the Head and his members. From this it follows that every liturgical celebration, because it is an action of Christ the priest and of his Body, which is the Church, is a sacred action surpassing all others. No other action of the Church can equal its efficacy by the same title and to the same degree.''[7]

That is Christ seen in the perspective of the Church's worship. In the Constitution on the Church the Council went deeper, considering Christ in relation to the very essence and existence of the Church. Ch. I presents the mystery in a Trinitarian setting. Having summarized the intention of the Father it proceeds to treat of the Son's role thus: ''The Son, accordingly, came, sent by the Father who, before the foundation of the world, chose us and predestined us in him for adoptive sonship. For it is in him that it pleased the Father to restore all things (cf. Eph 1:4-5, 10). To carry out the will of the Father, Christ inaugurated the kingdom of heaven on earth and revealed to us his mystery; by his obedience he brought about our redemption.''[8]

This soteriological approach allows for development of the idea of the Church and the kingdom as identical, a train of thought that reverts to the person of Christ in his different aspects: ''The miracles of Jesus also demonstrate that the kingdom has already come on earth: 'If I cast out devils by the finger of God, then the kingdom of God has come upon you' (Lk 11:20; cf. Mt 12:28). But principally the kingdom is revealed in the person of Christ himself, Son of God and Son of Man, who came 'to serve and to give his life as a ransom for many' (Mk 10:45). When Jesus, having died on the Cross for men, rose again from the dead, he was seen to be constituted as Lord, the Christ, and as Priest forever (cf. Acts 2:36; Heb 5:6; 7:17-21), and he poured out on his disciples the Spirit promised by the Father (cf. Acts 2:23). In the explanation of the various images used to describe the Church, occasional reference is necessarily made to Christ. This is especially so, with extended explanation in regard to the Mystical Body (see article Head of the Church).

Having chosen the Pauline idea of the People of God as basic to its teaching, the Council sought to relate it to Christ. ''That messianic people has as its head Christ 'who was delivered up for our sins and rose again for our justification' (Rom 4:25), and now having acquired the name which is above all names, reigns gloriously in heaven.''[10] This headship is shown to bring the faithful into relationship with the great privileged offices traditionally attributed to Christ. For the priesthood and prophetic office the treatment is clearly formulated: ''Christ the Lord, high priest taken from among men (cf. Heb 5:1-5), made the new people 'kingdom of priests to God, his Father' (Rev 1:6; cf. 5:9-10). The baptized, by regeneration and the anointing of the Holy Spirit, are consecrated to be a spiritual house and a holy priesthood, that through all the works of Christian men they may offer spiritual sacrifices and proclaim the perfection of him who has called them out of darkness into his marvelous light (cf. 1 Pet 2:4-10). Therefore, all the disciples of Christ, persevering in prayer and praising God (cf. Acts 2:42-47) should present themselves as a sacrifice, living, holy and pleasing to God (cf. Rom 12:1). . . . Though they differ essentially and not only in degrees, the common priesthood of the faithful and the ministerial or hierarchical priesthood are nonetheless ordered one to another; each in its own proper way shares in the one priesthood of Christ.''[11] ''The holy People of God share also in Christ's prophetic office; it spreads abroad a living witness to him, especially by a life of faith and love and by offering to God a sacrifice of praise, the fruit of lips praising his name (cf. Heb 13:15). The whole body of the faithful who have an anointing that comes from the holy one (cf. 1 Jn 2:20, 27) cannot err in matters of belief.''[12]

When it comes to Christ's kingship (qv), the Council is less emphatic. Whereas Pius XI (qv) in his Encyclical *Quas Primas* (qv) proclaimed the rights of Christ the King in civil society, the wording in the conciliar text is about ''citizens, who are taken from all nations, (who) are of a kingdom whose nature is not earthly but heavenly.'' ''Since the kingdom of Christ is not of this world (cf. Jn 18:36), the Church or People of God which establishes this kingdom does not take away anything from the temporal welfare of any people. Rather, she fosters and takes to herself, insofar as they are good, the abilities, the resources and customs of peoples. In so taking them to herself she purifies, strengthens and elevates them.'' It is then, after something akin to neutrality in regard to the rights of Christ the King in civil society has been formulated, that we read of the universality which Christ bestows on his Church: ''The Church indeed is mindful that she must work with that king to whom the nations were given as an inheritance (Ps 2:8) and to whose city gifts are brought (cf. Ps 71 [72] :10; Is 60:4-7; Rev 21:24). This character of universality which adorns the People of God is a gift from the Lord himself whereby the Catholic ceaselessly and efficaciously seeks for the return of all humanity and all its good under Christ the Head in the unity of his Spirit.''[13]

The ecclesial theology which is unfolded in the subsequent chapters of the Constitution have a continuing thread of reference to Christ, up to the chapter on Our Lady, who is presented in the mystery of Christ and the Church. In this section there is much insistence on the unique mediation of Christ as mother of men. "Mary's function," we are told, "in no way obscures or diminishes this unique mediation of Christ, but rather shows its power." We also read that "the predestination of the Blessed Virgin as Mother of God was associated with the incarnation of the divine Word."[14]

Of the documents promulgated during the fourth session of the Council, the Constitution on Divine Revelation, as has been already suggested, is the one which will repay study. The doctrine of revelation is Trinitarian in structure. It is brought to us by the mission of the Son—the concept of mission is a key one in conciliar teaching: "After God had spoken many times and in various ways through the prophets, 'in these last days he has spoken to us by a Son' (Heb 1:1-2). For he sent his Son, the eternal Word who enlightens all men, to dwell among men and to tell them about the inner life of God. Hence Jesus Christ, sent as 'a man among men' (*Epistle to Diognetus,* c. 7, 4, *Patres Apostolici,* I, 403) 'speaks the words of God' (Jn 3:34), and accomplishes the saving work which the Father gave him to do (cf. Jn 5:36; 17:4). As a result, he himself—to see him is to see the Father (cf. Jn 14:9)—completed and perfected Revelation and confirmed it with divine guarantees. He did this by the total fact of his presence and self-manifestation—by words and works, signs and miracles, but above all by his death and glorious resurrection from the dead, and finally by sending the Spirit of truth. He revealed that God was with us, to deliver us from the darkness of sin and death, and to raise us up to eternal life. The Christian economy, therefore, since it is the new and definite covenant, will never pass away; and no new public revelation is to be expected before the glorious manifestation of our Lord, Jesus Christ (cf. 1 Tim 6:14; Tit 2:13)."[15] In dealing with the transmission of divine revelation the Council restates its basic position in this context: "Therefore, Christ the Lord in whom the entire Revelation of the most high God is summed up (cf. 2 Cor 1:20; 3:16–4:6) commands the apostles to preach the Gospel, which had been promised beforehand by the prophets, and which he had fulfilled in his own person and promulgated with his own lips."[16]

The idea of mission (qv) is found, too, in the decrees on the Church's missionary activity and on the ministry and life of priests, while in the Pastoral Constitution on the Church in the Modern World, a Christian anthropology is briefly sketched. The theological basis for missionary activity is also Trinitarian: "Jesus Christ was sent into the world as the true Mediator between God and men. Since he is God, all the fullness of the divine nature dwells in him bodily (Col 2:9); as man he is the new Adam, full of grace and truth (Jn 1:14) who has been constituted head of a restored humanity. So the Son of God entered the world by means of a true incarnation that he might make men sharers in the divine nature; though rich, he was made poor for our sake, that by his poverty we might become rich (2 Cor 8:9). The Son of Man did not come to be served, but to serve and to give his life as a ransom for many, that is for all (cf. Mk 10:45). The Fathers of the Church constantly proclaim that what was not assumed by Christ was not healed (see article Origen). Now Christ took a complete human nature just as it is found in us poor unfortunates, but one that was without sin (cf. Heb 4:15; 9:28)."

The theology of this passage is more profound than what has so far been seen, with an echo of Chalcedon (qv), allusion to divinization and the suggestion of Christ the new Adam (qv). The decree on the ministry and life of priests repeats the teaching of the Constitution on the Church.

The outline of Christian anthropology in the Pastoral Constitution evokes the Pauline doctrine of the new Adam (though Paul speaks of the "last Adam," 1 Cor 15:45), and the doctrine of the image: "In reality it is only in the mystery of the Word made flesh that the mystery of man truly becomes clear. For Adam, the first man, was a type of him who was to come. Christ the Lord, Christ the new Adam, in the very revelation of the mystery of the Father and of his love, fully reveals man to himself and brings to light his most high calling. It is no wonder, then, that all the truths mentioned so far should find in him their source and their most perfect embodiment. He who is the 'image of the invisible God' (Col 1:15) is himself the perfect man who has restored in the children of Adam that likeness to God which had been disfigured ever since the first sin. Human nature, by the very fact that it was assumed, not absorbed, in him, has been raised in us also to a dignity beyond compare. For by his incarnation, he, the Son of God, has, in a certain way, united himself with each man. He worked with human hands, he thought with a human mind. He acted with a human will, and with a human heart he loved. Born of the Virgin Mary, he has truly been made one of us, like to us in all things except sin."[18]

There follows a brief account of Christ's work of redemption and of the benefits accruing from it to the Christian, "conformed to the image of the Son, who is the first-born of many brothers." Later the conciliar text returns to consider "Christ: Alpha and Omega." Here it comes near to teaching the absolute primacy (qv) of Christ: "The Word of God, through whom all things were made, was made flesh, so that as a perfect man he could save all men and sum up all things in himself. The Lord is the goal of human history, the focal point of the desires of history and civilization, the center of mankind, the joy of all hearts, and the fulfillment of all aspirations. It is he whom the Father raised from the dead, exalted and placed at his right hand, constituting him judge of the living and the dead. Animated and drawn together in his Spirit we press onwards on our journey towards the consummation of history which fully corresponds to the plan of his love: 'to unite all things in him, things in heaven and things on earth' " (Eph 1:10).[19]

A magnificent theological panorama inviting continuing study and scrutiny.

---

[1]Cf. *The Christ of Vatican II*, St. Paul Publications, Boston, 1968; B. de Margerie, S.J., "Vatican II," in *Christ for the World, The Heart of the Lamb*, Chicago, 1973, 228–56; H. Hernandez Cirre, O.F.M.Cap., "El primado universal de Cristo a la luz del Vaticano II," *Estudios Franciscanos* 69 (1968) 5–40; A. de Villalmonte, O.F.M.Cap., "El 'Mysterium Christi' del Vaticano II en perspectiva escotista," *Naturaleza y Gracia* 13 (1966) 215–68; R. Rosini, O.F.M., *Il Cristocentrismo di Giovanni Duns Scoto e la dottrina del Vaticano II*, Rome, 1967; B. Sesboué, S.J., "Vatican II," in *Jésus Christ dans la tradition de l'Eglise*, Paris, 1982, 181–94; T. Gertler, *Jesus Christ: Die Antwort der Kirche auf die Frage nach dem Menschsein. Eine Untersuchung zu Funktion und Inhalt der Christologie im ersten Teil der Pastoral Konstitution Gaudium et Spes des Zweiten Vaticanischen Konzils*, Leipzig, 1986; [2]*Constitution on Divine Revelation*, 2; [3]Art. 2; [4]*Ibid.*; [5]Art. 5; [6]Art. 7; [7]*Ibid.*; [8]Art. 3; [9]Art. 5; [10]Art. 9; [11]Art. 10; [12]Art. 12; [13]Art. 13; [14]Art. 56; [15]Art. 4; [16]Art. 7; [17]On the Missionary Activity of the Church, art. 3; [18]On the Church in the Modern World, art. 22; [19]Art. 45.

VON BALTHASAR, HANS URS (1905–1988)

B.'s unusual life story and his profound impact and increasing influence on Catholic thought give importance to his theology of Jesus Christ.[1] It permeates all the vast corpus which he produced, joins the great fundamental truths of the centuries and in places throws up surprising new intuitions, analyses, or synthetic summaries. The great key concepts in his theological composition, the aesthetic and the *Theodramatik,* demand a considerable mental adjustment from most of his readers. He was resolutely opposed to a cleavage between theology and spirituality and was convinced that since Christ is the center of all creation, all things must be enlightened by and derive meaning from his mystery. B. expressed new insights, breathed new life into themes that had been

left in a certain state of immobility; he proposed an original interpretation of the kenosis (qv) of Christ, was stark in his realistic interpretation of the "descent into hell," elevated the Resurrection to a peak point in all human striving and history. His theology of history offers a reading of all this in a way which as the Biblical Commission said, "avoids the too restricted conclusions of Idealists and Materialists."

Few if any writers of our or any time could draw on sources as vast and varied as nourished B.'s works: the Fathers, in particular Origen, St. Gregory of Nyssa, St. Augustine, St. Maximus the Confessor, the great theologians through the ages, the great mystics and saints, contemporary writers from widely different cultures and backgrounds. His Christology, along with that of K. Barth (qv) is thus described by the Biblical Commission: "In each synthesis the more recent results of biblical criticism are not neglected; each one makes use of the entire Bible to present a systematic synthesis. Jesus of Nazareth and the Christ of faith are merely two aspects intimately joined to make up the self-revelation of God in human history. This revelation is clearly disclosed and made evident only *through faith* (K. Barth). According to H. U. von Balthasar, the 'kenosis' Christ, manifested in his absolute obedience to the Father, even unto death on the cross, reveals an essential characteristic of the life of the Trinity itself; at the same time it brings about the salvation of sinful humanity, as he undergoes the experience of death for it. . . . But according to H. U. von Balthasar, who advocates a contemplation of God by a mode that he calls 'aesthetic,' rational reflection, historical investigation, and the involvement of human liberty governed by love coalesce in the very mystery of Easter itself. In this way a *theology of history* is sketched out that avoids the too restricted conclusions of Idealists and Materialists."[2]

B.'s Christology is so rich and manifold that quotation risks distorting his sense, weakening his perspective. Throughout all his thinking, Jesus is central, the "absolute singular," the revelation, even the "language of God." Moreover there is the danger of losing his originality. Thus on Jesus the fulfillment of Israel, he writes: "The Christ-event is understood as the fulfillment of 'all the promises of God' (2 Cor 7:19; Heb 7:1-2). This is understood in a concrete way because all the promises and all faith in them, from the very beginning, have been aimed at resurrection from the dead. Abraham was the first to believe the promise. He believed in a God 'who brings the dead back to life and calls into being what does not exist' (Rom 4:17). By so doing he set up and unleashed a dynamic process that was to go far beyond the symbolic confirmation of his act of faith; he received the son of promise although 'his body was past fatherhood—he was a hundred years old—and Sarah too old to become a mother' (Rom 4:19). This faith in a God who can raise the dead resounds like a general bass tone beneath all the single promises to Israel.''[3]

This insight is matched by another, equally original and probing: ''in its center the Christ-event, as superabundant fulfillment of the Old Testament covenant-event, is even less a doctrine than the covenant. It is the absolute saving act of God, the miracle of the infallible and yet free covenant agreement between God and humanity which, before all verbalization by the Church, in the sovereign disposition of God's deed and laws, is something set forth once and for all; God's word no longer on lips, no longer as proclaimed mandate which promises or judges or blesses, but Word in flesh, in the realization of the spiritual and psychological, of what is thought and intended—right down to the fingernails, down to the heart opened and poured out. However important may be what is said before and after the cross, or about its looking towards the event or reflecting on it, compared with the reality, with the event itself, it is of secondary importance. An endless number of things can be said about this, but all spoken words taken together never equal the accomplished Word, let alone replace, supersede, or get beyond it.''[4]

On the challenge of the Incarnation, B. writes: ''Rather, what sets Christianity apart from other religions is the scandalous claim that the one who bears all names and yet is without name, who as the scripture says, 'is everything' (Sir 43:27), has once and for all declared himself identical with a tiny something or someone in the vast cosmos and among the swarming millions of humanity—identical with someone who then can make such monstrously exclusive statements about himself as 'I am the door . . . all who have come before me are thieves and robbers' (Jn 10:7f) and 'No one knows the Father but the Son and he to whom the Son will reveal it' (Mt 11:27). Of course, once one has admitted that the 'all' can become identical with the tiny 'someone,' then one will be compelled to accept such unbearably intolerant claims on the part of this 'someone.' ''[5]

B. comes to grips with the need for a dogmatic formula, one which will not supplant Chalcedon (qv) but make it accessible. ''Where God says to a spiritual subject who that subject is for him, the eternally abiding and true God; where God says to it in the same breath why it exists—thus bestowing on it its divinely attested mission—at that point it can be said of a spiritual subject that it is a person. But that has taken place once, archetypically, in Jesus Christ,

who was given his eternal 'definition'—'You are my beloved son'—when his unique and universal mission was bestowed on him from time immemorial, and with it the most precise knowledge of who he is, not only for God, but also from the beginning with God (Jn 1:1). Yes, it must be said that the combination of an exact definition of the personal uniqueness and the universal meaning of this uniqueness which lies in the mission of Jesus is the incontrovertible expression of his divinity. It is this way because it is a matter of mission, of received divinity, but which there is no contradiction in itself only if it is not merely God's sharing with a creature but the giving over of divinity to one who is God (*Deum de Deo*).''

B. goes on to relate this reality to the idea of person: ''Everything which, besides Jesus, still merits a claim on the title 'person' can raise it only on the basis of a relation to him and derivation from him. There can be no talk about the identity between 'I' and mission, as it exists in Jesus, in regard to any other person; but only of the endowing of their spiritual subjectivity with a part or aspect of his universal mission. Jesus lives his human consciousness completely as mission; he has in the Holy Spirit the mandate from the Father to reveal the essence of God and God's attitude towards human beings. And not just onesidedly (as represented so gladly these days), merely as God's taking the part of sinners and the needy, but especially in as much as he reveals all the other qualities of God in his sensible human existence: God's wrath (e.g., over the sinful desecration of his place of cult), God's disgust at having to endure so long among these people without understanding, God's grief and tears at Jerusalem's refusal to accept his invitation, indeed one can even say, God's abandonment of sinners in the cry of abandonment on the Cross, and so forth.''[7]

The passages which follow this one must be read to form an idea of the amazing wealth and originality of B.'s thinking. Let these words indicate his originality: ''We must, according to biblical revelation, avoid splitting the Son of God, as he exists in his mission, into the one who fulfills his mandate on earth and the one who meanwhile abides unchanged in heaven and observes the one who is sent. The one sent is one single unity who abides in time as eternal one. His allowing himself to be disposed of from the form of God into the 'form of a slave' and 'human likeness' (Phil 2:6f) is an event which involves him as the eternal Son.''[8]

On the Eucharist as a revelation of Christ and the Father, B. writes: ''The passivity of the Passion, with chaining, scourging, nailing, piercing, is the expression of a most highly active will to self-sacrifice which precisely for this reason, transcends the limits of self-determination into the limitlessness of the pure letting-oneself-be-determined. On the other hand, such a will to sacrifice which in the Eucharistic gesture of delivering oneself among the disciples donates itself beyond all confines of human finitude, would really appear to be Promethean hubris if it were not already itself the expression of a prior act of being determined and disposed of. This Paul and John see exactly when they depict the whole self-giving of Jesus to his own and to the world as the concreteness of the self-giving of the Father who, out of love for the world he created and in fidelity to the covenant he has entered into with it, gives what is most precious to him, his Son (Rom 8:32; Jn 3:16). . . . This is clear: the human reality of Jesus (this 'flesh and blood' or his 'life' [Jn 10:15]) is, because of becoming man, already predisposed for Eucharist, insofar as it is the personified gift of God to the world. And the realization of this self-giving in the Lord's Supper, passion, and Resurrection (qqv) is nothing other than the actuation of this always intended, really planned and begun self-giving.'' [9]

There has been much discussion about B.'s theory on the descent "into hell," the *Triduum mortis*, which strongly resembles that of Adrienne von Speyr (qv). He has to be read fully on the subject and fairly evaluated.[10] He once wrote that since he did not belong to any theological school he was not a subject for academic dissertations. There is scarcely any theologian living who has prompted so many. One deals with his Christology and appeared with a preface written by himself.[11]

[1]For bibliography, cf. lists issued by Johannesverlag, Einsiedeln, 1975, 1980; excellent anthology in *The von Balthasar Reader*, eds., M. Kehl, S.J., W. Loser, S.J., tr. R. J. Daly, S.J., F. Lawrence, T. and T. Clark, Edinburgh, 1982, repr. with permission of the publisher; cf. M. O'Carroll, *Veni Creator Spiritus*, A Michael Glazier Book, Collegeville, 1990, 228–30; P. Escobar, *Zeit und Sein Jesu Christi bei Hans Urs von Balthasar*, Diss., Institut Catholique, Paris, 1973; H. Heinz, *Der Gott des Je-mehr, Der christologische Ansatz Hans Urs von Balthasar*, Frankfurt/Bern, 1975; G. Marchesi, *La Cristologia di Hans Urs von Balthasar*, Rome, Gregorian University, *AGreg* 207 (1977); J. Riches, ed., *The Analogy of Beauty. The Theology of Hans Urs von Balthasar*, Edinburgh, 1986; id., *The Modern Theologians*, I, 237–54; [2]Text tr. J. Fitzmyer, S.J., *Scripture and Christology*, London, 1986, 1.1.10.1 p. 16f; editor's comment, 88f; [3]*Warum ich noch ein Christ bin*, 35, *Reader*, 166; [4]*Spiritus Creator*, 54, *Reader*, 162; [5]*Klarstellungen*, 39, *Reader*, 195; [6]*Theodramatik*, II 32, 190, 206, *Reader* 132; [7]*Ibid.*; [8]*Ibid.*, *Reader*, 135; [9]*Neue Klarstellungen*, 68, *Reader*, 144; [10]Cf. *Reader*, 153; Pneuma und Institution, 67–70; [11]"The Paschal Mystery," *Mysterium Salutis*, XII; [11]G. Marchesi, *op. cit.*.

VON SPEYR, ADRIENNE (1902–1967)

If mystics (qv) are to be heard on the theology of Jesus Christ, a first claimant in modern times for such a contribution would be Adrienne von Speyr.[1] Her life, closely united with that of the giant of modern theology, Hans Urs von Balthasar (qv), was, even among mystics, rather singular. Twice married, a convert from Protestantism, a medical practitioner, she was the recipient of extraordinary mystical graces. In particular, with no formal theological training, she transmitted, again in a highly singular manner, an immense corpus of biblical commentary, which is replete with insights profound, stimulating and even provocative. Her method of composition was to dictate, at an exceptional speed, her intuitions and interpretations of important biblical texts, to Hans Urs von Balthasar, who took all this down in shorthand. In the end she had dictated sixteen thousand pages. Not only biblical commentary, but treatises on a variety of theological themes. Here we are concerned solely with what she taught about Jesus Christ.

Her upbringing in La Chaux de Fonds where her father practiced medicine, and in Bale where she lived with her mother after his early death, did not appear to dispose her towards Catholicism. Dissatisfaction with the teaching and practice in regard to the Eucharist and a keen appreciation of the Sacrament of Penance, not available to her, brought her, with the direction of Von Balthasar, to the Church; she was conditionally baptized in 1940. Thereafter "it is a cataract of mystical graces which breaks on Adrienne von Speyr, and in this storm apparently unloosed without plan, she felt herself impelled in every direction at once."[2] She was frequently visited by the Blessed Virgin (whom she had first seen in 1917), and by several saints, especially St. John and St. Ignatius; she worked miracles of healing (though a constant victim of illness, eventually losing her sight); had the gift of prophecy, and each year went through the Passion of Christ as a personal experience.

With Hans Urs von Balthasar, A. founded a secular institute, and in the choice of patron her theological orientation is manifest; her mystical experience gave her a keen existential sense of Christ, so St. John is chosen "because he is the most profound interpreter of the mystery of Christ," "the theologian par excellence"; John presents "Jesus as the Obedient One to the Father through love 'to the end,' in the Spirit whom he possesses 'without measure' he reveals love."[3]

It is in the four volumes of commentary on St. John's Gospel—over two thousand pages—that her theological and mystical insights are to be found. Her central idea is the obedience of Christ as the means of our Redemption; his mission to "redeem the word and bring it back to the Father, "to gather into one the children of God who are scattered abroad" (Jn 11:52). He is the Mediator (qv) between God and men, the "bridge" which crosses the abyss between him and them. He comes to set mankind in a genuine relationship with him who is its Creator, Father, Model, to turn back the face of creation to the Father.

Christ's obedience, the Son's obedience, is an absolute "Yes," without measure, without condition, without reservation, to the will of the Father. "What matters above all to him is obedience to the Father, this threefold consonance of love between the Father, the Son and the Spirit, this unity which manifests itself therein and at every moment demands his absolute obedience. . . . It is an obedience ever new, so strong that it will admit what is proper to himself only if what is proper to the Father and the Spirit are also within it."[4]

"The whole mysticism of Adrienne von Speyr," wrote Hans Urs von Balthasar, "had its center in the Christological obedience (which was thereby soteriological) which, true to the ancient theological tradition, is the revelation in human form of the eternal love of the divine Son for his eternal Father, who eternally begot him through love."[5]

A.'s intuitions were in this context both existential and experiential. Von Balthasar thought that what she thus discovered in Christ's obedience "was the most unheard-of part of her entire mission," "the greatest gift Adrienne received and bequeathed to the Church."[6] We are here evidently in the presence of a subtle, very profound theory, which Balthasar himself sought to justify with proper theological method in his work on the Paschal Mystery. Jesus' descent to the kingdom of the dead appears as the final stage of his obedience: "By this solidarity with sinners in their extreme state, Jesus accomplishes to the end the saving will of the Father. It is absolute obedience which goes beyond life . . ."[7] A. sees in this state a special manifestation of love: "It is the absolute perfection of love hidden, become inaccessible: the highest point of pure obedience seeking love where it is not. It is the ultimate in what the Father and the Son demand of each other in love." What love of the Father "the presence of the dead Christ among the dead represents."[8]

A. contends that the vision of hell given to the Son is the answer of the Father's love to the proof Jesus gave of his love on the Cross: "The Father answers the Son, and his answer is to show him hell. If the Son, through love for the Father and for men, carried the Cross, the Father, through love for the Son and for men, created hell. . . . Hell thus unveiled, as the Son sees it, is proof that the Father has accepted the Son's death on the Cross."[9] The suffering and torment that hell represents for Christ is unspeakable—a day for which there is no word, a place with nothing to grasp, a road without issue. Hell is the non-presence of love, the total rejection of God's name. Here, nonetheless the Son must seek the Father in the certitude that he will not find him: "The Father, recalling the Son to him, simultaneously sends him in the opposite direction, to where he will certainly himself not be found. This is the unfathomable mystery of Holy Saturday: the Son not being able to seek the Father in love, must seek him where he is not. The Father is not simply hidden, disappeared as on the Cross, but the Son is now obliged to plunge into what is opposed to the Father, to where but one thing is sure: the absence of the Father."[10]

The Father is the stranger in hell—the stranger to the Son. It is complete isolation, the silence of death, darkness without issue, the most radical negation of love, that which is wholly opposed to it, into which Christ must enter fully—this is the way the Father leads the Son to him, that he may see the realization of the work of Redemption: "sin dissolving into chaos."[11] On the Cross he died to dispense life; here he can give nothing, for "all is death and objection." He who is "the Light of the world" (Jn 8:12) is plunged into abysmal darkness; he who is the Word experiences absolute silence; he who is Love finds himself at the heart of non-love. Whereupon Christ must enter on the fullness of light, he regains the possession of the Father: the Resurrection (qv) suddenly takes place.

[1]Works relevant to our subject: *Die Bergpredigt, Betrachtungen über Matthäus V-VII,* 1948; *Die Abschiedsreden. Betrachtungen über das Johannesevangelium Kap 13–17,* 1948; *Das Wort wird Fleisch. Betrachtungen über das Johannesevangelium Kap 1-5,* 1949; *Die Streitreden. Betrachtungen über das Johannesevangelisum Kap 6–12; Geburt der Kirche, Betrachtungen über das Johannesevangelium, Kap 18–22; Gleichnisse des Herrn,* 1966; *Dienst der Freude. Betrachtungen über den Philipperbrief,* 1951; *Passion nach Matthäus,* 1957; *Die Magd des Herrn,* 1960; *Christlicher Stand,* 1982; posthumous works: *Kreuz und Hölle, Erde und Himmel,* 3 vols., all published by Johannesverlag, Einsiedeln; French tr. of some works, esp. the Johannine commentaries, ed., Lethielleux, 'Le Sycomore,' Paris; on A. v. Speyr, cf. Hans Urs von Balthasar, *Adrienne von Speyr et sa mission théologique,* 3rd ed., Paris, 1985; id., *L'Institut St. Jean,* Paris, 1986; B. Albrecht, "Une femme dans l'Eglise," A. v. Speyr, *Vie Consacrëe,* January 15, 1975, 34–44; T. de Roucy, S.J.M., *Adrienne von Speyr, Théologienne du Toujours-Plus,* Chiry-Ourscamp, 1990; *DSp,* s. v. XIII, B. Albrecht; [2]H. U. von Balthasar, *Adrienne von Speyr et sa mission théologique,* 26; [3]H. U. von Balthasar, *L'Institut St. Jean,* 98, 99; [4]*Dienst der Freude,* 68, 69; *Adrienne von Speyr,* 146; [5]*Adrienne von Speyr,* 48; [6]*Op. cit.,* 72; [7]*La gloire et la Croix,* II, 2, Paris, 1975, 199; [8]*Johannesevangelium IV,* 144; *Adrienne von Speyr,* 180; [9]*Kreuz und Hölle, Adrienne von Spehr,* 180; [10]*Johannesevangelium IV,* 257; *Adrienne von Speyr,* 180; [11]H. U. von Balthasar, Introduction to the posthumous works, in *A. v. Speyr, Das Allerheiligenbuch,* 22.

W

WOMEN, JESUS AND

The Savior's attitude toward women has been well summarized in the Roman document on the admission of women to the priesthood: "Jesus Christ did not call any woman to become part of the Twelve. If he acted in this way, it was not in order to conform to the customs of his time, for his attitude towards women was quite different from that of his milieu, and he deliberately and courageously broke with it.

"For example, to the great astonishment of his disciples, Jesus converses publicly with the Samaritan woman (cf. Jn 4:27); he takes no notice of the state of legal impurity of the woman who had suffered from hemorrhage (cf Mt 9:20-22); he allows a sinful woman to approach him in the house of Simon the Pharisee (cf. Lk 7:37f.); and by pardoning the woman taken in adultery, he means to show that one must not be more severe towards the fault of a woman than towards that of a man (cf. Jn 8:11). He does not hesitate to depart from the Mosaic law in order to affirm the equality of the rights and duties of men and women with regard to the marriage bond (cf. Mk 10:2-11; Mt 19:3-9).

"In his itinerant ministry, Jesus was accompanied not only by the Twelve but also by a group of women: 'Mary, surnamed the Magdalene, from whom seven demons had gone out, Joanna, the wife of Herod's steward Chusa, Susanna, and several others who provided for them out of their own resources' (Lk 8:2-3). Contrary to the Jewish mentality, which did not accord great value to the testimony of women, as Jewish law attests, it was nevertheless women who were the first to have the privilege of seeing the risen Lord, and it was they who were charged by Jesus to take the first paschal message to the Apostles themselves (cf. Mk 28:7-10; Lk 24:9-10; Jn 20:11-18), in order to prepare the latter to become the official witnesses to the Resurrection."[1]

One should still add to this not altogether adequate summary the entirely astonishing innovation made by the Eternal Son of God in choosing a woman, his Mother, to be his closest associate in his lifework, to be with him, through the ages, a mighty source of inspiration, intercession, mediation, renewal. Since Jesus was born of a virginal Mother, yet was thoroughly male, there is something of a mystery in his inheritance. Certainly his closeness to this woman through long years before his public ministry, especially after the death of St. Joseph, molded his mentality, his features, his very speech. His character (qv) derived something that was special from this sublime companionship. It prompted probably his ease in taking women as the subjects of his discourse and parables (qv)—the housewife and the leaven, the lost groat, the ten virgins, the widow and the judge, the widow's mite, the wife of the seven brothers, harlots and the kingdom of heaven, the Queen of the South, the widow of Sarepta, two women grinding at the mill, the mothers whose hour is come. One would be led on to develop a theology of woman, a subject which must wait for a further volume in this series of encyclopedias, *Gloria Deo.*

Pope John Paul II, in the Apostolic Letter, *Mulieris Dignitatem,* August 15, 1988, in part V, entitled "Jesus Christ," deals with these topics: "They marvelled that he was talking to a woman"; women in the Gospel; the woman caught in adultery; guardians of the Gospel message; first witnesses of the

Resurrection; important intuitions and suggestions.

The Pope has spoken twice on Our Lady and The Last Supper, on one occasion saying she was not present, later (in a Holy Thursday Letter to priests) that the gospels do not make it clear that she was present.

----

[1]*Inter insigniores,* October 15, 1976, *Vatican II,* 2, ed. A. Flannery, O.P., 334; cf. M. Faulhaber, *Women in the Bible,* tr., ed., B. Keogh, Westminster, Maryland, 1955; P. Ketter, *Christ and Womankind,* London, 1957; G. G. Blum, "Das Amt des Frau in NT," *NT* 7 (1964); P. Ketter, *Christus und die Frauen,* I and II, Stuttgart, 1949/50; A. Adam, *Christus und die Frau,* Ettal, 1951; G. Blaqueau, *La Grace d'être femme,* Paris, 1980; L. Boff, *The Maternal Face of God,* London, 1987; E. Schüssler-Fiorenza, *In Memory of Her,* London, 1984; M. S. van Leeuwen, *Gender and Grace,* Leicester, 1990; Bauer, III, 988–991; cf. article R. R. Reuther; B. Witherington, III, "Women in the Ministry of Jesus," *SNTS,* Cambridge, 1984, 198–211; J. Jeremias, "The Life of Discipleship—The Place of Women," in *New Testament Theology,* I, London, 1971, 223–27; F. Martin, "Feminist Hermeneutics: An Overview," in *Communio,* 18 (1991) 144–63; 398–424; A. Loaders, "Feminist Theology," in *The Modern Theologians* II, 235–52.

WORD OF GOD, CHRIST THE

The word *logos* occurs very frequently in the gospel of St. John.[1] What stimulates theological thinking incessantly is the application of the term to Jesus Christ. This occurs directly or indirectly in a few texts, but they are laden with meaning: Rev 19:13; 1 Jn 1:1, and especially Jn 1:1 and 1:14. Though the affinity with Philo Judaeus and Stoicism is apparent, these texts can be sufficiently interpreted in the light of OT usage—though Philo who used the word fourteen hundred times in his extant writings, certainly arouses interest, interest which probably has been best expressed by J. D. G. Dunn: "In the end of the day the Logos seems to be nothing more for Philo than God himself in his approach to man, God himself insofar as he may be known to man."[2]

The Revelation passage occurs in an eschatological context, described in the language characteristic of that book: conflict ensuing in defeat and condemnation of the malicious; the leader of the forces of righteousness, a rider on a white horse, has, among other names, that of the Word of God: "He is clad in a robe dipped in blood and the name by which he is called is the *Word* of God."

The reference in 1 Jn is within the opening passage descriptive of God's revelation in Christ—a passage beloved of Newman and chosen in part by Vatican II to introduce the important document on Divine Revelation as follows: "Hearing the word of God with reverence and proclaiming it confidently, this most sacred Synod takes its direction from these words of St. John . . ."[3] The whole passage is: "That which was from the beginning, which we have heard, which we have seen with our eyes, which we have looked upon and touched with our hands, concerning the Word of life—the life was made manifest, and we saw it, and testify to it, and proclaim to you the eternal life which was with the Father and was made manifest to us—that which we have seen and heard we proclaim also to you, so that you may have fellowship with us; and our fellowship is with the Father and with his Son Jesus Christ" (1 Jn 1:1-3).

The most important text, however, is Jn 1:14: "And the *Word* became flesh and dwelt among us, full of grace and truth; we have beheld his glory, glory as of the only Son from the Father." The words assume, of course, the statement made in the opening verses: "In the beginning was the Word, and the Word was with God, and the Word was God. He was in the beginning with God; all things were made through him, and without him was not anything made that was made. In him was life and the life was the light of men" (1:1-4).

This, as Grillmeier (qv) comments, taken with 1:14, is "the most penetrating description of the career of Jesus Christ that has been written." He notes that 1:14 was to become the "most influential text in the history of Dogma." We have a startling identity between "revelation" and "revealer." Grillmeier writes a sentence which strikingly and almost literally anticipates Vatican II: "The office of 'revealer' is so closely bound up with the person of Jesus that Christ himself becomes the embodiment of revelation."—Vatican II, "Christ is the Mediator and fullness of all revelation."[4]

There are as yet unplumbed depths in the conjunction of three ideas in the Prologue: the Word was God; through him all things were made; he became flesh. Creation and Incarnation are bound together and in that mighty synthesis the gospel of Jn is unfolded. C. H. Dodd puts it thus: "The Prologue is an account of the life of Jesus under the description of the eternal Logos and its relations with the world and with man, and the rest of the gospel an account of the Logos under the form of a record of the life of Jesus."[5] Dodd sees the two as bound together by the powerful formula, "the Word became flesh." It succinctly and finally explains the relation of the Logos to man and his world, and it summarizes the significance of Jesus' life.

This is very true, but it leaves still for investigation and explanation the relationship between the Logos as mediator of God's creative power and the union of all this incalculable might with the "flesh," not merely union, but "becoming." We are here at the very heart of the Christ mystery, event, proclamation. The Logos is God speaking with his utmost power, acting creatively by his speaking, the eternal Son who manifests the Father, whose being spans the vast universe of creation through his initial impact, and the immeasurable being of the Godhead by his total identity with that supreme reality. The more the human mind enters into this "Light of the World," the more it is dazzled by its effulgence, made conscious of depth upon depth in its mystery. "However much the human encounter with God had been experienced as personal address, it had not been conceived in terms of a person distinct from God. But now in John the word of God is identified with a particular historical person, whose pre-existence as a person with God is asserted throughout. Now the Christian conception of God must make room for the person who was Christ, the Logos incarnate." Thus, as a biblical theologian recalling other Johannine texts, 1:14; 1:18; 10:30; 14:28, J. D. G. Dunn (qv) concludes: "In a real sense the history of Christological controversy is the history of the Church's attempt to come to terms with John's Christology—first to accept it and then to understand and re-express it. The latter task will never end."[6]

It will end for the blessed finally called to the kingdom after the judgment and thus will fully be perceived the justifiable centrality of the Logos in all Christian thinking, the primacy (qv) of the Logos incarnate over all God's wonderful creation.

---

[1]Cf. biblical commentaries on Scripture passages, esp. Jn 1:14; biblical dictionaries, s.v., Word or Logos, A. Feuillet and P. Grelot in *Dictionary of Biblical Theology,* ed., X. Léon-Dufour, 1967, 587–89; J. L. McKenzie, *Dictionary of the Bible,* 1966, 940–41; esp. G. Kittel, *TDNT* IV, 69ff (G. Kittel, A. Debrunner, H. Kleinknecht, O. Procksch, G. Quell, G. Schrenk); J. Rendel Harris, *The Origin of the Prologue to St. John's Gospel,* London, 1917; *id.,* "Athena, Sophia and the Logos," *Bulletin of the John Rylands Library* 7 (1922/23) 56f; M. E. Boismard, O.P., "Dans le sein du Père," *RB* 61 (1952) 23–39; *id., Le Prologue de Saint Jean,* Paris, 1953 (English tr., Westminster, Maryland, 1957); esp. C. H. Dodd, *Interpretation of the Fourth Gospel,* Cambridge, 1953, 263–85; S. de Ansejo, "¿Es un himno a Cristo el Prologo de san Juan," *EstBib* 15 (1956) 223–77, 381–427; R. Schnackenburg, "Logoshymnus und Johanneische Prolog," *Biblische Zeitschrift,* N.F. 1 (1957); O. Cullmann, *The Christology of the New Testament,* London, 1959, 249–69; A. Grillmeier, S.J., *Christ in Christian Tradition,* London, 1964, 29–35; *id., Der Logos am Kreuz,* Munich, 1956; W. Pannenberg, *Jesus, God and Man,* London, 1968, 158–87; E. Haenchen, "Probleme des Johanneischen Prologs," *ZTK* 60 (1963) 313f; J. D. G. Dunn, *Christology in the Making,* 2nd ed., London, 1989, 213–50; J. Jeremias, "Zum Logos-Problem," *ZNW* 59 (1968) 82–85; B. Jendorff, *Der Logosbegriff,* Frankfurt, 1976; A. Heron, " 'Logos, Image, Son': Some Models and Paradigms in early Christology," *Creation, Christ and Culture, Studies in Honor of T. F. Torrance,* ed., R. W. A. McKinney, Edinburgh, 1976, 43–62; C. T. R. Hayward, "The Holy Name of the God of Moses and the Prologue of St. John's Gospel," *NTS* 25 (1978–79) 16–32; M. Rissi, "Die Logoslieder im Prolog des vierten Evangeliums," *TZ* 31 (1975) 321–36; A. Feuillet, "Le prologue du quatrième évangile," *Étude de théologie johannique,*

Burges, 1968; H. Gese, "Der 'Messias' und 'Der Johannesprolog,' *Zur biblischen Theologie: Altestamentliche Vorträge,* Munich, 1977, 128–51, 152–201; P. Borgen, "Observations on the Targumic Character of the Prologue of John," *NTS* 16 (1969–70) 288–95; *id.,* "Logos was the True Light," *NovT* 14 (1972) 115–30; M. McNamara, "Logos of the Fourth Gospel and Memra of the Palestinian Targum," *ExpT* 79 (1967–68), 115–17; [2]*Op. cit.,* 228; [3]*Constitution on Divine Revelation,* art. 1; [4]*Ibid.,* art. 2; [5]*Op. cit.,* 285; [6]*Op. cit.,* 250.

WORDS OF JESUS, IPSISSIMA VERBA

Allied with the problem of the "Jesus of History" (qv) is that of the sayings of Jesus.[1] It is largely a question for biblical scholars, for theologians can take the words attributed to Jesus as part of the inspired word of God, leaving research to the specialists, eventually profiting by it. Most readers have noted the difference between the synoptic gospels and the discourses in the fourth gospel. Modern critical historians have extended the scope of examination and evaluation to all that is reported as spoken by Jesus. The difficulty is caused by a) the fact that Jesus left no written work, and b) the interval of some thirty years which elapsed between his life and the written gospels. How to retrieve his exact words? Oral tradition was important in his world as a means of transmission. In communities which drew life from it, it was controlled by leaders. We owe enlightenment on this factor to the Swedish school who reacted against the excesses of Form Criticism (qv). The comparative method has been much used, i.e., the search for dissimilarity between sayings of Jesus and Judaism, between Jesus and the post-paschal Christian community. There is not agreement on how the criterion should be applied, nor on others suggested. Nor on results to date. Comparison with Judaism must now take account of what we more fully understand, the Jewishness (qv) of Jesus. We must not attribute exceptional creative power nor an arbitrary attitude to the early Christians. The suggestion is sometimes that they did considerable editing, even invention. B. Gerhardsson would contend that the transmission of the oral content was carefully monitored. J. Jeremias has proposed and himself exemplified a method to supplement the comparative approach: an examination of language and style. Sayings of Jesus reported in the gospel of Thomas and elsewhere, with allegations in the popular press of fresh discoveries, come within the competence of specialists in the whole area of the apocryphal gospels.

---

[1]C. F. Burney, *The Poetry of Our Lord,* Oxford, 1925; G. Dalman, *Jesus-Jeschua,* Leipzig, 1922, Supplement, 1929, repr. Darmstadt, 1967; *id., Die Worte Jesu,* 2nd ed., Leipzig, 1930, repr. Darmstadt, 1960, ET *The Words of Jesus,* Edinburgh, 1902; J. Jere-

mias, *The Central Message of the New Testament,* London, 1965; *id., New Testament Theology,* London, 1971, 1–41; H. Riesenfeld, *The Gospel Tradition and its Beginnings,* London, 1957; B. Gerhardsson, *Memory and Manuscript,* London/Uppsala, 1961; F. C. Grant, "The Authenticity of Jesus' Sayings" in *Neutestamentliche Studien für R. Bultmann,* Berlin, 1954, 137–43; M. Black, *An Aramaic Approach to the Gospels and Acts,* Oxford, 2nd ed., 1967; T. W. Manson, *The Sayings of Jesus,* London, 1949; P. Perkins, *NJBC,* 1065–68; C. H. Henkey, *NCE* II, 404–14; J. Jeremias, *The Unknown Sayings of Jesus,* 2nd ed., London, 1964; J. D. Crossan, *Sayings Parallels,* Philadelphia, 1986; J. Doresse, "The Gospel According to Thomas" in *The Secret Books of the Egyptian Gnostics,* London, 1960, 333–78, with commentary.

WOUNDS OF OUR LORD, THE

Jn 19:37 applies to Jesus in his Passion the words of Zech 12:10: "when they look on him whom they have pierced." Ps 21 (22):16f. has a similar theme, "They have pierced my hands and feet—I can count all my bones."[1] The Liturgy of the Passion takes up the Servant Oracle, Is 53:5, "But he was wounded for our transgressions, he was bruised for our iniquities; upon him was the chastisement that made us whole, and with his stripes we are healed." The kind of wounds went with the mode of death Jesus suffered, crucifixion given to outcasts and slaves, the socially degraded. There are implicit references to the event in Lk 24:39; Gal 2:20; Rev 1:7. Jn 20:25, 27, is explicit, "Unless I see in his hands the print of the nails, and place my finger in the mark of the nails, and place my hand in his side, I will not believe. . . . Put your finger here, and see my hands; and put out your hand, and place it in my side; do not be faithless but believing."

This emphasis on the corporeal has a doctrinal aspect, the answer to Docetism (qv), and significantly, in the context of the bodily description, we have the confession of faith, "My Lord, and my God" (Jn 20:28). The theology of the Redemption which emphasizes the shedding of Jesus' blood (cf. Eph 1:7) (qv) must have the Wounds in focus; through them the blood was shed. So they take us into the very mystery of his redemptive death. They are the signs of his utter generosity, of his loving us to the end.

The Wounds are again important for the apologetics of the bodily resurrection. They direct attention to an undeniable reality. They acquire a special splendor in the glorified body of Christ, a special aspect of his total beauty, beauty of soul and beauty of body, for the traditional image of the Savior shows rays of light shining from the Wounds. In the history of spirituality, of mysticism, the urge of great followers of Christ to identify with him in his Passion directs their thought especially to the Wounds. This has, in certain cases like St. Paul, St. Francis, Teresa Neumann, Marthe Robin, especially Padre Pio, the longest enduring instance, a visible reproduction of the Passion marks, the Stigmata, as they are called. In its ultimate significance this phenomenon, which must be accurately studied, implies a view of solidarity between the Redeemer and redeemed in the Mystical Body, and has interest for the elaboration of a theology of history: time here is a factor to be especially judged. This is a domain of the exception, but not of the abnormal.

There has been much attention to the manifold symbolism of one particular sacred Wound, the piercing of the side of the dead Christ. The symbolism of water and blood leads into mystic sponsal worlds, recalling the marriage of the Lamb (Rev 22:1; 21:9-10), of the nuptial union of Christ and his Church, sealed on Calvary, therefore of the new Adam and the new Eve, that is, the Church coming forth from the side of the dead Christ. Finally, there has been a typology linking the water and the blood with the sacraments of Baptism and the Eucharist, or again a pointer to the two baptisms, water: the Sacrament; blood: martyrdom. So many concyclic trends of the symbolic, still more perhaps to be discovered, for this is the central mystery of the universe, Incarnation, termination of one form of human existence to open another, this one shared indefinitely.

[1] J. P. Bruni and J. P. Schanz, *NCE,* XIV, 1035–37; E. Glotin, "The Wounded Heart of Jesus Christ," *Lum* V 16 (1961) 713–34; A. Lefevre, "Die Seitenwunde Jesu," *Geist und Leben* 33 (1960) 86–96; A. F. Sava, "The Wounds of Christ," *CBQ* 16 (1954) 438–43; *LTK,* X, "Wunden Christi."

About the Author

Michael O'Carroll, C.S.Sp., is an internationally respected theologian and educator. He has written widely and well, over the past three decades, on theological and ecumenical topics. He is also the author of the much acclaimed works *Theotokos: A Theological Encyclopedia of the Blessed Virgin Mary; Trinitas: A Theological Encyclopedia of the Holy Trinity; Corpus Christi: An Encyclopedia of the Eucharist;* and *Verbum Caro: An Encyclopedia on Jesus, the Christ.*